Concussion in Professional Team Sports: Time for a Harmonised Approach?

Alexandra Veuthey

Concussion in Professional Team Sports: Time for a Harmonised Approach?

Springer

Alexandra Veuthey
Neuchâtel, Switzerland

ISBN 978-981-15-1978-9 ISBN 978-981-15-1979-6 (eBook)
https://doi.org/10.1007/978-981-15-1979-6

This Springer imprint is published by the registered company Springer Nature Singapore Pte Ltd.
The registered company address is: 152 Beach Road, #21-01/04 Gateway East, Singapore 189721, Singapore

Abstract: The risk of athletes sustaining concussion while participating in professional team sports raises two serious concerns both nationally and internationally. First, concussion in sport carries a public health risk, given that injured athletes may have to deal with significant long-term medical complications, with some of the worst cases resulting in chronic traumatic encephalopathy (CTE). Secondly, sports governing bodies are now exposed to the risk of financial and reputational damage as a consequence of legal proceedings being filed against them. A good example of this, among many other recent examples, is the case of the United States of America's National Football League (NFL), the governing body for American football, which, in 2015, committed to pay USD1 billion to settle a class action lawsuit filed by its former professional players.

This thesis examines how to most efficiently reduce these public health and legal risks and proposes a harmonised solution across sports and legal systems.

Foreword by Dr Julian Bailes

I am specialised in the field of neurosurgery and both the short and long-term impact of brain injury on cognitive function. I serve as Chairman of the Department of Neurosurgery and Co-Director of NorthShore Neurological Institute at NorthShore University HealthSystem in Chicago, as well as Clinical Professor of Neurosurgery at the University of Chicago Pritzker School of Medicine. I have been involved in neurological sports medicine at the professional, collegiate, and youth levels. I am the former physician of the American football team the Pittsburgh Steelers. Since 1992, I have been the neurological consultant to the National Football League Players Association (NFLPA) and contributed to the National Football League (NFL)'s acknowledgement of the link between head injuries and chronic traumatic encephalopathy (CTE). In 2015, my work and that of my team was portrayed in the movie 'Concussion'.

I first met Dr Alexandra Veuthey at an international brain injury conference in 2016. We discussed her ongoing doctoral thesis, in particular the scope for harmonisation in the regulation of concussion in professional team sports. Interestingly, when Dr Veuthey formed her research proposal at the beginning of 2014, and then formally started her research one year later, American football and the NFL were the main focus of concussion issues, research, and controversy. Now, with the engagement of Dr Veuthey and other international researchers, the science of concussion, the brain's reaction to cranial impacts and repetitive blows, and the potential for cumulative effects are better understood and appreciated around the world. The prospect for brain injury is also now realised to be not only in American football, but in numerous other sports in which contact may occur, including football (soccer), rugby, ice hockey, and others. The emerging and exploding evidence, both from laboratory investigations and clinical studies of athletes from various sports, begin to define the myriad of issues regarding repetitive mild traumatic brain injury (mTBI). Thanks to dedicated researchers from around the world, the knowledge of mechanisms of injury, symptom complexes, and treatment paradigms start to emerge, which guides sports actors in the care of athletes with mTBI. The most effective diagnostic modalities and therapeutic plans are now increasingly being utilised and, in fact, are still evolving. It is essential for sports organisations and governments to have the most in-depth, comprehensive, and consistent policies. The publication of Dr Veuthey's thesis will further contribute to the recognition and implementation of harmonised policies to best assist all those who are involved in protecting and caring for athletes.

Chicago, IL Julian E. Bailes

Acknowledgements

I would like to acknowledge that this thesis was prepared with, and made possible by, the financial support of the University of Melbourne Law School. In addition, I would like to thank my main supervisor, Mr Hayden Opie, Prof. Jack Anderson (who replaced him down the track), my co-supervisor, Prof. John Tobin, as well as my external supervisors, Mr Paul Hayes and Dr Peter Harcourt. My sincere thanks also go to the librarians and academic staff of the University.

Finally, I am grateful for the unfailing support of my parents (in particular my father, who would have liked so much to witness the completion of my thesis) and of my friends, Madalina Diaconu, Alec Drion, Damon Luo, Garry Mann, Alexandra Mot, Brett Osler, Ana Maria Palacio, Jade Patterson, Heather Pereira, and Paulo V. da Costa.

Declaration

I, Alexandra Veuthey, declare that:

1. This thesis comprises only my original work towards the requirements of a Ph.D.
2. Due acknowledgement has been made in the text to all other material used.
3. The thesis is fewer than the maximum word limit in length, exclusive of tables, maps, bibliographies, and appendices.

Alexandra Veuthey, February 2019

Contents

Abbreviations and Acronyms

1st, 2nd, 3rd, 4th, etc.	First, second, third, fourth, etc.
&	Ampersand (and)
£	British pound
AAA	Australian Athletes Alliance
AAF	Adverse Analytical Findings
AAN	American Academy of Neurology
AAP	Australian Associated Press
ABC	Australian Broadcasting Corporation
Above n	Above footnote (1, etc.)
ADAMS	Anti-Doping Administration and Management System
ADRV	Anti-Doping Rule Violation(s)
AFL	Australian Football League
AFLPA	Australian Football League Players' Association
AIBA	Association Internationale de Boxe Amateur (International Amateur Boxing Association)
AIBA AOB Competition Rules	AIBA Open Boxing Competition Rules (2017)
AIS	Australian Institute of Sport
AIOWF	Association of International Olympic Winter Sports Federations
Ali Act	*Muhammad Ali Boxing Reform Act of 2000* (United States)
ALS	Amyotrophic Lateral Sclerosis
AMA	Australian Medical Association
ANOC	Association of National Olympic Committees
AP	Associated Press
APOE	Apolipoprotein
ARAF	All-Russia Athletics Federation

ARD	Arbeitsgemeinschaft der öffentlichrechtlichen Rundfunkanstalten der Bundesrepublik Deutschland (Association of Public Broadcasters of the Federal Republic of Germany)
ARLC	Australian Rugby League Commission
Art(s)	Article(s)
ARU	Australian Rugby Union
ASADA	Australian Sports Anti-Doping Authority
ASC	Australian Sports Commission
ASF	Association Suisse de Football (Swiss Football Association)
ASM Clermont	Association Sportive Montferrandaise Clermont (Sports Association of Montferrand, Clermont)
ASOIF	Association of Summer Olympic International Federations
ASUA	Amateur Swimming Union of the Americas
AUD	Australian dollar
BBC	British Broadcasting Corporation
BBBC	British Boxing Board of Control
BCCA or BC Court of Appeal	British Columbia Court of Appeal (Canada)
BCSC	British Columbia Supreme Court (Canada)
BMJ	BMJ (formerly: British Medical Journal)
BMJ Open Sport and Exercise Medicine	BMJ Open Sport and Exercise Medicine (affiliated to BMJ)
Cantu guidelines	Medical guidelines drafted by Dr Robert Cantu (Journal of Athletic Training, 2001)
CAD	Canadian dollar
CAS	Court of Arbitration for Sport
CBA(s)	Collective Bargaining Agreement(s)
CBC	Canadian Broadcasting Center
CBF	Confederação Brasileira de Futebol (Brazilian Football Confederation)
CBS	Columbia Broadcasting System
CC	*Código Civil (Civil Code)* (Brazil)
CC	*Code civil* (*Civil Code*) (Switzerland)
CCC	Canadian Concussion Collaborative
CD Cal	United States District Court for the Central District of California
CDC	Centers for Disease Control and Prevention
Cert.	Certification
CETS	Council of Europe Treaty Series
CFL	Canadian Football League
CFLPA	Canadian Football League Players' Association
CFSA	Canadian Freestyle Ski Association

Cir.	Circuit (United States Court of Appeals, 1st Circuit, etc.)
CISG	Concussion in Sport Group
CLR	Commonwealth Law Reports (Australia)
CMS	Colorado Medical Society
Cmt.	Comment
CNN	Cable News Network
CO	*Code des Obligations* (*Code of Obligations*) (Switzerland)
Colo. Court	Colorado Court (United States)
CONCACAF	Confederation of North, Central American and Caribbean Association Football
CONMEBOL	*Confederación Sudamericana de Fútbol* (South American Football Confederation)
Council of Europe Convention On Safety, Security and Services	*Council of Europe Convention on an Integrated Safety, Security and Service Approach at Football Matches and Other Sports Events* (2017)
CSAE	Children's Sports Athletic Equipment Safety Bill (United States)
CSTE	Center for the Study of Traumatic Encephalopathy
CT	Computed tomography
CTE	Chronic Traumatic Encephalopathy
CTE Center	Chronic Traumatic Encephalopathy Center
Cth	Commonwealth
DC United	District of Columbia United (Football Club)
DC Superior Court	Superior Court of the District of Columbia (United States)
D.D.C.	United States District Court for the District of Columbia
DePaul-LCA Journal of Art and Entertainment Law	DePaul-LCA Journal of Art and Entertainment Law (in collaboration with Chicago Lawyers for the Creative Arts)
Dir.	Director
DLR	Dominion Law Reports (Canada)
D Minn	United States District Court for the District of Minnesota
Dr(s)	Doctor(s)
DTI	Diffusion Tensor Imaging
DVD	Digital Versatile Disc
E-book	Electronic book
Ed	Edition (1st edition, etc.)
Ed(s)	Editor(s)
ED Mo	United States District Court for the Eastern District of Missouri

EEG	Electroencephalogram
eg	Exampli gratia (for instance)
EPCR	European Professional Club Rugby
EPL	English Premier League
ERISA	*Employee Retirement Income Security Act of 1974* (United States)
ESPN	Entertainment and Sports Programming Network
Et al	Et alia (and others)
Et seq	Et sequens (and what follows)
EU GDPR	*European Union's General Data Protection Regulation*
EU IDB	European Union Injury Database
European Convention on Spectator Violence	*European Convention on Spectator Violence and Misbehaviour at Sports Events and in Particular at Football* (1985)
FAPL	Football Association Premier League
FDDNP (scan)	2-(1-{6-[(2-[fluorine-18]fluoroethyl)(methyl) amino]-2-naphthyl}-ethylidene)malononitrile (scan)
FED.R.CIV.P.	*Federal Rules of Civil Procedure* (United States)
FEI	Fédération Equestre Internationale (International Federation for Equestrian Sports)
FENAPAF	Federação Nacional dos Atletas Profissionais de Futebol (National Federation of Professional Football Athletes)
FFA	Football Federation Australia
FHSAA	Florida High School Athletic Association
FIBA	Fédération Internationale de Basketball (International Basketball Association)
FIFA	Fédération Internationale de Football Association (International Federation of Association Football)
FIFA TMS	FIFA Transfer Matching System
FIFPro	International Federation of Professional Footballers
FINA	Fédération Internationale de Natation (International Swimming Federation)
FIS	Fédération Internationale de Ski (International Ski Federation)
FIU Law Review	Florida International University Law Review
F-MARC	FIFA Medical Assessment and Research Center
FSB	Federalnaya Sluzhba Bezopasnosti (Russian Federal Security Service)
F. Supp.	Federal Supplement (West Publishing)
GAA	Gaelic Athletic Association
GABA	Gamma-aminobutyric acid

GAISF	Global Association of International Sports Federations
GE	General Electric
HIA	Head Injury Assessment
HNGN	Headlines & Global News
House Comm. on Energy and Commerce	United States House Committee on Energy and Commerce
House Comm. on the Judiciary	United States House Committee on the Judiciary
H.R. (Bill)	Bill originated in the House of Representatives (Congress, United States)
IAAF	International Association of Athletics Federations
IADA	International Anti-Doping Agreement
Ibid	Ibidem (of the same source)
IB Times	International Business Times
ICC	International Cricket Council
ICHIRF	International Concussion and Head Injury Research Foundation
IDB-FDS	Injury Database (JAMIE) Full Data Set
ie	Id est (in other words)
IFAB	International Football Association Board
IFAF	International Football American Federation
IF(s)	International Federation(s)
IIHF	International Ice Hockey Federation
ImPACT	Immediate Post-Concussion Assessment and Cognitive Testing
IOC	International Olympic Committee
IOM	Institute of Medicine
IRB	International Rugby Board
IRFU	International Rugby Football Union
ISC	International Standard on Concussion
ISCCS	International Standard for Code Compliance by Signatories
ISL	International Standard for Laboratories
ISPPPI	International Standard for the Protection of Privacy and Personal information
ISTI	International Standard for Testing and Investigations
ISTUE	International Standard for Therapeutic Use Exemptions
ITA	Independent Testing Agency
JAMA Neurology	Journal of the American Medical Association of Neurology
JAMIE	Joint Action on Monitoring Injuries in Europe
LAA	*Loi fédérale sur l'assurance-accidents* (*Swiss Federal Law on Accident Insurance*)

LC, Lugano Convention	*Lugano Convention on Jurisdiction and Enforcement of Judgments in Civil and Commercial Matters* (1988)
LMRA	*Labor Management Relations Act of 1947* (United States)
Macolin Convention	*Convention on the Manipulation of Sports Competitions*
MEO(s)	Major Event Organisation(s)
MCI	Mild Cognitive Impairment
MDL	Multi-District Litigation
M.D. Pa.	United States District Court for the Middle District of Pennsylvania
Minn Stat	Minnesota Statutes (United States)
MLB	Major League Baseball
MLBPA	Major League Baseball Players Association
MLS	Major League Soccer
MLSPA	Major League Soccer Players Association
MLS SABH	MLS Player Substance Abuse and Behavioral Health Program and Policy (incorporated in 2015 CBA)
MMQB	Monday Morning Quarterback (Sports Illustrated)
MPR	Minnesota Public Radio
Mr	Mister
MRI	Magnetic resonance imaging
mTBI	Mild traumatic brain injury
NADO(s)	National Anti-Doping Organisation(s)
NAD Scheme	*National Anti-Doping Scheme* (Australia)
N. Am. Soccer League	North American Soccer League
NATA	National Athletic Trainers' Association
NBC	National Broadcasting Company
NCAA	National Collegiate Athletic Association
NCCSIR	National Center for Catastrophic Injury Research
N.D. Cal.	United States District Court for the Northern District of California
N.D.Ill.	United States District Court for the Northern District of Illinois
New York Convention	*New York Convention of 10 June 1958 on the Recognition and Enforcement of Foreign Arbitral Awards*
NFL	National Football League
NFL HNSMC	NFL Head, Neck and Spine Medical Committee
NFL MTBI Committee	NFL Mild Traumatic Brain Injury Committee
NFLPA	National Football League Players Association
NIH	National Institutes of Health
NHL	National Hockey League

NHLPA	National Hockey League Players' Association
NIOSH	National Institute for Occupational Safety and Health
No or Nr	Number
NOC(s)	National Olympic Committee(s)
NPA	Employment and Industrial Relations National Practice Area (Australia)
NRC	National Rugby Championship
NRL	National Rugby League
NSW	New South Wales
NSWSC	New South Wales Supreme Court (Australia)
NY CPLR	New York Civil Practice Law and Rules (United States)
NYSBA Entertainment, Arts and Sports Law Journal	New York State Bar Association Entertainment, Arts and Sports Law Journal
NZHC	New Zealand High Court
OHL	Ontario Hockey League
Olympic Code	Olympic Movement Code on the Prevention of the Manipulation of Competitions (2015)
Olympic Unit	Olympic Movement Unit on the Prevention of the Manipulation of Competitions
Ont. S.C.J.	Ontario Superior Court of Justice (Canada)
OSHA	Occupational Safety and Health Administration
OSHA	*Occupational Safety and Health Act of 1970* (United States)
Oswald Commission	IOC Commission chaired by Denis Oswald (in charge of looking into alleged doping violations by individual Russian athletes at the 2012 and 2014 Olympic Games)
P. or pp.	Page(s)
PA Cons Stat	Pennsylvania Consolidated Statutes (United States)
PAG	Pan-Arab Games
PBS	Public Broadcasting Service
PBSA	*Professional Boxing Safety Act of 1996* (United States)
PennRecord	Pennsylvania Record
PET scan	Positron Emission Tomography scan
PFA	Professional Footballers' Association
Ph.D.	Doctor of Philosophy
PILA	*Federal Act on Private International Law* (1987)
Prod.	Producer
PSCA	Pitch Side Concussion Assessment
Pt	Point
PT in Motion	Physical Therapy in Motion (American Physical Therapy Association)
Pty Ltd	Proprietary Limited

QB	Queen's Bench Division (England)
QCCS	Superior Court of Quebec (Canada)
QJM: An International Journal of Medicine	Quarterly Journal of Medicine: An International Journal of Medicine
Qld	Queensland
RADO(s)	Regional Anti-Doping Organisation(s)
RLIF	Rugby League International Federation
RLPA	Rugby League Players Association
ROC	Russian Olympic Committee
Rowan's Law	*Rowan's Law (Concussion Safety)*, 2018 (Ontario, Canada)
Rugby-7s	Rugby union, variant (seven players instead of 15)
Rugby-13s	Rugby league (13 players)
RUPA	Rugby Union Players' Association
RUSADA	Russian Anti-Doping Agency
RUSAF	Russian Athletics Federation
S.A.	Sociedade Anônima (limited liability company)
SANZAAR	South Africa, New Zealand, Australia and Argentina Rugby
SBC	Statutes of British Columbia (Canada)
SB Nation	Sports Blog Nation
SBS	Special Broadcasting Service
SCAT	Sport Concussion Assessment Tool (SCAT 1, etc.)
S.C.C.	Supreme Court of Canada
Schmid Commission	IOC Commission chaired by Samuel Schmid (in charge of investigating allegations of institutionalised doping in Russia)
SDE	Supporters Direct Europe
S.D.N.Y.	United States District Court for Southern District of New York
S.D. Ohio	United States District Court for the Southern District of Ohio
SFL	Swiss Football League
SFT	Swiss Federal Tribunal
SGB(s)	Sports Governing Body(ies)
SIHF	Swiss Ice Hockey Federation
SIHL	Swiss Ice Hockey League
SJ	Semaine Judiciaire (Judicial Week)
SMA	Sports Medicine Australia
S.O.	Statutes of Ontario (Canada)
TEAM	Targeted Evaluation and Active Management
The ANZSLA Commentator	The Australian and New Zealand Sports Law Association Commentator
The FA	The English Football Association
TSN	The Sports Network
TUE(s)	Therapeutic Use Exemption(s)

TV	Television
U-20	Under 20 (years old)
UCC	*Uniform Commercial Code* (United States)
UCL Institute of Neurology	University College London, Institute of Neurology
UEFA	Union of European Football Associations
UNESCO	United Nations Educational, Scientific and Cultural Organization
UNESCO Convention on Doping	*International Convention against Doping in Sport*
UNESCO IOS Evaluation Office	UNESCO Internal Oversight Service Evaluation Office
UNODC	United Nations Office on Drugs and Crime
UNTS	United Nations Treaty Series
UOL Esporte	Universo Online Esporte
US	United States of America
USA Today	United States of America Today
USBA	United States Boxing Administration
USC	United States Code
US Dist. LEXIS	LEXISNexis database for United States District Court
USD	United States dollar
US Soccer	United States Soccer Federation
USTA	United States Tennis Association
USAWP	USA Water Polo
UK	United Kingdom
V or vs	Versus
Vic	Victoria
Vol.	Volume
WA	Western Australia
WAtoday	Western Australia Today
WADA	World Anti-Doping Agency
WADC	World Anti-Doping Code
Wash Rev Code	Washington Revised Code (United States)
WCA	World Championships in Athletics
WGRZ	World Greatest Radio; Z=2 refers to virtual channel and former analog channel
WL	Westlaw
WRU	Welsh Rugby Union
WSSA	World Sports Safety Agency
WWE	World Wrestling Entertainment
WWR	Western Weekly Reports (Canada)
Zackery Lystedt Law	*Youth sports—Concussion and head injury guidelines—Injured athlete restrictions* (Washington, United States)

Chapter 1
Introduction

Doubt is an improvement on denial.

Louise Ackermann, Les pensées d'une solitaire, 1903.

I The Growing Problem

Concussion is a serious issue for both current and retired professional athletes, and is emerging as one of the biggest threats—if not the biggest threat—to player safety. A recent controversy arose in American football, where a wave of suicides, along with the intervention of the United States (US) Congress and the judicial system, informed public opinion of the potential long-term medical complications associated with multiple instances of head trauma and concussion. These complications, long denied by the National Football League (NFL), include memory loss, impulsive anger-control problems, disorientation, depression and dementia (symptoms notably associated with a degenerative disease called 'Chronic Traumatic Encephalopathy' ('CTE')).

In 2012, the NFL was sued in a consolidated class action involving nearly 5000 former professional players. This class action, based on torts (negligence and fraud), was settled in 2015 for USD1 billion. The litigation even caught the attention of the President at the time, Barack Obama, who indicated in an interview with

---

This thesis is published in the version accepted by the University of Melbourne Law School on 26 July 2019, apart from minor amendments (mainly related to typography and formatting). The thesis builds on previous research work on concussion undertaken by the author. In order not to exceed the maximum word limit, this previous work is not quoted in the footnotes. For the same reasons, references to other authors in the footnotes are limited to the strict minimum. However, all sources that were relied upon are listed in the bibliography.

A. Veuthey, *Concussion in Professional Team Sports: Time for a Harmonised Approach?*, https://doi.org/10.1007/978-981-15-1979-6_1

'The New Republic' in 2013 that if he had a son, he would have 'to think long and hard before [he] let him play football'.[1]

After the NFL case had been brought out into the open, the controversy surrounding concussion continued to increase and expand.

Numerous Sports Governing Bodies (SGBs) were sued in the US and Canada. This includes, for professional team sports, the National Hockey League (NHL), the Fédération Internationale de Football Association (FIFA), USA Water Polo (USAWP),[2] and the Canadian Football League (CFL). Some of these legal proceedings were definitively dismissed on procedural grounds, whereas others are still pending. New proceedings are expected in Australia, against the National Rugby League (NRL) and the Australian Football League (AFL).

Multiple CTE cases have also been diagnosed, notably in ice hockey, football, Canadian football, baseball, and rugby union.

These new revelations may only be the 'tip of the iceberg'. They highlight the two-fold risks of sports concussion: the risk of immediate and long-term injury to professional athletes and the related legal (financial and reputational) risk to SGBs.

This thesis seeks the best solution to address these two-fold risks. Recognising that the current regulation of concussion is insufficiently coordinated and effective, it proposes a harmonised solution across sports and legal systems.

II Scope

The medical and legal information now being derived from sports concussion and its consequences is vast and rapidly evolving. It emerges in a wide variety of sports, different levels of sporting competition, across international boundaries, and people versed in numerous disciplines and skills.

---

[1]Franklin Foer and Chris Hughes, 'Barack Obama is not Pleased – The President on his Enemies, the Media and the Future of Football', *The New Republic*, 27 January 2013 (<https://newrepublic.com/article/112190/obama-interview-2013-sit-down-president>).

[2]USAWP oversees an emerging professional men's league (see Chapter 3, Section ID2(a)). It is, therefore, classified in 'professional team sports'.

Because of the large scale of the concussion problem (highlighted by an extensive survey of litigation and literature), this thesis proposes to focus on professional team sports, excluding elite[3] and grassroots sports,[4] as well as individual sports.[5]

This thesis focuses more specifically on SGBs and governments. SGBs at the professional level (as actors at the top of the pyramidal structure of sport) and governments (as holders of legislative, executive and judicial powers) are the most influential and best positioned to take effective measures. In addition, governments' intervention is justified by the public health issues involved.

On the jurisdictional front, the legal proceedings filed against SGBs, over their management of concussion, involve multiple complex legal issues, which have, so far, mainly been examined through the lens of common law countries[6] and tort law. The best illustration of this can be found in the NFL litigation that, even though it did not lead to a judgment, is a landmark case.[7] The negligence-based claims contended

[3]Elite sport (which notably covers semi-professional and/or college sport) is also affected by the concussion controversy. For instance, at the end of 2014, the National College Athletics Association (NCAA), which is the main collegiate athletic organisation in the US, was named as a defendant in a class action lawsuit. A settlement is currently being discussed. Added to this are legal proceedings brought directly against certain universities themselves. The exclusion of elite sport is, however, due to its very unique structure and possible differences in the medical care provided.

[4]Grassroots, and/or young sport levels, are not spared from the concussion controversy. Recent examples include the lawsuits against FIFA and USAWP (lawsuits that, although filed against professional SGBs, involved youth athletes), Pop Warner and numerous high schools in the US, legal proceedings in Ireland, as well as various incidents in the US and Canada (which led to the adoption of youth concussion laws). The exclusion of grassroots and/or youth sport is, however, justified by its very specific environment, which is considerably different from that in professional sport, both in terms of financial resources and the level of players' monitoring involved. In addition, young players need to be protected and cared for in a particularly cautious manner due to their potential longer recovery timeframe, as well as their lower maturity and legal independence level.

[5]Individual sports are also affected by the concussion controversy. Apart from boxing, and its longstanding history with concussion-related medical issues, wrestling is a good example of this. Several former wrestlers have already been diagnosed with CTE. Several class actions have been filed in the US against World Wrestling Entertainment (WWE), all of which were dismissed at first instance. Appeals are currently pending. Other combat sports, such as mixed martial arts, are also particularly at risk. Finally, sports deemed to be less violent, such as skiing, ski jumping, Formula 1, surfing or tennis, are not spared. Among the most recent examples are the lawsuits filed in 2015 against the Canadian Freestyle Ski Association (CFSA) (still pending) and the United States Tennis Association (USTA) (settled in 2018). The exclusion of individual sports is, however, justified for several reasons, mainly by the fact that comparisons between individual and team sports (and, hence, the related suggestions for improvements in the regulation of concussion) would prove to be too difficult. Individual sports such as combat sports differentiate themselves from the sports examined as part of this thesis, in that they do not only imply incidental contacts, but are inherently violent by nature and may culminate in a 'knock out'. Conversely, other less violent individual sports often imply specific types of liability issues, due for instance to defective equipment or playing surface-related injuries.

[6]In particular the US, Canada (which is governed by common law, apart from the Province of Quebec), Australia and, to a lesser extent, England.

[7]See Chapter 3, Sections IA2(a) et seq.

by the plaintiffs are particularly interesting, since they were later re-used in numerous subsequent proceedings,[8] and show how future cases may be argued. A good example of a negligence claim can be found in the very first class action complaint filed in 2011 against the NFL (*Easterling*), which included, among others, the following pleadings:[9]

(a) Failing to warn of the risk of unreasonable harm resulting from repeated concussions;
(b) Failing to disclose the special risks of long term complications and return to play;
(c) Failing to disclose the role that repeated concussions has in causing chronic life-long cognitive decline;
(d) Failing to promulgate rules and regulations to adequately address the dangers of repeated concussions and a return to play policy to minimise long-term chronic cognitive problems;
(e) Misrepresenting pertinent facts that players needed to be aware of to make determinations of the safety of return to play;
(f) Concealing pertinent facts;
(g) Failing to adopt rules and reasonably enforce those rules to minimise the risk of players suffering debilitating concussions; and,
(h) Other acts of negligence and carelessness that may materialize during the pendency of the action.[10]

The plaintiffs' main assertion was that the NFL had breached its duty of care to the players by failing to protect them with league-wide procedures for handling concussion and to warn them about the potential long-term risks. This assertion raises the question of the existence and extent of the necessary components of tort liability, namely a duty of care owed by SGBs, a breach of that duty, causation and damage.[11] It also requires the examination of more specific defences and concepts, such as voluntary assumption of risk, contributory negligence, pre-emption/lack of jurisdiction of state courts, class certification, statutes of limitations, private insurance, or even workers' compensation and medical negligence. Additionally, it provides a basis for similar discussions in civil law countries that apply much more codified and rigid precepts through the law of delict, in line with the Roman law tradition. Tort law and delict law-related issues are defined and analysed below,[12] as

[8]See eg, Chapter 3, Sections IB2(a), IC2(b) and ID2(b).

[9]*Easterling et al v National Football League* (Pennsylvania Eastern District Court, 2:2011cv05209, 18 August 2011).

[10]Class action first amended complaint of 11 October 2011, p. 15, paragraph 47. This complaint is available on the 'NFL Concussion Litigation' website (<http://nflconcussionlitigation.com/?page_id=18>).

[11]For the US, see eg, *Restatement (Third) of Torts (2010)*, section 6 cmt. b; *Sandage v. Bankhead Enters.*, Inc., 177 F.3d 670, *675* (8th Cir. 1999), *cert. denied, 528* U.S. 1019 (1999).

[12]See Chapter 3, Sections IA2 et seq (including subsequent case studies).

they arise, in order to facilitate an understanding of the current and future litigation filed against SGBs. However, they are not the primary concern of this thesis.[13] Rather, the thesis is designed to investigate a harmonised medico-regulatory approach aimed at, ultimately, significantly reducing the public health risks associated with concussion and its related litigation.[14]

[13]For further reading, see the dozens of articles published in North America in relation to the NFL, NHL, FIFA, USAWP and CFL litigation (mentioned in the relevant footnotes and/or Bibliography). While some of these articles provide a general analysis, others focus on one specific issue [for the latter, see eg, Tracey B Carter, 'From Youth to Collegiate Athletics to Professional Leagues: Is There Really "Informed Consent" by Athletes Regarding Sports-Related Concussions' (2015) 84 *University of Missouri-Kansas City Law Review* 331, 331–72 (Tracey B Carter, 'Consent'); Christopher C French, 'A Battle for NFL vs Insurance Industry Re: Concussion Liabilities' (2016) 53 *San Diego Law Review* 901, 901–47; Joseph Giametta, 'In re National Football League Concussion Litigation: An Examination of the Merits of Class Action and Certification' (2017) 20 *Quinnipiac Health Law Journal* 231, 213–42; William B Gould IV, 'Football, Concussion and Preemption, The Gidiron of National Football League Litigation' (2012) 8 *FIU Law Review* 55, 55–69; John Guccione, 'Moving Past a Pocket Change Settlement: The Threat of Preemption and How the Loss of Chance Doctrine Can Help NFL Concussion Plaintiffs Prove Causation' (2014) 22 *Journal of Law and Policy* 907, 907–56; Jessica Leigh Hawley, 'Class Certification Issues: In re: National Football League Concussion Injury Litigation' (2016) 6 *Pace Intellectual Property, Sports & Entertainment Law Forum,* 185, 185–211; Kelly A Heard, 'The Impact of Preemption in the NFL Concussion Litigation' (2013) 68 *University of Miami Law Review* 221, 221–49; Heather McGillivray, 'Where is the Awareness in Concussion Awareness: Can Concussed Players Really Assume the Risk in a Concussed State?' (2014) 21 *Jeffrey S Moorad Sports Law Journal Sports Law Journal* 529, 529–76; Michelle M Modery, 'Injury Time-Out: Justifying Workers' Compensation Awards to Retired Athletes with Concussion-Caused Dementia' (2011) 84 *Temple Law Review* 247, 247–82; Sheila B Scheuerman, 'The NFL Concussion Litigation: a Critical Assessment of Class Certification' (2012) 8 *FIU Law Review* 81, 81–105; Michael Telis, 'Playing Through the Haze: The NFL Concussion Litigation and Section 301 Preemption' (2014) 102 *The Georgetown Journal* 1841, 1841–68]. For other juridictions, see eg, Richard Bunworth, 'Egg-Shell Skulls or Institutional Negligence? The Liability of World Rugby for Incidents of Concussion Suffered by Professional Players in England and Ireland' (2016) 16 *International Sports Law Journal* 82, 82–98 (about England); Annette Greenhow, 'Concussion Policies of the National Football League: Revisiting the "Sport Administrator's Charter" and the Role of the Australian Football League and National Rugby League in Concussion Management' (2011) *Sports Law eJournal* 1, 1–18 (<https://research.bond.edu.au/en/publications/concussion-policies-of-the-national-football-league-revisiting-th>) (Greenhow, 'Charter'); Michael Legg, 'National Football League Players' Concussion Injury Class Action Settlement' (2015) 10 *Australian and New Zealand Association Sports Law Journal* 47, 60–5; James McIntyre, 'Getting Schooled in the Hard Knocks of Concussion Liability' (2017) 99 *The ANZSLA Commentator* 2 (all three about Australia); Alexandra Veuthey, 'Quelle protection pour les athlètes blessés? Analyse du cas de la National Football League à la lumière du droit suisse' (27 January 2014) *Jusletter* (online review) Rz 1, 1–59 (Veuthey, 'Droit suisse') (about Switzerland). Finally, see the numerous sports law books that are dedicated, in whole or in part, to the law of negligence/delict in sport (including concussion) and insurance (eg, Matthew Mitten et al., *Sports Law and Regulation: Cases, Material and Problems* (Wolters Kluwer, 4th ed, 2017) Chapter 11, 857–973, in particular 929–31 (Mitten et al., 'Cases'); David Thorpe et al., *Sports Law* (Oxford University Press, 3rd ed, 2017) Chapter 5, 221–330, in particular 281–90 and Chapter 6, 290–330, in particular 299–301).

[14]See in particular Chapters 5 and 6.

III The Need for Harmonisation

The harmonisation of regulatory regimes is the process of creating common standards in a specific field. It seeks to 'effect an approximation or co-ordination of different legal provisions or systems by eliminating major differences and creating minimum requirement standards'.[15] It differs from unification, which aims to implement one single system.[16]

Harmonisation is an important feature of modern legal systems, and permeates all areas of law.[17] It promotes legal certainty and efficiency, allowing the establishment of clear and consistent rules, which are often essential in an increasingly globalised world.[18] Yet its necessity must be assessed in light of the particular area that is under examination.[19]

The need for harmonisation in sport has been acknowledged for a long time. This is not surprising, since sport is played on an international basis, and crosses domestic boundaries. It poses both universal issues (which expand across countries and sports around the world) and technical issues (which are mostly encountered in sport, and demand specialised skills). It necessitates a global vision and specialist knowledge.

Because modern sport operates internationally across legal and institutional boundaries, an effective response to the public health and legal risks of sports concussion, which now manifest on a large scale, requires a harmonised and consistent approach from SGBs and governments.

This thesis proposes a series of innovative reforms to achieve a harmonised regulatory framework. These reforms include an International Standard on Concussion (the 'ISC'), a supporting international convention ('*UNESCO Convention*'),[20] a new World Sports Safety Agency ('WSSA') and some limited enforcement mechanisms.

[15]WJ Kamba, 'Comparative Law: A Theoretical Framework' (1974) 23 *International and Comparative Law Quarterly* 485, 501.

[16]Mads Andenas, Camilla Baasch Andersen and Ross Ashcroft, 'Towards a Theory of Harmonisation', in Mads Andenas and Camilla Baasch Andersen (eds), *Theory and Practice of Harmonisation* (Edward Elgar Publishing, 2012) 572, 577.

[17]Ibid, 573–4.

[18]On this last point, see ibid, 573.

[19]Martin Boodman, 'The Myth of Harmonization of Laws' (1991) 39 *The American Journal of Comparative Law* 699, 702 and 706.

[20]'UNESCO' stands for the 'United Nations Educational, Scientific and Cultural Organization'.

IV Originality and Significance

The originality of this thesis lies in the fact that, until today, the relevant legal writing has generally confined itself to considering questions related to concussion in sport in a compartmentalised manner, that is to say within each sport and/or country. No author has analysed the question, in a thorough and extensive manner, from a comparative angle, nor has anyone considered the possibility of proposing a harmonised solution across sports and legal systems.

The issue is of great and broad significance from public health, legal, economic and social viewpoints. The main beneficiary stakeholders are the hundreds of thousands of former, current and future professional athletes who have sustained, or may potentially sustain concussion. The seriousness of the situation and the need for action to prevent more athletes from being injured should be self-evident. It is essential to quickly stem the scourge that is currently taking place. Added to the human cost is the risk of lawsuits, which have the potential to affect SGBs' reputations and impact them financially.

Additionally, by maintaining the status quo, SGBs run the risk of having domestic courts or legislatures impose rules on them. This would cause a loss of control of SGBs over the rules governing their respective sports with, as a consequence, the organisation of international competitions being rendered more complex or even restricted.

Furthermore, if sport loses its aura among the general public as a healthy activity, this could result in decreasing participation. From a long-term perspective, should the concerns surrounding the potential effects of concussion become even more persistent and publicised, the worst-case scenario could be the end of contact sport. An appropriate reaction of SGBs would help, with the support of the governments, to avoid this scenario.

The different solutions suggested as part of this thesis are likely to have practical utility. In particular, these solutions could be adopted by SGBs and governments, which are currently experiencing great difficulty in dealing with this growing issue.

V Structure

Chapter 2 provides a general medical overview of sports concussion, with a special emphasis on the current state of medical science and the medical guidelines published by medical organisations and other related groups. Initially starting from a definition of concussion, it then examines the question of symptoms and levels of concussion, together with other related issues (such as return-to-play decisions). Difficulties related to the diagnosis, treatment and prevention of concussion are then presented. There follows a description of the 'second-impact syndrome', the potential long-term effects associated with multiple instances of concussion and the areas for further research. The chapter ends with an outline of the future key medical-related challenges. Medical science is the starting point of the actual enquiry, but could also potentially be part of the solution. Medical guidelines are vital to the science. Both elements can inform and contribute to the development of an international standard.

Chapter 3 consists of national case studies, which describe and analyse the current regulation of sports concussion. It collects, examines and analyses the data obtained from the different countries and sports selected.

The national case studies focus on selected professional team sports and countries which have a history of, or potential for, CTE and litigation: US (American football, ice hockey, football, water polo, baseball); Canada (Canadian football); Australia (rugby, Australian Rules football); Switzerland (football, ice hockey); England (football) and Brazil (football).

The same chronological structure is used throughout the national case studies, with an emphasis on two main pillars: 'public health' (related to the prevention and management of concussion) and 'legal risks' (related to litigation and compensation). The 'public health' part puts into perspective, on the one hand, the incidence, causes, types and short/long-term effects of concussion on injured athletes and, on the other hand, the diverse responses of SGBs and governments. The 'legal risks' part examines the incidence and nature of (or potential for) legal proceedings against SGBs. These legal proceedings are currently solved in an uncoordinated way, based on the tort law/delict remedies specific to each country.

This comparative examination shows first that the concussion controversy has recently manifested on a large scale, immediately requiring the implementation of a harmonised solution across sports and legal systems. It then highlights some emerging good practices as well as perceived shortcomings, and indirectly exposes the means by which the concussion issue could be better regulated worldwide from a legal and public health perspective.

Chapter 4 identifies, briefly evaluates and summarises the common themes, good practices and existing shortcomings resulting from the data collected in Chapter 3. A series of tables is compiled to assist in this task.

Chapter 5 examines how the different harmonised regulatory mechanisms regulating doping, match-fixing and spectator violence could, by analogical reasoning, provide some guidance in relation to the means by which the regulation of sports concussion might be improved and harmonised in terms of public health and legal risks. It also explains what lessons could be drawn from these related fields, in particular in terms of predictable challenges. Finally, it proposes a harmonised framework for the regulation of concussion from the perspective of public health and legal risks.

Chapter 6 concludes the thesis by a way of a summary of the main findings of the research.

VI Latest Developments and Updates

This thesis is based on a research proposal formed at the beginning of 2014, and formally started at the beginning of 2015. At the time, the concussion controversy in professional team sports was, as indicated above, mainly associated with American football. However, since then, the countries and sports it has affected have grown exponentially. The responses of SGBs and, to a lesser extent, governments, have also developed very quickly. Emerging features of a harmonised approach have been devised or refined.

This rapid evolution testifies to the relevance of the argument and ideas developed as part of this thesis. It also constitutes a real challenge to keep up to date. This thesis deals with the situation regarding concussion as at 31 October 2018.

Chapter 2
Medical Overview

> Science is an endless story. The question is not to find out who is right and who is wrong. The goal is progress.
>
> Stephen and Lucy Hawking, George and the Big Bang, 2011.

I Outline

Concussion has historically been associated with loss of consciousness, or even other forms of visible injuries, such as fractures. The advancement of medical science around knowledge of the brain has shed light on a more complex issue, revealing new dimensions of concussion and ways to manage it. At the heart of the controversy is the neurodegenerative brain disease CTE, which is now believed to have the potential to affect a broad population of athletes.

This chapter provides a general medical overview of sports concussion, with special emphasis on the current state of medical science and the medical guidelines published by medical organisations and other relevant groups. It starts from the definition of concussion, and then examines the question of symptoms and levels of concussion, together with other related issues (such as return-to-play decisions). Difficulties confronting the diagnosis, treatment and prevention of concussion are then presented. There follows a description of the 'second-impact syndrome', the potential long-term effects associated with multiple instances of concussion and the areas for further research. The chapter concludes with an outline of the future key medical-related challenges.

A. Veuthey, *Concussion in Professional Team Sports: Time for a Harmonised Approach?*, https://doi.org/10.1007/978-981-15-1979-6_2

II Definition and Incidence

There is no single, precise definition of 'concussion'.[1] Since the early 2000s in particular, numerous attempts at a definition have been made, by commentators and medical organisations.[2] One of the most commonly accepted definitions is provided by the 'Concussion in Sport Group' (CISG), which brings together various SGBs and organises conferences at regular intervals, with the financial support of the International Olympic Committee (IOC), World Rugby, FIFA, the International Ice Hockey Federation (IIHF) and the International Federation for Equestrian Sports (FEI).[3] According to the 5th 'Consensus Statement on Concussion in Sport', published by this group (2018), concussion is defined as 'a traumatic brain injury induced by biomechanical forces'.[4]

Although the terms 'mild traumatic brain injury' (mTBI) and 'concussion' are often used interchangeably in the sporting context and the medical literature, others use these terms to refer to different injury constructs.[5] Health care professionals may tend to describe a concussion as a mTBI because it is usually not life threatening.[6] However, it remains true that the effects of concussion can be serious, all the more so in cases of repeated traumas.[7]

A concussion generally arises from a direct blow to the head, face or neck. It may also follow an indirect blow elsewhere on the body with an 'impulsive' force transmitted to the head.[8] This can occur in any sport or leisure activity. It is estimated that 3.8 million sports or leisure related incidents of concussion occur each year in

---

[1] James P Kelly and Jay H Rosenberg, 'Diagnosis and Management of Concussion in Sport' (1997) 48 *Neurology* 575, 575–6.

[2] See eg, Amy Bernstein, 'Into the Red Zone: How the National Football League's Quest to Curb Concussions and Concussions-Related Injuries Could Affect Player's Recovery' (2012) 22 *Seton Hall Journal of Sports and Entertainment Law* 271, 277–8; Dave Ellemberg, *Les commotions cérébrales dans le sport* (Les Editions Québec-Livres, 2013) 35–8; Alexander N Hecht, 'Legal and Ethical Aspects of Sports-Related Concussions: the Merrill Hoge Story' (2002) 12 *Seton Hall Journal of Sports and Entertainment Law* 17, 22–3.

[3] To date, five conferences have been organised: in Vienna (2001), Prague (2004), Zurich (2008 and 2012) and Berlin (2016). See this chapter, Section III.

[4] Paul McCrory et al., 'Consensus Statement on Concussion in Sport: The 5th International Conference on Concussion in Sport Held in Berlin, October 2016' (2018) 51 *British Journal of Sports Medicine* 838, 839 (McCrory et al., '5th Consensus').

[5] Ibid, 839.

[6] Centers for Disease Control and Prevention (CDC) (<https://www.cdc.gov/headsup/basics/concussion_whatis.html>).

[7] See this chapter, Section VII. For clarification purposes, the medical complications discussed here do not result strictly from concussion, but from head trauma. However, the term 'concussion' has been used widely by commentators in this context, and is now part of common language. Consequently, it will be referred to throughout the thesis.

[8] McCrory et al., '5th Consensus', above n 4, 839.

the US,[9] costing USD76.5 billion to governments.[10] These figures include 300 000 sports-related incidents of concussion treated in hospitals, together with an equal number of cases treated by general practitioners.[11] This tendency is more pronounced in Australia, where hospitalisations related to concussion from sport (3000 yearly) radically underestimate the incidence of concussion in the community.[12] As few as one in every four people, who experience concussion, will seek medical advice, let alone hospital attention, and then only if their symptoms persist.[13] The number of unreported concussions in sport may be much higher than that reported, due to the absence of official statistics.[14] In this context, players are more at risk of concussion in contact sports.[15]

Generally, a concussion results in the rapid onset of short-lived impairment of neurological function or symptoms, which resolves spontaneously.[16] The acute clinical symptoms largely reflect a functional disturbance rather than a structural injury.[17] As such, no abnormality is seen on standard structural neuroimaging studies.[18]

Finally, a concussion results in a graded set of clinical symptoms and signs, as well as functional impairment.[19]

---

[9]Erika A Diehl, 'What's All the Headache?: Reform Needed to Cope with the Effects of Concussions in Football' (2010) 23 *Journal of Law and Health* 83, 88.

[10]Tracey B Carter, 'Consent', above n 13 in Chapter 1, 346 and 348.

[11]Diehl, above n 9, 88.

[12]Brain Injury Australia, *Policy Paper: Concussion in Sport*, October 2012, 3 (<https://www.braininjuryaustralia.org.au/wp-content/uploads/CONCUSSIONpolicypaperFINAL.pdf>).

[13]Ibid.

[14]Ibid.

[15]Diehl, above n 9, 89. See also Christopher C Giza, 'Summary of Evidence-Based Guideline Update: Evaluation and Management of Concussion in Sport, Report of the Guideline Development Subcommittee of the American Academy of Neurology' (2013) 80 *Neurology* 2250, 2251–2.

[16]McCrory et al., '5th Consensus', above n 4, 839.

[17]Ibid.

[18]Standard structural neuroimaging studies include magnetic resonance imaging (MRI), computed tomography (CT) and electroencephalogram (EEG). See McCrory et al., '5th Consensus', above n 4, 839.

[19]Paul McCrory et al., 'Sports Concussion', in Brukner et al. (eds), *Brukner & Khan's Clinical Sports Medicine* (McGraw-Hill Australia, 5th ed, 2017, Vol. I, 'Injuries', Part B) 296, 300 (McCrory et al., 'Concussion').

III Symptoms, Grades of Concussion and Other Related Issues

Symptoms of concussion vary, and may include loss of consciousness.[20] The initial signs may include headaches, nausea, amnesia, balance problems, slurred speech and dizziness.[21] Excessive mood swings or personality changes may also occur.[22] Some patients complain about light or noise sensitivity, numbness or tingling, a sensation of feeling slowed down or 'in a fog'.[23] Difficulty with concentration and memory, visual problems and sleep disturbance are also listed.[24]

Historically, over 40 methods have been described to measure the grade of a concussion.[25] There was little agreement about which was the best.[26] This was particularly problematic in the field of sport, as return-to-play and return-to-practice[27] decisions were frequently based on evaluations usually made by team doctors employing one of these methods.[28]

Amongst medical associations and experts, the most common guidelines were those published by the American Academy of Neurology (AAN),[29] the Colorado Medical Society (CMS)[30] and the neurosurgeon expert Robert C Cantu,[31] all of which classified concussion on the basis of three grading scales (mild, moderate and severe). The AAN and CMS guidelines measured the severity of concussion by assigning a grade to the concussion at the time of the injury.[32] Both emphasised loss of consciousness and post-traumatic amnesia over other symptoms.[33] The Cantu guidelines placed less weight on loss of consciousness as a potential predictor of

[20]For more details, see eg, McCrory et al., '5th Consensus', above n 4, 839–40.

[21]Ibid.

[22]Ibid.

[23]Ibid.

[24]Ibid.

[25]Diehl, above n 9, 89.

[26]Ibid.

[27]'Return-to-practice' will be used in this thesis as a synonym for 'return-to-sport' (including any type of sport).

[28]Diehl, above n 9, 89.

[29]American Academy of Neurology, 'Practice Parameter, The Management of Concussion in Sports (Summary Statement), Report of the Quality Standards Subcommittee of the American Academy of Neurology' (1997) 48 *Neurology*, 581, 581–5.

[30]Colorado Medical Society, *Report of the Sports Medicine Committee, Guidelines for the Management of Concussions (Revised)* (Colorado Medical Society, 1991).

[31]Robert Cantu, 'Posttraumatic Retrograde and Anterograde Amnesia, Pathophysiology and Implications in Grading and Safe Return to Play' (2001) 36 *Journal of Athletic Training* 244, 244–8 (Cantu, 'Amnesia').

[32]For more details, see American Academy of Neurology, above n 29, 581–5; Colorado Medical Society, above n 30.

[33]Ibid.

subsequent impairment and additional weight on the overall persistence of symptoms.[34]

Grading methods have little by little been abandoned by the medical community.[35] In 2013, the AAN three-grading scale guidelines were formally removed and replaced by new guidelines.[36] The new guidelines mainly focus on specific risk factors, which can increase or decrease concussion-related consequences.[37] They recommend concussion be assessed in each athlete individually.[38] The CMS and the Cantu guidelines have also been superseded.[39]

At its 2nd 'International Conference on Concussion in Sport' (2004), in which expert Robert C Cantu participated,[40] the CISG confirmed the trend already decided three years earlier in Vienna.[41] It maintained in its 'Summary Statement' that the grading methods should be abandoned, in favour of a 'simple' or 'complex' classification.[42] In 2008, the CISG renounced the simple versus complex terminology.[43] However, it has since then kept the concept that most concussions heal in a short period (usually not more than 14 days), with a potential longer recovery time for children and teenagers.[44]

Usually concussion symptoms will resolve within a few days but can persist several weeks following an injury.[45] Occasionally, they last for over three months

---

[34]Cantu, 'Amnesia', above n 31, 244–8.

[35]See eg, W P Meehan, *Kids, Sports and Concussion* (Praeger, 2011) 26.

[36]Giza, above n 15, 2250–7, in particular 2250–1.

[37]These guidelines assert that ongoing clinical symptoms, concussion history, and younger age help identify those at risk for post-concussion impairments. Risk factors for recurrent concussion include history of multiple concussions, particularly within 10 days of initial injury. Concussion exposure and possible genetic predisposition (Apolipoprotein, APOE ε4 genotype) are particularly emphasised as risks factors for neurobehavioral impairment: Giza, above n 15, 2250–7, in particular 2250. Other guidelines, such as the CISG's guidelines, question the role of genetic predisposition in this matter: McCrory et al., '5th Consensus', above n 4, 841–2. For other potential risk factors, see this chapter, Section VII and Chapter 3, Section IA1(h), footnote 228.

[38]Giza, above n 15, 2250–7, in particular 2250.

[39]The obsolete nature of the CMS guidelines was acknowledged by the CMS: email from Chet Steward (Senior Director, Division of Health Care Policy, CMS) to author, 4 March 2015. About the Cantu guidelines, see this chapter, Section III, footnote 31.

[40]Robert C Cantu is one of co-authors of the 'Summary Statement' summarising the main findings of this conference.

[41]McCrory et al., '5th Consensus', above n 4, 197.

[42]P McCrory et al., 'Summary and Agreement Statement on the 2nd International Conference on Concussion in Sport, Prague 2004' (2005) 39 *British Journal of Sports Medicine* 196, 197 (McCrory et al., '2nd Consensus').

[43]P McCrory et al., 'Consensus Statement on Concussion in Sport: The 3rd International Conference on Concussion in Sport Held in Zurich, November 2008' (2009) 43 *British Journal of Sports Medicine* 76, 77 (McCrory et al., '3rd Consensus').

[44]McCrory et al., '5th Consensus', above n 4, 840 and 842–8.

[45]Kristina M Gerardi, 'Tackles that Rattle the Brain' (2011) 18 *Sports Lawyers Journal* 181, 186.

but these will generally resolve within a year.[46] Symptoms lasting longer than a year are unusual.[47]

There is a strong connection between the evaluation of concussion and return-to-play and return-to-practice decisions. The AAN's guidelines contain recommendations in this regard.[48] According to these guidelines, individuals supervising athletes should prohibit a concussed athlete from returning to play and practice until a licensed health care provider has judged that the concussion has resolved.[49] In addition, the athlete must be asymptomatic and off medication.[50] Complete retirement from playing should even be considered in the most serious cases that are usually associated with multiple instances of concussion.[51]

The 5th 'Consensus Statement on Concussion in Sport' (2017) contends that return-to-play should not occur on the day of a concussive injury.[52] It also provides a graduated and progressive return-to-practice protocol, according to which each athlete should continue to proceed to the next level if asymptomatic at the current level.[53] Usually each step lasts 24 hours.[54] An athlete will take approximately one week to reach full recovery once he or she is asymptomatic when at rest and under provocative exercise.[55] If post-concussion symptoms appear during rehabilitation, the athlete should return to the previous asymptomatic level and try to progress again after a further 24-hour period at rest.[56]

IV Diagnosis and Treatment

Diagnosis can be difficult, since concussion does not always manifest in an obvious or consistent way. Many patients may not be aware of their symptoms, or pay little attention to them.[57] The diagnosis may be further impeded in professional athletes,

---

46 Ibid, 186.

47 Ibid.

48 Giza, above n 15, 2254.

49 Ibid.

50 Ibid.

51 Ibid, 2254–5.

52 McCrory et al., '5th Consensus', above n 4, 843.

53 Ibid, 844.

54 Ibid.

55 Ibid.

56 Ibid.

57 Jennifer Ann Heiner, 'Concussions in the National Football League: Jani v Bert Bell/Pete Rozelle NFL Player Ret. Plan and Legal Analysis of the NFL's 2007 Concussion Management Guidelines' (2008) 18 *Seton Hall Journal of Sports and Entertainment* Law 255, 266; Andrew D Hohenstein, 'Team Physicians: Adhering to the Hippocratic Oath or Just Plain Hypocrites?' (2009) 19 *Marquette Sports Law Review* 579, 604–5.

who may not self-report concussive symptoms in order to keep on playing or to avoid appearing 'weak'.[58]

In addition, as already mentioned,[59] traditional neuroimaging techniques are generally not helpful. Their results frequently come back normal, even in cases of a severe concussion.[60]

Consequently, as things stand at present, the observations of the family, coaches and in particular team physicians, remain crucial during the days and weeks following an injury.[61]

Several guidelines, such as those of the AAN and the CISG, contain or refer to the various practice parameters currently available regarding symptom checklists, standardised assessments of concussion, and neuropsychological assessments.[62]

Standardised assessments receive particular attention. In many team sports, team physicians use sideline assessment tools.[63] The most utilised sideline assessment tool is the physical and cognitive test battery[64] called the 'Sport Concussion Assessment Tool' (SCAT), which is aimed at evaluating players immediately after a violent physical contact. The SCAT was produced as a result of the 2nd 'International Conference on Concussion in Sport' (2004).[65] Now in its 4th version (SCAT 5),[66] this test includes an initial exclusion of severe injury using the Glasgow Coma Scale,[67] followed by the observation and documentation of concussion symptoms and signs,[68] including neurocognitive and balance functions.[69] It can be performed in about 10 minutes.[70]

---

58 Diehl, above n 9, 90.

59 See this chapter, Section II.

60 Roger W Byard and Robert Vink, 'The Second impact Syndrome' (2009) 5 *Forensic Science, Medicine and Pathology* 36, 36.

61 Diehl, above n 9, 91.

62 Giza, above n 15, 2252; McCrory et al., '5th Consensus', above n 4, 839–41.

63 For concrete examples, see Chapter 3, Sections IA1(e) et seq (including subsequent case studies).

64 The term 'test battery' refers in the medical literature to a series of tests that are used together for the one purpose. In the case of the SCAT, there are several tests that assess different aspects of brain function.

65 McCrory et al., '2nd Consensus', above n 42, 198–201.

66 The various components of the SCAT 5 are described in more details in the accompanying documents of the latest 'Consensus Statement on Concussion in Sport' (2017) (<https://bjsm.bmj.com/content/early/2017/04/28/bjsports-2017-097506SCAT5>).

67 The Glasgow Coma Scale is the scale used for the extensive examination of head injuries. It is aimed to compare serial examinations of an injured athlete. Its score is based on numerically grading eye opening, motor response, and verbal response. It directly relates to the athlete's recovery prognosis: Michael Kent, *The Oxford Dictionary of Sports Science & Medicine* (Oxford University Press, 2006, 3rd ed), ad 'Glasgow Coma Scale', 231.

68 Kewin Guskiewicz et al., 'Evidence-Based Approach to revisiting the SCAT 2: Introducing the SCAT 3' (2013) 47 *British Journal of Sports Medicine* 289, 289 (Guskiewicz et al., 'SCAT 3').

69 Ibid, 289.

70 See accompanying documents of the latest 'Consensus Statement on Concussion in Sport' (2017) (<https://bjsm.bmj.com/content/early/2017/04/28/bjsports-2017-097506SCAT5>).

Screening computerised cognitive tests such as the 'Immediate Post-Concussion Assessment and Cognitive Testing' (ImPACT) and CogSport are widely used by team physicians once the game is over.[71] These tests, which can take up to 25 minutes, provide an additional neurocognitive assessment tool and service and are medically accepted as state-of-the-art practice.[72]

Team physicians may sometimes be assisted, or even replaced by other medical contributors (such as athletic trainers and independent doctors) to complete these tasks. Athletic trainers have long been active in this field in North America,[73] where the National Athletic Trainers' Association (NATA) has even provided them with specific medical guidelines.[74] The appearance of independent doctors is more recent.[75] It aims to mitigate the potential conflict of interest of team physicians and athletic trainers who owe loyalty both to the club that employs them, and the players they must treat.[76]

The primary treatment of concussion is rest and staged exercise, with an emphasis on prevention (aimed at managing the risk of re-injury).[77]

V Prevention

With regard to protective equipment, the AAN's guidelines indicate that it is highly probable that headgear use has a protective effect on concussion incidence in rugby.[78] These guidelines suggest that there is no compelling evidence that mouth guards protect athletes from concussion.[79] Current data is insufficient to support or refute the efficacy of protective football (soccer) headgear. The superiority of one type of football helmet over another in preventing concussion is controversial.[80]

The CISG's guidelines express a more conventional view by maintaining that there is limited evidence currently available demonstrating that protective equipment

---

[71] For more details, see ImPACT's website (<https://www.impacttest.com/about/>, <https://concussioncareresources.com/topic/impact-baseline-testing/>); and CogState's website (<https://www.cogstate.com/clinical-practice/concussion/>).

[72] For more details, see ImPACT's website (<https://www.impacttest.com/about/> and <https://concussioncareresources.com/topic/impact-baseline-testing/>).

[73] See eg, Chapter 3, Section ID1(a).

[74] See Broglio, Steven P, et al., 'National Athletic Trainers' Association Position Statement, Management of Sport Concussion' (2014) *Journal of Athletic Training* 245, 245.

[75] See Chapter 3, Sections IA1(e) et seq (including subsequent case studies).

[76] See Chapter 3, Section IA2(b).

[77] See eg, McCrory et al., '5th Consensus', above n 4, 840 and 842. For a detailed description of other possible treatments, see Ellemberg, above n 2, 209–33.

[78] Giza, above n 15, 2252.

[79] Ibid.

[80] Ibid. This appears to be a reference to helmets used in American and Canadian football.

can prevent concussion.[81] It recognises that changing the rules of play may be beneficial in some instances and emphasises the important role of player education.[82]

While helmets are traditionally considered with suspicion by medical experts,[83] convincing innovations in this field (helmet sensors,[84] new helmets concepts)[85] could reverse this trend. The same is true for mouthguards, which might be able to reduce concussive forces applied to the brain.[86]

VI 'Second-Impact Syndrome'

The 'second-impact syndrome' was first described in the literature in 1973, after the death of two young athletes.[87] Nevertheless, it was only in 1984 that the scientific community commonly adopted this term. Since then, 'second-impact syndrome' has been recognised as a rare complication, possibly leading to significant injury or death.[88] This secondary concussion condition occurs predominately in young individuals,[89] whose brains are still developing.[90] The proposed basis of this syndrome is that individuals who have sustained a second head injury before symptoms from the first have cleared[91] are at greater risk of further injury because of the first assault.[92] The second episode of trauma may not necessarily be severe.[93] It may occur during the same game or competition, or within days or weeks.[94] Affected

[81]McCrory et al., '5th Consensus', above n 4, 845.

[82]Ibid.

[83]Ibid.

[84]If they were to reach a sufficient level of reliability, they could help to efficiently detect blows to the head, while collecting reliable data for scientific purposes: Caleb Barker et al., 'NFL Concussions: The Current Situation and Policy Implications', A Section 6, Frontier Torts White Paper (Harvard Law School, 2012) 1, 42 (<http://learning.law.harvard.edu/frontiertorts/wp-content/uploads/2013/04/NFL-Concussions-White-Paper-2.pdf>).

[85]Ellemberg, above n 2, 243; Diehl, above n 9, 118.

[86]Diehl, above n 9, 117.

[87]Nicholas M Wetjen, Mark A Pichelmann and John LD Atkinson, 'Second Impact Syndrome: Concussion and Second Injury Brain Complications' (2010) 211 *Journal of the American College of Surgeons* 553, 553.

[88]Ibid, 553.

[89]Byard and Vink, above n 60, 37.

[90]Gavin A Davis and Laura K Purcell, 'The Evaluation and Management of Acute Concussion Differs in Young Children' (2014) 48 *British Journal of Sports Medicine* 98, 98–101.

[91]Byard and Vink, above n 60, 36; Robert C Cantu and Alisa D Jean, 'Second-Impact Syndrome and a Small Subdural Hematoma: An Uncommon Catastrophic Result of Repetitive Head Injury with a Characteristic Imaging Appearance' (2010) 27 *Journal of Neurotrauma* 1557, 1557.

[92]Byard and Vink, above n 60, 36.

[93]Cantu and Jean, above n 91, 1557.

[94]Ibid.

individuals often appear stunned but conscious. They are usually able to walk off the field on their own, before collapsing to the ground and showing evidence of respiratory failure within minutes of the event.[95]

In recent years, many medical experts have strongly questioned the existence of this syndrome.[96] According to these experts, it is more likely that a single impact of any severity, either alone or in combination with genetic predisposition, have resulted in this uncommon complication.[97]

Although somewhat controversial, the 'second-impact syndrome' has driven many of the current return-to-play guidelines following concussion.[98]

VII Long-Term Effects

The association between head trauma in sport and long-term neurodegenerative conditions, such as CTE (formerly referred to as 'punching syndrome' or 'dementia pugilistica') was first made in boxing, where investigations date back nearly a century.[99] The disease's potential ability to affect a broader population of athletes beyond boxing has come to public attention and been extensively studied only more

---

[95]Byard and Vink, above n 60, 37.

[96]See eg, Paul McCrory, Gavin Davis and Michael Makdissi, 'Second-Impact Syndrome or Cerebral Swelling After Sporting Head Injury' (2012) 11 *Current Sports Medicine Reports* 21, 21–3. See also Diehl, above n 9, 92.

[97]Ibid.

[98]McCrory, Davis and Makdissi, above n 96, 21. For more details about return-to-play guidelines, see this chapter, Section III.

[99]One of the first publications on the topic was a 1928 paper by Martland who called the condition he observed in boxers, 'punch drunk'. Martland hypothesized that the symptoms he observed at clinical examination (such as tremors, slowed movement, confusion, and speech problems) resulted from the repeated blows to the head that these fighters received during their careers: Harrison S Martland,'Punch Drunk' (1928) 15 *Journal of the Medical American Association* 1103, 1103–7. In 1937, Millspaugh outlined the disease marked by motor deficits and cognitive dysfunction under the name 'dementia pugilistica', as he too observed the disorder primarily in boxers: JA Millspaugh, 'Dementia Pugilistica' (1937) 35 *US Naval Medical Bulletin* 297, 297–303. In the only large-scale study of boxers to date, published in 1969, Roberts investigated 250 boxers from a cohort of 16 781 boxers in the United Kingdom (UK) and found 37 with neurological lesions (referred to as CTE), suggesting an overall prevalence of 17%: AH Roberts, *Brain Damage in Boxers: A Study of the Prevalence of Traumatic Encephalopathy Among Ex-Professional Boxers* (Pitman, 1969). In 1973, a group led by Corsellis described the typical neuropathological findings of dementia pugilistica after post-mortem examinations of the brains of 15 former boxers: JA Corsellis, CJ Bruton and D Freeman-Browne, 'The Aftermath of Boxing' (1973) 3 *Psychological Medicine* 270, 270–303. Subsequent forensic examinations confirmed these findings: see eg, JF Geddes et al., 'Neuronal Cytoskeletal Changes Are An Early Consequence Of Repetitive Head Injury' (1999) 98 *Acta Neuropathologica* 171, 171–8.

recently.[100] The full extent of long-term effects of head trauma on all athletes, as well as the exact role of other potential risk factors (such as genetic predisposition, medical illness, the use of illicit substances, alcohol consumption and age) remains unknown.[101] This absence of knowledge is accentuated in regard to the recently identified occurrence of CTE.[102]

The doubts of the scientific community are also reflected in some medical guidelines. The CISG's guidelines remain very conservative in this regard. They state that the causal link between exposure to contact sports and CTE still needs demonstrating.[103] Other guidelines, such as the AAN's guidelines, express a different view. They acknowledge, at least implicitly, causation across a broad range of professional sports,[104] it being noted that the frequency, intensity and mechanism of how a concussion, or even a sub-concussion,[105] occurs differs from one sport to another.[106] In any event, as it will be discussed later, convincing scientific studies postulating in favour of the acknowledgement of an extensive causal link are accumulating day by day.[107]

CTE is a progressive neurodegenerative brain disease found in people with a history of repetitive head trauma.[108] It triggers progressive degeneration of the brain tissue, including the build-up of a toxic protein called tau.[109] Typical symptoms of CTE include memory loss, confusion, impaired judgment, emotional instability,

---

[100] Ann C McKee 'Chronic Traumatic Encephalopathy in Athletes Progressive Tauopathy after Repetitive Head Injury' (2009) 68 *Journal of Neuropathology & Experimental Neurology* 709, 709 (McKee, 'Head Injury'); Joseph C Maroon et al., 'Chronic Traumatic Encephalopathy in Contact Sports, A Systematic Review of All Reported Pathological Cases' (February 2015) 10(2) *PlosOne* 1, 2.

[101] About the full extent of long-term effects of head trauma, see Roya Saffari, Lawrence S Chin and Robert C Cantu, 'From Concussion to Chronic Traumatic Encephalopathy: A Review' (2012) 6 *Journal of Clinical Sport Psychology* 352 and 358. Concerning the role of other risk factors, see the criticism raised by some medical experts, mentioned in Chapter 3, Section IA1(h), footnote 228.

[102] Concerning the role of other risk factors, see the criticism raised by some medical experts, mentioned in Chapter 3, Section IA1(h), footnote 228.

[103] McCrory et al., '5th Consensus', above n 4, 844.

[104] Giza, above n 15, in particular 2253.

[105] A sub-concussion is a minor head trauma that does not result in a known or diagnosed concussion on clinical grounds. Usually due to a cranial impact, it may also occur with rapid acceleration/deceleration of the body or torso. It has its greatest effect through repetitive occurrences whereby cumulative exposure becomes deleterious: Julian E Bailes et al., 'Role of Subconcussion in Repetitive Mild Traumatic Brain Injury, A Review' (2013) 119 *Journal of Neurosurgery* 1235, 1236.

[106] In the same vein, see McKee 'Head Injury', above n 100, 709. See also Chapter 3, Sections IA1 et seq.

[107] See Chapter 3, Sections IA1(b) et seq and IA1(h) et seq. About individual sports, see footnote 5 in Chapter 1.

[108] Robert A Stern et al., 'Clinical Presentation of Chronic Traumatic Encephalopathy' (2013) 81 *Neurology* 1122, 1122.

[109] Ibid, 1222.

erratic behaviour, impulsive anger-control problems and depression.[110] More advanced stages can include dementia or Parkinson's disease.[111] At present, CTE can only be diagnosed by post-mortem neuropathological analysis.[112]

Links between multiple head injuries and Alzheimer's disease have also been discussed within the scientific community.[113] Alzheimer's disease is a progressive brain disorder.[114] It is characterised by memory disturbances, along with the loss of other brain functions that affect the accomplishment of daily tasks.[115] It is associated with the destruction of brain cells and is the most common cause of dementia.[116]

Similarly, connections between multiple head injuries and Amyotrophic Lateral Sclerosis (ALS), commonly referred to as 'Lou Gehrig's disease',[117] have been reported.[118] ALS is a type of motor neurone disease with atrophy of skeletal muscles of the body,[119] resulting in difficulty speaking, swallowing and eventually breathing.[120]

Finally, possible links with other medical conditions, such as schizophrenia, brain tumours and epilepsy, have recently been noted.[121]

---

[110] Joseph M Hanna, 'Concussions May Prove to Be a Major Headache for the NFL' (2012) 84 *New York State Bar Association Journal* 10, 12 (Hanna, 'NFL'); ibid, 1122–3.

[111] Ibid.

[112] Christine Baugh et al., 'Chronic Traumatic Encephalopathy: Neurodegeneration Following Repetitive Concussive and Subconcussive Brain Trauma' (2012) 6 *Brain Imaging and Behavior* 244, 244.

[113] See eg, Robert Graham et al. (eds), *Sports Related Concussion in Youth, Improving the Science, Changing the Culture* (National Academy of Science, 2014) 223.

[114] Gerardi, above n 45, 188.

[115] Ibid.

[116] Ibid.

[117] See Chapter 3, Section ID1(a).

[118] For a summary of the medical literature, see Rudy J Castellani, 'Chronic Traumatic Encephalopathy: A Paradigm in Search Evidence' (2015) 95 *Laboratory Investigation* 576, 581–2.

[119] National Institute of Neurological Disorders and Stroke (NINDS) (<https://www.ninds.nih.gov/Disorders/Patient-Caregiver-Education/Fact-Sheets/Motor-Neuron-Diseases-Fact-Sheet>).

[120] Ibid.

[121] About the possible links between concussion and schizophrenia, see eg, Charlene Molloy et al., 'Is Traumatic Brain Injury A Risk Factor for Schizophrenia? A Meta-Analysis of Case-Controlled Population-Based Studies' (2011) 37 *Schizophrenia Bulletin* 1104, 1104–10. About concussion and brain tumours, see eg, S Dehghani et al., 'Intracranial Meningioma At the Site of a Previous Cranial Penetrating Trauma Due to Shrapnel' (2014) 25 *Journal of Craniofacial Surgery* 125, 125–7. About concussion and epilepsy, see eg, Réjean M Guerriero, Christopher C Giza and Alexander Rotenberg, 'Glutamate and GABA Imbalance Following Traumatic Brain Injury' (May 2015) 15(5) *Current Neurology and Neuroscience Reports* 1, 1–11.

VIII Areas for Further Research

Potential for significant improvement exists regarding the diagnosis of concussion, which could in the near future be detected with certainty through new kinds of neuroimaging devices,[122] or even blood tests.[123] Researchers also hope to use new tests based on eye movements to bring increased accuracy to the diagnosis of concussion.[124]

Pilot studies are currently being conducted in order to diagnose CTE in living patients by using Positron Emission Tomography (PET) scans.[125] Longitudinal studies related to the clinical symptoms of CTE in living individuals should also be undertaken.[126]

One can expect further studies on the exact influence of other risk factors that could potentially lead to CTE.[127] The effects of a single concussion (in relation to the 'second-impact syndrome'),[128] sub-concussion,[129] and the interaction of concussion and sub-concussion, together with the positions and contacts the most at risk, require further attention.[130] The same is true about the possible links between concussion and schizophrenia or even brain tumours.[131] Finally, the issue of concussion in women needs further investigation.[132]

---

[122]ML Lipton et al., 'Robust Detection of Traumatic Axonal Injury in Individual Mild Traumatic Brain Injury Patients: Intersubject Variation, Change Over Time and Bidirectional Changes in Anisotropy' (2012) 6 *Brain Imaging & Behaviour* 329, 329–42; Timothy B Meier et al., 'Recovery of Cerebral Blood Flow Following Sports-Related Concussion' (2015) 72 *JAMA Neurology* 530, 530–8.

[123]See eg, MJ Wadas et al., 'Detection of Traumatic Brain Injury Protein Biomarkers With Resonant Microsystems' (December 2017) 1(6) *Sensors Letters* 1, 1–4.

[124]Uzma Samadani et al., 'Eye Tracking Detects Disconjugate Eye Movements Associated with Structural Mild Traumatic Brain Injury and Concussion' (2015) 32 *Journal of Neurotrauma* 548, 548–56.

[125]See eg, Benet Omalu et al., 'Postmortem Autopsy-Confirmation of Antemortem [F-18]FDDNP-PET Scans in a Football Player With Chronic Traumatic Encephalopathy' (2018) 82 *Neurosurgery* 237, 237–46 (Omalu et al., 'Scans').

[126]Longitudinal studies would be particularly useful with regard to domestic violence issues (see Chapter 3. Section IA1(g)). See also the shortcomings raised by the judge in charge of the NFL settlement in relation to the clinical study of CTE (Chapter 3, Section IA2(a)(v), footnote 337).

[127]Concerning the role of other risk factors, see this chapter, Section VII, as well as the criticism raised by some medical experts, in Chapter 3, Section IA1(h), footnote 228.

[128]For more details about this topic, see this chapter, Section VI.

[129]Chad A Tagge et al., 'Concussion, Microvascular Injury, and Early Tauopathy in Young Athletes after Impact Head Injury and an Impact Concussion Mouse Model' (2018) 141 *Brain* 422, 452. These authors contend that early exposure to sub-concussion may induce early CTE brain pathologies.

[130]Ellemberg, above n 2, 51, 70–2 and 279.

[131]For more details about this topic, see this chapter, Section VII.

[132]Ellemberg, above n 2, 157–74. This author underlines that so far, scientific research on concussion has mainly been focused on a population of adult males (ibid, 157). See also Carrie

IX Outline of the Key Related Challenges

The medical issues surrounding concussion are multiple and challenging. Efforts to address concerns about public health and the appropriate legal and regulatory responses to concussion will require the comprehension of a number of complex medical and even technological matters. This thesis argues that central to those efforts will be the harmonisation of relevant laws and regulations.

Current medical guidelines provide a starting point for harmonisation, and the development of an international standard. They are currently used by SGBs to enact their own regulations, in particular their concussion management protocols.[133] They also provide very limited guidance regarding the rules of play, research and education.[134] However, the fact remains that there is no real current consensus concerning the guidelines to be applied.[135] With divergent opinions regarding the definition, prevention, diagnosis, management and even long-term effects of concussion, the biggest challenge to achieving harmonisation will be to at least develop or extract some principles on which to move forward bearing in mind the diversity of legal jurisdictions and sports.

The CISG's guidelines seem to have little by little gained some ground and are increasingly seen as being the main authority in this regard at an international level,[136] due to the level of expertise, diverse nationalities, key insights and powerful interest groups represented by the stakeholders involved. However, these guidelines must be viewed with caution.[137] First, they are designed by experts on behalf of SGBs, which are likely to be brought under court scrutiny in case of alleged mismanagement. They are prepared without the input from a wide range of perspectives, such as governments, athletes' advocates and medical associations. Although not prepared with the intention of being used in a court of law to assess the required standard of care, the fact remains that they raise problems in terms of independence.[138] This issue is particularly sensitive when it comes to the link between head

Arnold, 'Concussion in Women' (2014) 13 *The Lancet* 136, 136–7, who highlights the high rates of concussion in women, which could be explained by hormonal reasons, differences in the upper body, but also by the fact that women are more likely to report their symptoms.

[133]See Chapter 3, Sections IA1(e) et seq (including subsequent case studies).

[134]See this chapter, Sections V and VII.

[135]In the same vein (about football in the UK), see Gavin A Davis and Michael Makdissi, 'Concussion Tests: Clarifying Potential Confusion Regarding Sideline Assessment and Cognitive Testing' (2012) 46 *British Journal of Sports Medicine* 959, 959.

[136]See Chapter 3, Sections IA1(e) et seq (including subsequent case studies) and Chapter 4, Section IIIB.

[137]Most of the articles that follow were published before the publication of the latest version of the CISG's guidelines (2018; Online First 2017). However, the criticism that they express is still relevant.

[138]Note that members of the CISG's Medical Committee disclosed 132 potential conflicts of interest at the CISG's conference in Berlin (2016) [Peter Keating, 'Why Does it Seem Like Nobody Cares about Female Concussion', *ESPN*, 5 July 2017 (<http://www.espn.com/espnw/sports/article/19775123/why-does-seem-cares-female-concussions>)].

trauma and CTE, which the CISG's guidelines, unlike other guidelines, do not acknowledge.[139]

Secondly, attention has been drawn in the medical literature to the theoretical (rather than operational) approach used by the CISG's guidelines when determining the existence of concussion.[140] This theoretical approach is problematic when it comes to determine which injuries should be considered as concussion for the purposes of injury surveillance.[141] The same is true about the exact time when the SCAT should be conducted.[142] Similarly, the CISG's guidelines have endorsed clinical decisions as being the basis for concussion diagnosis without providing any information about the typical validity or reliability of concussion diagnosis (suggesting gaps regarding the sensitivity and specificity of the test).[143] Also, the extent to which any given sign or symptom, or combination thereof, is typically associated with a clinical diagnosis of concussion being made is not clearly determined.[144]

Furthermore, some experts have highlighted the current confusion in practice between sideline assessment and cognitive testing.[145] They note, in particular, that the primary goal of sideline assessment tools, such as the SCAT, developed by the CISG, is to assist with the diagnosis of concussion on sidelines, with a secondary use of monitoring recovery over time.[146] These tests should be used in addition to a medical assessment; not as stand-alone instruments.[147] While they contain some brief cognitive screening tools, they are not a complete cognitive assessment.[148] The next level of cognitive testing involves screening computerised cognitive tests, such as ImPact and CogSport.[149] These test batteries are not suitable for on-field diagnosis of concussion, but are screening tools for cognitive assessment.[150] They have utility in monitoring athletes diagnosed with concussion, especially when used with baseline pre-season assessment.[151] They are not as reliable as the ultimate level of

[139]See this chapter, Section VII.

[140]Kenneth Lincoln Quarie and Ian Robert Murphy, 'Towards an Operational Definition of Sports Concussion': Identifying a Limitation in the 2012 Zurich Consensus Statement and Suggesting Solutions' (2014) 48 *British Journal of Sports Medicine* 1589, 1589–91.

[141]Ibid, 1589–90. As to the nature and process of injury surveillance, see Chapter 3, Sections IA1 (h) et seq (including subsequent case studies).

[142]Ibid, 1590.

[143]Ibid.

[144]Ibid.

[145]Davis and Makdissi, above n 135, 959.

[146]Ibid.

[147]Ibid.

[148]Ibid.

[149]Ibid.

[150]Ibid.

[151]Ibid. Baseline tests consist of memory exercises given to players before suffering from a concussion to determine the level of their cognitive ability. These tests are repeated once a concussion has occurred. The two results are compared, in order to determine when players can

cognitive testing, the formal neuropsychological assessment performed by an expert neuropsychologist.[152]

Confusion in the assessment of concussion is not surprising, given the fact that the CISG's guidelines, like other guidelines, are still struggling to reach their target audience.[153] According to a study published in 2012 regarding return-to-play practices in professional football in the United Kingdom (UK), 27.8% of the respondents were not aware of the CISG's guidelines.[154] The same ignorance regarding medical guidelines has been observed in Australian rugby.[155] To this day, the main path for the dissemination of the CISG's guidelines is through published statements in leading peer-reviewed journals aimed at sports medicine professionals.[156] The difficulty remains as to how to disseminate efficiently, and on a large-scale, the correct information about concussion management to players, coaches and health providers.[157]

The CISG's guidelines have also raised controversy within the medical profession regarding their alleged absence of evidence-based management strategies and unattainable rehabilitation goals.[158] Thus, some commentators consider that concussed players should be forced to wait more than one week before getting back into competition.[159]

A final remark about the content of the CISG's guidelines is that, like other guidelines, they do not refer to an important parameter of concussion prevention and scientific understanding: injury surveillance.[160] In particular, they do not indicate what data could be collected, how that might occur and the conditions under which

return to play: Heiner, above n 57, 262; Hecht, above n 2, 50. The tests are reliable, as long as players do not cheat by intentionally scoring lower on the initial test.

[152]Davis and Makdissi, above n 135, 959.

[153]In the same vein, see Caroline F Finch and Peta White, 'The New Concussion in Sport Guidelines Are here. But how do We Get them out there?' (2017) 51 *British Journal of Sports Medicine* 1734, 1734.

[154]Jo Price, Peter Malliaras and Zoe Hudson, 'Current Practices in Determining Return to Play following Head Injury in Professional Football in the UK' (2012) 46 *British Journal of Sports Medicine* 1000, 1001.

[155]Alex Donaldson et al., 'Translating Guidelines for the Diagnosis and Management of Sports-Related Concussion into Practice' (2016) 10 *American Journal of Lifestyle Medicine* 120, 122.

[156]Finch and White, above n 153, 1734.

[157]Ibid, 1734–5.

[158]For more details, see eg, Neil Craton and Leslie Oliver, 'Time to Re-think the Zurich Guidelines?: A Critique on the Consensus Statement on Concussion in Sport: The 4th International Conference on Concussion in Sport, Held in Zurich, November 2012' (2014) 24 *Clinical Journal of Sports Medicine* 93, 93–5.

[159]Bunworth, above n 13 in Chapter 1, 92.

[160]McCrory et al., '5th Consensus', above n 4, 838–47 (a contrario). About other guidelines, see eg, Giza, above n 15, 2250–7 (a contrario).

the data might be stored, retrieved and shared.[161] They are also silent on the possible financial support to be provided to concussed players.[162]

Apart from the question of the choice and the content of medical guidelines to be applied, the next significant challenge, in terms of harmonisation, will be how SGBs interpret these guidelines and adapt them to their own sporting codes. Medical guidelines operate in a fairly general way. Their implementation in a specific sporting context will require more guidance, in order to achieve high standards from a public health perspective, and ensure the wellbeing of athletes. Some SGBs (11 in total),[163] made an important step in this direction by meeting in Dublin in 2017. This meeting led to the publication, in 2018, of an 'implementation paper' aimed at harmonising the interpretation of the CISG's guidelines, discuss impediments to implementation, exchange information on current practice and identify areas for collaboration among team contact and collision sports.[164] This paper is, however, primarily intended to summarise current practices.[165] It only makes a few recommendations, and does not provide definitive authority.[166] It leaves various grey areas (starting with the person in charge of players' assessment), and is deprived from the support of important federations, such as FIFA.[167]

Similarly, even if the use of medical guidelines could facilitate the harmonisation process, they are not exhaustive in terms of areas covered, and are not intended to be. This raises the question of who fills the gaps, if necessary, and how. Conversely, medical guidelines might potentially conflict with the legal standards created by governments.[168]

Finally, the harmonisation process will have to accommodate the uncertainty linked to current medical scientific and technological knowledge, together with the lack of long-term data. This uncertainty can be observed at all stages of the medical

---

[161] Ibid.

[162] Ibid.

[163] These 11 SGBs include the AFL, the Gaelic Athletics Association (GAA), Hockey Canada, the IIHF, the International Ski Federation (FIS), the NCAA, the NFL, the NHL, the NRL, The English Football Association (The FA) and World Rugby. They were accompanied by a few international federation (IF) observers, such as the International Cricket Council (ICC), the International Basketball Federation (FIBA) and FIFA.

[164] Jon S Patricios et al., 'Implementation of the 2017 Berlin Concussion in Sport Group Consensus Statement in Contact and Collision Sports: A Joint Position Statement from 11 National and International Sports Organisations' (2018) 52 *British Journal of Sports Medicine* 635, 635.

[165] Ibid, 635.

[166] Ibid, 635–41.

[167] Ibid. FIFA, which only took part in the Dublin meeting as an observer (see this chapter, footnote 163), did not co-author nor adhere to this paper. It is expected that the paper will be completed with additional harmonisation initiatives, including a follow-up meeting at the end of 2018, and increased collaboration in the area of video surveillance [Gavin A Davis et al., 'International Study of Video Review of Concussion in Professional Sports' (September 2018; Online First) *British Journal of Sports Medicine* 1, 1 and 6].

[168] See eg, the youth concussion laws/guidelines discussed in Chapter 3, Sections IA1(f), IIA1 and IIB1(a).

process, from the prevention of concussion to the determination of its long-term effects. The new medical scientific and technological developments[169] will have to be followed closely.

[169]See this chapter, Sections V and VIII.

Chapter 3
National Case Studies

> Your work suggests. . .that football is a dangerous sport, and that if 10 per cent of mothers in this country would begin to perceive football as a dangerous sport, that is the end of football.
>
> Joseph Maroon, an NFL doctor, to Dr Bennet Omalu, after being confronted with Omalu's research on the link between American football and long-term neurological issues; reported in the movie 'Concussion', 2015.

Chapter 3 comprises national case studies, which depict and analyse the current regulation of concussion in sport. It describes, examines and analyses the data collected from a number of selected countries and sports. It forms the backbone of this thesis, as it not only analyses the current state of the situation but also enables the initiation of a reflection on the reforms to be conducted.

The national case studies focus on selected professional team sports and countries that have a history of, or potential for, CTE and litigation:

(1) US (American football, ice hockey, football, water polo, baseball);
(2) Canada (Canadian football);
(3) Australia (rugby, Australian Rules football);
(4) Switzerland (football, ice hockey), England (football) and Brazil (football).[1]

The national case studies include two distinct categories of sports: those governed by International Federations (IFs) and those under the authority of sports leagues.[2] IFs have, by definition, an international influence. They create a common set of rules that trickle down to national levels, and organise international competitions. They are part of the Olympic Movement, and recognise the jurisdiction of the Court of Arbitration for Sport (CAS) by means of arbitration clauses contained in their

---

[1]The case studies mainly focus on professional men's sports, which have until now attracted most of the concussion controversy. Nevertheless, their lessons may also apply to women's sports, within the available financial means.

[2]The case of ice hockey is quite unique, since it is governed by an IF (the IIHF), apart from in North America, where the NHL is competent.

A. Veuthey, *Concussion in Professional Team Sports: Time for a Harmonised Approach?*, https://doi.org/10.1007/978-981-15-1979-6_3

respective regulations. Sports leagues, primarily in North America, govern, in most cases, their national competitions autonomously.[3] They evolve outside the Olympic Movement,[4] negotiate their rules with players' associations through the process of collective bargaining[5] and resolve their disputes by means of specific arbitration mechanisms. Both IFs and sports leagues may, however, take action on player safety, and concussion in particular, through the rules of play, rules of the game[6] and concussion protocols, financial support for injured athletes,[7] education, research and data collection.

In relation to the case studies, the same chronological structure is used, with specific attention on two main pillars: 'public health' (related to the prevention and management of concussion) and 'legal risks' (related to litigation and compensation). The 'public health' part puts into perspective, on the one hand, the incidence, causes, types and short/long-term effects of concussion on injured athletes and, on the other hand, the diverse responses of SGBs and governments. The 'legal risks' part examines the incidence and nature of (or potential for) legal proceedings against SGBs.

The chapter demonstrates that the concussion controversy has recently manifested on a large scale and, therefore, requires the implementation of a harmonised solution across sports and legal systems. It also emphasises some emerging good practices as well as perceived shortcomings, and thereby indirectly displays the means by which the concussion issue could be better regulated worldwide from both a legal and public health perspective. It allows in particular gathering information about the potential content of an international standard (aimed at establishing the regulatory duties and practical actions expected by SGBs) and its related international convention (aimed at clarifying the supportive role of governments).

---

[3]The most notable exception is Major League Soccer (MLS), which is hierarchically subject to FIFA. In addition, there are pseudo-IFs (International Football American Federation/IFAF, Rugby League International Federation/RLIF), which do not exercise authority over their respective leagues in practice.

[4]It should be noted that certain leagues might sometimes allow their athletes to participate in the Olympic Games on the basis of agreements negotiated with the IOC. Such is the case of the NHL, which may be joined by MLB in the future.

[5]Collective bargaining refers to the negotiations undertaken between an employer and the representatives of organised employees to determine the conditions of employment. These negotiations usually result in a contract, entitled 'collective bargaining agreement' (CBA) [Bryan A Garner (ed), *Black's Law Dictionary* (Thomson Reuters, 10th ed, 2014) ad 'collective bargaining', and 'collective bargaining agreement', 320].

[6]The rules of play govern the ways in which a sport is played and define its essence (eg, the ban imposed on football players to use their hands). The rules of the game have a broader meaning, as they include, for instance, substitution rules.

[7]This thesis only aims to give an overview of the financial support provided to injured athletes. Moreover, it will not examine ancillary issues, such as private insurance concluded on behalf of athletes.

I United States of America (US)

A American Football: The National Football League (NFL)

American football provides by far the most high profile and furthest reaching example of the incidence of concussive episodes in professional team sports to date, both in terms of public health and legal risks. This state of affairs stems from the relevantly scientifically confirmed high-risk nature of American football,[8] and the reluctance of the major professional league, the NFL, to acknowledge and seriously address the issue until quite recently;[9] but also from the involvement of the US state and federal governments, and the use of litigation aimed at providing compensation for injured players and their families, which led to the payment of a record sum by the NFL.

The position is best understood by commencing with a chronological description of the evolution of scientific knowledge juxtaposed with the remedial measures gradually taken by the NFL and the US state and federal governments. The starting point is the concern expressed from the early 1900s about the dangers of American football, as well as the measures adopted in response by the NFL from the mid-1940s. It will emerge that the excessively reassuring position put forward by the NFL for decades, based on its very controversial internal studies, has definitively been swept away by the progress of science from the mid-2000s. This was followed by the beginning of US state and federal governments' involvement and the end of the NFL's denial.

This chronological account is followed by an examination of legal issues, through the lens of liability. The analysis extends from the first legal procedures filed by former professional players in the late-2000s against the NFL (subsequently consolidated into a single class action lawsuit) to a settlement in the mid-2010s. The potential liability of other contributors is also briefly discussed.

The section ends with a summary of the main findings. It explains to what extent and how the NFL case study justifies and informs the conceptualisation of a more harmonised, collaborative solution aimed at better regulating the public health and legal risks associated with concussion across sports and legal systems. In that regard, some key points to emerge from the NFL experience may be briefly stated as follows:

The NFL case study sheds light on numerous short and long-term medical complications associated with concussion in American football. These medical complications, which have also started to be documented in other sports, are illustrated by the increasing volume of players' suicides, violent behaviour and

[8]The expression 'scientifically confirmed hig-risk nature' is used throughout this thesis to refer to sports in which there have been confirmed diagnoses of CTE.

[9]The IFAF, continental associations, and USA Football, the national governing body for American football in the US, will not be examined. They have very limited authority at the international and professional levels respectively.

early retirements, as well as by the numerous CTE cases recently established by autopsy. They greatly demonstrate the need for a proactive and consistent public health approach. The analysis of the NFL's and the US state and federal governments' responses in this regard, which manifested, on the one hand, through various new safety rules and other measures of concussion management and, on the other hand, through Congressional, regulatory and other practical interventions, is evidently of interest for American football. Due to the general experience gained and the sometimes transversal nature of the governments' intervention, this analysis is also relevant for other SGBs and countries, which are currently having great difficulty tackling this issue, often in isolation. It will, therefore, crucially contribute to the discussion related to the adoption of a harmonised public health regulatory framework. This contribution will be made both from a negative and positive perspective, the NFL and the US governments having delayed action, before taking measures that, despite a number of shortcomings, are now moving in the right direction.

The analysis of the NFL concussion litigation, and in particular the class action commenced in 2012, provides lessons in terms of legal risks. On an unprecedented scale (nearly 5000 plaintiffs involved) and media coverage, it resulted in 2015 in a USD1 billion settlement, and was the trigger for subsequent legal proceedings filed against other SGBs. It shows to what extent SGBs, like the NFL, are exposed to the legal (financial and reputational) risks associated with concussion. Against the backdrop of medical controversies with sometimes unclear legal consequences, it also demonstrates the legal complexity and flaws of such litigation, and illustrates the now widespread legal uncertainty that this thesis seeks to address.

More broadly, the NFL case study highlights a series of key relationships that, by their reactive, or even competitive and adversarial nature, negatively affect the interests of all the stakeholders involved, and underline the need to ensure harmony at an international level.

1 Chronology

(a) The Position of the NFL before the National Public Controversy

American football has been regarded as a dangerous sport for almost as long as it has been played.[10] In the early 1900s, President Theodore Roosevelt, known for being a tough man, expressed his disquiet in this regard, urging radical reforms to the rules of play, or even a ban of football.[11] In a study of injuries in American football and other sports published in 1952,[12] a sports medicine expert from Harvard University

---

[10]Greenhow, 'Charter', above n 13 in Chapter 1, 1.

[11]Gerardi, above n 45 in Chapter 2, 154.

[12]Augustus Thorndike, 'Serious Recurrent Injuries of Athletes – Contraindications to Further Competitive Participation' (1952) 247 *New England Journal of Medicine* 554, 554.

highlighted the potential risks of concussion. He opined that football players sustaining more than three instances of concussion or with more than momentary loss of consciousness should not be exposed to further body-contact trauma.[13] The study, which was in line with warnings previously issued by the American Football Coaches Association, paved the way for a substantial body of medical literature mindful of players' protection.[14]

It was not until the 1940s that the NFL made significant changes to player safety, when it made helmet use compulsory in 1943 with transitory arrangements allowing some flexibility until 1947.[15] The helmets, made of padded leather, were later replaced by polymer helmets, to which a facemask was added.[16] In the 1960s and 1970s, new rules of play were put in place, such as the prohibition against grabbing another player's facemask, the head slap,[17] and the use of helmets as weapons.[18]

In 1996, referees were required to call in-game personal fouls by defenders for helmet-to-helmet hits[19] with a view to better protecting quarterbacks.[20] Six years later, this prohibition was extended to all players.[21]

Meanwhile, players were becoming bigger, stronger and quicker, leading to more frequent and rougher contacts.[22]

In response to the growing concern for player safety and concussion, the NFL established, in 1994, the Mild Traumatic Brain Injury ('MTBI') Committee with the stated goal of studying the causes and effects of concussion on its players.[23] This Committee was chaired by Dr Elliot Pellman, a rheumatologist and New York Jets' associate team physician.[24] Under Dr Pellman's supervision, the MTBI Committee published a thirteen-part study.[25] This study, based on data collected between 1996 and 2001, pointed out the assumed causes of concussion (such as helmet hits and

---

[13]Ibid, 555–6.

[14]This literature was summed up by the plaintiffs in the context of the class action that will be discussed further (see this chapter, Section IA2(a)(iv), in particular footnote 292. This footnote refers to the amended master complaint, [pp. 23–32, paragraphs 108–47] and amended class action complaint [pp. 22–30, paragraphs 89–127], which recount chronologically the main developments in this matter).

[15]Ira Berkow, *Giants Among Men: Y.A., L.T., the Big Tuna and Other New York Giants Stories* (Triumph Books, 2015) 87; Gerardi, above n 45 in Chapter 2, 154.

[16]Gerardi, above n 45 in Chapter 2, 218.

[17]A headslap occurs when an opposing player, mainly on the defensive side of the ball, takes his hand and slaps the offensive player on the helmet.

[18]Jeremy P Gove, 'Three and Out: the NFL's Concussion Liability and How Players Can Tackle the Problem' (2012) 14 *Vanderbilt Journal of Entertainment and Technology Law* 649, 656–7.

[19]A 'hit' is a common expression to describe physical contact of a violent kind in the US.

[20]Heiner, above n 57 in Chapter 2, 271.

[21]Ibid.

[22]Gerardi, above n 45 in Chapter 2, 191 and 193.

[23]Gove, above n 18, 658.

[24]Ibid, 659.

[25]Greenhow, 'Charter', above n 13 in Chapter 1, 5.

tackles),[26] as well as the positions deemed most vulnerable in terms of absolute risks (defensive secondaries) and relative risks (quarterbacks and wide receivers).[27] More controversially, the study determined that there was no increased risk after multiple instances of concussion and no slower recovery period for players with a history of concussion.[28] It stated that most concussed players could 'quickly' return to play,[29] and highlighted the fact that returning to play during the same game did not involve a significant risk of a second injury in that same game or during the season.[30] Players' baseline test scores were also outlined, with allegedly no measurable differences in the testing conducted before the season started and after a concussion occurred.[31]

The scientific community was highly critical of Dr Pellman's lack of competence and independence.[32] It rejected the findings of the study, in particular those related to the effects of concussion on players (and the prescribed management requirements resulting from it). This was on account of it being in total contradiction with the research published previously by numerous other experts in the field.[33]

This strong criticism, as well as the increased number of early retirement cases among professional players due to multiple instances of concussion,[34] did not change the position of the NFL. The NFL kept on referring to its own findings, even going so far as to subsequently using its controversial study to create its first concussion guidelines.[35]

The pressure on the NFL, from the scientific community, increased.

---

[26]Elliot J Pellman et al., 'Concussion in Professional Football: Epidemiological Features of Game Injuries and Review of the Literature, Part 3' (2004) 54 *Neurosurgery* 81, 81, 85 and 87 (Pellman, 'Part 3').

[27]Ibid, 81 and 84–5. Absolute risks refer to the total number of concussions sustained for each position, while relative risks relate to the concussion rate per 100-game positions.

[28]Elliot J Pellman et al., 'Concussion in Professional Football: Repeat Injuries, Part 4' (2004) 55 *Neurosurgery* 860, 869 (Pellman, 'Part 4).

[29]Ibid, 860.

[30]Elliot J Pellman et al., 'Concussion in Professional Football: Players Returning to the Same Game, Part 7' (2005) 56 *Neurosurgery* 79, 79 (Pellman, 'Part 7').

[31]Elliot J Pellman et al., 'Concussion in Professional Football: Neuropsychological Testing, Part 6' (2004) 55 *Neurosurgery* 1290, 1298 (Pellman, 'Part 6').

[32]Gove, above n 18, 649 and 658–9.

[33]The criticism by the scientific community towards the MTBI's thirteen-part study was expressed by means of commentaries and right of reply published in the medical literature. For more details, see Heiner, above n 57 in Chapter 2, 261–4.

[34]Note that these early retirement cases, which really started to draw the attention of observers in the early 2000's [see, eg, Hecht, above n 2 in Chapter 2, 19], were mainly motivated by persistent symptoms of post-concussion syndrome [Gerardi, above n 45 in Chapter 2, 192]. As a result of scientific advancements (see eg, this chapter, Sections IA1(b) and IA1(h)) and growing awareness of potential long-term trauma associated with multiple instances of concussion, instances of early retirements have increased, reaching an unprecedented number.

[35]See this chapter, Section IA1(c). See also Bernstein, above n 2 in Chapter 2, 283.

(b) Game-Changing Science (2005–8)

In 2005, forensic examinations undertaken by two renowned neuropathologists, Dr Bennet Omalu (then affiliated to the University of Pittsburgh) and Dr Robert Cantu (co-founder of the Sports Legacy Institute of Boston), confirmed the fears of the scientific community.[36] Drs Omalu and Cantu found that multiple instances of concussion can lead to depression and early-onset dementia.[37] They analysed the brain tissue of three deceased former NFL players: Mike Webster, Terry Long, and Andre Waters.[38]

Mike Webster, a former Pittsburgh Steelers center, died in 2002, aged 50, from a heart attack.[39] Terry Long, an alumnus of the Steelers, died in 2004, aged 45, from drinking antifreeze.[40] Andre Waters, ex-Philadelphia Eagles safety, died two years later from a self-inflicted gunshot to the head at the age of 44.[41]

These three players shared a history of multiple instances of concussion.[42] After their retirement from sport, each had experienced symptoms of sharply deteriorated cognitive function and psychiatric symptoms such as paranoia, panic attacks and depression.[43] Based on medico-legal examination, Drs Omalu and Cantu concluded

---

[36]See this chapter, Section IA1(a). See also Greenhow, 'Charter', above n 13 in Chapter 1, 4, footnote 25.

[37]Bennet I Omalu et al., 'Chronic Traumatic Encephalopathy in a National Football League Player' (2005) 57 *Neurosurgery* 128, 128 and 130–2 (about the 'Mike Webster' case) (Omalu et al., 'NFL Player I'); Bennet I Omalu et al., 'Chronic Traumatic Encephalopathy in a National Football League Player: Part II' (2006) 59 *Neurosurgery* 1086, 1086 and 1090–1 (about the 'Terry Long' case) (Omalu et al., 'NFL Player II)'; Bennet I Omalu et al., 'Chronic Traumatic Encephalopathy (CTE) in a National Football League Player: Case Report and Emerging Medicolegal Practice Questions' (2010) 6 *Journal of Forensic Nursing* 40, 40 and 43–5 (about the 'Andrew Waters' case) (Omalu et al., 'NFL Player III'). See also Robert C Cantu, 'Chronic Traumatic Encephalopathy in the National Football League' (2007) 61 *Neurosurgery* 223, 223 (Cantu, 'CTE') (about the three cases).

[38]Omalu et al., 'NFL Player I', above n 37, 128–34 (about the 'Mike Webster' case); Omalu et al., 'NFL Player II', above n 37, 1086–92 (about the 'Terry Long' case); Omalu et al., 'NFL Player III', above n 37, 40–6 (about the 'Andrew Waters' case). See also Cantu, 'CTE', above n 37, 223–5 (about the three cases).

[39]Omalu et al., 'NFL Player I', above n 37, 223.

[40]Omalu et al., 'NFL Player II', above n 37, 1087–8. See also Cantu, 'CTE', above n 37, 223.

[41]Omalu et al., 'NFL Player III', above n 37, 41–2. See also Cantu, 'CTE', above n 37, 223.

[42]Omalu et al., 'NFL Player I', above n 37, 129 (about the 'Mike Webster' case); Omalu et al., 'NFL Player II', above n 37, 1087 (about the 'Terry Long' case); Omalu et al., 'NFL Player III', above n 37, 41 (about the 'Andrew Waters' case). See also Cantu, 'CTE', above n 37, 223 (about the three cases).

[43]Omalu et al., 'NFL Player I', above n 37, 129 (about the 'Mike Webster' case); Omalu et al., 'NFL Player II', above n 37, 1087–8 (about the 'Terry Long' case); Omalu et al.,'NFL Player III', above n 37, 41–2 (about the 'Andrew Waters' case). See also Cantu, 'CTE', above n 37, 223 (about the three cases).

that CTE caused by multiple instances of concussion had contributed to the players' deaths.[44] Their brain tissue was severely affected, the medical transcripts even likening Water's brain to that of an octogenarian or nonagenarian Alzheimer's patient.[45]

These clinical studies, which were confirmed shortly afterwards by further studies performed by the same experts (2007),[46] constituted a significant turning point in relevant medical understanding.[47] They were also soon supported by other researchers.

In 2005, Dr Kevin Guskiewicz (University of North Carolina) conducted a survey on more than 2550 former NFL athletes.[48] He found that athletes who had suffered at least three episodes of concussion in their careers had a fivefold prevalence of Mild Cognitive Impairment (MCI) diagnosis compared to those who had no history of concussion.[49]

Finally, in 2008, Dr Ann McKee (Boston University School of Medicine) studied the brain tissue of deceased NFL alumni John Grimsely and Tom McHale.[50] John Grimsely, ex-Houston Oilers linebacker, died in 2008 from an accidental gunshot wound at 46 years old.[51] Thomas McHale, ex-Tampa Bay Buccaneers offensive guard, died during the same year at 45 years old, due to an apparent drug overdose.[52] Dr McKee discovered clear signs of CTE on both players.[53] She also acknowledged that the risk of developing CTE increased after several head injuries.[54]

These studies, all coming to the same conclusion, did not seem to make the NFL excessively concerned.

---

[44]Omalu et al., 'NFL Player I', above n 37, 128 and 130–2 (about the 'Mike Webster' case); Omalu et al., 'NFL Player II', above n 37, 1086 and 1090–1 (about the 'Terry Long' case); Omalu et al., 'NFL Player III', above n 37, 40 and 43–5 (about the 'Andrew Waters' case). See also Cantu, 'CTE', above n 37, 223 (about the three cases).

[45]Omalu et al., 'NFL Player III', above n 37, 44 (about the 'Andrew Waters' case). See also Cantu, 'CTE', above n 37, 223 (about the three cases).

[46]See eg, the case of Justin Strzelczyk, who died in a car accident in 2004 at the age of 36. For more details, see Joel Michael Ugolini, 'Even a Violent Game has its Limits: a Look at the NFL's Responsibility for the Behavior of its Players' 39 (2007) *University of Toledo Law Review* 41, 50.

[47]In the same vein, see eg, Hanna, 'NFL', above n 110 in Chapter 2, 11.

[48]Kevin M Guskiewicz et al., 'Association between Recurrent Concussion and Late-Life Cognitive Impairment in Retired Professional Football Players' (2005) 57 *Neurosurgery* 719, 719–22 (Guskiewicz et al., 'Impairment').

[49]Ibid, 722.

[50]McKee 'Head Injury', above n 100 in Chapter 2, 710.

[51]Boston University, 'Football And Progressive Brain Damage: Tom McHale Of NFL Suffered From Chronic Traumatic Encephalopathy When He Died In 2008' *ScienceDaily*, 27 January 2009 (<www.sciencedaily.com/releases/2009/01/090127165938.htm>).

[52]Ibid.

[53]McKee, 'Head Injury', above n 100 in Chapter 2, 710.

[54]Ibid, 732.

(c) The Reaction of the NFL (2005–8)

Despite the medical evidence, the MTBI Committee kept on denying any causal link between head trauma and later-life cognitive decline.[55] It claimed that more research was necessary to reach a definitive conclusion.[56]

In response to Dr Omalu's report on the first CTE case, MTBI members Ira Casson, Elliot Pellman and David Viano wrote a letter to the editor of the *Neurosurgery* journal, asking that the article in question be removed.[57] The subtext of their letter, referring pejoratively to Dr Omalu, was clear: 'We own this field. We are not going to bow to some no-name Nigerian with some bullshit theory'.[58]

Simultaneously, MTBI Committee member Mark Lovell criticised the results of Dr Guskiewitz's study as being unreliable, since they were based on subjective statements.[59]

During its first Concussion Summit in June 2007, the NFL produced and disseminated a brochure aimed at players that simply indicated that 'there is no magic number for how many concussions is too many'.[60] Furthermore, following the publication of Dr McKee's findings in 2009, Dr Casson maintained that current research on the subject was unreliable and inconclusive.[61]

Contrary to its constant denials, the NFL announced various adjustments to player safety. As a result, in June 2007, the NFL adopted its first concussion guidelines, based on previous highly controversial publications of the MTBI Committee.[62] In spite of this obvious resort to the past, the guidelines introduced a few positive steps. These included the establishment of a standardised baseline testing for all players, as well as the implementation of a whistle blower system allowing anyone to report to the league when a concussed player was pressured to practise or play against medical advice.[63] Finally, the team medical personnel was urged not to let a concussed player return to the field during the same game if there had been loss of consciousness.[64]

---

[55] Greenhow, 'Charter', above n 13 in Chapter 1, 7.

[56] Ibid.

[57] Joseph Hanna and Daniel Kain, 'NFL's Shaky Concussion Policy Exposes the League to Potential Liability Headaches' (Fall 2010) 28(3) *Entertainment and Sports Lawyer* 9, 9.

[58] This remark was attributed to MTBI members by many authors. See eg, ibid, 9.

[59] Hanna and Kain, above n 57, 9.

[60] Ibid.

[61] Ibid, 9-10.

[62] See this chapter, Section IA1(a). See also Bernstein, above n 2 in Chapter 2, 283.

[63] Gerardi, above n 45 in Chapter 2, 222–3.

[64] Ibid, 223.

These new measures were accompanied by minor rule changes, such as the introduction of increased penalties in case of a block below the waist against an eligible receiver in the protection zone (pocket area).[65]

In 2007, the NFL devoted funds for retired players diagnosed with dementia through the '88 Plan'.[66] The '88 Plan' was introduced as an amendment to the 2006 NFL Collective Bargaining Agreement (CBA).[67] It was named after the 88 jersey worn by Hall of Famer John Mackey, who had suffered from dementia in his early 50s until his death in 2011.[68] Redeveloped in the 2011 CBA and still in force,[69] it provides reimbursement for former players' medical, residential and home care costs.[70] The latest version of the Plan also covers ALS and Parkinson's disease, and establishes higher monetary caps.[71] So far, it has distributed over USD92 million to former players and their families.[72]

Ironically, the NFL sought to profit from the release of a new video, being the latest in a series of video programs glorifying head-banging hits.[73]

Finally, in 2008, the NFL stiffened financial penalties in instances of unnecessarily rough hits.[74]

This paradoxical attitude, whereby the NFL denied any causal link between multiple instances of concussion and later life cognitive decline, and glorified aggressive plays, while taking concrete measures to remedy the situation, did not escape the scrutiny of the US Congress.

---

[65]According to Rule 3, Section 26 of the 2018 NFL Rulebook, '[t]he pocket area is the area between the outside edges of the normal tackle positions on each side of the center extending backward to the offensive team's end line. After the ball leaves the pocket area, this area no longer exists'. For the NFL Rulebook, see the NFL website (<http://www.nfl.com/kickoff/story/09000d5d801e3eb1/article/new-rules-for-2007> and <https://operations.nfl.com/media/3277/2018-nfl-rulebook_final-version.pdf>).

[66]Bernstein, above n 2 in Chapter 2, 292–3.

[67]Hanna and Kain, above n 57, 13.

[68]Bernstein, above n 2 in Chapter 2, 292–3.

[69]Note that the duration of the 2011 NFL CBA runs from 2011 to 2020. This CBA (dated August 2011) is available on the NFL website (<https://nfllabor.files.wordpress.com/2010/01/collective-bargaining-agreement-2011-2020.pdf>). The '88 Plan' remained in effect despite the final settlement concluded in 2015 between the NFL and the players [see this chapter, Sections IA2 and IA2(a)(v), in particular footnote 252. This footnote refers to the final settlement and its approval memorandum, which expressly indicates on p. 20 that the benefits that players are entitled to under their CBAs are not compromised].

[70]Modery, above n 13 in Chapter 1, 267–8.

[71]See NFL CBA, Art. 58. See also Art. 65, which introduced a new disability benefit, specifically dealing with neuro-cognitive disorders. This article applies to early stage cognitive disorders, and supplements the '88 Plan' benefits.

[72]Email from Andrew Jo (NFL Manager, Retired Player Program) to author, 11 September 2018.

[73]Paul M Barrett, 'Will Brain Injury Lawsuits Doom or Save the NFL?', *Bloomberg*, 21 February 2013 (<http://www.bloomberg.com/news/articles/2013-01-31/will-brain-injury-lawsuits-doom-or-save-the-nfl>).

[74]Diehl, above n 9 in Chapter 2, 112–13.

(d) Congressional Hearing (2009)

The controversy, fuelled by media pressure and new players' suicides,[75] continued to grow. The debate reached a boiling point in September 2009, after the release of a study by the University of Michigan.[76] This study, commissioned by the NFL, concluded that former NFL players were diagnosed with Alzheimer's disease (or other memory-related diseases) vastly more often than the general population.[77] This included a rate of 19 times the normal rate for men aged from 30 to 39 years old.[78]

A few weeks after release of the study, the Congress announced that it would hold a hearing on this issue.[79] The hearing took place in October 2009, in the presence of Congress representatives, NFL executives, players and doctors.[80] Among the 16 experts that came to testify, Dr Cantu's presence was particularly influential.[81] Dr Cantu, whose testimony was interpreted as critical towards the NFL, summed up the main findings of his forensic examinations, as well as subsequent clinical studies.[82] Dr McKee, who also testified in the Congressional Hearing, displayed images of brains of deceased football players diagnosed with CTE.[83]

Asked on several occasions about whether multiple instances of head trauma could contribute to early onset brain impairment, NFL Commissioner Roger Goodell

---

[75]Note the suicide of former defensive lineman Atlanta Falcons Shane Dronett, aged 38. In 2006, Dronett began to exhibit symptoms of paranoia, confusion, fear, and rage. The removal of a brain tumour, in 2007, did not improve the situation. In January 2009, he confronted his wife with a gun. As she ran away for safety, he turned the gun on himself. After his death, it was determined that he had suffered from CTE [Stephanie Smith, 'Ex-Falcons Lineman Had Brain Disease Due to Concussions', *CNN*, 1 April 2011 (<http://edition.cnn.com/2011/HEALTH/04/01/brain.concussion.dronett/index.html?hpt=Sbin>) (Stephanie Smith, 'Falcons')].

[76]This study, based on phone surveys conducted in late 2008 over 1063 NFL retired players, has not been peer-reviewed. It was firstly brought to the attention of the general public by Alan Schwarz, 'Dementia Risks Seen in Players in N.F.L Study', *The New York Times*, 29 September 2009 (<http://www.nytimes.com/2009/09/30/sports/football/30dementia.html?pagewanted=all&_r=0>) (Alan Schwarz, 'Dementia').

[77]Alan Schwarz, 'Dementia', above n 76.

[78]Ibid.

[79]Gerardi, above n 45 in Chapter 2, 211.

[80]Ibid.

[81]Legal Issues Relating to Football Head Injuries (Part I): Hearing Before the House Comm. on the Judiciary, 111th Cong. 66–71 and 86 (2010) (Testimony of Dr C. Cantu, Chief of Neurosurgery Service and Director, Sports Medicine, Emerson Hospital, Concord, MA). The minutes of the Congressional Hearing is available on the Judiciary House's website (<http://judiciary.house.gov/_files/hearings/printers/111th/111-82_53092.PDF>).

[82]See this chapter, Section IA1(b). See also ibid, 66–71 and 86.

[83]Legal Issues Relating to Football Head Injuries (Part I): Hearing Before the House Comm. on the Judiciary, 111th Cong. 153–68 (2010) (Testimony of Dr Anne C. McKee, Associate Professor, Neurology and Pathology, Boston University School of Medicine).

refused to comment.[84] He deferred to medical expertise on this question.[85] The committee then played a recording of an interview of another NFL representative and leading voice on this issue, Dr Casson, absent on this occasion, denying all potential links between multiple head injuries and dementia.[86]

Several Congress representatives raised complex legal issues. Implicitly referring to the doctrine of voluntary assumption of risk, whereby players are taken to accept the risks of injuries inherent in sport,[87] representative John Conyers insisted on the fact that brain damage was not the type of risk that players and their families would associate with the game of football.[88]

Representative Linda Sanchez drew parallels between the NFL's position and the tobacco industry's denial of the link between cigarette consumption and ill health effects.[89] Sanchez encouraged Commissioner Goodell to get ahead on this issue, at least to cover the NFL legally.[90] She seemed thereby to suggest that the NFL might avoid tobacco-like liability just by issuing adequate warning to players.[91]

Another Representative, Maxine Waters, whose husband had played in the NFL, called for revoking the NFL's antitrust exemption.[92]

These criticisms were taken into account by the NFL, which seemed to finally admit the seriousness of the concussion issue.

[84]Legal Issues Relating to Football Head Injuries (Part I): Hearing Before the House Comm. on the Judiciary, 111th Cong. 85–6 (2010) (Inquiry of Rep. Conyers, Chair, House Comm. on the Judiciary).

[85]Ibid.

[86]Legal Issues Relating to Football Head Injuries (Part I): Hearing Before the House Comm. on the Judiciary, 111th Cong. 113 (2010) (Statement of Rep. Linda Sanchez, Member, House Comm. on the Judiciary).

[87]The doctrine of voluntary assumption of risk (also known as 'volenti non fit injuria') is common in many different legal systems. It finds its expression in different laws. For more details about this doctrine, see this chapter, Section IA2(a)(ii)(iv) and footnote 287, as well as Sections IC2 (b) and ID2(b).

[88]Legal Issues Relating to Football Head Injuries (Part I): Hearing Before the House Comm. on the Judiciary, 111th Cong. 1 (2010) (Statement of Rep. John Conyers, Member, House Comm. on the Judiciary).

[89]Legal Issues Relating to Football Head Injuries (Part I): Hearing Before the House Comm. on the Judiciary, 111th Cong. 116 (2010) (Statement of Rep. Linda Sanchez, Member, House Comm. on the Judiciary).

[90]Ibid.

[91]Hanna and Kain, above n 57, 10.

[92]Legal Issues Relating to Football Head Injuries (Part I): Hearing Before the House Comm. on the Judiciary, 111th Cong. 95 (2010) (Statement of Rep. Maxine Waters, Member, House Comm. on the Judiciary). Like baseball, ice hockey and basketball, American football is statutorily exempt from US antitrust laws for the purpose of collectively selling the rights to television broadcasts of games [*Sports Broadcasting Act of 1961* (15 USC § 1291-5)]. A threat to end this exemption would imperil the NFL's ability to broadcast, and subsequently its revenues.

(e) Remedial Measures Taken by the NFL to Protect Players after the Congressional Hearing (2009–18)

The NFL reacted shortly after the 2009 Congressional Hearing by taking several remedial measures.[93] First, the NFL, through its spokesperson, Greg Aiello, acknowledged the existence of a link between multiple instances of concussion and 'long-term problems'.[94]

Secondly, MTBI Committee co-chairmen, Dr Casson and Dr David Viano, were replaced by neurologists Dr H. Hunt Batjer and Dr Richard G. Ellenbogen to preside over the newly created NFL Head, Neck and Spine Medical Committee ('HNSMC').[95]

Thirdly, the NFL partnered with the Center for the Study of Traumatic Encephalopathy ('CSTE'), resulting from the joining of the Sports Legacy Institute and the Boston University School of Medicine, and now known as the Chronic Traumatic Encephalopathy Center (CTE Center)[96] by making a donation of USD1 million.[97] Following this, current and former athletes from the US and elsewhere were actively urged to posthumously donate their brain to the Center.[98]

Finally, the NFL promulgated stricter concussion management policies.[99] All 32 clubs received a memorandum stating that any concussed player should not return to the field on the same day in case of serious symptoms, including inability to remember assignments, persistent dizziness or headaches.[100] The clubs were also required to make an independent doctor available to examine players and determine whether they should return-to-practice after a head injury.[101] This memorandum was then incorporated into a formal protocol, whose latest version is adapted from the 5th CISG's statement (2017).[102]

---

93 Hanna, 'NFL', above n 110 in Chapter 2, 13.

94 Ibid.

95 Ibid, 13 and 17.

96 The CSTE subsequently changed its name due to changes with its partner organisation, the Concussion Legacy Foundation (formerly the Sports Legacy Foundation). The CSTE was a formal affiliation between the Sports Legacy Institute and the Boston University that has now been dissolved to allow a wider breadth of concussion related research. The research programs and staff remain the same [email from Patrick Kiernan (Research Assistant, CTE Center) to author, 11 September 2015].

97 Hanna, 'NFL', above n 110 in Chapter 2, 13.

98 Note that to date, over 3000 current and retired athletes have pledged to posthumously donate their brain to the CTE Center [email from Lisa McHale (Director of family relations, Concussion Legacy Foundation) to author, 6 September 2018].

99 Bernstein, above n 2 in Chapter 2, 286.

100 Ibid.

101 Ibid.

102 This protocol, entitled 'National Football League Head, Neck and Spine Committee's Concussion Diagnosis and Management Protocol' (2018), is available on the NFL website (<https://www.playsmartplaysafe.com/wp-content/uploads/2018/08/nfl-concussion-protocol-2018.pdf>).

At the end of 2009, the NFL began a series of programs to test new helmets.[103] Among these was the highly publicised program related to helmet sensors.[104] In February 2015, the NFL suspended this pilot-study, due to 'unreliable data collected' and data protection concerns.[105] Nevertheless, this suspension did not put into question the investigations by the NFL of equipment. These investigations have benefitted, since October 2014, from the support of a subcommittee of the HNSMC ('Engineering Subcommittee').[106] In 2010, the NFL also committed through collective bargaining to dedicate at least USD11 million yearly to medical research.[107]

In July 2010, the NFL produced and disseminated an informative brochure aimed at explaining the potential risks associated with multiple head injuries to its players.[108] The NFL's educational intervention then extended to other stakeholders and levels of competition. The best example of this is the 'Heads Up' Program, launched jointly in 2013 by the NFL and USA Football, youth football's governing body.[109] This program, whose claimed benefits are contested,[110] consists of a series of courses for coaches to learn better safety procedures and proper tackling drills. In 2016, the National Football League Players Association (NFLPA) launched an educational video on concussion for its players.[111]

Prior to the 2011 season, the NFL amended the rules of play concerning kick-offs, with the view to better protecting returners.[112] Large fines and suspensions were also put in place for helmet-to-helmet hits.[113] These measures were followed, two years

---

[103]Gerardi, above n 45 in Chapter 2, 219 and 231.

[104]For more details, see Mike Florio, 'NFL Moving Closer to Using Helmet Sensors', *NBC Sports*, 4 September 2013 (<http://profootballtalk.nbcsports.com/2013/09/04/nfl-moving-closer-to-using-helmet-sensors/>) (Florio, 'Helmets').

[105]Ken Belson, 'N.F.L Suspends Use of Helmet Sensors', *The New York Times*, 19 February 2015 (<http://www.nytimes.com/2015/02/20/sports/football/nfl-suspends-use-of-helmet-sensors.html?_r=0>) (Belson, 'Helmets').

[106]For more details, see eg, Daniel Kaplan, 'Engineers to Assist NFL with Injury Prevention', *SportsBusinessDaily*, 23 February 2015 (<http://www.sportsbusinessdaily.com/Journal/Issues/2015/02/23/Leagues-and-Governing-Bodies/NFL-engineers.aspx>).

[107]NFL CBA, Art. 12, section 5.

[108]Hanna, 'NFL', above n 110 in Chapter 2, 17.

[109]Alan Schwarz, 'N.F.L.-Backed Youth Program Says It Reduced Concussion. The Data Disagrees.', *The New York Times*, 27 July 2016 (<http://www.nytimes.com/2016/07/28/sports/football/nfl-concussions-youth-program-heads-up-football.html?nytmobile=0&_r=0&mtrref=undefined>) (Alan Schwarz, 'Youth Program').

[110]Ibid.

[111]Pauline Anderson, 'AAN, NFLPA Launch a Video on Concussion for Players', *Medscape*, 7 September 2016 (<https://www.medscape.com/viewarticle/868529>) (paywall) (Pauline Anderson, 'AAN').

[112]Gove, above n 18, 657–8 and 689–90.

[113]Bernstein, above n 2 in Chapter 2, 282.

later, by various new safety rules, including the ban of helmet-first tackles.[114] In addition, more protection was gradually given to players unable to protect themselves, such as quarterbacks in the act of throwing.[115] In 2015, the NFL gave 'defenceless player protection' to the intended receiver of a pass in the immediate continuation action following an interception or potential interception.[116] In 2016, the NFL passed an automatic ejection rule for repeated unsportsmanlike conduct fouls in a game, such as throwing a punch or kicking an opponent.[117] The evolution of the rules of play continued into the beginning of the 2018 season, when the NFL made all helmet-to-helmet contact illegal with the possibility of ejection.[118]

In February 2011, the HNSMC indicated that they would implement a standardised sideline concussion assessment protocol.[119] This protocol was derived from the SCAT 2, as described in the 3rd CISG's statement (2008).[120]

In December 2011, the NFL set up an injury video review system, with spotters who have athletic and medical knowledge, and independent from clubs,[121] placed in each stadium in order to help monitor players' head injuries.[122] First considered as simple advisors, they received greater power in March 2015, and are now allowed to stop a game if it appears necessary.[123]

---

[114]This means that runners and defenders are now prohibited from lowering their heads and hitting with their helmets when outside of the tackle box—the area of the field between the two offensive tackles.

[115]For more details about the 2013 changes in the NFL rules, see Michael David Smith, 'NFL Officiating Video Stresses New "Crown of the Helmet" Rule', *NBC Sports*, 6 August 2013 (<http://profootballtalk.nbcsports.com/2013/08/06/nfl-officiating-video-stresses-new-crown-of-the-helmet-rule/>) (Michael David Smith, 'Crown'). See also Matt Slater, 'NFL Safety Boss Says the League Could Ban Helmets One Day', *BBC*, 18 June 2015 (<http://www.bbc.com/sport/0/american-football/33167457>).

[116]For more details about the 2015 new rules, see Michael David Smith, 'NFL Passes Five Player Safety Rules', *NBC Sports*, 24 March 2015 (<https://profootballtalk.nbcsports.com/2015/03/24/nfl-passes-five-player-safety-rules/>) (Michael David Smith, 'Safety').

[117]Marc Sessler, 'NFL Passes Automatic Ejection Rule for 2016 Season', *NFL*, 23 March 2016 (<http://www.nfl.com/news/story/0ap3000000646837/article/nfl-passes-automatic-ejection-rule-for-2016-season>) (and related hyperlinks).

[118]Alex Kozora, 'NFL Rule Change Now Makes Head To Head Contact Illegal', *'Steelers Depot'*, 27 March 2018 (<https://steelersdepot.com/2018/03/nfl-rule-change-now-makes-head-to-head-contact-illegal-possible-ejection/>).

[119]Hanna, 'NFL', above n 110 in Chapter 2, 17.

[120]See Chapter 2, Sections III and IV.

[121]NFL's spotters must have athletic training experience of at least 10 years, have a valid certification by NATA, and have professional (or major college) sports experience. Additionally, NFL's spotters must not have been employed by an NFL team as a head athletic trainer, nor have been employed by an NFL team in the last 20 years [for more details, see NFL website (<https://operations.nfl.com/the-game/gameday-behind-the-scenes/atc-spotters/>)].

[122]NFL website (<https://operations.nfl.com/the-game/gameday-behind-the-scenes/atc-spotters/>).

[123]Ibid.

In July 2012, NFL Commissioner Goodell announced the development of an IPad application.[124] This application, aimed at helping evaluate whether a player had effectively suffered a concussion,[125] may possibly override the electronic software 'ImPACT', historically used in the NFL.[126]

In January 2013, the NFL adopted a new rule, starting with the 2013 season, imposing an independent neurologist on the sidelines for all games in order to assist team physicians with the evaluation and treatment of head injuries.[127]

Also early 2013, the NFLPA pledged USD100 million grant to Harvard Medical School for a 10-year study aimed at researching the health problems associated with playing football.[128] In September 2013, the NFL donated USD30 million to the Foundation for National Institutes of Health (NIH) to help medical research on brain injuries.[129] In a report published in 2016, the NFL was accused by Congressional investigators of trying to pressure the NIH and attempting to intervene in the choice of the researchers involved in one of the financially supported projects.[130] The NFL reportedly restricted the NIH from using USD16 million of its USD30 million grant to fund a CTE Center study led by Dr Robert Stern, who was publicly critical of the league.[131] The NFL never paid the remaining sum,[132] which marked a break with both the NIH and the CTE Center.

In 2013, the NFL and General Electric (GE) also launched a four-year, USD60 million collaboration called the 'Head Health Initiative'. The initiative aim is to

---

[124]Hanna, 'NFL', above n 110 in Chapter 2, 17.

[125]Ibid.

[126]Ibid.

[127]Bill Bradley, 'Independent Concussion Specialists Ready to Work NFL Sidelines', *NFL*, 3 September 2013 (<http://www.nfl.com/news/story/0ap1000000237739/article/independent-concussion-%20specialists-ready-to-work-nfl-sidelines>).

[128]Note, however, that the use of this donation, or even the donation itself, was subsequently called into question by the NFLPA [Joseph M Hanna, 'The Real Story Behind the NFL's Player Association "$100 Million Research Grant" to Harvard Medical School', *Sports and Entertainment Law Insider*, 13 March 2014 (<http://sportslawinsider.com/the-real-story-behind-the-nfl-players-association-100-million-research-grant-to-harvard-medical-school/>) (Hanna, 'Grant')].

[129]Elizabeth O'Connell, 'NFL Announces Latest Partnership with International Concussion and Head Injury Research Foundation', *SportTechie*, 28 October 2015 (<http://www.sporttechie.com/2015/10/28/nfl-announces-latest-partnership-international-concussion-head-injury-research-foundation/>).

[130]US House of Representatives, Committee on Energy and Commerce, Ranking Member Franck Pallone Jr, Democratic Staff Report, 'The National Football League's Attempt to Influence Funding Decisions at the National Institutes of Health', May 2016 (<https://democrats-energycommerce.house.gov/sites/democrats.energycommerce.house.gov/files/Democratic%20Staff%20Report%20on%20NFL%20NIH%20Investigation%205.23.2016.pdf>).

[131]Lindsay Gibbs, 'NFL Ends Concussion Research Partnership $16 Million Short of $30million Commitment', *Think Progress*, 29 July 2017 (<https://thinkprogress.org/nfl-nih-end-concussion-research-8a5750ecf3fb/>).

[132]Ibid.

accelerate diagnosis and improve treatment for brain injuries by finding new technologies and innovations.[133] It has already provided financing for various projects, including the development of padding technology aimed at making synthetic turf safer and softer.[134] In September 2016, the NFL initiated 'Play Smart', a program to drive progress in the prevention, diagnosis and treatment of head injuries, enhance medical protocols and further improve the way the game is taught and played.[135] The program began with a pledge of USD100 million in support for independent medical research and engineering advancements.[136]

In May 2015, NFL Commissioner Goodell announced the creation of a new part-time position, a chief health and medical advisor, to oversee the league's health policies.[137] The person appointed for the role was Betsy Nabel, a cardiologist, president of Brigham and Women's Hospital in Boston and a professor of medicine at Harvard Medical School.[138] Nabel's first task was to lay the foundations, together with the NFLPA, of a new game day concussion protocol for all the 32 clubs to address the diagnosis and management of concussion.[139] This protocol introduced heavy fines (up to USD150 000) and possible forfeiture of draft picks for clubs whose medical team members or other employees are not compliant.[140] It was then amended and updated on several occasions under the leadership of Dr Allen Sills, a neurosurgeon, who was appointed NFL Chief Medical Officer in 2017.[141]

In October 2015, the NFL sponsored a scientific meeting aimed at setting a national agenda on concussion treatment.[142] This meeting, whose scientific

---

[133] O'Connell, above n 129.

[134] Ken Belson, 'Concussion Report Highlights Field Maintenance', *The New York Times*, 29 December 2015 (<http://www.nytimes.com/2015/12/30/sports/football/concussion-report-highlights-field-maintenance.html>) (Belson, 'Field Maintenance').

[135] 'NFL Commitment to Player Health and Safety, A Letter from Commissioner Roger Goodell', *NFL*, 14 September 2016 (<https://www.playsmartplaysafe.com/commitment-letter/>).

[136] Ibid.

[137] Jenny Vrentas, 'NFL Safety is in her Hands', *MMQB*, 15 May 2015 (http://mmqb.si.com/2015/05/15/betsy-nabel-nfl-health-medical-concussions-head-injuries/#>).

[138] Ibid. For a critical view on this appointment, see David Steele, 'Goodell's New Medical Chief Isn't a Concussion Expert', *Sporting News*, 12 February 2015 (<http://snip.ly/RxOc#http://www.sportingnews.com/nfl/story/2015-02-12/elizabeth-nabel-nfl-medical-advisor-goodell-cardiologist-concussions-conflict-kraft-patriots>).

[139] Jesse Kirsch, 'New NFL Game Plan Looks to Tackle Head Injuries', *ABC News*, 13 September 2015 (<http://abcnews.go.com/Sports/nfl-game-plan-tackle-head-injuries/story?id=33387925>).

[140] 'NFL, NFLPA Announce Policy to Enforce Concussion Protocol', *NFL*, 25 July 2016 (<http://www.nfl.com/news/story/0ap3000000676669/article/nfl-nflpa-announce-policy-to-enforce-concussion-protocol>).

[141] See eg, Reuters, 'Concussion Protocol Altered after Recent Missteps', *Reuters*, 24 September 2017 (<https://www.reuters.com/article/us-football-nfl-concussion/concussion-protocol-altered-after-recent-missteps-idUSKBN1EI0JV>) (Reuters, 'Protocol').

[142] Amy Nordrum, 'NFL Underwrites Scientific Meeting to Set National Agenda for Concussion Treatment', *International Business Times*, 14 October 2015 (<http://www.ibtimes.com/nfl-underwrites-scientific-meeting-set-national-agenda-concussion-treatment-2137145>) (Nordrum,

independence was questioned by some commentators due to its ties to the NFL,[143] was organised in Pittsburgh, and regrouped about 30 US leading concussion clinicians and researchers.[144] The new medical directions discussed during this conference resulted in an agreed statement.[145] Present experts began to outline a new approach that could question the prevailing view that rest for players is the main treatment for brain injuries.[146] However, there was no consensus on which other treatment would be the most appropriate.[147] The experts also identified six types of concussions, depending on which part of the brain is affected.[148]

The NFL is also focusing on international cooperation. Apart from its participation in the CISG's meetings (and the Dublin meeting),[149] it organises the 'NFL Think Tank'. The Think Tank serves as a platform for SGBs to propose cutting edge ideas for research collaborations and to share best practice and progress.[150] Its latest meeting was hosted in October 2015 in London.[151] On this occasion, the NFL reiterated its commitment to research,[152] through the announcement of a partnership with the International Concussion and Head Injury Research Foundation (ICHIRF).[153]

In parallel to the measures mentioned above, the NFL launched an extensive lobbying campaign in order to lead the federal government and the states to intervene into this matter.[154]

'National Agenda'); Amy Nordrum, 'Concussions Are Treatable, Experts Conclude at NFL-Sponsored Scientific Meeting', *International Business Times*, 16 October 2015 (<http://www.ibtimes.com/concussions-are-treatable-experts-conclude-nfl-sponsored-scientific-meeting-2144801?utm_content=buffer66d04&utm_medium=social&utm_source=linkedin.com&utm_campaign=buffer>) (Nordrum, 'NFL-Sponsored Meeting').

[143]Nordrum, 'National Agenda', above n 142.

[144]Ibid.

[145]Michael W Collins et al., 'Statements of Agreement From the Targeted Evaluation and Active Management (TEAM) Approaches to Treating Concussion Meeting Held in Pittsburgh, October 15-16 2015' (2016) 79 *Neurosurgery* 912, 912–29.

[146]Ibid.

[147]Ibid, 922.

[148]Ibid, 920-1.

[149]See Chapter 2, Sections II and IX.

[150]O'Connell, above n 129.

[151]Ibid.

[152]The research undertaken and/or sponsored by the NFL, as well as other steps aimed at better protecting players, are summed up in the NFL Annual Player Health and Safety Reports. For the 2018 report (and previous reports), see the NFL ('Play Smart') website (<https://www.playsmartplaysafe.com/newsroom/reports/nfl-annual-player-health-and-safety-reports/>).

[153]O'Connell, above n 129.

[154]Associated Press, 'Youth Concussion Laws Lack Bite', *ESPN*, 28 January 2015 (<http://espn.go.com/nfl/story/_/id/12242612/youth-concussion-laws-pushed-nfl-lack-bite-according-associated-press-analysis>) (Associated Press, 'Youth Concussion Laws').

(f) Remedial Measures Taken by the Federal Government and States to Protect Players after the Congressional Hearing (2009–18)

Following the Congressional Hearing, the federal government and the states have been active, and their focus has been on youth and college sport.

Fifty-one youth concussion state laws, primarily targeting children, were adopted over the course of five years (one in each state and one in the District of Columbia).[155] These laws are all designed (or supposed to be designed) on the same four key principles, established by an initial bill passed in Washington state in 2009.[156] This bill, which is now a law (the '*Zackery Lystedt Law*'),[157] requires education for coaches, players' removal from games in case of suspicion of head injury, a written clearance to return, and the signature of an information form by both parents and players.[158]

The initial bill also contained provisions that were not considered by experts as mandatory key principles aimed at being incorporated in other state legislations. A good example of this is section 1 of the bill, which provided legal immunity from liability for compliant schools in case of injury or death of a player due to action or inaction of persons employed by or under contract with the sports program. This section was not incorporated in the final statute. However, it was used as a source of inspiration for other laws, such as Ohio, which grants immunity from liability for all persons associated with youth athletics, unless there is wilful or wanton misconduct.[159]

In 2015, an Associated Press analysis of these laws, albeit praising the efforts made, highlighted a few issues.[160] At that time, only 21 laws had all of the four mandatory requirements of the model legislation.[161] One-third of the laws made no specific reference to which ages were covered.[162] Even fewer laws explicitly referred to interscholastic sport and recreational leagues (Pop Warner, Little League).[163] Furthermore, some laws only referred to public schools, while others did not specify

[155]Ibid.

[156]'House Bill 1824' [H.R. 1824, 61st Leg. (Wa. 2009)].

[157]This law (Wash. Rev. Code § 28A.600.190) was named after a 13-year old football player who suffered serious sequelae following a haemorrhage due to a concussion.

[158]House Bill 1824 [H.R. 1824, 61st Leg. (Wa. 2009)], section 2.

[159]Ohio Rev Code Ann. § 3313.539.

[160]Howard Fendrich and Eddie Pells, Associated Press, 'States Youth Concussion Laws Vary in Strength', *Albuquerque Journal*, 30 January 2015 (<http://www.abqjournal.com/533408/sports/states-youth-concussion-laws-vary-in-strength.html>).

[161]Ibid.

[162]Ibid.

[163]Ibid.

anything at all.[164] Finally, almost all lacked consequences for non-compliant schools.[165]

This last criticism confirmed previous analysis undertaken on the basis of intermediate data, which highlighted that enforcement of youth sports concussion laws was largely non-existent, due to the absence of such language in the laws and uncertainty about under whose purview the enforcement falls.[166]

Lessons from implementation, research developments and knowledge about best practice resulted in states gradually adding components to strengthen or streamline their concussion-related laws.[167] Many states have already amended their original law, for instance, by adding provisions regarding concussion-data collection,[168] while others have introduced bills to ban youth tackle football.[169] The efficacy of these laws still needs assessing. They seem, to date, to have led to an increase in concussion rates, which may be caused by a range of factors, including increased awareness and better identification[170] or, conversely, a lack of compliance.[171]

Several bills, aimed at regulating youth safety/equipment and management of concussion at federal level did not make it through the Congress.[172]

In 2014, the Centers for Disease Control and Prevention (CDC)[173] was charged by the Institute of Medicine with the task of setting up a surveillance system of sports-related concussion in youth sport.[174] The CDC is currently undertaking a

---

[164]Ibid.

[165]Ibid. This unsurprisingly led to a lack of compliance in practice among US states, as confirmed by several studies [see eg, Maria Kajankova et al., 'Response of School Districts to the New York State Concussion Awareness and Management Act: Review of Policies and Procedures' (2017) 87 *Journal of School Health* 409, 409–15].

[166]Kerri McGowan Lowrey and Stephanie R Morain, 'State Experiences in Implementing Youth Sports Concussion Laws: Challenges, Successes, and Lessons for Evaluating Impact' 2014 (42) *Journal of Law, Medicine and Ethics* 290, 290–6, in particular 295.

[167]Francis X Shen, Are Youth Sports Concussion Statutes Working? (2018) 56 *Duquesne Law Review* 7, 10.

[168]Ibid. This author refers to the examples of Connecticut and Vermont.

[169]De Caro and Kaplen atttorneys' website (<https://brainlaw.com/youth-tackle-football/>).

[170]Jingzhen Yang et al., 'New and Recurrent Concussions in High School Athletes before and after Traumatic Brain Injury Laws', 2005–16 (2017) 107 *American Journal of Public Health* 1916, 1918.

[171]See this chapter, Section IA1(f), footnote 165.

[172]Among these bills are the Children's Sports Athletic Equipment Safety Bill (CSAE), the Concussion Treatment and Care Tools Bill (ConTACT), the Protecting Student Athletes from Concussion Bill and the Youth Sports Concussion Bill.

[173]The CDC, formed in 1946, is the leading national public health institute of the US. It maintains several departments concerned with occupational safety and health. For more details about the CDC's organisation, see <http://www.cdc.gov/about/organization/cio.htm>.

[174]This initiative comes in the wake of the work undertaken by the National Center for Catastrophic Injury Research (NCCSIR) and of other various existing surveillance systems, such as the NCAA Injury Surveillance System. It follows the recommendations of a report released in 2013 by the Institute of Medicine (IOM) [Graham et al., above n 113 in Chapter 2, 285–6].

small-scale pilot of the surveillance system.[175] Data collection for the pilot is expected to be completed in 2019.[176] In the longer term, the system is expected to provide the first truly comprehensive national representative estimates of concussion among children and adults.[177]

Simultaneously, the White House hosted a Summit on Youth Concussion in Sport, during which key stakeholders, including the NFL and the National College Athletics Association (NCAA), declared their commitment to expand research and data collection.[178] On this occasion, private-public partnerships were also highlighted.[179]

Still in 2014, the US Congress, again,[180] stepped into the matter, by holding a hearing on sports safety.[181] It discussed the innovations made by the NFL and other US sports leagues (including the NHL, and various leagues governing youth sport), equipment manufacturers and the medical community.[182] In March 2016, a round-table discussion on concussion was convened by the US House of Representatives' Committee on Energy and Commerce.[183] It was the opportunity for Jeff Miller, NFL vice-president for health and safety, to assert the now unequivocal position of the league, by acknowledging the link between the practice of American football and CTE.[184] Following this roundtable, it was revealed that the NFL had recently given nearly USD300 000 in campaign contributions to the members of the Committee, exposing the links between the league and political representatives.[185]

---

[175]Email from Matthew Breiding (Team Lead, Division of Unintentional Injury Prevention, CDC) to author, 29 November 2018.

[176]Ibid.

[177]Ibid.

[178]The White House, Office of the Press Secretary, 'Fact Sheet: President Obama Applauds Commitments to Address Sports-Related Concussions in Young People', *The White House*, 29 May 2014 (<https://www.whitehouse.gov/the-press-office/2014/05/29/fact-sheet-president-obama-applauds-commitments-address-sports-related-c>) (The White House, 'Young People').

[179]Ibid.

[180]For previous and subsequent Congressional interventions, see this chapter, Sections IA1(d), IA1(e), IA1(f) and IA1(g), footnote 221.

[181]Improving Sports Safety: A Multifaceted Approach: Hearing Before the House Comm. on Energy and Commerce, 113th Cong. 1 (2014). The minutes of this Congressional Hearing can be retrieved from Heinonline.

[182]Ibid, 2.

[183]Steve Fainaru, 'NFL Acknowledges, for First Time, Link between Football, Brain Disease', *ESPN*, 16 March 2016 (<http://espn.go.com/espn/otl/story/_/id/14972296/top-nfl-official-acknowledges-link-football-related-head-trauma-cte-first>).

[184]Ibid.

[185]Elliott Almond, 'NFL is Funding Campaigns of Lawmakers Reviewing Concussion Issue' *Mercury News*, 23 March 2016 (<http://www.mercurynews.com/sports/ci_29676270/nfl-funds-campaigns-lawmakers-reviewing-concussions>).

On a more general level (not restricted to sport), the Obama administration announced in 2013 the implementation of the 'White House Brain Initiative'.[186] This initiative, the scale of which was expanded in 2014,[187] is a collaborative, public-private research 'think-tank' with the goal of supporting the development and application of innovative technologies that can create a dynamic understanding of brain functioning.[188]

Meanwhile, the controversy continued to grow.

(g) Latest News, Domestic Violence and Other Offences

In December 2009, Cincinnati Bengals wide receiver, Chris Henry, 26 years old, was killed in an automobile accident.[189] Uncertainty still remains on whether Henry fell down or jumped out of a moving pickup truck.[190] When Dr Omalu and Dr Julian Bailes (then affiliated to the West Virginia University) performed an autopsy on his brain, they discovered signs of CTE.[191] Such a finding shocked researchers for two reasons. Henry had never reported a concussion during his four years of active play in the NFL nor during his years at West Virginia University.[192] Additionally, although he was the twenty-second confirmed case of CTE in American football, he was the first player diagnosed at such a young age, while still active in the NFL.[193]

In February 2011, former Chicago Bears defenseman, Dave Duerson, fatally shot himself in the chest, at the age of 50.[194] Prior to his death, he left specific instructions to his family. He asked that his brain be donated to research in order to be analysed, presumably to confirm his self-diagnosed suspicions.[195] Duerson had suffered from deteriorating cognitive symptoms that he thought were due to CTE.[196] In May 2011, the CSTE[197] confirmed Duerson's fears by stating that he had 'indisputable'

---

[186] The White House, Office of the Press Secretary, 'Fact Sheet: Brain Initiative', *The White House*, 2 April 2013 (<https://www.whitehouse.gov/the-press-office/2013/04/02/fact-sheet-brain-initiative>) (The White House, 'Brain Initiative').

[187] The White House, Office of Science and Technology Policy, 'Fact Sheet: Obama Administration Proposes Over $300 Million in Funding for the Brain Initiative', *The White House*, February 2015 (<https://obamawhitehouse.archives.gov/sites/default/files/microsites/ostp/brain_initiative_fy16_fact_sheet_ostp.pdf>) (The White House, 'Support').

[188] The White House, 'Brain Initiative', above n 186.

[189] Modery, above n 13 in Chapter 1, 247.

[190] Hanna, 'NFL', above n 110 in Chapter 2, 16–17.

[191] Ibid.

[192] Hanna and Kain, above n 57, 14.

[193] Hanna, 'NFL', above n 110 in Chapter 2, 17.

[194] Ibid, 17–18.

[195] Ibid.

[196] Ibid.

[197] See this chapter, Section IA1(e), footnote 96.

evidence of CTE in his brain tissue.[198] These findings led his estate to file a wrongful death action against the NFL.[199]

Further, in April of 2012, former Atlanta Falcon safety, Ray Easterling, 62 years old, died due to a self-inflicted gunshot wound to the chest.[200] Over the last 20 years of his lifetime, Easterling struggled to cope with various typical CTE symptoms, including severe memory impairment, personality changes, tremors, and eventually dementia.[201] He was the lead plaintiff in the first class action concussion lawsuit registered against the NFL.[202]

Shortly thereafter, legendary NFL veteran, Junior Seau, passed away at 43 years old in similar circumstances after suffering from recurring insomnia and depression.[203] In early 2013, Seau's family donated his brain to science.[204] At autopsy, it was found that Seau's brain showed evidence of CTE.[205] Seau's family subsequently filed a wrongful death lawsuit against the NFL and helmet manufacturer Riddell.[206]

Finally, in December 2012, Kansas City Chiefs linebacker, Jovan Belcher, aged 25, shot his girlfriend to death, before committing suicide in front of team officials and coaches.[207] Belcher's body was exhumed one year after his death.[208] In September 2014, the media revealed the findings of neuropathologist Piotr Kozlowski, hired by court-appointed attorneys representing the interests of Belcher's young daughter in a lawsuit filled against the Kansas City Chiefs.[209] Dr Kozlowski detected toxic protein tau in the dead player's hippocampus, which suggests that Belcher also suffered from CTE.[210]

---

198 Hanna, 'NFL', above n 110 in Chapter 2, 17–18.

199 Mike Florio, 'Duerson Estate Sues for Wrongful Death', *NBC Sports*, 23 February 2012 (<http://profootballtalk.nbcsports.com/2012/02/23/duersons-estate-sues-nfl-for-wrongful-death/>) (Florio, 'Duerson').

200 Hanna, 'NFL', above n 110 in Chapter 2, 17–18.

201 Ibid.

202 See Chapter 1, Section II and this chapter, Section IA2.

203 Associated Press, 'Junior Seau's Family Sues NFL for Wrongful Death after CTE Diagnosis' *The Guardian*, 24 January 2013 (<https://www.theguardian.com/sport/2013/jan/23/junior-seau-family-sues-nfl-cte>) (Associated Press, 'Junior Seau').

204 Ibid.

205 Ibid.

206 Ibid. Seau's doctor was also sued by California state medical board for improper drug prescription, and got probation in 2017.

207 Sean D O'Brien and Kenneth Ferguson, 'Traumatic Brain Injury and the Law: Introduction' (2015) 84 *University of Missouri-Kansas City Law Review* 287, 288.

208 Michael O'Keefe, 'Former Chief Player Jovan Belcher Showed Signs of CTE in Postmortem Brain Exam', *New York Daily News*, 29 September 2014 (<http://www.nydailynews.com/sports/football/chiefs-player-jovan-belcher-showed-signs-cte-post-mortem-brain-exam-article-1.1957229>) (O'Keefe, 'Jovan Belcher').

209 Ibid.

210 Ibid.

In September 2013, former San Diego Chargers safety, Paul Oliver, aged 29, committed suicide by a self-inflicted gunshot.[211] Oliver shot himself in front of his wife and his two young boys, ending several years of domestic violence and terror.[212] It was later determined that he suffered from CTE, caused by repeated concussions he endured during his football playing career.[213] One year after Oliver's death, his widow and sons filed a wrongful death lawsuit against the NFL.[214]

Belcher and Oliver's cases marked the beginning of another concern. Since 2013, the question of suicides within the NFL has been supplanted in the headlines by another issue: the instances of domestic violence (and other violent offences) committed by certain players and veterans. This issue, correlated with impulse control, is also linked—at least likely partly—to medical conditions due to multiple instances of concussion.[215] It involves third-party victims, most of the time part of the player's immediate circle of family and acquaintances.

---

[211]Rich Phillips, 'Former Football Player Paul Oliver Shot Himself in the Head, Police Says', *CNN*, 3 October 2013 (<http://edition.cnn.com/2013/10/02/us/georgia-football-player-suicide/index.html>).

[212]Ibid.

[213]Edvard Pettersson, 'NFL Sued by Widow of Chargers Paul Oliver After Suicide', *Bloomberg Business*, 24 September 2014 (<http://www.bloomberg.com/news/articles/2014-09-24/nfl-sued-by-san-diego-chargers-paul-oliver-s-widow-after-suicide>).

[214]Ibid. For a general overview of the claims lodged against the NFL, as well as a direct access to the relevant submissions, see the 'NFL Concussion Litigation' website (<http://nflconcussionlitigation.com/?page_id=18>). Note that in addition to the cases mentioned as part of this chapter, numerous other players' suicides that occurred during the same period were not formally and publicly associated with CTE. This uncertainty on the potential causes of the death is notably due to the fact that forensic examinations were not systematically carried out. Similarly, some CTE diagnoses were reported in scientific journals without disclosing the names of the players in question. Finally, a very small number of examinations did not lead to a CTE diagnosis (on this last point, and for recent statistics about CTE diagnosis, see this chapter, Section IA1(h)).

[215]As already mentioned, impulse control problems are part of the list of the typical symptoms attributable to CTE (see chapter VII) [For some comments on this potential causal link, see Dr Ann McKee's analysis, retranscribed in Michael O'Keefe, 'Boston University Finds Possible Link Between Traumatic Brain Injuries and Domestic Violence', *New York Daily News*, 18 October 2014 (<http://www.nydailynews.com/sports/football/study-cte-linked-domestic-violence-article-1.1978936>)]. The personality of the players, as well as the use of doping substances and other drugs, notably among others, may also be considered. Interestingly, a study of the University of Texas and Florida State found that the arrest rate for NFL players is lower than the one of the general population in the US. However, and surprisingly, this study does not take domestic abuse instances into account [Alex Piquero et al., 'The National Felon League? A Comparison of NFL Arrests to General Population Arrests' (2015) 43 *Journal of Criminal Justice* 397, 397–403]. It would be particularly useful to undertake extensive comparative longitudinal studies on the general rates of domestic violence in NFL players and the general population, and/or in the concussive and non-concussive population.

Offences of all kinds committed by football players are certainly not something new.[216] However, the cases which had previously come to light in the media had not yet reached such a severe, or widespread level.[217]

The most publicised domestic violence (and child abuse) cases are, among others, these of running backs Ray Rice (Baltimore Ravens), Adrian Peterson (Minnesota Vikings) and Jonathan Dwyer (Arizona Cardinals) as well as defensive ends Ray McDonald (San Francisco 49ers), Greg Hardy (Carolina Panthers) and Ezekiel Elliott (Dallas Cowboys)[218] To this must be added cases of various allegations or convictions for rape,[219] or even the commission of other violent criminal offences.[220]

Although the regulation of domestic violence is beyond the scope of this thesis, such incidents show the large spectrum of issues posed by concussion, and should raise a red flag for SGBs.[221]

---

[216]For a summary of violent behaviours of NFL players in and outside sports fields, see Alexandra Veuthey, *Concussion in the National Football League: What Can We Learn?* (E-book, Weblaw, 2013) chapter III A.6 and footnote 288 (Veuthey, 'NFL') as well as this chapter, Section IA2(b), footnote 387.

[217]At the end of 2014, Jerry Angelo, a former NFL executive, revealed that teams did not discipline players in 'hundreds and hundreds' of domestic violence incidents during his 30 years in the league (Josh Peter, 'Former NFL Exec: Team Hid "Hundreds" of abuse incidents', *USA Today*, 9 October 2014, <http://www.usatoday.com/story/sports/nfl/2014/10/09/jerry-angelo-chicago-bears-national-football-league/16981865/>). Additionally, according to data released in 2014, 21 of 31 NFL teams employed a player with a domestic or sexual violence charge in 2013 (Amy E Bonomi, 'Dear NFL: Put Your Money Where All the Concussions are', *The Huffington Post*, 29 July 2014, <http://www.huffingtonpost.com/amy-e-bonomi/dear-nfl-put-your-money-where-all-the-concussions-are_b_5630392.html?utm_hp_ref=sports&ir=Sports>).

[218]For more details about these cases, see eg, 'Concerns about Violence Spread in the NFL', *SBS*, 15 September 2014 (<http://www.sbs.com.au/news/article/2014/09/15/concerns-over-violence-spread-nfl>); Michael David Smith, 'Cardinals Deactivate Dwyer After Domestic Violence Arrest', *NBC Sports*, 17 September 2014 (<http://profootballtalk.nbcsports.com/2014/09/17/cardinals-deactivate-dwyer-after-domestic-violence-arrest/related/>) (Michael David Smith, 'Domestic Violence'); Sarah Hardy, 'A Comprehensive Timeline of Ezekiel Elliott's Domestic Violence Case', *SBNation*, 30 November 2017 (<https://www.sbnation.com/2017/8/29/16151642/ezekiel-elliott-timeline-domestic-violence-police-report-nfl-suspension-appeal>).

[219]See eg, the cases of Brandon Marshall (allegations of rape, 2014); Darren Sharper (numerous convictions for aggravated rapes, 2015–16); Dana Stubblefield (charges of rape, 2016); Jameis Winston (charges of rape, settlement 2016); Claude Norman Spillmann (conviction of rape, 2016); Ray McDonald (charges of rape, dismissed 2017) and Kellen Winslow II (charges of rapes, 2018).

[220]See eg, among numerous examples, the cases of Aaron Joseph Hernandez (conviction of murder, 2017, followed by his suicide, a CTE diagnosis and a lawsuit filed by his daughter against his former club); Titus Young (various convictions including burglary, assault and felony battery, 2013–15); and Anthony McClanahan (charges of kidnapping, murder, 2017). McClanahan now blames CTE for his behaviour.

[221]The NFL has well understood it, as its domestic violence policy not only provides for sanctions, but also for clinical evaluation, education and counselling for players, and assistance for the victims [for more details about US sports leagues domestic violence policies, see Martin Tate, 'Wake up Call: How the Ray Rice Incident Opened the Public's Eyes to Domestic Violence in Professional Sports and the Need for Change' (2017) 24 Sports Law Journal 183, 183]. It may be noted that the

(h) The Latest Scientific Research

Recent research in the field of concussion has confirmed the findings previously established by Boston University.[222]

For instance, a study undertaken in 2011 by American researchers of various institutional affiliations on 100 active and retired NFL players acknowledged that these individuals face a significantly higher risk of subsequently suffering from dementia.[223] In 2011 and 2012, studies of the Center for Brain Health at the University of Texas, respectively of the University of North Carolina, focusing on retired NFL players, confirmed the link between multiple head injuries and depression.[224] In 2015, a study of the Southwestern Medical Center at the University of Texas evaluated the relationship between hippocampal volume, memory performance and the influence of concussion history on 28 retired NFL players with and without MCI.[225] It highlighted that players who experience concussion alongside loss of consciousness may be at increased risk of brain shrinkage in the hippocampus of the brain, leading to memory abnormalities later in life.[226] More recently, in 2016, a study of the Florida Center for Headaches and Sports Neurology, based on Diffusion Tensor Imaging (DTI) combined with memory tests, found that 43% of the 40 NFL veterans examined showed signs of brain injury.[227]

However, criticism was simultaneously raised against the Boston University's studies by some medical experts, some affiliated with SGBs. These experts accuse

---

US Congress also intervened several times into this matter [see eg, House Judiciary Democrats' website (<https://democrats-judiciary.house.gov/press-release/sports-leagues-respond-judiciary-democrats-letter-domestic-violence-policies>); Howard Fendrich, 'Members of Congress Ask NFL to Hold Teams Accountable For Domestic Abuse', *The Huffington Post*, 24 February 2015 (<http://www.huffingtonpost.com/2015/02/24/2-members-of-congress-wri_n_6744810.html?utm_hp_ref=sports&ir=Sports>) (Fendrich, 'Congress')].

[222] See this chapter, Section IA1(b).

[223] Daniel G Amen et al., 'Impact of Playing American Professional Football on Long-Term Brain Function' (Winter 2011) 23(1) *Journal of Neuropsychiatry & Clinical Neuroscience* 98, 98–106.

[224] John Hart Jr et al., 'Neuroimaging of Cognitive Dysfunction and Depression in Aging Retired National Football League Players' 2013 (70) *JAMA Neurology* 326, 326–35; ZY Kerry et al., 'Nine Year Risk of Depression Diagnosis Increases with Increasing Self-Reported Concussions in Retired Professional Football Players' (October 2012) 40(10) *American Journal of Sports Medicine* 2206, 2206–12.

[225] Jeremy F Strain et al., 'Imaging Correlates of Memory and Concussion History in Retired National Fotball League Athletes' (2015) 72 *JAMA Neurology* 773, 773–80.

[226] Ibid, in particular 773 and 779.

[227] Kim Bellware, 'Nearly Half of Living NFL Veterans Show Signs of Brain Injury: Study' *The Huffington Post*, 12 April 2016 (<http://www.huffingtonpost.com.au/entry/nfl-veterans-brain-injury_us_570c19f0e4b014223249f6b8?ir=Sports&section=australia&utm_hp_ref=sports>). The study's authors have now expanded their evaluations, and plan to publish their findings in a peer-reviewed journal during 2019 [email from Dr Francis Conidi (Neurologist, Florida) to author, 3 September 2018].

the Boston researchers of assuming too easily the causal link between multiple instances of concussion and CTE,[228] or at least knowingly exaggerating the extent of the issue in order to promote their own careers.[229] The fact remains that new and strong evidence continues to accumulate. According to the latest results released in 2017 by the US Brain Bank Depository, affiliated to Boston University, and chaired by neuropathologist and neurologist Ann McKee, 110 out of 111 NFL players examined were found to have CTE.[230] Researchers in Boston have now examined the brain tissue of 202 American (and Canadian) football players who, before their deaths, played the game professionally, semi-professionally, in college or in high school. Of that sample, 177 players, or 87%, tested positive for CTE.[231] These results were followed in 2018 by a study of the same University, which highlighted that in addition to violent collisions, repeated minor head trauma (sub-concussion) that occurs regularly in football may pose great risk to players.[232] This finding is particularly alarming for linemen, who come into contact with one another on every play of a game.[233] Boston University's work must be placed in perspective with the

---

[228]For instance, during the 4th CISG's conference held in Zurich in 2012, some experts, notably affiliated with the IOC and FIFA, highlighted that Boston researchers have limited their studies to individuals who were significantly impaired before their deaths, thus distorting statistics. They cautioned that there was not enough data to assess the risk of playing American football (or other team sports). In addition, they questioned whether other factors, such as genetic predisposition, medical illness, the use of illicit substances, alcohol, and age, may have led, or at least contributed to the appearance of the disease [Steve Fainaru and Mark Fainaru-Wada, 'Study: New Cases of CTE in Players', *ESPN*, 3 December 2012 (<http://espn.go.com/espn/otl/story/_/id/8697286/boston-university-researchers-discover-28-new-cases-chronic-brain-damage-deceased-football-players>) (Fainaru and Fainaru-Wada, 'CTE']. Their concerns were subsequently incorporated in the 4th CISG's statement, and reiterated during the 2016 CISG's conference in Berlin and its 5th statement [see Paul McCrory et al., 'Consensus Statement on Concussion in Sport: The 4th International Conference on Concussion in Sport Held in Zurich, November 2012' (2013) 47(5) *British Journal of Sports Medicine* 250, 254 (McCrory et al., '4th Consensus'); and Chapter 2, Section VII]. In the same vein, see eg, Gavin A Davis, Rudolph J Castellani and Paul McCrory, 'Neurodegeneration in Sport' (2015) 76 *Neurosurgery* 643, 643–56, in particular 645–6 and 653; Andrew Gardner, Grant L Iverson and Paul McCrory, 'Chronic Traumatic Encephalopathy in Sport: A Systematic Review' (2014) 48 *British Journal of Sports Medicine* 84, 84 and 86–9, in particular 89; Maroon et al., above n 100 in Chapter 2, 1–16, in particular 11–12. These authors notably point out the lack of accounting for premorbid data, and comorbidity factors, which might contribute to or confound neuropathological findings.

[229]Ibid. In the same vein, see also Mark Fainaru-Wada and Steve Fainaru, *The League of Denial: The NFL, Concussions, and the Battle for Truth* (2013, Crown Archetype), in particular 324–39 (Fainaru-Wada and Fainaru, 'Denial'). Although highly critical towards the NFL and its handling of the concussion crisis, this book acknowledges the existence of a certain competition between US researchers.

[230]Jesse Mez at al, 'Clinicopathological Evaluation of Chronic Traumatic Encephalopathy in Players of American Football' (2017) 318 *Journal Of American Medical Association* 360, 361.

[231]Ibid.

[232]Tagge et al., above n 129 in Chapter 2, 422.

[233]About the vulnerability of linemen, see eg, Ann C McKee et al., 'The Spectrum of Disease in Chronic Traumatic Encephalopathy' (2013) 136 *Brain* 43, 59 (McKee et al., 'Spectrum').

first study released following the 'Play Smart' initiative, previously mentioned.[234] The study consisted of a video review of the 459 known instances of concussion that occurred over the 2015 and 2016 seasons.[235] It showed that concussion mostly affects defensive secondaries (cornerbacks), and are primarily due to helmet-to-helmet hits or helmet-to-body hits.[236] It also highlighted the risks of tackles.[237] The 2017 NFL Injury Data Report[238] is also of interest. It gives account of 200 physician-diagnosed instances of concussion during regular season games (out of a total of 291)—the highest rate of concussion since the NFL started to share its data in 2012.[239]

It is now logical to examine the legal activities and implications involved.

2 Legal Activities and Implications

The events described above were not without repercussions for the NFL. In recent years, thousands of former NFL players have filed suits across the US against the league and helmet manufacturers.[240] Among the legal proceedings that have attracted the most attention from legal commentators, are the *Maxwell*[241] and *Easterling*[242] claims, lodged in Los Angeles and Pennsylvania.

In June 2012, all of these lawsuits were combined into one single consolidated class action and multi-district litigation (which encompassed nearly 5000 plaintiffs)[243] in the US District Court for the Eastern District of Pennsylvania.[244] The

[234] See this chapter, Section IA1(e).

[235] Cindy Boren, 'The NFL Studied Every Concussion over Two Seasons. What Happens Next May Be up to Manufacturers', *The Washington Post* (<https://www.washingtonpost.com/news/early-lead/wp/2017/11/09/the-nfl-studied-every-concussion-over-two-seasons-what-happens-next-may-be-up-to-manufacturers/?noredirect=on&utm_term=.aafa26b0f89a>).

[236] Ibid.

[237] Ibid.

[238] NFL Injury Data Report (2017) (<https://www.playsmartplaysafe.com/newsroom/reports/2017-injury-data/>).

[239] This number covers pre-season and regular season practices and games.

[240] Joseph M Hanna, 'Paying the Piper: NFL's Concussion Policy Results in Huge Class Action Lawsuit', *'Mosessport'*, 15 August 2012 (<http://www.mosessport.com/Paying_the_Piper_-_NFL_s_Concussion_Policy_Results_in_Huge_Class_Action_Lawsuit.pdf>) (Hanna, 'Class Action').

[241] *Maxwell et al v National Football League et al* (Superior Court of California, County of Los Angeles, BC 465842, 19 July 2011.

[242] See Chapter 1, Section II and this chapter, Section IA1(g).

[243] 'NFL Concussion Litigation' website (<http://nflconcussionlitigation.com/?page_id=274>).

[244] In re: *National Football League Players' Concussion Injury Litigation*, MDL No. 2323. Plaintiffs filed a master administrative class action complaint for medical monitoring and a master administrative long-form complaint on 7 June 2012. They filed an amended master administrative long-form complaint on 17 July 2012 and an amended class action complaint on 6 January 2014. These documents are partly available on the 'NFL Concussion Litigation' website (<http://

NFL and the football helmet manufacturer Riddell were named as defendants in the proceedings.[245] In August 2012, the NFL filed a motion to dismiss the class action on pre-emption grounds, aimed at contesting the competence of the state court.[246] Written submissions were exchanged until early 2013.[247] Oral arguments on the motion to dismiss were held in April 2013.[248] In July 2013, prior to ruling on the motion to dismiss, the Court ordered the parties to engage in mediation.[249] In April 2015, after several failed attempts,[250] a final settlement,[251] concluded between the NFL and the former players, was endorsed by the presiding judge,[252] leaving Riddell as the only defendant in the procedure.[253]

This section examines the potential liability of the NFL in closer detail against the background of the abovementioned proceedings. It describes the legal path that was

---

nflconcussionlitigation.com/?page_id=18>) and fully available via the Bloomberg database (access on subscription).

[245]Riddell was only named as a defendant in the master administrative long-form complaints, that is to say in the mass actions. It was not involved in the master administrative class action complaints for medical monitoring [ibid].

[246]The NFL filed a motion to dismiss the master administrative class action complaint for medical monitoring and the amended master administrative long-form complaint on 30 August 2012. These documents are available on the 'NFL Concussion Litigation' website (<http://nflconcussionlitigation.com/?page_id=18>). In US law, federal pre-emption is the invalidation of a US state law or regulation that conflicts with federal law [see Garner, above n 5, 1369 and this chapter, footnote 269].

[247]Plaintiffs filed their opposition to the motion on 31 October 2012, the NFL filed a reply memorandum of law on 17 December 2012, and plaintiffs filed a sur-reply memorandum of law on 28 January 2013. These documents are available on the 'NFL Concussion Litigation' website (<http://nflconcussionlitigation.com/?page_id=18>).

[248]Paul D Anderson, 'Exclusive: Concussion Kickoff—Oral Arguments held in NFL Concussion Litigation', *'NFL Concussion Litigation'*, 10 April 2013 (<http://nflconcussionlitigation.com/?p=1423>) (Paul D Anderson, 'Kickoff).

[249]Paul D Anderson, 'Judge Brody Orders Mediation', *'NFL Concussion Litigation'*, 8 July 2013 (<http://nflconcussionlitigation.com/?p=1467>) (Paul D Anderson, 'Mediation').

[250]On 29 August 2013, the parties signed a settlement term sheet setting forth the material terms of a settlement agreement. The content of this initial agreement is summed up in the press release of the Alternative Dispute Resolution Center of 29 August 2013 (<http://static.nfl.com/static/content/public/photo/2013/08/29/0ap2000000235504.pdf>). The proposed settlement of 6 January 2014, as well as its revised versions, are available on the 'NFL Concussion Litigation' website (<http://nflconcussionlitigation.com/?page_id=18>). See also the 'NFL Concussion Settlement' website, where the main court documents related to the settlement procedure are available (<https://www.nflconcussionsettlement.com/CourtDocs.aspx>).

[251]Ibid.

[252]See final settlement approval order and judgment of 22 April 2015 and its accompanying approval memorandum. See also the amended final order and judgment of 8 May 2015 and the order clarifying paragraph 16 of the amended final order and judgment of 11 May 2015. These documents are available on the 'NFL Concussion Settlement' website (<https://www.nflconcussionsettlement.com/CourtDocs.aspx>).

[253]See this chapter, Section IA2(b).

instrumental in reaching a settlement, as well as the specific terms of this settlement. Finally, it briefly discusses the potential liability of other contributors.

(a) The Potential Liability of the NFL

(i) Legal Arguments against the NFL

In their amended class action complaint of 6 January 2014,[254] the plaintiffs sought unspecified financial damages and medical monitoring for neurological disorders.[255] They set out different counts of legal claims in torts.[256] These included negligence and fraud-based claims.[257]

The negligence-based claims focused on an allegation that the NFL breached its duty of care to its players by failing to warn them about, and protect them from, the long-term health problems associated with concussion.[258]

The fraud-based claims centered on the affirmative actions the NFL allegedly took to conceal and/or misrepresent the connection between concussion and long-term medical complications.[259]

The NFL had several possible defences.

(ii) Possible Defences

In the US, discussion has been rife about the filing of a class action and legal commentators have been quick to analyse possible defences available to the NFL.[260] These defences related to the justiciability and the merits of the class action.

---

[254]See this chapter, Section IA2, footnote 244.

[255]Amended class action complaint, pp. 76–7 (Prayer for Relief).

[256]Amended class action complaint, pp. 52–76, paragraphs 250–389.

[257]Ibid.

[258]Amended class action complaint, pp. 62–72, paragraphs 307–68. See also pp. 73–5, paragraphs 373–85 (negligent hiring and retention).

[259]See amended class action complaint, in particular pp. 56–61, paragraphs 274–306 and p. 60, paragraph 298. These paragraphs refer to the research that the NFL voluntarily funded and produced from 1994, through the MTBI Committee, in total contradiction with the scientific data available for decades in relation to the risks associated with head trauma [referred to on pp. 13–16, paragraphs 54–64 and pp. 22–30, paragraphs 89–127]. See also p. 76, paragraphs 386–9 (civil conspiracy and fraudulent concealment).

[260]Greenhow, 'Charter' above n 13 in Chapter 1, 13. Note that most of these writings were published before the class action occurred, or at an early stage of the proceedings. Consequently, they are not related to the defences available in Pennsylvania in particular, but are intended to be general. As most of the defences raised are typically common law defences, it has little bearing on the legal proceedings in general. If appropriate, some comments have, however, been added in the footnotes.

To the notable exception of the statute of limitations,[261] the issue of justiciability was then extensively discussed by the parties during the proceedings.[262] This was not the case on the merits, which was not the object of a full formal exchange of written submissions or oral pleadings,[263] leaving more room for speculation.[264]

(iii) Justiciability

In its motion to dismiss of 30 August 2012,[265] the NFL asked, as several commentators had forecast,[266] for the dismissal of the class action on pre-emption grounds.[267] The NFL argued that the case fell under its own regulations (in particular its CBAs),[268] which contain numerous provisions on warnings and player safety, as well as an arbitration clause.[269]

In their opposition to the motion of 31 October 2012,[270] the plaintiffs contended that their claims fell outside the provisions of the CBAs.[271]

---

[261] See this chapter, Section IA2(a)(iii).

[262] Ibid.

[263] See this chapter, Section IA2(a)(iv) (a contrario).

[264] There is no doubt that settlement negotiations presented an opportunity for the parties to evaluate the legitimacy of their respective claims and defences [in the same vein, see eg, initial proposed settlement agreement of 1 January 2014, Recitals, H (incorporated in subsequent agreements); final settlement approval memorandum of 22 April 2015, p. 9]. The analysis of the arguments related to the merits, performed as part of these negotiations, remains confidential. Reference will mainly be made to the legal commentaries for this issue. Some references to the plaintiffs' submissions will also be indicated, as these have partly anticipated sensitive problems from being raised further in proceedings. Conversely, the NFL's submissions strictly rely on pre-emption grounds.

[265] See this chapter, Section IA2, footnote 246.

[266] See eg, Hanna, 'NFL', above n 110 in Chapter 2, 13.

[267] Motion to dismiss, pp. 1–35.

[268] For the 2011 NFL CBA, see this chapter, Section IA1(c), footnote 69.

[269] Motion to dismiss, pp. 6–11 and 14–32. The NFL moved to dismiss the plaintiffs' claims under section 301 of the *Labor Management Relations Act (LMRA)*, 29 USC §185 [Motion to dismiss, p. 14]. In support, the NFL invoked extensive precedent of preempted cases [Motion to dismiss, in particular ii-iv], among which *Duerson* and *Maxwell* [*Duerson v National Football League*, N.D. Ill, 2012 WL 1658353; *Maxwell v National Football League* (C.D. Cal., No. 11-CV-08394, 8 December 2011), Order; concussion lawsuits that were subsequently incorporated into the class action), *Stringer* (*Stringer v National Football League*, 474 F. Supp. 2d 894 (S.D. Ohio 2007); heat stroke death during a training camp) and *Williams* (*Williams v National Football League*, 582 F.3d 863 (8th Cir. 2009); use of steroids)].

[270] See this chapter, Section IA2, footnote 247.

[271] Opposition to the motion, pp. 2 and 34–5. The plaintiffs argued that their claims arose from historical actions [Opposition to the motion, p. 2]. They rejected the applicability of the precedent invoked by the NFL [Opposition to the motion, pp. 28–33], while trying to take advantage of the argument of precedent of non-preempted cases, some of which, such as *Kline*, did not concern specifically the NFL [Opposition to the motion, in particular p. 12; see also *Kline v Security Guards*, Inc., 386 F.3d 246 (3d Cir. 2004); use of electronic surveillance over employees]. Additionally, the plaintiffs asserted that many of them were not covered under the CBAs, none of which were in force before 1968 and between 1987 and 1993 [Opposition to the motion, p. 9].

The parties' arguments were further developed in their reply memorandum of law and sur-reply memorandum of law of 17 December 2012 and 28 January 2013,[272] before being raised again during the hearing on 10 April 2013.[273]

The state of these discussions lay in the issue as to whether the class action could progress before the state court, or if the plaintiffs should seek arbitration.[274]

The NFL did not argue that the plaintiffs had lost their right to sue as a result of the expiration of the statutory limitations period.[275] This ground could have conflicted with the 'discovery rule', aimed to apply to latent injuries. Under this rule, a cause of action does not accrue until plaintiffs know, or reasonably should have known, that they were injured with latent injuries as a result of defendant's conduct.[276]

(iv) Merits

Should the proceedings have continued before state court or arbitration, the NFL could have raised several defences on the merits.[277]

The NFL might first have alleged that, in the absence of a special relationship, it had no legal duty to warn players and/or protect them from the potential long-term

[272]See this chapter, Section IA2, footnote 247.

[273]On this occasion, the key discussion focused on the binding precedent *Kline* (see this chapter, Section IA2(a)(iii), footnote 271). The plaintiffs tried to rely closely on *Kline*'s facts and reasoning to argue that pre-emption was inappropriate [sur-reply memoranda of law, p. 13]. In contrast, the NFL tried to distinguish the facts of the class action from *Kline* [reply memoranda of law, p. 7]. The same issue emerged throughout the hearing, whose summary and audio recording are available on the 'NFL Concussion Litigation' website: Paul D Anderson, 'Kickoff', above n 248.

[274]Telis, above n 13 in Chapter 1, 1844–5.

[275]Note that the NFL would not have been precluded from raising this argument later in the proceedings [see Rule 12(b) of the *Federal Rules of Civil Procedure* (*FED.R.CIV.P.)* a contrario]. For more details about the statutory limitations period in Pennsylvania, see Title 42, Part VI, Chapter 55 of the *Pennsylvania Statutes* (PAS Cons Stat). Section 5524, which covers any injury claims (Subpart 2) as well as fraud/deceit claims (subpart 7) would have applied. This section provides for a two-year statute of limitations.

[276]The 'discovery rule' has been long established by US courts [in Pennsylvania, see eg, *Beauty Time Inc v VU Skin System*, 118 F3d 140 (3d Cir. 1997); this case tolls statutes for various types of cases, and refers to the fact that a cause of action does only starts when the plaintiff knows, or through the exercise of reasonable diligence should have known, of the injury and its cause].

[277]The NFL defences would have in essence remained the same, regardless of the jurisdiction. However, the remedies usually afforded to players under the NFL's arbitration process include contract damages, injunctive relief, fines, and specific performance [Art. 15 section 2c of the NFL CBA]. Conversely, tort law generally allows for the recovery of compensatory, and sometimes punitive damages [*Restatement (Second) of Torts* (1979), sections 904–8]. On this topic, see also Telis, above n 13 in Chapter 1, 1846.

risks associated with head injuries.[278] Courts have indicated that NFL players are employees of their teams, and not the league.[279] Even in the absence of an employment relationship, the players could have emphasised the NFL's voluntary creation of its internal Concussion Committee. This might have created a duty for the NFL to exercise reasonable care, as the players relied on its recommendations.[280]

The NFL could also have argued that the players had contributed to their own injuries by failing to report their concussive conditions, and returning to play before becoming symptom free.[281] This defence may have been supported by a survey of the Associated Press of 2009, in which 30 of 160 NFL players had admitted that they either failed to report or underreported concussion symptoms, and returned to play despite them.[282] Nevertheless, this behaviour most probably finds its grounds in the 'macho attitude' that prevails in American football,[283] as well as in the NFL's contractual scheme itself.[284] Indeed, NFL contracts do not guarantee players' payments beyond the season in which an injury occurs.[285] To this is added the fact that,

---

[278]Hanna, 'NFL', above n 110 in Chapter 2, 13; and motion to dismiss, p. 20, where the NFL contends that the assessment of a duty of care, if any, would depend on the interpretation of the CBAs.

[279]See eg, *N. Am. Soccer League v NFL*, 670 F.2d 1249, 1252 (2d Cir. 1982). Contra: Heiner, above n 57 in Chapter 2, 280–92. Note that if one followed this author's opinion—and chose to distance himself/herself from the current American jurisprudence—this might lead to a discussion in relation to the workers' compensation system. This system is a form of insurance providing limited wage replacement, medical and like benefits, and in some cases, lump sum benefits to employees injured in the course of employment in exchange for mandatory relinquishment of the employee's right to bring a common-law cause of action against his or her employer [for a detailed analysis of this issue, see Modery, above n 13 in Chapter 1, 247–82].

[280]Hanna, 'NFL', above n 110 in Chapter 2, 13; opposition to the motion, pp. 1–3, 15 and 25; and sur-reply memorandum, pp. 1, 6, 8 and 28. The plaintiffs raised similar arguments during the hearing, just as the audio recording confirms (see this chapter, Section IA2(a)(iii), footnote 273). See also amended class action complaint, p. 20, paragraphs 84–5.

[281]Hanna, 'NFL', above n 110 in Chapter 2, 14. For a legal definition of the contributory-negligence doctrine, see Garner, above n 5, ad 'contributory-negligence doctrine', 403.

[282]Hanna, 'NFL', above n 110 in Chapter 2, 14.

[283]See eg, Bernstein, above n 2 in Chapter 2, 308. In the same vein, see amended master complaint, p. 3, paragraph 10, pp. 11–15, paragraphs 50–66, in particular p. 14, paragraphs 61–2, pp. 64–5 paragraphs 335–6 and p. 67, paragraphs 353–5; opposition to the motion, pp. 2, 5 and 14–15; and sur-reply memorandum, in particular p. 6. See also amended class action complaint, p. 10, paragraph 39 and p. 12, paragraph 49.

[284]Hanna, 'NFL', above n 110 in Chapter 2, 14.

[285]2011 NFL CBA, Appendix A. In addition, the grievance hearing process in player contract disputes, regulated by the NFL CBA, is likely to deter a player to disclose his concussion symptoms. Team management might call the trainer as a witness to testify against the player filing the grievance, in order to demonstrate that the player did not pass the physical examination administered by the club physician at the beginning of the pre-season training camp [Art. 44 of the 2011 CBA)]. In the same vein, see amended master complaint, p. 14 paragraph 62 and p. 23 paragraph 107; amended class action complaint, p. 21, paragraph 88.

under certain circumstances, players might not be capable of determining if they are able to return to play, due to the trauma suffered.[286]

The NFL could have raised the argument of the doctrine of voluntary assumption of risk.[287] This doctrine implies that players knew, or should have known, the potential risk of later-life cognitive decline associated with playing football.[288]

The NFL could have pointed to a number of other causes that might have contributed to deceased NFL players' cognitive decline, such as steroids, drug abuse, or even injuries sustained in lower leagues ('but for' standard).[289] This standard is applied with certain flexibility in practice.[290] Taking such a defence would have turned on each individual case. It would also have amounted to questioning the reliability of respectable and well-established studies,[291] for which NFL accepted their legitimacy, at least in principle, in 2009.[292]

---

[286]Tracey B Carter, 'Consent', above n 13 in Chapter 1, 35. Note that contributory negligence is a partial defence. Even if players had been found contributorily negligent, they could still have recovered damages in the State of Pennsylvania, which adheres to comparative negligence principles. Their financial recovery would have been reduced by the degree of their fault, but not prohibited, as long as their fault did not reach 51% [*Pennsylvania Comparative Negligence Law*, PA Cons Stat §7102].

[287]Hanna, 'NFL', above n 110 in Chapter 2, 14. For a legal definition of the doctrine of voluntary assumption of risk, see Garner, above n 5, ad 'assumption of (the) risk', 149. This doctrine is very close to the principle of contributory negligence. However, it is a distinct and complete defence. As discussed in this section, '[a]ssumption of risk involves a plaintiff's actual knowledge of danger and intelligence acquiescence in it, whereas contributory negligence is a matter of plaintiff's fault or departure of standard of reasonable conduct' [Hanna, 'NFL', above n 110 in Chapter 2, 16]. Where a defendant can establish the doctrine of voluntary assumption of risk, they are absolved from liability [Natasha Schot, 'Negligent Liability in Sport' (2005) *Sports Law e-Journal* 1, 5 (<http://classic.austlii.edu.au/au/journals/SportsLaweJl/2005/1.html>)].

[288]Ibid. In the same vein (implied), see amended master complaint, in particular p. 2, paragraph 6 and p. 55, paragraph 276 (where the plaintiffs declare that the NFL failed to warn and protect them and concealed the connection between concussion and long-term chronic brain injury), p. 18, paragraph 85 and p. 19 paragraph 89 (where the plaintiffs highlight that the NFL's scientific knowledge was superior to theirs); opposition to the motion, in particular p. 22; and sur-reply memorandum, in particular pp. 16 and 24, footnote 19. See also amended class action, in particular p. 2, paragraph 3 and p. 16, paragraph 66.

[289]Hanna, 'NFL', above n 110 in Chapter 2, 14.

[290]Ibid.

[291]See this chapter, Section IA1(b).

[292]See this chapter, Section IA1(e). In the same vein (implied), see amended master complaint, pp. 23–32, paragraphs 108–47 (where the plaintiffs offer a chronological account of the state of science) and p. 47, paragraph 234 (where the plaintiffs point out the NFL's acknowledgement of the link between multiple concussions and brain damage); opposition to the motion, pp. 7–8. See also amended class action, pp. 22–30, paragraphs 89–127 and p. 43, paragraphs 199–200.

Finally, defence attorneys might have argued that a player's acceptance of the '88 Plan'[293] indemnified the NFL against any future civil liability.[294] However, the section related to the '88 Plan' does not contain any indemnification language.[295] The implementation of this plan might, conversely, constitute an implicit acknowledgment of responsibility by the NFL.[296]

(v) Prospects of Success and Settlement Procedure

The methods adopted by the NFL are open to criticism in many respects. For decades, the NFL entrenched itself behind its own studies, though criticised by the scientific community.[297] Since at least 2005, the NFL has been aware of medical examinations linking football head impacts with later-life cognitive decline.[298]

Despite this, little has been done to protect players' health until the intervention of Congress in 2009.[299] The players were left in ignorance of the potential risks they assumed.[300] These failings were likely to provide the basis for the liability of the NFL. This is, in any case, what the broad principles of justice would have required.

As the legal literature emphasised, 'the NFL [was] most vulnerable to players who experienced concussions between the 2005 widespread publication of the risks of concussions and the NFL's adoption of stricter guidelines and issuance of warnings in 2010. During this period, the NFL appear[ed] most culpable by first contesting the findings of scientists and ultimately, reversing course in its treatment of concussions'.[301]

If convincing evidence showed that the NFL failed to implement adequate measures early enough,[302] the league had, however, various potential persuasive

[293] See this chapter, Section IA1(c).

[294] Hanna, 'NFL', above n 110 in Chapter 2, 15.

[295] Ibid.

[296] Andrew B Carrabis, 'Head Hunters: the Rise of Neurological Concussions in American Football and its Legal Implications' (2011) 2 *Harvard Journal of Sports & Entertainment Law* 371, 380. See also the discussions of the parties with regard to the '88 Plan' and other benefit provisions [amended master complaint, p. 56, paragraph 282 and p. 61, paragraph 317; motion to dismiss, p. 29; opposition to the motion, 26, reply memorandum, pp. 23–4 and sur-reply memorandum, p. 19; amended class action, p. 27, paragraph 115].

[297] See this chapter, Sections IA1(a) et seq; Heiner, above n 57 in Chapter 2, 261–4.

[298] See this chapter, Section IA1(b); Hanna, 'NFL', above n 110 in Chapter 2, 13 and 19.

[299] See this chapter, Sections IA1(a) et seq; Greenhow, 'Charter', above n 13 in Chapter 1, 5 and 7 (a contrario).

[300] See this chapter, Sections IA1(a) et seq; Hanna, 'NFL', above n 110 in Chapter 2, 13 and 19.

[301] Cerra, 'Unringing the Bell: Former Players Sue NFL and Helmet Manufacturers over Concussion Risks in Maxwell v NFL' (2012) 16 *Michigan State University Journal of Medicine & Law* 265, 294 (in the specific case of the Maxwell's suit, whose reasoning is, however, relevant for the 2012 class action).

[302] Gove, above n 18, 676, 680–4; Hanna, 'NFL', above n 110 in Chapter 2, 13.

defences to the class action.[303] Among these, CBA pre-emption and contributory negligence were considered as particularly solid by legal commentators.[304]

At that time, there had been very few cases in the US brought against SGBs for failure to comply with their legal duty of care to protect players from harm.[305] The unique nature of the class action litigation made any attempt at comparison difficult.

The complexity of the case and legal uncertainty could have resulted in very long proceedings.[306] This prospect probably discouraged the plaintiffs, some of whom were already impaired, and possibly in a difficult financial situation, coping with uncovered medical treatment costs, including nursing and/or home care.

Similarly, the discovery process had the potential of irreparably damaging the image of the NFL.[307] This could have resulted in indirect substantial financial loss in ticketing, TV rights and/or even sponsoring, not to mention the possible impact at lower levels.[308]

These considerations presumably led the parties to seek a settlement. At the end of August 2013, it was announced that the NFL had agreed to pay out USD765 million over 20 years to settle the class action.[309] This amount included a cap of USD675 million Monetary Award Fund for the players and their families, the remainder having to be paid to baseline medical tests, research and awareness campaigns.[310]

---

[303]See this chapter, Sections IA2(a)(ii) et seq; Hanna, 'NFL', above n 110 in Chapter 2, 13 and 19.

[304]About pre-emption, see eg, Heard, above n 13 in Chapter 1, 233 and 243–4; Telis, above n 13 in Chapter 1, 1846 and 1866–8. About contributory negligence, see eg, Hanna, 'NFL', above n 110 in Chapter 2, 14. Note, however, that the pre-emption argument has been rejected in the NHL concussion litigation (see this chapter, Section IB2(a)(i)).

[305]Most of the cases relating to the legal duty of care to protect players concern other contributors (mainly at amateur level), such as schools, coaches and doctors [for more details, see Mitten et al., 'Cases', above n 13 in Chapter 1, 857–973]. However, a few cases (some of which, such as *Williams* and *Stringer*, were discussed in relation to the admissibility of the class action against the NFL; see this chapter, Section IA2(a)(iii), footnote 269; see also *Dent v National Football League*, N.D. Cal., 2014 US Dist. LEXIS 174448 (painkillers)) are worth mentioning. These cases could have shed some light into the foregoing issue, in particular regarding the extent and scope of the legal duty of the NFL to protect its players, as opposed to the doctrine of voluntary assumption of risk. They constitute the background of the decisions ruled in the FIFA and USAWP litigation (see this chapter, Sections IC2(b) and ID2(b)).

[306]Certain experts considered that this litigation would not even have reached court for years (due to the controversy regarding the jurisdiction of the state courts), some speculating as far in the future as 2018. For more details, see Pete Strom, 'Will Concussions Bankrupt the NFL?', *'Strom Law Firm'* website (<http://stromlaw.com/6459/will-concussions-bankrupt-the-nfl/#>).

[307]Heard, above n 13 in Chapter 1, 241. For a definition of the 'discovery process', see this chapter, Section IA2, footnote 595.

[308]Cerra, 'above n 301, 294 (in the specific case of the Maxwell's suit, whose reasoning is, however, relevant for the 2012 class action).

[309]Alternative Dispute Resolution Center, above n 250, 1.

[310]Ibid, Summary of the key terms of the agreement (attached to the press release), pp. 1–2.

The initial settlement proposal did not satisfy the presiding judge.[311] In January 2014 and February 2015, the judge refused to endorse both the original and the revised settlement, and required various amendments in order to better protect the players' interests.[312]

A final settlement agreement,[313] without any cap, was approved in April 2015,[314] and the class certification granted.[315] According to first estimates, this settlement was expected to cover up to 21 000 now-retired NFL players (1700 of whom were already deceased)[316] over 65 years[317] and cost about USD1 billion in total to the NFL.[318] Finally, 18 400 players and relatives registered within the imposed deadline to receive benefits.[319] More than USD675 million dollars in claims have already been approved, out of a total that could reach USD1.89 billion, according to attorneys for players.[320]

As described in detail in the final document setting out the agreement between the parties and its 132-page accompanying approval memorandum,[321] the settlement provides payments to former players suffering from a range of neurological conditions.[322] The settlement also establishes a Baseline Assessment Program of USD75

[311]In the US, Rule 23e *FED.R.CIV.P.*, which relates to class actions proceedings, requires the court's approval for the signature of a settlement.

[312]For more details about these amendments, see final settlement approval memorandum, pp. 10–12 and pp. 21–3.

[313]See this chapter, Section IA2, footnote 250.

[314]See final settlement approval order and judgment of 22 April 2015 and its accompanying approval memorandum. See also the amended final order and judgment of 8 May 2015 and the order clarifying paragraph 16 of the amended final order and judgment of 11 May 2015.

[315]Class certification allows one or more members of a class to sue (or be sued) as representative parties on behalf of all members. It is governed by Art. 23 (a) and (b) *FED.R.CIV.P.*

[316]Final settlement approval memorandum, p. 24. See also Steven J Silver, 'NFL Concussion Litigation Moves Closer to a Resolution' (2015) 13(5) *World Sports Law Report* (online review). This author refers to the estimate of plaintiffs' expert (Thomas Vasquez, 'NFL Concussion Liability Forecast', Report, 10 February 2014, pp. 3 and 14, available at <http://nflconcussionlitigation.com/wp-content/uploads/2014/09/6167-Special-Master-Report.pdf>).

[317]Final settlement, Art. VI, section 6.10, p. 38; final settlement approval memorandum, pp. 10, 36, 74, 90 and 125.

[318]Silver, above n 316. See also Vasquez, above n 316, 33.

[319]Rachel Graf, 'More Than 18K Players Register For NFL Concussion Settlement', *'Consider The Consumer'*, 7 August 2017 (<https://considertheconsumer.com/consumer-news/18k-push-nfl-concussion-settlement>).

[320]AAP, 'NFL Concussion Claims Eclipse $675 Mark', *Brisbane Times*, 31 July 2018 (<https://www.brisbanetimes.com.au/sport/nfl/nfl-concussion-claims-eclipse-675m-mark-20180731-p4zujd.html>) (AAP, 'NFL').

[321]See this chapter, Section IA2, footnote 252.

[322]Final settlement, Art. VI, sections 6.1–6.10, pp. 31–8; final settlement approval memorandum, pp. 14–17.

million aimed at monitoring retired players' health, and determining if they are eligible for monetary awards.[323] It includes a USD10 million fund meant to improve players' awareness about their legal rights and, more generally, the long-term risks associated with concussion.[324]

The settlement provides cash awards for six Qualifying Diagnoses: Level 1.5 Neurocognitive Impairment; Level 2 Neurocognitive Impairment; Alzheimer's Disease; Parkinson's Disease; ALS; and Death with CTE.[325] The Level 1.5 and 2 Neurocognitive Impairments are essentially mild and moderate dementia that cause a loss of cognitive and functional capabilities, such as holding a job or performing household chores.[326]

The application of the settlement is not restricted to the players involved in the class action. The settlement applies to any player who retired before 7 July 2014 and to the families of players with CTE who died between 1 January 2006 and 22 April 2015,[327] with the exception of those who exercised their rights to opt-out.[328]

If a former player is diagnosed with any of the aforementioned disorders, he is entitled to the following payouts regardless of causation: Level 1.5 Neurocognitive Impairment—USD1.5 million; Level 2 Neurocognitive Impairment - USD3 million; Parkinson's Disease—USD3.5 million; Alzheimer's Disease—USD3.5 million; Death with CTE—USD4 million; and ALS—USD5 million.[329]

Although the amounts outlined (and notably the USD765 million discussed on a preliminary basis) represent a lot of money, criticism of the settlement did not take long to emerge. Some commentators pointed out that the sums promised by the NFL should be put into perspective with its annual revenues (USD10 billion at that time),

---

[323]Final settlement, Art. V, sections 5.1–5.5, pp. 20–1; final settlement approval memorandum, pp. 18–19.

[324]Final settlement, Art. VII, sections 12.1–12.2, p. 64; final settlement approval memorandum, pp. 19–20.

[325]Final settlement, Art. VI, section 6.3, pp. 32–3; final settlement approval memorandum, p. 15.

[326]Final settlement, Exhibit A1, pp. 2–4. See also Silver, above n 316.

[327]Final settlement, Art. II, section 2.1, p. 14 and Art. VI, sections 6.1–6.4, pp. 31–4; final settlement approval memorandum, pp. 12–13, 16–17 and 122–4. Any eligible representative claimant of a deceased retired player who died prior to 1 January 2006 will receive a monetary award only if he can show that his wrongful death or survival claim would not be barred by the statute of limitations under applicable state law. Such a claimant could in all likelihood invoke the 'discovery rule'. Under this rule, a cause of action does not accrue until plaintiffs know or reasonably should have known that they were injured with latent injuries as a result of the defendant's conduct. Applied to CTE, which can currently only be diagnosed post-mortem, this should mean that the limitation period should not start running before the death of the athlete in question [see ibid.; about the statute of limitations and the 'discovery rule', see this chapter, Section IA2(a)(iii), and footnotes 275–6; about the diagnosis of CTE, see Chapter 2, Section VII].

[328]Final settlement, Art. I, section 1.1, p. 4 and Art. II, section 2.1, p. 12; final settlement approval memorandum, pp. 63 and 131–2.

[329]Final settlement, Exhibit A5, p. 11; final settlement approval memorandum, p. 15.

regretting that the league could escape litigation and, therefore, avoid having to explain its failures.[330]

Similarly, despite actuarial calculations made by the NFL during the negotiations, according to which 28% of the retired players would develop brain impairment,[331] a relatively small number of players (3600, according to the plaintiffs' expert)[332] may in fact receive payment. This is primarily due to the medical conditions that are actually covered by the settlement. The most contentious of the Qualifying Diagnoses is CTE.[333] In the absence of a test able to diagnose CTE with certainty in living individuals,[334] only a former player's estate can qualify for a payment, subject to a post-mortem diagnosis of CTE by a board of certified neuropathologists.[335] In other words, as things stand, any player with mood and behavioural symptoms, supposedly living with CTE, will not qualify for a monetary award.[336] In theory, the settlement leaves the prospect of possible modifications by the parties 'in good faith' to the Qualifying Diagnosis in case of advancement of science.[337]

Another issue with the settlement concerns attorneys' fees (related to negotiations), which the NFL agreed not to contest up to USD112.5 million.[338] The approval of such high fees made some commentators say that players' lead counsels were colluding with the NFL.[339]

---

[330]See eg, Heard, above n 13 in Chapter 1, 246.

[331]Howard Flurh et al., 'Report of the Segal Group to Special Master Perry Golkin', 2014, p. 13, (<http://nflconcussionlitigation.com/wp-content/uploads/2014/09/6168-NFL-Report-to-Special-Master.pdf>).

[332]Vasquez, above n 316, 3–4.

[333]Final settlement approval memorandum, p. 78.

[334]See Chapter 2, Sections VII and VIII.

[335]Final settlement, Art. VI, section 6.3, p. 33; final settlement approval memorandum, p. 14.

[336]Final settlement, Art. VI, section 6.3, p. 33 (a contrario); final settlement approval memorandum, pp. 14 (a contrario), 79 and 83.

[337]Final settlement, Art. VI, section 6.6, p. 35; final settlement approval memorandum, p. 79. In her final settlement approval memorandum (pp. 79–83), Judge Brody emphasised the limits of the current state of scientific and medical knowledge regarding CTE. The judge asserted that clinical study of CTE (led by Dr Ann McKee and Robert Stern) was in its infancy. She insisted on the fact that researchers had only been able to reconstruct the symptoms of about half of the subjects while alive, all the more since they referred to family members' statements, instead of medical professionals. The judge also pointed out the possibility of selection bias, making it difficult to infer the incidence of CTE in the general population, or even among players. Referring to the 4th CISG's statement, she highlighted that other risk factors needed further investigating. She concluded that because of these limitations, it was not possible to determine accurately the symptoms someone with CTE would suffer from during their life.

[338]Final settlement, Art. XXI, sections 21.1–21.2, pp. 77–8; final settlement approval memorandum, pp. 21 and 30.

[339]According to objectors, these high fees gave players' attorneys more of an incentive to reach a deal and not hold out for a better benefits package on behalf of the players. This argument was, however, denied by Judge Brody [Final settlement approval memorandum, pp. 31–2].

Moreover, awards can be reduced to satisfy government liens[340] and based on a player's age and the number of seasons he played in the NFL and its former affiliate leagues (World League of American Football and NFL Europe).[341] For instance, a person who played fewer than five 'eligible seasons' in the NFL will see his award decrease potentially by more than half.[342] Yet the average NFL career is only 3.5 years.[343]

Finally, the settlement excludes from its scope players who retired as of 7 July 2014 and the estates of players diagnosed with CTE who died after 22 April 2015. These exclusions allow some uncertainty to persist for future claims while, in the second hypothesis, the potentially compensatory injuries might have been caused a few decades ago.[344]

Mainly due to the sticking point about CTE compensation, 208 class members opted out of the settlement and 205 objectors filed 83 written objections.[345] Others, such as the Seau family, opted out because they wanted to force the NFL to give explanations about its alleged wrongdoing.[346]

Based on these objections, several appeals were filed in the 3rd Circuit Court of Philadelphia.[347] In April and June 2016, these appeals were dismissed[348] and the

---

[340] Federal and state law allow the Medicare and Medicaid programs to recoup any health insurance payments made to an insured if a third party is found responsible for the underlying injury [Final settlement approval memorandum, pp. 15–16].

[341] The World League, later renamed the NFL Europe League, was a professional American football league that operated between 1991 and 2007, and whose season culminated with the World Bowl. It was subsequently backed by the NFL [For more details, see the NFL website (<http://www.nfl.com/news/story/09000d5d801308ec/article/nfl-europa-closes>)]. About the determination of monetary awards and related reductions, see final settlement, Art. II, section 2.1, p. 9, Art. VI, section 6.7, pp. 36–7 and Art. XI, section 11.3, pp. 60–3; final settlement approval memorandum, pp. 15–16.

[342] Final settlement, Art. II, section 2.1, p. 9 and Art. VI, section 6.7, p. 36; final settlement approval memorandum, pp. 15–16.

[343] Silver, above n 316.

[344] For more details, see Paul D Anderson, 'Stabler's Death is a Stark Reminder About the Settlement Deficiencies' *'NFL Concussion Litigation'*, 10 July 2015 (<http://nflconcussionlitigation.com/?p=1756>) (Paul D Anderson, 'Settlement'), who discusses this issue through the case of deceased former NFL player and plaintiff Ken Stabler.

[345] Final settlement approval memorandum, p. 21.

[346] Silver, above n 316. It may be noted, however, that the Seau family reached a settlement with the NFL in October 2018.

[347] In re: *NFL Players Concussion Injury Litigation,* No. 15-2206. The parties' submissions and the audio recording of the related hearing of 19 November 2015 are available on the *'NFL Concussion Litigation'* website: Paul D Anderson, 'NFL Concussion Litigation Oral Argument Set for Nov. 20', *'NFL Concussion Litigation'*, 9 October 2015 (<http://nflconcussionlitigation.com/?p=1764>) (Paul D Anderson, 'Oral Argument'); Paul D Anderson, 'Third Circuit Oral Argument Published', *'NFL Concussion Litigation'*, 23 November 2015 (<http://nflconcussionlitigation.com/?p=1827>) (Paul D Anderson, 'Third Circuit').

[348] Ken Belson, 'Appeals Court Affirms Landmark N.F.L. Concussion Settlement', *The New York Times*, 18 April 2016 (<http://www.nytimes.com/2016/04/19/sports/football/nfl-concussion-

request for rehearing denied.[349] The appellate judges concluded that the settlement, although perfectible, benefited the greater good among players and was fair.[350] In December 2016, the US Supreme Court upheld this decision, clearing the way for payouts to begin.[351]

However, this may not be totally the end of the controversy for American football. Issues surrounding the settlement remain regarding the allocation of attorneys' fees[352] and NFL compensation payouts.[353] In addition, the NFL is currently embroiled in litigation in the New York Supreme Court against its insurers over who will ultimately bear these fees and compensation payouts.[354] Finally, new individual concussion lawsuits have been filed against the NFL, either by players who opted out the settlement or retired after 7 July 2014.[355]

Together with the NFL, other contributors could potentially be held liable in cases of medical complications associated with multiple instances of concussion.

---

lawsuit.html?_r=0>) (Belson, 'Appeals Court I')—which contains a link to the judgment of the 3rd Circuit Court of Philadelphia of 18 April 2016.

[349]Joseph M Hanna, 'Third Circuit Denies Rehearing NFL Concussion Settlement, Compensation Forthcoming' *Sports and Entertainment Law Insider*, 9 June 2016 (<http://sportslawinsider.com/third-circuit-denies-rehearing-nfl-concussion-settlement-compensation-forthcoming/>) (Hanna, 'Third Circuit').

[350]Judgment of 18 April 2016, pp. 69–70.

[351]Ken Belson, 'N.F.L. Concussion Settlement Payments Can Begin After Supreme Court Defers', *The New York Times*, 12 December 2016 (<https://www.nytimes.com/2016/12/12/sports/football/nfl-concussion-settlement-payments-supreme-court.html>) (Ken Belson, 'Supreme Court').

[352]Joseph M Hanna, 'NFL Concussion Litigation Settlement Results in a Flurry of Objections', *Sports and Entertainment Law Insider*, 1 May 2017 (<http://sportslawinsider.com/nfl-concussion-litigation-settlement-results-in-a-flurry-of-objections/>) (Hanna, 'Objections'). For this procedure, see In Re: *NFL Players' Concussion Injury Litigation*, No. 18-02724.

[353]See eg, Ken Belson, 'Debilitated Players Accuse N.F.L. of Stalling on Settlement Payments', *The New York Times*, 13 November 2017 (<https://www.nytimes.com/2017/11/13/sports/football/nfl-concussion-lawsuit.html>) (Belson, 'Settlement'). According to the settlement (p. 119), class members, co-lead class counsel and the NFL parties may appeal the claims administrator's decision as to whether a class member is entitled to a monetary award. This appeal right gave rise to another procedure (In re: *National Football League Players' Concussion Injury Litigation* (Specified Ancillary Matters), No 2:18-md-02323).

[354]French, above n 13 in Chapter 1, 901–47. For these procedures, see Alterra America Insurance Co. v. National Football League, No. 652813/2012 and Discover Property & Casualty Co. v. National Football League, No. 652933/2012.

[355]See eg, Patrick Finley, 'Ex Bear Safety Craig Stelz Suing the NFL over Concussions: Report', *Chicago Sun Times*, 30 March 2018 (<https://chicago.suntimes.com/sports/ex-bears-safety-craig-steltz-suing-nfl-over-concussions-report/>).

(b) The Potential Liability of Other Contributors

Other contributors worth mentioning include helmet manufacturers (Riddell still being sued in the legal proceedings in Pennsylvania)[356] and retailers, the NFLPA, but also the clubs and their employees (team physicians and coaches) or even the players themselves.

This issue is beyond the scope of this study and only a few points of US law and questions of interest related to American football will be raised in this context.[357]

In the US, the case law against helmet manufacturers and retailers is extensive.[358] Liability may arise under the *Uniform Commercial Code (UCC)*[359] and strict liability principles (in particular the *Second* and *Third Restatements of Torts*).[360]

In the legal proceedings in Pennsylvania, the football helmet manufacturer Riddell was named as a defendant primarily because of its advertisements. These advertisements indicated that Riddell helmets reduced the risk of concussion by 31% compared to other manufacturers, a statement which is now highly questionable.[361] As with the NFL,[362] a finding of liability could have negative financial and reputational consequences for Riddell.[363] Riddell may, therefore, be inclined to seek out a settlement.[364]

---

[356]As mentioned previously (see this chapter, Section IA2 and footnote 245), the settlement between the NFL and the former players does not include Riddell.

[357]Numerous concussion lawsuits have recently been filed in this respect in other sports and countries. A few examples are mentioned further in this thesis (see eg, this chapter, Sections IIB2 (b) and IIC2).

[358]For more details about the US jurisprudence in this area, see eg, Brian James Mills, 'Football Helmets and Product Liability' (2001) 8 *Sports Lawyers Journal* 153, 153–80. For a more recent case, see Associated Press, 'Colo. Court Finds Riddell Negligent in Helmet Suit', *CBS*, 14 April 2013 (<http://www.cbsnews.com/8301-201_162-57579537/colo-court-finds-riddell-negligent-in-helmet-suit/>) (Associated Press, 'Riddell').

[359]A helmet is a 'good' under the *UCC* [Art. II, section 2-103 (2002)]. Consequently, liability for defective helmets may arise from express or implied warranties under the *UCC* [Art. II, in particular section 2-313 (2002)].

[360]The *Second Restatement of Torts (1965)* (section 402A) provides for strict liability in tort in case of goods in a defective condition, unreasonably dangerous for the consumer or his property. The *Third Restatement (1997)* (section 2) retains strict liability only for manufacturing defects, and adopts a negligence standard for defective design and warning/misinformation defects.

[361]Amended master complaint, p. 76, paragraph 392. More generally, the plaintiffs' arguments are based on strict liability for design and manufacture defect, failure to warn and negligence [For more details, see the amended master complaint, pp. 73–82, paragraphs 383–425].

[362]See this chapter, Section IA2(a)(v).

[363]Concerning the financial consequences, see Cerra, above n 301, 294 (in the specific case of the Maxwell's suit, whose reasoning is, however, relevant for the 2012 class action). This author argues in particular that 'if Riddell was negligent in its helmet design and manufacture then any football player who used these helmets could sue on a similar basis'.

[364]In the same vein, see Hanna, 'NFL', above n 110 in Chapter 2, 19. Upon Judge Brody's request, nothing has been revealed about the settlement discussions between Riddell and the plaintiffs [order of 29 August 2013, whose content is reproduced in Associated Press, 'Judge Order on NFL

The NFLPA was not spared from litigation. In July 2014, several former NFL players sued the association in two separate lawsuits in Missouri.[365] They alleged that the NFLPA knowingly and fraudulently concealed evidence linking concussion to long-term neurological damage over the last several decades.[366] The players, whose lawsuits were subsequently consolidated before the Missouri District Court, sought financial compensation and medical monitoring.[367] However, in August 2015, their consolidated putative class action was dismissed, because it was considered as pre-empted by CBAs.[368]

The lawsuit filed in December 2013 by Jovan Belcher's daughter representatives against The Kansas City Chiefs[369] was a reminder that the clubs are also subject to being sued. This finding is actually not as obvious as it seems. By their system of protection of workers (workers' compensation system),[370] many US states prevent the players from taking legal action against their employer clubs.[371] The compensation one can get from this system, if appropriate, is capped at a low amount and there is often a limitation period from the date the person last worked for the employer.[372]

The same kind of difficulties might also occur with regard to a club's employees (eg, team physicians and coaches), usually also covered by this system according to the 'co-employee doctrine',[373] and whose liability is often difficult to establish.

Concussion Settlement', 29 August 2013 (<http://www.nfl.com/news/story/0ap1000000235517/printable/judges-order-on-nfl-concussion-settlement>) (Associated Press, 'Order')].

365 For more details about the *Ballard* case, see Joseph M Hanna, 'Former Players Accused Union of Conspiring to Conceal Risks of Head Injuries' *Sports and Entertainment Law Insider*, 21 July 2014 (<http://sportslawinsider.com/former-nfl-players-accused-union-of-conspiring-to-conceal-risks-of-head-injuries//>) (Hanna, 'Union'). For more details about the *Smith* case, see Terez A Paylor, 'Three Former KC Chiefs Join Neil Smith in Lawsuit Against NFLPA', *The Kansas City Star*, 12 August 2014 (<http://www.kansascity.com/sports/nfl/kansas-city-chiefs/article1207242.html>).

366 For more details, see Brett Emison, 'More Players Join Lawsuits Against NFLPA', *The Legal Examiner* (Kansas City), 13 August 2014 (<http://kansascity.legalexaminer.com/head-brain-injuries/more-players-join-concussion-lawsuits-against-nflpa//>).

367 Ibid.

368 *Ballard v National Football League Players' Association* (ED Mo) (2015) WL 4920329.

369 See this chapter, Section IA1(g).

370 For more details about the workers' compensation system, see this chapter, Section IA2(a)(iv), footnote 279.

371 Hanna, 'NFL', above n 110 in Chapter 2, 19; Modery, above n 13 in Chapter 1, 275. In states where professional players are covered by workers' compensation, the legal immunity of clubs is nearly absolute [see eg, sections 303 and 308.1 of the *Pennsylvania Workers' Compensation Act* (§ 481 and 565 PA Cons Stat); *Dean v Handy & Harmon*, 961 F. Supp. 798 (M.D. Pa. 1997)]. See eg, section 308.1 of the *Pennsylvania Workers' Compensation Act* (§ 565 PA Cons Stat).

372 This period may be short, such as in the state of Pennsylvania. In this state, occupational diseases are covered if the disability occurred within 300 weeks following the last employment [Section 301C(2) of the *Pennsylvania Workers' Compensation Act,* PA Cons Stat § 411(2)].

373 Matthew J Mitten, 'Team Physicians as Co-Employees: A Prescription That Deprives Professional Athletes of an Adequate Remedy for Sports Medicine Malpractice' (2005) 50 *Marquette University Law School Review* 211, 214, footnotes 19–20 (Mitten, 'Team Physicians').

Team physicians must adhere to certain legal standards of care, set within the sports medicine industry.[374] They may face a conflict of interest due to the competing loyalties they owe to the team that employs them and to the athletes they must treat.[375] If the occasion arises, athletes could bring a civil action for malpractice.[376] If such a lawsuit is filed, it may face many obstacles,[377] but past experience has demonstrated that a finding of liability is not inconceivable.[378]

The issue of the responsibility of coaches, who sometimes interfere in medical decisions and put pressure on injured players to return to play too early, was discussed publicly when 'the concussion case' came to light.[379] Several high-profile players, such as former New England Patriots player Ted Johnson and Washington Redskins player DeSean Jackson (formerly playing for Philadelphia Eagles) expressed their negative experiences in this area.[380] Liability could be found if a coach engaged in negligent or reckless conduct which harms a player, even if acting without intent to injure him.[381] However, as just noted,[382] players might have difficulty succeeding in a tort-based civil action.[383] These types of lawsuits are rare at the professional level.[384] Apart from the legal difficulties, this might be

---

[374]Hohenstein, above n 57 in Chapter 2, 583. See also Matthew J Mitten, 'Emerging Legal Issues in Sports Medicine' (2002) 76 *Saint John's Law Review* 5, 9–13 (Mitten, 'Legal Issues').

[375]For more details about this issue, see Steve P Calandrillo, 'Sports Medicine Conflicts' (2005) 50 *Saint Louis University Law Journal* 185, 185–210.

[376]Brian Lipsky, 'Dealing with the NFL's Concussion Problems of Yesterday, Today and Tomorrow' (2008) 18 *Fordham Intellectual Property, Media and Entertainment Law Journal* 959, 971–2.

[377]Hohenstein, above n 57 in Chapter 2, 584–95. This author discusses in particular the legal issues that athletes must overcome to circumvent the impediments to imposing civil liability on team physicians through malpractice actions [ibid, 585]. See also Mitten, 'Legal Issues', above n 374, 31–7 and 42–7.

[378]The best example of this is the *Hoge v Munsell* case. After suffering two instances of concussion in seven weeks that resulted in permanent injury and ended his football career, Merrill Hoge sued the Chicago Bears' physician. He was awarded USD1.45 million for the two remaining years on his NFL contract and USD100 000 for pain and suffering following a jury's decision. This decision was, however, reversed on appeal, before being settled under confidential terms [for more details, see Hecht, above n 2 in Chapter 2, 17–64, in particular 25–30].

[379]Timothy Davis, 'Tort Liability of Coaches for Injuries to Professional Athletes: Overcoming Policies and Doctrinal Barriers' (2008) 76 *University of Missouri Kansas City Law Review* 571, 571.

[380]For more details about Ted Johnson's and DeSean Jackson's stories, see Gove, above n 18, 651–2 and 670–1.

[381]Davis, above n 379, 572.

[382]See this chapter, Section IA2(b).

[383]See eg, Davis, above n 379, 572. This author discusses the main defences that might impede a player's ability to pursue its state claims [ibid, 572, 587–96].

[384]Ibid, 576.

explained by the 'macho culture' previously mentioned,[385] which may incline players to follow coaching directives, even if potentially harmful.[386]

Finally, NFL players have often been undisciplined or even violent on sports fields.[387] A player who causes an injury to an opponent through an infringement of the rules of play can be held liable before civil courts in many states.[388] In principle, this should not be different for a concussion. However, unless the concussion causes immediate damage, the player is unlikely to be held liable, as it would become difficult to show causation.[389] Criminal liability could also theoretically come into the picture, but is very rarely acknowledged in practice.[390]

Based on what has been discussed so far, the next part explores some of the options for domestic reforms within the sports sector and state law.

3 Lessons and Significance

Short and long-term medical complications associated with concussion in American football are numerous. They are illustrated by the numerous players' suicides, violent behaviours and early retirements, but also by the post-mortem diagnosis of CTE in most of the players examined by leading experts.[391] These medical complications, which have also started to be scientifically documented in other sports,[392] highlight the need for a proactive and consistent public health approach.

The analysis of the NFL's and the US state and federal governments' responses in this regard is evidently of interest for American football. Due to the general experience gained and the sometimes transversal nature of the governments' intervention, this analysis is also relevant from a broader perspective, namely for other SGBs and countries, which are currently having great difficulty tackling this issue, often in isolation. It will, therefore, crucially contribute to the discussion related to the adoption of a harmonised public health regulatory framework. This is

[385]See this chapter, Section IA2(a)(iv).

[386]Davis, above n 379, 577–9.

[387]The example of the 'Bounty Scandal' is particularly explicit. This scandal concerned several New Orleans Saints defensive players, who were found to have operated a slush fund that paid out bonuses (or 'bounties'), for in-game performance in violation of NFL rules. The pool operated from 2009 to 2011. Amongst other things, Saints players allegedly earned bonuses for inflicting injuries on opposing players that forced them to miss games. After investigations, several coaches and players were suspended by the NFL [For more details about this case, see Hanna, 'NFL', above n 110 in Chapter 2, 16].

[388]For concrete examples (but with a special focus on young athletes), see Diehl, above n 9 in Chapter 2, 97–9.

[389]Hanna, 'NFL', above n 110 in Chapter 2, 16.

[390]For a few examples involving criminal liability issues in sport, see Matthew Mitten et al., 'Cases', above n 13 in Chapter 1, 887–99.

[391]See this chapter, Sections IA1(a) et seq.

[392]See this chapter, Sections IB1 et seq (including subsequent case studies).

particularly true regarding the implementation of an international standard and related convention.

The NFL's management of the concussion issue was open to criticism in many ways, and has for long been a perfect example of what not to do in terms of transparency and (in)action.[393] They finally reacted through the adoption of various appropriate measures, many of which were adopted after the intervention of the Congress in 2009.[394] Although there is still room for improvement, the NFL's current efforts in the management of concussion are in the process of creating the necessary conditions to reach a satisfactory outcome. These efforts should not be tarnished by the high number of head injuries reported for the 2017 season,[395] which may be due, at least partly, to a better identification and awareness. It is yet to be seen the success of each measure in the long term. The new standards will probably have to be adapted, and new measures taken, in order to achieve optimal results.

The NFL's intervention has manifested through rules of play, rules of the game, medical protocols, financial support for injured athletes, education, research and data collection.

The NFL understood well that the amendment of the rules of play constituted a key measure when it came to the improvement of player safety, and the prevention of concussion in particular. Therefore, it gradually introduced numerous rules of play changes.[396] However, it remains true that American football is still extremely violent. At this stage, various rules of play may still be amended in order to minimise the violence and frequency of contacts to the head.[397] Rule amendments should build on the current, albeit rare, studies available in relation to the positions and activities/contacts the most at risk in the matter of concussion. These studies seem to identify quarterbacks, wide receivers and defensive secondaries as particularly exposed positions to violent hits, but also highlight the high risk of repeated sub-concussion for linemen.[398] They also point to tackles, as well as helmet-to-helmet and helmet-to-body hits.[399] The positions deemed the most at risk undeniably need to be better protected through relevant targeted amendments. An example, among other possible amendments aimed at minimising helmet-related contact, would be the elimination of the three-point stance for linemen, and its replacement with lineman in an upright, two-point stance, with no hands on the ground.[400]

---

[393]See this chapter, Sections IA1(a) et seq.

[394]See this chapter, Sections IA1(d) and IA1(e).

[395]See this chapter, Section IA1(h).

[396]See this chapter, Sections IA1(a) et seq.

[397]Gerardi, above n 45 in Chapter 2, 230–1; Hecht, above n 2 in Chapter 2, 60–1.

[398]See this chapter, Section IA1(h).

[399]Ibid.

[400]This amendment would force players to block with their arms and their hands, not headfirst with their helmets. For more details, see eg, Gerardi, above n 45 in Chapter 2, 230–1.

A more radical solution, currently considered by the NFL,[401] would consist of purely and simply abandoning mandatory helmet use. Measures aimed at better securing tackles could also be of interest. Amendments of the rules of play could even extend to other positions and activities/contacts, as illustrated by the recent discussions related to the possible elimination of kickoffs.[402] The reduction of the number of players, or bigger fields, could also be beneficial by bringing down the frequency of collisions, knowing however that this would alter the physicality of the game and, therefore, face strong opposition.[403] In relation to enforcement, referees should avoid the 'culture of tolerance' that still predominates in American football. Stricter fines and suspensions could be instituted for players who recklessly cause helmet-to-helmet contacts or prove to be violent.[404] The amount of the fines imposed could then be reinvested in the improvement of concussion management and research.[405]

Too many injuries occur during training.[406] Amendments aimed at decreasing or eliminating full-contact practices might, like in college sport (Ivy League)[407] and Canadian football,[408] help better protect players' health.[409] However, a limitation of

[401] Slater, above n 115. This announcement followed the abandonment, in 2013, by the International Amateur Boxing Association (AIBA), of mandatory helmet use [for more details, see Anna Hodgekiss, 'Headgear for Amateur Boxers to Be Banned in Bid to Reduce Head Injuries' *Daily Mail Australia*, 16 March 2013 (<http://www.dailymail.co.uk/health/article-2293803/Headgear-boxers-banned-bid-REDUCE-head-injuries.html>; for AIBA current regulations, see Art. 21 of AIBA Open Boxing (AOB) Competition Rules (effective as of 26 April 2017) (<http://d152tffy3gbaeg.cloudfront.net/2015/02/AIBA-AOB-Competition-Rules-April-26-2017.pdf>)].

[402] These discussions are relevant for special teams, namely the units that are on the field during kicking plays. For more details, see John Breech, 'Roger Goodell Admits that a Key NFL Play Could Be Eliminated Soon', 14 September 2016, *CBS Sports* (<http://www.cbssports.com/nfl/news/roger-goodell-admits-that-a-key-nfl-play-could-be-eliminated-soon/?ET_CID=12593&ET_RID=46461995&ttag=allsportsdailyheadline30914201 6>).

[403] In the same vein, see Christian Red, 'Meet the Doctors Trying to Solve NFL's CTE Issue' *New York Daily News*, 6 November 2017 (<http://www.nydailynews.com/sports/football/meet-doctors-solve-nfl-cte-issue-article-1.3613902>).

[404] In the same vein, see Gove, above n 18, 690.

[405] In the same vein, see Barker et al., above n 84 in Chapter 2, 42. These authors go, however, further, by discussing the creation of a specific trust fund to benefit players suffering from consequences of head trauma. According to the NFL CBA, fines and suspensions are currently imposed on players on the basis of the NFL On-Field Code of Conduct and Schedule of Fines. The amounts gathered are then allocated to the Players Assistance Trust Fund and charitable organisations [NFL CBA, Art. 46, sections 1d and 5c; about forfeiture of salary, see Art. 4, section 9].

[406] See this chapter, Section IA1(h).

[407] For more details, see Ken Belson, 'Ivy League Moves to Eliminate Tackling at Football Practices', *The New York Times*, 1 March 2016 (<http://www.nytimes.com/2016/03/02/sports/ncaafootball/ivy-league-moves-to-eliminate-tackling-at-practices.html?emc=edit_th_20160302&nl=todaysheadlines&nlid=50808085&_r=2>) (Belson, 'Ivy League').

[408] See this chapter, Section IIA1.

[409] A reduction or elimination of full-contact practices (also referred to as 'padded practices') would decrease the opportunities of receiving concussive hits [for more details, see Barker et al., above n 84 in Chapter 2, 38]. Currently, the NFL CBA allows up to 14 padded practices per team during the

contact, restricted to training only, will not solve the problem on its own, and could even make inexperienced players more vulnerable during official matches.

Similarly, the NFL introduced improvements in player safety through new rules of the game and concussion protocols, in line with the CISG's guidelines (and their implementation paper).[410] Baseline testing, the obligation for the clubs to make independent doctors available to examine concussed players before returning to practice, the introduction of concussion spotters and independent neurologists on sidelines, together with the extensive use of video,[411] also constitute positive measures. Here, again, these measures will need to be strictly enforced. The recent implementation of sanctions (fines, forfeiture of draft picks) for clubs whose medical team members or other employees are not compliant with the game day concussion protocol[412] is a step in the right direction.[413] The next step could consist of additional sanctions (loss of premiership points for clubs, deregistration of staff), while the amount of the fines imposed could be used to improve concussion management and research. In order to further mitigate the potential conflict of interest of team physicians,[414] who remain in charge of the day-to-day management of players' health, some adjustments could be considered. Among them, the hiring of doctors directly by the NFLPA or by the NFL itself, or the negotiation by reputable physician groups of healthcare provision agreements that stress the independence of their medical judgment, would be worth discussing.[415] Other improvements may include the adoption of measures aimed at mandating testing for any borderline hit.[416]

In an environment dominated by bargaining agreements, negotiations between the NFL and the NFLPA are of particular importance. It is also through the CBA that significant financial improvements were implemented in the past. A good example of this is the '88 Plan', which provides reimbursement for former players' medical and custodial care costs.[417] Other amendments to the CBA could, together with the amendment of standard contracts, allow the NFL to provide better contractual

regular season. The distinctive feature of these practices lies in the fact that players are required to wear helmets and shoulder pads [NFL CBA, Art. 24].

[410]See Chapter 2, Section IX, footnote 164, and this chapter, Section IA1(e).

[411]See this chapter, Section IA1(e).

[412]Ibid.

[413]See however Paul D Anderson, 'NFL to Enforce Concussion Protocol Violations', '*NFL Concussion Litigation*', 26 July 2016 (<http://nflconcussionlitigation.com/?p=1900>) (Paul D Anderson, 'NFL'). This author argues that the NFL new policy, although included in a separate document, is subject to the CBA process in order to bar players from filing malpractice lawsuits against team physicians and force them to seek arbitration.

[414]See Chapter 2, Section IV and this chapter, Section IA2(b).

[415]For more details, see Calandrillo, above n 375, 208–10.

[416]A borderline hit is one that does not necessitate that a player leaves the field but still may require further investigation based on the expertise of a doctor as observer. Borderline hits are currently considered below the threshold for investigation and are thus not investigated adequately [Barker et al., above n 84 in Chapter 2, 40].

[417]See this chapter, Section IA1(c).

security.[418] The first measure to take would be to guarantee the players' salary payment beyond the year when the injury occurred, in order to prevent players from hiding their symptoms by fear of losing their income.[419]

Additionally, the NFL made a first step towards the education of its players, coaches, doctors and even the general public, by acknowledging the causal link between head impacts and cognitive impairment, evasively, in 2009, and more peremptorily, in 2016.[420] This acknowledgement was then solidified through concrete educational and informational initiatives, launched at the professional, college and youth levels. A whistle-blower system, allowing anyone to report to the league when a concussed player is pressured to practice or play against medical advice, was also implemented.[421] Although praiseworthy, the NFL's efforts should be intensified and pursued in the long-term to have any hope of changing mindsets, and the 'macho culture' that still prevails.[422] In order to establish a coherent approach, the NFL, television commentators and broadcasters should also avoid glorifying illegal hits and violent collisions.[423]

Finally, the NFL has, for a long time, been very active in the field of medical (or even technological) research and data collection. The NFL's involvement in this field started in 1994, with the creation of the MTBI Committee, which published controversial internal studies, before being replaced by the HNSMC in 2009.[424] It then continued through the creation of sub-committees and specialised positions, the publication of injury reports, the participation of NFL representatives in CISG's meetings (and the Dublin meeting) and other international and domestic roundtables.[425] To this are added a partnership with the CTE Center (broken up since then) and the allocation of numerous generous research grants and sponsorships, in line with the commitment taken through collective bargaining.[426] Although issues related to the independence and quality of the NFL research, and to the competence (or even integrity) of the people involved, originally identified,[427] do not seem of the same magnitude anymore, some recurring concerns still need to be addressed. This is demonstrated by the appointment, in 2015, of a cardiologist (instead of a neurologist) to the position of chief health and medical advisor.[428] It

[418]Evidence rules related to the grievance process in contractual disputes could also be amended, in order to abolish, under certain circumstances, the possibility for a club trainer to testify against his player. See this chapter, Section IA2(a)(iv) and footnote 285.

[419]Ibid.

[420]See this chapter, Section IA1(e).

[421]See this chapter, Section IA1(c).

[422]See this chapter, Sections IA2(a)(iv) and IA2(b).

[423]In the same vein, see Gerardi, above n 45 in Chapter 2, 232. See also this chapter, Section IA1(c).

[424]See this chapter, Sections IA1(a) and IA1(e).

[425]See Chapter 2, Section IX, footnote 163 and this chapter, Section IA1(e).

[426]See this chapter, Section IA1(e).

[427]See this chapter, Section IA1(a).

[428]See this chapter, Section IA1(e).

is also demonstrated by the recent accusations made against the NFL, as attempting to influence external research by putting pressure on some institutions to which it had allocated a grant, or by sponsoring conferences.[429] Added to this, are the revelations that the NFL would have knowingly maintained ties with political representatives in order to retain control of their decisions.[430] Furthermore, the NFL must coordinate its efforts, and ensure not to get into a process in which it allocates grants and makes new proposals for the sole purpose of restoring its reputation. If it fails to do so, it runs the risk of its concussion management becoming incoherent and counter productive. This risk is illustrated by the conference held in Pittsburgh in 2015 that, in addition to the independence issues it raised due to its sponsorship by the NFL,[431] led to the publication of a controversial agreed statement. This statement does not only interpret or adapt the CISG's guidelines, to which the NFL has to a great extent agreed with, but proposes a new definition of concussion, as well as new treatments. It questions the main principles adopted until then.[432]

The US state and federal governments' action to stem the public health risks associated with concussion for its part really started only in early 2000s, and has hitherto mainly focused on youth and college sport. It is divided into four main axes: legislation, Congressional interventions, research and data collection.

All 50 US states, and the District of Columbia, have adopted youth concussion laws. This legislative process, previously discussed,[433] could provide for possible basic lines of action at the professional and international levels. High standard safety measures, education and awareness should ideally start at a high level. They could then trickle down to grassroots level,[434] while bearing in mind that the competent entities do not have the same financial resources at their disposal. Government intervention would be justified in this regard by the major public health issues raised and would also require appropriate action from the NFL and other SGBs. The willingness to avoid new judicial proceedings, might, certainly, in itself, constitute a good incentive to act. However, given the NFL's and some others SGBs' massive annual revenues,[435] it would ensure these do not put up with costs and damages related to possible concussion lawsuits instead of putting in place an efficient and comprehensive preventive action.

---

[429]Ibid.

[430]Ibid.

[431]Ibid.

[432]Ibid. For a comprehensive analysis of these issues, and other suggestions for improvement, see Christopher R Deubert et al., *Promoting and Protecting the Health of NFL Players: Legal and Ethical Analysis and Recommendations'* (Report, Harvard Law School, 2016); Christopher Deubert, Glenn I Cohen and Holly Fernandez Lynch, *Comparing Health Related Policies and Practices in Sports, the NFL and Other Professional Leagues* (Report Harvard Law School, 2017).

[433]See this chapter, Section IA1(f).

[434]Heard, above n 13 in Chapter 1, 248.

[435]About the NFL, see this chapter, Section IA2(a)(v). About other leagues, see this chapter, Section IIA, footnote 1053.

For the record, the law passed in 2009 in Washington,[436] and which was used as a model by other states, contains four key measures: education for coaches, players' removal from the game in case of suspicion of head injury, a written clearance to return, and the signature of an information form by both parents and players. Some state laws were then gradually amended, in order to incorporate new measures, such as provisions regarding concussion-related data collection, while some bills aimed at banning youth tackle football are awaiting approval.[437] At the federal level, bills[438] aimed at regulating youth safety/equipment and management of youth concussion did not make it through the Congress. As for the professional level, the most relevant example is the *Professional Boxing Safety Act of 1996 (PBSA)*, as amended by the *Muhammad Ali Boxing Reform Act of 2000 ('Ali Act')*.[439] Professional boxing, besides the specificities linked to the nature of the sport, has the unique characteristic of not being governed by any league/association, or subject to any collective bargaining process.[440] The *PBSA*[441] establishes general minimum health safety standards: physical examination by a physician prior to each match, presence of an ambulance and physician at ringside, as well as appropriate health insurance.

Youth concussion laws and the *PBSA* provide us with lessons regarding the major pitfalls to avoid, notably in relation to enforcement. As it has been mentioned,[442] a great number of youth concussion laws do not provide for sanctions in the case of infringement, nor clearly state whom they target and who must enforce them. An exemption from liability for compliant schools was discussed as part of the work undertaken in preparation of the model legislation, and was used as a source of inspiration by some states. The *PBSA* is, for its part, more accurate. It provides for a range of civil and criminal sanctions starting with a fine and going as far as imprisonment for non-compliant contributors, such as managers, promoters, match-makers, licensees or even, to a lesser extent, boxers themselves.[443] Primary responsibility for enforcing the *PBSA* rests with the US Department of Justice and its many attorney's offices across the country. Since its adoption, the *PBSA* has been facing recurrent enforcement problems, principally attributed to the absence of a federal oversight of the boxing industry, coupled with the absence of a central sports

[436]See this chapter, Section IA1(f).

[437]Ibid.

[438]Ibid.

[439]While the *PBSA* was originally aimed at better protecting professional boxers within the ring, its reform was intended to protect the rights and welfare of boxers by putting a stop to certain exploitative, oppressive, and unethical business practices outside the ring [Brad Ehrlichman, 'Is this Corner: An Analysis of the Federal Boxing Legislation' (2011) 34 *Columbia Journal of Law and The Arts* 421, 421].

[440]See section 2(1) of the *Muhammad Ali Boxing Reform Act* (2000).

[441]15 USC § 6304.

[442]See this chapter, Section IA1(f).

[443]15 USC § 6309.

governing body, or even to terminology inaccuracies.[444] No exemption from liability is provided for.

Youth concussion laws and the *PBSA* also illustrate two different doctrines, the first having the effect of applying to all sports, and the second only aiming at boxing. A standard with a general scope would have the advantage of regulating the situation in all sports at a professional level. By virtue of its nature, it could allow a less focused action than a standard whose scope would be limited to one sport only.

Finally, the bills aimed at tackling youth football serve as a reminder that similar intervention by federal governments at the professional level could disrupt international competitions, which depend on the existence of harmonised rules.

The government also intervened several times through its Congress. The most noteworthy Congressional intervention, which was the trigger for a series of positive measures taken by the NFL, is the hearing that took place in 2009.[445] Other similar hearings/roundtables aimed at initiating discussion on concussion in American football or, more broadly, sports safety, followed in 2014 and 2016.[446] Added to this is, in 2016, a report by Congress members shedding light on some of the NFL's questionable practices in connection with research.[447] These interventions are undeniably an effective way to lead the NFL to act. However, they will only have an optimal effect when any link between the NFL and political representatives has disappeared.[448]

The best illustration of the government's involvement in research is the work undertaken by leading experts at the CTE Center in Boston.[449] This forensic research, and related Brain Bank Depository, made it possible to identify and centralise dozens of CTE diagnoses.[450] Mainly focused on deceased American football players, it needs to be further developed to other sports in the US and worldwide. Other examples of the government's involvement in research include grants, partnerships and concussion summits.[451]

---

[444]Various attempts to solve these issues have been made. Last in time, the Professional Boxing Amendments Act of 2013, which proposed the creation of the United States Boxing Administration (USBA), a federal regulatory agency to oversee the sport, was introduced in August 2014 before the Congress. However, it was not enacted. The *Professional Boxing Safety Enhancement Act* of 2018, which is aimed at providing additional minor safety standards, was introduced into the Congress in 2018.

[445]See this chapter, Section IA1(d).

[446]See this chapter, Sections IA1(f) and IA1(g).

[447]See this chapter, Section IA1(e).

[448]About this issue, see this chapter, Section IA1(f).

[449]The CTE Center receives funding from the NIH, but also accepts private donations [for more details, see the CTE Center website (<https://www.bu.edu/cte/about/> and <https://www.bu.edu/cte/financial-support/>); see also this chapter, Section IA1(e) and footnote 96].

[450]See this chapter, Section IA1(h).

[451]See this chapter, Section IA1(f).

In addition to the Brain Bank Depository, data collection will also be facilitated by the new provisions of some youth concussion laws, previously mentioned,[452] and the surveillance system of sports-related concussion in youth sport that is currently being put in place by the CDC.[453] This system is, in the longer run, expected to provide national representative estimates of concussion, and may include information on adults.[454] Although these efforts must be praised, they remain focused on the US, and highlight the need for a better centralisation of data worldwide. They also illustrate the potential conflicts that may arise between medical guidelines, previously discussed,[455] and the legal standards created by governments, which will be appropriate to keep in mind when proposing a harmonised solution across sports and legal systems.

Moreover, the example of the CDC, whose main goal is to protect public health and safety,[456] is a reminder that the protection of players' health should also be ensured through the application of the general legislation. Occupational health and safety laws could be used to force the NFL,[457] and its teams, to pay more attention to this issue. A deep involvement of the CDC would be valuable in this regard, knowing however that the CDC has no binding powers against the different contributors involved, such as the NFL and other SGBs.[458] The silence of agencies created in 1970 under the *Occupational Safety and Health Act*,[459] such as the Occupational Safety and Health Administration (OSHA)[460] and the National Institute for Occupational Safety and Health (NIOSH)[461] also appears surprising.[462] Similarly, criminal law should be applied more rigorously on sporting fields,[463] which should not constitute lawless areas.

On a broader level, the examination of the NFL case study from a public health perspective brings to light various key relationships—medical professionals, researchers, SGBs, governments, players and their representative unions. These

---

452 Ibid.

453 Ibid.

454 Ibid.

455 See Chapter 2, Sections I et seq.

456 See this chapter, Section IA1(f) and footnote 173.

457 Even if US jurisprudence does not currently recognise an employment relationship between the leagues and the players (see this chapter, Section IA2(a)(iv)), the NFL could be concerned indirectly by these laws, as it usually holds negotiations on behalf of the clubs.

458 For more details about the CDC's competences, see <http://www.cdc.gov/about/organization/mission.htm>.

459 29 USC § 651 et seq.

460 The OSHA is part of the US Department of Labour. Its mission is to assure safe and healthy working conditions for working employees by setting and enforcing standards and by providing training, outreach, education and assistance.

461 The NIOSH is part of the CDC within the US Department of Health and Human Services. It is responsible for conducting research and making recommendations for the prevention of work-related injuries and illnesses.

462 In the same vein (about the OSHA), see Heard, above n 13 in Chapter 1, 249.

463 See this chapter, Section IA2(b).

relationships are essentially reactive (the NFL having previously primarily reacted periodically to the progress of science and US governments' interventions), or even competitive and adversarial in parts. By their nature, they can be an obstacle to the optimum protection of players, and show the need for a more harmonised, collaborative and evidence-based approach to public health risks, as proposed in this thesis. In addition to enabling players to benefit from optimum protection, such an approach would benefit other stakeholders. It would allow the medical community to work more efficiently, SGBs to better exercise their regulatory role and protect their most visible and valuable assets and US governments to reduce health care costs.

The analysis of the NFL concussion litigation, and in particular the class action commenced in 2012 before the US District Court in Pennsylvania,[464] allows us to draw conclusions in terms of legal risks. This class action aimed to recover compensation for injured players and their families. On an unprecedented scale and media coverage, it resulted in 2015 in a USD1 billion settlement,[465] and was the trigger for subsequent legal proceedings filed against other SGBs.[466] By its adversarial nature, it shows to what extent SGBs, like the NFL, are exposed to the legal (financial and reputational) risks associated with concussion. It demonstrates the legal complexity of concussion litigation, likely to extend over a long period and discourage already weakened plaintiffs.[467] It also illustrates the now widespread legal uncertainty that this thesis seeks to address.

The legal uncertainty related to the NFL litigation resulted from the absence of similar precedents,[468] and the difficulty to assess the parties' arguments, making the outcome difficult to predict. On the one hand, the NFL did little to inform its players and protect their health until the intervention of Congress in 2009.[469] These failings were likely to provide the basis for the liability of the NFL. This is, in any case, what the broad principles of justice would have required.[470] On the other hand, NFL players would have encountered various hurdles.[471] Players remain vulnerable, from a legal point of view, in litigation. A good example of this is the assessment of the existence of a duty of care giving rise to liability in torts. More generally, players' apparent legal vulnerability is due to the multiple defences at the disposal of potentially liable contributors.[472]

By taking consistent action upstream and clarifying the public health expectations and requirements, establishing a more harmonised, collaborative approach to legal risks and a possible exemption from liability for compliant SGBs, an international

[464] See this chapter, Sections IA2 et seq.

[465] See this chapter, Section IA2(a)(v).

[466] See this chapter, Sections IA2 et seq (including subsequent case studies).

[467] See this chapter, Section IA2(a)(v).

[468] Ibid, and footnote 305.

[469] See this chapter, Sections IA1(a) et seq.

[470] See this chapter, Section IA2(a)(v).

[471] See this chapter, Sections IA2(a)(ii) et seq.

[472] Ibid.

standard, together with its accompanying convention, would help control legal uncertainty. This legal uncertainty is not in anyone's best interests. In the NFL case, both the NFL and the players benefitted, for the reasons mentioned above,[473] from avoiding legal proceedings. US governments (here confined to a judicial role) could save in costs of justice. The medical and scientific community/evidence (that somewhat faded away during the class action, due to the absence of discussions, at least public, on the merits, but whose importance re-emerged during the settlement),[474] could avoid being undermined when it comes to interpreting the knowledge and doubts of science in legal terms.

A more harmonised, collaborative approach would not exempt governments, and courts in particular, from implementing a fair judicial framework, considering notably that tort law would subsidiarily come into the picture again, in case of non-compliance.[475]

The NFL, like other SGBs being at the top of the sports pyramidal structure,[476] is in the best position to protect the players, in terms of regulations and educational campaigns. It should, therefore, be subject to high standards. A broad sense of the concept of 'special relationship' leading to a duty of care should be recognised by courts. Once the existence of a duty of care is established, the potential liability could be assessed in light of the proposed international standard and previous case law.

Courts must ensure that defences, such as pre-emption, are not distorted from their initial purpose. They must act expeditiously and prevent them from being used for delaying purposes in order to exert undue pressure on plaintiffs.[477] Other principles, such as the doctrine of voluntary assumption of risk and contributory negligence,[478] should not be extended too far, at risk of indirectly lowering, or even annihilating the standard of care potentially applicable in practice.[479] Improvements could even go beyond the field of tort law and SGBs. For example, the current workers' compensation system in the US, which often bars players from suing their employer clubs without valuable consideration (in return for a payment capped at a low amount, subject to a short limitation period from the termination of the working relationship),[480] is open to criticism. In the field of sport, it does not allow the

---

[473]See this chapter, Section IA3.

[474]See this chapter, Sections IA2(a)(iv) et seq and footnote 337.

[475]See Chapter 5, Section VIC3 and Chapter 6, Section II.

[476]See this chapter (introductory remarks).

[477]For more details about the possible delays caused by the resolution of jurisdiction issues, see this chapter, Section IA2(a)(v), and footnote 306.

[478]See this chapter, Section IA1(d), and footnote 87, as well as Section IA2(a)(iv), and footnote 287.

[479]As already mentioned, in the US, players who are considered to have contributed to their injury can still recover damages in states that adhere to comparative negligence principles (their financial recovery being reduced by the degree of their fault, but not prohibited). This is not the case for players who are deemed to have accepted the risks they ensured, the doctrine of voluntary assumption of risk absolving the defendant from liability (see this chapter, Section IA2(a)(iv) and footnotes 286–7).

[480]See this chapter, Section IA2(b).

achieving of the goal it was originally created to reach, namely the protection of players' interests.[481] This may lead the lawmaker to adapt this system to the specificities of professional sport. Possible adaptations include the implementation of a special legal regime for professional athletes, and/or the creation of a complementary governmental compensation scheme.[482]

In the NFL case, the judicial framework was not tested. Yet, it presumably indirectly influenced the outcome, by leading the parties to seek a settlement.[483]

The settlement prevented a judicial examination of the parties' arguments and, therefore, led to a reduced level of transparency. Despite the substantial amounts involved, which tend to confirm the legitimacy of the allegations issued by the plaintiffs, the settlement leaves legal commentators with unanswered questions. It also leaves room for uncertainty regarding future cases. It is foreseeable that players who practised football after the settlement (and the NFL's unequivocal acknowledgment of the causal link between head trauma and later-life cognitive decline) will have to face the doctrine of voluntary assumption of risk; however, cases of players who died subsequently are more complex.[484]

The settlement could be used as a guide for pending or future concussion lawsuits against other SGBs.[485] But it deprives us from the legal clarity that could have resulted from a judgment. Unlike a judgment, it will not have a persuasive effect for other common law courts facing similar cases. Nevertheless, even in the absence of a finding of liability, the psychological effects of this settlement should not be underestimated. The concussion issue has now become a real hot spot, forcing the main sports contributors, researchers and even the governments to question player safety further.

However, much remains to be done, as the analysis of the situation in other sports will demonstrate. This is particularly true for ice hockey, football, water polo and baseball in the US, which are the subject of the next sections.

---

[481] Ibid.

[482] A federal compensation scheme exists for instance in the US for victims of 9/11 (under the *Air Transportation Safety and System Stabilization Act of 2001*) and for employees victims of black lung (under the *Black Lung Benefits Act of 1973*).

[483] See this chapter, Section IA2(a)(v).

[484] About the settlement and the acknowledgement of the NFL, see this chapter, Sections IA1(f) and IA2(a)(v). Former players are, for obvious legal and medical reasons (related to good faith and the often latent nature of their injuries), in a more favourable legal position to complain about the health repercussions associated with concussion. However, the fact that individuals have subsequently continued to play, despite their knowledge of the potential risks, should not deprive them of the right to benefit from a good standard of care. This is true from a general perspective, but above all in specific instances of mismanagement.

[485] In the same vein, see Silver, above n 316.

B Ice Hockey: The National Hockey League (NHL)

Ice hockey is the second major sport for consideration. This section first provides a chronological account of the evolution of scientific knowledge about concussion in ice hockey and the responses of the NHL and US governments. It then analyses the potential liability of the NHL.[486] This examination reveals that the NHL is currently facing, albeit on a smaller scale, public health and legal risks similar to those encountered by the NFL. These risks are illustrated by the scientifically confirmed dangerous nature of ice hockey, and its potential short and long-term health repercussions among professional ice hockey players, as well as the class action that was filed in 2014 against the NHL, which comprised more than 200 plaintiffs.

Nevertheless, the NHL and NFL class actions had different outcomes. While the NFL class action ended up in a USD1 billion settlement,[487] the NHL class action was stopped in 2018 due to the judge's refusal to grant class certification, forcing the plaintiffs to pursue their claims individually. Unlike the NFL, the NHL still refuses to admit any causal link between concussion and later-life medical complications. This refusal influences its concussion management practices and reverberates in its legal strategy, which may, however, become more flexible in the future, in the context of the recently opened settlement negotiations. The general measures taken by US governments following the controversy generated by the NFL case are equally applicable to the NHL. In addition, there have been some minor interventions from a member of the US Congress in the specific context of ice hockey.

The section ends with a summary of the main findings. It describes how the NHL case study justifies and contributes to the conceptualisation of a harmonised legal framework aimed at better regulating the public health and legal risks related to concussion across sports and legal systems. In that regard, some key points to be drawn from the NHL experience may be summed up as follows.

Short and long-term medical complications associated with concussion in ice hockey are exemplified by early retirements, as well as by five CTE cases diagnosed among former NHL players. The NHL's management of the concussion issue has evolved constantly and is not without its merits. It has demonstrated a moderate willingness to change the rules of play to improve safety, expand medical care and adopt a number of labour relations and educational measures to address specific concerns. Nonetheless, it remains less proactive than the management of other sports federations governing ice hockey or even other sports. Reminiscent of that of the NFL a few years ago, it will undoubtedly need to be modified in order to ensure better player safety.

---

[486]The NHL is not a member of the IIHF. Consequently, the IIHF's regulatory activity will be discussed in a separate section (IIC1). USA Hockey, the national governing body for ice hockey in the US, will not be examined. It has only limited authority at the professional level, and was not sued in the class action.

[487]See this chapter, Section IA2(a)(v).

The analysis of the class action that was filed against the NHL, and which ended in the middle of the discovery process, confirms the lessons drawn from the NFL case study in terms of legal risks. One thus finds again the elements discussed previously—legal (financial and reputational) risks, legal complexity and associated legal uncertainty, difficulty in translating the doubts of science for legal purposes and possible shortcomings in tort law. The discovery process temporarily allowed a real debate over the connection between head injuries and CTE. It now gives way to great uncertainty.

More broadly, the NHL case study confirms the reactive, competitive and adversarial nature of the key relationships previously identified, which negatively affects the interests of all the stakeholders involved, and highlights the need to ensure harmony at an international level.

1 Chronology

Violence, sometimes leading to players' accidental deaths, has been part of ice hockey since at least the early 1900s.[488] The NHL has endured its share of controversies. The league consists of franchised professional ice hockey clubs located in the US and Canada.[489] It grew out of Canada into the US, where it exported its culture of toughness.[490] Prominent incidents include that of Minnesota North Star player Bill Masterton, who died in 1968 from a brain injury after his head hit the ice during a game.[491] In 1999, former Rochester Americans player Craig Fisher lost a significant part of his motor skills after a concussion resulting from a shoulder check by an opposing player.[492] Similarly, in 2009, Ron Duguay, born in 1957, and a NHL player from 1977 to 1989, revealed that he had failed many memory tests as a result of repeated blows to the head and cannot remember his playing days.[493]

The first significant measure taken by the NHL in response to head injury concerns was the introduction of mandatory helmet use in 1979,[494] adopted in

[488]A People's History - Episode 1: A Simple Game. Dir. Laine Drewery, prod. Wayne Chong. DVD. Canadian Broadcasting Corporation/Radio- Canada, 2006.

[489]For more details, see the NHL website (<http://www.nhl.com/ice/teams.htm?nav-tms-main>).

[490]John Barnes, *The Law of Hockey* (LexisNexis, 2010) 200 and 371–6 (Barnes, 'Hockey').

[491]First believed to be due to a single hit, Masterton's death was subsequently attributed by some medical experts, such as neuropathologist Charles Tator, from the Krembil Neuroscience Institute in Toronto, to a possible second-impact syndrome [Randy Starkman and Rob Cribb, 'Star Investigation: What Really Killed NHL's Bill Masterton', *The Star*, 28 May 2011 (<http://www.thestar.com/sports/hockey/2011/05/28/star_investigation_what_really_killed_nhls_bill_masterton.html>); about the Second-Impact Syndrome, see Chapter 2, Section VI].

[492]Gerardi, above n 45 in Chapter 2, 210–11.

[493]Ibid, 211.

[494]Website Hockey Draft Central (<http://www.hockeydraftcentral.com/1979/79facts.html>).

spite of the strong opposition of the National Hockey League Players' Association (NHLPA).[495] The scope of this rule was restricted by a special clause allowing hockey's veterans (who had signed their contracts before 1 June 1979) to choose whether or not they wanted to wear helmets.[496]

In 1981, the NHL incorporated a standard contract clause in its CBA entitling injured players to receive their full remaining salary as long as they were unable to perform, until contract expiration.[497] This clause, which is notable because it eliminated the need for players to hide their symptoms for fear of losing their income, was then repeated in subsequent CBAs.[498]

Dating back to 1996, the NHL gradually introduced a stricter supplemental discipline standard to punish illegal hits in all circumstances in which a player is deemed to have intentionally directed contact to an opponent's head.[499]

In 1997, the NHL, in collaboration with the NHLPA, launched a comprehensive 'Concussion Program'.[500] In order to mark the beginning of this program, the NHL adopted its first concussion management protocols,[501] and initiated baseline testing for all players.[502] It also created a 'Concussion Study Group', headed by orthopaedic surgeon and then Pittsburgh team physician Charles Burke, to research and study brain injuries affecting its players, based on the records maintained by team doctors and trainers.[503] In 2007, the Concussion Study Group, unable to conclude the analysis of the data collected, was disbanded and re-formed under a new name, the 'Concussion Working Group', and new leadership, namely neuropsychologist Ruben Echemendia.[504] In its current form, this working group consists of physi-

[495]Carter Anne McGowan, 'The Other Skate Drops: The NHL Concussion Lawsuit' (2014) 25 *NYSBA Entertainment, Arts and Sports Law Journal* 23, 29.

[496]Website Hockey Draft Central (<http://www.hockeydraftcentral.com/1979/79facts.html>).

[497]See eg, Exhibit 2E of the 1981 NHL CBA.

[498]See eg, Exhibit 1 of the 2013-22 NHL CBA. This CBA is available on the NHL's website (<http://www.nhl.com/nhl/en/v3/ext/CBA2012/NHL_NHLPA_2013_CBA.pdf>).

[499]See this chapter, footnote 584, which refers to NHL Commissioner Gary Bettman's letter to US senator Richard Blumenthal of 22 July 2016 [in particular pp. 19–20].

[500]For more details, see the NHL website (<https://www.nhl.com/news/frequently-asked-questions-about-concussions/c-551900>).

[501]Ibid.

[502]Ibid.

[503]Ibid. See also Rick Westhead, 'NHL Concussion Study Group Folded Without Any Conclusions After Leadership Worries, PA "Roadblocks" ', *TSN*, 29 March 2016 (<http://www.tsn.ca/nhl-concussion-study-group-folded-without-any-conclusions-after-leadership-worries-pa-roadblocks-1.461185>) (Westhead, 'Leadership').

[504]Westhead, 'Leadership', above n 503. According to this article, which refers to unsealed emails, the Concussion Study Group's members were not fully committed to their task, for which they were not remunerated. This absence of payment also seems to show that this project was not a matter of priority for the NHL.

cians, neuropsychologists, former NHL players, and representatives from the NHL and the NHLPA.[505]

The NHL Concussion Program also brought in an educational component. The NHL launched campaigns aimed at informing its players, club personnel and on-ice game officials about the signs and symptoms of concussion, and the risks of going back to the ice too quickly.[506] In addition, the NHL supported and assisted in the development of educational programs for youth ice hockey players.[507]

From 1999 onward the NHL adopted policies and regulations aimed at making the playing area safer, prior to forming a NHL/NHLPA Environment Subcommittee.[508]

These measures, however, failed to reassure researchers mindful of ice hockey players' protection.[509] Furthermore, ice hockey play gradually became faster and more violent, most concussions in the NHL being caused by checks to the head, body checking[510] at high speed, fights and, to a lesser extent, rough incidental contact (involving sticks, pucks or collisions).[511] As a result, concussion-related incidents, which sometimes led to instances of early retirements,[512] continued to escalate.

---

[505]For more details, see University of Calgary's website (<https://www.ucalgary.ca/news/utoday/april18-2011/concussion>).

[506]Improving Sports Safety: A Multifaceted Approach: Hearing Before the House Comm. on Energy and Commerce, 113th Cong. 8-9, 13, 18-9, 186 (2014) (Statement of William L Daly, Deputy Commissioner, NHL).

[507]Ibid, 14.

[508]Ibid, 12-13 and 18.

[509]As highlighted in the amended consolidated class action complaint (see this chapter, Section IB2, footnote 590 and Section IB2(a)(i), footnote 602), research on safety in professional ice hockey has historically been conducted by several medical institutes, and is now developing under the leadership of the Mayo Clinic, in Minnesota (about this Clinic, see also further in this chapter, Sections IB1 and IIC1).

[510]The difference between body checking and check to the head lies in the contact zone: body checking is a shoulder-to-shoulder contact while a check to the head implies a shoulder-to-head (or even elbow-to-head) contact.

[511]See eg, Gerardi, above n 45 in Chapter 2, 210. See also Andrew W Kuhn and Gary S Solomon, 'Concussion in the National Hockey League: A Narrative Review of the Literature' (2015) 1 (1) *Concussion* 1, 2-3; Laura Donaldson, Mark Asbridge and Michael D Cusimano, 'Bodychecking Rules and Concussion in Elite Hockey' (2013) 8(7) *PlosOne* 1, 4 (<http://www.ncbi.nlm.nih.gov/pmc/articles/PMC3714233/pdf/pone.0069122.pdf>); Michael G Hutchison et al., 'A Systematic Video Analysis of National Hockey League (NHL) Concussions, Part II: How Concussions Occur in the NHL' (2015) 49 *British Journal of Sports Medicine* 552, 552–3 (Hutchison et al., 'Hockey') (and previous publications).

[512]See this chapter, Section IB2, in particular footnote 590. This footnote refers to the amended consolidated class action complaint, which recounts chronologically how class representatives have been harmed, violent incidents that documented the NHL knowledge, and recent career ending instances of concussion [see eg, pp. 9–23, paragraphs 27–87, pp. 61–72, paragraphs 244–75, pp. 99–100, paragraphs 371–7]. For other examples of concussions and violent behaviours within the NHL, see Jennifer A Wood, 'Dirty Game: Trusting the National Hockey League to Play Judge, Jury and Executioner' (2012) 13 *Texas Review of Entertainment and Sports Law* 185, 185–98.

In 2009, Reggie Fleming became the first NHL player to be tested and diagnosed with CTE, after his death at the age of 73 following a stroke and heart attack.[513] This CTE case was quickly followed by those of three other former NHL players (Bob Probert, aged 45, and Rick Martin, aged 59, who both died of heart problems; and Derek Boogaard, aged 28, who died of a drug and alcohol overdose).[514] All four cases were diagnosed by researchers from Boston University.[515] Three of them (Fleming, Probert and Boogaard) were enforcers—players purposefully placed on teams for their physicality and fighting ability in order to protect teammates.[516] A fifth CTE case was diagnosed in 2015 by researchers from the Krembil Research Institute in Toronto.[517] This was Steve Montador who, while not generally categorised as an enforcer, still fought more than 60 times during his NHL career.[518] The causes of Montador's death were not made public, but he had revealed during his lifetime that he suffered from depression, among other symptoms, following his retirement due to concussion in 2013.[519] Between 2016 and 2018, the CTE cases of former NHL players Larry Zeidel and Jeff Parker (both enforcers), and of four junior ice hockey players, were released by Boston University.[520] This evidence of the link between concussion in ice hockey and CTE, in conjunction with a Canadian qualitative study highlighting the long-term negative impact of repeated concussions

[513]Gerardi, above n 45 in Chapter 2, 209.

[514]Sheryl Ubelacker, 'NHL Hockey Concussions Take Centre Ice', *The Huffington Post* (<http://www.huffingtonpost.ca/2011/12/19/nhl-hockey-concussions_n_1158403.html>).

[515]For more details, see McKee et al., 'Spectrum', above n 233, 48.

[516]Melanie Romero, 'Check to the Head: The Tragic Death of NHL Enforcer, Derek Boogaard, and the NHL's Negligence – How Enforcers Are Treated as Second-Class Employees' (2015) 22 *Jeffrey S Moorad Sports Law Journal Sports Law Journal* 271, 272 and 276. See also Sean Fitzgerald, 'List of NHL Enforcers Who Have Passed Away Gets Longer', *The Star*, 22 September 2015 (<https://www.thestar.com/sports/hockey/2015/09/22/list-of-nhl-enforcers-who-have-passes-away-gets-longer.html>).

[517]John Branch, 'Steve Montador Had C.T.E.; Family to Sue N.H.L.' *The New York Times*, 12 May 2015 (<http://www.nytimes.com/2015/05/13/sports/hockey/steve-montador-had-brain-trauma-family-to-sue-nhl.html?_r=0>).

[518]Fitzgerald, above n 516.

[519]Mark Lazerus, 'Former Blackhawks Defenseman Steve Montador Dead at 35', *The Chicago Suntimes*, 15 February 2015 (<http://chicago.suntimes.com/sports/former-blackhawks-defenseman-steve-montador-dead-at-35/>).

[520]Concussion Legacy Foundation's website (<https://concussionfoundation.org/about/media/press-releases/former-nhl-player-jeff-parker-diagnosed-cte>).

on retired NHL players' lives,[521] did not prevent more conservative medical experts from expressing their scepticism.[522]

Faced with this situation, the NHL considered that a warning about CTE to its players would be, 'at best, premature and potentially dangerous.'[523] From 2011, the NHL launched new educational campaigns aimed at reassuring players and briefing them on CTE due to 'misinformation' in the media and medical literature.[524] Surprisingly, the NHLPA was involved in these campaigns.[525]

Despite this reassuring position, and the expressed will of NHL Commissioner Gary Bettman not to over-legislate head hits,[526] the NHL took some measures in a hurry. In addition to enforcing longstanding existing rules of play, such as the prohibition of charging,[527] cross-checking[528] high-sticking,[529] and slashing,[530] and more stringently penalising dangerous contact,[531] the NHL installed a stricter rule

[521]Jeffrey G Caron et al., 'Effects of Multiple Concussions on Retired National Hockey League Players' (2013) 35 *Journal of Sports & Exercise Physiology* 168, 168. This study used a small sample size of five retired NHL players who had suffered multiple concussions. Based on interviews, it showed that all players' lives were significantly impacted (through headaches, visual disturbances and forgetfulness). Interestingly, the players also reported hiding their concussion symptoms from coaches and medical staff.

[522]For a critical opinion, see eg, Ozan Toy, Mill Etienne and Ronald Bogdasarian, 'Consequences of Traumatic Brain Injury in Male Ice Hockey Players' (P5.319)' (2014) 82 *Neurology* No 10 Supplement.

[523]See this chapter, footnote 584, which refers to NHL Commissioner Gary Bettman's letter to US senator Richard Blumenthal of 22 July 2016 [in particular pp. 2 and 17].

[524]Ibid.

[525]Ibid.

[526]Commissioner Bettman notably made such statement in the margins of a 2011 Congressional panel discussion on encouraging American kids to get into ice hockey, and in the wake of Montreal Canadiens player Max Pacioretty being hospitalised with a severe concussion and fractured vertebra. For more details, see The Canadian Press, 'Pacioretty Injury Part of the Game: Bettman', *CBC Sports*, 10 March 2011 (<http://www.cbc.ca/sports/hockey/pacioretty-injury-part-of-game-bettman-1.1008959>) (The Canadian Press, 'Pacioretty').

[527]Charging refers to the action of a player who, as a result of the distance travelled, violently checks an opponent in any manner [Rule 42.1 of the 2018-19 NHL Rulebook]. The NHL Rulebook is available on the NHL's website (<http://www.nhl.com/nhl/en/v3/ext/rules/2018-2019-NHL-rulebook.pdf>).

[528]Cross-checking occurs when a player checks an opponent by using the shaft of his stick with both hands [See Rule 59.1 of the 2018-19 NHL Rulebook].

[529]High-sticking occurs when a player intentionally or inadvertently plays with his stick above the height of the shoulders or above the cross bar of an ice hockey goal [See Rule 60.1 and 80.1 of the 2016-17 NHL Rulebook].

[530]Slashing is the act of a player swinging his stick at an opponent, whether contact is made or not [Rule 61.1 of the 2018-19 NHL Rulebook]. These four infractions pre-existed the creation of the NHL, although the exact wording of their definition, and the penalties handed to offenders, have evolved over time [For more details, see Iain Fyffe, *On His Own Side of the Puck* (2014, self-published), who analyses the codes of ice hockey rules from major hockey leagues from across the US and Canada from 1875 to 1915].

[531]See this chapter, Section IB1.

regarding checks to the head for the 2010–11 season. This new rule,[532] which made targeting an opponent's head from the lateral or blindside illegal, was supposed to preserve both the player's health and the physicality of the game.[533] However, it proved insufficient, with many players being victims of serious concussions due to 'legal checks'.[534] Thus, a further change occurred for the 2011–12 season. The 'lateral or blindside' provision was removed, potentially making any hit to the head illegal, regardless of the direction from which it is delivered.[535] However, the revised rule, still criticised for its lack of efficiency, provides for an exception for the checker based on specific circumstances, notably when the opponent puts himself in a vulnerable position.[536]

The NHL distances itself from the IIHF and governing bodies for junior levels, such as the Ontario Hockey League (OHL). The IIHF and the OHL fully banned this practice in 2009 and 2006 respectively.[537] They regularly inflict long suspensions to the recalcitrant players.[538]

These new measures did not prevent the NHL from featuring violent hits and fights in commercials for the game, and other advertising, on its website.[539] Additionally, no review was carried out regarding body checking that, although prohibited in women's ice hockey and some youth leagues,[540] are still considered as part of the game in men's ice hockey.

In 2011, the NHL published a report summing up the conclusions of its study initiated in 1997.[541] This report, prepared in collaboration with the University of Calgary in Canada, released the number of instances of concussion sustained by

---

[532] Rule 48 of the 2010–11 NHL Rulebook.

[533] Jeff Klein, 'With Stricter Rule on Hits to the Head, Some N.H.L. Stars Are Split on a Full Ban', *The New York Times*, 19 September 2011 (<http://www.nytimes.com/2011/09/20/sports/hockey/nhls-top-stars-weigh-in-on-hits-to-the-head.html?pagewanted=all>) (Jeff Klein, 'NHL').

[534] Donaldson, Asbridge and Cusimano, above n 511, in particular 1 and 3.

[535] Rule 48 of the 2011–12 NHL Rulebook. Note that this rule remained unchanged for the subsequent seasons (see eg, 2018–19 NHL Rulebook).

[536] Ibid. About the lack of efficiency of this rule, see Donaldson, Asbridge and Cusimano, above n 511, in particular 1 and 5.

[537] For the current regulations, see Rule 124 of the 2018–22 IIHF Rulebook; Rule 48.1 of the 2017–18 OHL Rulebook. These documents are available on the IIHF and OHL websites (<https://www.iihf.com/IIHFMvc/media/Downloads/Rule%20Book/IIHF_Official_Rule_Book_2018_Web_v2.pdf; <http://ontariohockeyleague.com/ohl-rule-book/>).

[538] For recent suspensions, see eg, the OHL website (<http://ontariohockeyleague.com/article/ohl-announces-disciplinary-action-28>). See also Rule 48.2-4 of the OHL Rule Book and Rule 124 i-iii of the IIHF Rulebook.

[539] See this chapter, Section IB2, footnote 590, which refers to the amended consolidated class action complaint filed against the NHL on 15 January 2016 [in particular, p. 86].

[540] While the prohibition of body checking is a feature of women's ice hockey, its application at the youth level depends on each league.

[541] Brian W Benson et al., 'A Prospective Study of Concussions Among National Hockey League Players During Regular Season Games: The NHL-NHLPA Concussion Program' (2011) 183 *Canadian Medical Association Journal* 905, 905–11 (Benson et al., 'Hockey').

NHL players over the period 1997–2004 (559 physician-diagnosed, regular season, in-game concussions in seven years, namely an average of 80 concussions per year).[542] These statistics, though leaving aside pre-season games and practice, are an interesting source of guidance, particularly because since 2008, NHL teams are no longer required to disclose the specific nature of players' injuries.[543] Moreover, the report indicated that the majority of concussions were sustained by wingers (closely followed by defensemen and centremen), and highlighted the vulnerability of centremen in relative terms.[544] Similar trends were reported by independent studies, which highlighted, however, the risk of underreporting.[545]

Unlike the NFL's internal study,[546] the NHL report[547] remains silent on the causes of concussion (which are, however, the subject of subsequent publications).[548] While acknowledging the need to pay attention to post-concussion symptoms,[549] the report also did not expressly discuss the general[550] and emerging ice hockey-specific medical literature[551] related to the causal link between head trauma and cognitive decline.[552]

Simultaneously to the release of its study, the NHL created a Department of Player Safety, the first of its kind, at least for any American professional league.[553] This department proposes rule changes to enhance safety, reviews safety issues

[542] Benson et al., 'Hockey', above n 541, 906.

[543] Joe Delessio, 'Injury Status: Unknown', *Sports on Earth*, 26 February 2013 (<http://www.sportsonearth.com/article/41962374/the-nhls-injury-policy-forces-fans-and-the-media-to-speculate-wondering-why-for-example-the-new-york-rangers-rick-nash-has-been-out-for-over-a-we>).

[544] Considering that centremen are less numerous on the ice than other players, they are in fact twice as likely to sustain a concussion [Benson et al., 'Hockey', above n 541, 907].

[545] See eg, Jason Izraelszki, 'Concussions in the NHL: A Narrative Review of the Literature' (2014) 58 *The Journal of the Canadian Chiropractic Association* 346, 347–50. See also Kuhn and Solomon, above n 511, 2; Alexander Ruhe, Axel Gänsslen and Wolfgang Klein, 'The Incidence of Concussion in Professional and Collegiate Ice Hockey: Are We Making Progress? A Systematic Review of the Literature' (2014) 48 *British Journal of Sports Medicine* 102, 104–5.

[546] See this chapter, Section IA1(a).

[547] Benson et al., 'Hockey', above n 541, 905–11.

[548] See this chapter, Section IB1, and footnote 511, which notably refers to Hutchison et al., 'Hockey', 552–3.

[549] Benson et al., 'Hockey', above n 541, 905–11.

[550] See this chapter, Sections IA1(b) and IA1(h).

[551] See this chapter, Section IB1.

[552] Benson et al., 'Hockey', above n 541, 905–11. The report also remains silent on other issues, such as the efficiency of helmets in the prevention of concussion. However, the Head of the NHL/NHLPA Concussion Working Group, Dr Reuben Echemendia, indicated in an interview published on the NHL website in 2011, that, in his opinion, helmets are inefficient for preventing concussion (<https://www.nhl.com/news/frequently-asked-questions-about-concussions/c-551900>).

[553] For more details about this department, see the NHL website (<http://www.nhl.com/ice/eventhome.htm?location=/playersafety>).

related to equipment and environment and suspends and fines players as a disciplinary matter.[554]

Again in 2011, the NHL changed its concussion protocols (henceforth codified in a single document)[555] to require an examination off the ice and bench, in a location referred to as a 'quiet room', by the on-site team physician (rather than a trainer).[556] The concussed player could return to the ice if he was symptom free, returned to his brain baseline[557] and passed the SCAT 2 test.[558] In 2013, the NHL re-amended its concussion protocols to state that concussed players could not return to the same game in which the concussion occurred.[559] This amendment was aimed at complying with the recommendations of the CISG,[560] whose meetings (including the Dublin meeting) have all been attended by members of the NHL Concussion Program.[561] Other meetings attended sporadically by NHL representatives include the NFL Think Tanks and the Ice Hockey Summits organised by the Mayo Clinic in Minnesota, with the support of the IIHF.[562]

In 2012, the NHLPA partnered with 'Smashfest', a new annual charity event aimed at raising funds for research on brain injuries and rare cancers.[563] Since its inception, this event has raised more than CAD500 000 for the benefit of various foundations.[564] To this, various other grants have been added, such as a

---

[554]Ibid.

[555]The NHL codified its then-current policies and protocols into a single document in 2010, the essential components of which were first established in 1997 [See this chapter, footnote 584, which refers to NHL Commissioner Gary Bettman's letter to US senator Richard Blumenthal of 22 July 2016, in particular p. 13].

[556]For more details about this revision, see Dan Rosen, 'New Concussion Protocol Goes Into Effect Tonight', *NHL*, 16 March 2011 (<http://www.nhl.com/ice/news.htm?id=556289>) (Rosen, 'Protocol'). See also Improving Sports Safety: A Multifaceted Approach: Hearing Before the House Comm. on Energy and Commerce, 113th Cong. 15 (2014) (Statement of William L Daly, Deputy Commissioner, NHL).

[557]See Chapter 2, Section IX and footnote 151.

[558]See Chapter 2, Section IV.

[559]Improving Sports Safety: A Multifaceted Approach: Hearing Before the House Comm. on Energy and Commerce, 113th Cong. 15 (2014) (Statement of William L Daly, Deputy Commissioner, NHL).

[560]See Chapter 2, Sections II et seq.

[561]Improving Sports Safety: A Multifaceted Approach: Hearing Before the House Comm. on Energy and Commerce, 113th Cong. 9 and 13 (2014) (Statement of William L Daly, Deputy Commissioner, NHL); see also Chapter 2, Section IX, footnote 163.

[562]About the NFL Think Tanks, see this chapter, Section IA1(e). About the Mayo Clinic, see this chapter, Section IB1, footnote 509 and Section IIC1. References to the participation of NHL representatives in these meetings can be found in relevant press releases and newspaper articles. See also amended class action complaint, p. 59, paragraph 237.

[563]For more details, see the NHLPA's website (<https://www.nhlpa.com/be-a-player/in-the-community/smashfest>).

[564]NHLPA Staff, 'Smashfest Raises Over $500 000 in First five Years For Concussion and Rare Cancer Research', *NHLPA*, 22 July 2016 (<http://www.nhlpa.com/news/smashfest-raises-over-500000-in-first-five-years-for-concussion-rare-cancer-rese>) (NHLPA Staff, 'Smashfest').

CAD500 000 challenge gift allocated in 2015 to support concussion research at Western University in London, Ontario.[565]

Prior to the 2013–14 season, the NHL instituted a so-called 'hybrid icing' rule, aimed at reducing the risk for potentially dangerous collisions into the end walls.[566]

At the same time, the NHL introduced changes related to equipment. Under the auspices of the newly created NHL/NHLPA Protective Equipment Subcommittee, and against the advice of the NHLPA,[567] the NHL mandated the use of face shields by all incoming players.[568] It adopted a rule penalising players who remove their helmets in an on-ice fight,[569] without fully banning the act of fighting,[570] as the IIHF and the NCAA do.[571]

Prior to the 2015/2016 season, the NHL made the presence of concussion spotters mandatory in each stadium.[572] These spotters, although modelled on the NFL's system,[573] were not required to have medical training, and were employed by the home teams.[574] One year later, the NHL amended its concussion protocols to introduce 'central league spotters'.[575] These new spotters have athletic and medical

---

[565] NHLPA Staff, 'NHLPA Gift to Support Concussion Research Announced at See The Line', *NHLPA*, 12 August 2015 (<http://www.nhlpa.com/news/nhlpa-gift-to-support-concussion-research-announced-at-see-the-line>) (NHLPA Staff, 'Gift').

[566] Pursuant to the new rule, icing plays are whistled prior to players reaching the end walls, thereby and for all intent and purposes avoiding player contact and collisions on icing plays [for more details about this revision, see Dan Rosen, 'Hybrid Icing Tops List of Rule Changes for 2013-14', 1 October 2013 (<https://www.nhl.com/news/hybrid-icing-tops-list-of-rule-changes-for-2013-14/c-684940>) (Rosen, 'Rule Changes')].

[567] McGowan, above n 495, 29.

[568] Mike Brophy, 'NHL, NHLPA Agree on Mandatory Visors', *NHL*, 5 June 2013 (<https://www.nhl.com/news/nhl-nhlpa-agree-on-mandatory-visors/c-672983>). See also Improving Sports Safety: A Multifaceted Approach: Hearing Before the House Comm. on Energy and Commerce, 113th Cong. 9 and 19 (2014) (Statement of William L Daly, Deputy Commissioner, NHL).

[569] Rosen, 'Rule Changes', above n 566.

[570] See Rule 46.2 of the 2013-14 NHL Rulebook. Note that this rule remained unchanged for the subsequent seasons (see eg, 2018-19 NHL Rulebook).

[571] See Rule 141 of the 2014-18 IIHF Rulebook and Rule 48 of the 2016-17 and 2017-18 NCAA Ice Hockey Rules and Interpretations.

[572] Dan Rosen, 'NHL, NHLPA Bolster Concussion Evaluation Process', *NHL*, 15 September 2015 (<https://www.nhl.com/news/nhl-nhlpa-bolster-concussion-evaluation-process/c-779135>) (Rosen, 'Process'); Shayna Goldman, 'Hit or Miss: NHL Appoints Concussion Spotters', *SportTechie*, 25 September 2015 (<http://www.sporttechie.com/2015/09/25/hit-miss-nhl-appoints-concussion-spotters/>) (Goldman, 'Concussion Spotters').

[573] See this chapter, Section IA1(e).

[574] Goldman, 'Concussion Spotters', above n 572.

[575] NHL Public Relations, 'NHL Updates Concussion Protocols', *NHL*, 12 October 2016 (<https://www.nhl.com/news/nhl-updates-concussion-protocol/c-282571624>). See also Shayna Goldman, 'The NHL Adds "Central Spotters" to Concussion Protocols', *SportTechie*, 28 September 2016 (<http://www.sporttechie.com/2016/09/28/sports/nhl/the-nhl-adds-central-spotters-to-concussion-protocol/>) (Goldman, 'Central Spotters'). The NHL Concussion Evaluation and Management

knowledge, and are independent from clubs.[576] Assisted by ‘in-arena league spotters’, they observe games via live broadcast from NHL headquarters in New York.[577] They have the power to order a club to submit its player to medical evaluation by team doctors.[578] The NHL can levy fines if a team is not compliant.[579] Post-concussion evaluation by a neuropsychologist was also mandated before return-to-practice.[580] In 2018, the protocols were updated in order to incorporate the latest recommendations of the CISG.[581]

Conversely, the NHL’s position on the causal link between head trauma and cognitive decline evolved little. Over the course of decades, the NHL remained silent on the subject, and only responded to inquiries by saying that ‘further research is required’.[582] More recently, the NHL, facing legal proceedings,[583] was forced to take a formal position. The latest public example of the NHL’s (and NHLPA’s) denial is to be found in the reply, in July 2016, of NHL Commissioner Bettman to questions submitted one month earlier by US senator, inquiring about the effects of concussion in ice hockey.[584] This exchange of views, which then extended to the potential responsibility of the NHL in funding research,[585] also illustrates the increasing US federal government’s involvement in the concussion issue, and adds to other state and federal interventions described previously as part of the NFL section.[586]

Protocol (2016–17) is available on the NHLPA’s website (<http://cdn.agilitycms.com/nhlpacom/2016-17_ConcussionProtocol.pdf>).

[576]Ibid.

[577]Ibid.

[578]Ibid.

[579]Ibid.

[580]Ibid.

[581]NHL Concussion Evaluation and Management Protocol (2017–18) (unpublished, but copy on file with author).

[582]See this chapter, Section IB2, footnote 590, which refers to the master administrative long-form and class action complaint filed against the NHL on 20 October 2014 [in particular, p. 91], as well as to the amended consolidated class action complaint filed against the NHL on 15 January 2016 [in particular, pp. 5 and 28].

[583]See this chapter, Sections IB2 et seq.

[584]NHL Commissioner Gary Bettman’s letter to US senator Richard Blumenthal of 22 July 2016 can be consulted on The New York Times’ website (<http://www.nytimes.com/interactive/2016/07/26/sports/hockey/27hockey-doc.html?_r=0/>).

[585]Jonas Siegel, ‘NHL’s Gary Bettman Brushes off Attack from US Senator over Concussion’, *The Star*, 17 August 2016 (<https://www.thestar.com/sports/hockey/2016/08/17/gary-bettman-nhl-stance-on-concussions-sends-wrong-message-us-senator.html>).

[586]See this chapter, Sections IA1(d), IA1(e), IA1(f), IA1(g), footnote 221 and Section IA3. Among these interventions, numerous general interventions—youth concussion laws, research (CTE Center in Boston; also mentioned in this section), grants, partnerships and concussion summits—are also relevant for the NHL.

2 Legal Activities and Implications

As some legal commentators had forecasted,[587] the sequence of events described above resulted in judicial proceedings against the NHL. From 2013 onward, dozens of former NHL players have filed suits across the US against the league.[588] Among the procedures were the *Christian*, *Leeman* and *LaCouture* claims, lodged in Minnesota, Columbia and New York.[589]

In October 2014, all of these suits were combined into one class action in the US District Court of Minnesota.[590] This class action encompassed more than 200 plaintiffs, but could potentially have covered the estimated 5000 living former NHL players, as well as deceased players' estates.[591] In November 2014, the NHL filed motions to dismiss the class action based on statutes of limitations and pre-emption grounds.[592] In March 2015, the presiding judge rejected the NHL's motion to dismiss related to the statutes of limitations.[593] In May 2016, the judge took the

[587]See eg, Veuthey, 'NFL', above n 216, 39.

[588]See eg, Joseph M Hanna, 'Lawsuits Becoming a Headache for NHL as Fourth Concussion Suit is Filed' *Sports and Entertainment Law Insider*, 1 August 2014 (<http://sportslawinsider.com/lawsuits-becoming-a-headache-for-nhl-as-fourth-concussion-suit-is-filed/>) (Hanna, 'NHL').

[589]*Christian v. National Hockey League* (D. Minn., No. 0:14-cv-01140-SRN-JSM, 15 April 2014); *Leeman v. National Hockey League* (D.D.C., No. 1:13-cv-01856-KBJ, 25 November 2013); *LaCouture v. National Hockey League* (S.D.N.Y., No. 1:14-cv-02531-SAS, 9 April 2014). All plaintiffs alleged that the NHL did not do enough in the matter of prevention, and hid the medical long-term related risks related to concussion. For more details about these lawsuits, as well as other lawsuits, see Hanna, 'NHL', above n 588; Joseph M Hanna, 'Minnesota Will Play Host to NHL Concussion Litigation', *Sports and Entertainment Law Insider*, 23 August 2014 (<http://sportslawinsider.com/minnesota-will-play-host-to-nhl-concussion-litigation/>) (Hanna, 'Minnesota'). For a general overview of the claims lodged against the NHL, as well as a direct access to the relevant submissions, see the Bloomberg database (access on subscription). See also the 'NHL Concussion Litigation' website (<https://www.nhlconcussionlitigation.com/information.html>), where some submissions are available.

[590]In re: *National Hockey League Players' Concussion Injury Litigation*, MDL No. 2551. Plaintiffs filed a master administrative long-form and class action complaint on 20 October 2014. They filed an amended consolidated class action complaint on 15 January 2016. These documents are available on the 'NHL Concussion Litigation' website (<http://www.nhlconcussionlitigation.com/information.html>). See also *Veitch v. National Hockey League* (D. Minn., No 0:16-cv-02683, 9 August 2016), which is part of the same litigation.

[591]Associated Press, 'Former Players in Concussion Lawsuit Seek Deposition from Bettman', *The Global and Mail*, 26 March 2015 (<http://www.theglobeandmail.com/sports/hockey/former-nhl-players-in-concussion-lawsuit-seek-deposition-from-bettman/article23642872>) (Associated Press, 'Deposition').

[592]The NHL filed motions to dismiss the master administrative long-form and class action complaint on 18 November 2014. See also the NHL's answer and administrative defences to plaintiffs' second amended class action complaint of 1 December 2016, which sums up a total of 26 defences that the NHL may raise subsequently in response to the former players' claim. These documents are available via the Bloomberg database (access on subscription).

[593]In re: *National Hockey League Players' Concussion Injury Litigation* (D Minn, MDL No. 14-2551, 25 March 2015), Court memorandum opinion and Order denying motion to dismiss

same steps with the NHL's motion to dismiss related to pre-emption.[594] Simultaneously, written submissions were exchanged as part of the discovery process.[595] In July 2018, the judge denied the plaintiffs' bid to attain class action status.[596] Two months later, it was reported in the media that the parties had been ordered to enter settlement negotiations.[597]

This section first examines the potential liability of the NHL in closer detail against the background of the above-mentioned proceedings. In order to avoid repetition, it compares the NHL class action and that of the NFL, previously discussed[598] and just highlights their main differences. It then analyses the consequences of the judge's refusal to grant class certification, and settlement negotiations.

(Court memorandum opinion I). This court memorandum opinion and order was issued after the motion was fully briefed [plaintiffs had filed their opposition to the motion on 9 December 2014 and the NFL had filed a reply memorandum of law on 23 December 2014], and the matter heard on 8 January 2015. The court memorandum opinion is available on the 'NHL Concussion Litigation' website (<http://www.nhlconcussionlitigation.com/information.html>). The other documents are partly available on the same website, and fully available via the Bloomberg database (access on subscription).

594In re: *National Hockey League Players' Concussion Injury Litigation*, (D Minn, MDL No. 14-2551, 18 May 2016), Court memorandum opinion and Order denying motion to dismiss (Court memorandum opinion II). This court memorandum opinion and order was issued after the motion was fully briefed [plaintiffs had filed their opposition to the motion on 9 December 2014 and the NFL had filed a reply memorandum of law on 23 December 2014], and the matter heard on 22 March 2016. The court memorandum opinion is available on the 'NHL Concussion Litigation' website (<http://www.nhlconcussionlitigation.com/information.html>). The other documents are partly available on the same website, and fully available via the Bloomberg database (access on subscription).

595The discovery process, in the US law and other common law countries, is a pre-trial procedure in a lawsuit in which each party, through the law of civil procedure, can obtain evidence from the other party by means of discovery devices. The primary discovery devices are interrogatories, depositions, requests for admissions and requests for production [Garner, above n 5, ad 'Discovery', 564]. The parties' submissions related to the discovery process are numerous. They can be found via the Bloomberg database (access on subscription).

596In re: *National Hockey League Players' Concussion Injury Litigation* (D Minn, MDL No. 14-2551, 13 July 2018), Court memorandum opinion and Order denying class certification (Court memorandum opinion III). This court memorandum opinion and order was issued after the exchange of numerous submissions between the parties and the matter was heard on 16 March 2018. The court memorandum opinion is available on the 'NHL Concussion Litigation' website (<http://www.nhlconcussionlitigation.com/information.html>). The parties' submissions are partly available on the same website, and fully available via the Bloomberg database (access on subscription).

597John Wawrow, 'NHL, Former Players in Mediation for Concussion Lawsuit', *CBC*, 11 September 2018 (<https://www.cbc.ca/sports/hockey/nhl/nhl-former-players-in-mediation-for-concussion-lawsuit-1.4819212/>).

598See this chapter, Sections IA2 et seq.

(a) The Potential Liability of the NHL in the Class Action

(i) Legal Arguments against the NHL and Possible Defences

In their amended class action complaint of 15 January 2016,[599] former NHL players sought unspecified financial damages and medical monitoring for neurological disorders.[600] The arguments invoked (negligence and fraud), the questions raised and the scientific evidence referred to were in essence similar to those discussed in the context of the legal proceedings against the NFL.[601] Additional emphasis was placed on the few CTE cases diagnosed in ice hockey.[602]

However, the NHL's defence differed somewhat from that of the NFL, both regarding the procedure and the merits. Thus, unlike the NFL,[603] the NHL argued that the plaintiffs' claims were time-barred.[604] The argument did not convince the presiding judge, who determined that the issue of whether the limitation periods had (started to) run was a question of fact that could not be resolved in a motion to dismiss and should be subject to discovery.[605] The NHL, like the NFL,[606] argued that the plaintiffs' claims fell within the scope of the CBAs and their related arbitration clauses[607] and were, therefore, pre-empted.[608] Again, this argument did not satisfy the judge, who asserted that the possible existence of a duty of care

---

599 See chapter IB2, footnote 590.

600 Amended class action complaint, pp. 125–6 (Prayer for Relief).

601 For the NHL, see amended class action complaint, in particular pp. 44–58, paragraphs 182–230 and pp. 110–25, paragraphs 412–77. For the NFL, see this chapter, Section IA2(a)(i) and footnotes 258–9. Note, however, that the plaintiffs invoke fraudulent concealment by omission, and do no argue that the NHL took affirmative actions to cloud science.

602 Amended class action complaint, pp. 43–4, paragraphs 178–81 and pp. 58–61, paragraphs 231–43.

603 See this chapter, Section IA2(a)(iii).

604 Motion to dismiss (statutes of limitations), pp. 3–18. The NHL argued that the plaintiffs' claims were time barred under the statutes of limitations of Minnesota [Minn Stat § 541.05; six years], District of Columbia [DC Code § 12-301(8); three years] and New York [NY CPLR 214(5); three years]. In its motion, the NHL also argued that the plaintiffs' claims for negligent misrepresentation by omission and fraud by omission/failure to warn should be dismissed because they were not pleaded with particularity [pp. 18–29]. Finally, they raised jurisdiction issues related to the medical monitoring claim [pp. 30–3].

605 Court memorandum opinion (I), pp. 11–13. About the 'discovery process', see this chapter, Section IA2, footnote 595. The judge, Susan Richard Nelson, also rejected the other arguments raised by the NHL (see this chapter, Section IB2(a)(i), footnote 604 and Court memorandum opinion (I), pp. 17–31 and 31–3).

606 See this chapter, Section IA2(a)(iii).

607 For the 2013-22 NHL CBA, see this chapter, Section IB1, footnote 497.

608 Motion to dismiss (pre-emption), pp. 1–38. The NHL argued that the plaintiffs' claims are pre-empted by federal labour law pre-emption [section 301 *LMRA*]. The pre-empted cases relied upon by the NHL are the same as those invoked by the NFL in its motion to dismiss (see this chapter, Section IA2(a)(iii), footnote 269), apart from *Boogaard v NHL*, 126 F. Supp. 3d 1010 (N.D.Ill.2015).

outside the CBA, and in particular the fact that the NHL could enact rule changes independently of the NHLPA, required further analysis.[609] Although acknowledging implicitly that NHL players were all unionised during their playing careers[610]—another point of divergence with the NFL case[611]—the judge also noted that the plaintiffs were retired players who were no longer subject to collective bargaining.[612]

Unlike the NFL,[613] the NHL still contests the state of the science regarding the link between head trauma and brain impairment, as well as its relevance for ice hockey.[614] The NHL's position pushed other possible responses to the claim (absence of duty of care, doctrine of voluntary assumption of risk, contributory negligence)[615] into the background.[616] The NHL firmly refused to compromise,[617] which led the parties to enter a discovery process.[618]

The NHL's denial was a central part of the discovery process. For instance, in October 2015, the NHL asked the US District Court of Minnesota to force the plaintiffs to admit that studies cited in their suit contain 'significant limiting language or other caveats'.[619] The plaintiffs maintained their position.[620] In March 2016, the NHL asserted that the plaintiffs should be subject to an independent medical

---

[609]Court memorandum opinion (II), pp. 3, 30–3 and 47.

[610]Court memorandum opinion (II), pp. 3 and 32–3. See also motion to dismiss (pre-emption), pp. 1–3.

[611]See this chapter, Section IA2(a)(iii), footnote 271.

[612]Court memorandum opinion (II), pp. 3 and 32.

[613]See this chapter, Sections IA1(e) and IA1(f).

[614]See this chapter, Section IB1.

[615]See this chapter, Section IA2(a)(iv), where these defences are considered within the context of the NFL litigation.

[616]The issue of the duty of care is discussed in the NHL motion to dismiss related to the statutes of limitations, where the NHL argues that the plaintiffs failed to establish the existence of such a duty in their fraud-based claims [see motion to dismiss, pp. 22–5]. It is also discussed in the NHL motion to dismiss related to pre-emption, where the NHL contends that the assessment of a duty of care, if any, would depend on the interpretation of the CBAs [see motion to dismiss, p. 15]. While contributory negligence may potentially constitute a solid defence for the NHL, the doctrine of voluntary assumption of risk would be more difficult to argue. This defence would indeed imply that players knew, or should have known, the potential risk of later-life cognitive decline associated with playing ice hockey (see this chapter, Section IA2(a)(iv) and footnote 287) , risk that the league is still striving to deny.

[617]According to some newspapers, this was confirmed by a recent internal memo circulating around the NHL headquarters, which indicated that the NHL and Commissioner Gary Bettman felt 'no desire' to engage in settlement discussions (Cal Setar, 'NHL Feels "No Desire" to Settle Concussion Lawsuit' (REPORT), *HNGN*, 1[er] October 2015 (<http://www.hngn.com/articles/135746/20151001/nhl-feels-no-desire-to-settle-concussion-lawsuit-report.htm>).

[618]For a definition of the 'discovery process', see this chapter, Section IA2, footnote 595.

[619]Memorandum in support re 234 motion of 5 October 2015, pp. 5–11; Memorandum in support re 239 motion of 5 October 2015, pp. 2 and 8.

[620]Response in opposition re 234 motion of 22 October 2015, in particular p. 12; Response in opposition re 239 motion of 22 October 2015, p. 7.

examination,[621] which was subsequently done,[622] despite the plaintiffs' objections.[623] In January 2017, the NHL tried to compel the Boston University researchers to hand over confidential materials related to their CTE studies in an attempt to discredit their work,[624] but were knocked back two months later.[625]

Simultaneously, following a motion by Canadian television's W5, a weekly newsmagazine series, certain discovery documents, in particular some of the NHL's internal emails, were unsealed and made public.[626] These emails revealed the existence of diverging views on CTE[627] and a strong 'macho culture' among NHL executives.[628] They also further highlighted the sometimes ambiguous role of the NHLPA in player safety, illustrated by its long-held opposition to the banning of fighting.[629] A new set of emails with similar content was released one year later, causing further embarrassment to the NHL.[630]

(ii) A Closer Look at the Parties' Situation

The NHL's alleged carelessness, which appears to a greater extent when in contrast to the examination of the responses of other sports federations governing ice

---

[621]Memorandum in support re 400 motion of 29 February 2016, in particular p. 33.

[622]See notably order and memorandum of 29 March 2016, p. 1, and the controversy that ensued (discussed in subsequent submissions).

[623]Response in opposition re 400 motion of 10 March 2016, pp. 1–3.

[624]NHL Motion to compel production of documents from the Boston University CTE Center of 19 January 2017, pp. 1–2.

[625]In re: *National Hockey League Players' Concussion Injury Litigation* (D Minn, MDL No. 14-2551, 26 April 2017), Court memorandum opinion and Order denying bid to access documents, p. 31 (Court memorandum opinion IV). The Minnesota federal judge overseeing the case rejected most of the league's request but did allow it to get materials related to ice hockey players.

[626]For some comments about this case, and a direct link to the W5's motion, see Ryan Lake, 'The Effects of Fighting in Ice Hockey: An Overview of the Ongoing NHL Concussion Litigation', *Lawinsport*, 19 April 2016 (<http://www.lawinsport.com/sports/item/the-effects-of-fighting-in-ice-hockey-an-overview-of-the-ongoing-nhl-concussion-litigation?category_id=152>) (paywall).

[627]See eg, Rick Westhead, 'Link between Fighting, Concussions, "Personal Tragedies" Discussed in Unsealed NHL' Emails', *TSN*, 28 March 2016 (<http://www.tsn.ca/link-between-fighting-concussions-personal-tragedies-discussed-in-unsealed-nhl-emails-1.460651?smid=tw-nytsports&smtyp=cur>) (Westhead, 'Fighting').

[628]See eg, Mary Clarke and Pat Iversen, 'The Most Interesting and Damning Details from the Unsealed Documents in the NHL Concussion Lawsuit', *SB Nation*, 30 March 2016 (<http://www.sbnation.com/nhl/2016/3/30/11333286/nhl-concussion-lawsuit-unsealed-emails-gary-bettman-colin-campbell>).

[629]See eg, Westhead, 'Fighting', above n 627. See also 'NHLPA Chief Seeks Ban on Hits to Head', *NHL*, 9 March 2009 (<https://www.nhl.com/news/nhlpa-chief-seeks-ban-on-hits-to-head/c-413060>).

[630]See eg, Rick Westhead, 'NHL Doctor Slams "Situational Ethics" on Concussions in Unsealed Lawsuit Documents', *TSN*, 28 March 2017 (<http://www.tsn.ca/nhl-doctor-slams-situational-ethics-on-concussions-in-unsealed-lawsuit-documents-1.708729>) (Westhead, 'Documents').

hockey,[631] or even other sports,[632] might have led to a finding of liability. Although not binding on the merits, the judge's rejection of the NHL motions to dismiss,[633] allowing the discovery process (and its related million dollars of legal fees) to move forward, was a step in this direction. The NHL had various potential solid defences to the class action.[634] Unlike the NFL, they could in particular have invoked the recent judgment related to the concussion litigation filed against FIFA, which will be discussed later.[635] This judgment, whose scope must be viewed in perspective, tends to deny the existence of SGBs' duty of care in the context of sports injuries.[636]

However, the NHL's constant and strong denial of the link between head trauma and brain impairment changed the terms of the debate, by shifting it to the medical field. It remains to be seen what evidence the discovery process could still have brought, and how the presiding judge of the case would have interpreted the doubts related to the state of science in legal terms.

The NHL seemed in any case determined to take advantage of these doubts,[637] based on conservative opinions expressed in this regard, both from a general point of view[638] and in connection with ice hockey.[639]

These issues will never be resolved as part of the class action, due to the judge's refusal to grant class certification to the plaintiffs.

---

[631] See this chapter, Section IB1.

[632] See this chapter, Sections IA1(c) et seq (including subsequent case studies).

[633] See this chapter, Section IB2(a)(i).

[634] See this chapter, Section IB2(a)(i) and footnote 616. See also McGowan, above n 495, 28–30. This author discusses various possible defences to the *Leeman* complaint (which was subsequently incorporated into the class action), including pre-emption and causation. She also considers that the NHL did not engage in any fraud or malfeasance, notably due to the efforts undertaken and the public nature of the medical studies on which the plaintiffs base their claims. For a more nuanced opinion (about the *Boogard case*, whose general reasoning is also relevant for the class action), see John J Miller and Tom T Wendt, 'The Concussion Crisis in the National Hockey League' (2015) 9 *Journal of Contemporary Athletics* 1, 2–6, in particular 5–6.

[635] See this chapter, Section IC2(b).

[636] Ibid.

[637] See in particular the discovery process, described above (in this chapter, Section IB2(a)(i)), as well as NHL Commissioner Gary Bettman's letter to US Senator Richard Blumenthal of 22 July 2016, above n 584, pp. 5–12.

[638] See the shortcomings expressed by some medical experts with regard to American football and other sports (in Chapter 2, Section VII, this chapter, Section IA1(h) and footnotes 228–9), as well as by Judge Brody at the end of the settlement procedure in the NFL litigation (see this chapter, Section IA2(a)(v), footnote 337).

[639] See the shortcomings expressed by some medical experts with regard to ice hockey (in this chapter, Section IA1 and footnote 522), as well as the amended class action complaint filed against the NHL (in this chapter, Sections IA2 et seq, footnotes 590 and 601). This complaint refers, to a large extent, to the medical literature related to American football, paving the way for the NHL to insist on the very unique nature and dangerousness of this sport.

(b) The Judge's Refusal to Grant Class Certification, Consequences and Settlement Negotiations

The judge refusal to grant class certification, which occurred in July 2018, is justified by 'widespread differences in applicable state laws' that govern the kind of medical monitoring sought by the players as a remedy, which were likely to pose 'significant case management difficulties'.[640]

This represents a major blow for the plaintiffs, who will now face major costs and duplication of legal effort in pursuing their claims as individuals rather than as a class. The outcome of these claims is difficult to predict, as it may vary based on the arguments and situation of each plaintiff, and the applicable state law.

In September 2018, lawyers for the NHL confirmed they had entered settlement negotiations, following the court's order.[641] The details of the negotiations are confidential. Officially, the NHL still denies the merits of the claims.[642]

Simultaneously, the parties decided to seek bellwether trials[643] through the multi-district litigation.[644] They will have to choose four cases among the 140 lawsuits that have been filed to date to head to trial in the spring or summer of 2019.[645] After that, discovery will take place over a period of 150 days.[646]

3 Lessons and Significance

Short and long-term medical complications associated with concussion in ice hockey are exemplified by early retirements, as well as by the five CTE cases diagnosed among NHL players.[647] Like for the NFL,[648] these medical complications highlight the need for a proactive and consistent public health approach.

---

[640]See court memorandum opinion (III), p. 45. The judge based its judgment on Art. 23(b)(3) *FED. R.CIV.P*, which allows for class certification where 'the court finds that the questions of law or fact common to class members predominate over any questions affecting only individual members, and that a class action is superior to any other available methods for fairly and efficiently advocating the controversy'.

[641]Wawrow, above n 597.

[642]Ibid.

[643]The primary value of bellwether trials is that they allow both the defendant and plaintiffs to test legal theories in courts. They are generally used as a precursor to a settlement. For a legal definition, see Garner, above n 5, ad 'bellwether trial', 184.

[644]Rick Westhead, 'NHL, Plaintiffs Agree Concussion Lawsuits Should Kick Off with Four Trials', TSN, 26 September 2018 (<https://www.tsn.ca/nhl-plaintiffs-agree-concussion-lawsuits-should-kick-off-with-four-trials-1.1181451>) (Westhead, 'Trials').

[645]Ibid.

[646]Ibid.

[647]See this chapter, Section IB1 and footnote 512.

[648]See this chapter, Section IA3.

The analysis of the NHL's and the US state and federal governments' responses in this regard is of interest for ice hockey in general, as well as for other SGBs and countries. It is, therefore, relevant in view of the adoption of a harmonised public health regulatory framework.

The NHL's management of the concussion issue, although constantly evolving and not without certain positive aspects, remains less proactive than that of other sports federations governing ice hockey,[649] or even other sports.[650] It is at the moment seriously hindered by the NHL's inflexible position, which focuses most of its efforts on peremptorily denying any link between head trauma and brain impairment.[651] This situation, which is reminiscent of that of the NFL a few years ago,[652] will undoubtedly need to be modified in order to ensure better player safety.

The NHL's intervention has taken shape by the adoption of measures related to the rules of play, rules of the game, medical protocols, financial support for injured players, education, research and data collection.

Although the NHL has made amendments to its rules of play, especially during the last few years,[653] further obvious measures—already applied by other leagues[654]—could be taken to minimise the violence and frequency of contact. These measures, notably called for by the plaintiffs in the pending class action against the NHL[655] and the researchers in charge of identifying measures to be given priority at the end of the Ice Hockey Summits,[656] include the elimination of checks to the head and fighting, as well as body checking policy changes.[657] Checks to the head, fights and body checking are pointed out by the current studies available on the causes of concussion and CTE.[658] Current studies do not clearly identify the position that is the most at risk for concussion in absolute terms (wingers being closely followed by defensemen and centremen).[659] However, they do highlight the vulnerability of centremen in relative terms,[660] as well as the overrepresentation of enforcers in the CTE cases diagnosed,[661] offering again some guidance concerning

[649]See this chapter, Sections IA1 and IB2(a)(ii).

[650]See this chapter, Sections IA1(e) et seq (including subsequent case studies).

[651]See this chapter, Sections IB1 and IB2(a)(i)

[652]See this chapter, Sections IA1(a) et seq.

[653]See this chapter, Section IB1.

[654]Ibid.

[655]Amended class action complaint, pp. 6–7, paragraphs 20–1, p. 8, paragraph 23, p. 60 paragraph 241, pp. 80–2, paragraphs 297–306, pp. 101–4, paragraphs 383–90 and p. 116, paragraph 437.

[656]For more details, see Aynsley M Smith et al., 'Ice Hockey Summit II: Zero Tolerance for Head Hits and Fighting' (2015) 14 *Current Sports Medicine Reports* 135, 135–44, in particular 135 and 142 (Aynsley M Smith, 'Summit').

[657]Ibid. In the same vein, see Lake, above n 626; Jon Heshka, 'Brain Injuries: A Shot Across the NHL's Bow' (2012) 36 *Law Now* 35, 36 (Heshka, 'NHL').

[658]See this chapter, Section IB1.

[659]Ibid.

[660]Ibid, and footnote 544.

[661]See this chapter, Section IB1.

possible improvements in player safety, and the need to better protect certain categories of players (or even, to purely and simply renounce enforcers) through the adoption of new rules of play. These new rules should be implemented with the full support of the NHLPA, which historically has been reluctant to embrace rule changes,[662] and strictly enforced by referees. Stricter fines and suspensions could be instituted for players who prove to be violent. The amount of the fines imposed could then be reinvested in the improvement of concussion management and research.[663]

The NHL introduced improvements in player safety through new rules of the game and concussion protocols, which are in line with the latest CISG's guidelines (and their implementation paper).[664] The introduction of baseline testing, the examination of concussed players by on-site team physicians in a 'quiet room', as well as of concussion spotters (whose instructions are now mandatory for clubs, subject to sanctions),[665] are also positive steps. Other amendments may include the adoption of measures aimed at mandating testing for any borderline hit.[666] Modelled on the NFL,[667] the NHL could simplify its concussion spotter policy[668] (which, because of the numerous actors involved, is likely to create communication problems). It could also mandate the presence of neurologists and/or independent doctors during games. Here, again, the protocols will need to be strictly enforced. Like for the NFL,[669] clubs whose employees are not compliant (regardless of concussion spotters' instructions) could be penalised. The mandatory intervention of a neuropsychologist before return-to-practice is also worth mentioning. Additional measures aimed at improving the day-to-day management of players' health, and mitigating the potential conflict of interest of team physicians,[670] could be considered.

The NHL also introduced improvements in player safety and welfare through a better financial coverage. Particularly worth mentioning is the standard contract clause entitling injured players to receive their full salary until the expiration of their contract.[671] Nonetheless, more could be done, such as the establishment of a NFL-like '88 Plan'[672] aimed at providing reimbursement for former players' medical and custodial care costs.

---

[662]Ibid.

[663]According to the NHL CBA, fine money and forfeited salary are currently allocated to the Players' Emergency Assistance Fund [NHL CBA, Art. 18.16(c]), aimed at helping players who are in financial distress, due to various reasons, such as health issues or mismanagement.

[664]See Chapter 2, Section IX, footnote 164, and this chapter, Section IB1.

[665]See this chapter, Section IB1.

[666]For a definition of 'borderline hit', see this chapter, Section IA3, footnote 416.

[667]See this chapter, Section IA1(e).

[668]See this chapter, Section IB1.

[669]See this chapter, Section IA1(e).

[670]See Chapter 2, Section IV and this chapter, Section IA2(b).

[671]See this chapter, Section IB1.

[672]See this chapter, Section IA1(c).

The NHL launched educational and information initiatives on concussion at the professional and youth levels.[673] These initiatives were, however, mainly aimed at reassuring players by concealing the full extent of the potential short and long-term medical risks associated with concussion.[674] They will have low impact on player safety as long as the NHL—and the NHLPA, whose role is supposed to ensure the protection of players' interests—do not fully acknowledge these risks. It is, therefore, hoped that the NHL follows the NFL's example[675] on this point. Like in the NFL,[676] a whistle-blower system allowing anyone to anonymously report any concussion-related incident could be implemented. The current 'macho culture', stretching as far as NHL executives,[677] would also need closure.

Lastly, the NHL has for a long time been active in the field of medical (or even technological) research and data collection. The NHL's involvement in this field started in 1997, with the creation of the Concussion Study Group (renamed 'Concussion Working Group' in 2007) and the publication of internal studies.[678] It then continued through the creation of sub-committees and the participation of NHL representatives in CISG's meetings (including Dublin) and, to a lesser extent, in other international and domestic roundtables.[679] Major issues related to the independence and quality of the NHL research, and to the lack of specific competence and transparency of the people involved, need to be addressed. This is demonstrated by the incapacity of the Concussion Study Group to conclude the analysis of the data collected until its dissolution, in 2007, and by the absence of neurologists within it, both in its initial and restructured composition.[680] It is also illustrated by the incomplete nature of its internal studies, which remain silent on the causal link between head trauma and cognitive decline.[681] The fact is that there are diverging views on this topic among NHL executives,[682] which are suppressed, for now, by Commissioner Bettman. Once these issues are resolved, the NHL could ally with the NHLPA[683] to support financially independent external research, ensure a more regular participation of its representatives in international meetings, or even strengthen its internal research by the implementation of retired players' surveys. In order to improve transparency, the NHL could also reinstate the obligation for

---

[673]See this chapter, Section IB1.

[674]Ibid.

[675]See this chapter, Section IA1(f).

[676]See this chapter, Section IA1(c).

[677]See this chapter, Section IB2(a)(i). About the macho culture existing among ice hockey players, see this chapter, Section IB1, footnote 521.

[678]See this chapter, Section IB1.

[679]See Chapter 2, Section IX, footnote 163, and this chapter, Section IB1.

[680]See this chapter, Section IB1.

[681]Ibid.

[682]See this chapter, Section IB2(a)(i).

[683]See this chapter, Section IB1.

clubs to disclose the nature of players' injuries[684] and publish formal annual injury reports, possibly inspired by the format of those released by the NFL.[685]

The US governments' involvement in the concussion issue is illustrated here by the questions sent by a US senator to the NHL in 2016, inquiring about the effects of concussion in ice hockey and the potential responsibility of the NHL in funding research.[686] These questions add to other state and federal interventions described previously as part of the NFL section.[687] Although a good number of these interventions are, due to their general nature, also relevant for ice hockey (and other sports),[688] the fact remains that governmental efforts could be intensified in a targeted manner. Thus, a Congressional hearing on the potential risks and management of head injuries in ice hockey could trigger positive measures, in the same manner as the hearing targeting American football in 2009.[689] The forensic research undertaken at Boston University, until now mainly focused on American football players,[690] could be expanded in order to give a more accurate picture of the extent of CTE diagnosis in ice hockey. CTE diagnoses made outside the US, such as that made at the Krembil Neuroscience Institute in Toronto in 2015,[691] highlight the risk of data fragmentation and the need for a better centralisation of data worldwide.

More broadly, the examination of the NHL case study from a public health perspective returns attention to the key relationships (including medical professional and researchers, SGBs and governments, players and their representative unions) identified as part of the NFL chapter.[692] These reactive, competitive and adversarial relationships, fuelled by the NHL's constant and strong denial of the link between head trauma and brain impairment,[693] do not allow players to benefit from optimum protection. They legitimise once again the more harmonised, collaborative approach to public health risks proposed in this thesis.

The analysis of the class action that was filed by former players against the NHL in the US District Court of Minnesota confirms the lessons drawn from the NFL case study in terms of legal risks.[694] One thus finds again the elements discussed previously[695]—legal (financial and reputational) risks, the legal complexity (auguring long litigation) and associated legal uncertainty, the adversarial nature

---

[684]Ibid.

[685]See this chapter, Section IA1(h).

[686]See this chapter, Section IB1.

[687]See this chapter, Sections IA1(d), IA1(e), IA1(f), IA1(g), footnote 221 and Section IA3. See also this chapter, Section IB1.

[688]See this chapter, Section IB1, footnote 586.

[689]See this chapter, Sections IA1(d) et seq.

[690]See this chapter, Sections IA1(b) and IA1(h). About ice hockey, see this chapter, Section IB1.

[691]See this chapter, Section IB1.

[692]See this chapter, Section IA3.

[693]See this chapter, Section IB1.

[694]See this chapter, Section IA3.

[695]Ibid.

of the relationships involved, the difficulty in translating the doubts of science for legal purposes, and the possible shortcomings in tort law. The fears of a long litigation and the difficulties related to the doubts of science, driven by the discovery process and the rigid approach adopted by the NHL,[696] were particularly exacerbated here. The judge refusal to grant class certification[697] only added uncertainty to the whole process. This substantiates, here again, the need for establishing a more harmonised, collaborative approach to legal risks.

C The World Game in the US: Association Football

Football, also known as soccer in the US, is the third major sport for consideration. This section first provides a chronological account of the evolution of scientific knowledge about concussion in football and the responses of the four main entities governing professional football in the US and of US governments. Those four entities are FIFA, the Confederation of North, Central American and Caribbean Association Football (CONCACAF), the United States Soccer Federation (also known as US Soccer) and Major League Soccer (MLS). This section then analyses the potential liability of those four entities and goes on to reveal that they are currently facing, albeit on a smaller scale, public health and legal risks similar to those encountered by the NFL and the NHL. The medical risks are illustrated by the scientifically confirmed dangerous nature of football, and its potential short and long-term health repercussions among professional football players. The legal risks are reflected in the class action that was filed against FIFA and US Soccer. As for FIFA, the action was dismissed in 2015 on grounds related to lack of jurisdiction and failure to state a recognised basis of claim. In regard to US Soccer, there was a settlement involving the banning of headers by children under 10 years old in the US.

Football presents some different issues because of the sports' international organisational structure and the nature of the game. As the most popular sport in the world with 240 million participants[698] and 211 member associations,[699] football has the particular feature of being led by a powerful IF (FIFA) and five continental associations (for North and Central America, CONCACAF). Within the US, regulatory responsibilities are divided between a national federation (US Soccer) affiliated with FIFA, CONCACAF and MLS, which is a professional men's league.

---

[696] See this chapter, Sections IB1 and IB2(a)(i).

[697] See this chapter, Sections IB2(a)(ii) and IB2(b).

[698] See FIFA website (<http://www.fifa.com/news/y=2003/m=4/news=how-many-people-play-football-worldwide-86821.html>).

[699] See FIFA website (<http://www.fifa.com/associations>). Each member association 'is responsible for organising and supervising football in all of its forms in its ***country***' [emphasis added] (2018 FIFA Statutes, Art. 11.1). The FIFA statutes are available on FIFA website (<https://resources.fifa.com/image/upload/the-fifa-statutes-2018.pdf?cloudid=whhncbdzio03cuhmwfxa>).

Similarly, football is unique in its relationship to concussion because part of the game involves heading the ball. Also, physical contact between players is mainly incidental rather than an accepted method of play. These essential characteristics influence the methodology of concussion management, as well as the scope for its improvement. Subsidiary characteristics involve the almost absence of protective equipment (apart from shin pads) and the limited number of substitutions during a game, with no possibility to return.[700] The general measures taken by US governments following the controversy generated by the NFL case are equally applicable to entities governing football in the US. In addition, there has been a minor intervention from two members of the US Congress in the specific context of football.

The section ends with a summary of the main findings. It describes how the US football case study justifies and contributes to the conceptualisation of a harmonised legal framework aimed at better regulating the public health and legal risks related to concussion across sports and legal systems. In that regard, some key points to be drawn from the US football experience may be summed up as follows.

Short and long-term medical complications associated with concussion in football are exemplified by instances of early retirement, as well as by the few CTE cases found in former football players in the US and elsewhere. FIFA's approach to concussion management, although seemingly more open than that of the NHL and, in the past, of the NFL, is nonetheless chilling when it comes to acknowledging a possible link between head trauma and brain impairment. The same is true for the other football entities examined. Numerous efforts have already been made at the international and domestic levels through the implementation of various safety rules and other measures of concussion management. The ability of FIFA, which sits on the top of the football governance pyramid and, to a lesser extent, of its confederations, to provide the necessary hierarchical impetus, will now be essential for constructing better and more harmonised player safety standards.

The analysis of the class action filed against FIFA and US Soccer confirms the lessons drawn from the NFL and the NHL case studies in terms of legal risks. One finds again the elements discussed previously—legal (financial and reputational) risks, legal complexity and associated legal uncertainty, difficulty of attaching legal significance to medical knowledge that is uncertain and possible shortcomings in tort law. In addition, it demonstrates that what happens in US football has the potential to be more complex and far-reaching than for the NFL and NHL by virtue of the immense popularity and scale of football internationally. It also highlights the risk of rules imposed on SGBs by courts, inconsistent outcomes that can result from tort litigation, as well as the excessively litigious nature of US society.

More broadly, the US football case study confirms the reactive, competitive and adversarial nature of the key relationships previously identified, which negatively

---

[700]Return substitutions are only permitted at the grassroots/recreational levels, subject to the agreement of the relevant national associations (2018-19 Laws of the Game, Rule 3/2). The Laws of the Game are available on FIFA website (<https://img.fifa.com/image/upload/khhloe2xoigyna8juxw3.pdf>).

affects the interests of all the stakeholders involved, and highlights the need to ensure harmony at an international level.

1 Chronology

The analysis of the concussion issue in US professional football first requires the examination of the regulatory activity of the four major entities: FIFA, CONCACAF, US Soccer and MLS. FIFA is the world football's governing body and, as such, defines and regulates the main orientations of football worldwide.[701] CONCACAF is one of the five continental football governing bodies recognised by FIFA.[702] At the domestic level, US Soccer and MLS share their authority. US Soccer serves as the football governing body for both professional and grassroots levels in the US.[703] In practice, its authority at the professional level is mainly focused on competitions that are not covered by MLS, such as competitions involving national teams. MLS is the professional sports league for men's football. It consists of franchised professional football clubs located in the US and Canada,[704] and is distinguished by being organised as a 'single entity' (which results in a direct employment relationship with its players).[705] Formally, MLS is an affiliate member of US Soccer,[706] which itself is a member of FIFA and CONCACAF.[707] These four entities have not been subject to the same level of concussion controversy as the NFL[708] and the NHL.[709] They are nonetheless exposed to varying degrees.[710]

Although football is usually not deemed to be violent, its practice is not without risks. Discussion about the possible long-term medical complications of concussion in football has been more frequent and insistent in the scientific field since the beginning of the 2000s.[711] While some studies acknowledge the link between

---

[701]For more details, see 2018 FIFA Statutes, Art. 2.

[702]2018 FIFA Statutes, Art. 22.

[703]2018-19 US Soccer Bylaws, Section 102. US Soccer Bylaws are available on US Soccer website (<https://www.ussoccer.com/about/governance/bylaws>).

[704]For more details, see the MLS website (<https://www.mlssoccer.com/nav/team-news>).

[705]MLS is a limited liability corporation. Instead of team owners, the league has operator-investors. Some of these operator-investors may run more than one of the league's 14 teams. As a result, players are hired by MLS, sign a contract with the league, and then are assigned to the various teams rather than being direct employees of a team [Glenn Wong, *Essentials of Sports Law* (Praeger, 4th ed, 2010) 15].

[706]See 2018-19 US Soccer Bylaws, Section 102; and US Soccer website (<http://www.ussoccer.com/about/affiliates>).

[707]2018-19 US Soccer Bylaws, Section 103.

[708]See this chapter, Sections IA1 et seq and this chapter, Sections IA2 et seq.

[709]See this chapter, Sections IB1 and IB2 et seq.

[710]See this chapter, Sections IC1 and IC2 et seq.

[711]Andrew Rutherford et al., 'Do UK University Football Club Players Suffer Neuropsychological Impairment as a Consequence of their Football (Soccer) Play?' (2009) 31 *Journal of Clinical &*

football concussion and brain impairment, others reach opposite conclusions.[712] Furthermore, the effects of sub-concussions, due to multiple headers,[713] are controversial, notably because of the difficulty distinguishing concussive and sub-concussive effects.[714]

Even though this area requires further investigation,[715] several recent international studies performed by neuropathologists show that brain injury in football caused by repeated blows to the head is attracting increased attention. In 2002, the death of Jeff Astle, a former legendary striker for the English national team and club West Bromwich Albion, who died aged 59, was attributed by a local coroner to an 'industrial disease' (believed to be Alzheimer's disease) brought on by repeatedly heading the ball.[716] In 2014, the Alzheimer's diagnosis originally given to Astle was altered to CTE by Dr Willie Stewart, a neuropathologist at Glasgow's Southern General Hospital in Scotland.[717] This new diagnosis came a few months after the first CTE case ever diagnosed in a football player, namely semi-professional player Patrick Grange, examined by Boston researchers after his death of ALS in 2012 at the age of 29.[718] It was followed by the case of former captain of the Brazilian national football team Hilderaldo Luis Bellini, and that of an anonymous donor who played for 16 years at the professional level in the UK. Bellini died from various medical complications in 2014, aged 83, and was diagnosed with CTE based on a joint post-mortem examination by researchers from the Universities of Boston,

Experimental Neuropsychology 664, 664. For older studies, see J Dvorak, A Junge and P McCrory, 'Head Injuries' (2005) 39 (Supplement 1) *British Journal of Sports Medicine* 1, 1.

712 For an illustration of this contradiction, see eg, Ammar Al-Kashmiri and J Scott Delaney, 'Head and Neck Injuries in Football (Soccer)' (2006) 8(3) *Trauma* 189, 189 and 192 (these authors argue that the incidence and possibly effects of concussion in football are similar to other contact sports such as American football and ice hockey, and call for more research in this area); Rutherford et al., above n 711, 664–81, in particular 664–6 (these authors support the view that there is, to date, no reliable evidence towards this direction).

713 Part of playing the game involves striking the ball with the head. That can lead to repetitive and strong blows to the head, for instance if the head is used to stop a ball kicked powerfully by another player or from a fast falling goal kick.

714 Al-Kashmiri and Delaney, above n 712, 192; Rutherford et al., above n 711, 664–6. For a recent study (2018) which tends to acknowledge the link between headers and brain impairment, see Walter F Stewart et al., 'Heading Frequency Is More Strongly Related to Cognitive Performance than Unintentional Head Impacts in Amateur Soccer Players' (2018) Vol. 9 Art. 240 *Frontiers of Neurology* 1, 1 (Stewart et al., 'Soccer').

715 Al-Kashmiri and Delaney, above n 712, 192; Rutherford et al., above n 711, 664 and 678–9.

716 Catherine Norwood, 'Clear Heads Needed on Concussion in Sport' (August 2012) 58(39) *Chronicle of Higher Education*, Monash Supplement 20.

717 Ben Pepper, 'Jeff Astle Died from "Boxing" Brain Injury', *Lexology*, 3 June 2014 (<https://www.lexology.com/library/detail.aspx?g=7779a299-7a91-49e2-8405-b629b1549351>) (paywall).

718 Ann C McKee et al., 'The Neuropathology of Sport' (2014) 127 *Acta Neuropathologica* 29, 29–51 (McKee et al., 'Neuropathology').

California and Sao Paulo.[719] The case of the anonymous donor is little documented.[720]

Against this background, the 2014 World Cup, organised under the auspices of FIFA, attracted much controversy when several concussed players were immediately allowed to return to the field,[721] or simply did not undergo any physical assessment.[722] It led two members of the US Congress to send a letter to FIFA.[723] This letter, criticising FIFA's concussion management and urging the organisation to take adequate action, adds to other state and federal interventions described previously as part of the NFL section.[724] The 2014 World Cup also triggered the filling of a class action against FIFA.[725] The concussion controversy was given further impetus in 2016, when it was revealed that at least three of England's 1966 World Cup winning team had been diagnosed with Alzheimer's.[726] In 2017, four more CTE diagnosis, including a former English Premier League (EPL)'s player, were released by the UCL Institute of Neurology in London.[727] FIFA declared these findings inconclusive.[728]

[719] Lea T Grinberg et al., 'Chronic Traumatic Encephalopathy Presenting as Alzheimer's Disease in a Retired Soccer Player' (2016) 54 *Journal of Alzheimer's Disease* 169, 169–74.

[720] Chadwick Hales et al., 'Late Stage CTE Pathology in a Retired Soccer Player with Dementia' (2014) *Neurology* 2307, 2307.

[721] For more details, see John T Wendt and John J Miller, ' "Ref, Is This the Final?" Concussion Issues at the 2014 FIFA Men's World Cup: A Case Study' (2015) 25 *Journal of Legal Aspects of Sport* 1, 2–4. Interestingly, these authors report that several of the players concussed during the 2014 World Cup 'appeared to be unconcerned about their head injuries and more concerned about the greater glory of winning in the competition' [see ibid, 3].

[722] For more details, see Michael D Cusimano et al., 'Assessment of Head Collision Events During the 2014 FIFA World Cup Tournament' (2017) 317 *Journal of the American Medical Medical Association* 2548, 2548–9.

[723] This letter, sent by Bill Pascrell Jr and Thomas Rooney, members of the US House of Representatives, to former FIFA President Sepp Blatter, is available on the New York Daily News website (<http://www.nydailynews.com/blogs/iteam/congress-tells-fifa-act-concussions-blog-entry-1.1869314>).

[724] See this chapter, Sections IA1(d), IA1(e), IA1(f), IA1(g), footnote 221 and Section IA3. Among these interventions, numerous general interventions—youth concussion laws, Congressional hearing on sports safety, research (CTE Center in Boston; also mentioned in this section), grants, partnerships and concussion summits – are also relevant for FIFA and other football governing bodies.

[725] See this chapter, Section IC2(b).

[726] Sam Peters, 'After Three 1966 Heroes Are Revealed to Have Dementia, Jeff Astle's Family Ask Why the FA Have Yet to Tackle Sport's Silent Scandal', *MailOnline*, 16 April 2016 (<http://www.mailonsunday.co.uk/sport/concussion/article-3543806/After-three-1966-heroes-revealed-dementia-Jeff-Astle-s-family-ask-FA-tackle-sport-s-silent-scandal.html>).

[727] Helen Ling et al., 'Mixed Pathologies, Including Chronic Traumatic Encephalopathy Account for Dementia in Retired Association Football (Soccer) Players' (2017) 133 *Acta Neuropathologica* 337, 337–52 (Ling, 'Pathologies').

[728] George Flood, 'FIFA Respond to Latest Football Dementia Study as FA Welcome New Research', *IB Times*, 15 February 2017 (<https://www.ibtimes.co.uk/fifa-respond-latest-football-dementia-study-fa-welcome-new-research-1606735>).

US Soccer (also named as a defendant in the class action)[729] and MLS were not spared either. Several high-profile players had to retire due to concussion from 2009, including former US international and New England player Taylor Twellman.[730] In 2015, former high-school football player Curtis Baushke, aged 24, was diagnosed with CTE.[731]

US Soccer and its affiliate member, MLS, are subject to world football's governing body FIFA and continental association CONCACAF.[732] Accordingly, the analysis of the management of concussion in football should start at the top of the sports pyramid.

In 1994, FIFA established the FIFA Medical Assessment and Research Center (F-MARC).[733] While F-MARC's major focus is on injury prevention, the first step was the determination of the frequency, characteristics and mechanisms of injury in football.[734] Several different studies were carried out under the supervision of Dr Jiri Dvorak, who was at the time FIFA's Chief Medical Officer and a consultant neurologist at Zurich's Schulthess Clinic.[735] From 1998, F-MARC performed injury surveillance at all FIFA competitions and football competitions of the Olympic Games.[736] This system, based on report-forms sent to team physicians,[737] did not only prove useful for football, but also paved the way for the IOC injury surveillance system.[738] Head and neck injuries being quickly identified as the most frequent injuries in football,[739] this issue, already regularly discussed in the scientific community in connection with the narrower question of concussion, logically fell within

[729] See this chapter, Section IC2(b).

[730] Associated Press, 'MLS Discusses Concussion Protocol', *ESPN*, 7 January 2012 (<http://www.espn.com/sports/soccer/news/_/id/7436065/mls-medical-staffers-target-concussion-protocol>) (Associated Press, 'MLS'). See also this chapter, Section IC2(a), footnote 796.

[731] Dan Barry, 'An Athlete Felled by Concussions, despite Playing a "Safer" Sport', *The New York Times*, 21 June 2015 (<https://www.nytimes.com/2015/06/22/sports/an-athlete-felled-by-concussions-despite-playing-a-safer-sport.html?ref=international&_r=1>).

[732] See 2018 FIFA Statutes, in particular Arts. 10 et seq., and 22 et seq; 2018-19 US Soccer Bylaws, Section 103.

[733] See FIFA website (<http://www.fifa.com/development/medical/about-us/f-marc/index.html>).

[734] See FIFA website (<http://www.fifa.com/development/medical/about-us/f-marc/frequency-and-characteristics-of-injury.html>).

[735] Dr Dvorak left FIFA in November 2016. His position has remained unfilled since then [email from Alexis Weber (Head of Medical and Anti-Doping, FIFA) to author, 26 November 2018].

[736] See eg, Astrid Junge et al., 'Football Injuries during FIFA Tournaments and the Olympic Games, 1998-2001' (2004) 32 (Supplement 1) *American Journal of Sports Medicine* 80S, 80S-9S (Junge et al., 'Football Injuries'); Astrid Junge and Jiri Dvorak, 'Injury Surveillance in World Football Tournaments 1998-2012' (2013) 47 *British Journal of Sports Medicine* 782, 782–8 (Junge and Dvorak, 'World Football').

[737] Ibid.

[738] Astrid Junge et al., 'Injury Surveillance in Multi-Sport Events: The International Olympic Committee Approach' (2008) 42 *British Journal of Sports Medicine* 413, 414 (Junge, 'Multi-Sport Events').

[739] Ibid.

one of F-MARC's priority research areas. In the mid-2000s, one of F-MARC's studies identified elbow-to-head-contacts as the primary cause of head and neck injuries in football,[740] a trend already highlighted by other studies, which also pointed out the dangerousness of head-to-head contacts,[741] and the particular vulnerability of goalkeepers and defenders.[742] This observation prompted the introduction, prior to the 2006 World Cup, of a new rule penalising elbowing to the head with red cards, meaning ejection from the field.[743] This new rule is in line with previous safety measures, such as the gradual weight reduction of balls (when wet) [744] and, in 1998, the introduction of red cards for tackles from behind.[745]

F-MARC also published targeted studies, dedicated to concussion and sub-concussion only. These studies were an opportunity to highlight the lack of a proven link between the practice of football and cognitive impairment, while also stressing the current scientific uncertainty related to possible long-term cognitive consequences.[746] This position corresponds to that stated in the medical guidelines of the CISG,[747] in which FIFA has, from the beginning, played an active part, exemplified by both its financial and scientific support.[748] The CISG's guidelines and related tools are also published on FIFA's website,[749] readily available to its members and the general public. Conversely, FIFA has not endorsed the CISG's implementation paper.[750]

Simultaneously, F-MARC introduced a worldwide injury prevention program for amateur football players ('The 11'), then further developed into a complete warm-up program ('The 11+').[751]

---

[740] CW Fuller, A Junge and J Dvorak, 'A Six-Year Prospective Study of the Incidence, Aetiology and Causes of Head and Neck Injuries in International Football' (2005) 39 (Supplement 1) *British Journal of Sports Medicine* 1, 3–9.

[741] For a summary of the current studies, see Michael L Levy et al., 'Concussions in Soccer: A Current Understanding' (2012) 78 *World Neurosurgery* 535, 536–7.

[742] See eg, Al-Kashmiri and Delaney, above n 712, 190; Michael Nilsson et al., 'Head and Neck Injuries in Professional Soccer' (2013) 23 *Clinical Journal of Sports Medicine* 255, 255 and 258.

[743] See FIFA website (<http://www.fifa.com/development/medical/about-us/f-marc/index.html>).

[744] Dvorak, Junge and McCrory, above n 711, 1.

[745] See FIFA website (<http://www.fifa.com/development/news/y=1998/m=3/news=fifa-crack-down-tackle-from-behind-70380.html>).

[746] See eg, J Dvorak, Junge and McCrory, above n 711, 1–2; Truls M Straueme-Naesheim et al., 'Do Minor Head Impacts in Soccer Cause Concussive Injury? A Prospectice Case Control Study' (2009) 64 *Neurosurgery* 719, 723–4.

[747] See Chapter 2, Section VII.

[748] It should be noted that former FIFA Chief Medical Officer Jiri Dvorak was part of the CISG's Scientific Committee from 2001 (date of its creation) to 2016.

[749] See FIFA website (<https://www.fifa.com/development/news/y=2016/m=11/news=fifa-helps-concussion-issue-move-forward-2847636.html> and <https://resources.fifa.com/image/upload/concussion-recognition-tool-5.pdf?cloudid=y9y5fpwji70rtzyefdoa>).

[750] See Chapter 2, Section IX, footnote 164.

[751] See FIFA website (<http://www.fifa.com/development/medical/about-us/f-marc/index.html>).

In 2014, a year marked by various controversies in the football world and elsewhere,[752] FIFA announced the launch of a collaborative project with the University-Hospital Zurich's Clinic of Neurology and Zurich's Schulthess Clinic.[753] This project was led during the 2014–15 season by Dr Nina Feddermann, a F-MARC member and doctor within these clinics.[754] It consisted of neurological and neuropsychological examination of male and female players from teams in Switzerland's highest football leagues.[755] Building on a pilot-project started in 2013, it was primarily aimed at determining the most appropriate treatment and return-to-play timeline for players who have sustained head injuries.[756] Data on depression was also collected.[757] Still in 2014, FIFA launched a similar collaborative study with the Hamburg Medical School, targeting former male and female players of Germany's highest football leagues.[758] This study then formed the basis of a wider project, entitled 'Head In the Game'.[759] This international, multicentre project was launched in the Netherlands, US and Germany with the support of FIFA and US Soccer.[760] Its first aim is to evaluate the long-term effects of head injuries on elite football players in terms of mental and physical health, based on surveys and various examination methods, such as neuroimaging.[761]

Concurrently, FIFA representatives attended international meetings on concussion in the US, such as the NFL Think Tanks.[762]

---

[752]See this chapter, Sections IA1(g) and IA2 et seq (including subsequent case studies).

[753]See FIFA website (<http://www.fifa.com/development/news/y=2014/m=8/news=fifa-kooperationsprojekt-zum-thema-gehirnerschutterung-im-fussball-24199-2420132.html>).

[754]Dr Feddermann is a doctor within the University-Hospital Zurich's Clinic of Neurology and Zurich's Schulthess Clinic. She is the Head of the Swiss Concussion Center, also affiliated to these clinics.

[755]See FIFA website (<http://www.fifa.com/development/news/y=2014/m=8/news=fifa-kooperationsprojekt-zum-thema-gehirnerschutterung-im-fussball-24199-2420132.html>).

[756]Ibid.

[757]For more details, see Astrid Junge and Nina Feddermann-Demont, 'Prevalence of Depression and Anxiety in Top-Level Male and Female Football Players' (2016) 2(1) *BMJ Open Sport and Exercise Medicine* (online article).

[758]See FIFA website (<http://fifa.pressfire.net/newsletter/newsletter?id=2611&html=1>).

[759]See 'Head in the Game' website (<http://hitg.study/> and <http://hitg.study/team/>).

[760]See 'Head in the Game' website (<http://hitg.study/about/>) and (<http://hitg.study/partners/>).

[761]See 'Head in the Game' website (<http://hitg.study/about//>). The first findings of this project can eg, be found in: Birgit Prinz, Jiri Dvorak and Astrid Junge, 'Symptoms and Risk Factors of Depression during and after the Football Career of Elite Female Players' (2017) 2(1) *BMJ Open Sport and Exercise Medicine* (online article); A Prien et al., 'Health Problems in Elite Female Football Players: Prevalence and Risk Factors' (2017) 27 *Scandinavian Journal of Medicine & Science in Sports* 1404, 1404–10 (Prien et al., 'Football').

[762]See eg, Ben Klayman, 'Concussion Treatment, Diagnosis Focus of World Sports Conference', *Reuters*, 22 October 2015 (<http://www.reuters.com/article/us-sport-concussions-idUSKCN0SG18520151022>); Gary Mihoces, 'FIFA Doctor at NFL Summit "not Alarmed" by Soccer's Concussion Data', *USA Today*, 25 August 2014 (<http://www.usatoday.com/story/sports/nfl/2014/08/25/nfl-fifa-concussion-think-tank-world-cup-christoph-kramer/14574077/>) (Mihoces, 'FIFA').

In addition, FIFA amended its competition rules in order to allow the referee to stop the game for three minutes in case of a suspected concussion, and to enable the relevant team doctor to complete an on-field assessment.[763] The referee can only allow the injured party to continue playing with the authorisation of the team doctor, who makes the final decision.[764] This new rule is applicable in World Cup qualifying games and, in collaboration with the Union of European Football Associations (UEFA), in European Championship qualifiers, Champions League and Europa League matches, but not yet at the domestic level.[765] Its geographical scope is intended to be gradually extended. Other confederations, such as CONCACAF and its South American counterpart, CONMEBOL,[766] have already incorporated this rule (coupled with the use of the SCAT, developed by the CISG) into their own regulations.[767] The possibility for teams to use video replay to assist team doctors in this context was also approved.[768]

While minimising the importance of the issue of concussion in football (only 12 instances of concussion reported during the five last men's World Cups, 1998–2014),[769] FIFA continued with remedial action. In 2016, FIFA relaxed its substitution rules, which limit, in principle, the number of substitutes to three during a game,[770] and are potentially problematic in that they create a temptation to keep a concussed player on the field. It allowed a fourth substitution in extra time as an experiment conducted at the Olympic Football Tournaments, the FIFA U-20

---

[763]See FIFA website (<http://www.fifa.com/development/news/y=2014/m=9/news=fifa-s-medical-committee-proposes-new-protocol-for-the-management-of-c-2443024.html>).

[764]Ibid.

[765]See FIFA and UEFA tournaments regulations, available on the respective websites of each association. See also Mike Collett, 'FIFA Medical Officer Wants Strict New Rules on Concussion', *Reuters*, 9 September 2014 (<http://www.reuters.com/article/us-soccer-medical-concussion-idUSKBN0H422C20140909>).

[766]The Confederación Sudamericana de Fútbol.

[767]See eg, 2017 CONCACAF Gold Cup Regulations, Arts. XI (8) and (9); 2016 CONMEBOL and CONCACAF Copa Americana Centenario Regulations, Chapter X, Art. 8. The first regulations are available on CONCACAF website (<https://res.cloudinary.com/concacaf-production/image/upload/v1498764762/goldcup-prod/assets/2017_Regulations_English_Edition.pdf>). The second regulations are on file with author.

[768]For more details about video replay, see eg Amar Toor, 'Soccer's Rule Makers Consider Video Replay for Head Injuries', *The Verge*, 10 November 2016 (<http://www.theverge.com/2016/11/10/13582510/instant-replay-soccer-concussion-ifab>).

[769]Astrid Junge and Jiri Dvorak, 'Fotball Injuries during the 2014 FIFA World Cup' (2015) 49 *British Journal of Sports Medicine* 601, 601 (Junge and Dvorak, 'FIFA'). Official statistics for the 2018 World Cup have not yet been published.

[770]2018-19 Laws of the Game, Rule 3/2.

Women's World Cup in Papua New Guinea and the FIFA Club World Cup in Japan.[771] It then expanded it to the 2018 Men's World Cup.[772]

FIFA's confederations and member associations are required to respect its Statutes, Regulations and Laws of the Game.[773] This principle has the effect of limiting their regulatory authority. However, the Laws of the Game sometimes allow some variation in their application. This is, for example, the case, in the event of a prior agreement of the parties involved, for the number of substitutions allowed in friendly games or national championships.[774] Similarly, some adjustments (size, weight and material of the ball) may occur for youth, veteran footballers and for players with disabilities.[775] In addition, the CISG's guidelines, although published on FIFA's website,[776] have not been recognised by the formal adoption of concussion protocols. They constitute, therefore, only general recommendations, without binding force, which confederations and national federations still have to interpret and adapt, when appropriate, to the characteristics of football.[777] Finally, the scope of some measures, incorporated in competition rules, is limited to specific tournaments.

CONCACAF has rarely made use of its regulatory authority. With the exception of the incorporation into some of its regulations of FIFA's new three-minute rule for on-field assessment (based on the SCAT) in case of a suspected concussion, mentioned above,[778] it has not publicly announced any substantive measures.

MLS has been more proactive. In 2010, following the early retirements of several high-profile players due to concussion,[779] MLS created a nine-member Concussion Committee, chaired by Ruben Echemendia, already involved in the NHL Concussion Working Group.[780] In 2011, MLS adopted its first concussion protocol, based on four key principles: baseline testing for all players, removal from field when a brain injury is suspected, evaluation by team physicians and no return-to-play until the player is symptom free.[781] The revised version of this protocol recommends the use of a modified version of the SCAT 3 and of the baseline (ImPACT) test.[782]

---

[771]See FIFA website (<http://www.fifa.com/about-fifa/news/y=2016/m=3/news=fifa-executive-committee-approves-key-priorities-to-restore-trust-in-f-2771049.html>).

[772]Sports Joe website (<https://www.sportsjoe.ie/football/fifa-come-senses-fourth-substitutes-extra-time-152892>).

[773]See 2018 FIFA Statutes, Arts. 11/4a and b, 14/1d and h and 22/3a.

[774]2018-19 Laws of the Game, Rule 3/2.

[775]2018-19 Laws of the Game, Modifications to the Laws of the Game.

[776]See this chapter, Section IC1.

[777]See this chapter, Section IC.

[778]See this chapter, Section IC1.

[779]Ibid, and this chapter, Section IC2(a), footnote 796.

[780]Associated Press, 'MLS', above n 730. This Committee was subsequently extended to 12 members, among which leagues' and players' representatives, athletic trainers and physicians. About the NHL/NHLPA Concussion Working Group, see this chapter, Section IB1.

[781]Associated Press, 'MLS', above n 730.

[782]2015 MLS CBA, Exhibit 12, p. 2; 2016 MLS Medical Policies and Procedures Manual, Sections 8A and 12 B (all unpublished, but copy on file with author).

It grants team physicians absolute powers for on-field assessment, and the ultimate authority to decide when a player is fit to return-to-practice (based on the assessment of a neuropsychologist, whose opinion is only advisory, and not communicated to the player).[783] The protocol is attached to the MLS CBA,[784] which also grants protection to injured players during the period of their contract, with the risk of default at the end of the year in the rare event of a semi-guaranteed contract.[785] In 2012, MLS held its first Medical Symposium on player safety.[786] The experience was repeated in 2015, in conjunction with US Soccer.[787] MLS and US Soccer also participated in the Summit on Youth Concussion in Sport held in 2014 at the White House,[788] previously mentioned.[789] These joint efforts were notably aimed at leading a coordinated effort on concussion management and prevention initiatives. Finally, MLS has, through the years, undertaken a range of research on medical issues and collected data on players' injuries, including concussion, without publicly disclosing its findings.[790]

For its part, US Soccer created a 'Concussion Management Program' for national team players, including pre-injury baseline testing with post-injury follow-up evaluations, return-to-play protocols (based on a 'modified SCAT 2' and the electronic software ImPACT) and education.[791] In 2016, US Soccer unveiled its new 'Concussion Initiative'. This initiative, implemented at the youth level in the US, allowed US Soccer to terminate the legal proceedings instituted against it.[792] It includes the implementation of educational campaigns, more uniform concussion management and return-to-play protocols, the amendment of substitution rules (in the form of an additional 'concussion substitute' not counting against the team's total number of allowed substitutions during the game),[793] and the prohibition of headers by children

[783] 2015 MLS CBA, Exhibit 12, pp. 2–3 and 5.

[784] 2015 MLS CBA, Exhibit 12.

[785] MLS CBA, Art. 9, Section 9.2; and Art. 18, Section 18.6(b), which states that contracts for players who are at least 24 years old and have completed at least 1 MLS guaranteed service year are automatically fully guaranteed against injuries.

[786] Associated Press, 'MLS', above n 730.

[787] US Soccer website (<https://www.ussoccer.com/stories/2015/01/06/12/22/150106-ussoccer-mls-medical-symposium>).

[788] See MLS website (<https://www.mlssoccer.com/post/2014/05/29/mls-us-soccer-participate-healthy-kids-and-safe-sports-concussion-summit-white-house>).

[789] See this chapter, Section IA1(f).

[790] Email from Bob Foose (Executive Director, MLS Players Union) to author, 4 January 2017. See also the 2016 MLS Medical Policies and Procedures Manual (unpublished), *Glossary of Terms and Abbreviations*, which requires clubs to report any players' injuries to the league.

[791] US Soccer website (<http://cd03.ussoccer.com/development-academy/resource-center/sports-medicine>).

[792] US Soccer website (<http://www.ussoccer.com/about/recognize-to-recover/concussion-guidelines/player-safety-campaign>) and (<http://www.ussoccer.com/about/recognize-to-recover/concussion-guidelines>).

[793] US Soccer website (<http://www.ussoccer.com/about/recognize-to-recover/concussion-guidelines/player-safety-campaign-faqs>).

under 10 years old.[794] Like MLS, US Soccer's activity also includes unpublicised study and data collection related to concussion.[795]

2 Legal Activities and Implications

(a) Major League Soccer (MLS)

MLS, unlike its clubs,[796] has never been a party to a concussion lawsuit. Should this occur, it would be interesting to see how a judge would assess MLS's potential liability. As already mentioned,[797] it only has limited regulatory room to manoeuvre. Additionally, due to its 'single entity' nature,[798] it could at the same time theoretically be subject to a heightened duty of protection in tort law (negligence) due to its special relationship to players,[799] while being protected by workers' compensation laws that, in many US states, bar employees from suing their employer.[800]

Although MLS has been spared for now, this is not the case with FIFA and US Soccer, which had to face legal proceedings in 2014.

---

[794]Ibid.

[795]Email from Hughie O'Malley (Manager, Sports Medicine Administration, US Soccer) to author, 9 January 2017.

[796]Two MLS clubs have recently received concussion lawsuits. In 2012, former international and DC United player Bryan Namoff sued his former club and medical team before the D.C. Superior Court, alleging that his career ended prematurely because they negligently allowed him to play while he was still suffering from concussion-related symptoms. In 2014, former international and Portland Timbers player Eddie Johnson filed a similar complaint in Oregon state court. Namoff's lawsuit was found to be barred by workers' compensation laws in 2015. Johnson's lawsuit is still pending (in an amended version). For more details, see Steven Goff, 'Namoff's Lawsuit was Dismissed', *The Washington Post*, 14 January 2015 (<https://www.washingtonpost.com/news/soccer-insider/wp/2015/01/14/namoffs-lawsuit-was-dismissed/>); Jamie Goldberg, 'Portland Timbers no Longer Defendant in Eddie Johnson's Concussion Lawsuit, *The Oregonian*, 19 January 2017 (<https://www.oregonlive.com/timbers/index.ssf/2017/01/portland_timbers_no_longer_a_d.html>) (Goldberg, 'Lawsuit').

[797]See this chapter, Sections IC and IC1.

[798]See this chapter, Section IC1.

[799]Ibid. For a discussion of this issue within the context of the NFL litigation, see this chapter, Sections IA2(a)(ii) and IA3.

[800]See this chapter, Section IA2(a)(iv), footnote 279, and Section IA2(b).

(b) The Class Action against the Federation Internationale of Football Association (FIFA) and US Soccer

In August 2014, several current and former youth football players and parents filed a class action lawsuit against FIFA in the US District Court for the Northern District of California.[801] Unlike the NFL[802] and the NHL[803] litigation, the plaintiffs invoked the torts of negligence and breach of voluntary undertaking,[804] with the exception of fraud.[805] In the absence of actual damage,[806] they did not seek monetary damages, but called for a more cautious management and monitoring of concussion by way of injunctive relief.[807]

In January 2015, FIFA filed a motion to dismiss the class action,[808] based on four main grounds: lack of personal matter jurisdiction, lack of subject matter jurisdiction, failure to state a recognised basis of claim and failure to join to the action the International Football Association Board (IFAB)[809] as a necessary party. As an alternative plea, FIFA filed an accompanying motion to dismiss or compel arbitration (in relation to the possible jurisdiction of the CAS, in place of the state courts).[810]

---

[801] *Mehr et al. v. Fédération Internationale de Football Association et al*, U.S. District Court, Northern District of California, No. 14-03879. Plaintiffs filed a class action complaint on 27 August 2014. This document is available via the Bloomberg database (access on subscription).

[802] See this chapter, Section IA2(a)(i).

[803] See this chapter, Section IB2(a)(i).

[804] The 'voluntary undertaking doctrine' comes from section 323 of the *Restatement (Second) of Torts* (1965). It provides that those who take voluntary measures to protect others are responsible for ensuring that those measures are carried out successfully and that no additional harm comes to those relying on those held duties. For more details, see eg, Sam C Ehrlich, 'Gratuitous Promises: Overseeing Athletic Organizations and the Duty of Care' (2018) 25 *Jeffrey S Moorad Sports Law Journal Sports Law Journal* 1, 2–3, 16–20 and 22–4 (this author examines this issue in light of the FIFA and USAWP litigation).

[805] Class action complaint, pp. 126–30, paragraphs 423–44.

[806] Class action complaint, in particular pp. 12–16, paragraphs 38–54.

[807] Class action complaint, in particular p. 10, paragraph 32, pp. 126–31, paragraphs 423–51 and p. 131 (Request for Relief).

[808] FIFA filed a motion to dismiss the complaint on 30 January 2015. This document is available via the Bloomberg database (access on subscription).

[809] According to Art. 7 of the 2018 FIFA Statutes, IFAB is a Swiss organisation that convenes once a year to discuss the Laws of the Game. The sole responsibility for the Laws of the Game lies with IFAB, which is composed of FIFA (with four votes) and the four British associations (England, Scotland, Wales, and Northern Ireland) with one vote apiece. Thus, FIFA, with its four votes, cannot unilaterally modify the Laws.

[810] FIFA filed an accompanying motion to dismiss or compel arbitration on 30 January 2015. This document is available via the Bloomberg database (access on subscription). In some other common law jurisdictions, such a motion to dismiss may be pleaded as a 'motion to dismiss the action on the grounds of justiciability'.

The lawsuit was dismissed in July 2015.[811] The US District Court agreed with FIFA's first three main defence grounds.[812] The Court declined jurisdiction due to the claim's insufficient connection with California, and the failure to identify any harm linked to the alleged breaches.[813] Interestingly, it also expressed a conventional view as to SGBs' and players' responsibility and the voluntary assumption of risk while engaging in sports activities.[814] It noted in particular that '[a] defendant has no duty to protect a plaintiff against risks inherent in a particular sport voluntarily played by the plaintiff, since those who participate in a sporting activity that poses an inherent risk of injury generally assume the risk that they may be injured while doing so'.[815] The Court did not consider it necessary to examine FIFA's fourth main ground.[816] The Court emphasised, however, several times in its decision, that the responsibility for the Laws of the Game lies with IFAB.[817] FIFA's accompanying motion to dismiss or compel arbitration was also not considered.[818]

The decision was initially challenged by the plaintiffs,[819] but the appeal was later withdrawn.[820] It is notable because, at the time, there was no other legal authority concerning the potential liability of SGBs for concussion in the US.[821] The scope of this decision, must, however, be put into perspective and considered with regard to its specific context (organisational structure of the entities involved, absence of CBA and of fraud allegations, hypothetical damage and the fact that football is not generally acknowledged as a particularly violent sport).[822] In addition, the

[811]*Mehr et al. v. Fédération Internationale de Football Association et al* (N.D., Cal, 16 July 2015, No. 14-cv-3879-PJH), Order granting motion to dismiss (Order I). This document is available via the Bloomberg database (access on subscription).

[812]Order (I), pp. 7–19, pp. 19–29, and pp. 29–44.

[813]Ibid, pp. 7–19 and pp. 19–29.

[814]Under Californian law, the analysis of a possible failure to state a recognised basis of claim implies the examination of four elements: duty of care, breach, causation and damage [Order (I), p. 32].

[815]Order (I), p. 34.

[816]Ibid, p. 44.

[817]Ibid, pp. 16 and 27. See also this chapter, Section IC2(b), footnote 809.

[818]In the absence of jurisdiction, the Court formally denied the motion [Order granting motion to dismiss, p. 45]. Note that the alleged jurisdiction of the CAS, based notably on Arts. 11/4 c and 57 et seq. of the 2018 FIFA's Statutes, implied the exhaustion of all internal remedies.

[819]*Rachel Mehr et al. v. Federation Internationale de F* et al, No. 15-16622 (9th Cir. Aug 17, 2015).

[820]The appeal was voluntarily dismissed with prejudice following the stipulation of the parties [see *Mehr et al. v. Fédération Internationale de Football Association et al* (9th Cir, No. 15-16622, 22 September 2015), Order granting request for dismissal (Order II); this document is available via the Bloomberg database (access on subscription)].

[821]See this chapter, Section IA2(a)(v), and footnote 305. For a more recent decision (in water polo), see this chapter, Section ID2(b).

[822]See this chapter, Sections IC, IC1 and IC2(b).

decision comes from a lower court and is based on jurisdictional and procedural grounds.[823] More generally, it may appear somewhat inconsistent, as it assumes that football players know the long-term medical risks associated with concussion, which FIFA still strives to deny.[824]

US Soccer, together with various US youth football associations, were also named as defendants in the class action.[825] The complaint against those defendants was settled in 2015,[826] following the adoption of the US Soccer Concussion Initiative, mentioned above.[827]

3 Lessons and Significance

Short and long-term medical complications associated with concussion in football are exemplified by instances of early retirement, as well as by the few CTE cases found in football players in the US and elsewhere.[828] Like for the NFL and the NHL,[829] these medical complications highlight the need for a proactive and consistent public health approach. The need for consistency in the management of concussion in football presents itself with even more urgency, due to the popularity of this sport worldwide.[830]

The analysis of the responses of FIFA, CONCACAF, US Soccer and MLS, together with those of the US state and federal governments in this regard is of interest for football in general, as well as for other SGBs and countries. This analysis will be particularly useful for the sports played under the umbrella of an IF and/or organised with a dual structure of a national governing body and a professional league at the domestic level. It will enrich the discussion related to the adoption of a harmonised public health regulatory framework.

FIFA's approach to concussion management, although seemingly more open than that of the NHL[831] and, in the past, of the NFL,[832] is also nonetheless chilling when

---

[823]See this chapter, Section IC2(b). In the same vein, see also Order granting motion to dismiss, pp. 7, 8 and 18.

[824]See this chapter, Section IC1.

[825]Class action complaint, pp. 21–7.

[826]For more details, see the 'Joint Statement Regarding Concussion Lawsuit Resolution' published by the parties involved on the US Soccer website (<http://www.ussoccer.com/about/recognize-to-recover/concussion-guidelines/player-safety-campaign>).

[827]See this chapter, Section IC2(b).

[828]See this chapter, Sections IC1 and IC2(a), footnote 796.

[829]See this chapter, Sections IA3 and IB3.

[830]See this chapter, Section IC.

[831]See this chapter, Section IB1.

[832]See this chapter, Sections IA1(a) et seq.

it comes to acknowledging a possible link between head trauma and brain impairment.[833] The same is true for the other football entities examined, including MLS, whose Concussion Committee relies in part on advisors and experts also active within the NHL.[834] While numerous efforts have already been made at the international and domestic levels,[835] the ability of FIFA and, to a lesser extent, of its confederations, to provide the necessary hierarchical impetus, will be essential to the construction of better and more harmonised player safety standards.

FIFA's intervention includes the adoption of measures related to the rules of play, rules of the game, medical guidelines, education, research and data collection. The following paragraphs provide an analysis and critical evaluation of the intervention.

FIFA, together with IFAB, has amended its rules of play several times in order to make the game safer.[836] Even though the point has been reached where the practical scope for FIFA to reform the rules to further reduce impacts to players' heads is relatively limited (most of contact between football players is incidental, and headers are an integral part of football), some measures could be considered. FIFA could, for instance, take a tougher position towards head to head contact, which has been identified by numerous studies as a significant cause of concussion,[837] and which could be sanctioned by a red card.[838] It could also investigate ways to better protect defenders and goalkeepers, which have been identified at high risk for concussion.[839] The new rules should be strictly enforced by referees. Like for the NFL and the NHL,[840] heavy financial penalties could be levied (at least for international competitions),[841] and stricter suspensions could be instituted for players who prove to be violent. The amount of the fines imposed could then be reinvested in the improvement of concussion management. The impact of headers could be reduced by the use of even lighter balls, associated with appropriate training techniques.[842] The issue of headers by children should be investigated further and its regulation harmonised worldwide (knowing that, for the time being, headers by children under 10 years old are considered as dangerous and prohibited in the US, but not elsewhere).[843]

---

[833]See this chapter, Section IC1.

[834]See this chapter, Sections IB1 and IC1.

[835]See this chapter, Section IC1.

[836]Ibid.

[837]Ibid.

[838]In the same vein, see Levy et al., above n 741, 536.

[839]See this chapter, Section IC1.

[840]See this chapter, Sections IA1(e), IA3, IB1 and IB3. About MLS, see Art. 20, Section 20.2 of the CBA.

[841]In the same vein, see Levy et al., above n 741, 536.

[842]Training techniques could help players head the ball in a less dangerous way, and develop their neck muscles. This issue is currently ignored by the FIFA '11+' warm up program [see this chapter, Section IC1], which is moreover only designed for the grassroots level.

[843]See this chapter, Section IC2(b).

FIFA also introduced improvements in player safety by adopting new rules of the game and contributing financially and scientifically to the development of the CISG's guidelines.[844] Notwithstanding that this contribution is problematic in terms of scientific independence,[845] and does not include the CISG's implementation paper,[846] it helped lay the necessary foundations for a more consistent management of concussion. Similarly, FIFA's new three-minute rule for on-field assessment in case of a suspected concussion (to which supporting analysis by video was added)[847] must be praised. As suggested in the class action complaint,[848] the next step consists of the adoption of concussion protocols by FIFA. These protocols would be an integral part of FIFA regulations and interpret current medical guidelines. They would contribute to the implementation of concussion management best practice during international football competitions, but also, by a trickle down effect,[849] at the domestic level. The introduction of the three-minute rule for on-field assessment has not completely solved the situation. In addition to its limited scope, this new rule mainly relies on referees (not sufficiently trained for this issue) and team doctors (potentially subject to a conflict of interest).[850] Moreover, the time allocated is not sufficient for a complete assessment,[851] and comes into conflict with FIFA strict substitution rules.[852] In order to address these shortcomings, various amendments could be considered, such as the introduction of NFL-like independent doctors and/or neurologists on sidelines, and concussion spotters.[853] An easing of substitution rules could also be introduced (in the form of a fourth substitute, in line with the experiments conducted by FIFA,[854] an additional 'concussion substitute' not counting against the team's total number of allowed substitutions during the game, as practised by US Soccer,[855] or a temporary substitute, as suggested by the International Federation of Professional Footballers (FIFPro)).[856]

---

[844]See this chapter, Section IC1.

[845]See Chapter 2, Section IX and this chapter, Section IX.

[846]See Chapter 2, footnote 164, and this chapter, Section IX.

[847]See this chapter, Section IC1.

[848]Class action complaint, in particular p. 10, paragraph 32, and pp. 78–9, paragraphs 238–9.

[849]See this chapter, Section IC1.

[850]See Chapter 2, Section IV and this chapter, Section IA2(b) and ibid.

[851]See Chapter 2, Section IV.

[852]See this chapter, Section IC.

[853]See this chapter, Section IA1(e).

[854]See this chapter, Section IC1. While allowing more flexibility for coaches, a fourth substitute would not avoid with certainty, in situations where all substitutions have already been made, that a player would not stay on the field after sustaining a concussion.

[855]See this chapter, Section IC1. This would contribute to better player protection. However, it would also leave the door open for possible abuse, as a player could feign an injury to get around the rules and allow a fresh player to take his place. Safeguards could be implemented to reduce this possibility. For instance, the player who is suspected of having a concussion (and is, therefore, substituted) could be forced to sit out the following week.

[856]This would ensure that a team is not prejudiced by having a player assessed (if that player is not concussed). Here, there would also be a risk of abuse. To address this risk, the temporary

In addition to on-field assessment, it will be necessary to ensure that issues such as baseline testing,[857] graduated timeline for return-to-practice[858] and, more generally, medical care (out of competition),[859] are appropriately regulated and interpreted.

Once the content of medical protocols has been set, another stumbling block will be their enforcement. FIFA will have to show the right example during its competitions. As the next step, it will have to make sure that member associations and leagues follow its example, if necessary, through the development of a monitoring system aimed at assuring, controlling and enforcing its procedures. As suggested by FIFPro, this system could be modelled on FIFA Transfer Matching System (TMS),[860] and require each national association/league to submit its protocols and detailed reports on concussed players to FIFA.[861] Sanctions could be imposed on associations and leagues, or even, like for the NFL,[862] on clubs that are not compliant.

FIFA launched several general educational initiatives, and emphasised the importance of training techniques.[863] However, FIFA is still reluctant to admit any link between playing football and cognitive impairment.[864] It has not yet implemented educational programs aimed at better informing its players about the short and long-term medical risks associated with concussion.[865] This gap ought to be filled. Additionally, a NFL-like whistle blower system[866] could be considered. The 'macho culture' that still prevails in football[867] would also need to end.

---

substitution could count towards the allotted three substitutions. In addition, if a coach has already used his three substitutions, the player who is suspected of having a concussion (and is, therefore, substituted) could be forced to sit out the following week [for more details, see Jake Cohen, 'How Effective is FIFA's Concussion Protocol', *Lawinsport*, 8 October 2014, (<http://www.lawinsport.com/sports/football/item/how-effective-is-fifa-s-concussion-protocol>) (paywall), who discusses the CISG's guidelines and FIFPro's recommendations; see also the class action complaint, in particular p. 10, paragraph 30 and p. 119, paragraph 386, which highlight the rigidity of FIFA's substitution rule without taking sides with a specific alternative]. For examples of concussion substitutes in other sports, see this chapter, Sections IIB1(a) and IIB2(a).

[857]See Chapter 2, Sections IV and IX.

[858]See Chapter 2, Section III.

[859]Ibid. The intervention of independent doctors for return-to-practice decisions might notably be useful.

[860]FIFA TMS is an electronic system that has monitored all international transfers of players since 2010 (<https://www.fifatms.com/>).

[861]For more details about FIFPro's proposal, see Cohen, above n 856. Note that this proposal does not presuppose the adoption of concussion protocols by FIFA and/or its continental associations.

[862]See this chapter, Section IA1(e).

[863]See this chapter, Section IC1.

[864]Ibid.

[865]Ibid.

[866]See this chapter, Section IA1(c).

[867]See this chapter, Section IC1, footnote 721.

FIFA has for a long time been prominent in the field of medical research and data collection. Following the creation of F-MARC in 1994, FIFA published numerous studies on the frequency, characteristics and mechanisms of head injury in football.[868] To this add a few articles on concussion and sub-concussion only, as well as various research projects carried out jointly with partner institutions.[869] Since 1998, FIFA has performed injury surveillance (including head injuries) at all its competitions and football competitions of the Olympic Games.[870] In addition, it contributed financially and scientifically to the development of the CISG's guidelines (helping to lay the necessary foundations for a more consistent management of concussion, while highlighting problems in terms of scientific independence), and sent its representatives to international meetings on concussion in the US.[871] FIFA will now have to strengthen its internal research and data collection with a stronger focus on concussion and, possibly, the centralisation and publication of concussion-related statistics not only for all international competitions but also domestic competitions.[872] Retired players' surveys could be implemented in collaboration with continental and national federations. FIFA's internal research could also be better targeted to explore technological solutions,[873] if necessary with the support of specific sub-committees. Moreover, FIFA will have to support financially independent external research, with a particular focus on concussion, sub-concussion and their related long-term risks. Such support would contribute to changing the mentality and practices within FIFA, which is still reluctant to acknowledge a possible link between head trauma and brain impairment.[874]

Lastly, even if FIFA is not bound by any CBA, it could, if needed, facilitate the adoption of a NFL-like '88 Plan'[875] aimed at providing reimbursement for former players' medical and custodial care costs. FIFA could in particular negotiate a deal

---

[868] See this chapter, Section IC1.

[869] Ibid.

[870] Ibid.

[871] Chapter 2, Section IX, ibid, and this chapter, Section IC3.

[872] This centralisation could be achieved through a monitoring system such as that proposed by FIFPro [see this chapter, Section IC3] or, failing that, through the participation of clubs, as it is the case for the NFL and, to a lesser extent, the NHL [see this chapter, Sections IA1(h) and IB1].

[873] FIFA's research in this area, led from 1994 to 2016 by Dr Dvorak, has until now been mainly restricted to very few literature reviews on the efficacy of protective equipment preventing concussion [see Brian Benson et al., 'Is Preventive Equipment Useful in Preventing Concussion? A Systematic Review of the Literature' (2009) 43 (Supplement 1) *British Journal of Sports Medicine*, 56, 56–67 (Benson et al., 'Prevention'); see also Christopher Withnall et al., 'Effectiveness of Headgear in Football' (2005) 39 (Supplement 1) *British Journal of Sports Medicine* 40, 40–8, based on controlled laboratory tests conducted in relation to the effectiveness of headgears in football]. Issues related to football pitches (composition of the surface, structure, etc) would also need further exploring.

[874] See this chapter, Section IC1.

[875] See this chapter, Section IA1(c).

with FIFPro, aimed at encouraging or even requiring national SGBs to set up such a Plan. When necessary, it could also support SGBs financially.

The examination of the lower levels of governance reveals that CONCACAF's intervention is, for the time being, limited to rough outlines of measures, which lie between the rules of the game and medical protocols. These measures consist of the incorporation of FIFA's new three-minute rule for on-field assessment (based on the SCAT) into some of CONCACAF's regulations.[876] They are just waiting to be extended, in partnership with FIFA, with the main aim being the adoption of binding concussion protocols. Other possible areas of cooperation between FIFA and CONCACAF include former players' medical care and data collection. This cooperation would benefit from being supplemented by each of them taking their own individual initiatives in the fields of education and research.

MLS' intervention includes the adoption of measures related to the rules of the game, concussion protocols, financial support for injured athletes, education, research and data collection. Besides the creation of a Concussion Committee in 2010, these measures comprise the adoption, one year later, of concussion protocols (in line with the CISG's guidelines, but characterised by an extreme reliance of team physicians), awareness campaigns and the participation in medical symposia and concussion summits.[877] They are complemented by unpublicised internal medical research and reports on concussion and other types of injuries.[878] In addition to this is the protection granted to injured players through the CBA, which can vary according to whether the player's contract payments are fully guaranteed or semi-guaranteed against injury (the first hypothesis being, by far, the most common).[879]

US Soccer's intervention has taken shape by the adoption of measures related to the rules of play, rules of the game, medical protocols, education and research. These measures, mostly focused on elite and youth levels, first result from the 'Concussion Management Program' and 'Concussion Initiative' recently implemented by US Soccer, as well as from its participation in medical symposia and concussion summits.[880] They are supplemented by other projects, such as 'Head in the Game', as well as unpublicised internal studies and reports on concussion and other types of injuries.[881]

It will now be up to MLS and US Soccer to follow FIFA's regulatory and, where appropriate, data collection instructions, as suggested above,[882] and to intensify and better publicise their efforts in research and education. In addition, MLS should

---

[876]See this chapter, Section IC1.

[877]Ibid.

[878]Ibid.

[879]Ibid.

[880]Ibid.

[881]Ibid.

[882]See this chapter, Section IC3.

allow all injured players, without distinction, to receive their full salary until the expiration of their contract.

The US governments' involvement in the concussion issue is illustrated here by the letter sent by two members of the US Congress to FIFA, in 2014, criticising FIFA's concussion management, and urging the organisation to take adequate action.[883] This letter adds to other state and federal interventions described previously as part of the NFL section.[884] Although a good number of these interventions are, due to their general nature, also relevant for football (and other sports),[885] government efforts could be intensified in a targeted manner. Thus, like for American football,[886] a Congressional hearing on the potential risks and management of head injuries in football could be held. The forensic research undertaken at Boston University, until now mainly focused on American football players,[887] could be expanded in order to give a more accurate picture of the extent of CTE diagnosis in football. CTE diagnoses made outside the US, such as that made at the Glasgow's Southern General Hospital in Scotland in 2014,[888] illustrate the risk of data fragmentation and the need for a better centralisation of data worldwide. More broadly, the discussions related to FIFA's involvement in the CISG and the independence issues that it raises[889] highlight, once again, the importance, in research as in other fields, not to abandon SGBs to their fate, at the expense of player safety.

Similarly, the examination of the US football case study from a public health perspective returns attention to the key relationships (including medical professional and researchers, SGBs and governments) identified as part of the NFL and NHL chapters.[890] These relationships are slightly less reactive, competitive and adversarial than those surrounding the NFL and the NHL,[891] due to, notably, the more proactive role that has long been played by FIFA in the management of concussion.[892] However, they do not allow players to benefit from optimum protection. They legitimise once again the need for a more harmonised, collaborative approach to public health risks as proposed in this thesis.

Although its scope must be taken into account,[893] the recent decision ruled by the US District Court of California in the context of the class action filed against FIFA

[883] See this chapter, Section IC1.

[884] See this chapter, Sections IA1(d), IA1(e), IA1(f), IA1(g), footnote 221 and Section IA3. See also this chapter, Section IC1.

[885] See this chapter, Section IC1, footnote 724.

[886] See this chapter, Section IA1(d).

[887] See this chapter, Sections IA1(b) and IA1(h). About football, see this chapter, Section IC1.

[888] See this chapter, Section IC1.

[889] See this chapter, Section IC3

[890] See this chapter, Sections IA3 and IB3.

[891] Ibid.

[892] See this chapter, Section IC1.

[893] See this chapter, Section IC2(b).

and other entities over the management of concussion is a notable case in this area in the US. The analysis of the FIFA litigation confirms the lessons drawn from the NFL and NHL case studies in terms of legal risks.[894] One thus finds again, the elements discussed previously[895]—legal (financial[896] and reputational) risks, the legal complexity and associated legal uncertainty, the adversarial nature of the relationships involved, the difficulty in translating the doubts of science for legal purposes, and the possible shortcomings in tort law.

Furthermore, the Californian football class action illustrates some particular legal complexities and shortcomings. First, unlike the litigation involving the NFL and NHL,[897] in the football class action the court was dealing with a major international sports federation that, in the case of FIFA, has members from 211 countries.[898] The US District Court, like any court, had to decide the technical question of whether FIFA's connections with the legal jurisdiction were sufficiently strong for the particular court to exercise authority over FIFA. Although the court dismissed the action on this ground,[899] a different result would lead to the larger issue of the appropriateness of a domestic court that has the limited geographical authority of one country deciding points that may have an impact on how a sport is played and managed in those 211 other countries worldwide. The potential for mischief is hinted at by the settlement of the class action against US Soccer whereby the rules of play were changed in the US to prohibit players under 10 years of age from heading the ball.[900] Had the court possessed jurisdiction over FIFA (and IFAB), the outcome might have been a worldwide change of the rules of play so that a child in Egypt, Malaysia, Sweden, etc would not be allowed to head the ball. The desirability of a US court (or any other local court) making a ruling of such international effect is questionable. Also, there is the scope for conflicting court rulings in different countries. Such scenarios place FIFA in an awkward position because maintaining uniform rules of play worldwide is one of its key roles.[901]

Second, the ad hoc nature of tort litigation often results in outcomes that are seemingly difficult to reconcile and thereby contribute to the appearance of inconsistency.[902] On the one hand, the governing body of American football, the NFL, agreed to a USD1 billion court approved settlement for players injured from concussion.[903] On the other hand, the governing body of football, FIFA, avoided

[894]See this chapter, Sections IA3 and IB3.

[895]Ibid.

[896]In this instance, the plaintiffs did not seek monetary damages. However, FIFA would still have to have paid its own legal fees, which were probably substantial.

[897]See this chapter, Sections IA2 et seq and IB2 et seq.

[898]See this chapter, Sections IC and IC2(b).

[899]See this chapter, Section IC2(b).

[900]See this chapter, Sections IC1 and IC2(b).

[901]See this chapter, Sections IC and IC1.

[902]In jurisdictions where there are juries, inconsistent outcomes may be more prevalent.

[903]See this chapter, Section IA2(a)(v).

any responsibility when the class action against it was dismissed.[904] Those respective outcomes can be explained by technical legal reasons and the specific circumstances of each case.[905] However, the perception can arise easily that players suffering concussion-related injuries arising from not dissimilar mechanisms in a general sense have differing legal rights to compensation according to the sport they play or which jurisdiction is deciding the matter.

Third, it could be said that the class action against FIFA and US Soccer reflects the less desirable features of a litigious society in the US. The plaintiffs appear not to have suffered any physical harm[906] but, bearing in mind the developments emerging from the NFL and NHL controversies,[907] and the progress of science regarding concussion in football,[908] took the position that they might be exposed to harm unless the practices in football changed. Such activity has the potential to create unnecessary legal uncertainty, and negatively affects the interests of the stakeholders involved.

D Other Sports: Baseball and Water Polo

Baseball and water polo are the final sports examined as part of the US case studies. Following the same structure as the previous case studies, this section provides an interesting combination: while both sports have both been subject to some level of concussion controversy, they are characterised by very different individual circumstances and responses.

Baseball and water polo are notably distinguished by their different nature of play, popularity, financial resources and organisational structure. Baseball is a bat-and-ball sport with incidental contact, requiring not only batting but also fielding. Embedded in US popular and commercial culture, it is dominated by a professional men's league, Major League Baseball (MLB). Water polo is a sport with a high degree of physicality and aggressive play, which traces its origins to an 'aquatic form of rugby'.[909] It is often seen as being an Olympic/college style participation sport with little fan following and limited financial resources. It still aspires to evolve, as demonstrated by the example of USAWP and its emerging professional men's league. Organised in a pyramid structure, it also includes the International Swimming Federation (FINA) and the Amateur Swimming Union of the Americas (ASUA). Moreover, these sports have experienced

[904]See this chapter, Section IC2(b).

[905]See this chapter, Sections IA1 et seq, IA2(a) et seq, IC1 and IC2(b).

[906]See this chapter, Section IC2(b).

[907]See this chapter, Sections IA1(b), IA1(h) and IB1.

[908]See this chapter, Section IC1.

[909]See Hagens Bermans' website (<https://www.hbsslaw.com/cases/usa-water-polo>).

controversy in different ways. Baseball has one CTE case established by autopsy as well as instances of early retirement, but has, until now, been spared from litigation. Conversely, water polo, although tarnished by various concussion-related incidents, which in at least one case led to early retirement, does not have any confirmed CTE case. However, it is facing legal proceedings that, in 2016, saw the defendant, USAWP, escape liability in first instance on procedural grounds. An appeal is currently pending. The responses provided also differ. MLB has recently put in place substantial measures of concussion management. In contrast, entities governing water polo have taken a course of relative inaction, which may well contribute to the worsening of the polemic in the near future. Governments have not taken any specific measures, with the exception of a failed legislative initiative in the state of Minnesota aimed at forcing the disclosure and re-examination of a former baseball player's medical records.

This section gives a representative and useful insight for sports that, without being on the same scale as 'the Big Three' (American football, ice hockey and football),[910] are nonetheless exposed. It illustrates two different trends that can potentially exist among those sports with, on the one hand, a proactive approach (represented by baseball) and, on the other hand, a 'wait-and-see' approach (represented by water polo). It shows the diversity of sports environments that may be encountered not only at the international level but also within the same country. It underlines, once again, the conflictive nature of the relationships at stake and the need for a proactive and consistent public health and legal risks approach, while auguring the possible hurdles that such an approach may face.

1 Baseball

(a) Chronology

MLB, which consists of franchised professional baseball clubs located in the US and Canada,[911] were exposed to controversy as early as 1920, when player Ray Chapman died after being hit in the head by a pitch.[912] His death quickly triggered the elimination of the spitball[913] and, after decades of discussion, the introduction of

[910]See this chapter, Sections IA1 et seq, IB1 et seq and IC1 et seq.

[911]See MLB's website (<http://mlb.mlb.com/team/>).

[912]Paul Lukas, 'Alex Torres and the History of Headgear in Baseball', *ESPN*, 23 April 2015 (<http://www.espn.com/mlb/story/_/id/12741917/uni-watch-history-headgear-mlb-alex-torres>).

[913]A spitball is an illegal baseball pitch in which the ball has been altered by the application of saliva, petroleum jelly, or some other foreign substance. This technique alters the wind resistance and weight on one side of the ball, causing it to move in an atypical manner, or slip out of the pitcher's fingers.

mandatory protective helmets for batters and catchers.[914] In 1939, legendary baseball star Lou Gehrig, who suffered several well-publicised instances of head trauma,[915] was forced to retire at age 36 and died two years later from a neurodegenerative disease believed to be ALS (since then also commonly referred to as 'Lou Gehrig's disease').[916] Gehrig's case returned to the forefront in 2010, following the publication of a new medical article suggesting, like for CTE, the existence of a causal link between ALS and repetitive head injury.[917] In 2012, Minnesota state legislators vowed to pass new legislation in order to force the disclosure and re-examination of Gehrig's medical records in light of new scientific knowledge.[918] The effort was finally abandoned due to the impossibility of performing an autopsy.[919]

Simultaneously, head injury-related issues in baseball became more and more publicised. Starting in the early 2000s, serious incidents, sometimes going so far as to force players into early retirement, regularly made headlines.[920]

As a result, MLB adopted its first basic concussion protocols in 2007.[921] In 2011, MLB, learning from the experience of the NFL, which was already mired in turmoil,[922] took further measures. These measures were facilitated by the replacement of Dr Elliot Pellman (well known for his controversial role within the NFL)[923] by Dr Gary Green as a Medical Director.[924] The 2007 protocols were replaced by more comprehensive protocols, designed by the newly created 'MLB Mild Trau-

---

[914] Lukas, above n 912. This rule is now set out in Art. 3.08 of the 2018 MLB Official Baseball Rules. The MLB Rules are available on the MLB website (<http://mlb.mlb.com/documents/0/8/0/268272080/2018_Official_Baseball_Rules.pdf>).

[915] Mike Kaszuba, 'What's to Learn from Lou Gehrig's Death?', *Star Tribune*, 9 October 2012 (<http://www.startribune.com/what-s-to-learn-from-lou-gehrig-s-death/172581481/?c=y&page=all&prepage=1#continue>).

[916] See Chapter 2, Section VII.

[917] Ann C McKee et al., 'TDP-43 Proteinopathy and Motor Neuron Disease in Chronic Traumatic Encephalopathy' (2010) 69 *Journal of Neuropathology and Experimental Neurology* 918, 918–29 (McKee et al., 'Motor Neurone Disease').

[918] Kaszuba, above n 915.

[919] Ibid. Gehrig's remains were cremated.

[920] The most prominent examples of early retirements include those of players Mike Mattheny, in 2007, and Ryan Freel, in 2010, which will be discussed later in this section.

[921] Nathaniel Grow, 'Imagining a MLB Concussion Lawsuit', *Fangraphs*, 18 February 2015 (<http://www.fangraphs.com/blogs/imagining-an-mlb-concussion-lawsuit/>).

[922] See this chapter, Sections IA1(g) and IA2 et seq.

[923] See this chapter, Section IA1(a).

[924] Michael S Schmidt, 'BATS; M.L.B. Names New Medical Director', *The New York Times*, 15 April 2010 (<https://archive.nytimes.com/query.nytimes.com/gst/fullpage-9404E6DE1438F936A25757C0A9669D8B63.html>).

matic Brain Injury Committee' and other experts (including neurologists).[925] The 2011 protocols introduced baseline testing for all players.[926] They also set standardised procedures for on-field assessment by athletic trainers and, if necessary, by club doctors.[927] They mandated clearance for return-to-activity from both the MLB's Medical Director and the players' association (MLBPA)'s concussion expert and, in case of a disagreement, from an independent expert.[928] Finally they established a seven-day disabled list for concussion, which was added to the customary 15-day and 60-day disabled lists.[929] The revised version of the 2011 protocols is available as an annex to the new 2017–21 MLB CBA.[930] These protocols recommend the use of the SCAT 3 and of the baseline (ImPACT) test.[931] They refer to the NATA guidelines,[932] but are also globally in line with the 2012 CISG's guidelines.[933] In case of injury, the CBA states that players are entitled to receive the 'unpaid balance of their full salary for the year in which the injury was sustained'.[934] However, this clause is often nullified in practice and, as a result, most contracts are fully guaranteed against injuries.[935]

The MLB's efforts were complemented by the launch of educational initiatives (distribution of concussion information sheets to professional players, information sessions for team staff, and use of major events as a platform to educate youth players).[936] Simultaneously, MLB representatives attended various international

[925]MLB, press release, 29 March 2011 (<http://mlb.mlb.com/content/printer_friendly/mlb/y2011/m03/d29/c17181944.jsp>); and Attachment 36 of the 2012-16 MLB CBA (on file with author).

[926]Ibid.

[927]Ibid.

[928]Ibid.

[929]Ibid. This measure aims to allow concussion to clear, to prevent players from returning prematurely and to give clubs a full complement of players in one's absence. Any player on the seven-day disabled list for more than 14 days will automatically and retroactively be transferred to the 15-day disabled-list, effective with the first day of the initial placement, and with the prior 14 days applying to the initial 15-day maximum term.

[930]See 2017-21 MLB CBA, Attachment 36, p. 258. The 2017-21 MLB CBA is available on the MLB players' association (MLBPA)'s website (<http://www.mlbplayers.com/pdf9/5450407.pdf>).

[931]2017-21 MLB CBA, Introduction, pp. 258–62; see also pp. 263–5 (more specifically about the SCAT 3).

[932]2017-21 MLB CBA, Art. VIII, p. 58; Introduction, pp. 258 and 262.

[933]Deubert, Cohen and Fernandez Lynch, above n 432, 75 (about the previous version of the CBA). Note that in baseball, not only players, but also umpires are exposed to the risk of concussion. Umpires are, therefore, part of the MLB's concussion strategy (baseline testing, protocols for on-field assessment and return-to-activity).

[934]Once workers' compensation payments have been deducted [2017-21 MLB CBA, Art. IX, p. 38].

[935]Deubert, Cohen and Fernandez Lynch, above n 432, 182 (about the previous version of the CBA).

[936]Jake Cohen and Sean Cottrell, 'An Overview of Concussion Protocols Across Professional Sports Leagues', *Lawinsport*, 5 November 2014 (<http://www.lawinsport.com/features/item/an-

symposia on concussion.[937] A web-based medical record system, aimed at complementing the long-standing MLB disabled list data, was also set up.[938] It formed the basis for a study conducted by MLB's Medical Director, Dr Green, which listed a total of 41 instances of concussion in MLB during the 2011 and 2012 seasons, among which 36 during games, mainly affecting catchers.[939] These figures can be put into perspective with those provided by the disabled list, which excludes, however, off-season, spring season and post-season.[940] The disabled list highlighted 11 instances of concussion for both 2011 and 2015.[941] The 2016 statistics were not released, but were 'approximately consistent with 2015'.[942] A rise was observed for 2017, 'mainly ascribed to an increased recognition and utilisation of the disabled list'.[943]

In 2013, former MLB player Ryan Freel, who had retired three years earlier following numerous instances of concussion, became the first baseball player diagnosed with CTE.[944] Freel's case, examined by Boston researchers after his suicide in 2012 at the age of 36,[945] provided again the basis for discussion within the scientific community.[946] It also led MLB to release a statement, indicating that they are working with experts 'to remain proactive on concussions and head injuries.'[947]

---

overview-of-concussion-protocols-across-professional-sports-leagues#major-league-baseball-mlb-click-here-for-mlb-protocols>) (paywall).

937 References to the participation of MLB representatives in these symposia can be found in relevant press releases and newspaper articles.

938 Stan Conte, Christopher L Camp and Joshua S Dines, 'Injury Trends in Major League Baseball over 18 Seasons: 1998-2015' (2016) 45 *American Journal of Orthopedics* 116, 117.

939 Gary A Green, et al., 'Mild Traumatic Brain Injury in Major and Minor League Baseball Players' (2015) 43 *American Journal of Sports Medicine* 1118, 1118–21.

940 Email from Michael Teevan (Vice-President, MLB Communications) to author, 11 October 2018.

941 Joe Schwarz, 'Major League Baseball and the Concussion Problem', *Viva El Birdos*, 2 February 2016 (<http://www.vivaelbirdos.com/2016/2/2/10892078/major-league-baseball-and-the-concussion-problem>) (Joe Schwarz, 'MLB').

942 Email from Michael Teevan (Vice-President, MLB Communications) to author, 28 February 2017.

943 Email from Michael Teevan (Vice-President, MLB Communications) to author, 11 October 2018.

944 'Ryan Freel Had CTE, Parents Say', *ESPN*, 16 December 2013 (<http://www.espn.com/mlb/story/_/id/10142581/cte-present-ryan-freel-killed-self-report-says>).

945 McKee et al., 'Neuropathology', above n 718, 40.

946 During his lifetime, Freel suffered from various illnesses such as bipolar, hyperactivity and impulse-control disorders, depression and anxiety. He is also believed to have used steroids, which brings us back to the current medical controversy related to a possible association between CTE and drug abuse [see Chapter 2, Sections VII and this chapter, Section IA1(h), footnote 228].

947 Stephanie Smith and Dan Moriarty, 'First Major League baseball Player Diagnosed with CTE', *CNN*, 16 December 2013 (<https://edition.cnn.com/2013/12/15/health/baseball-ryan-freel-cte-suicide/index.html>).

Prior to the 2014 season, MLB banned home plate collisions in order to better protect catchers (vulnerable due to their position) from concussion.[948] No measures were taken regarding other players, who are also exposed to concussion caused by contact with batted balls, pitches and collisions.[949]

At the same time, MLB and the MLBPA funded helmet manufacturers to develop safer standards of helmets, for an undisclosed but 'substantial' amount.[950]

(b) Legal Activities and Implications

MLB has, to date, not been a defendant in any concussion litigation. The outcome of such litigation would be difficult to predict. It would likely proceed along the same lines as the litigation involving other US leagues, namely the NFL and the NHL.[951] However, the probable absence of a culture of concealment, the proactive approach adopted, and the smaller possibility of actual damage due to the fact that baseball is not a very violent sport have more in common with other litigation, in particular that of FIFA.[952]

(c) Lessons and Significance

Short and long-term medical complications associated with concussion in baseball manifest by early retirements, as well as by one CTE case diagnosed in a MLB player in 2013.[953]

While MLB's active involvement in concussion management only started in 2011, MLB, with the benefit of the insight of the NFL's concussion controversy, reacted—to its credit—before being directly affected by a CTE case or a concussion lawsuit. Although there is still room for improvement, the recent efforts by MLB

---

[948]In baseball, blocking the plate is a technique performed by a catcher to prevent a runner from scoring, leading to rough physical contact. It is now banned by MLB, except when the catcher already has possession of the ball. For more details, see Ed Molina, 'After Ryan Freel's CTE PostMortem Diagnosis, MLB's Ban on Home Plate Collision is the Right Move for Player Safety' Latinone, 16 December 2013 (<http://www.latinone.com/articles/2114/20131216/ryan-freel-cte-postmortem-diagnosis-mlb-ban-home-plate-collisions.htm>). See also 2018 MLB Official Baseball Rules, Art. 6.01(i).

[949]Leslie E Schwindel et al., 'Epidemiology and Outcomes of Concussions in Major League Baseball' (2014) 2 *Annals of Orthopedics and Rheumatology* 1022, 1022–4.

[950]William Weinbaum, 'Pitchers to Debut New Protective Headwear in Spring Training', *ESPN*, 12 February 2016 (<http://www.espn.com/mlb/story/_/id/14765775/mlb-players-association-work-together-develop-more-protective-pitching-hat>).

[951]See this chapter, Sections IA2(a) et seq and IB2(a) et seq. See also Grow, above n 921.

[952]See this chapter, Section IC2(b).

[953]See this chapter, Section ID1(a).

concerning the management of concussion are undeniably headed in the right direction.

MLB's intervention includes measures related to the rules of play, rules of the game, medical protocols, financial support for injured athletes, education, research and data collection.

MLB gradually amended its rules of play in order to improve player safety. Further amendments could be considered, in order to better protect catchers (vulnerable due to their position) or even other players, who too often sustain concussion due to contact with batted balls, pitches and collisions.[954] Possible options available to MLB include the introduction of longer suspensions for pitchers who throw intentionally at a batter's head,[955] alongside heavier fines, which could then be reinvested in player safety.[956]

MLB introduced new rules of the game and medical protocols. These improvements include the implementation of baseline testing for all players, standardised procedures for on-field assessment (based on the SCAT 3) and clearance for return-to-activity (based on forms, with the possible intervention of an independent expert in case of disagreement) as well as the creation of a seven-day disabled list.[957] MLB's policy for return-to-activity is of particular interest when it comes to improving day-to-day management of players' health, and dealing with the potential conflict of interest of team physicians[958] off-field. Possible areas of consideration relate to the predominant role of athletic trainers in players' assessment, who often substitute themselves for team doctors, and the use of SCAT 5.[959] The CISG's guidelines could also expressly be referred to, instead of the NATA guidelines.[960] Modelled on the NFL,[961] MLB could also mandate the presence of concussion spotters, neurologists and/or independent doctors during games. Here, again, these measures will need to be strictly enforced. Like for the NFL,[962] clubs whose employees are not compliant could be penalised.

---

954 Ibid.

955 The typical punishment for a pitcher found to have intentionally thrown at a batter's head is a suspension for fewer than 10 games. Yet starting pitchers only throw once every five days, so with clever scheduling of an appeal, a pitcher can serve his suspension while effectively missing no games [for more details, see Adam Felder, 'Battering the Batter', *The Atlantic*, 5 May 2015 (<https://www.theatlantic.com/entertainment/archive/2015/05/no-more-battering-the-batter/391991/>); see also 2018 MLB Official Baseball Rules, Art. 6.02(c)(9)].

956 In the MLB, the money from fines goes to the Baseball Assistance Team, which helps former players in financial need, or other philanthropic groups [2017-21 MLB CBA, Attachment 54, p. 331].

957 See this chapter, Section ID1(a).

958 Ibid.

959 Ibid.

960 Ibid.

961 See this chapter, Section IA1(e).

962 Ibid.

MLB granted protection to injured players through its CBAs, which state that players are entitled to receive the unpaid balance of their full salary for the year in which the injury was sustained.[963] Even if most contracts are now fully guaranteed in practice,[964] this protection could be expressly upgraded in order to provide full salary to all injured players until the expiration of their contract. Other measures, such as the establishment of a NFL-like '88 Plan'[965] aimed at providing reimbursement for former players' medical and custodial care costs, may subsequently be considered, depending on the evolution of forensic medicine related to concussion in baseball and based on need.

MLB also launched educational initiatives on concussion at the professional and youth levels.[966] These measures need only to be developed, with the aim of informing players better about the risks encountered, and ending the macho culture that generally prevails in sport. Like in the NFL,[967] a whistle-blower system for concussion-related incidents could be put in place.

Finally, MLB took measures related to research and data collection, including the creation of a 'Mild Traumatic Brain Injury Committee', formed by neurologists and other experts who regularly take part in international symposia, a grant aimed at improving helmet safety and the maintenance of internal concussion statistics.[968] MLB may now contemplate further developing its medical and technological research activities, both internally and externally, and publishing annual injury reports, possibly inspired by the format of those released by the NFL.[969]

The only government intervention related to baseball was the 2012 failed initiative of Minnesota state legislators aimed at unsealing Gehrig's medical records.[970] Like for American football,[971] the US Congress could step in through a Congressional hearing. The forensic research undertaken at Boston University[972] could also further focus on baseball players, in order to study the real extent of CTE in baseball.

The legal risks surrounding MLB have for the time being not materialised in concussion litigation.[973] The outcome of such litigation would be difficult to predict.[974]

---

[963]See this chapter, Section ID1(a).

[964]Ibid.

[965]See this chapter, Section IA1(c).

[966]See this chapter, Section ID1(a)

[967]See this chapter, Section IA1(c).

[968]See this chapter, Section ID1(a).

[969]See this chapter, Section IA1(h).

[970]See this chapter, Section ID1(a).

[971]See this chapter, Section IA1(d).

[972]See in particular this chapter, Sections IA1(b) and IA1(h).

[973]See this chapter, Section ID1(b).

[974]Ibid.

More broadly, the baseball case study confirms the multiplicity of the various relations at stake.[975] These relations, here also, regrettably manifest by a relatively reactive and conflictive nature. Nonetheless, MLB seems to have acted more in the wake of the NFL concussion controversy rather than following a tumult directly affecting baseball.

2 Water Polo

(a) Chronology

The analysis of the concussion issue in US professional water polo requires the examination of the regulatory activity of three major entities: FINA, ASUA and USAWP. FINA oversees competitions in various aquatic sports worldwide, including water polo.[976] ASUA is the Continental Association for the Americas.[977] USAWP serves as the water polo governing body for all levels in the US. It oversees national team competitions, various championships and a recent semi-professional men's national league, expected to further develop into a professional league.[978] USAWP is subject to the authority of FINA and ASUA,[979] and must respect their regulations. Variations, at least minor, seem, however, to be tolerated in practice.[980]

Concussion in water polo had not attracted international news media attention until the months leading up to the 2012 Olympic Games in London when the Canadian women's water polo team suffered a 'concussion epidemic'.[981] Eight of the 20 players suffered concussion or concussion-related symptoms, including backup goalie Marissa Jansens, who was finally forced into retirement.[982] US water polo was not spared either. Collegiate player Karoline Krumpholz suffered

---

[975]See this chapter, Sections IA3, IB3 and IC3.

[976]2017 FINA Constitution, Art. C5/E (available on FINA website, < https://www.fina.org/sites/default/files/1._fina_constitution_approved_by_the_fina_congress_on_22.07.2017_final.pdf>).

[977]2015 ASUA Constitution, Chapter I, Art. 1 (available on ASUA website, <https://www.teamunify.com/uana/UserFiles/File/Bylaws/UANA-CONSTITUCION2011(EngSept).pdf>).

[978]2015 USAWP Zone Policies and Procedures, Art. 1 Section 1 and Art. 2 Section 3 (available on USAWP's website, <http://grfx.cstv.com/photos/schools/uswp/genrel/auto_pdf/2015-16/misc_non_event/USAWPZonePolicies_Procedures.pdf>). About the men's national league and its development prospects, see Vikram Muller, 'Cal Men's Water Polo Athletes Participate in USA Water Polo National League Championship' *The Daily Californian*, 3 May 2016 (<http://www.dailycal.org/2016/05/03/cal-mens-water-polo-athletes-participate-in-usa-water-polo-national-league-championship/>).

[979]2017 FINA Constitution, Art. C7.3; 2015 ASUA Constitution, Chapter III, Art. 8.

[980]For concrete examples, see the Southern Pacific Zone of USA Water Polo (SOPAC)'s website (<http://www.sopacwp.com/Resources/Documents/2013NewRulesPOE.pdf>).

[981]See eg, Randy Starkman, 'Concussion Epidemic Hits Women's Water Polo Team before Olympic Qualifier' *The Star*, 1 April 2012 (<https://www.thestar.com/sports/olympics/2012/04/01/concussion_epidemic_hits_womens_water_polo_team_before_olympic_qualifier.html>).

[982]Ibid.

from persistent concussion-related symptoms after a concussion sustained in 2011.[983] Four years later, a class action lawsuit was filed against USAWP by a mother on behalf of the class and her 16-year-old daughter, who had experienced similar symptoms.[984]

FINA has not taken any substantial measures in response to these events. However, FINA has, through the years, monitored players' injuries during the Olympic Games and World Championships. Although the results are not published, FINA admitted in 2017 having recently noticed a 'remarkable increase' of concussion in water polo.[985] Furthermore, it posted a video on concussion on its website, which reflects some of the main principles established by the CISG[986] regarding diagnosis (including the SCAT), treatment and return-to-play.[987] It also discussed the issue during its 2016 World Aquatic Convention in Windsor, Canada.[988] ASUA has so far not adopted any specific measure of concussion management.[989]

USAWP adopted a 'Concussion Policy' in 2011.[990] Provided that the referee decides to stop the game,[991] this policy prescribes an initial medical evaluation on the sideline by an individual trained in concussion management in accordance with the SCAT 2.[992] If the player fails the test, the policy prohibits return-to-play on the same day and requires a follow up with the team physician as well as the notification

---

[983]Steve Jansen and Gus Garcia-Roberts, 'Concussion Take a Terrible Toll on America's Young Athletes', *LaWeekly*, 18 August 2011 (<http://www.laweekly.com/content/printView/2171689>).

[984]See this chapter, Section ID2(b).

[985]Email from Johan Lefebvre (FINA Anti-Doping Department) to author, citing FINA Sports Medicine Committee, 15 February 2017. Multiple attempts to obtain an indication for the increase and precise time covered have not been successful. For a preliminary answer, see Annika Prien et al., 'Injury and Illness in Aquatic Sport: How High is the Risk? A Comparison of Results from three FINA World Championships' (2017) 51 *British Journal of Sports Medicine* 278, 278–83 (Prien et al., 'Aquatic Sport'). This article, however, only outlines certain trends, without providing accurate features about concussion in water polo.

[986]See Chapter 2, Sections III and IV.

[987]Email from Johan Lefebvre (FINA Anti-Doping Department) to author, citing FINA Sports Medicine Committee, 15 February 2017. This video has since then been removed from FINA website, possibly in view of its updating.

[988]Ibid.

[989]Email from Gregory Eggert (Media Officer, ASUA) to author, 9 February 2017.

[990]The Policy has not been published. For more details, see this chapter, Section ID2(b), footnote 1013, which refers to the second amended class action complaint [in particular pp. 26–7, paragraph 92].

[991]According to Art. 25/1 of the 2017-21 FINA and 2015-18 USAWP Water Polo Rules, the referee is competent to stop the game (for a maximum of three minutes) in case of a suspected concussion (or any other injury). These rules are available on FINA and USAWP websites (<https://www.fina.org/sites/default/files/2017_2021_wp_rules_07022018_colour.pdf>; <http://grfx.cstv.com/photos/schools/uswp/genrel/auto_pdf/2015-16/misc_non_event/2015_2017Rules.pdf>).

[992]See this chapter, Section ID2(b), footnote 1013, which refers to the second amended class action complaint [in particular p. 27, paragraph 93]. The individual trained in concussion management can be either an athletic trainer, osteopathic physician, emergency medical technician, doctor of chiropractic or doctor of medicine.

of the coach.[993] Intended to apply to the US national teams, the policy does not appear to have been properly notified to those people who were meant to implement it or widely used in practice.[994]

In 2013, USAWP introduced a provision in its Code of Conduct prohibiting athletes, coaches and referees from ‘encouraging an athlete to return to play prematurely following a serious injury (eg, a concussion) and without the clearance of a medical professional.’[995]

In 2014, USAWP partnered with the University of California/Irvine to conduct a joint study on the incidence of concussion in water polo.[996] This study, the first of its kind in water polo, took the form of a survey sent to USAWP members.[997] It showed that an alarming rate of respondents (36%) reported sustaining at least one concussion while playing water polo.[998] It highlighted the vulnerability of goalies, which are at high-risk of being hit by a ball.[999] It also noted that field players were subject to frequent contacts with other players, particularly elbows to the head.[1000] Players wear lightwear caps, but these are mainly aimed at facilitating their identification and protecting ears from impacts.[1001]

Simultaneously, USAWP made information on concussion (definition, link to CDC’s Facts Sheets) available on its website,[1002] and discussed the issue of concussion internally during its ‘Leadership Summit.’[1003]

---

[993]Ibid. This notification is subject to the athlete’s consent to share medical information.

[994]See this chapter, Section ID2(b), footnote 1013, which refers to the second amended class action complaint [in particular pp. 26–7, paragraphs 92–4 and pp. 36–7, paragraphs 116–18].

[995]For more details, see USAWP’s Athletes’ and Coaches’ Codes of Conduct ad ‘Sportsmanship’, Section 2/b. See also Referees’ Code of Conduct, Rules 7 and 12 (no date mentioned). These Codes are available on USAWP website (<https://usawaterpolo.org/sports/2018/11/28/resources-codes-conduct-html.aspx>).

[996]Robert S Blumenfeld, ‘The Epidemiology of Sports-Related Head Injury and Concussion in Water Polo’ (June 2016) 7(98) *Frontiers in Neurology* 1, 11.

[997]Ibid, 1-2.

[998]Ibid, 1 and 4. This percentage, which is based on the answers of 1500 water polo players from all levels (out of a total of 44 000 members), is beyond the concussion prevalence observed in self-reported studies in other contact sports (see eg, NCAA, *Self-Reported Concussion among NCAA Student Athletes, Executive Summary*, February 2014 (<https://www.ncaa.org/sites/default/files/Concussion%20%20GOALS%20Exec%20Summary_Feb_12_2014_FINALpost_0.pdf>).

[999]Ibid, 1 and 4–5.

[1000]Ibid, 1–2 and 4–5.

[1001]2017-21 FINA and 2015-18 USAWP Water Polo Rules, Arts. 4/1-4/4.

[1002]See USAWP’s website (<https://usawaterpolo.org/sports/2018/12/19/safety-policies.aspx#head-section>).

[1003]See this chapter, Section ID2(b), footnote 1013, which refers to the second amended class action complaint [in particular p. 35, paragraphs 110–12].

(b) Legal Activities and Implications

FINA and ASUA have, to date, never been sued as part of a concussion lawsuit. This is not the case with USAWP, which is currently facing legal proceedings.

In February 2015, plaintiff Mayall, on behalf of a proposed class of current and former water polo players, including her injured 16-year-old daughter H.C., brought a class action lawsuit against USAWP before the US District Court for the Central District of California.[1004] Similar to the FIFA litigation,[1005] also filed in California, the plaintiff invoked negligence and breach of voluntary undertaking, with the exception of fraud.[1006] She sought monetary damages for her daughter and, more generally, called for a more cautious management and monitoring of concussion by USAWP.[1007]

Procedural issues related to the legal capacity of the plaintiff to represent her daughter[1008] prompted the filing of an amended class action complaint.[1009] In March 2016, this amended complaint was dismissed for failure to state a recognised basis of claim.[1010] Reflecting the order made in the FIFA case,[1011] the court relied on the absence of a general duty of care of sports federations to prevent injury to players and the voluntary assumption of risk while engaging in sports activities.[1012] The plaintiff responded with a second amended class action complaint aimed at overcoming dismissal by shifting the focus of the negligence claim from the sports federation's duty of care to prevent injury to its players, to its duty of care to prohibit a concussed player's same-day return-to-play. However, that was no more successful and the action was dismissed in August 2016.[1013]

[1004]*Alice Mayall v. USA Water Polo*, U.S. District Court, Central District of California, No. 8:15-cv-00171. Plaintiffs filed a class action complaint on 3 February 2015. This document is available on the Hagens Berman's law firm website (<https://www.hbsslaw.com/cases/usa-water-polo>).

[1005]See this chapter, Section IC2(b).

[1006]Class action complaint, pp. 69–77, paragraphs 199–231.

[1007]Ibid.

[1008]See USAWP's motion to dismiss of 1 April 2015 (together with subsequent submissions); and *Alice Mayall v USA Water Polo* (CD Cal, No 8:15-cv-00171, 4 May 2015), Order granting motion to dismiss (Order I). These documents are available via the Bloomberg database (access on subscription).

[1009]See amended class action complaint of 8 July 2015. This document is available on the Hagens Berman's law firm website (<https://www.hbsslaw.com/cases/usa-water-polo>).

[1010]For more details, see USAWP's motion to dismiss of 7 August 2015; and *Alice Mayall v USA Water Polo* (CD Cal, No 8:15-cv-00171, 8 June 2015), Order granting motion to dismiss (Order II). These documents are available via the Bloomberg database (access on subscription).

[1011]See this chapter, Section IC2(b).

[1012]Order (II), pp. 7–8.

[1013]For more details, see second amended class action complaint of 12 May 2016; USAWP's motion to dismiss of 26 May 2016; and *Alice Mayall v USA Water Polo,* (CD Cal, No 8:15-cv-00171, 30 March 2016), Order granting motion to dismiss (Order III). These documents are available via the Bloomberg database (access on subscription).

In September 2016, the plaintiff initiated an appeal procedure before the US Court of Appeals for the Ninth Circuit.[1014] In March 2018, the plaintiff urged the US Court of Appeals to revive the lawsuit, arguing the US District Court wrongfully tossed out the class action without appropriately examining the duty of care.[1015] As at 31 October 2018, a decision is pending.

(c) Lessons and Significance

No CTE cases have to date been diagnosed in water polo. Short and long-term medical complications associated with concussion in this sport are, however, illustrated by several recent incidents reported by the media in the US and elsewhere, one of which at least led to early retirement.[1016]

FINA and ASUA do not so far seem to have been able to get a grip on the issue of concussion.[1017] Unsurprisingly, this lack of leadership is reflected at lower levels of water polo governance,[1018] making the need for coordinated and swift action even more apparent.

FINA has confined its efforts, so far, to limited measures regarding rules of the game, medical guidelines, education and data collection.

These efforts, which have been mentioned above as consisting of unpublished monitoring of concussion incidents at international competitions, an informational video (based on the CISG's guidelines) and internal discussions with some stakeholders,[1019] appear insubstantial compared with the responses of other SGBs, especially in the US.[1020] Similar to other SGBs, FINA should consider amending its rules of play to better protect its players: if not goalies (regularly hit by balls), at least field players, which too often sustain concussion from elbows to the head.[1021] A wider prohibition of elbowing could, for instance, be instituted and more strictly enforced.[1022] Similar to the NFL and NHL, heavy fines could be imposed,[1023] and then possibly contribute to the improvement of concussion management. FINA, or at the very least, its continental associations, will also have to adopt and ensure the

[1014] *Alice Mayall v. USA Water Polo*, 9th Cir., No. 16-56389. All the relevant documents are available via the Bloomberg database (access on subscription).

[1015] The audio recording of oral argument is available on the Court of Appeals' website (<https://www.ca9.uscourts.gov/media/view_video.php?pk_vid=0000013285>).

[1016] See this chapter, Section ID2(a).

[1017] Ibid.

[1018] Ibid.

[1019] Ibid.

[1020] See this chapter, Sections IA1(c) et seq (including subsequent case studies).

[1021] See this chapter, Section ID2(a).

[1022] According to Arts. 21/12 and 21/14 of the 2017-21 FINA and 2015-18 USAWP Water Polo Rules, only elbowing backwards may currently be considered as an 'act of brutality' leading to the exclusion from the remainder of the game, without any possibility of substitution for four minutes.

[1023] See this chapter, Sections IA1(e), IA3, IB1 and IB3.

enforcement of binding concussion protocols, based on current international best practice.[1024] The first step will be to prevent potentially concussed players from remaining or returning to the field during a game, and that the main responsibility of game stoppage does not continue to be at the sole discretion of the referee.[1025] NFL-like independent doctors and/or neurologists and concussion spotters could be introduced[1026] (knowing that their function should be adapted to the playing area). In addition to on-field assessment, it will be necessary to ensure that issues such as baseline testing,[1027] graduated timeline for return-to-practice[1028] and, more generally, medical care (out of competition),[1029] are appropriately regulated. Furthermore, FINA should implement educational programs aimed at better informing its players about the short and long-term medical risks associated with concussion and contribute thereby to end the macho culture that generally prevails in sport. FINA could also set up a NFL-like whistle-blower system[1030] allowing anyone to anonymously report any concussion-related incident. Finally, FINA should get involved in the field of medical and technological research, both internally and externally, and ensure a systematic and publicised concussion reporting for international and national competitions.

Further measures, such as a NFL-like Plan aimed at covering former players' medical and custodial care costs, may subsequently be required, in the event that CTE cases were to be discovered in water polo.

ASUA has so far not adopted any specific measure of concussion management.[1031] When necessary, it should support FINA. Possible areas of cooperation between FINA and ASUA include the implementation of binding concussion protocols and data collection. This cooperation would benefit from being supplemented by each of them taking their own individual initiatives in the fields of education and research.

At the domestic level, USAWP has struggled to fill the void left by FINA and ASUA by taking measures related to the rules of the game, concussion protocols, education, research and data collection. In 2011, USAWP adopted concussion protocols (supplemented in 2013 by specific rules governing athletes, coaches and referees' conduct).[1032] As alleged in the class action filed in 2015 against

[1024] See Chapter 2, Sections II et seq.

[1025] See this chapter, Section ID2(a).

[1026] See this chapter, Section IA1(e).

[1027] See Chapter 2, Sections IV and IX.

[1028] See Chapter 2, Section III.

[1029] Ibid. The intervention of independent doctors for return-to-practice decisions might notably be useful.

[1030] See this chapter, Section IA1(c).

[1031] See this chapter, Section ID2(a).

[1032] Ibid.

USAWP,[1033] these protocols are open to criticism (no baseline testing nor stepwise return-to-practice protocol, interruption of the game left to the referee's discretion, no specific medical background required for those who assess players). They have a limited scope and do not seem to be strictly applied in practice. Similarly, USAWP's emerging efforts in education, research and data collection (information on website, internal discussions and joint study of the incidence of concussion in water polo)[1034] do not compensate for the absence of educational campaigns, coherent research policies and systematic concussion reporting. Once FINA and ASUA have acted upstream, USAWP will then be able to follow their regulatory and data collection instructions, and intensify its efforts in research and education. Particular attention will also need to be paid on monetary compensation for injured players (eg, loss of income), whether by contract or, in the medium-term, by the conclusion of a CBA.

US Governments have not yet taken any measures targeting specifically water polo. Similar to American football,[1035] the US Congress could step in through a Congressional hearing. The forensic research undertaken at Boston University[1036] could also be expanded to water polo players, in search of the first proven CTE case in water polo.

The class action filed in 2015 against USAWP has (so far) been similar in essence to the previous litigation examined (in particular the litigation involving FIFA and US Soccer).[1037] It corroborates the lessons learned from them in terms of legal risks, as well as the conflictive nature of the relationships at stake.[1038] Interestingly, and in contrast to other sports previously examined,[1039] this class action has not triggered any substantial measures of concussion management.[1040]

3 Final Remarks

Water polo and baseball are two sports that seem to be completely opposed at first glance, due to their different nature of play, popularity, financial resources and organisational structure.[1041] Their only commonality may lie in the limited level of concussion controversy that they have experienced so far, which, however,

[1033]See in particular class action complaint, p. 5, paragraphs 12–15, pp. 13–14, paragraphs 46–7, pp. 54–5, paragraphs 145–9, p. 57, paragraph 156, pp. 66–7, paragraphs 185–90, pp. 70–3, paragraphs 204–13; amended class action complaint, pp. 6–7, paragraphs 14–19, p. 38, paragraphs 117–20, pp. 42–8, paragraphs 137–59; second amended class action complaint, pp. 26–7, paragraphs 92–4, pp. 36–7, paragraphs 116–18 and pp. 42–3, paragraphs 134–9.

[1034]See this chapter, Section ID2(a).

[1035]Ibid.

[1036]See in particular this chapter, Sections IA1(b) and IA1(h).

[1037]See this chapter, Sections IA2(a) et seq, IB2(a) et seq and IC2(b).

[1038]See in particular this chapter, Sections IA3, IB3 and IC3.

[1039]See this chapter, Sections IA1(e), IB1 and IC1.

[1040]See this chapter, Section ID2(a).

[1041]See this chapter, Section ID.

manifests in different ways. Water polo does not count any official CTE case for the time being, but is facing legal proceedings.[1042] Conversely, baseball has one official CTE case, but has until now been spared from litigation.[1043] The responses provided also differ. MLB has recently put in place substantial measures of concussion management.[1044] In contrast, entities governing water polo have taken the course of relative inaction.[1045] This is all the more regrettable since concussion in water polo might soon emerge as a more significant issue, as the first statistics recently published[1046] suggest. Similarly, governments have not taken any specific measures, with the exception of a failed legislative initiative in the state of Minnesota.[1047]

The parallel review of water polo and baseball is representative and insightful for other US sports that, without being on the same scale as the three other sports previously discussed,[1048] are nonetheless exposed. It illustrates the diversity of sports environments and responses that can exist not only at the international level but also within the same country. It underlines once again the conflictive nature of the relationships involved and the need for a proactive and consistent public health and legal risks approach, while auguring the possible impediments that such an approach may face.

II The Rest of the World

A Canada: Canadian Football

Canada is linked to the US concussion controversy through its franchised clubs in the NHL, MLS and MLB.[1049] Added to that is the case of Canadian football, chosen here to illustrate the issue of concussion in Canada. Canadian football is a modified form of American football.[1050] It is governed by a professional men's league, the CFL, sometimes considered as the anteroom of the NFL, or even a second-class

---

[1042] See this chapter, Sections ID2(a) and ID2(b).

[1043] See this chapter, Sections ID1(a) and ID1(b).

[1044] See this chapter, Section ID1(a).

[1045] See this chapter, Section ID2(a).

[1046] Ibid, and footnote 998, which refer to the joint study of USAWP and the University of California/Irvine. See also the reference, in the same sub-section, to FINA's unpublished statistics which, by the association's own admission, have recently highlighted a 'remarkable increase' of concussion in water polo.

[1047] See this chapter, Section ID1(a).

[1048] See this chapter, Sections IA1 et seq, IB1 et seq and IC1 et seq.

[1049] See this chapter, Sections IB1, IC1 and ID1(a).

[1050] Differences between American and Canadian football include field size and game rules. For more details, see Marika Washchyshyn, 'Is the Canadian Football League Safer than the NFL?' *Complex Sports*, 25 November 2015 (<http://au.complex.com/sports/2015/11/cfl-concussions>).

league offering an alternative to players who have failed to achieve the highest levels.[1051]

The CFL, due to its limited size,[1052] is not subject to the same level of concussion controversy as the NFL. The CFL, however, has been sued by former professional players in two separate legal proceedings, and has several recognised CTE and early retirement cases. Similarly, while the CFL has recently taken valuable measures of concussion management, they are not on the same scale as those of the NFL. Although this is due, in part, to more limited financial means,[1053] it also indicates an insufficient awareness of the problem and its possible long-term repercussions, which the CFL still strives to deny. The action of the Canadian governments is along the same lines, with interesting initiatives taken mainly at the grassroots levels that are still waiting to be developed.

This section confirms that the concussion issue goes beyond US borders and sports. It shows that the CFL does not give the same degree of attention to its players as the NFL, suggesting a two-speed player safety for two professional sports with similar characteristics. This inconsistency is further accentuated by the examination of the two concussion lawsuits that have been filed by former players against the CFL: one individual lawsuit (*Bruce*) and one class action lawsuit (*Allen & Banks*). Unlike the proceedings instituted in the US,[1054] these cases have (so far) failed to overcome the state courts' reluctance to interfere with internal issues of sports governance. Moreover, they involve various other defendants who were supposed to be responsible for player safety, confirming the conflictive nature of the relationships identified in previous case studies[1055] and the need for a more consistent and harmonised approach. The arbitration claim filed in 2018 by the Canadian Football League Players' Association (CFLPA) against the league, aimed at compensating injured players and requiring specific rule and policy changes, shows for its part the risks for SGBs to have rule changes imposed on them by courts.

1 Chronology

The CFL launched a 'Concussion Campaign' to promote awareness, prevention, management and research in 2011, in the wake of the NFL controversy.[1056] The CFL Commissioner at the time, Mark Cohon, announced the distribution of flyers and

[1051] Andrew Bucholtz, 'John Cornish Retiring at 31 Should be Another CFL Concussion Wake Up Call' *Yahoo Sports*, 2 December 2015 (<https://ca.sports.yahoo.com/blogs/cfl-55-yard-line/jon-cornish-retiring-at-31-should-be-another-cfl-concussion-wake-up-call-201104913.html>).

[1052] For more details about the CFL's structure and teams, see its website (<https://www.cfl.ca/>).

[1053] For a comparison of the revenues between US and Canadian leagues, see Deubert, Cohen and Fernandez Lynch, above n 432, 14.

[1054] See this chapter, Sections IA2(a)(ii), IB2(a)(i), IC2(b) and ID2(b).

[1055] See this chapter, Sections IA3 et seq (including subsequent case studies).

[1056] See this chapter, Sections IA1(e) and IA2.

posters to hundreds of thousands of athletes, kids and coaches, and released a series of new measures for all teams, inspired by the CISG's guidelines.[1057] These new measures included the use of the SCAT 2 by athletic therapists and medical staff, minimum baseline cognitive testing (IMPaCT) for all CFL rosters during training camps,[1058] the prohibition of return-to-play during the same game for concussed players and a stepwise return-to-practice timeline.[1059] They formed the basis for the adoption of formal concussion protocols[1060] with, in case of non-compliance, fines going up to CAD25 000.[1061] Commissioner Cohon also declared that the league would keep accurate records (for internal purposes) by using a computerised system, and support research.[1062]

The CFL's commitment to support research materialised during the same year through a partnership with the Krembil Neuroscience Institute in Toronto and neuropathologist Charles Tator.[1063] This partnership, commonly referred to as the 'Sports Concussion Project', is aimed to last until 2021.[1064] It advertises to both current and former players to take part in clinical studies and donate their brains.[1065] Its first findings were released in 2013, with the publication by Dr Tator and his team of an article based on autopsies performed on six former CFL players. Although entitled 'The Absence of Chronic Traumatic Encephalopathy in Retired Players with Multiple Concussions and Neurological Symptomatology',[1066] this article states that three of the six players examined had CTE.[1067] In addition, the three other donors had ALS, Alzheimer's disease, and Parkinson's disease.[1068] At the end of 2015, newspapers reported that half of the 18 brains analysed as part of the Sports Concussion Project had CTE,[1069] figures that Dr Tator, who is being sued alongside

---

[1057]Email from Kevin McDonald (CFL Vice President of Player Safety) to author, 10 August 2017.

[1058]Ibid.

[1059]Ibid.

[1060]The CFL protocols have not been published, but a summary is available on the CFL Alumni Association's website (<http://www.cflaa.ca/wp-content/uploads/2014/07/CFL-PLAYER-SAFETY-AND-CONCUSSION-MANAGEMENT.pdf>).

[1061]Emails from Kevin McDonald (CFL Vice President of Player Safety) to author, 9–10 August 2017.

[1062]Ibid.

[1063]Chris Zelkowich, 'Canadian Football Tackles Concussions Head-On', *The Toronto Star*, 4 May 2011 (<https://www.pressreader.com/canada/toronto-star/20110504/282595964479675>).

[1064]For more details, see the Toronto General and Western Hospital Foundation's website (<https://www.tgwhf.ca/stories/tag/concussion/>).

[1065]Ibid.

[1066]Lili-Naz Hazrati et al., 'The Absence of Chronic Traumatic Encephalopathy in Retired Players with Multiple Concussions and Neurological Symptomatology' (2013) 7 *Frontiers in Human Neuroscience* 1, 1 (<https://www.ncbi.nlm.nih.gov/pmc/articles/PMC3662898/>).

[1067]Ibid, 1 and 3–8.

[1068]Ibid.

[1069]Washchyshyn, above n 1050.

the CFL and other defendants,[1070] now refuses to confirm and update.[1071] These findings are complemented by Boston University researchers' studies,[1072] from which it is sometimes difficult to retrieve data for Canadian football solely, as numerous athletes examined played both in the NFL and the CFL.[1073]

This controversy was further fuelled by the early retirements of several of CFL players due to persistent concussion-related symptoms.[1074] In response, the CFL partnered with the NFL to gradually develop and implement the King-Devick Test[1075] as a complement to the SCAT.[1076] The first results of this partnership were shared during international concussion symposia.[1077]

Simultaneously, the adoption of a new CBA enabled pre-existing rights, such as salary payment until the end of the season for injured players, to be confirmed.[1078] CFL also commenced a 'Concussion Awareness and Management' program aimed at educating players ranging from youth to professional levels on concussion symptoms and management.[1079] Despite this program, a survey showed that the overwhelming majority of CFL players who had sustained a concussion in 2015 had decided not to seek medical attention and to hide their symptoms.[1080]

In 2016, the CFL revised its concussion protocols, with the introduction of spotters as the main novelty, inspired by the NHL system, during games and the

[1070]See this chapter, Section IIA2.

[1071]Email from Dr Charles Tator (Neuropathologist, Krembil Institute) to author, 24 March 2017. Note that in May 2018, Dr Leila Hazrati, a neuropathologist with the Krembil Institute team, indicated during a symposium that the brains of about 40 high level professional and amateur athletes had been analysed from 2011 to 2017. According to her, 'only a small portion of cases' had CTE (<https://www.uhn.ca/KNC/Research/Projects/Canadian_Concussion_Centre/Documents/KNC_RES_6th_Symposium_Summaries.pdf/>).

[1072]See eg, Mez et al., above n 230, 360 and 362–3, who report seven CFL players with CTE.

[1073]Ibid.

[1074]See eg, Bucholtz, above n 1051.

[1075]CFL Staff, 'CFL Teams Partner with NFL on Concussion Testing', *CFL*, 6 August 2015 (<https://www.cfl.ca/2015/08/06/cfl-teams-and-nfl-partner-on-concussion-testing/>).

[1076]Washchyshyn, above n 1050.

[1077]See eg, the 2015 NFL Think Tank [Klayman, above n 762]. See also the CISG's conferences, in which Dr Tator took part as a member of the Scientific Committee.

[1078]CFL CBA (2014-19), Appendix AA, Paragraph 11 p. 132, as well as previous CBAs. The 2014-19 CBA is available on the BC Bargaining's website (<http://www.bcbargaining.ca/content/1665/CFL_CFLPA.pdf>).

[1079]CFLPA, media release, 22 August 2014 (<https://cflpa.com/concussion-prevention-in-the-cfl/>).

[1080]Jeffrey Scott Delaney et al., 'Why Professional Football Players Chose not to Reveal their Concussion Symptoms during a Practice or Game ' (2018) 28 Nr 1 *Clinical Journal of Sports Medicine* 1, 1. One hundred and six of the 454 respondents (23.4%) believed they had suffered a concussion during their previous football season and 87 of the 106 (82.1%) did not seek medical attention for a concussion at least once during that season (ibid, 1).

possibility for players to consult independent physicians for a second opinion when a concussion has been diagnosed.[1081] The CFL continued its momentum by adopting new rules of play (prohibition of pushing blockers through gaps in the offensive line, expansion of the definition of 'peel-back' block).[1082] Additionally, the CFL launched a joint initiative with its players' association, the CFLPA, to collect data on the diagnosis of concussion and players' understanding of symptoms.[1083] Nevertheless, new CFL Commissioner Jeffrey Orridge and his team hastened to tell the media that scientific findings linking head trauma and brain disease were inconclusive.[1084] With this, they indicated that instances of concussion (40 during the 2016 season,[1085] believed to be mainly caused by another player's head or helmet)[1086] only represented a small proportion of the total number of injuries recorded by team physicians and were decreasing.[1087] These comments drew widespread criticism in the media and Commissioner Orridge stepped down shortly afterwards for unspecified reasons.[1088] In 2017, the CFL updated its concussion protocols in order to include the SCAT 5[1089] and prohibited all regular season full-contact practices.[1090]

[1081] CFL, media release, 28 April 2016 (<https://press.cfl.ca/new-canadian-football-league-player-health-and-safety-measures-for-2016-season>). Like for the NHL, CFL spotters monitor games from a command centre, are video-assisted and can stop the game when required. They have a variety of football backgrounds (former players, therapists), undergo training from the CFL and are independent from clubs (email from Kevin McDonald (CFL Vice President of Player Safety) to author, 9 August 2017).

[1082] CFL, media release, 28 April 2016. It means that players are not allowed anymore to push blockers through gaps in the offensive line on single point or field goal attempts. In addition, any offensive player is prohibited from blocking an opponent low anywhere on the field when he is moving towards his own goal line, not just those players that start the play in the 'close line play area', commonly referred to as the tackle box.

[1083] CFL, media release, 28 April 2016.

[1084] The Canadian Press, 'Sports Legends Push for National Standard for Concussion Treatment', *CBC Sports*, 6 December 2016 (<http://www.cbc.ca/sports/concussions-protocol-canada-conference-1.3883604>) (The Canadian Press, 'Standard').

[1085] Justin Robertson, 'How Canadians Are Helping in the Fight Against Concussion in Sport', *Vice Sports*, 6 March 2017 (<https://sports.vice.com/en_ca/article/how-canadians-are-helping-in-the-fight-against-concussions-in-sport>).

[1086] The only available studies relate to college sport. See eg: J Scott Delaney, 'Mechanisms of Injury for Concussions in University Football, Ice Hockey and Soccer' (2014) 24 *Clinical Journal of Sport Medicine* 233, 233.

[1087] Robertson, above n 1085.

[1088] 'CFL Commissioner Jeffrey Orridge to Step Down in June', *AP News*, 12 April 2017 (<https://apnews.com/4c175dee8f604151a8f9d210c0bdbc43/cfl-commissioner-jeffrey-orridge-step-down-june>).

[1089] See 2017 CFL concussion protocols (unpublished, but copy on file with author); see also email from Kevin McDonald (CFL Vice President of Player Safety) to author, 9 August 2017.

[1090] Dave Naylor, 'CFL Immediately Ends Full-Contact Practices', *TSN*, 13 September 2017 (<http://www.tsn.ca/cfl-to-announce-immediate-end-to-full-contact-practices-1.855515>).

In 2018, a study undertaken by the McMaster Department of Psychiatry, based on brain imaging, showed signs of brain damage in former CFL players, with an average of 20% reduction in the mass of cerebral cortex.[1091] In response, the CFL provided a written statement where it reiterated its commitment to 'develop a culture of health and safety across the league'.[1092]

Canadian governments took various measures, with a focus on youth/grassroots sport. In 2014, the Province of Ontario introduced a policy/program memorandum on concussions requiring school boards to develop protocols and giving them rough directions in this regard.[1093] In 2016, Ontario passed legislation[1094] that paved the way for a possible youth concussion law.[1095] In March 2018, the Ontario enacted Canada's first concussion safety legislation, known as *Rowan's Law*.[1096] *Rowan's Law* and its proposed regulations impose a number of requirements on sport organisations in the province regarding concussion prevention, detection, management and awareness. These requirements include the creation, promulgation and implementation of concussion awareness resources,[1097] codes of conduct[1098] and removal-from-sport protocols.[1099] It also proposes to create different classes of sports organisations and impose different requirements on them through regulations.[1100] Various bills were also discussed in other provinces and at the federal level, without being implemented.[1101]

[1091] Steve Buist, 'Collision Course: A Spectator Report on the Science of Hard Head Knocks', *The Spectator*, 30 August 2017 (<https://www.thespec.com/news-story/7525066-collision-course-a-spectator-report-on-the-science-of-hard-head-knocks/>). The study involved 22 former CFL players, who were compared to a 'healthy' cohort. It will be published in *Clinical Neurophysiology* in 2019 [information provided by John Connolly, Professor & Senator William McMaster Chair and part of the research team, 19 October 2018].

[1092] Ibid.

[1093] This memorandum is available on the Ontario Ministry of Education's website (<http://www.edu.gov.on.ca/extra/eng/ppm/158.pdf>). It highlights five main pillars: awareness, prevention, identification, diagnosis and training [ibid, 3]. A similar memorandum was subsequently published in Quebec.

[1094] *Rowan's Law Advisory Committee Act*, 2016, S.O. 2016, chapter 11 [repealed 2016, chapter 11, section 3].

[1095] The law mandated the creation of a Committee to determine on how to best act on the 49 recommendations from the coroner's inquest. Its report, published in 2017, is available at <https://www.ontariocanada.com/registry/showAttachment.do?postingId=27186&attachmentId=37751>.

[1096] *Rowan's Law (Concussion Safety)*, 2018, S.O. 2018, chapter 1. This law was named after a 17-year old rugby player, Rowan Stringer, who passed away in 2013 after being tackled to the ground by an opponent. Coroner's inquest later attributed her death to second-impact syndrome.

[1097] *Rowan's Law*, Art. 2.

[1098] *Rowan's Law*, Art. 3.

[1099] *Rowan's Law*, Art. 4.

[1100] *Rowan's Law*, Art. 7(2).

[1101] For more details, see Kelly Russell et al., 'Legislation for Youth Sport Concussion in Canada: Review, Conceptual Framework and Recommendations' (2017) 44 *The Canadian Journal of*

Simultaneously, the Canadian Concussion Collaborative (CCC),[1102] which regroups leading sports health organisations, produced a guide to help schools and related entities implement protocols.[1103] In 2016, national charity Parachute, a CCC member, received part of a CAD1.4 million-governmental funding[1104] to undertake a 'Concussion Protocol Harmonisation Project'.[1105] This project has already led to the publication, at the end of 2017, of (non mandatory) national guidelines on concussion in sport.[1106] These very detailed guidelines are intended to complement the CISG's guidelines on various areas in the prevention, recognition, diagnosis and management of concussion.[1107] They create the foundation for a more consistent approach to concussion for all recreational sports activities across the country.[1108] The Governor General of Canada[1109] also stepped in by holding a conference on concussion in youth sport.[1110]

The sole governmental initiatives targeting specifically professional sport were conducted at the instigation of the CFLPA. In 2016, the CFLPA submitted a brief to the Alberta government asking them to review the province workers' compensation laws with the view to including professional athletes.[1111] Follow-up meetings were organised one year later with government representatives to discuss how to improve concussion education and the lack of ongoing rehabilitation support for injured players.[1112]

Neurological Sciences 225, 225–34. Several new bills were examined subsequent to this article, such as in Manitoba.

[1102] Canadian Concussion Collaborative (<http://casem-acmse.org/education/ccc/>).

[1103] 'Leading Canadian Health Organizations Produce a Guide to Help Sport and School Organizations Implement Concussion Management Protocols', press release, *Lawinsport,* 7 September 2016 (<https://www.lawinsport.com/sports-law-news/item/leading-canadian-health-organizations-produce-a-guide-to-help-sport-and-school-organizations-implement-concussion-management-protocols>) (paywall).

[1104] Vicki Hall, 'Federal Government Announces $1.4M Investment to Develop National Concussion Management Guidelines', *The National Post*, 24 October 2016 (<http://news.nationalpost.com/sports/federal-government-announces-1-4m-investment-to-develop-national-concussion-management-guidelines>).

[1105] For more details about this project, see Parachute's website (<http://www.parachutecanada.org/injury-topics/item/2231>).

[1106] For more details about these guidelines, see the Parachute's website (<http://www.parachutecanada.org/injury-topics/item/canadian-guideline-on-concussion-in-sport>).

[1107] Ibid.

[1108] Ibid.

[1109] The Governor General represents the Queen in Canada.

[1110] Faraz Damji and Shelina Babul, 'Improving and Standardizing Concussion Education and Care: a Canadian experience' (2018; Online First) *Concussion* 1, 3.

[1111] CFLPA, media release, 23 August 2016 (<https://cflpa.com/35293-2/>).

[1112] CFLPA, media release, 26 April 2017 (<https://cflpa.com/why-the-1playaway-push-for-expanded-rehab-coverage-matters-to-the-cfls-players/>).

2 Legal Activities and Implications

In 2014, Arland Bruce, a former CFL wide receiver, filed a concussion lawsuit against the CFL in the Supreme Court of British Columbia for unspecified damages.[1113] Bruce, who also briefly played in the NFL, had to retire in 2013 due to persistent concussion-related symptoms.[1114] He alleged two main legal claims in tort, namely negligence and its sub-set, negligent misrepresentation.[1115] He argued that the CFL took insufficient steps to make the game safer.[1116] In addition not to warn players about the long-term medical risks associated with concussion, the CFL also misled them as to the severity of those risks.[1117] Former CFL Commissioner Cohon, all nine teams, the CFL Alumni Association and its director, as well as Dr Charles Tator and the Krembil Neuroscience Institute were also named as defendants.[1118]

In 2016, the Supreme Court of British Columbia declined jurisdiction.[1119] Taking on the defendants' main argument,[1120] it declared that the claim is subject to the grievance and arbitration procedures under the CBA.[1121] The British Court of Appeal upheld this decision one year later.[1122] It also noted in its judgment that the suit had been discontinued against Dr Tator, the CFL Alumni Association and its director, since they were not bound by the CBA.[1123] The plaintiff applied to the Supreme Court of Canada for leave to appeal in August 2016.[1124] In March 2018, the Supreme Court refused to hear the case.[1125] Unable to take his case to court, Bruce filed a concussion-related grievance one month later against the CFL and five

[1113] *Bruce v Mark Steven Cohon et al*, No. 145512. Plaintiffs filed a notice of civil claim on 16 July 2014. This document is available on 'The Concussion Blog' (<https://theconcussionblog.com/2014/07/16/filed-claim-arland-bruce-iii-v-cfl-entities/>).

[1114] Notice of civil claim, paragraphs 101–19, pp. 17–19.

[1115] Ibid, paragraphs 13–18, pp. 34–6.

[1116] Ibid.

[1117] Ibid.

[1118] Ibid, paragraphs 2–28, pp. 2–5.

[1119] *Bruce v Cohon* 2016 BCSC 419.

[1120] The defendants' responses to the civil claim are available on 'The Concussion Blog' (https://theconcussionblog.com/2014/09/23/terry-ott-canadian-concussion-law-suit-begins-its-slow-crawl-to-resolution/https://theconcussionblog.com/2014/07/16/filed-claim-arland-bruce-iii-v-cfl-entities/>).

[1121] *Bruce v Cohon* 2016 BCSC 419.

[1122] *Bruce v Cohon* 2017 BCCA 186.

[1123] *Bruce v Cohon* 2017 BCCA 188, paragraph 3.

[1124] *Arland Richard Bruce v Mark Steven Cohon*, Leave to appeal refused, March15, 2018 (S.C.C.). See also Supreme Court of Canada's website (<https://www.scc-csc.ca/case-dossier/info/dock-regi-eng.aspx?cas=37696>).

[1125] Ibid.

teams.[1126] An arbitrator will be selected and a hearing date set during spring 2019.[1127]

On the heels of the Bruce lawsuit, two other former CFL players, Eric Allen and Korey Banks, filed a concussion class action against the CFL in the Ontario Superior Court for CAD200 million.[1128] Allen, who suffered from brain impairment, died a few months later, age 66, in hospice care.[1129] Banks turned towards coaching after 10 gruelling seasons in the CFL and a brief stint in the NFL.[1130] The class action is based in essence on the same arguments as the Bruce lawsuit, and targets the same initial defendants, to the exclusion of the CFL Alumni Association and its director.[1131] It encompasses more than 200 plaintiffs, and was put on hold waiting for the outcome of the Bruce lawsuit regarding the jurisdiction of Canadian courts.[1132] As at 31 October 2018, the class action is still pending, but no submissions have been filed by the parties,[1133] suggesting that the case is either in abeyance, suspended or dormant.

The CFLPA seems to have taken the lead. It has recently filed grievance against the league, in order to ask an arbitrator to compensate injured players and impose specific rule and policy changes.[1134]

Canadian Courts have often been mindful of players' protection,[1135] and this protection should be found equally in arbitration. However, the questions raised in

---

[1126]Gord Holder, 'Arland Bruce Files Concussion-Related Grievance Against CFL and Five Teams', *Ottawa Sun*, 6 April 2018 (<https://ottawasun.com/sports/football/cfl/arland-bruce-files-concussion-related-grievance-against-cfl-and-five-teams>) (Holder, 'Bruce').

[1127]Gord Holder, 'Head Injuries and the CFL: Grievance and Class-Action Suit Still Pending', *Ottawa Citizen*, 21 November 2018 (<https://ottawacitizen.com/sports/football/cfl/head-injuries-and-the-cfl-grievance-and-class-action-suit-still-pending>) (Holder, 'CFL').

[1128]The submissions in *Allen and Banks* have not been published. A summary of this class action and the parties' arguments can be found in Jon Heshka, 'Sports Law Expert Takes Closer Look at $200 Million CFL Concussion Lawsuit' (2015) *Professional Sports and the Law* 17, 17–19 (Heshka, 'CFL').

[1129]Chris Sokoloski, 'Howard High Legend Dead at 66', *South Strand News*, 29 October 2015 (<http://www.southstrandnews.com/news/howard-high-legend-dead-at/article_89835109-9e05-5a2f-80b7-edf0f19cee38.html>).

[1130]Jodie Wagner, 'Football: Santaluces Withdraws Coaching Offer to Korey Banks Amid FHSAA Probe' *PalmBeachPost*, 19 January 2017 (<http://highschoolbuzz.blog.palmbeachpost.com/2017/01/19/football-santaluces-withdraws-coaching-offer-to-korey-banks-amid-fhsaa-probe/>).

[1131]Heshka, 'CFL', above n 1128, 18.

[1132]Gord Holder, 'Former CFLer Receiver Carrying Through with his Concussion-Related Lawsuit' *Ottawa Citizen*, 27 January 2017 (<http://ottawacitizen.com/sports/football/cfl/former-cfler-receiver-carrying-through-with-his-concussion-related-lawsuit>) (Holder, 'Receiver').

[1133]Email from Rebecca Nagy (Assistant Trial Coordinator, Ontario Superior Court of Justice) to author, 10 November 2018.

[1134]The Canadian Press, 'CFL Players' Association Files Grievance Against League over Safety', *CBC*, 2 March 2018 (<http://www.cbc.ca/sports/football/cfl/cfl-players-association-grievance-safety-1.4585843>) (The Canadian Press, 'Grievance').

[1135]See the cases mentioned in this chapter, Section IIA2, footnotes 1138 and 1139. See also *Zacchardo v Chartis Insurance Company of Canada* 2016 QCCS 398. Junior ice hockey player

the Bruce, Allen & Banks and CFLPA concussion cases are unprecedented on the territory,[1136] and their resolution remains uncertain. In addition to the objections related to jurisdiction, the CFL will have similar defences to the claims as the NFL and other US SGBs.[1137] The assessment of the existence of a duty of care giving rise to liability in tort will be central.[1138] Another question will be to what extent head shots are risks that are inherent to Canadian football and whether or not players consent to, or voluntarily assume, the risks associated with such contact.[1139] Discussions related to contributory negligence and causation will play an important role, in an environment still dominated by macho culture and that, like Bruce and Bank,[1140] saw many players temporarily attempting to prove their worth in the NFL. Finally, the various statutes of limitations[1141] may also be raised.

3 Lessons and Significance

The recent CTE and early retirements cases in Canadian football raise serious public health concerns that now go beyond US borders and sports. The CFL has recently

Zacchardo received CAD8 million from an opponent and its insurance company after becoming quadriplegic following a violent hit.

[1136]Similar cases have been examined in the US (see this chapter, Sections IA2(a) et seq, IB2(a) et seq, IC2(b) and ID2(b)). While the NFL settlement will only deploy its effects between the parties, judgments ruled in the other concussion litigation will have a persuasive effect for Canadian courts.

[1137]See this chapter, Sections IA2(a)(ii), IB2(a)(i), IC2(b) and ID2(b).

[1138]The most famous precedent regarding duty of care and player safety in Canada is *Robitaille v Vancouver Hockey Club Ltd* (1981) 124 D.L.R. (3d) 228. Professional ice hockey player Robitaille had successfully sued his team for requiring him to continue playing with a neck and shoulder injury that ultimately resulted in a disabling spinal cord injury. In 2016, Robitaille, who also experienced concussion, joined the concussion class action filed against the NHL (see this chapter, Sections IB2 et seq). No equivalent exists regarding the duty of care of a professional sports organisation. See however *Smith v Horizon Aero Sports Ltd* [1981] 130 D.L.R. (3d) 91 B.C.S.C., involving a participant rendered paraplegic after falling from a tree where she landed during her first parachute jump. The court found that the Canadian Sport Parachuting Association, sued among other defendants as the body certifying parachute instructors, was not liable; and *Levita v Crew* (2015), 2015 CarswellOnt 13326 (Ont. S.C.J.), where a player and the relevant league were found not liable following a fractured tibia sustained by the plaintiff during a recreational ice hockey game.

[1139]The leading Canadian authority on the extent to which violent contact can be consented to and considered part of the game is *Agar v Canning* [1965] 54 W.W.R. 302. During the course of a senior ice hockey game, Canning hit Agar in the face with a hockey stick, resulting in severe injuries, including Agar's loss of one eye. The judge recalled that players accept the possibility of injury when they play contact sports. However, he considered that the injury suffered by the plaintiff in this case exceeded what a player could legitimately consent to.

[1140]See this chapter, Section IIA2.

[1141]Limitations in Ontario are dealt with in the *Limitations Act 2002*, S.O. 2002, chapter 24, Schedule B. The basic period is two years (from the knowledge of the essential elements of the claim) (section 4) and the ultimate period is 15 years (from the occurrence of the act or omission) (section 15(2)). The equivalent legislation in British Columbia is the *Limitation Act 2012*, S.B.C. 2012 chapter 13.

taken some valuable measures regarding concussion management, which seem to have translated into a decrease of concussion instances.[1142] However, the CFL suffers, by comparison to its NFL counterpart,[1143] at all regulatory levels.

The CFL initiated a few amendments in its rules of play (prohibition of pushing blockers through gaps in the offensive line, expansion of the definition of 'peel-back' block) and eliminated full-contact practices in order to improve player safety.[1144] These initiatives should be extended by further measures, based on the current body of scholarship related to the most dangerous contacts and positions in American football,[1145] as well as more targeted new studies.

The CFL also adopted concussion protocols and new rules of the game. These protocols and rules are aligned with the CISG's guidelines and best practice (including SCAT 5, IMPaCT, pre-season baseline testing, and stepwise return-to-practice). They provide for the intervention of spotters and, when requested by a concussed player, of an independent physician before return-to-practice.[1146] Based on the experience of the NFL and, when necessary, of other leagues,[1147] the functioning of spotters could be fine-tuned,[1148] and supplemented by the presence of independent doctors during games. A compulsory independent process for return-to-play could be implemented.

Additionally, the CFL granted financial protection to injured players through its CBAs. Injured players are entitled to receive their salary until the end of the season during which the injury was sustained.[1149] Improved coverage and benefits (payment of salary beyond the end of the season, creation of a NFL-like '88 Plan')[1150] could be provided.

Similarly, the CFL launched educational initiatives on concussion at the professional and youth levels.[1151] These initiatives should be enhanced and expanded to include possible long-term effects of concussion, which remain contested by the CFL.[1152] Like in the NFL,[1153] a whistle-blower system could be introduced.

Finally, the CFL took measures related to research and data collection. These measures include a partnership with the Krembil Neuroscience Institute in Toronto

---

[1142] See this chapter, Section IIA1.

[1143] See this chapter, Sections IA1(c) et seq.

[1144] See this chapter, Section IIA1.

[1145] See this chapter, Section IA1(h).

[1146] See this chapter, Section IIA1.

[1147] See this chapter, Sections IA1(e), IB1 and IIB2(a).

[1148] Like the NFL (see this chapter, Section IA1(e)), CFL spotters, who currently operate from a command centre, could for instance be placed in all stadiums, in order to ease communication between all the stakeholders.

[1149] See this chapter, Section IIA1.

[1150] See this chapter, Section IA1(c).

[1151] See this chapter, Section IIA1.

[1152] Ibid.

[1153] See this chapter, Section IA1(c).

(which involves both clinical and forensic studies, supervised by Dr Tator), participation in international meetings and symposia on concussion, and the maintenance of concussion statistics for internal purposes.[1154] Unfortunately, Dr Tator is currently subject to a potential conflict of interest due to the legal proceedings instituted against him.[1155] Consequently, the CFL's research may have to be reoriented. Data collection could be improved by the publication of NFL-like concussion reports.[1156]

The action of Canadian governments is illustrated by *Rowan's Law*, and the regulatory efforts of the CCC.[1157] *Rowan's Law*, enacted by Ontario, is the only youth concussion legislation in Canada.[1158] It imposes the creation, promulgation and implementation of concussion awareness resources, codes of conduct and removal-from-sport protocols.[1159] It also proposes to create different classes of sports organisations and to impose different requirements on them through regulations.[1160] The CCC's efforts have led to the drafting of (non mandatory) concussion guidelines for all recreational sports activities across the country.[1161] These guidelines seek to provide a complementary perspective to the SGBs' regulatory activities, and particularly to the CISG's guidelines. *Rowan's Law* and the regulatory efforts of the CCC highlight the potential risk of conflicts, not only between the standards set by the SGBs and governments, but also between those set by governments of different countries. Therefore, they demonstrate the need for a more harmonised approach. They could also inspire the creation of measures at professional and international levels. In the absence of a US-like Congress allowing the holding of specific hearings,[1162] Canadian governments would be well advised to support medical research. They could also consider the hand that is extended to them by the CFLPA regarding player welfare and the application of workers' compensation to professional sport.[1163] One can, however, recall that such a system, as applied in the US, should be adapted to the reality of professional sport.[1164]

On the procedural front, the two concussion lawsuits that have been filed by former professional players against the CFL[1165] substantiate the cross-border nature

[1154]See this chapter, Section IIA1.

[1155]See this chapter, Section IIA2.

[1156]See this chapter, Section IA1(h).

[1157]The CCC is not entitled to receive governmental funding. However, as mentioned earlier (see this chapter, Section IIA1), leading sports health organisations regrouped within it, have, just like Parachute, recently received substantial public funds. Therefore, one can consider that, indirectly, Canadian governments act through them.

[1158]See this chapter, Section IIA1.

[1159]Ibid.

[1160]Ibid.

[1161]Ibid.

[1162]In Canada, the Parliament can mainly act through Parliamentary Committees, Royal Commissions/Commissions of Inquiry and Independent inquiries.

[1163]See this chapter, Section IIA1.

[1164]See this chapter, Sections IA2 and IA3.

[1165]See this chapter, Section IIA2.

and legal complexity of the concussion controversy. Unlike the proceedings instituted in the US,[1166] these cases have (so far) failed to overcome the state courts' reluctance to interfere with sports matters.[1167] Moreover, they comprise various other defendants who were supposed to be responsible for player safety, bringing light again on the conflictive nature of the relationships identified in previous case studies[1168] and the need for a more consistent and harmonised approach. Finally, the arbitration claim filed in 2018 by the CFLPA against the league, aimed at compensating injured players and requiring specific rule and policy changes,[1169] shows the risks for SGBs to have rule changes imposed on them by courts.

B Australia: Rugby Codes and Australian Rules Football

Australia cherishes three sports with frequent contacts: rugby union, rugby league and Australian Rules football. This section begins with a review of the situation in rugby union, before analysing jointly rugby league and Australian Rules football.

Rugby union is a popular international full-contact sport involving 15 players in each team (in the traditional game format; but only seven in the modified version of the game: Rugby-7s), who have to score as many points as possible by carrying, passing, kicking, and grounding the ball.[1170] Rugby union is governed by an IF, World Rugby, which is very active in concussion management and even harmonisation. World Rugby is supported at the lower levels of governance by continental and national associations (in this case, Oceania Rugby and Rugby Australia (formerly known as the Australian Rugby Union, the ARU)), as well as various transnational consortiums, such as SANZAAR (which consists of the rugby unions of Australia, Argentina, Japan, New Zealand and South Africa).

Rugby league (or Rugby-13s) is close to rugby union, but emerged as an independent sport following a schism in the late nineteenth century[1171] that saw it develop its own technical specifics[1172] and emerge as a professional sport.[1173] Australian Rules football is often considered to have been derived from rugby or Gaelic football, but also, due to the importance of its foot play, from football or even

[1166]See this chapter, Sections IA2(a)(ii), IB2(a)(i), IC2(b) and ID2(b).

[1167]See this chapter, Section IIA2.

[1168]See this chapter, Sections IA3 et seq (including subsequent case studies).

[1169]See this chapter, Section IIA2.

[1170]Andrew J Gardner et al., 'A Systematic Review and Meta-Analysis of Concussion in Rugby Union' (2014) 44 *Sports Medicine* 1717, 1718 (Gardner et al., 'Rugby Union').

[1171]Ibid.

[1172]In addition to a different number of players, rugby league has notably its own peculiarities regarding tackles, scrums and scoring [for more details, see eg, Ian Tuckey, 'What is the difference Between Rugby League and Rugby Union?', *The Sun*, 3 March 2017(<https://www.thesun.co.uk/sport/2238885/what-is-the-difference-between-rugby-union-and-rugby-league/>)].

[1173]For more details, see Gardner et al., 'Rugby Union', above n 1170, 1718.

Aboriginal jousts.[1174] Both codes have a limited geographical scope: Rugby league is mainly played in Australasia and, to a lesser extent, Pacific Islands and Europe,[1175] while Australian Rules football is only organised in professional form in Australia.[1176] These codes self-govern in practice. Thus, the AFL and the NRL have the power to individually set up their rules in Australia. They have used that power to adopt numerous safety rules and other concussion management measures that echo each other.

Rugby union, rugby league and Australian Rules football have recently all been subject to considerable public attention, following reports of numerous concussion-related incidents, which have sometimes led to early retirement. However, unlike the sports examined previously, they have so far been spared from CTE diagnosis (with the exception of 2 CTE diagnoses in rugby union, whose scientific validity is contested by World Rugby). This may be explained by the proactive approach of the SGBs involved, the different nature of the game, but also by the very low number of forensic examinations undertaken. Australian governments' action mainly consists in the funding of educational measures and concussion guidelines for grassroots sport. There has to date been no reported concussion litigation against a major SGB in Australia. The noose seems, however, to be tightening: pre-trial proceedings were filed against the NRL in 2017, and a concussion class action is expected against the AFL during 2019.

This section shows that the concussion issue goes beyond North American borders and sports. It describes numerous concussion management measures, embedded in a relatively harmonious and collaborative environment, though not entirely devoid of conflicts. It demonstrates that even the most proactive SGBs are not immune from litigation, due to alleged failures from the past. It confirms the need for a more global and harmonised approach.

1 Rugby Union

(a) Chronology

The analysis of the concussion issue in Australian professional rugby union requires the examination of the regulatory activity of four major entities: World Rugby, Oceania Rugby, SANZAAR and Rugby Australia. World Rugby is the international

[1174]The exact origins of Australian Rules football have generated enormous controversy among sports historians, who sometimes see it as a sport marked by British influence, and sometimes as an indigenous sport [for more details, see eg, Roy Hay, 'A Tale of Two Footballs: The Origins of Australian Football and Association Football Revisited' (2010) 13 *Sport in Society* 952, 952–69].

[1175]Tim Gabbett et al., 'Applied Physiology of Rugby League' (2008) 38 *Sports Medicine* 119, 120.

[1176]For lower levels, see the AFL website (<http://www.aflcommunityclub.com.au/index.php?id=607>).

governing body for rugby union. It sets the main orientations of rugby union worldwide and oversees numerous competitions, including the World Cups.[1177] Oceania Rugby is the Continental Association for Oceania.[1178] SANZAAR is a consortium that operates transnational tournaments (Super Rugby, Rugby Championship).[1179] Rugby Australia serves as the governing body for rugby union in Australia.[1180] It oversees national team competitions and the National Rugby Championship (NRC).[1181] Rugby Australia is subject to the authority of World Rugby, Oceania Rugby and SANZAAR,[1182] and must respect their regulations.

World Ruby has worked for many years on the issue of injuries through its research and data collection activities. It regularly publishes statistics on injuries and sometimes more specifically on concussion in peer-reviewed journals, showing for instance 24 physician-diagnosed instances of concussion during the 2015 men's World Cup (a figure steadily increasing, and mainly affecting backs).[1183] Additionally, World Rugby has sponsored the CISG since 2004,[1184] directly contributed to the consensus statement in 2012,[1185] and endorsed the recent Dublin implementation paper.[1186] World Rugby also sent its representatives to other international symposia, such as the NFL Think Tank.[1187] Simultaneously, it amended the rules related to scrums and encouraged greater vigilance in relation to the refereeing of spear tackles.[1188]

[1177]For more details, see World Rugby Handbook (2017), Section 2, By-Law 3 and Section 3, Regulation 17.3.3. This Handbook is available on World Rugby website (<https://www.world.rugby/handbook>).

[1178]Oceania Rugby Constitution (2018), Arts. 3.1 and 3.2 (unpublished, but copy on file with author).

[1179]For more details, see SANZAAR's website (<http://www.sanzarrugby.com/about-sanzar/>).

[1180]Rugby Australia (ARU) Constitution (2016), Art. 2.1 (a) (unpublished, but copy on file with author).

[1181]See Rugby Australia website (<http://www.rugbyaustralia.com.au/wallabies/Home.aspx>).

[1182]See eg, World Rugby Handbook (2015), Section 3, Regulation 2; Oceania Rugby Constitution (2018), Arts. 5.1 and 5.5.

[1183]Colin W Fuller et al., 'Evaluation of World Rugby Concussion Management Process: Results from Rugby World Cup 2015' (2017) 51 *British Journal of Sports Medicine* 64, 64 and 66.

[1184]McCrory et al., '3rd Consensus', above n 43 in Chapter 2, 81. Note that World Rugby acknowledges its contribution since 2008 only (email from Dr Martin Raftery (World Rugby Chief Medical Officer) to author, 1 June 2017).

[1185]McCrory et al., '4th Consensus', above n 228, 250. Dr Martin Raftery, was a member of the CISG's Scientific Committee in 2012 but stood down in 2016 due to what he considered to be a conflict of interest (email from Dr Martin Raftery (World Rugby Chief Medical Officer) to author, 1 June 2017).

[1186]See Chapter 2, Section IX, footnote 164.

[1187]See eg, Gary Mihoces, 'NFL Think Tank has Sports "Pooling Resources" *USA Today* in Concussion Battle', 25 August 2014 (<https://www.usatoday.com/story/sports/2014/08/25/nfl-concussions-olympics-fifa-soccer-nhl-ncaa/14593579/>) (Mihoces, 'NFL Think Tank').

[1188]IRB Staff, 'IRB Issues Statement on "Tip or Spear" Tackle', 16 October 2011 (<http://www.rugby.com.au/news/2016/02/10/irb-issues-statement-on-tip-or-spear-tackle>).

In 2011, World Rugby intensified its efforts amid concussion controversies in the US and elsewhere.[1189] New measures were facilitated by the nomination of a new Chief Medical Officer, Dr Martin Raftery, who set concussion as a priority as soon as he took office.[1190] In 2012, a concussion working group, formed by Dr Raftery, team physicians, a player representative and independent concussion experts (including neurologists) was established to implement protocols.[1191] Although it lost one of its members following disagreements,[1192] this group quickly introduced the Pitch Side Concussion Assessment (PSCA).[1193] When initially trialled, in 2012-13, the PSCA allowed potentially concussed players to be temporarily replaced during five minutes, and return to play if they passed an examination involving answering questions and a physical balance test.[1194] In 2014, the PSCA was renamed 'Head Injury Assessment' (HIA) to include all types of head injuries, not only concussion.[1195] The time for temporary replacement was also increased from five to 10 minutes.[1196] The HIA is currently based on a reformatted SCAT 5 and recommends the use of pre-season baseline testing (preferably CogSport).[1197]

Since 2015, the HIA has been enshrined, in principle, in the Laws of the Game.[1198] However, SGBs and tournament organisers that want to access it must seek approval, annually based, via an online form.[1199] Approval is subject to a range of supportive measures, such as untoward incident review groups, real-time pitch-side video and independent match-day doctors to assist or even supervise team doctors for international competitions (or a similar means of review).[1200] Online educational modules for all medical staff and informative sessions for players and team management are also part of mandatory standards,[1201] and are supplemented by

---

[1189] See this chapter, Sections IA1(e), IA2 et seq (including subsequent case studies).

[1190] Martin Raftery and Ross Tucker, 'Implementing a Worldwide Concussion Program, The World Rugby Strategy to Secure Player Welfare' (2016) 5 *Aspetar* 50, 50.

[1191] Ibid, 52.

[1192] Dr Barry O'Driscoll resigned in 2012 due to what he felt were grave inadequacies. Since then, he has continued to criticise World Rugby's concussion management in the media.

[1193] Raftery and Tucker, above n 1190, 52–3.

[1194] Ibid, 53.

[1195] Ibid, 54.

[1196] Ibid. Since 2017, players who undertake an off-field screening under the HIA cannot return to the game before this 10-minute break has elapsed.

[1197] World Rugby's website (<http://playerwelfare.worldrugby.org/concussion/>).

[1198] For the current regulations, see World Rugby, Laws of the Game, Rugby Union (2018), in particular Law 3.27. These Laws are available on World Rugby website (<https://laws.worldrugby.org/>).

[1199] This online form is available on World Rugby's website (<http://playerwelfare.worldrugby.org/concussion/>).

[1200] Ibid. Independent doctors may override team doctors' decisions and immediately and permanently remove a player from the field.

[1201] See online form.

larger-scale initiatives led by World Rugby.[1202] In addition, recommended player welfare standards were introduced related to concussion and general medical issues.[1203] Compliance is ensured via online forms, central checking of online education database and contracts with tournaments.[1204] World Rugby reserves the right to review individual cases.[1205]

The HIA is currently used in 22 worldwide professional and elite adult tournaments, including World Cups, Olympic Games, Super Rugby and national competitions.[1206] It is complemented by mandatory graduated return-to-practice protocols.[1207]

Concurrently, World Rugby conducted a video analysis of more than 600 instances of concussion.[1208] This analysis, the findings of which were published in a peer-reviewed journal, confirmed the dangerousness of tackles, already highlighted in previous studies.[1209] It showed that 76% of instances of concussion occurred during tackles (a majority of which were sustained by the tackler),[1210] far exceeding the concussion rate during other phases of play, such as rucks and scrums.[1211] It triggered the introduction of increased sanctions for high tackles in 2016.[1212]

Despite these efforts, the world of rugby was not spared from controversy, both at the international and domestic levels. In addition to numerous early retirements, two CTE cases were discovered in rugby in 2014.[1213] These cases involved former Australian professional rugby union player Barry Tizza and Irish semi-professional

---

[1202] Raftery and Tucker, above n 1190, 51.

[1203] See online form.

[1204] Raftery and Tucker, above n 1190, 54–5.

[1205] Email from Liam McTiernan (Head of Regulations and Compliance, European Professional Club Rugby, EPCR) to author, 22 March 2017. See also the controversy that arose during the 2015 Six Nations Tournament, which is discussed further in this section.

[1206] Emails from Dr Martin Raftery (World Rugby Chief Medical Officer) to author, 22 March 2017, 9 June 2017 and 17 October 2018.

[1207] Raftery and Tucker, above n 1190, 55.

[1208] Ross Tucker et al., 'A Video Analysis of Head Injuries Satisfying the Criteria for a Head Injury Assessment in Professional Rugby: A Prospective Cohort Study' (2017) 51 *British Journal of Sports Medicine* 1147, 1147–8 and 1151.

[1209] Ibid, 1147.

[1210] Ibid, 1147, 1149 and 1151.

[1211] Ibid, 1148. Note that rucks and tackles are somewhat related. A ruck typically takes place after a tackle and is where one or more players from each team, who are on their feet, in physical contact, close around the ball on the ground.

[1212] See World Rugby's website (<http://www.worldrugby.org/news/213339>).

[1213] For case reports, see McKee et al., 'Neuropathology', above n 718, 41–2 and 44; W Stewart et al., 'Chronic Traumatic Encephalopathy: A Potential Late and Under Recognized Consequence of Rugby Union? (2016) 109 *QJM: An International Journal of Medicine* 11, 11–15 (Stewart et al, 'Rugby Union').

ruby union player Kenny Nuzum, examined respectively by Boston researchers and Scottish neuropathologist Willie Stewart.[1214] In 2015, World Rugby was accused of attempting to influence a study on the long-term effects of head injuries that it had commissioned from the Auckland Institute of Technology.[1215] In an attempt to relieve the polemic, World Rugby published a statement indicating that it was 'difficult to draw robust conclusions about the links between rugby and long-term cognitive health issues' and highlighting the need for 'further in-depth research'.[1216]

At the lowest levels of governance, Oceania Rugby, SANZAAR and Rugby Australia follow World Rugby's regulations. On this basis, Rugby Australia in particular adopted its own concussion protocols, and applies for the use of the HIA annually.[1217] Match-day doctors are present for Super Rugby and national team competitions,[1218] and concussion education is delivered to players by Rugby Australia Chief Medical Officer, with a focus on awareness, symptoms, treatment and return-to-play.[1219] Financial coverage for injured players is regulated through the CBA, which ensures that they receive their 'total remuneration package' until the expiration of their contract.[1220] Rugby Australia also took part in recent meetings gathering representatives of all four Australian football codes with the view to implementing the CISG's guidelines and harmonise practices.[1221] Its teams use a monitoring system through the high performance staff to monitor and track injuries and wellbeing data for internal purposes.[1222]

[1214] Ibid.

[1215] Daniel Schofield, 'The Big Read: Sport Must Come Clean over Risks of Concussion', *New Zealand Herald*, 11 July 2016 (<http://www.nzherald.co.nz/sport/news/article.cfm?c_id=4&objectid=11672511>).

[1216] 'Rugby Study Points to Link Between Concussion and Brain Function', *BBC*, 28 July 2015 (<http://www.bbc.com/sport/rugby-union/33686163>). Debate even expanded to youth sport when, in 2017, erroneous and misleading representation of injury statistics, aimed at reassuring parents, were pointed out by Australian medical experts, forcing World Rugby to amend its website [Joe Piggin and Allyson Pollock, 'World Rugby's Erroneous and Misleading Representation of Australian Sports Injury Statistics' (2017) 57 *British Journal of Sports Medicine* 1108, 1108; World Rugby's website (<http://www.worldrugby.org/news/142105>)].

World Rugby's website (<http://www.worldrugby.org/news/142105>).

[1217] Rugby Australia's protocols are unpublished; email from Dr Martin Raftery (World Rugby Chief Medical Officer) to author, 1 June 2017.

[1218] See Rugby Australia Medical Policy (2017), Art. 4.1, which refers to SANZAAR's Super Rugby Tournament Manual and World Rugby Regulations. This policy is available on Rugby Australia website (<http://www.rugbyau.com/about/codes-and-policies/all-codes-and-policies>).

[1219] Email from Toby Duncan (Chief Executive Officer, Australian Rugby Union Players' Association) to author, 15 May 2017.

[1220] This financial protection is limited to players who sustained injury as a result of performing their contractual obligations [Rugby Australia CBA (2018-20), Schedule C, Art. 17.2, p. 8 (unpublished, but copy on file with author)].

[1221] Email from Dr Peter Harcourt (AFL Chief Medical Officer) to author, 2 February 2018.

[1222] Email from Toby Duncan (Chief Executive Officer, Australian Rugby Union Players' Association) to author, 9 August 2017.

Rugby Australia can count on the support of the Rugby Union Players Association (RUPA). RUPA is grouped, together with the NRL and AFL players' associations (RLPA and AFLPA), in the Australian Athletes Alliance (AAA).[1223] The AAA has a strong commitment to the issue of sports injuries, and concussion in particular. In 2014, the AAA called for an overhaul of workers' compensation laws, which exclude professional athletes in Australia.[1224] It even proposed a national plan, which contained three main points: payment of all medical costs arising from employment; payment of salary for up to 104 weeks in case of injury; and a career ending injury lump sum based on age and salary.[1225] Despite the lack of support that its plan received, the AAA was not discouraged. In 2016, it created a concussion working group, with the hope of contributing to the unification of policy and ensuring greater transparency and independence in research and management.[1226] It is currently working towards a cross-code longitudinal study on concussion.[1227]

The federal government did not show much interest for concussion management and research, despite repeated calls from former labour politician and Australian Rules football player Justin Madden.[1228] An AUD-200 000 grant was, however, allocated in 2016 to researchers at the University of Melbourne for a project aimed at improving the management of concussion.[1229] This grant was completed by the creation of a government-funded website.[1230] The said website brings together information on concussion for the general public.[1231] It was launched in partnership with the Australian Institute of Sport (AIS) and the Australian Medical Association

---

[1223]AAA's website (<http://www.ausathletesall.com.au/member-associations>).

[1224]Nicola Berkovic, 'Australian Athletes Alliance Calls for Workers Compensation Law Revamp', *The Australian*, 18 July 2014 (<http://www.theaustralian.com.au/business/legal-affairs/australian-athletes-alliance-calls-for-workers-compensation-law-revamp/news-story/a3c63526e3b0ee86cdff402e5fde2ba8>) (paywall).

[1225]Presentation Laura Sigal (AFLPA), Melbourne Law School, 25 November 2015; adequacy and currency of information reconfirmed by Ms Sigal orally on 19 October 2018.

[1226]AAA's website (<http://www.ausathletesall.com.au/content/aaa-launches-concussion-working-group>).

[1227]Jon Ralph, 'AFL to Fund a Minimum of $250 000 a Year for Concussion Research', *News. Com*, 22 June 2017 (<http://www.news.com.au/sport/afl/afl-to-fund-a-minimum-of-250000-a-year-for-concussion-research/news-story/e95fe084d1bc8f9637acbf51ea00ea0b>) (Ralph, 'AFL').

[1228]See eg, Jon Pierik, 'Madden Ready to Donate Brain to Help Injury Research', *The Age*, 15 May 2012 (<http://www.theage.com.au/afl/afl-news/madden-ready-to-donate-brain-to-help-injury-research-20120514-1yn2w.html>) (Pierik, 'Madden').

[1229]Lanai Scarr, 'Health Minister Greg Hunt has Unveiled $125Million of Fuding into Medical Research Projects', *The Herald Sun*, 3 February 2017 (<http://www.heraldsun.com.au/news/national/health-minister-greg-hunt-has-unveiled-125-million-of-funding-into-medical-research-projects/news-story/8684f9a1c3017059ff7bf650215172a4>) (paywall).

[1230]For more details, see 'Concussion in Sport' website (<https://concussioninsport.gov.au/>).

[1231]Ibid.

(AMA), both known for their scepticism regarding a possible link between head injuries and CTE.[1232]

Simultaneously, the states of Western Australia and New South Wales funded the development of (non mandatory) concussion guidelines.[1233] These brief guidelines, drafted by Sports Medicine Australia (SMA) state branches and sports departments, are part of a broader scheme to improve concussion identification and handling, as well as education in children's sport and/or at grassroots level.[1234] They are in line with the CISG's guidelines, and must be complied with by sports organisations that want to receive state funding.[1235]

(b) Legal Activities and Implications

No concussion lawsuit has so far been filed against World Rugby, Oceania Rugby, SANZAAR or Rugby Australia. However, there has been a recent increase of legal activity related to sports injuries in rugby union. World Rugby had to face a legal action for negligence instituted in the late 1990s before the High Court of Australia by two amateur rugby players rendered quadriplegic after participating in poorly executed scrums.[1236] Although World Rugby escaped liability,[1237] this case showed that SGBs were not untouchable, and paved the way for subsequent legal proceedings.[1238]

On a different note, World Rugby was indirectly involved in a litigation stemming from a concussion incident that occurred during the Six Nations Tournament

[1232]The AIS and AMA have published a joint position statement on concussion in sport that, on p. 8, denies the link between head injuries and CTE (<https://concussioninsport.gov.au/position-statement>).

[1233]For more details about the New South Wales initiatives, see NSW's government website (<https://sport.nsw.gov.au/news/20170806-concussion-guidelines>) and (<https://sportandrecreation.nsw.gov.au/sites/default/files/sma-concussion-in-sport-policy.pdf>); for more details about the Western Australia initiatives, see 'Sport Concussion Australia' website (<https://sportconcussion.com.au/>); Sports Medicine Australia (WA)'s website (<http://sma.org.au/state-branches/wa/programs/concussion-in-sport-project/>) (and related links) (this link is not active anymore, but the relevant documents are on file with the author).

[1234]Ibid.

[1235]On this latter point, see the WA's sports department website (<https://www.dsr.wa.gov.au/support-and-advice/research-and-policies/policies/concussion-in-sport>).

[1236]*Agar v Hyde (2000)* 201 CLR 552.

[1237]The two plaintiffs sued, more specifically, the Board members of World Rugby (formerly known as the International Rugby Football Union, IRFU). They contended that they had breached a duty of care by not amending the rules of play to remove unnecessary risks. The High Court rejected this claim, stating that they did not owe such a duty. It notably highlighted the plaintiffs' acceptance of the inherent risks of the sport by virtue of their voluntary participation [*Agar v Hyde (2000)* 201 CLR 552, 600-1, paragraphs 127-8].

[1238]See eg, *Haylen v New South Wales Rugby Union Ltd [2002]* NSWSC 114; *Green v Australian Rugby Football League Ltd and Ors* [2002] NSWSC 749; *Woods v Multisport Holdings* (2002) 208 CLR 460 (all cases confirm in essence *Agar v Hyde*).

organised in 2015 under its auspices in Wales.[1239] While World Rugby finally cleared the Welsh Rugby Union (WRU)'s medical and coaching staff, as well as the match-day doctor of wrongdoing after an investigation,[1240] numerous media were very critical of the parties concerned.[1241] As a result, media company Fairfax and one of its journalists were sued in the New Zealand High Court for alleged defamatory statements.[1242] The case was finally settled by mediation.[1243]

This trend towards litigation, coupled with the forthcoming concussion litigation against the AFL and possibly, the NRL,[1244] as well as recently greater public awareness related to the concussion issue and wave of litigation overseas,[1245] opens the door to speculation. While the levels of controversy and possible concealment in Australian sports, such as rugby union, are in no way comparable to those sometimes observed in North America,[1246] the possibility of concussion litigation against an entity governing rugby union in Australia cannot be ruled out. In this case, common-law concepts similar to those in the US[1247] and Canada[1248] would apply. Plaintiffs would also have to face the Australian courts' past reluctance to hold SGBs liable in cases of injury litigation arising from inherently dangerous contact sports.[1249] This reluctance has historically been justified by the absence of a general duty of care of SGBs and the voluntary participation of amateur athletes, deemed to accept the risks related to the activity in which they take part.[1250] These elements need, however, to be revisited in light of the evolution of society and the recent public awareness about sports safety, as well as the structural changes that occurred in the organisation of international sport.[1251] In addition, they may be assessed with

[1239] For more details, see Jack Anderson, 'The Legal Implications of Concussion in Contact Sports', *Lawinsport*, 12 September 2016 (<https://www.lawinsport.com/articles/item/the-legal-implications-of-concussion-in-contact-sports?category_id=112>) (paywall) (Jack Anderson, 'Contact Sports').

[1240] Ibid.

[1241] See eg, Paul Rees, 'George North's Concussion Damaged Him and the Image of Rugby Union', *The Guardian*, 12 February 2015 (<https://www.theguardian.com/sport/2015/feb/12/breakdown-george-north-wales-concussion>).

[1242] See *Gatland v Fairfax New Zealand Limited* [2016] NZHC 970 (preliminary decision).

[1243] The settlement included the publication of a retraction and apology by Fairfax in the online and print version of the Dominion Post on 21 August 2016 [see press release, 'Clarification: WRU Concussion', *Stuff*, 21 August 2016 (<https://www.stuff.co.nz/sport/rugby/international/83256246/clarification-wru%2D%2Dconcussion>)].

[1244] See this chapter, Section IIB2(b).

[1245] See this chapter, Sections IA2 et seq, IB2 et seq, IC2(b), ID2(b) and IIA2.

[1246] See eg, this chapter, Sections IA1(a) et seq and IB1.

[1247] See in particular this chapter, Sections IA2(a) et seq, IB2(a) et seq and IC2(b).

[1248] See this chapter, Section IIA2.

[1249] See this chapter, Section IIB1(b), as well as footnotes 1237 and 1238.

[1250] See this chapter, Section IIB1(b), footnote 1237.

[1251] On this latter point, see *Agar v Hyde*. This landmark case, discused above in this section (and footnote 1237), did not formally target World Rugby directly, but the members of its Board. This specificity, due to the legal structure of World Rugby at that time, undeniably influenced the opinion

more flexibility in professional sport, due to the substantial resources available to SGBs and the athletes' willingness to keep their means of livelihood.[1252] Not to mention that head hits depart from other types of injuries in terms of consent, due to the controversial nature of their potential long-term risks.[1253] The short deadlines imposed by Australian statutes of limitations would be an additional hurdle to be overcome by the plaintiffs.[1254] Finally, the jurisdiction of the state courts, which are traditionally in charge of personal injury claims, should be confirmed.[1255]

(c) Lessons and Significance

The recent discovery of the first CTE cases in Australian and Irish rugby union, together with early retirements,[1256] confirm that the concussion issue is not restricted to North America. It raises serious public health concerns worldwide. World Rugby has well understood this, since it has tried to include its numerous safety measures in a global and harmonised context. World Rugby's action should not be tarnished by the high and steadily increasing number of head injuries reported during international tournaments,[1257] which may be due, at least partly, to a better identification and awareness.[1258] Although revealing some shortcomings, World Rugby's efforts must be praised and should be pursued in all sectors of concussion management. The same is true for lower levels of governance.

World Rugby amended its rules of play in order to better protect players' heads and necks during tackles and scrums.[1259] Despite this, rugby union remains a particularly violent sport. This violence could be mitigated by a stricter enforcement of existing rules.[1260] New rules could also be adopted in relation to the most

---

of the judges, who highlighted that individuals had very little authority to amend the rules themselves [*Agar v Hyde (2000)* 201 CLR 552, in particular 580, paragraph 78].

[1252]In the same vein, see the window left open in *Agar v Hyde* [*Agar v Hyde (2000)* 201 CLR 552, 561 and 584, paragraphs 13 and 91].

[1253]See Chapter 2, Sections VII and this chapter, Section IA1(h) and footnote 228.

[1254]See eg, *Limitations Act 1958* (Vic), section 27D, which provides that an action shall not be brought after the expiration of a period of three years from the date on which the cause of action is discoverable by the plaintiff; and 12 years from the date of the act or omission alleged to have resulted in the death or personal injury concerned. About other types of statutory defences, see McIntyre, above n 13 in Chapter 1, 2. This author discusses the materialisation of an obvious risk of a dangerous recreational activity, which is embedded in the legislation of some Australian states.

[1255]The possible jurisdiction of CAS or other arbitration mechanisms established under CBAs for personal injury claims has not been explored at a practical level in Australia.

[1256]See this chapter, Section IIB1(a).

[1257]Ibid.

[1258]In the same vein, see Fuller et al., above n 1183, 64, who support their viewpoint by highlighting the fact that overall injury rates in rugby have remained unchanged over the same period.

[1259]See this chapter, Section IIB1(a).

[1260]In the same vein, see Tom English, 'Rugby's Concussion Reviews "Are not Fit for Purpose", Says Brain Expert', *BBC*, 21 April 2017 (<http://www.bbc.com/sport/rugby-union/39630540>).

dangerous phases of the game, such as tackles, rucks and scrums,[1261] with the view to better protecting backs, identified as being at high-risk for concussion.[1262] They could be coupled with other measures, such as better education and training techniques to maximise injury reduction.[1263]

Furthermore, World Rugby adopted detailed rules of the game and concussion protocols inspired by the CISG's guidelines (and their implementation paper).[1264] World Rugby's protocols include the HIA, based on a reformatted SCAT 5, and its related concussion substitute, which provides for a 10-minute break for sideline player assessment.[1265] The use of HIA is rooted in the Laws of the Game, and can be applied for via an online form.[1266] Its authorisation is subject to the implementation of a range of supportive measures (incident review groups, pitch-side video, independent match-day doctors for international competitions or a similar means of review).[1267] World Rugby's protocols also provide for a mandatory stepwise return-to-practice process, and include recommended medical and player welfare standards.[1268] While these protocols could still be improved (extension of the duration for sideline player assessment, greater presence of independent doctors at rugby match games, introduction of concussion spotters),[1269] they constitute a noteworthy effort of harmonisation. It would be desirable for this effort to continue, by means of a more automatic and widespread application. In addition, compliance could be enhanced, if necessary through the development of a more systematic and stricter monitoring system aimed at assuring, controlling and enforcing the procedures.[1270]

Interestingly, online educational modules for all medical staff and information sessions for players and team management are also part of World Rugby's mandatory standards to access the HIA,[1271] allowing a centralisation of concussion education. The fact remains that education could be further improved by changing the

---

This article quotes Dr Willie Stewart, who maintains that the recent strict rules adopted by World Rugby are counterbalanced by a greater laxity of referees.

1261See this chapter, Section IIB1(a).

1262Ibid. For more details about possible changes, see Tucker et al., above n 1208, 1150–1; Owen Slot, 'Rugby Needs Confidence and Proof it is not a Health Risk', *The Australian*, 5 September 2017 (<http://www.theaustralian.com.au/sport/the-times-sport/rugby-needs-confidence-and-proof-it-is-not-a-health-risk/news-story/aa38a4200bff5e93a80013cda06a59be>) (paywall).

1263In the same vein, see Tucker et al., above n 1208, 1150–1.

1264See Chapter 2, Section VIII, footnote 164 and this chapter, Section IIB1(a).

1265See this chapter, Section IIB1(a).

1266Ibid.

1267Ibid.

1268Ibid.

1269In the same vein, see eg, Bunworth, above n 13 in Chapter 1, 90, who even discusses the possibility of permanent removal for players suspected of being concussed.

1270In the same vein, see English, above n 1260. This article quotes Dr Willie Stewart, who questions the efficiency of current World Rugby's concussion incident reviews.

1271See this chapter, Section IIB1(a).

cultural attitude towards concussion in rugby.[1272] This change should start with World Rugby, which still denies any link between multiple head injuries and later-life cognitive decline.[1273] A NFL-like whistle-blower system[1274] could also be implemented.

Finally, World Rugby has undertaken numerous efforts regarding both internal and external research, with the view to improving the management of head injuries and investigating their potential long-term effects.[1275] These efforts should be pursued, and cleansed, once and for all, from pressure and independence-related problems, which seem to persist despite the withdrawal of World Rugby's scientific contribution to the CISG.[1276] Similarly, initiatives related to data collection during international tournaments[1277] should continue. They could extend to domestic competitions through a centralised system,[1278] and would benefit from being shared with a wider audience, for instance through NFL-like concussion reports.[1279]

Additional measures (eg, NFL-like '88 Plan' aimed at covering former players' medical and custodial care costs[1280]) may also be required depending on the evolution of the debate.

At lower levels of governance, Oceania Rugby, SANZAAR and Rugby Australia are following the trend.[1281] In addition to the rules of play, Rugby Australia applies World Rugby's concussion protocols and related-educational standards.[1282] It provides contracts that are fully guaranteed against injuries, and takes part in meetings between the four Australian football codes, aimed at implementing international best practice in the most efficient and harmonised way.[1283] It is also linked to the AAA,[1284] which has initiated numerous proposals and initiatives related to concussion (national plan for injured athletes' compensation, concussion working group, cross-code longitudinal study on concussion).[1285] All these efforts should be pursued and enhanced. In addition, Rugby Australia should fill gaps in its concussion management,[1286] by getting involved in research and publishing its injury related data.

[1272]Ibid.

[1273]Ibid.

[1274]See this chapter, Section IA1(c).

[1275]See this chapter, Section IIB1(a).

[1276]See ibid, and footnote 1185.

[1277]See this chapter, Section IIB1(a).

[1278]See this chapter, Section IC3.

[1279]See this chapter, Section IA1(h).

[1280]See this chapter, Section IA1(c).

[1281]See this chapter, Section IIB1(a).

[1282]Ibid.

[1283]Ibid.

[1284]Ibid.

[1285]Ibid.

[1286]Ibid.

Australian governments do not have much involvement in the matter. Their action to date has been mainly manifested in educational measures (including a website, launched in partnership with contributors known for their scepticism regarding a possible link between head injuries and CTE) and concussion guidelines for grassroots sport.[1287] Scientific research on concussion is neglected, with the funding of only one research project intended to improve concussion management.[1288] More funding should be provided to improve the understanding of concussion and its long-term effects. Some further thought needs to be given to the legitimacy and possible content of a workers' compensation system for professional athletes, in the wake of the negotiations undertaken by the AAA. An intervention of the Australian Parliament into the issue of concussion could also be considered.[1289]

Although entities governing professional rugby union in Australia have probably increased their efforts in order to avoid a crisis such as the one that occurred in North America,[1290] it must be recognised that they have created a more proactive and collaborative environment. This also applies to the legal risks, since these entities have so far been spared from concussion litigation.[1291] However, it may be only a matter of time. Should that be the case, they could benefit from a favourable position at common law, which, however, still needs to be confirmed for professional sport and the very specific issue of concussion.[1292]

2 Rugby League and Australian Rules Football

(a) Chronology

The analysis of the concussion issue in Australian professional rugby league and Australian Rules football requires the examination of the regulatory activity of the NRL (which acts formally through the Australian Rugby League Commission, ARLC)[1293] and the AFL.[1294]

[1287] Ibid.

[1288] Ibid.

[1289] Such an intervention could, for instance, take the form of an inquiry by a Senate Committee.

[1290] See this chapter, Sections IA1(d) et seq and IA2 et seq (including subsequent case studies).

[1291] See this chapter, Section IIB1(b).

[1292] Ibid.

[1293] The ARLC is in charge of organising the NRL competition, and of liaising with the RLIF [ARLC's Constitution, Art. 6; unpublished]. However, the ARLC and the NRL have the same Chief Executive Officer/administration and references externally are almost invariably to the NRL, rather than to the ARLC. Consequently, and for the sake of simplification, it will be referred to as the NRL in this section.

[1294] Although a pseudo-international structure (headed by the RLIF) exists in rugby league, it has very little concrete influence. The RLIF's authority is restricted in practice to the organisation of international competitions and the adoption of the Laws of the Game, which the NRL can adapt for its own competitions due to the existence of a 'local clause'. This situation is explained by historical

The NRL's involvement in concussion management is believed to have started during the 2000s, through internal and external research activities.[1295] The NRL has so far shown little inclination to comment on its internal research. However, independent experts that the league commissioned to conduct research projects have recently made their findings public—including neurosurgeon Richard Parkinson (and his team) and neurophysiologist Alan Pearce. Dr Parkinson's study, based on retroactive analysis of injury reports collected during 15 years for a NRL team, showed a significant increase in the incidence of concussion.[1296] It also highlighted the vulnerability of forwards and, more generally, the dangerousness of tackles and collisions.[1297] Dr Pearce's cognitive and motor tests, performed on a cohort of retired NRL players, revealed signs of brain damage.[1298]

In 2008, the NRL began to conduct an injury surveillance system and internal injury reviews.[1299] While data is not published, they reported in 2018, upon request, an annual average incidence of 5.5 instances of concussion per team (namely 88 for 2017 and 86 for 2018, including pre-season).[1300] After a brief upward trend in 2015, these figures are now relatively stable.[1301]

The NRL's stance on concussion management gained momentum in 2011, as the controversy was in full swing in the US,[1302] with the introduction of mandatory concussion protocols, based on the CISG's guidelines.[1303] In 2013, these protocols were amended to prohibit return-to-play during the same game for concussed players

reasons, in particular the fact that rugby league has mainly and almost exclusively developed in Australia (see this chapter, Section IIB), resulting in the grip of Australian sports administrators on this sport.

[1295] Emails from Dr Paul Bloomfield (NRL Chief Medical Officer) to author, 28 April and 10 July 2017. Dr Bloomfield is not certain of the exact timeframes.

[1296] Jason Savage et al., 'The Incidence of Concussion in a Professional Australian Rugby League Team, 1998-2012' (2013) *Journal of Sports Medicine* 1, 1–2 and 4–6 (<https://www.hindawi.com/journals/jsm/2013/304576/>).

[1297] Ibid, 1 and 4–5. As underlined by the authors, the vulnerability of forwards had already been shown in previous studies. The dangerousness of collisions and tackles does not seem to have been subject to an accurate review, but was confirmed by a subsequent study based on a small cohort of players [see Andrew J Gardner et al., 'A Preliminary Video Analysis of Concussion in the National Rugby League' (2015) 29 *Brain Injury* 1182, 1182–3 (Gardner et al., 'Rugby League')].

[1298] Alan Pearce et al., 'Neurophysiological and Cognitive Impairment following Repeated Sports Concussion Injuries in Retired Professional Rugby League Players' (2018) 32 *Brain Injury* 498, 498 and 501–2 (Pearce, 'Rugby League').

[1299] Email from Dr Paul Bloomfield (NRL Chief Medical Officer) to author, 28 April 2017.

[1300] Email from Dr Paul Bloomfield (NRL Chief Medical Officer) to author, 9 November 2018.

[1301] The numbers of diagnosed concussions were lower in 2014, but different rules/criteria were in place then [ibid].

[1302] See eg, this chapter, Sections IA1(g) and IA2 et seq.

[1303] The NRL concussion protocols are not freely available to the public. For more details, see Greenhow, 'Charter', above n 13 in Chapter 1, 15 and 17.

and adopt the SCAT 3, used in addition to CogSport (including pre-season baseline testing).[1304] In 2014, the protocols were supplemented by a specific HIA and temporary concussion substitute, which allows teams to use their substitute as an interchange player for a 15-minute period while a concussion assessment is taking place.[1305] The number of interchanges was also reduced several times to avoid congestion on the field and reduce the risk of injury.[1306] In 2017, the protocols were updated to take the latest CISG's guidelines into account, including the SCAT 5.[1307] Although players' physical assessment still lies with team doctors, match-day doctors with access to video monitors were instituted in 2014 for State of Origin competitions.[1308] Since 2017, match-day doctors have been assisted by a concussion spotter.[1309] For a short period of time, spotters had the power to rule out a player from competing if video replay showed serious symptoms,[1310] but since 2018, they can only refer him to be assessed by team doctors.[1311] An independent process for return-to-practice, including neuropsychological tests, was also implemented for players who sustain two or more head injuries during a season.[1312]

Since 2014, clubs' non-compliance with NRL's protocols has been sanctioned by fines, the amount of which varies according to the Executive Committee's discretion.[1313] The highest sanctions were imposed in 2017 when, following various incidents, three clubs were issued breach notices and fines for a total of AUD350 000 (among which AUD150 000 were confirmed and AUD200 000 suspended with

---

[1304]Greenhow, 'Charter', above n 13 in Chapter 1, 15 and 17; Tony Webeck, 'Concussion Guidelines Explained', *NRL*, 14 March 2014 (<http://www.nrl.com/concussion-guidelines-explained/tabid/10874/newsid/76791/default.aspx>).

[1305]Webeck, above n 1304.

[1306]See eg, 'NRL to Conduct Interchange Rule Review to Reduce "Big Collisions", *ABC*, 24 March 2015 (<http://www.abc.net.au/news/2015-03-25/nrl-to-conduct-interchange-rule-review-to-reduce-27big-collisio/6346064?section=sport>).

[1307]Email from Dr Paul Bloomfield (NRL Chief Medical Officer) to author, 12 November 2018.

[1308]Michael Carayannis, 'State of Origin: NRL Appoints Independent Doctor to Help avoid Concussion Headache', *The Sydney Morning Herald*, 23 May 2014 (<http://www.smh.com.au/rugby-league/league-news/state-of-origin-nrl-appoints-independent-doctor-to-help-avoid-concussion-headache-20140523-zrmh9.html>).

[1309]NRL, media release, 24 May 2017 (<http://www.nrl.com/independent-expert-to-assess-origin-concussions/tabid/10874/newsid/107120/default.aspx>).

[1310]Ibid.

[1311]Adam Pengilly, 'States back in Charge of Concussion Calls', *The Sydney Morning Herald*, 31 May 2018 (<https://www.smh.com.au/sport/nrl/states-back-in-charge-of-concussion-calls-20180531-p4zimm.html>).

[1312]David Riccio, 'NRL Beef Up Concussion Protocols Following Series of Ugly Head Knocks', *The Daily Telegraph*, 29 June 2017 (<http://www.dailytelegraph.com.au/sport/nrl/teams/nrl-beef-up-concussion-protocols-following-series-of-ugly-head-knocks/news-story/d0b7ec049b4f0e48f5df64f6906b6bb1>) (paywall).

[1313]Email from Dr Paul Bloomfield (NRL Chief Medical Officer) to author, 28 April 2017.

one-year probation after the appeal procedure).[1314] However, in 2018, the NRL announced that it would not automatically make concussion breaches public anymore.[1315] Other types of sanctions, such as deregistration of trainers and doctors and loss of premiership points for teams are also regularly discussed, but to date have not been enforced.[1316]

Simultaneously, the NRL took a harsher position on lift tackles that, without being fully prohibited, were subject to a more stringent enforcement.[1317] It also banned shoulder charges to the head, and then all types of shoulder charges where players use a certain amount of force.[1318]

Since 2016, the NRL has provided education to its players on concussion via a specific video, associated presentation and posters.[1319] Coaches, football managers and referees are also instructed in a similar way.[1320] A video, available on the NRL website[1321] and online modules on concussion for all levels of the game complete the picture.[1322]

Finally, injured players are generally entitled to receive their full salary until the end of their contract.[1323] In addition, they can receive a lump-sum fee for career-ending injuries through a hardship fund (AUD3 million per year) that was established as part of the 2018-22 CBA.[1324]

[1314] See NRL, media release, 6 April 2017 (<http://www.nrl.com/nrls-head-injury-protocol-sanctions/tabid/10874/newsid/105412/default.aspx>).

[1315] Russell Kennedy, 'The NRL to Keep Concussion Breaches Secret', *Lexology*, 31 May 2018 (<https://www.lexology.com/library/detail.aspx?g=d6cd4a3e-ddc9-410b-83ea-2b63fa1b7543&utm_source=lexology+daily+newsfeed&utm_medium=html+email+-+body+-+general+section&utm_campaign=australian+ihl+subscriber+daily+feed&utm_content=lexology+daily+newsfeed+2018-06-01&utm_term=>) (paywall).

[1316] See eg, Brad Walter, 'NRL Clubs Face Loss of Competition Points Over Concussion Breaches', *WAtoday*, 23 March 2015 (<http://www.watoday.com.au/rugby-league/league-news/nrl-clubs-face-loss-of-competition-points-over-concussion-breaches-20150323-1m5v3k.html>) (Walter, 'NRL').

[1317] Dan Walsh, 'NRL Cracks Down on lifting Tackles', *NRL*, 16 April 2014 (<http://www.nrl.com/nrl-cracks-down-on-lifting-tackles/tabid/10874/newsid/77691/default.aspx>).

[1318] AAP, 'NRL to Tighten Shoulder Charge Law', *SBS*, 6 August 2015 (<http://www.sbs.com.au/news/article/2015/08/06/nrl-tighten-shoulder-charge-law?utm_source=Clearinghouse+for+Sport&utm_campaign=9a73618d6e-Daily_Sports_News_5_August_20158_4_2015&utm_medium=email&utm_term=0_3515f1cde2-9a73618d6e-316686657>) (AAP, 'NRL').

[1319] Email from Dr Paul Bloomfield (NRL Chief Medical Officer) to author, 28 April 2017.

[1320] Ibid.

[1321] For more details, see the NRL website (<https://playnrl.com/trainer/concussion/>). This video is a short version of the video shown to professional players.

[1322] Email from Dr Paul Bloomfield (NRL Chief Medical Officer) to author, 28 April 2017.

[1323] Email from Dr Paul Bloomfield (NRL Chief Medical Officer) to author, 9 November 2018. The NRL standard player contract is part of the NRL CBA (2018-22), which is not freely available to the public.

[1324] 'NRL Announces Historic CBA Deal', NRL website, 3 November 2017 (<https://www.nrl.com/news/2017/11/03/nrl-announces-historic-cba-deal/>).

The AFL's concussion management is quite similar, but started a couple of years earlier. The AFL has undertaken research on concussion since 1985, and then more intensively since the creation of the AFL Research Board in 1999.[1325] Further impetus was given in 2010 through the creation of a 'Concussion Working Group'.[1326] This group includes AFL Chief Medical Officer Peter Harcourt, assisted by Hawthorn team physician Michael Makdissi, neuropsychologist/lawyer David Maddocks, neurologist Paul McCrory and neurosurgeon Gavin Davis.[1327] These medical experts, who are in their majority known for their scepticism regarding the link between head injuries and brain impairment,[1328] have taken on numerous research projects on behalf of the AFL.[1329]

Some of these projects are ongoing. A good example of this is a project led since 2013 by Drs McCrory and Davis, in partnership with the Florey Institute and the AFLPA.[1330] Aimed at studying the long-term effects of concussion, it started by an extensive survey of former AFL players.[1331] A small cohort was then selected for further tests (such as MRIs) with the avowed aim to carry out, in a more distant future, a series of post-mortem examinations.[1332] Intermediate conclusions, which were released as part of the meetings organised between the four Australian football codes,[1333] indicate that 30% of some 700 respondents believe that past brain injuries are now negatively affecting their life.[1334] This percentage is, as interpreted by Dr

---

[1325]AFL Information Paper, 'Responsible Approach to Concussion in the AFL', May 2012, p. 1. This document is available on the AFL website (<http://www.aflcommunityclub.com.au/fileadmin/user_upload/Coach_AFL/Injury_Management/ResponsibleApproachConcussionintheAFL.pdf>).

[1326]Ibid, 2.

[1327]Ibid.

[1328]Dr McCrory is the leading voice of the AFL Concussion Working Group casting doubt on the growing evidence linking head injuries and brain impairment. He notably declared in 2014 that CTE is an 'almost non existent media beat up' (<http://www.abc.net.au/radionational/programs/backgroundbriefing/concussion-games/5497562>). His position is reiterated in his publications, some of which are co-authored with Dr Davis (see eg, this chapter, footnote 228). In addition, Drs McCrory, Davis and Maddocks were part of the 2016 CISG's Scientific Committee, whose statement reflects the same scepticism (see ibid, and Chapter 2, Section VII).

[1329]AFL Information Paper, 'Responsible Approach to Concussion in the AFL', May 2012, pp. 4–5. See also presentation Patrick Clifton, AFL Concussion Neurology Network, Melbourne, 12 August 2016.

[1330]Presentation Paul McCrory and Gavin Davis, AFL Concussion Neurology Network, Melbourne, 12 August 2016.

[1331]Ibid.

[1332]Ibid.

[1333]Ibid. See also this chapter, Section IIB1(a).

[1334]Ibid. This study shows higher rates than a survey currently being performed by La Trobe University in conjunction with the AFLPA, whose intermediate results show that one in 10 retired players suffered after-effects stemming from head knocks sustained during their careers (Grant Baker and Michael Warner, 'Research Shows Full Extent of Concussion Problem within AFL', *The Herald Sun*, 30 August 2016 (<http://www.heraldsun.com.au/sport/afl/more-news/research-shows-full-extent-of-concussion-problem-within-afl/news-story/7556a0ea7a5d1b72ebd79384f66f07ce>) (paywall).

McCrory, fuelled by the media and other risk factors, such as excessive alcohol consumption.[1335] To date, only one autopsy has been performed, without revealing any signs of CTE.[1336] This project is now competing with the new Australian Sports Brain Bank, launched in 2018 at the University of Sydney's Brain and Mind Centre, in partnership with the Concussion Legacy Foundation in Boston.[1337] The University of Sydney has already persuaded several former professional athletes (including AFL, NRL and rugby union players) to pledge to donate their brain to science.[1338]

In addition, there is the ongoing research by Murdoch University into helmet sensors, as well as by Dr Pearce,[1339] whose previous studies on former AFL players, using cheat-proof brain stimulation testing in conjunction with a battery of psychological assessments, have already revealed the prolonged impact traumatic injury may wreak on the brain.[1340] New studies are expected to follow: In July 2017, the AFL committed, through collective bargaining, to spend at least AUD250 000 annually on concussion research, which the league intends to fund, at least partly, through Tribunal fines.[1341]

The AFL has conducted continuous injury surveillance since the mid-1990s.[1342] In 2017, the AFL published a summary of its concussion audit (2011–17).[1343] They reported an annual average incidence of seven instances of concussion per team for 2017 (namely 126 per year, including pre-season).[1344] The highest incidence was found in 2012, with almost 10 instances of concussion per team (180 per year).[1345]

In early 2000, the AFL initiated a series of rule of play changes to protect players from head and neck injuries.[1346] This included numerous changes, with a primary

---

[1335] Presentation Paul McCrory and Gavin Davis, AFL Concussion Neurology Network, Melbourne, 12 August 2016.

[1336] Presentation Zee Arain, AFL Concussion in Football Conference, Melbourne, 23 March 2017.

[1337] University of Sydney's website (<https://sydney.edu.au/news-opinion/news/2018/03/27/head-first%2D%2Dsports-brain-bank-launched.html?cid=em_se-apr-2018>).

[1338] Ibid.

[1339] Presentation Paul McCrory and Gavin Davis, AFL Concussion Neurology Network, Melbourne, 12 August 2016.

[1340] See eg, Alan J Pearce et al., 'The Long Term Effects of Sports Concussion on Retired Australian Football Players: A Study Using Transcranial Magnetic Stimulation' (2014) 31 *Journal of Neurotrauma* 1139, 1139–45 (Pearce, 'Australian Football').

[1341] Nathan Schmook and Lee Gaskin, 'Players Get 20 Per Cent Pay Rise in New CBA', *AFL*, 20 June 2017 (<http://www.afl.com.au/news/2017-06-20/players-get-20-per-cent-pay-rise-in-new-cba>).

[1342] AFL Information Paper, 'Responsible Approach to Concussion in the AFL', May 2012, p. 1.

[1343] See 2017 AFL Injury Survey, p. 18. This document is available on the AFL website (<http://www.afl.com.au/staticfile/AFL%20Tenant/2017AFLInjuryReport.pdf>).

[1344] 2017 AFL Injury Survey, p. 18.

[1345] Ibid.

[1346] For more details, see AFL Information Paper, 'Responsible Approach to Concussion in the AFL', May 2012, p. 3; AFL Concussion Neurology Network, 12 August 2016.

focus on tackles[1347] that, along with marking contests and bumps, regularly stir up controversy, regardless of the players' position.[1348]

The AFL has been involved in education since 2002,[1349] and adopted its first concussion protocols in 2006.[1350] The AFL protocols and associated rules of the game have evolved over time,[1351] and are similar in essence to those of the NRL,[1352] with two notable exceptions: the absence of temporary concussion substitute (that, after being introduced in 2011, was withdrawn in 2015 because it became potentially redundant with a 4-man bench)[1353] and the exclusive reliance on team doctors, for both on-field and off-field assessment.[1354] Protocols infringement can result in fines up to AUD50 000.[1355]

Furthermore, the negotiation of a new CBA in 2017 was the occasion for the AFL to further improve the financial protection of injured players, already ensured to receive their salary until the end of their contract in case of unavailability.[1356] The new model for career-ending payouts provides for an easier threshold for receiving money that does not discriminate against degenerative or pre-existing injuries.[1357] It benefits from a new pool of AUD4 million per year.[1358]

[1347] Ibid.

[1348] In the same vein, see Michael Makdissi and Gavin Davis, 'Using Video Analysis for Concussion Surveillance in Australian Football' (2016) 19 *Journal of Science and Medicine in Sport* 959, 961.

[1349] Email from Dr Peter Harcourt (AFL Chief Medical Officer) to author, 31 March 2017.

[1350] The AFL concussion protocols are not freely available to the public. For more details, see AFL Concussion Neurology Network, 12 August 2016.

[1351] Ibid.

[1352] AFL Concussion protocols 2017-18 (unpublished, but copy on file with author); AFL Information Paper, 'Responsible Approach to Concussion in the AFL', May 2012, p. 3.

[1353] For more details, see Jon Pierik, 'Sports Doctor Peter Larkins Calls for AFL to Consider Concussion Substitute', *The Age*, 29 May 2017 (<http://www.theage.com.au/afl/afl-news/sports-doctor-peter-larkins-calls-for-afl-to-consider-concussion-substitute-20170529-gwfjun.html>) (Pierik, 'AFL').

[1354] AFL teams do not take part in State of Origin competitions anymore, which are used by the NRL as a trial for match-day doctors. Similarly, the AFL does not resort to independent doctors for return-to-practice. However, the AFL has an external auditing of head injury and concussion management [email from Dr Peter Harcourt (AFL Chief Medical Officer) to author, 4 February 2018].

[1355] Email from Dr Peter Harcourt (AFL Chief Medical Officer) to author, 4 February 2018.

[1356] See AFL CBA (2017-22), Art. 21, as well as previous CBAs. The CBA is available on the AFL website (<http://www.aflplayers.com.au/wp-content/uploads/2017/08/2017-2022-CBA.pdf>).

[1357] See AFL CBA (2017-22), Art. 41, as opposed to previous CBAs.

[1358] See AFL CBA (2017-22), Art. 42 and Schedule B, Nr 7.

Both the NRL and the AFL can count on the strong support of their players' associations.[1359] As already mentioned,[1360] these associations are linked to the AAA, which has played a particularly active role in the field of concussion in recent years. NRL and AFL representatives regularly take part in the CISG's conferences. They have recently attended the Dublin meeting[1361] and other international symposia,[1362] whose best practice is then rediscussed and implemented at the domestic level.[1363]

(b) Legal Activities and Implications

The NRL and the AFL have never been reported defendants in concussion litigation. Nevertheless, the noose is tightening against these two SGBs. Two NRL clubs are being sued over their concussion management.[1364] One of these lawsuits includes pre-trial proceedings against the NRL.[1365] In addition, in 2016, the AFL had to face compensation claims by two players based on its insurance scheme (CBA) after their careers were cut short from successive instances of concussion.[1366] While these claims were first denied (as they did not fit the payout definition of the previous CBA), a confidential agreement, involving hundreds of thousands of dollars, was finally reached in 2017.[1367] Simultaneously, a website was created by a veteran player agent, with the view to finding players willing to file a concussion class action

[1359]One can note in this regard that current RLPA's Chief Executive Officer, Ian Prendergast, a former AFL player, who also spent beforehand six years as a General Manager of the AFLPA (2009–15), is particularly sensitive to the issue of concussion, which he himself experienced during his career.

[1360]See this chapter, Section IIB1(a).

[1361]See Chapter 2, Section IX, footnote 163.

[1362]References to the participation of NRL and AFL representatives in these conferences and symposia can be found in relevant press releases and newspaper articles.

[1363]See this chapter, Sections IIB1(a) and IIB2(a), which refer to the meetings organised by the four Australian football codes.

[1364]Former NRL player James McManus filed a lawsuit against the Newcastle Knights in 2017. He invoked various incidents that led to his early retirement in 2016 due to multiple instances of concussion. During the same year, Brett Horsnell, who played professionally from 1989 to 1998, did the same against the Parramatta Eels, claiming in addition that he possibly suffers from CTE [see eg, Brent Read, 'Brett Horsnell to Claim that he Suffers from Disease that Cost NFL a Billion', *The Australian*, 13 May 2017 (<http://www.theaustralian.com.au/sport/nrl/brett-horsnell-to-claim-he-suffers-from-disease-that-cost-nfl-a-billion/news-story/00691cc2cdff35ebfa5c7ad22cec2d64>); and *McManus v Knights Rugby League Pty Ltd* [2017] NSWSC 1101].

[1365]Ibid.

[1366]Jonno Nash and Charlie Happell, 'Front and Centre: Concussion in AFL Remains a Critical Issue', *ESPN*, 11 May 2017 (<http://www.espn.com.au/afl/story/_/id/19355678/front-centre-head-concussion-remains-critical-issue-afl>).

[1367]Ibid.

against the AFL.[1368] Media reports suggest that a class action is likely to be filed in the Federal Court during 2019, with John Platten and John Barnes, who played in the AFL in the 1980–90s, as possible lead plaintiffs.[1369] More than 70 former players are currently being screened.[1370]

Concussion litigation against the NRL and the AFL would face the same legal difficulties as those discussed for the entities governing rugby union in Australia (duty of care, voluntary assumption of risk, unfavourable position at common law—at least for grassroots sport—, statutes of limitations).[1371] However, such litigation would be even more hypothetical, in the absence of any recognised CTE case in rugby league and Australian Rules football.

Lawyers representing former AFL players have suggested that the 'AFL has known for 40 years about the dangers associated with allowing concussed players to continue to play'.[1372] This claim constitutes an attempt to assimilate the AFL litigation to the NFL litigation. It could face the lower level of controversy and possible concealment often presented as characterising Australian sport,[1373] and will have to be proven through discovery. It may also involve questions around workplace matters involving players and the AFL.[1374] Proceedings could then fall under the Employment and Industrial Relations National Practice Area (NPA), incorporating proceedings 'substantially of a character of employment and/or industrial relations'.[1375]

[1368] Jon Ralph, 'Peter Jess Says He Has Players with Evidence to Sue Over Concussion Management', *The Herald Sun*, 26 February 2016 (<http://www.heraldsun.com.au/sport/afl/more-news/peter-jess-says-he-has-players-with-evidence-to-sue-their-club-over-concussion-management/news-story/44e5f99663e5641139e04eac4f77d741>) (paywall) (Ralph, 'Peter Jess'). A concussion class action could be envisaged in Australia based on the *Federal Court of Australia Act 1976* (Cth) Pt IVA, *Supreme Court Act 1986* (Vic) Pt 4A, *Civil Procedure Act 2005* (NSW) Pt 10 and *Civil Proceedings Act 2011* (Qld) Pt 13A.

[1369] Stuart Honeysett, 'Former Hawthorn Premiership Winner and Brownlow Medallist John Platten Joins AFL Concussion Lawsuit', *Nine*, 28 November 2017 (<https://wwos.nine.com.au/afl/former-hawthorn-browlow-medallist-john-platten-joins-afl-concussion-lawsuit/7e1b5173-cfc7-4a73-ad7b-105dac7c60e7>).

[1370] 'Peter Gordon Doesn't Believe a Concussion Class Action against the AFL Would Be Successful', *The Herald Sun*, 14 September 2018 (<https://www.news.com.au/sport/afl/peter-gordon-doesnt-believe-a-concussion-class-action-against-the-afl-would-be-successful/news-story/2b774aafaf84e6a86c3bb1de9eb1d5b6>).

[1371] See this chapter, Section IIB1(b).

[1372] Honeysett, above n 1369.

[1373] See this chapter, Section IIB1(b).

[1374] Greenhow, Annette, 'A Knock to the Head', *Law Institute of Victoria Journal*, 3 April 2018 (<https://www.liv.asn.au/Staying-Informed/LIJ/LIJ/April/A-knock-to-the-head>) (paywall) (Greenhow, 'Knock').

[1375] Ibid.

(c) Lessons and Significance

The concussion issue in the AFL and NRL is exemplified, in terms of public health, by many concussion-related incidents, which sometimes led to early retirement cases.[1376] The AFL and, with a certain time lag, the NRL, have responded to those concerns by numerous measures that echo each other. These measures go in the right direction and could be extended further. They allowed a stabilisation of the number of concussion instances, after a slight peak,[1377] probably due, at least partly, to a better identification and awareness.[1378]

The AFL and the NRL amended their rules of play in various sectors of the game, with an emphasis on tackles.[1379] The AFL and the NRL adopted concussion protocols aligned with the CISG's guidelines and best practice (including SCAT 5, pre-season baseline testing/Cogsport, and stepwise return-to-practice).[1380] They regularly discuss their content and implementation during international and domestic cross-code meetings (as was the case with the recent Dublin meeting).[1381] They protected injured players against termination and hazards caused by early retirement.[1382] In addition, they launched educational campaigns, undertook internal research and commissioned a few external studies on concussion.[1383] They also gathered concussion-related statistics for internal purposes.[1384] Both benefit from the strong support of their players' associations and the AAA.[1385]

Possible room for improvement first appears when comparing the two codes. The research undertaken by the AFL seems to be more advanced.[1386] It also takes a longer-term perspective, given the fact that it could lead to the creation of a brain bank.[1387] Its continuity and financing are also well thought out, since the AFL has recently committed to spend at least AUD250 000 annually, which will be funded, at least partly, through Tribunal fines.[1388] The NRL stands out because of its concussion protocols. These protocols include a concussion substitute, independent match-day doctors and spotters for State of Origin competitions, an independent process

[1376] See this chapter, Section IIB2(a).

[1377] Ibid.

[1378] Indeed, like for rugby union (see this chapter, Section IIB1(c), footnote 1258), other types of injuries remained stable during the same period [email from Dr Peter Harcourt (AFL Chief Medical Officer) to author, 4 February 2018].

[1379] See this chapter, Section IIB2(a).

[1380] Ibid.

[1381] See Chapter 2, footnote 163, this chapter, Section IIB1(a), and ibid.

[1382] See this chapter, Section IIB2(a).

[1383] Ibid.

[1384] See this chapter, Section IIB2(a).

[1385] See this chapter, Sections IIB1(a) and IIB2(a).

[1386] See this chapter, Section IIB2(a).

[1387] Ibid.

[1388] Ibid.

return-to-practice for players concussed several times, and heavy fines imposed in case of non-compliance – unfortunately these fines are not automatically communicated publicly anymore.[1389]

More generally, both codes should consider further amending their rules of play in order to better protect players, with a main focus on tackles[1390] and, possibly, other dangerous contact and positions to be determined by more comprehensive studies. Independent doctors and spotters could be introduced for all games. Education efforts could be enhanced, bearing in mind the potential long-term medical risks associated with head injuries, and supplemented by setting up an NFL-like whistle blower hotline.[1391] Internal research should avoid any real of perceived bias and presuppositions, and be completed with more independent medical and technological studies. NFL-like concussion reports[1392] could be published. Depending on the evolution of the situation, a NFL-like '88 Plan'[1393] could be put in place in order to cover former players' custodial and medical care costs.

Finally, observations made in relation to rugby union regarding the lack of involvement of Australian governments can be repeated here.[1394] The same goes for the legal framework applicable in case of litigation, and the general environment prevailing in Australian sport.[1395] The pre-trial proceedings against the NRL,[1396] as well as the forthcoming class action against the AFL,[1397] will have to be followed closely.

3 Final Remarks

This section shows that the concussion issue has implications beyond the borders of North America. It reveals numerous measures of concussion management, facilitated by a relatively cooperative environment, which nonetheless has its share of medical and legal disputes (factual and speculative). It demonstrates that even the most proactive SGBs are not immune from litigation, due to alleged past failures. It confirms the need for a more global and harmonised approach.

1389 Ibid.

1390 Ibid.

1391 See this chapter, Section IA1(c).

1392 See this chapter, Section IA1(h).

1393 See this chapter, Section IA1(c).

1394 See this chapter, Section IIB1(a).

1395 See this chapter, Section IIB1(b). See also Section IIB2(b).

1396 See this chapter, Section IIB2(b).

1397 Ibid.

C Other Countries: Switzerland, England, Brazil

This section concludes the case studies by examining concussion in football for three countries: Switzerland, England and Brazil, with the example of ice hockey also included for Switzerland.

While there is no reported concussion litigation against a SGB in those countries, England and Brazil have already been notified of CTE diagnoses in football. Switzerland remains exposed due to its position in the global sporting environment as it hosts the headquarters of the majority of IFs.

Faced with this situation, the competent SGBs with, at the forefront, FIFA, discussed in detail as part of the US case studies, and the IIHF, briefly referred to in opposition to the more lax practices of the NHL, adopted numerous measures of concussion management. These measures share similarities in terms of content and room for improvement. The concerned national SGBs are just starting to realise the potential impact of the issue.

This is also the case for governments. The British government has recently made notable progress, while Brazilian and Swiss governments lag behind.

The following discussion of the experience of these three countries confirms that the concussion controversy is now on a world scale, and requires a more coordinated response. It also reminds us of the importance for SGBs and governments to be proactive, to ensure the greatest possible protection of athletes.

1 Switzerland: Football and Ice Hockey

Switzerland has not had any reported CTE diagnosis or concussion litigation, with the exception of criminal[1398] and insurance claims. Insurance claims have highlighted, in particular, the potential long-lasting effects of sports concussion, and the legal issues that they raised in terms of legal standing (illness, accident) and causality.[1399]

[1398] See STF 134 IV 26, *Andrew McKim vs Kevin Miller* [in 2007, Miller, a former professional ice hockey player, was convicted of physical harm to his opponent by the District Court of Zurich; he also had to pay significant civil damages following the separate civil action of Swiss insurance company Allianz].

[1399] See eg, Cantonal Insurance Court of Fribourg, *Sandy Jeannin vs HDI-Gerling*, 27 July 2017 [in 2015, Jeannin, a professional ice hockey player, had to retire due to multiple instances of concussion; he made a claim on his accident insurer and received partial benefits; the accident insurer ceased payment on the basis that his claim fell outside the definition of 'accident' under Swiss insurance law; he appealed the decision; his appeal was partly upheld by the Cantonal Insurance Court of Fribourg in July 2017, before being settled; email from Alexandre Zen-Ruffinen, (lawyer for the player) to author, 9 October 2018].

Switzerland is worth examining, because of the presence on its territory of almost 70 international sports organisations (the majority of which are, like the IOC, FIFA, UEFA, the IIHF or FINA, recognised by the Olympic Movement) and CAS.[1400] As a country of civil law tradition, it also provides insight into how civil law countries address the issue of concussion.

The two most popular team sports in Switzerland are football and ice hockey. Swiss football is governed by the Swiss Football Association (ASF) and the Swiss Football League (SFL).[1401] The ASF and SFL operate under the general umbrella of FIFA, previously discussed in detail,[1402] and UEFA.[1403] UEFA introduced the FIFA three-minute rule in its own competitions.[1404] It also just set up a concussion working group and invited research proposals to study the risk of heading the ball in young players.[1405]

In addition to complying with FIFA and UEFA rules and having collaborated with FIFA on one of its research projects,[1406] the ASF and SFL have also taken a few initiatives of their own. These initiatives include sending letters to team doctors and referees (reminding them of the existence of the CISG's guidelines and of the exclusive competence of team doctors to perform on-field assessments in the Swiss Championship).[1407] They also require team doctors to have a postgraduate diploma in sports medicine (which usually involves training on concussion) and to participate in annual colloquia.[1408] Finally, a contract template is made available to the different teams.[1409] It refers to the provisions of the *Swiss Code of Obligations*

1400 For more details about the IFs headquartered in Switzerland, see Heinz Rütter and Christian Schmidt, *The Economic Importance of International Sports Organisations in Switzerland*, Report, 2013 (<http://www.fifa.com/mm/document/affederation/footballgovernance/02/22/25/11/international_sports_organisations_report_en_ok_neutral.pdf>); Claude Stricker and Amandine Bouzigue, *The Economic impact of International Sports Organisations in Switzerland* (2008–13), Report, 2015 (<https://www.aists.org/sites/default/files/publication-pdf/aists_economic_impact_study-english-web.pdf>). About CAS, see (<http://www.tas-cas.org/en/index.html>).

1401 See ASF statutes (2013), Art. 2 (<http://www.football.ch/fr/Portaldata/1/Resources/dokumente/offizielle_dokumente_/2013/juli/STATUTEN_F_20130507.pdf>); SFL statutes (2018), Arts. 2-3 (<https://www.sfl.ch/fileadmin/user_upload/Statuts_SFL_300518.PDF>).

1402 See this chapter, Sections IC et seq.

1403 ASF statutes, Arts. 4-5; SFL statutes, Art. 5.

1404 See this chapter, Section IC1.

1405 UEFA, press release, 18 May 2017 (<http://www.uefa.com/insideuefa/protecting-the-game/medical/news/newsid=2470859.html?redirectFromOrg=true>).

1406 See this chapter, Section IC1.

1407 Phone call from Dr Roland Grossen (ASF Medical Commission President) to author, 19 April 2017.

1408 Ibid.

1409 See SFL website (<http://www.football.ch/sfl/fr/Portaldata/2/Resources/reglemente_f/Contrat_de_travail_joueur.pdf>).

(CO) and the *Swiss Federal Law on Accident Insurance (LAA)* regarding players' salary in case of incapacity.[1410]

Swiss ice hockey is run by the Swiss Ice Hockey Federation (SIHF) and the Swiss Ice Hockey League (SIHL), which are themselves hierarchically subject to the IIHF.[1411] The IIHF's longstanding strict rules regarding checks to the head and fights have already been mentioned as opposed to those, more lax regulations, of the NHL.[1412] The IIHF's collaboration with the Mayo Clinic in the organisation of the Ice Hockey Summits was also referred to.[1413] Nevertheless, the IIHF's concussion management also incorporates additional measures, which are somewhat reminiscent of those of other international SGBs, such as FIFA and, above all, World Rugby;[1414] the IIHF provides its scientific and financial support to the CISG.[1415] Additionally, it has medical regulations in place, including brief concussion protocols designed for international competitions.[1416] These protocols are unique in that compliance is overseen by medical supervisors who, since 2016, have also fulfilled the task of concussion spotters.[1417] In each country, chief medical officers are in charge of implementing good practices and education at the domestic level.[1418] Finally, injury surveillance has been conducted during international tournaments since 1998.[1419] Reports published in peer-reviewed journals outline trends relatively similar to those of the NHL with, however, the primary challenge not being the establishment of the rules themselves, but rather their enforcement.[1420]

Emerging efforts can also be identified on a domestic level in Switzerland, where a Concussion Task Force has been created.[1421] This Task Force has published various documents related to concussion management, loosely inspired by the

---

[1410] SFL contract template, Arts. 22-3 (<http://www.football.ch/sfl/fr/Portaldata/2/Resources/reglemente_f/Contrat_de_travail_joueur.pdf>).

[1411] See SIHF statutes (2017), Arts. 2-3 (<https://www.sihf.ch/media/8331/sihf_statuts.pdf>). The SIHL does not have its own legal personality, but is subject to the IIHF as a member of the SIHF.

[1412] See this chapter, Section IB1.

[1413] Ibid.

[1414] See this chapter, Sections IC1 and IIB1(a).

[1415] The IIHF has co-organised the CISG's conferences since 2001. Its Chief Medical Officer, Dr Mark Aubry, has been a member of the CISG's Scientific Committee since then [M Aubry et al., 'Summary and Agreement Statement on the 1st International Conference on Concussion in Sport, Vienna 2001' (2002) 36 *British Journal of Sports Medicine* 6, and subsequent statements].

[1416] IIHF Medical Regulations (2019), pp. 11–12; IIHF Medical Care Guide (2018), p. 35.

[1417] IIHF Medical Care Guide (2018), p. 33; IIHF Medical Regulations (2019), p. 12; IIHF Medical Regulations (2016), p. 17.

[1418] Phone call from Dr Mark Aubry (IIHF Chief Medical Officer) to author, 11 May 2017.

[1419] Ibid. See also IIHF Medical Regulations (2019), p. 11; IIHF Medical Care Guide (2018), p. 20.

[1420] See eg, Markku Tuominen et al., 'Concussion in the International Ice Hockey World Championships and Olympic Winter Games between 2006 and 2015' (2017) 51 *British Journal of Sports Medicine* 244, 244, 247 and 251, who point out that the majority of concussion cases result from illegal contact.

[1421] For more details, see SIHF brochure (2009) (<http://www.sihf.ch/media/4925/siha-broschuere-concussion-ed-24-11-09-2.pdf>).

CISG's guidelines, including a check-up list in case of hit and return-to-play protocols, intended for the multiple use of team doctors, players and coaches.[1422] It also conducts information campaigns for team physicians, coaches and athletes.[1423] The most common breaches of playing rules found by the Disciplinary Committee are published and explained in the form of videos, with an educational perspective.[1424] Finally, research and data collection are undertaken for internal purposes.[1425]

So far, no government initiative has occurred.

The filing of a concussion lawsuit against a SGB in Switzerland is currently speculative. This hypothesis, however, cannot be excluded, in view of the importance of Switzerland on the world sports stage, coupled with the growing controversy at the international level.[1426] This controversy has already indirectly affected the country, through the class action brought against FIFA in the US.[1427]

Since class actions do not exist in Switzerland,[1428] players who consider themselves aggrieved would be forced to sue their governing bodies separately. The first issue to be resolved would be the jurisdiction of the courts. The statutes and regulations of FIFA/UEFA and the IIHF, as well of their Swiss member associations,[1429] contain, like all international Olympic federations,[1430] arbitration clauses in favour of CAS. These clauses are relatively broadly worded, and could potentially be applied. In the absence of an election of law by the parties, CAS would apply Swiss law, on the basis of its rules of procedure.[1431] If there are no arbitration clauses, or even more restrictive clauses, then one should turn to the state courts. In the event that the plaintiff is domiciled abroad, the rules of private international law[1432] may also intervene. These rules provide for a special regime for contractual

---

[1422] Ibid.

[1423] The Task Force notably collaborates with the Schafhauser Foundation (<http://www.respect.sihf.ch/media/1047/respect_my_head_-_brochure_pour_l_entra_neur.pdf>).

[1424] See the SIHF's website (<http://www.sihf.ch/fr/disciplinary/videos/>).

[1425] Email from Claudia Weber (SIHF Youth Sport and Development Officer) to author, citing SIHF Medical Committee, 7 May 2017. See also SIHF injury report form 2018 to 2019 (<http://www.sihf.ch/de/medical/injury-report/?cache=false>).

[1426] See this chapter, Sections IA1(b) et seq (including subsequent case studies) and IIC1.

[1427] See this chapter, Section IC2(b).

[1428] Veuthey, 'Droit suisse', above n 13 in Chapter 1, Rz 41.

[1429] For football, see FIFA statutes, Arts. 57 et seq.; UEFA statutes, Arts. 61 et seq.; ASF statutes, Arts. 89 et seq.; SFL statutes, Arts. 56 et seq. For ice hockey, see IIHF statutes, Arts. 60 et seq.; SIHF statutes, Arts. 114 et seq. These statutes are available on these SGBs' respective websites.

[1430] See interview of Matthieu Reeb, CAS General Secretary, in: *Le Temps*, 5 August 2016 (<https://www.letemps.ch/sport/2016/08/05/sportifs-ont-pris-lhabitude-dexplorer-toutes-voies-reglementaires-possibles>).

[1431] Code of Sports-Related Arbitration (CAS Code, 2017), Rule 45. The CAS Code is available on CAS' website (<http://www.tas-cas.org/fileadmin/user_upload/Code_2017_FINAL__en_.pdf>).

[1432] *Federal Act on International Private Law* (1987) (*PILA*); *Lugano Convention on Jurisdiction and Enforcement of Judgments in Civil and Commercial Matters* (1988) (*Lugano Convention, LC*).

and delictual (torts) actions,[1433] likely to lead to the jurisdiction of Swiss state courts and, hypothetically, the application of Swiss law.

Assuming that Swiss law is applicable, the type of liability would determine the relevant provisions of the *CO*. In the absence of a contract between the players and the various SGBs, the provisions on delicts (torts)[1434] would likely be retained[1435] with, as a requirement, the fulfilment of four conditions: unlawful act/omission, damage, causality between the unlawful act and the damage, and fault attributable to the defendant.[1436] These provisions provide for a relatively short statute of limitations period, which may be exploited by the SGBs sued.[1437] Like in common law countries,[1438] the SGBs in question could also put forward the contributory fault of the players,[1439] the doctrine of voluntary assumption of risk,[1440] or even a possible interruption of the causal link.[1441]

In the absence of legal authority concerning the potential liability of SGBs for concussion in Switzerland, the provisions of the *CO* should, where appropriate, be examined in light of the general case law on sports injuries. This case law is, for the moment, very limited.[1442] In any event, it augurs restricted damages.[1443]

[1433] *PILA*, Arts. 2, 33, 112 et seq and 129 et seq.; *LC*, Arts. 2 et seq. and 5 et seq.

[1434] Arts. 41 et seq. *CO*.

[1435] This interpretation is supported by SFT 121 III 350 (*Fédération Suisse de Lutte Amateur vs Grossen*), where the Swiss Federal Tribunal applied the law of delict to a dispute between a Swiss wrestler and his federation in relation to selection criteria for the 1989 World Championships.

[1436] Art. 41/1 *CO*.

[1437] See Art. 60/1 *CO*. This article provides for a basic period of one year (from the date on which the injured party became aware of the loss/damage and of the identity of the person liable) and an ultimate period of 10 years (after the date on which the loss/damage was caused). In June 2018, the Swiss Parliament passed a revision of the statute of limitations. A special category of damages was created, namely personal injuries, to which a basic limitation period of three years and an ultimate limitation period of 20 years will apply in the future. The revision should come into force during 2019. It does not provide for special transitional provisions for cases that have already become statute-barred. [For more details, see the Swiss Parliament's website (<https://www.parlament.ch/en/ratsbetrieb/suche-curia-vista/geschaeft?AffairId=20130100>)].

[1438] For the US, see in particular this chapter, Sections IA2(a)(ii), IB2(a)(i), and IC2(b). For Canada, see this chapter, Section IIA2.

[1439] Art. 44 *CO*.

[1440] For more details about the application of this theory in civil law, see eg, Manon Simeoni and Pierre Wessner, 'L'acceptation du risque en responsabilité civile, un concept à géométrie variable dans la pratique de sports', in Antonio Rigozzi, Dominique Sprumont and Yann Hafner (eds), *Mélanges en l'honneur de Denis Oswald* (Helbing & Lichtenhahn, 2012) 259, 259–90.

[1441] Art. 41/1 *CO*.

[1442] Landmark cases have so far focused on the (civil or criminal) liability of players. See eg, *Lucien Favre & Gabet Chapuisat*, judgment of the Indictment Chamber of Geneva of 1 September 1986 (SJ 1987 119), upheld on appeal by the Court of Justice of Geneva on 1 March 1988; CAS 2013/A/3280, *Eishockey club Olten & Keller vs Schnyder & SIHF*.

[1443] At the very least for moral suffering. For the rest, the damage would be calculated based on the concrete loss suffered by the victim.

2 England: Football

England, and more generally, the UK, also has its share of concussion controversies in various sports. For example, a former English rugby league player, who sustained a career-ending concussion in 2013, is currently suing his former club's team doctors for an alleged clinical negligence.[1444] However, it is football that is the most relevant to the question examined in this thesis (professional sport and SGBs).

English football is governed by The Football Association (The FA) and the English Premier League (EPL),[1445] in compliance with the regulatory scheme set at the international level by FIFA and UEFA,[1446] explained above.[1447] The FA and the EPL were first publicly confronted with the concussion issue through the case, mentioned above,[1448] of former international English player Jeff Astle, who died in 2002, aged 59, after a long decline.

Astle's widow was convinced from the outset that her husband's death was linked to football practice, and headers in particular.[1449] Her battle was met with indifference in England—The FA and the EPL only answering her inquiries by sending laconic letters and free tickets.[1450] The case started, however, to gain momentum from 2014, following Astle's formal diagnosis of CTE and the filing of the concussion class action against FIFA in the US.[1451]

In 2015, The FA became the first football national association to adopt concussion protocols.[1452] The protocols reflect the CISG's guidelines and international best practice (including the prohibition of return-to-play during the same game for concussed players, SCAT 3, pre-season baseline testing, stepwise return-to-

[1444]The player, Cillian Willis, filed a lawsuit against the Sale Sharks and its team doctors in 2016. The lawsuit was discontinued against the Sale Sharks 'without any payment of compensation' in 2018, but is still pending against the team doctors [Rob Bleaney, 'Cillian Willis to Sue Sale Sharks Over Concussion Which Ended His Career', *The Guardian*, 23 August 2016 (<https://www.theguardian.com/sport/2016/aug/23/cillian-willis-sue-sale-sharks-concussion-saracens>); Sale Sharks' website (<https://www.salesharks.com/2019/01/08/club-statment-cillian-willis/>)]. This case is not an exception in Europe. Similar litigation, involving professional rugby union player Jamie Cudmore and its former club, ASM Clermont, is currently pending in France.

[1445]See The FA Handbook 2018-19, Introduction by the Chairman and Professional Game Board, Part A 1.1 (<http://handbook.fapublications.com/#!/book/26>); House of Commons, Culture, Media and Sport Committee, *Football Governance* (2010-12) (<https://publications.parliament.uk/pa/cm201012/cmselect/cmcumeds/792/792i.pdf>), and previous inquiries.

[1446]The FA Handbook 2018–19, Rules of the Association, Part A 1(b).

[1447]See this chapter, Sections IC1 and IIC1.

[1448]See this chapter, Section IC1.

[1449]Brett Gibbons, 'Jeff Astle's Widow Accuses FA of "Lies" Over Albion Star's Death', *The Birmingham Mail*, 18 March 2014 (<http://www.birminghammail.co.uk/news/midlands-news/jeff-astles-widow-accuses-fa-6846102>).

[1450]Ibid.

[1451]See this chapter, Sections IC1 and IC2(b).

[1452]The FA's Concussion Guidelines (2015) (<http://www.thefa.com/get-involved/coach/concussion>) (23 August 2017); Peters, above n 726.

practice).[1453] Their peculiarity lies in the introduction of 'tunnel doctors', paid by the home team to assist team doctors by spotting potential instances of concussion and watching replays to assess the severity of incidents.[1454] Simultaneously, The FA announced the launch of educational campaigns, in conjunction with the EPL, aimed at making players and managers at all levels aware of the dangers of head injuries.[1455] The FA also indicated that it would employ its own doctor to conduct research and liaise with club medical staff on key medical matters.[1456] In 2017, after a failed first attempt, The FA, together with the Professional Footballers' Association (PFA), got involved in research.[1457] They invited independent researchers to submit proposals for a study on the prevalence of degenerative brain diseases among football players.[1458] In 2018, the study, titled 'Football's Influence on Lifelong Health and Dementia Risk' formally started, under the leadership of Dr Stewart, previously mentioned.[1459]

These measures, however, only temporarily alleviated the controversy, fuelled again by the revelation of numerous dementia cases among former football players, including four of the eight surviving outfield players of the 1966 World Cup-winning team,[1460] and newly recognised CTE cases in the UK.[1461]

The British government also put in place general measures primarily focused on grassroots and youth sport. In 2014, a group of experts led by labour politician Chris Bryant published a report on the issue of concussion in sport, highlighting various possible lines for action with, as a priority, a parliamentary inquiry.[1462] During the

---

1453 Richard Conway, 'Premier League to Introduce New Rules on Head Injuries', *BBC*, 5 August 2014 (<http://www.bbc.com/sport/football/28656263>).

1454 Ibid.

1455 Ibid.

1456 Ibid.

1457 In 2001, the FA and the PFA had already initiated a study focused on following a group of young football players over 10 years. The study was dropped after five years, due apparently to a lack of participants available in the long run. Its preliminary conclusions have never been published [Jeremy Wilson, 'Football's Brain Injury Risk No Lower Now than in the Past', *The Telegraph*, 31 May 2016 (<http://www.telegraph.co.uk/football/2016/05/31/footballs-brain-injury-risk-no-lower-now-than-in-the-past-warn-m/>) (Jeremy Wilson, 'Risk'); Jeremy Wilson, 'FA Finally Opens Study into Link between Football and Dementia in Victory for the Telegraph and Astle Family', *The Telegraph*, 30 March 2017 (<http://www.telegraph.co.uk/football/2017/03/30/fa-finally-opens-study-link-football-dementia-victory-telegraph/>) (Jeremy Wilson, 'Study')].

1458 Ibid.

1459 Anne Galland, 'Football Headers and Dementia: Five Minutes with Willie Stewart' (January 2018) Vol. 360 Issue 8137 *BMJ* 190, 190.

1460 Jeremy Wilson, 'FA Invites Jeff Astle's Daughter to Join Panel on Head Injuries', *The Telegraph*, 28 July 2016 (<http://www.telegraph.co.uk/football/2016/07/28/fa-invite-jeff-astles-daughter-to-join-panel-on-head-injuries/>) (Jeremy Wilson, 'Panel').

1461 See this chapter, Section IC1.

1462 The report also proposed other measures: a single set of concussion management protocols covering all sports, independent peer-reviewed research into concussion and British sport, a clear message that concussion can kill and better coordination between sports, schools, colleges and

same year, Bryant organised a parliamentary roundtable on the management of concussion in sport, and publicly expressed his fear of seeing a wave of concussion litigation in his territory.[1463] In 2016, an independent group was set up to lay down the foundations of a duty of care review, with the view to improving safety and welfare of sports participants.[1464] In 2018, an all-party parliamentary group found that schools, colleges, universities and even healthcare professionals lack understanding of sports-related brain injuries and urged the government to step up.[1465] This finding triggered a discussion about the need to adopt a simple set of protocols applying to every sport at every level across the UK.[1466]

The UK is also part of an interesting international project, the European Union Injury Database (EU IDB).[1467] This database, set up in 1999, is run by the European Commission.[1468] It regroups injury data (including concussion) collected in hospitals by 31 countries.[1469] It contributes to the standardisation of injury and accident surveillance and storage in the EU, through a codification manual/dictionary[1470] with various modules, related to sports activities (including amateur sport), work injuries (including professional sport), home injuries and transport. The UK's

---

doctors. In addition, it opened the debate as to whether restrictions should be placed on full contact and headers in youth rugby and football. A full version of the report is available on the Scribd's website (<https://fr.scribd.com/document/229341836/Concussion-Can-Kill-Call-for-Inquiry>).

[1463]John F Burns, 'In Europe, Echoes of America as Concussions Spur Debate', *The New York Times*, 5 April 2014 (<https://www.nytimes.com/2014/04/06/sports/in-europe-echoes-of-america-as-concussions-spur-debate.html>).

[1464]For more details, see the UK Government's website (<https://www.gov.uk/government/consultations/sport-duty-of-care-review-call-for-evidence>).

[1465]For more details, see All-Party Parliamentary Group, *Acquired Brain Injury and Neurorehabilitation, Time for Change,* Report, 2018 (<https://www.ukabif.org.uk/wp-content/uploads/2018/10/1533_40pp_APPG-on-ABI_Report_Time-for-Change_2018_AW_SINGLES_WEB.pdf>).

[1466]Jeremy Wilson, 'Exclusive: Single Protocol Needed to Treat Brain Injuries in Sport, Urges Report', *The Telegraph*, 9 October 2018 (<https://www.telegraph.co.uk/sport/2018/10/09/exclusive-single-protocol-needed-treat-brain-injuries-sport/>) (Jeremy Wilson, 'Protocol').

[1467]For more details, see the European Commission's website (<https://ec.europa.eu/health/data_collection/databases/idb_en>).

[1468]Ibid.

[1469]For more details, see Eurosafe's website, which publishes regular reports on the data collected (<http://www.eurosafe.eu.com/key-actions/injury-data/reports>). Among these 31 countries, 26 have provided full data.

[1470]The latest version of this Dictionary is available on the Eurosafe's website (<http://www.eurosafe.eu.com/uploads/inline-files/IDB%20JAMIE%20FDS%20Data%20Dictionary%20MAR14.pdf>).

contribution, although praiseworthy in principle, is currently deemed to be unsatisfactory, due to implementation and harmonisation issues on its own territory.[1471]

In the event that a concussion lawsuit or class action[1472] was to affect English sport, and football in particular, it would be assessed based on the common law principles examined as part of the previous case studies.[1473] Moreover, British state courts, called upon to judge the liability of SGBs in case of sports injuries, have so far been mindful of athletes' protection.[1474] The apparent restrictive nature of the UK statute of limitations could be mitigated by a fairly broad discretion given to judges.[1475] In the absence of a general CAS clause in The FA's regulations, a possible jurisdiction of CAS would be questionable, without being totally excluded.[1476]

3 Brazil: Football

Brazil was affected by the concussion controversy in 2014, when the former captain of the Brazilian football national team, Hilderaldo Bellini was diagnosed with CTE.[1477] A few football players were also in the news after returning to play despite a concussion, or being sidelined due to memory loss.[1478] Nevertheless, this did not

---

[1471] For more details, see Eurosafe's website, which gives regular updates on the IDB's implementation in relation to each country (<http://www.eurosafe.eu.com/key-actions/injury-data/reports>).

[1472] See eg, *Civil Procedure Rules & Practice Directions*, Part. 19.

[1473] See in particular this chapter, Sections IA2(a) et seq, IB2(a) et seq and IC2(b).

[1474] The landmark case is *Watson v BBBC* [2001] QB 1134. Watson, a professional boxer, spent 40 days in a coma and six years in a wheelchair following a knockout during a match in 1991. He sued the British Boxing Board of Control (BBBC). He claimed that the BBBC had been negligent in the rules it created in relation to medical facilities and assistance provided to boxers at ringside. Watson was awarded almost £1 million by the High Court and Court of Appeal, eventually reduced to £400 000 after a settlement agreement.

[1475] The *Limitation Act 1980* (UK) provides for a three-year limitation period for personal injury actions. This period normally starts to run from the date of the injury. However, in case of latent injuries, the 'date of knowledge', as defined by section 14, prevails. See also section 33, which gives the court a fairly broad discretion to disapply the three-year period.

[1476] To date, CAS has never used this argument to declare itself incompetent in a case involving The FA, finding the FIFA statutes (see this chapter, Section IIC1, footnote 1429), the order of procedure signed by the parties, or even their lack of objection to be a sufficient reason to review the case. However, it adopted a different approach in a case involving the EPL [see CAS 2005/A/952, *Ashley Cole v Football Association Premier League (FAPL)*].

[1477] See this chapter, Section IC1.

[1478] See eg, 'Uruguaio do Sao Paulo bate a cabeza, repeta cena da Copa e volta ao juogo', *UOL Esporte*, 2 August 2014 (<https://esporte.uol.com.br/futebol/campeonatos/brasileiro/serie-a/ultimas-noticias/2014/08/02/uruguaio-do-sao-paulo-bate-a-cabeca-repete-cena-da-copa-e-volta-ao-jogo.htm>); 'Miranda sofre concussão em choque com Alisson é cortado da Seleção Brasileira após perder memória', *Fox Sports*, 1 September 2017 (<https://www.foxsports.com.br/news/320799-miranda-sofre-concussao-em-choque-com-alisson-e-cortado-da-selecao-brasileira-apos-perder-memoria>); 'Marcelo encaminhado para o hospital com concussão cerebral', *Record*, 24 February

really raise the awareness level in Brazil, both from the point of view of SGBs and governments.

The Brazilian Football Confederation (CBF) holds the right to lead football in Brazil.[1479] It is a member of FIFA, previously examined in detail,[1480] and of CONMEBOL.[1481] While CONMEBOL has incorporated FIFA's three-minute rule in its competition regulations,[1482] the CBF has, to date, not undertaken any substantial measures in relation to concussion. However, the CBF has published a Brazilian translation of the CISG's guidelines (pocket version) on its website, designed to assist non-medically trained individuals to identify possible concussion at the community level.[1483] In addition, in 2014, it was forced by a court ruling to grant a minimum of three days between games of each team in order to allow players to recover and to reduce injuries.[1484] The Brazilian federal government adopted a general legislation (commonly referred to as *'Pelé Law'*, after Brazil's most famous football player) [1485] that regulates various aspects of sports law.[1486] The *Pelé Law* requires clubs to have an insurance policy that covers athletes' injuries or death during their employment.[1487] SGBs are also subject to compulsory insurance, but only for non-professional athletes participating in Olympic competitions.[1488] This obligation is likely to be extended soon to all athletes without exception.[1489]

Although the overwhelming majority of injury decisions in Brazil have been ruled against clubs and their medical staff (with a strong propensity to protect the injured party),[1490] a concussion lawsuit or class action[1491] against a SGB would also

---

2018 (<https://www.record.pt/futebol/futebol-nacional/liga-nos/rio-ave/detalhe/marcelo-encaminhado-para-o-hospital-com-concussao-cerebral>).

[1479]CBF statutes, Art. 1.

[1480]See this chapter, Sections IC et seq.

[1481]CBF statutes, Art. 1.

[1482]See this chapter, Section IC1.

[1483]CBF website (<https://cdn.cbf.com.br/content/201508/20150828190703_0.pdf>).

[1484]*Federação Nacional dos Atletas Profissionais de Futebol (FENAPAF) v Confederação Brasileira de Futebol (CBF)*, Labour Court of Campinas, 12 June 2017.

[1485]*Law 9615/98.*

[1486]For more details about the *Pelé Law* and other sports law legislation in Brazil, see Adolpho Julio Camargo de Carvalho, Chapter 3, Brazil in András Gurovits (ed), *The Sports Law Review* (Law Business Research, 2nd ed, 2016) 26, 26–35.

[1487]*Law 9615/98*, Art. 45.

[1488]*Law 9615/98*, Art. 82-B.

[1489]Legislative bill n° 531/2011, 'Anteprojeto da Lei Geral do Esporte Brasileiro', ad Art. 45. This bill, if accepted, would also introduce a joint liability regime between SGBs and clubs in case of accident or death.

[1490]For a summary of the case law, see Danielle Maiolini and Leila Barreto, '*Lesões no Esporte Profissional – a Jurisprudência Trabalhista sobre o Seguro Desportivo'* (2017) Nr 38 *Revista Síntese de Direito Desportivo* 81, 81–90, as well as previous commentaries published as part of the same review (eg, 2014, Nr 18).

[1491]The Labour Public Prosecutor's Office could propose a class action against a SGB before state courts based on Art. 83, II of *Complementary Law 75/93* and Art. 7, XXII of the *Constitution*. If

be possible. Again, it would be necessary to determine who, between state and arbitral tribunals, should be responsible, it being specified that the CBF only recognises the jurisdiction of CAS in the event of a dispute involving FIFA.[1492] Since Brazil is a civil law country, the provisions of the *Civil Code (CC)* on delicts would be relevant. These provisions incorporate the four usual conditions of delicts (unlawful act/omission, damage, causality, fault).[1493] In addition, they provide for a derogatory regime, called 'strict liability', which establishes an obligation to compensate the damage regardless of fault 'when the activity normally developed implies, by its nature, a risk to the rights of others'.[1494]

This means that SGBs that fail to take out insurance, or even to set appropriate measures of concussion management, are exposed to increased liability.[1495] However, as a defence, they could attempt to invoke the contributory fault of the players, the interruption of the causal link or even the doctrine of voluntary assumption of risk.[1496] The statute of limitations may also be relevant in specific instances.[1497]

4 Lessons and Significance

Switzerland, England and Brazil, examined in this section through the example of football, plus ice hockey in Switzerland, have all been made aware of the concussion controversy. This was manifested by the discovery of several CTE cases in England and Brazil. Switzerland's exposure is more hypothetical, since it mainly results from the presence of IFs on its territory, coupled with the growing controversy at the international level.[1498]

Various concussion management measures have been taken by the relevant international SGBs. The IIHF, known for its more proactive concussion

[1492]See CBF statutes (2015), Arts. 75 and 73. The new CBF statutes (2017) regulate arbitration at Arts. 122-34 and 158. They do not expressly refer to CAS anymore, but the logic remains the same, based on the 2018 FIFA Statutes, Arts. 57-9.

[1493]Art. 186 *CC*.

[1494]Art. 927 *CC*.

[1495]In the same vein (regarding the liability of a football club for the ankle injury of one of its players), see eg, *Thiago Dutra Regis v Joinville Esporte Clube*, Superior Labor Court, 7 March 2014. In this case, the Court considered that the absence of insurance, as required by the *Pelé Law*, represented an omission constituting an unlawful act giving entitlement to financial compensation under the rules of strict liability.

[1496]For contributory negligence and the interruption of the causal link, see Arts. 945 and 186 *CC*. The doctrine of voluntary assumption of risk could also be envisaged. However, it may come into conflict with Art. 2 of the *Labour Code*, according to which all risks related to the economic activity pursued shall be borne by the employer (regardless of causation).

[1497]See Art. 206 §3, V *CC*, which provides for a three-year deadline. According to the case law, this deadline only starts to run from the knowledge of the damage [see eg, *Altair da Silva v Sadia S.A*, Paraná Regional Labour Court, 28 September 2010].

[1498]See also the case of Sandy Jeannin (early retirement due to concussion) mentioned in this chapter, Section IIC1, footnote 1399.

management than the NHL, shares similarities with FIFA, in terms of overall vision and scope for progress. However, it is distinguished by some specific features, such as the existence of brief concussion protocols for international competitions, the implementation of which is ensured by its own medical supervisors/spotters.

The national SGBs concerned are only starting now to follow the move, after a longstanding ‘wait-and-see’ approach. The same is true for governments. The British government has recently made notable progress, while Brazilian and Swiss governments trail behind.

This section confirms that the concussion controversy is expanding worldwide, and requires a more coordinated response in order to better protect athletes. It also reminds us of the importance for SGBs and governments to act upstream, before incidences and consequences of concussive events cause more pain and suffering to athletes and more litigation.

Chapter 4
General Trends

> We cannot undo the past, but we are bound to pass it in review in order to draw from it such lessons as may be applicable to the future.
>
> Winston Churchill, House of Commons, 16 April 1936.

I Introduction

The national and sport cases studies, in Chapter 3, reveal much about the response of SGBs and governments to the growing issue of concussion in sport. Different levels of awareness and commitment to addressing the issue are evident and there is significant diversity in the nature of measures that have been implemented. Nonetheless, there is much that is common and there are early indications of co-ordinated action.

This chapter identifies and briefly evaluates the common risks, good practices, existing shortcomings and themes revealed by the data collected in the case studies.[1] It aims to indirectly expose means by which concussion could be better regulated from a public health and legal risk perspective.

The analysis commences with a tabular representation of the incidence of CTE diagnosis (confirmed by autopsy, and believed to result from head trauma) and CTE-related litigation activity on a country-by-country basis subdivided into sports. It then examines the responses of SGBs and governments, based on categories already outlined in the case studies.

For SGBs, their responses are divided into five broad categories:

(1) Rules of play;
(2) Rules of the game and medical/concussion protocols;

[1]Collective expressions such as 'SGBs' and 'governments' should be taken as references to those considered in the case studies only.

A. Veuthey, *Concussion in Professional Team Sports: Time for a Harmonised Approach?*, https://doi.org/10.1007/978-981-15-1979-6_4

(3) Financial support for injured athletes;
(4) Education; and
(5) Research and data collection.

A similar approach is taken for governments for which there are four categories:

(1) Legislative interventions and guidelines;
(2) Other Congressional and parliamentary interventions;
(3) Education; and
(4) Research and data collection.

Included among the responses of governments is the work of some private bodies which are not SGBs but which receive government support to address the concussion controversy.

The chapter then offers some general observations on access to documentation and transparency, the potential for conflicted interests among stakeholders and emerging features of a harmonised approach. It concludes with a summary of the main findings.

II General Overview of the Concussion Controversy

The following tables show the incidence of CTE diagnosis and CTE-related litigation activity on a country-by-country basis subdivided into sports.

American football, ice hockey, Canadian football, baseball and rugby union all have CTE diagnoses. Water polo, rugby league and Australian Rules football have so far been spared.

Numerous class actions have been filed against SGBs (NFL, NHL, FIFA, USAWP, CFL). Three of these class actions (NHL, CFL, USAWP) are still pending, while the others have led to various outcomes, ranging from the USD1 billion settlement for the NFL to the dismissal on procedural grounds for FIFA. Legal proceedings are expected against the NRL and the AFL.

– United States

Sports	CTE diagnoses	Litigation
American football	- 110 CTE diagnoses in former NFL players (2005–17); - 177 CTE diagnoses if high school (3), college (48), semi-professional sport (9) and CFL (7) included (2005–17).	- Class action vs the NFL, US District Court/Pennsylvania (2012); - Settlement (2015).
Ice hockey	- 7 CTE diagnoses in former NHL players (2009–18); - 4 CTE diagnoses in former junior players (2015–17).	- Class action vs the NFL, US District Court/Minnesota (2014); - Discovery process (ongoing).
Football	- 1 CTE diagnosis in former US semi-professional player (2012); - 1 CTE diagnosis in US individual who had played football in high school (2015); - 7 CTE diagnoses outside the US (see below, England (6) and Brazil (1)).	- Class action vs FIFA, US Soccer et al., US District Court/California (2014); - Order (dismissal) vs FIFA based on procedural grounds (2015); - Settlement with US Soccer (2015).
Baseball	- 1 CTE diagnosis in former MLB player (2013).	X
Water polo	X	- Class action vs USAWP, US District Court/California (2015); - Order (dismissal) based on procedural grounds (2016).

– Canada

Sports	CTE diagnoses	Litigation
Canadian football	- 9 CTE diagnoses in former CFL players (Canadian autopsies, 2013–15; no statistics released afterwards); - 7 CTE diagnoses in former CFL players (US autopsies).	- Lawsuit vs the CFL et al., Supreme Court of British Columbia (2014); - Judgment (dismissal) based on procedural grounds (2016); upheld by British Columbia Court of Appeal (2017) and the Supreme Court of Canada (2018). The plaintiff had to go to arbitration (pending); - Class action vs the CFL et al., Ontario Supreme Court (2015; currently on hold); - Grievance procedure between the CFL and the CFLPA (2018, pending).

- Australia

Sports	CTE Diagnoses	Litigation
Rugby union	- 1 CTE diagnosis in former ARU player (2014).[2]	X
Rugby league	X	X (but pre-trial proceedings vs the NRL; 2017)
Australian Rules football	X	X (but class action under preparation; 2017)

- Switzerland

Sports	CTE diagnoses	Litigation
Various (70 international sports federations only in the canton of Vaud—football and ice hockey examined as examples)	X	X

- England

Sports	CTE diagnoses	Litigation
Football	- 1 CTE diagnosis in former EPL and English national team player (2014; death already attributed to an 'industrial disease' in 2002); - 1 CTE diagnosis in former EPL player (2014); - 4 CTE diagnoses in former UK players, including a former EPL player (2017).	X

- Brazil

Sports	CTE diagnoses	Litigation
Football	- 1 CTE diagnosis in former Brazilian team player (2014).	X

The main conclusion to be drawn from the above tables is that the concussion controversy is expanding across countries and sports. It now manifests on a large scale, which contrasts with the measures still often taken in a compartmentalised manner by SGBs and governments.

[2]Another CTE case was found in rugby union in 2014 in a semi-professional ruby union player in Ireland.

III The Regulatory Activity of Sports Governing Bodies (SGBs)

A Rules of Play

The amendment of the rules of play constitutes a key measure for the prevention or reduction of concussion.

The vast majority of SGBs that have the authority to amend the rules of play of their sport have also acted in this direction, to varying degrees. The NFL is at the top of the scale (with dozens of changes in recent years). In contrast, FINA has not adopted any new rules.

Scope for progress still exists in all the sports examined. The more a sport may be regarded as violent (eg, American football), the greater its scope for progress. For sports where physical contact between players is mainly incidental (eg, football and baseball), there is less scope for progress through changing the rules of play. Considering the welfare of the players should outweigh any fear by administrators of changing the nature of the sport in question, and possibly making it less attractive for fans, by removing part of its physicality.

Sub-concussion, resulting from minor, repeated blows to the head, may also benefit from these amendments, as well as from specifically targeted rules. Technological innovation (eg, lighter balls) may in addition be valuable in football, where the issue of headers complicates the picture.

B Rules of the Game and Medical Guidelines/Concussion Protocols

Chapter 2 highlighted the diversity of the medical guidelines available to define, identify, treat and manage concussion. However, the CISG's guidelines have an increasing authority at the international level, despite issues related to their content and, more generally, their exclusive reliance on SGBs' scientific and financial contributions. This section focuses on the use of the CISG's guidelines in practice.

All the North American and Australian leagues have been inspired by the CISG's guidelines to establish their own concussion protocols (either in full, or, like the MLB, in conjunction with other guidelines). In rare cases, leagues (eg, MLS, MLB) have submitted these protocols to collective bargaining, by annexing them to their CBAs. IFs have also referred to the CISG's guidelines, either when setting up their own concussion protocols (eg, World Rugby, IIHF) or, at the very least, by means of recommendation (eg, FIFA, FINA). A few national entities have also acted, either to fill the regulatory gap left by their respective upper governing bodies (eg, The FA, USAWP), or to interpret the protocols of the aforementioned bodies (eg, Rugby Australia).

While an in-depth analysis of SGBs' protocols is rendered laborious by their difficulty of access in full, it should be noted that they are usually in line with the

CISG's guidelines (in their 2016 or previous versions). The main flaws were identified at the national levels (eg, USAWP), in particular in the absence of appropriate international leadership.

These protocols (and their related rules of the game) are, however, characterized by a certain lack of homogeneity.

Thus, while the SCAT, developed by the CISG, is endorsed by all SGBs for sideline assessments, it is often used under a modified form, and implemented in different ways. A few SGBs have introduced independent doctors (eg, NFL, World Rugby, NRL) and concussion/injury spotters (eg, NFL, NHL, CFL, IIHF). The aim is to assist or even supervise team physicians—whose conflict of interest has already been emphasized—[3] and improve concussion identification and management during games. Some leagues (eg, NFL, NHL, MLB, NRL) have also instituted an independent process for return-to-practice (involving a neuropsychologist). These mechanisms are sometimes limited to specific competitions and circumstances (eg, World Rugby, IIHF, NRL).

In some cases, the situation is further complicated by the presence, within medical teams, of athletic trainers/therapists, who may be tasked with helping, or even supplanting (eg, MLB), team physicians.

The use of video is becoming increasingly popular, either during games, or later on, to perform further analysis on the issue of concussion, including their number and causes.

Similarly, baseline testing (either IMPaCT or CogSport) is quite widespread. It appears to be complemented, on specific occasions, by neuropsychological assessments.

A few SGBs (eg, World Rugby, NRL, previously AFL) have also introduced a temporary concussion substitute in order to prevent injured players from remaining on the pitch for fear of seeing their team outnumbered, at least in some competitions (World Rugby). FIFA has preferred to adopt a more global approach, by conducting tests to soften its substitution rules. The option of a substitute not counting against the team's substitutions during the game was only applied at lower levels of football governance.

These differences are partly explained by the specificities of each sport (eg, rules and conditions of play, substitution practices),[4] or even by practical considerations (eg, financial means, number of matches during the regular season).[5] However, they

---

[3]See Chapter 2, Section IV and Chapter 3, Section IA2(b).

[4]Player assessment during a game will not be the same depending on whether a sport is practiced in the water, on grass or on the ice. Likewise, concussion substitutes are primarily beneficial for sports without an interchange bench with free flow of athletes, especially when there are a limited number of substitutions.

[5]In the same vein, see Deubert et al., above n 432 in Chapter 3, 53, footnote Y. These authors highlight that the difference between the NFL and NHL policies regarding independent doctors might be partly explained by practical reasons, in particular the number of games during the regular season (256 NFL games versus 1312 NHL games). The authors also provide an estimate of the revenues of the main US leagues (and the CFL)—ranging from USD14 billion for the NFL to USD200 million for the CFL [Ibid, 14], which may partly justify some disparities when compared to each other, but above all when put into perspective with other sports/countries with more limited financial means.

may also, in some cases, reflect different strategic approaches and sensitivities[6] that will have to be, as far as possible, reconciled, taking into account players' interests first and foremost.[7] Emerging harmonisation efforts have already been made in this direction by some SGBs, through the AAA, NFL Think Tanks and the Dublin meeting (which resulted in the publication of the CISG's implementation paper in 2018).

In addition to the issue of harmonisation, it is important to address compliance. Besides the presence of independent contributors, mentioned above, the establishment of a systematic review process, coupled with heavy fines against non-compliant clubs (eg, NFL, NRL), may have a positive effect in this regard. These fines have deterrent and punitive effects, and also represent a possible 'tied' source of funding for concussion management or research (eg, AFL). They could be coupled with the loss of points, or even the deregistration or suspension of responsible personnel.

Harmonisation and compliance issues are even more acute with regard to sports overseen by an IF, because of the multiple layers of governance involved.

The IFs examined (including World Rugby, the IIHF and FIFA, which are all members of the CISG) are at varying stages of progress in managing these issues. World Rugby, which has made available its HIA and related concussion substitute to its members, is the most advanced. However, World Rugby's HIA only applies on a voluntary basis, reducing its geographical scope. Moreover, compliance is not systematically monitored. Then follows the IIHF, which adopted a brief protocol, applicable only in competitions organised under its auspices, and whose compliance is controlled by its own spotters. FIFA and FINA simply refer to the CISG's guidelines as a recommendation.

C Financial Support for Injured Athletes

The review of the CBAs concluded by the North American and Australian leagues/unions offers various lessons regarding the financial support provided to injured athletes and its possible impact on player safety and welfare. Standard contracts (as vectors that can influence the behaviour of players, potentially inclined to hiding their symptoms by fear of losing their income) are of particular interest.

[6]The introduction of independent contributors for on-field and off-field player assessments presupposes the willingness to take away part of team doctors' prerogatives. Similarly, the institution of concussion substitutes and baseline testing implies the readiness to guard against the risks of cheating, to which adds, for concussion substitutes, the acceptance to alter the game (see Chapter 2, Section IX, footnote 151 and Chapter 3, Section IC3, footnotes 855 and 856).

[7]For instance, sports such as football (see Chapter 3, Sections IC1, IIC2 and IIC3) that do not facilitate the recommended 10 minutes off-field assessment for the SCAT should amend their regulations rather than expecting clinicians to compromise the concussion evaluation and, possibly, athlete safety.

In the US and Canada, players contracts tend to be fully guaranteed against injuries, with the exception of the NFL and CFL. The same trend was found in Australia.

Increased guaranteed compensation, as a way to protect player health, would be worth considering, while ensuring that the average duration of contracts is not reduced with the view to counteracting this protection.

With regard to health related benefits, the NFL '88 Plan', which covers medical, residential and home care costs of former players with dementia, Parkinson's or ALS, is worthy of attention. This is also the case of the Australian leagues' recent efforts aimed at facilitating the internal resolution of disputes related to early retirements due to concussion (through the payment of substantial lump sum fees, which do not discriminate against degenerative or pre-existing injuries).

These measures have undeniably been taken in response to a real need. The expediency of extending them to a wider international level, with or without adjustments and complementary measures, shall vary depending on the specific circumstances of each sport/country, as well as the development of medical science.

As things stand, SGBs that do not have CBAs act in a more opaque way. Nonetheless, they should also provide players with adequate compensation and benefits.

D Education

The majority of the SGBs have implemented campaigns aimed at educating professional players on concussion. These campaigns take various forms (eg, information sessions—including presentations and videos—brochures, posters, and diverse types of electronic resources), deployed alternatively or cumulatively. While the exact content of these campaigns is sometimes difficult to establish precisely, they appear to mostly focus on the short-term effects of concussion and their appropriate management (eg, treatment, return-to-play and practice). They teach players to recognise and take their symptoms into account, with the aim to raise awareness and reduce the macho culture in sport. They sometimes include grassroots sport, as well as additional contributors, such as medical staff and coaches.

All US, Canadian and Australian sports leagues are now actively involved in concussion education. Special mention goes to the NFL that has, in addition, set up a whistle blower system allowing anyone to report to the league when a concussed player is pressured to practice or play against medical advice. Conversely, IFs mainly leave educational tasks to their national associations (whose contribution substantially varies from one sport/country to another). A notable exception is World Rugby, which has incorporated an education component as part of its HIA, allowing thereby a certain centralisation of concussion education.

These initiatives are positive steps. Nevertheless, they still need to be enhanced and better coordinated in order to fully achieve their goals.[8]

---

[8]This is demonstrated by recent surveys (see Chapter 3, Sections IA2(a)(ii) and IIA1), which show that most NFL and CFL players are still inclined to hide their symptoms in order to continue to play.

In addition, information on the possible long-term medical risks associated with head trauma, and CTE in particular, seems to be regularly omitted. This is, however, not surprising, when one recalls that, with the exception of the NFL, all SGBs still refuse to acknowledge these risks. When provided, the relevant information may be problematic, as illustrated by the case of the NHL, which took the option of reassuring its players by disputing or even trying to discredit emerging science.

E Research and Data Collection

1 Research

Research, whether conducted internally or externally (eg, grants), has long been used by SGBs to better understand the causes and effects of concussion.

To date, all US, Canadian and Australian leagues conduct research on concussion. Some of them (eg, NFL, AFL) have even committed to spending a minimum amount on research through collective bargaining. The NFL is once again at the top of the rankings, with hundreds of millions of dollars spent on a wide range of medical and technological research activities (eg, creation of committees, sub-committees and specialised positions, internal studies, meetings and roundtables, grants, sponsorships and partnerships). At the other end, other leagues (eg, NHL, MLB, MLS) seem to have a much more limited contribution even when taking into consideration their revenues. However, this contribution is sometimes difficult to assess accurately, due to different communication/publication policies of those concerned.

IFs, such as FIFA, World Rugby and the IIHF, are heavily involved in research, whether through the CISG or other projects. FINA, again, is left behind. Some initiatives have also recently been reported at the national levels (eg, The FA).

These efforts contribute to a better understanding and management of concussion, and should be pursued and extended. Nevertheless, they are sometimes tarnished by issues related to the independence and quality of the research undertaken internally, or within the frameworks or partnerships. These issues range from simple preconceived ideas of some researchers (eg, AFL), to allegations of negligent misrepresentation (eg, CFL) or fraud/concealment (eg, NFL, NHL). Furthermore, there are accusations that some SGBs (eg, NFL, World Rugby) have attempted to influence external research by putting pressure on some institutions or researchers to whom they had allocated a grant.

In addition to potentially leading to biased results and slowing down the improvement of player safety, these issues have the disadvantage of damaging the reputation of the SGBs involved. They must be addressed, keeping in mind that while research is not to be kept secret, it should not be utilised by SGBs for self-promotion or simply to repair reputational damage.

Finally, the contribution of some IFs to the CISG, although welcome, remains nonetheless problematic in terms of scientific independence, because of the potential conflicts of interest that it implies.[9]

2 Data Collection

Data collection contributes to the understanding of the issue of concussion. It allows, to a certain extent,[10] the evaluation of the effectiveness of prevention strategies, in the long term, within one sport and comparisons between sports. The NFL has understood this well, since it publishes annual reports, including detailed concussion statistics for pre-season and regular season practices and games, by position/contacts.

Other SGBs in the US, Canada, Australia and Switzerland, also maintain concussion related-statistics. Nonetheless, these statistics are published extremely sparingly, if at all, making it difficult to discuss their content or draw conclusions. Additionally, assuming that they are accessible, their comparison may not be easy because of the predictable diversity of the methods, observation periods, number of games played, or even the definitions/thresholds, used.

Similar shortcomings exist concerning IFs. They restrict themselves, at best, to the holding of statistics related to their own competitions (eg, World Cups), which are generally published in peer-reviewed journals. They do not provide for vertical coordination (with their national associations, a few of which also collect data) or horizontal coordination (between sports). Broader data collection projects (eg, IOC injury surveillance system), which encompass all types of injuries, including concussion, are also worth mentioning.

The role of SGBs in data collection sometimes even extends beyond the life of the players, as with autopsy studies. This is illustrated by certain partnerships concluded with forensic medicine centres (eg, CFL, previously NFL).[11]

IV The Regulatory Activity of Governments

A Legislative Interventions & Guidelines

Governments' legislative efforts to improve the management of concussion on and off-field are few.

---

[9]See eg Chapter 2, Section IX.

[10]One should, however, be aware that better identification and awareness might distort statistics (see Chapter 3, Sections IA1(f), IA3 and IIB1(c)). In addition, that data must be collected accurately.

[11]See eg, the CTE Center, discussed further in this chapter (Section IVD).

The most active country is the US, where all 50 states and the District of Columbia adopted youth concussion laws over the course of five years (2009–14). These laws are all designed (or supposed to be designed) on the same four key tenets: education for coaches about concussion symptoms, players' removal from the game in case of suspicion of head injury, a written clearance to return, and the signature of a concussion information form by both parents and players.

Many states have then gradually made adjustments and added components to their concussion laws, including new provisions regarding concussion-data collection. Despite this, recent studies highlighted various flaws and inconsistencies between these laws, which still seem to prevent them from attaining their full effect.[12]

At the professional level, the most relevant example is boxing, governed by a federal law, which sets minimum general health safety standards.

In Canada, the Province of Ontario has had, since 2018, a youth concussion law. At the national level, sports health organisations, located within the CCC, have taken the initiative. Among them is the national charity Parachute that, in late 2017, made use of governmental funding to publish (non-mandatory) guidelines on concussion in sport. These very detailed guidelines are intended to complement the CISG's guidelines on various areas in the prevention, recognition, diagnosis and management of concussion. They create the foundation for a more consistent approach to concussion for all recreational sports activities across the country.

Simultaneously, two Australian states (New South Wales, Western Australia) issued brief general principles for concussion policy development. These principles, drafted by SMA (state branches) and sports departments, are part of a broader scheme to improve concussion identification and handling, as well as education in children's sport and/or at grassroots level. They are in line with the CISG's guidelines, and must be complied with by sports organisations that want to receive state funding.

All these interventions, although valuable, mainly target sport in general, and are insufficiently coordinated (either between each others, or with SGBs). They could provide possible basic lines of action and lessons for the management of concussion at the professional and international levels.

Finally, from a broader perspective, legislation was also used, or at least considered, to regulate issues as diverse as research (eg, failed legislative initiative in the state of Minnesota/US) and insurance (eg, *Pelé Law*/Brazil, workers' compensation/US, with ongoing discussions in Canada and Australia, which currently exclude professional athletes from any payments).

---

[12]These laws seem, to date, to have led to an increase in concussion rates, which may be caused by a range of factors, including a lack of compliance or, conversely, increased awareness and better identification (see Chapter 3, Section IA1(f)).

B Other Congressional/Parliamentary Interventions

Other forms of Congressional and parliamentary interventions regarding concussion or, more broadly, player safety, are relatively rare.

The only country that examined concussion and player safety under the main lens of professional sport is the US, where the Congress intervened several times through hearings and a roundtable (2009–16). Principal among these was the hearing that targeted American football in 2009, and which truly marked a turning point in the NFL's concussion management. Ancillary issues, such as NFL's questionable practices in connection with research, were also reviewed in 2016, through a report by Congress members.

In the UK, various working groups and a parliamentary roundtable were set up under the leadership of politicians (2014–18). Focused on grassroots and youth sport, they came out with a variety of recommendations, ranging from the launch of a parliamentary inquiry to the wide adoption of improved standards in the sports sector.

Given their possible impact, it is regrettable that governments do not use these types of interventions more often.

C Education

Governmental efforts in concussion education are just starting to emerge. Public and private entities, such as the CDC in the US, the CCC (and its members) in Canada and SMA in Australia have, directly or indirectly contributed, through their activities, to raise public awareness, with the financial support of governments. Public-private partnerships, such as that formed by the AIS/AMA in Australia, are also noteworthy. These entities should now further expand and coordinate their efforts, along with SGBs, without neglecting to take professional sport into consideration.

Interestingly, while most of these entities show moderation in publicly expressing their position about scientific issues, the AIS/AMA have expressly shared their scepticism regarding a possible link between head trauma and CTE.

D Research and Data Collection

Governments have recently taken an interest in concussion research and data collection.

The US is the most active. This is best illustrated by the CTE Center in Boston, which benefits from public and private funding (including that of the NIH and, previously, the NFL). The CTE Center has helped advance science on the possible long-term effects of concussion through multiple autopsies performed on former athletes from various sports and countries (with a main focus on former professional American football players). It has also developed a Brain Bank Depository, which facilitates data collection and storage.

The US involvement also extends to youth sports and/or grassroots, both in terms of research (grants, partnerships, concussion summits) and data collection (specific provisions in some youth concussion laws, CDC's surveillance system of sports-related concussion).

The US efforts are now starting to be emulated elsewhere in the world (Canada, Australia, England, Brazil), under the leadership of centres of excellence in forensic medicine.[13]

Canada and Australia also stand out through a variety of other initiatives (conferences, research funding aimed at improving concussion management), while the UK is part of an international injury database (EU IDB) that aims to allow a better standardisation of injury and accident surveillance and storage in the EU.

Governments' emerging efforts in research and data collection must be praised. However, despite these efforts (and those, aforementioned, of SGBs), there remain significant unanswered or disputed questions. Also, coordination of research and a centralised body for the collection and storage of data and knowledge worldwide are either limited or non-existent.

V General Observations and Issues

A Access to Relevant Documents and Transparency

The research effort for this thesis has, in many cases, encountered the reluctance by SGBs to publish or provide highly relevant documents and information.

While the wave of litigation in North America, along with the intervention of the US Congress, have, indirectly, forced the SGBs concerned to give account of their concussion management and divulge their practices, it has also made them defensive. Thus, SGBs that have been sued do not want to re-ignite controversy. SGBs that are being sued tend to refuse to communicate on matters that potentially relate to pending proceedings, whereas those that are not being sued fear possible litigation.

Elsewhere in the world, the environment is generally more cooperative. However, primary sources remain difficult to access.

This lack of transparency must be dealt with. In addition to its negative repercussions on the present research (the conclusions of which are, *de facto*, incomplete), it adversely affects, in a broader perspective, player safety. In particular, it prevents the formulation of constructive criticism and suggestions, as well as effective

[13]In Canada, Australia and England, these centres rely on private funding for their autopsies/research on concussion. They are discussed here for simplicity purposes.

cooperation between the different contributors concerned. It also gives the impression (rightly or wrongly) that the sports world has something to hide.

B Nature of the Relationships at Stake

The concussion issue involves the interaction of various contributors, including medical professionals, researchers, SGBs, governments, players and their representative unions.

In North America, most of the sports examined are characterized by reactive and/or competitive and adversarial relationships between these different contributors. The most obvious case is that of the NFL, which has for a long time simply reacted periodically to the progress of science and US governments' interventions. Mired in a class action, the league finally avoided a discovery process through the conclusion of a USD1 billion settlement with its former players.

This tension tends, to some extent, to ease as one moves away from North America, giving way to a more synergetic and proactive approach. Thus, like the AFL and the NRL, some SGBs have put in place substantial measures of concussion management without being implicated in confirmed CTE diagnosis or litigation.

The fact remains that even the most diligent SGBs could be accused of having dithered. Despite studies showing an association between head trauma and neurodegenerative conditions in boxing nearly 100 years ago,[14] all of the SGBs waited for controversy to break out in the NFL, or even to be on their doorstep, to take their first substantial measures of concussion management, or step up their efforts. Worse, others (a minority in the case studies, but likely symptomatic of a real deficiency on a global scale) have not yet taken any substantial measures. As a result, new legal procedures may well follow.

As already argued in detail,[15] this situation harms the interests of all the contributors concerned, in particular players (not protected in the most optimal and consistent way) and SGBs (which are currently facing increasing threats from litigation). It cannot continue indefinitely, and shows the need for a more harmonised, collaborative approach to public health and legal risks.

C Emerging Features of a Harmonised Approach

The harmonisation process of the regulation of concussion has, in reality, already begun. A few features of a harmonised approach have already started to emerge across sports and countries.

---

[14]See Chapter 2, Section VII.

[15]See Chapter 3, Sections IB1 et seq (including subsequent case studies).

The features of harmonisation initiated by SGBs are best illustrated by the CISG's guidelines (including the protocols and meetings intended to facilitate their implementation). Another good example is the adoption of new rules of play by IFs, which then apply to all levels of the game internationally. Research and data collection (eg, cross-codes studies, concussion surveillance during international tournaments) play a more marginal role.

The features of harmonisation brought about by governments comprise youth concussion laws/guidelines, concussion surveillance systems and brain banks. In principle, they do not go beyond national borders and focus mainly on youth sport and/or grassroots. There are, however, some exceptions (eg, CTE Center).

In addition, there are broader projects, which cover all types of injuries (eg, IOC surveillance system, EU IDB). Although pertaining to an individual/combat sport, the US federal boxing legislation also deserves mention.

These initiatives could constitute the starting point, or at the very least the source of inspiration for a stronger harmonised approach. In any case, they require development and better coordination.

VI Conclusion

The chapter shows once again that the concussion controversy is expanding, both in terms of public health and legal risks. It demonstrates that while SGBs and, to a lesser extent, governments, have recently made notable regulatory efforts, opportunities for further improvement exist in all sectors of interventions examined. It observes that current efforts take place within a framework still too often opaque, conflictive, defensive and self-centered (despite recent initiatives to remedy the situation). It confirms the need for the harmonised reforms to be discussed in the next chapter, and provides the foundation for their analysis.

Chapter 5
Harmonised Reforms

Tomorrow's reality [will] be made of yesterday's and today's Utopia.

André Gide, Fruits of the Earth, 1897.

I Introduction

Previous chapters demonstrated the pressing need for both greater awareness of the problem of sports-related concussion and a coordinated (harmonised) approach among sports and government authorities from both a public health and regulatory perspective. They highlighted shortcomings and good practices in the current management and regulation of concussion, as well as emerging features of a harmonised approach that could be built upon.

In view of these findings, this chapter adopts an innovative two-step approach.

In the first phase, this chapter seeks further guidance by examining the harmonised regulatory mechanisms that have been successfully introduced in doping, match-fixing and spectator violence,[1] all of which involve international arrangements.[2]

[1]This approach has received very little attention in academic literature. Only one (Canadian) academic article draws a parallel between the regulation of anti-doping and concussion. Nevertheless, it does not offer any comprehensive and clear conclusion [see Jon Heshka and Kris Lines, 'A Proposed New Approach to Regulating Brain Injuries in Sport' (2013) 3 *International Journal of Sport and Society* 141, 141–52]. In addition, another (Australian) article advocates for increased collaboration between Australian football codes over concussion, without, however, detailing the possible content of such collaboration, proposing harmonised rules or expanding the reasoning on the international scene [see Annette Greenhow and Jocelyn East, 'Custodians of the Game: Ethical Considerations for Football Governing Bodies in Regulating Concussion Management' (2015) 8 *Neuroethics* 65, 65–82].

[2]Smaller scale attempts of harmonised laws in the US and Canada (youth concussion laws) are dealt with in the case studies.

A. Veuthey, *Concussion in Professional Team Sports: Time for a Harmonised Approach?*, https://doi.org/10.1007/978-981-15-1979-6_5

These mechanisms have a very different philosophy, scope and geographical reach:

- The anti-doping system (known as the 'WADA system') was initiated in 1999 and is currently under review. It is grounded in the World Anti-Doping Code (WADC) and *International (UNESCO) Convention against Doping in Sport*, which involve more than 660 sports organisations and nearly 190 governments. It is headed by the World Anti-Doping Agency (WADA).
- The system against match-fixing was initiated in 2014 and is yet to come completely into force. It is grounded in the *European (Council of Europe) Convention on the Manipulation of Sports Competitions ('Macolin Convention')*, which is expected to involve nearly 60 countries. It is complemented by the Olympic Movement Code on the Prevention of the Manipulation of Competitions and its related Unit.[3] It is not overseen by any global agency or body, despite some initiatives in this respect.
- The system against spectator violence was initiated in 1985. It is grounded in the *European (Council of Europe) Convention on Spectator Violence and Misbehaviour at Sports Events and in Particular at Football Matches*, which is in the process of being replaced by a new convention. Mainly focused on the issue of European football hooliganism, it involves 42 countries as signatories (FIFA and UEFA are notably observers to the Convention). Like match-fixing, it is not overseen by any global agency or body.

This chapter argues that despite its disciplinary nature and other characteristics specific to doping, the WADA system must address similar issues as a regulatory system for concussion. Therefore, the WADA system appears to be the richest source of guidance for the reforms to be undertaken, both regarding their content and the foreseeable challenges that they may face. The systems against match-fixing and spectator violence could also provide limited guidance in this regard.

In the second phase, this chapter proposes a series of reforms to achieve a harmonised regulatory framework for addressing the public health and legal risks of concussion in sport. Briefly, these reforms consist of an international standard, a supporting international convention, a new international sports safety body and some limited enforcement mechanisms.

Chief among the proposed reforms is an International Standard on Concussion (ISC). The ISC would establish the regulatory mechanisms, duties and practical actions expected of IFs and sports leagues (including the rules of play, rules of the game and concussion management protocols, financial support for injured athletes, education, research and data collection). It could be given a legal foundation through an accompanying international convention, creating a private/public partnership inspired by the regulatory mechanisms existing in doping (ie, the WADC and the *UNESCO Convention*). In addition, a World Sports Safety Agency (WSSA),

[3]This Unit, entitled 'The Olympic Movement Unit on the Prevention of the Manipulation of Sports Competitions' is an administrative Unit of the IOC (see this chapter, Section IIIB3).

inspired by WADA, could be established. This would be responsible for overseeing the implementation and operation of the proposed reforms, and also advocating for the growing issue of sports safety. Where necessary, state courts, CAS or other arbitration courts could have jurisdiction to enforce these reforms.

This chapter shows how the current disparate arrangements could be harmonised and improved in order to most efficiently reduce the public health and legal risks associated with concussion. It acknowledges that this process will, in all likelihood, be long and potentially challenging.

The chapter is divided into five main parts. The first part provides an overview of the harmonised regulatory mechanisms in doping, match-fixing and spectator violence, and discusses their relevance for concussion. The second and third parts analyse these mechanisms in more depth, with a particular focus on doping, and summarise the main lessons to be learned for concussion. The fourth part makes the link between these lessons and the proposed reforms, which are then exposed in detail in the fifth part.

II Harmonised Regulatory Mechanisms in Doping, Match-fixing and Spectator Violence: Overview and Relevance for Concussion

A Doping

As this chapter will demonstrate in detail,[4] the WADA system is the most advanced international harmonised regulatory mechanism in sport to date. It is, therefore, a benchmark system. Moreover, it has immediate relevance when compared with the field of concussion, with which it shares substantial similarities.

First, until 1999 anti-doping was characterised by an absence of global strategy, despite early indications of coordinated action, mainly emanating from the medical field.[5] It showed in particular a weak collaboration between sports organisations and governments,[6] gradually subject to increased public scrutiny due to the death of athletes and judicial proceedings.[7] This situation is reminiscent of that of concussion,[8] which is now at the same turning point, and offers the same 'breeding ground' for reforms.

Secondly, anti-doping offers a global approach that is also needed for the regulation of concussion. Although the concussion controversy originated in one North American professional league, a global perspective is essential because of the

[4]See this chapter, Sections IIIA et seq.

[5]See this chapter, Section IIIA1.

[6]Ibid.

[7]See this chapter, Sections IIIA1, IIIA2(a) and footnote 37.

[8]See in particular Chapter 3, Sections IA1(b) et seq and IA2 et seq.

issue's on-going expansion across sports and countries.[9] Regardless of the differing levels of controversy and responses, there is a growing need to regulate and anticipate issues surrounding concussion in sports worldwide. More generally, it is worth noting the growing importance that the issue of sports safety should represent in the future, as sports participation is increasing in economically developing countries, in particular in Asia.[10]

Thirdly, anti-doping is based on public health imperatives, in that it aims in particular to protect athletes from the use of substances and methods with potentially serious consequences for their health.[11] By this public health aspect, anti-doping undeniably echoes the regulation of concussion.[12]

Finally, anti-doping pillars, outlined in WADA strategic plan,[13] solidify the link between the two genres. They include protecting the rights of athletes, assisting stakeholders with the implementation of programs, ensuring compliance, and strengthening the engagement of the sports movement and public authorities. They also comprise facilitating information and data management, promoting education initiatives and research, as well as good governance. These components are, again, transposable in essence to the area of concussion.[14]

In view of its intrinsic qualities, and the similarities it shares with concussion, the anti-doping system appears to be the most relevant source to draw upon for the reforms to be undertaken. It makes it possible not to start from scratch, but on the contrary to rely on an existing framework and the experience already gained in this field.

However, these similarities are offset by significant differences that call for a certain measure of caution. First, anti-doping, despite its public health component, mainly aims to ensure the integrity and fairness of competitions.[15] It is characterised by a strong disciplinary/punitive nature,[16] which contrasts with the essentially preventive, managerial and compensatory nature of the regulation of concussion.[17] Secondly, anti-doping is mainly led under the impetus of the Olympic Movement,[18] to the exclusion

---

[9]See Chapter 3, Sections IA1(b) et seq, IA2 et seq (including subsequent case studies) and Chapter 4, Section II.

[10]Three of the four largest countries by population (China, India and Indonesia) and five of the top 10 (with Bangladesh and Pakistan) are located in Asia ['World population review' website (<http://worldpopulationreview.com/countries/>)].

[11]See this chapter, Sections IIIA3(a)(i) and IIIA3(a)(ii).

[12]The public health aspect of the regulation of concussion is part of the research question of this thesis (set out in Chapter 1, Section I).

[13]WADA strategic plan 2015–19, p. 5. This document is available on WADA website (<https://www.wada-ama.org/sites/default/files/wada-strategic_plan-2015-en.pdf>).

[14]See in particular the reforms proposed further in this chapter (Sections VI et seq).

[15]For a recent illustration of the role that integrity and fairness of competitions can play in anti-doping, see this chapter, Section IIIA6(b)(ii).

[16]See this chapter, Sections IIIA3(a)(i) and IIIA5.

[17]See Chapter 3, Sections IA1(c) et seq and IA2(a)(i) et seq (including subsequent case studies).

[18]See this chapter, Sections IIIA2(a) et seq.

of many sports leagues[19] that, conversely, are highly involved in and affected by the concussion controversy.[20] Finally, doping is considered to be quite widespread across sports and countries at the professional level,[21] while concussion is, to date, still (too often) perceived as an emerging threat, mainly affecting contact sports.[22]

B Match-fixing and Spectator Violence

The only features that systems against match-fixing and spectator violence have in common with concussion are their link with sport, and in the case of spectator violence, some aspects related to safety.[23] They are characterised by their strong criminal nature, absence of a global approach, limited material scope, and lack of focus on athletes' health.[24] As a result, they can only provide limited guidance.

III Harmonised Regulatory Mechanisms in Doping, Match-fixing and Spectator Violence: In Depth Analysis

A Doping

1 A Brief History of Regulatory Intervention

The practice of enhancing athletic performance through foreign substances was known from the earliest Olympic Games.[25] However, the first regulatory response started only in the late 1960s, following the deaths of two cyclists from amphetamine abuse.[26] In 1967, the IOC established its Medical Commission, and quickly published its first 'List of Prohibited Substances' (1968).[27] This List was then expanded through several additional documents, including the 'International

[19]See this chapter, Section IIIA6(b)(i).

[20]See Chapter 2, Section IX, footnote 163, Chapter 3, Sections IA1(b) et seq (including subsequent case studies), this chapter, Sections IVC, VIB2, VIC4(a) and Chapter 6, Section IIIC.

[21]This can be seen from the impressive number of sports organisations and countries that have adhered to the WADA system, mentioned by way of introduction.

[22]This can be seen from the many SGBs that, like FINA, have still not taken any substantial measures of concussion management (see Chapter 3, Section ID and Chapter 4, Section VB).

[23]See this chapter, Sections IIIB et seq and IIIC et seq.

[24]Ibid.

[25]Charles Flint, Adam Lewis and Jonathan Taylor, 'The Fight Against Doping in Sport: the Regulatory Framework' in Adam Lewis and Jonathan Taylor, *Sport, Law and Practice* (Bloomsbury, 3rd ed, 2014) 135, 143.

[26]Ibid, 143.

[27]Ibid, 143–4.

Olympic Charter Against Doping in Sport' (1988) and the 'Medical Code relating to the Use of Drugs in Sport' (1994).[28]

These initiatives had limited success. There remained significant differences from sport to sport in terms of what was banned, what was permitted, and which sanctions were imposed.[29] This lack of harmonisation was seen as a substantial weakness, reflecting a lack of unity within the sports world in the face of the drug threat, and significantly undermining the fight against drugs in sport.[30] Therefore, in 1998, the IOC adopted a single unified 'Anti-Doping Code', which formed the basis for the WADC,[31] described below.[32]

The Council of Europe favoured the use of non-binding legal instruments ('Resolution Against the Use of Drugs in Sport' (1960), 'Anti-Doping Charter' (1984)) until 1989, which marked the adoption of the European *'Anti-Doping Convention'*.[33] In 1991, a group of interested countries (mainly from Scandinavia and the Commonwealth) signed an International Anti-Doping Agreement (IADA) outlining their commitment to cooperatively pursue and promote anti-doping in sport.[34]

Some links between sports and public authorities then began to take shape (recognition of the IOC anti-doping List by the *European Anti-Doping Convention*,[35] reuse of IADA's work by the IOC[36]).

Nevertheless, it was only when the IOC and governments formally and globally decided to join forces that the fight against doping really took off, leading to the system that is in place today.

2 The World Anti-Doping Agency (WADA)

(a) Creation and Mission

Following a series of doping incidents and judicial proceedings that befell the world of cycling around the 1998 Tour de France,[37] the IOC decided to convene a World

---

[28]Ibid, 144.

[29]Ibid.

[30]Ibid. See also Matthew J Mitten and Hayden Opie, '"Sports Law", Implications for the Development of international, Comparative law and Global Dispute Resolution', in Robert CR Siekmann and Janwillem Soek, *Lex Sportiva, What is Sports Law?* (Springer, 2012) 173, 181.

[31]Ibid.

[32]See this chapter, Section IIIA3(a)(i).

[33]Flint, Lewis and Taylor, above n 25, 143–4.

[34]For more details, see IADA website (<https://antidoping.no/english/international-cooperation/iada/>).

[35]*Anti-Doping Convention*, Arts. 2 and 11.

[36]IADA website (<https://antidoping.no/english/international-cooperation/iada/>).

[37]These incidents are usually referred to as the 'Festina affair'. The affair began when a whole host of doping products were found in the car of the Festina cycling team. An investigation quickly revealed systematic doping among the team, and brought the world of cycling into disrepute. The

Conference on Doping.[38] This Conference was held in Lausanne, Switzerland, in February 1999, and brought together all parties involved in the fight against doping.[39] It resulted in the Lausanne Declaration on Doping in Sport,[40] which provided for the creation of an independent international anti-doping agency, aimed to be operational for the 2000 Sydney Olympic Games.[41]

Based on the Lausanne Declaration, the World Anti-Doping Agency (WADA) was established in 1999 to coordinate the fight against doping in sport internationally.[42] Although set up under the initiative of the IOC, it also benefits from the support of intergovernmental organisations, governments and other public authorities.[43]

WADA's activities have expanded over time. They currently include scientific research, education, data storage/access, the development of anti-doping capacities, and the monitoring of the WADC—[44] the document harmonising anti-doping policies in all sports and countries.[45]

(b) Structure and Governance

WADA is a Swiss private law, non-profit foundation.[46] Its seat is in Lausanne, Switzerland and its headquarters are in Montreal, Canada.[47] Regional offices are located on each continent.[48]

---

main people involved, cyclists and their medical and sporting entourage, received suspended custodial sentences, fines and/or suspensions [for more details, see eg, Jean-François Quénet, *Un cyclone nommé dopage* (Broché, 1999)]. It should be noted that such a procedure, extending to cyclists, is very rare in the field of doping.

[38]WADA website (<https://www.wada-ama.org/en/who-we-are>).

[39]Ibid.

[40]The Lausanne Declaration is available on WADA website (<https://www.wada-ama.org/en/resources/general-anti-doping-information/lausanne-declaration-on-doping-in-sport>).

[41]Ibid.

[42]Ibid.

[43]Ibid.

[44]The WADC (2018) is available on WADA website (<https://www.wada-ama.org/en/resources/the-code/world-anti-doping-code>).

[45]WADA website (<https://www.wada-ama.org/en/who-we-are>). See also WADA statutes, Art. 4. The WADA statutes (2018) are available on WADA website (<https://www.wada-ama.org/en/resources/legal/revised-statutes>).

[46]WADA website (<https://www.wada-ama.org/en/governance>). See also WADA statutes, Art. 1.

[47]WADA website (<https://www.wada-ama.org/en/governance>). See also WADA statutes, Art. 2. According Art. 56 of the *Swiss Civil Code (CC)*, the seat of a legal entity (ie, its legal domicile) is located where its administration is carried out, unless otherwise stated. The headquarters are the central place where people in authority are stationed; especially the main offices used by a large company or organisation having at least several satellite locations [Garner, above n 5 in Chapter 3, ad 'Headquarters', 835].

[48]WADA website (<https://www.wada-ama.org/en/contact-us/regional-offices>).

WADA is composed of a Foundation Board, an Executive Committee, and several Advisory Committees.[49]

The Foundation Board is WADA's supreme decision-making body.[50] It defines the main strategic orientations to be implemented.[51] It comprises 38 members, composed equally of representatives from the Olympic Movement (IOC, international umbrella organisations,[52] Athletes' Commission) and governments.[53]

The Executive Committee is WADA's ultimate policy-making body.[54] It is tasked with the day-to-day management and running of the Agency, including the performance of activities and the administration of assets.[55] It comprises 12 members, which also equally represent the Olympic Movement and governments.[56]

Advisory Committees provide guidance for WADA's programs, through recommendations.[57]

WADA is headed by a President and a General Director. WADA's Presidency is a voluntary position, which alternates between the Olympic Movement and governments.[58] The General Director position is advertised externally.[59]

(c) Operation

WADA oversees the fight against doping internationally. Nevertheless, in practice, WADA delegates many of its operational aspects (eg, drug testing in and out of competitions, education programs, sanctions) to external stakeholders.[60] IFs are in the forefront of these stakeholders,[61] in addition to National Anti-Doping

---

[49]WADA website (<https://www.wada-ama.org/en/governance>). See also WADA statutes, Arts. 6-11.

[50]WADA website (<https://www.wada-ama.org/en/governance>). See also WADA statutes, Arts. 6-10.

[51]Ibid.

[52]Association of Summer Olympic International Federations (ASOIF), Association of International Olympic Winter Sports Federations (AIOWF), Global Association of International Sports Federations (GAISF), Association of National Olympic Committees (ANOC).

[53]WADA website (<https://www.wada-ama.org/en/governance>). See also WADA statutes, Art. 6.

[54]WADA website (<https://www.wada-ama.org/en/governance>). See also WADA statutes, Art. 11.

[55]Ibid.

[56]Ibid.

[57]Ibid.

[58]WADA website (<https://www.wada-ama.org/en/governance>). See also WADA statutes, Art. 7.

[59]WADA website (<https://www.wada-ama.org/en/media/news/2015-11/wada-appoints-olivier-niggli-as-new-director-general>).

[60]In the same vein, see WADA website (<https://www.wada-ama.org/en/anti-doping-community>).

[61]WADA website (<https://www.wada-ama.org/en/international-federations-if>). See also WADC, Art. 20.3.

Organisations (NADOs),[62] which themselves are regrouped in Regional Associations (RADOs).[63]

The IOC, National Olympic Committees (NOCs),[64] Major Event Organisations (MEOs)[65] and governments[66] also intervene on an ad-hoc basis.

WADA-accredited laboratories[67] complete the picture.

(d) Funding

WADA's funding is sourced, on a parity basis, from the Olympic Movement and governments of the world.[68] Its annual budget for 2018 amounts to a total of USD32 million.[69]

WADA's regional budget allocation for governments is as follows: Africa (0.5%); Americas (29%); Asia (20.46%); Europe (47.5%); and Oceania (2.54%).[70] Respective government representatives from each region on WADA Foundation Board are responsible for facilitating annual agreements within each region to determine the share of individual countries.[71] The WADA Executive Committee Member of the region usually leads this process.[72] This information is then provided each year to WADA by the Board members so that each country can be individually invoiced.[73]

The Olympic Movement has a policy of making payments to WADA only when governments make their payments, matching dollar for dollar contributions.[74]

[62]WADA website (<https://www.wada-ama.org/en/national-anti-doping-organizations-nado>). See also WADC, Art. 20.5.

[63]WADA website (<https://www.wada-ama.org/en/who-we-are/anti-doping-community/regional-anti-doping-organizations-rado>). See also WADC, Art. 21.3.

[64]WADA website (<https://www.wada-ama.org/en/olympic-paralympic-committees>). See also WADC, Arts. 20.1 and 20.2.

[65]WADA website (<https://www.wada-ama.org/en/major-event-organizations>). See also WADC, Art. 20.6.

[66]WADA website (<https://www.wada-ama.org/en/governments>). See also *UNESCO Convention*, discussed in this chapter, Section IIIA4.

[67]WADA website (<https://www.wada-ama.org/en/what-we-do/science-medical/laboratories>). See also WADC, Art. 6.

[68]WADA website (<https://www.wada-ama.org/en/funding>). See also WADA statutes, Art. 5.

[69]WADA website (<https://www.wada-ama.org/sites/default/files/resources/files/contributions_2018_20181219_en.pdf>).

[70]WADA website (<https://www.wada-ama.org/en/funding-by-governments>).

[71]Ibid.

[72]Ibid.

[73]Ibid.

[74]WADA website (<https://www.wada-ama.org/en/funding>).

WADA's funding represents only a small part of the total annual contribution of the Olympic Movement to the fight against doping.[75] According to figures released by the IOC in 2017, this contribution totals up to USD300 million (including USD180 million for drug testing only).[76]

3 The Main Texts Framing the Global Fight against Doping

(a) The World-Anti-Doping Code (WADC), International Standards, Model Rules and Guidelines

(i) The WADC

The WADC is the core document that harmonises anti-doping policies, rules and regulations within sport organisations and among public authorities around the world.[77] It was drafted by WADA, and then adopted in 2003 during the World Conference on Doping in Sport of Copenhagen (Denmark), following an extensive consultation process.[78]

The WADC came into effect on a global scale in 2004 for sports organisations, and in 2007 for governments.[79] It underwent two major reviews, in 2009 and 2015, and a minor review (related to compliance) in 2018.[80] It is set for a further review in 2021.[81] To date, it has been adopted by more than 660 sports organisations (including the IOC, all IFs, NOCs, MEOs and NADOs) and nearly 190 governments.[82] To this are added national associations and leagues, which are expected to adhere to the system through indirect mechanisms that will be discussed further below,[83] or upon invitation.[84]

---

[75] Nick Butler, 'Anti-Doping Claimed to Cost Sport $300 Million Each Year', *Inside the Games*, 16 March 2017 (<https://www.insidethegames.biz/articles/1048181/anti-doping-claimed-to-cost-sport-300-million-each-year>).

[76] Ibid.

[77] WADA website (<https://www.wada-ama.org/en/what-we-do/the-code>).

[78] WADA website (<https://www.wada-ama.org/en/what-we-do/the-code/2021-code-review>). See also Jean-Loup Chappelet and Brenda Kübler Mabbott, *The International Olympic Committee and the Olympic System*: The Governance of World Sport (Routledge, 2008) 143–4.

[79] About sports organisations, see WADA website (<https://www.wada-ama.org/en/what-we-do/the-code>). For governments, see this chapter, Section IIIA4.

[80] WADA website (<https://www.wada-ama.org/en/what-we-do/the-code>) and (<https://www.wada-ama.org/en/what-we-do/the-code/2021-code-review>). See also this chapter, Sections IIIA3 (a)(ii) and IIIA6(b)(ii).

[81] WADA website (<https://www.wada-ama.org/en/what-we-do/the-code>) and (<https://www.wada-ama.org/en/what-we-do/the-code/2021-code-review>).

[82] The list of WADC signatories is available on WADA website (<https://www.wada-ama.org/en/code-signatories>). For governments, see this chapter, Section IIIA4 and footnote 136.

[83] See this chapter, Section IIIA3(b).

[84] WADC, Art. 23.1.2.

The WADC is organised in four main parts. The first part is dedicated to doping control.[85] The second part relates to education and research.[86] The third part is about the roles and responsibilities of the sports organisations and the states involved.[87] Finally, the last part sets out the principles related to the acceptance of and respect for the WADC, in addition to the conditions for its modification or interpretation.[88]

The foundations for the fight against doping thus appear in the first part. This part starts with a definition of doping, and the list of circumstances and conduct that lead to it.[89] It then provides the principles for the determination of the list of prohibited substances and methods,[90] and clarifies the roles and responsibilities of the various actors in carrying out controls.[91] Finally, it outlines the rules related to sanctions and the management of positive tests results.[92]

Essential articles, such as those related to the definition of doping, the list of prohibited substances, or sanctions, are mandatory and must be strictly adhered to by sports organisations and governments.[93] Conversely, other articles are mandatory only in their principles but allow some flexibility for their implementation.[94] This is the case, for example, for hearing and sanctioning procedures.[95]

(ii) International Standards

The WADC works in conjunction with six International Standards that aim to foster consistency among anti-doping organisations in various areas: prohibited substances and methods; testing; laboratories; Therapeutic Use Exemptions (TUEs); protection of privacy and personal information; and compliance.[96]

First, the Prohibited List identifies the substances and methods prohibited in and out-of-competition, and in particular sports.[97] The substances and methods on the List are classified by different categories (eg, steroids, stimulants, gene doping).[98]

---

[85] WADC, Arts. 1-17.

[86] WADC, Arts. 18-19.

[87] WADC, Arts. 20-2.

[88] WADC, Arts. 23-5.

[89] WADC, Arts. 1-2.

[90] WADC, Art. 4.

[91] WADC, Art. 5.

[92] WADC, Arts. 6-7.

[93] WADC, Introduction and Art. 23.2.2.

[94] Ibid.

[95] Ibid.

[96] WADA website (<https://www.wada-ama.org/en/what-we-do/international-standards>). All International Standards can be downloaded from this webpage.

[97] WADA website (<https://www.wada-ama.org/en/what-we-do/international-standards>).

[98] Ibid.

The list is developed following several consultations; it is then published by WADA on October 1st and comes into force on January 1st of the following year.[99]

The International Standard for Testing and Investigations (ISTI) provides for the planning of controls and aims to maintain the integrity and identity of samples, from notifying the athlete to transporting samples for analysis.[100] It also incorporates provisions related to the management of information on athletes' whereabouts.[101]

The International Standard for Laboratories (ISL) aims to ensure the production of valid test results and evidentiary data and to achieve uniform and harmonised results from all accredited laboratories.[102] In addition, the ISL specifies the criteria that must be fulfilled by anti-doping laboratories to achieve and maintain their accreditation.[103]

The International Standard for Therapeutic Use Exemptions (ISTUE) specifies the conditions under which athletes may apply for TUEs that allow them to use prohibited methods or substances when their state of health justifies it.[104]

The International Standard for the Protection of Privacy and Personal information (ISPPPI) intends to ensure that all relevant parties involved in anti-doping in sport adhere to a set of minimum privacy protections when collecting, using and erasing[105] athlete personal information (eg, whereabouts, doping controls/results and TUEs).[106] These minimum privacy protections notably include the compliance with data protection and privacy laws, the proportionality of the information processed, the consent of the participant, the implementation of security safeguards and the prohibition of public disclosure (apart from listed exceptions).[107]

The ISPPPI refers to the Anti-Doping Administration and Management System (ADAMS).[108] ADAMS is a web-based database management system created in 2005 to allow the storage of data.[109] It facilitates the sharing of information amongst relevant organisations and enables them to coordinate their actions and decisions.[110] The security and confidentiality of the data collected is ensured through a multi-level

[99]WADA website (<https://www.wada-ama.org/en/what-we-do/the-prohibited-list>).

[100]WADA website (<https://www.wada-ama.org/en/what-we-do/international-standards>).

[101]Ibid. Professional athletes are required to submit timely and accurate information of their whereabouts for the purpose of locating them for random out-of-competition testing.

[102]WADA website (<https://www.wada-ama.org/en/what-we-do/international-standards>).

[103]Ibid.

[104]Ibid.

[105]Different retention times apply to the retention of personal information [ISPPPI, p. 16 and Annex A].

[106]Ibid.

[107]For more details, see Paul David, *A Guide to the World Anti-Doping Code* (Cambridge, 2017) 148–56.

[108]ISPPPI, p. 4.

[109]WADA website (<https://www.wada-ama.org/en/adams>).

[110]Ibid.

access system.[111] The fact remains that the collection of data implies privacy risks for athletes and their families, and requires regular updates. The latest version of the ISPPPI, effective from June 2018, reflects in particular the principles of the European Union's new *General Data Protection Regulation (EU GDPR).*[112]

Finally, the International Standard for Code Compliance by Signatories (ISCCS), effective from April 2018, sets out WADA's new compliance monitoring program.[113] The ISCCS aims to ensure that strong, WADC-compliant anti-doping rules and programs are applied and enforced consistently and effectively across all sports and all countries.[114] It outlines WADC signatories' rights and responsibilities, and the ways WADA supports them in achieving, maintaining and, where applicable, regaining WADC compliance.[115] It also provides for a process for determining and contesting non-compliance, as well as sanctions.[116]

It may be noted that additional standards are currently under preparation, including a standard for education.[117]

(iii) Model Rules and Guidelines

WADA has developed models of good practice called Model Rules since 2009 as well as guidelines that are of a recommendatory nature.[118]

Model Rules are aimed to assist sports organisations in drafting anti-doping rules in line with the WADC.[119]

Guidelines provide with recommended practices for several aspects of anti-doping programming.[120]

(b) Methods to Implement and Ensure Compliance with the WADC and International Standards

Once a sports organisation has accepted the WADC, it must enact rules or amend existing regulations to include its mandatory sections and general principles.[121] All

[111]Ibid.

[112]WADA website (<https://www.wada-ama.org/en/what-we-do/international-standards>).

[113]Ibid.

[114]Ibid.

[115]Ibid.

[116]Ibid.

[117]WADA website (<https://www.wada-ama.org/en/media/news/2018-06/wada-launches-second-phase-of-2021-code-review-process-and-first-phase-for>).

[118]WADA website (<https://www.wada-ama.org/en/model-rules-guidelines-and-protocols>). The Model Rules and Guidelines are available on this page.

[119]Ibid.

[120]Ibid.

[121]WADC, Introduction and Art. 20.

IFs have thus adopted anti-doping rules for their own competitions,[122] which allow them to claim, in return, to be part of the Olympic Program and receive Olympic funding.[123] Compliance is then ensured through WADA's new compliance monitoring program and related Standard, discussed above.[124]

National associations are required to follow the move, as a condition of maintaining the membership that binds them to their umbrella organisation and related funding.[125] Similar conditions apply for governmental funding.[126] Governmental pressure can be useful and even essential in the absence of an IF and/or international leadership. A good example of this is Australia, where major professional sports leagues (including the NRL and the AFL) have incorporated the WADC into their regulations.[127] They are indirectly bound by its provisions through a federal regulation, which they must respect or risk losing governmental funding.[128] Although they were opposed to applying the WADC at first, they finally yielded to the financial pressure and public opinion.[129]

The situation is more complex with regard to governments, which cannot be legally bound by documents of a private nature.[130] Accordingly, governments prepared the Copenhagen Declaration on Anti-Doping in Sport,[131] where they expressed their intention to formally recognise and implement the WADC and its related Standards through an international convention.[132]

---

[122]See this chapter, Section IIIA3(a)(i).

[123]Olympic Charter (2015), Arts. 25, 43, 45/3 and 59/1.2, available on the IOC website (<https://stillmed.olympic.org/Documents/olympic_charter_en.pdf>). See also WADC, Arts. 20.1.2 and 20.1.3.

[124]See this chapter, Section IIIA3(a)(ii).

[125]WADC, Arts. 20.3.2 and 20.3.9.

[126]See this chapter, Section IIIA4.

[127]AFL Anti-Doping Code (2015) (<http://s.afl.com.au/staticfile/AFL%20Tenant/AFL/Files/AFL%20Anti-Doping%20Code%202015-FINAL.pdf>); NRL Anti-Doping Policy (2015) (<https://playnrl.com/media/2308/2015-leagues-anti-doping-policy.pdf>).

[128]This is also the case of Rugby Australia, which must in addition adhere to the WADC due to its affiliation with World Rugby. See *Australian Sports Anti-Doping Authority (ASADA) Regulations 2006* and their Schedule 1, *the National Anti-Doping (NAD) Scheme,* Art. 2.04; and Australian Sports Commission (ASC)'s website (<https://www.sportaus.gov.au/integrity_in_sport/integrity_templates_and_principles#integrity_guidelines_for_directors_and_leaders_of_sporting_organisations>; < https://www.sportaus.gov.au/grants_and_funding>).

[129]For more detail, see Vanessa McDermott, *The War on Drugs in Sport: Moral Panics and Organizational Legitimacy* (Routledge, 2016) 17 and 107–42.

[130]WADA website (<https://www.wada-ama.org/en/who-we-are/anti-doping-community/governments>).

[131]The Copenhagen declaration is available on WADA website (<https://www.wada-ama.org/en/governments#CopenhagenDeclaration>).

[132]WADA website (<https://www.wada-ama.org/en/governments#CopenhagenDeclaration>).

This declaration of intent materialised in the adoption, in 2005, of the *International Convention against Doping in Sport*.[133]

4 *The International Convention against Doping in Sport*

The International Convention against Doping in Sport (commonly referred to as the '*UNESCO Convention*') is the first global treaty against doping in sport.[134] It was adopted unanimously by the 33rd UNESCO General Conference in 2005, and came into force in 2007, following the 30th ratification.[135] It has so far been ratified by nearly 190 countries.[136]

The *UNESCO Convention* is intended to commit governments domestically, and at the international level, to 'the fight against doping in sport', and obligates signatories to 'adopt appropriate measures' which 'may include legislation, regulation, policies or administrative practices'.[137]

Overall, there is a degree of flexibility as to how governments can comply with the Convention.[138] However, governments must take specific action to:

- Restrict the availability of prohibited substances or methods to athletes (except for legitimate medical purposes) including measures against trafficking;
- Facilitate doping controls and support national testing programmes;
- Withhold financial support from athletes and athlete support personnel who commit an anti-doping rule violation, or from sporting organisations that are not in compliance with the WADC;
- Encourage producers and distributors of nutritional supplements to establish 'best practice' in the labelling, marketing and distribution of products that might contain prohibited substances;
- Support the provision of anti-doping education to athletes and the wider sporting community.[139]

The Convention also provides a mechanism to assist governments to develop anti-doping education and prevention programmes through 'The Fund for the Elimination of Doping in Sport' managed by UNESCO.[140]

---

133 Ibid. This Convention is available on WADA website (<https://www.wada-ama.org/en/resources/world-anti-doping-program/unesco-international-convention-against-doping-in-sport>).

134 Ibid.

135 Ibid.

136 The list of *UNESCO Convention* ratifications is available on WADA website (<https://www.wada-ama.org/en/unesco-convention-ratifications>).

137 *UNESCO Convention*, Arts. 1 and 5.

138 UNESCO website (<http://www.unesco.org/new/en/social-and-human-sciences/themes/anti-doping/international-convention-against-doping-in-sport/>).

139 Ibid. See also *UNESCO Convention*, Arts. 7-12 and 19.

140 UNESCO website (<http://www.unesco.org/new/en/social-and-human-sciences/themes/anti-doping/international-convention-against-doping-in-sport/>).

The monitoring of compliance with the Convention is ensured by the Conference of Parties, which is held at UNESCO headquarters in Paris every two years.[141] Governments are required to provide a report that outlines all the measures they have taken to comply with the provisions of the Convention.[142]

5 The Court of Arbitration for Sport (CAS)

CAS is often referred to as the 'sport's supreme court'.[143] It aims to facilitate the settlement of sports-related disputes by means of procedural rules adapted to the specific needs of the sport world.[144]

CAS is based in Lausanne, Switzerland.[145] It officially came into existence in 1984, from the initiative of the IOC President at the time, Juan Antonio Samaranch.[146] Its creation was motivated by the desire to submit sports disputes to an institution offering specialised knowledge, rapid action and a low cost,[147] but also to standardise the case law ruled in this area,[148] subject to enforcement according to the *New York Convention*.[149]

CAS is composed of two permanent arbitration divisions: the Ordinary Arbitration Division, having general jurisdiction, and the Appeal Arbitration Division, responsible for the resolution of disputes relating to challenges to decisions made by internal bodies of sports organisations.[150]

---

[141]UNESCO website (<http://www.unesco.org/new/en/social-and-human-sciences/themes/anti-doping/conference-of-parties/>).

[142]Ibid.

[143]WADA website (<https://www.wada-ama.org/en/court-of-arbitration-for-sport>).

[144]Ibid. See also CAS website (<http://www.tas-cas.org/en/index.html>); and CAS Code, mentioned in Chapter 3, Section IIC1, footnote 1431.

[145]CAS Statutes, incorporated in CAS Code, S1.

[146]Matthieu Reeb, 'The Role and Functions of the Court of Arbitration for Sport (CAS)' in Ian Blackshaw, Robert CR Siekmann and Janwillem Soek (eds), *The Court of Arbitration for Sport 1984–2004* (TMC Asser Press, 2006) 31, 32.

[147]Ibid, 31. See also Richard McLaren, 'Twenty-Five Years of the Court of Arbitration for Sport: A Look in the Rear-View Mirror' (2010) 20 *Marquette Sports Law Review* 306 (McLaren, 'Twenty-Five Years').

[148]Richard McLaren, 'The Court of Arbitration for Sport: An Independent Arena for the World's Disputes' (2001) 35 *Valparaiso University Law Review* 381 (McLaren, 'Independent Arena').

[149]*New York Convention of 10 June 1958 on the Recognition and Enforcement of Foreign Arbitral Awards.*

[150]In practice, the Ordinary Arbitration Division particularly addresses commercial and contractual disputes (CAS Statutes, S20/a); the Appeal Arbitration Division, for its part, mainly deals with disciplinary disputes (CAS Statutes, S20/b). Both apply specifically tailored procedures. The 'Ordinary Arbitration Procedure', is characterised by a great deal of procedural autonomy conferred to the parties (CAS Statutes, R38-46). Conversely, the 'Appeals Arbitration Procedure' sets a series of time limits for each step of the procedure, in particular for filing a statement of appeal (21 days

CAS has potentially jurisdiction to arbitrate any sports-related disputes, provided that the parties have agreed to submit the dispute to it.[151] In doping, its jurisdiction is established in principle by the WADC.[152] It is then concretised in sports organisations' regulations through an arbitration clause (of general or specific scope).[153]

The WADC[154] designates CAS (Appeal Division) as the single authority of appeal against the sanctions imposed by international or national federations against international-level athletes for doping acts committed out of competition or during an international competition.

The right of appeal belongs to the sanctioned athlete, the relevant IF, the NADO of the athlete's country of residence or countries where the athlete is a national or licence holder, and WADA.[155] The IOC is also entitled to appeal in cases where the decision may have an effect in relation to the Olympic Games.[156]

The appeal procedure for doping cases involving other types of athletes or competitions is left to the discretion of NADOs.[157] In most cases, appeals are either to CAS or to a panel of arbitrators established under the relevant rules.[158] In any case, minimum procedural safeguards must be respected.[159]

Furthermore, since April 2018, CAS (Ordinary or Appeal Division) has been competent to review WADA's report of non-compliance by a signatory (and its related consequences), as well as conditions for reinstatement.[160]

CAS decisions are final and binding, subject to appeal to the Swiss Federal Tribunal (SFT) only on the grounds of public policy and procedural defects.[161]

---

from the receipt of the decision appealed against) and for the appointment of arbitrators (various deadlines) (CAS Statutes, R47-59).

[151]CAS Code, Art. 27. See also Rachelle Downie 'Improving the Performance of Sports Ultimate Umpire: Reforming the Governance of the Court of Arbitration for Sport' (2011) 12 *Melbourne Journal of International Law* 315, 317.

[152]WADC, Art. 13.2.1.

[153]See Chapter 3 (introductory remarks) and Section IIC1.

[154]WADC, Art. 13.2.1.

[155]WADC, Art. 13.2.3.

[156]Ibid.

[157]WADC, Art. 13.2.2.

[158]Thorpe et al., above n 13 in Chapter 1, 404.

[159]WADC, Art. 13.2.2.

[160]WADC, Art. 13.6 and Compliance Standard, pp. 3, 14 and 45–6. In case of disagreement, the signatory must notify WADA in writing within 21 days of its receipt of the notice from WADA. WADA shall then file a formal notice of dispute with CAS, and the dispute will be resolved by CAS Ordinary Division. If the signatory does communicate such dispute in writing to WADA, the notice will be deemed accepted and will automatically become a final decision enforceable. Any party that has the right to intervene in CAS proceedings (pursuant to Art. 23.5.7 WADC) is entitled to file an appeal with CAS within 21 days of WADA posting that decision on its website. The Appeal shall be resolved by the CAS Appeal Division.

[161]CAS Code, Rule 28; *PILA*, Arts. 190-1.

6 Evaluation: Main Advances, Pitfalls and Remedies

(a) Main Advances

WADA reflects the willingness of governments and the private sports movement to join their efforts to address one of the key regulatory challenges facing the world of sport.[162] This formal joint venture was then and remains an absolutely unique and remarkable partnership.[163] It is the recognition of the fact that governments and sports organisations must act together to fight doping and that neither sector can be successful without mutual collaboration and cooperation.[164]

WADA's key achievement is the adoption of the WADC (and the related *UNESCO Convention*, which make it binding for governments). The adoption of the WADC led to several significant advances in the global fight against doping in sport, including the formalization of certain rules, the clarification of stakeholder responsibilities and more predictable sanctions.[165] This new approach to anti-doping brought consistency to a previously disjointed system.[166]

Since its adoption in 2004, the WADC has proven to be a powerful and effective tool in the harmonisation of anti-doping efforts worldwide.[167] This is demonstrated by the large number of governments and sports that have accepted the WADC, and the growing case law of CAS supporting its main principles.[168]

Never before has a project generated such an adherence within the sports world. This trend also applies to governments, since the *UNESCO Convention* is the most successful convention in the history of UNESCO, in terms of rhythm of ratification after adoption.[169] It is also the second most ratified of all UNESCO Conventions.[170]

Nevertheless, the application of the WADC is not universal, as the example of North American sport illustrates.

---

[162] Flint, Lewis and Taylor, above n 25, 145.

[163] Ibid.

[164] UNESCO Director-General's Final Report on the Preparation of the International Convention Against Doping in Sport (Paris, February 2005), paragraph 7. This report is available on the UNESCO website (<http://unesdoc.unesco.org/images/0013/001388/138831e.pdf>).

[165] WADA website (<https://www.wada-ama.org/en/what-we-do/the-code>).

[166] Ibid.

[167] Ibid.

[168] Ibid.

[169] UNESCO website (<http://www.unesco.org/new/en/social-and-human-sciences/themes/anti-doping/international-convention-against-doping-in-sport/>).

[170] Ibid.

(b) Pitfalls and Remedies

(i) The North American Exception

While the US has ratified the *UNESCO Convention*, major US professional sports leagues (including the NFL, NHL, MLS and MLB, discussed above)[171] are not signatories of the WADC.[172] US professional sports leagues negotiate their own drug testing policies and procedures through collective bargaining.[173] These policies are deemed to be less stringent than those of other SGBs.[174] However, in recent years, they have been brought closer to WADA standards, thanks to political pressure and collaboration with WADA.[175]

Interestingly, the MLS, although hierarchically subordinated to FIFA,[176] proceeds the same way as other leagues. It negotiates its drug policy in the margins of WADA, whilst still drawing on its standards.[177]

The situation is similar in Canada, where the CFL and its players' association regularly hold talks on their drug policy.[178]

Even if increased collaboration between North American leagues and WADA could be considered, the 'North American exception' will remain so. It has, however, recently been eclipsed by another concern: the potential non-compliance of some signatories, illustrated by the Russian doping affair.

(ii) The Russian Doping Affair (2014) and WADA Anti-Doping Reforms

Independent Investigations

In December 2014, WADA launched an investigation under the leadership of founding president Dick Pound, after German broadcaster ARD reported widespread doping in Russian athletics.[179] Pound's investigation substantiated these

---

[171]See Chapter 3, Sections IA et seq, IB et seq, IC et seq and ID1.

[172]WADA website (<https://www.wada-ama.org/en/code-signatories> and <https://www.wada-ama.org/en/unesco-convention-ratifications>).

[173]For more details, see eg, Brent D Showalter, Steroid Testing Policies in Professional Sports: Regulated by Congress or Responsibility of the Leagues?' (2007) *Marquette Sports Law Review* 651, 651–78, in particular 655.

[174]Ibid, 664.

[175]Ibid, 656. See also WADA statement on Al Jazeera's documentary, 28 December 2015 (<https://www.wada-ama.org/en/media/news/2015-12/wada-statement-on-al-jazeera-documentary>).

[176]See Chapter 3, Sections IC and IC1.

[177]See MLS CBA, Arts. 12.1 and 12.2, and Exhibit 5. The MLS' list of prohibited substances (in-competition) mirrors in particular that of WADA.

[178]For more details, see CFL CBA, Art. 32; and CFL website (<https://www.cfl.ca/2015/05/05/cfl-drug-policy-glance/>).

[179]WADA, press release, 16 December 2014 (<https://www.wada-ama.org/en/media/news/2014-12/wada-announces-details-of-independent-commission>).

allegations,[180] and resulted in WADA ruling the Russian Anti-Doping Agency (RUSADA) non-compliant with the WADC.[181] The International Association of Athletics Federations (IAAF) also suspended the All-Russia Athletics Federation (ARAF) (now called the Russian Athletics Federation, RUSAF) indefinitely from world track and field events.[182]

In May 2016, WADA appointed Canadian law professor Richard McLaren to investigate allegations of state-sponsored doping in Russia, exposed in a documentary aired on the American television network CBS.[183] McLaren published two reports, in July and December 2016, which marked a turning point in the fight against doping.[184] The first report showed evidence of systematic state-sponsored subversion of the drug testing processes from 2010, with the view to protecting the best Russian athletes for the 2014 Olympic Winter Games in Sochi, Russia.[185] It highlighted the involvement of the Moscow and Sochi laboratories, the Russian ministry of Sport and the Russian Federal Security Service (FSB).[186] The second report confirmed and expanded on much of the evidence contained in the first report.[187] It also suggested that more than 1000 Russian athletes from summer and winter sports were involved in or benefited from this conspiracy.[188]

McLaren's first report was released one month before the 2016 Summer Olympic Games in Rio, raising the issue of the Russian athletes' participation in the competition. The IOC made the decision to let each IF resolve this issue.[189] Only the IAAF banned Russian athletes, with the exception of a few athletes (based outside the Russian system) allowed to compete as neutral competitors.[190]

---

[180]The results of this investigation, summed up in Pound's reports, are available on WADA website (<https://www.wada-ama.org/en/resources/world-anti-doping-program/independent-commission-report-1> and <https://www.wada-ama.org/en/resources/world-anti-doping-program/independent-commission-report-2>).

[181]WADA, press release, 18 November 2015 (<https://www.wada-ama.org/en/media/news/2015-11/foundation-board-media-release-wada-strengthens-anti-doping-worldwide>).

[182]IAAF, press release, 13 November 2015 (<https://www.iaaf.org/news/press-release/iaaf-araf-suspended>).

[183]WADA, press release, 19 May 2016 (<https://www.wada-ama.org/en/media/news/2016-05/wada-names-richard-mclaren-to-sochi-investigation-team>).

[184]These reports are available on WADA website (<https://www.wada-ama.org/en/resources/doping-control-process/mclaren-independent-investigation-report-part-i> and <https://www.wada-ama.org/en/resources/doping-control-process/mclaren-independent-investigation-report-part-ii>).

[185]McLaren report (I), pp. 10 and 18.

[186]Ibid.

[187]McLaren report (II), pp. 1–4.

[188]Ibid, pp. 2, 5 and 57 together with Appendix A.

[189]IOC, press release, 24 July 2016 (<https://www.olympic.org/news/decision-of-the-ioc-executive-board-concerning-the-participation-of-russian-athletes-in-the-olympic-games-rio-2016>).

[190]IAAF, press release, 17 June 2016 (<https://www.iaaf.org/news/press-release/iaaf-council-meeting-vienna>). This webpage contains a link to the IAAF Task Force interim report that formed the basis of this decision.

Simultaneously, the IOC set up two Commissions: the Oswald and Schmid Commissions.[191] The Oswald Commission, chaired by IOC Executive member Denis Oswald, was originally tasked to look into allegations related to the manipulation of samples given by Russian athletes at the 2014 Olympic Winter Games in Sochi, and to take appropriate sanctions.[192] Its mandate was subsequently expanded to include the 2012 Olympic Summer Games in London.[193] It has already led to dozens of Russian athletes being stripped off their medals and/or banned from the Olympics for life.[194] The Schmid Commission, chaired by former Swiss Confederation President Samuel Schmid, was established to examine the institutional conspiracy across summer and winter sports athletes who participated with Russian officials within the Ministry of Sport and its infrastructure.[195] It published a report[196] that confirmed the existence of a ‘systemic manipulation of anti-doping results’ at events including Sochi 2014.[197]

In December 2017, the IOC imposed a suspension on the Russian Olympic Committee (ROC) in addition to a fine of USD15 million.[198] It also banned Russian former sports minister Vitaly Mutko for life, and sanctioned a number of top sports officials.[199] Finally, it created a path for clean Russian athletes to compete in the 2018 Winter Olympic Games in Pyeongchang, South Korea, under a neutral Olympic flag.[200] This allowed 169 handpicked Russian athletes to participate in the Games.[201] No exceptions were made for the athletes sanctioned by the Oswald

[191] IOC’s website (<https://www.olympic.org/fight-against-doping/sochi-2014-investigations>).

[192] Ibid.

[193] IOC, press release, 9 December 2016 (<https://www.olympic.org/news/statement-of-the-ioc-regarding-the-independent-person-report>).

[194] IOC Fact Sheet, 22 December 2017 (<https://stillmed.olympic.org/media/Document%20Library/OlympicOrg/IOC/Who-We-Are/Commissions/Disciplinary-Commission/2017/IOC-re-analysis-programme-Sochi-2014-22-december-2017-1.pdf#_ga=2.35280545.1613046842.1515970842-402556292.1510806486>).

[195] IOC’s website (<https://www.olympic.org/fight-against-doping/sochi-2014-investigations>).

[196] The Schmid report is available on the IOC’s website (<https://stillmed.olympic.org/media/Document%20Library/OlympicOrg/IOC/Who-We-Are/Commissions/Disciplinary-Commission/IOC-DC-Schmid/IOC-Disciplinary-Commission-Schmid-Report.pdf#_ga=2.174085026.1613046842.1515970842-402556292.1510806486>).

[197] Schmid report, p. 28.

[198] IOC, press release, 5 December 2017 (<https://www.olympic.org/news/ioc-suspends-russian-noc-and-creates-a-path-for-clean-individual-athletes-to-compete-in-pyeongchang-2018-under-the-olympic-flag>).

[199] Ibid.

[200] Ibid.

[201] ‘Olympics: IOC Confirms 169 Russians Cleared to Compete in Pyeongchang’, *Reuters*, 28 January 2018 (<https://www.reuters.com/article/us-olympics-2018-russia-team/olympics-ioc-confirms-169-russians-cleared-to-compete-in-pyeongchang-idUSKBN1FG0Y6>).

Commission, despite some of them being cleared, at the last minute, by CAS due to lack of evidence.[202]

At the end of February 2018, the IOC lifted ROC's suspension with immediate effect.[203] It considered that it met the conditions for reinstatement, despite the discovery of two doping cases of Russian athletes during the Games.[204] WADA did the same with RUSADA in September 2018.[205] The IAAF maintained RUSAF's ban, a position that is currently being challenged before CAS.[206]

WADA Anti-Doping Reforms

The Russian doping affair has led anti-doping authorities, and WADA in particular, to reflect upon the future of the current anti-doping system. As mentioned above,[207] it has already prompted minor amendments of the WADC in relation to compliance, and the adoption of a new International Standard in this area. It also triggered a full review process, with a new WADC coming into force in 2021.[208]

The 5th and 6th Olympic Summits,[209] which are intended to be incorporated into broader stakeholders' consultations, already give a glimpse of the ongoing and

---

[202] CAS, media release, 1 February 2018 (<http://www.tas-cas.org/fileadmin/user_upload/Media_Release__decision_RUS_IOC_.pdf>); and IOC, press release, 5 February 2018 (<https://www.olympic.org/news/request-to-invite-15-athletes-and-coaches-to-pyeongchang-2018-for-the-olympic-athlete-from-russia-group-declined>). The power struggle between the IOC and CAS was finally resolved when CAS conceded, in a subsequent sentence, that the IOC was free to establish its own eligibility conditions, excluding in instances relating to discriminatory, arbitrary or dishonest practices (which were not applicable in this case) [CAS, media release, 9 February 2018 (<http://www.tas-cas.org/fileadmin/user_upload/Media_Release_AHD9_DecisionOG18_02_03.pdf>)]. Note that CAS used the same argument against another group of the athletes who, without being sanctioned by the Oswald Commission, contested the results of the vetting conducted by the IOC.

[203] IOC, press releases, 25 and 28 February 2018 (<https://www.olympic.org/news/decision-of-the-ioc-executive-board-2018-02-25> and <https://www.olympic.org/news/ioc-statement-2018-02-28>).

[204] Ibid.

[205] WADA, press release, 20 September 2018 (<https://www.wada-ama.org/en/media/news/2018-09/wada-executive-committee-decides-to-reinstate-rusada-subject-to-strict-conditions>).

[206] CAS, media release, 27 September 2018 (<http://www.tas-cas.org/fileadmin/user_upload/Media_Release_5921.pdf>).

[207] See this chapter, Sections IIIA3(a)(i) and IIIA3(a)(ii).

[208] See this chapter, Section IIIA3(a)(i).

[209] See Declaration of the 5th Olympic Summit, 8 October 2016, pp. 1–3, updated by the decisions of the IOC Executive Board of 16 March and 9 July 2017; and Declaration of the 6th Olympic Summit, 28 October 2017. All documents are available on the IOC website (<https://www.olympic.org/news/declaration-of-the-5th-olympic-summit>, <https://www.olympic.org/news/declaration-of-the-ioc-executive-board-1>, <https://www.olympic.org/news/the-international-olympic-committee-ioc-executive-board-eb-today-ended-its-first-day-of-meetings-in-lausanne-switzerland-with-several-updates-and-decisions-on-institutional-matters> and <https://www.olympic.org/news/communique-of-the-olympic-summit>).

future reforms.[210] The most significant proposed reform is the creation of an Independent Testing Agency (ITA) within WADA's framework to replace IFs and MEOs as the primary body responsible for drug testing.[211] This is part of an overarching attempt to address the conflicts of interest of IFs and MEOs, caught between two potentially antagonistic duties, the fight against doping (and its related scandals) and the promotion of their sport. Another key reform is the delegation of major anti-doping sanctions to CAS, which would act as a court of first instance.[212] To this are added specific governance reforms, such as the nomination of a neutral president and independent board members, aimed at strengthening WADA and avoiding internal conflicts of interest.[213] Further, a stronger representation of athletes within the sports movement, allowing them more influence in the decision-making process, is contemplated.[214]

All proposals are currently being examined. Some of these proposals have already been endorsed by WADA, and are on track.[215] It goes without saying that their full implementation would result in a substantial additional workload for both WADA and CAS, which should translate into an increased funding.[216] The IOC has already announced that the aforementioned USD15-million fine imposed on the ROC[217] will contribute to increasing the capacity and integrity of the new global anti-doping system.[218] Furthermore, the Olympic Movement is ready to step up its financial contribution, depending on the implementation of the proposed reforms and the results provided by WADA.[219] This could be partly achieved by transferring the pots of money each IF/MEO is currently spending on its own anti-doping operation to WADA, knowing that the amount in question would then in principle

---

[210] Stakeholders' consultations and comments can be consulted in gradual stages on WADA website (<https://www.wada-ama.org/en/media/news/2018-06/wada-launches-second-phase-of-2021-code-review-process-and-first-phase-for>).

[211] Ibid.

[212] Ibid.

[213] Ibid.

[214] Ibid.

[215] Thus, the ITA, which started its operations in June 2018, is expected to manage pre-games testing for the 2020 Olympic Summer Games in Tokyo (<https://www.olympic.org/news/independent-testing-authority-on-track> and <https://www.olympic.org/news/international-testing-agency-appoints-director-general>).

[216] Press Association, 'IOC Promises to Boost WADA's Funding if it Agrees to Anti-Doping Reform', *The Guardian*, 9 October 2016 (<https://www.theguardian.com/sport/2016/oct/08/ioc-wada-funding-anti-doping-reform>). Note that in May 2018, WADA Foundation Board endorsed an increase in WADA's budget for each of the next four years (2019–22) (<https://www.wada-ama.org/en/media/news/2018-05/wada-foundation-board-endorses-budget-increase-to-strengthen-agencys-capacity-to>).

[217] See this chapter, Section IIIA6(b)(ii).

[218] IOC, press release, 5 December 2017 (<https://www.olympic.org/news/ioc-suspends-russian-noc-and-creates-a-path-for-clean-individual-athletes-to-compete-in-pyeongchang-2018-under-the-olympic-flag>).

[219] Declaration of the 5th Olympic Summit, above n 209, p. 3.

have to be matched by governments.[220] Finally, the idea of imposing a small anti-doping levy on broadcasters and sponsors does not seem to have unanimous support.[221]

(iii) The University of Tübingen's and Harvard's Study (2017) and the International Olympic Committee (IOC)'s New Approach to Testing

The structural and operational issues brought to light by the Russian doping affair are not the only ones to undermine the smooth running of the fight against doping. The effectiveness of the 300 000 biological tests carried out annually under WADA's leadership[222] is also problematic. While only 1–2% of these tests result in Adverse Analytical Findings (AAF),[223] and even fewer in Anti-Doping Rule Violations (ADRV),[224] doping in sport is in all likelihood far more prevalent than that. This is suggested in a study by researchers from the Universities of Tübingen (Germany) and Harvard (US) published in 2017,[225] six years after being commissioned by WADA.[226]

The research is based on anonymous surveys carried out at two elite athletics competitions in 2011: the World Championships in Athletics (WCA) and the Pan-Arab Games (PAG).[227] It found that more than 43% of athletes questioned at WCA had doped in the past year, with the figure reaching over 57% for those at

[220] Press Association, above n 216.

[221] Ibid.

[222] WADA Anti-Doping Testing Figures Report 2017, pp. 1 and 6. This report, which includes Olympic sports, non-Olympic sports and non-ADAMS data, lists 4596 AAF from 322 050 samples in 2016 (compared with 4822 AAF from 300 565 samples in 2016). It is available on WADA website (<https://www.wada-ama.org/sites/default/files/resources/files/2017_anti-doping_testing_figures_en_0.pdf>).

[223] Ibid.

[224] WADA Anti-Doping Rule Violations (ADRV) Report 2016, p. 5. This report, which does not include non-ADAMS data, indicates that 44% of samples reported as AAF led to ADRV (sanctions). The difference between AAF and ADRV can be explained by various reasons, such as TUEs and possible multiple measurements performed on the same athlete [for more details, see WADA website (<https://www.wada-ama.org/sites/default/files/resources/files/2016_adrvs_report_web_release_april_2018_0.pdf> and (<https://www.wada-ama.org/en/questions-answers/ado-testing-statistics>)].

[225] Rolf Ulrich et al., 'Doping in Two Elite Athletics Competitions Assessed by Randomized-Response Surveys' (2018) 48 *Sports Medicine* 211, 211–19 [officially published in 2017 on 'First Online', but partly leaked to the media from 2013]. The surveys comprise 2167 athletes in total.

[226] Some commentators attribute this delay to the IAAF, which apparently tried to suppress the publication of this study. Others explain it as a result of pressure from WADA that, if it were to be confirmed, would raise problems in terms of transparency [Marina Nehme and Catherine Ordway, 'Governance and Anti-Doping: Beyond the Fox and the Hen House' in Ulrich Haas and Deborah Healey (eds), *Doping in Sport and the Law* (Hart Publishing, 2016) 207, 222].

[227] Ibid, 211 and 214.

PAG.[228] By contrast, biological tests at the events came back positive in just 0.5% of cases at WCA and under 4% at PAG.[229]

When these statistics are seen in conjunction with the annual cost of anti-doping tests for the Olympic Movement (USD180 million), outlined above,[230] they prompt scrutiny of the cost efficiency of WADA's anti-doping system.

The IOC has already partially recognised this issue. Despite increased volume, it conducted more targeted testing prior to the 2018 Winter Olympic Games. Particular attention was paid to at-risk disciplines and nationalities, top-ranked athletes, and suspicious changes in performance or adverse testing history.[231]

(iv) The UNESCO Internal Oversight Service (IOS)'s Report (2017) and its Related Reforms

Governments are not spared from difficulties either. This is demonstrated in a report of the UNESCO IOS Evaluation Office,[232] published in 2017, on the occasion of the 10-year anniversary of the *UNESCO Convention* entering into force.

This report first highlights the overall success, importance and relevance of the *UNESCO Convention*.[233] It then identifies several areas of possible improvement, including:

- Implementation of the Convention;
- Synergy between the anti-doping legal instruments available;
- Gender equality;
- Working methods of the Conference of Parties and Bureau;
- Monitoring compliance with the Convention;
- Resource mobilisation and/or allocation (Fund for the Elimination of Doping in Sport and Convention Secretariat);
- Horizontal integration between the Convention's mechanisms and UNESCO's other bodies.[234]

The report also makes numerous recommendations.[235] On this basis, the Secretariat, was charged, in 2018, to develop an action plan, including timeline, associated

---

[228]Ibid, 211 and 216.

[229]Ibid, 216.

[230]See this chapter, Section IIIA2(d).

[231]IOC, press release, 18 January 2018 (<https://www.olympic.org/news/already-over-14-000-doping-tests-conducted-to-safeguard-pyeongchang-2018>).

[232]IOS Evaluation Office, *Evaluation of UNESCO's International Convention against doping in sport*, Report, August 2017 (<http://unesdoc.unesco.org/images/0025/002587/258739E.pdf>).

[233]IOS Report, pp. 5 and 7–8.

[234]IOS Report, pp. 5–7.

[235]IOS Report, pp. 9–14.

costs, priority actions and required procedural changes, to be circulated to governments.[236]

Interesting initiatives, inspired by the IOS report and/or triggered by the Russian doping affair,[237] are already at various stages of development. This includes the establishment of a national public policy review (Policy Advice Project) to provide guidance and reform-oriented recommendations to governments;[238] the drafting of operational guidelines and a framework of consequences of non-compliance with the convention to reinforce the monitoring system;[239] and the drafting of model legislation and policies to encourage the sharing of information between public service agencies and anti-doping organisations.[240]

(c) Final Remarks

Despite its shortcomings and ongoing reforms, the current anti-doping system nonetheless demonstrates a remarkable effort of, and outcome for, harmonisation, and a significant achievement globally. It has also started to be emulated in other fields, such as match-fixing.

B Match-Fixing

Match-fixing is about to be regulated by a Council of Europe Convention, which is yet to come into force. To this is added the IOC 'Olympic Movement Code on the Prevention of the Manipulation of Competitions' and its related Unit, which has so far been preferred to the creation of a World Sports Integrity Agency.

1 Discussions Related to the Creation of a World Sports Integrity Agency

Since the early 2000s, some sports managers, betting experts and commentators voiced their support for the implementation of a unified strategy to fight against

---

[236]Conference of Parties to the International Convention against Doping in Sport, 25–26 September 2017, Resolution 6CP/15, p. 4 (<http://unesdoc.unesco.org/images/0025/002592/259298E.pdf>). The action plan was drafted but is not available to the public [email from Ekaterina Sediakina-Rivière (IOS, Associate Evaluation Specialist) to author, 1 March 2018].

[237]See this chapter, Section IIIA6(b)(ii).

[238]IOS Report, p. 13.

[239]Ibid.

[240]Ibid.

corruption, and match-fixing in particular.[241] They called for the creation of a World Sports Integrity Agency, modelled on, or even encapsulating WADA.[242]

This proposal, although initially put forward with hesitation, has gained momentum over time, due to the massive increase of legal and illegal sports betting around the world, coupled with various corruption scandals.[243] The proposal even received the support of WADA's then Director General, David Howman,[244] as well as legal scholars, which examined how it might operate, on the basis, for instance, of a WADA-like Code.[245] Nevertheless, it did not go further than the discussion stage, due to the absence of consensus within sports organisations.[246] The main concerns among sports organisations reluctant to embrace reforms were the loss of their prerogatives, the spectre of organised crime and law enforcement involvement, related negative exposure, as well as the issue of financing.[247]

This situation pushed governments to take the lead through the adoption of a European convention.

2 *The Convention on the Manipulation of Sports Competitions (Macolin Convention)*

The Convention on the Manipulation of Sports Competitions (Macolin Convention) is a legally binding convention elaborated by the Council of Europe.[248] It was opened for signature by member countries and, under restrictive conditions, non--members,[249] during the 13th Council of Europe Conference of Ministers Responsi-

---

[241]For more details, see eg, Jean-Loup Chappelet, 'L'Agence Mondiale Antidopage: Un nouveau régulateur des relations internationales sportives' (Autumn 2002) Nr 111 *Relations* Internationales 381, 400–1 (Chappelet, 'Agence'); Alexandra Veuthey, 'Match-Fixing and Governance in Cricket and Football: What is the Fix?' (2014) 14 *International Sports Law Journal* 82, 104–5 (Veuthey, 'Match-Fixing').

[242]Ibid.

[243]For more details about this evolution, see Jean-Loup Chappelet, 'The Olympic Fight Against Match-Fixing' (2015) 18 *Sport in Society* 1260, 1260 and 1266 (Chappelet, 'Match-Fixing'); Jean-Loup Chappelet, 'Beyond Governance: the Need to Improve the Regulation of International Sport' (2018) 21 *Sport in Society* 724, 724–5 (Chappelet, 'Governance').

[244]David Howman, 'Time for a World Sports Integrity Agency', statement from WADA director general following the European Union Sports Forum Budapest, 24 February 2011 (<https://www.wada-ama.org/en/media/news/2011-02/statement-from-wada-director-general-following-the-european-union-sports-forum>).

[245]See eg, Veuthey, 'Match-Fixing', above n 241, 104–5.

[246]Ibid, 104.

[247]Ibid, footnote 416.

[248]Council of Europe website (<https://www.coe.int/en/web/conventions/full-list/-/conventions/treaty/215>).

[249]Ibid.

ble for Sport in September 2014 in Macolin, Switzerland.[250] It has already been signed by 33 countries, of which three have already ratified it.[251] It will come into force as soon as it has been ratified by five countries.[252] Twenty-five more countries are expected to join, including the US, Canada and Australia.[253]

The Macolin Convention requires governments to create effective criminal standards and strengthen collaboration and mutual legal assistance in the fight against match-fixing.[254] It also makes recommendations regarding contacts with sports betting operators and sports organisations.[255]

The Convention aims to facilitate exchanges between the stakeholders, around three main axes: prevention, monitoring and investigation.[256] In a bid to achieve coordination, it provides common definitions, and requires governments to set up national platforms for effective ongoing detection of and response to match-fixing.[257] Interestingly, it calls on governments to use gathered information for risk assessment and risk management in cooperation with sports organisations and betting operators.[258] Its implementation and monitoring will be ensured by a follow-up Committee, which will be set up in due course.[259]

3 Recent Measures Taken by the International Olympic Committee (IOC)

The IOC, which has been active in the field of match-fixing since 2007,[260] finally decided to prioritise strengthening its internal structure and regulations.

In 2015, the IOC adopted an 'Olympic Movement Code on the Prevention of the Manipulation of Competitions' (Olympic Code),[261] This Code aims to provide the

---

[250]Council of Europe website (<https://www.coe.int/fr/web/secretary-general/speeches/-/asset_publisher/gFMvl0SKOUrv/content/13th-council-of-europe-conference-of-ministers-responsible-for-sport?_101_INSTANCE_gFMvl0SKOUrv_viewMode=view/%3E)>).

[251]Council of Europe website (<https://www.coe.int/en/web/conventions/full-list/-/conventions/treaty/215>).

[252]Ibid.

[253]Ibid.

[254]*Macolin Convention*, Arts. 15-28.

[255]*Macolin Convention*, Arts. 7-14.

[256]*Macolin Convention*, Arts. 4 and 12 (as well as the overall structure of the Convention).

[257]*Macolin Convention*, Arts. 3 and 13.

[258]*Macolin Convention*, Arts. 5 and 12.

[259]Explanatory report to the Council of Europe Convention on the Manipulation of Sports Competitions – CETS 215 –, 18 September 2014, pp. 31–2 (<https://rm.coe.int/CoERMPublicCommonSearchServices/DisplayDCTMContent?documentId=09000016800d383f>).

[260]From 2007 to 2014, the IOC's intervention took various forms (regulations, meetings, memoranda of understanding), before culminating in the establishment of an Olympic Monitoring System [Chappelet, 'Match-Fixing', above n 243, 1263–6].

[261]Olympic Movement Code on the Prevention of the Manipulation of Competitions (2015) (<https://stillmed.olympic.org/media/Document%20Library/OlympicOrg/IOC/Who-We-Are/Commissions/Ethics/Good-Governance/olympic_movement_code_on_the_prevention_of_the_

Olympic Movement with harmonised regulations to protect all competitions from the risk of manipulation.[262] It defines the different kinds of violations and minimum standards of disciplinary procedures, in compliance with the *Macolin Convention*.[263] It is compulsory for any sports organisation bound by the Olympic Charter.[264]

In 2017, the IOC established the 'Olympic Movement Unit on the Prevention of the Manipulation of Competitions' (Olympic Unit) as part of its IOC Ethics and Compliance Office.[265] This Unit aims to oversee the Olympic Movement's overall fight against match-fixing,[266] while letting each sports organisation conduct its own investigation and sanctioning.[267]

C Spectator Violence

Spectator violence is currently regulated by a 1985 Council of Europe Convention, which is in the process of being replaced by a new (updated) convention.

1 *The European Convention on Spectator Violence and Misbehaviour at Sports Events and in Particular at Football Matches (1985)*

The European Convention on Spectator Violence was elaborated by the Council of Europe in the wake of the Heysel disaster (Belgium) and the emergence of football hooliganism in Europe.[268] The Convention, which came into force in 1985, was signed and ratified by 41 states parties to the Council of Europe, as well as Morocco.[269] It grants an observer status to a few non-member states, football

manipulation_of_competitions-2015-en.pdf#_ga=2.37936038.447501667.1520204391-402556292.1510806486>).

262 IOC, press release of 17 December 2015 (<https://www.olympic.org/news/ioc-publishes-unprecedented-olympic-movement-code-for-preventing-competition-manipulation>).

263 Ibid.

264 Ibid. See also Olympic Charter, Art. 1.4 and Olympic Code, Art. 7.1.

265 IOC website (<https://www.olympic.org/prevention-competition-manipulation>).

266 Ibid.

267 Email from Ms Ingrid Beutler (IOC Integrity Manager) to author, 1 March 2018.

268 The Heysel disaster occured in 1985, during the European Cup final between Juventus (Turin) and Liverpool at Heysel stadium in Brussels. It cost the lives of 39 people, and led to a five-year blanket ban on English football teams at European competitions (<https://www.coe.int/en/web/sport/historical-background-of-the-convention>).

269 Council of Europe website (<https://www.coe.int/en/web/conventions/full-list/-/conventions/treaty/120/signatures?p_auth=X3Dgw3ot>).

governing bodies (FIFA, UEFA, EPL), Supporters Direct Europe (SDE) and Interpol.[270] It aims to prevent crowd violence and misbehaviour by spectators, and to ensure spectator safety during sports events, in particular football.[271] It centres around three main themes: prevention, cooperation and repression.[272]

A Standing Committee monitors the Convention based on annual reports drafted by governments, auto-evaluations and visits, which are then used as a basis for the preparation of country profiles.[273] The Committee also adopts recommendations and responds to new concerns.[274]

The Committee started to revise the original text of the Convention in 2012.[275] This is in the process of gradually being replaced by a new Convention.

2 *The Council of Europe Convention on an Integrated Safety, Security and Service Approach at Football Matches and Other Sports Events (2017)*

The Council of Europe Convention on Safety, Security and Services was opened for signature in July 2016 in France,[276] and came into force in November 2017.[277] Each state that wants to ratify the new Convention will automatically repeal the former one so that only one international standard applies.[278]

The Convention builds upon the work previously accomplished. However, it offers an enhanced integrated multi-agency approach, based on three independent pillars: safety, security and services.[279] It also establishes a new Committee on Safety and Security,[280] and recommends the use of risk assessment.[281] Finally, it takes into account the new best practice developed internationally since the adoption of the original Convention, as well as societal changes.[282]

---

[270]Council of Europe website (<https://www.coe.int/en/web/sport/standing-committee-of-the-european-convention-on-spectator-violence>).

[271]Council of Europe website (<https://www.coe.int/en/web/sport/violence-convention>).

[272]Europe Watchdog website (<https://www.europewatchdog.info/en/international-treaties/treaties_and_monitoring/sport_conventions/>).

[273]Ibid.

[274]Council of Europe website (<https://www.coe.int/en/web/sport/violence-convention>).

[275]Ibid.

[276]Ibid.

[277]Ibid.

[278]Ibid.

[279]Explanatory report of the Convention – CETS 218 – Integrated Safety, Security and Service Approach at Sports Events, 3 August 2016, p. 4. This report is available on the Council of Europe website (<https://rm.coe.int/CoERMPublicCommonSearchServices/DisplayDCTMContent?documentId=0900001680666d0d>).

[280]Explanatory report of the Convention, p. 5.

[281]Ibid, 11.

[282]Ibid, 2–3.

IV Lessons for Concussion

The harmonised mechanisms in doping, match-fixing and spectator violence have paved the way for similar concussion reforms. Doping, and to a lesser extent match-fixing and spectator violence, also offer useful guidance regarding the way such reforms should be undertaken, and the predictable challenges that they may face.

A Doping

The substantial similarities between doping and concussion (same 'breeding ground' for reforms, need for a global approach, public health aspects, identical general pillars)[283] have already been highlighted. The particularities of doping, which distinguish it from concussion (stronger focus on disciplinary measures than public health aspects, strong reliance on the Olympic Movement, established phenomenon)[284] have also been underlined.

The following sections build on these similarities and differences to accurately assess the possible contribution of the anti-doping system to concussion, component by component.

1 The World Anti-Doping Agency (WADA)

WADA represents an interesting starting point for the establishment of a World Sports Safety Agency (creation/mission, structure/governance, operation and funding). Some components (eg, specific duties, testing infrastructure, stakeholders) appear, however, to have a limited (if any) relevance, while others are missing.

---

[283]See this chapter, Section IIA.

[284]Ibid.

Components	WADA	Relevant	Irrelevant	Not covered
Creation and mission	Creation by IOC with the support of governments	✓		
	General duties	✓		
	Specific duties related to concussion/sports injuries			✓
Structure and governance	Legal form and bodies	✓		
	(Potential) headquarters, regional offices	✓		
	Equal representation of sports movement/ governments	✓		
	Representation leagues			✓
	Representation entities in charge of public health and/or player safety			✓
	Additional independent members + strong athletes' representation (forthcoming)	✓		
Operation	IOC, IFs (and member associations), governments	✓		
	Testing infrastructure (NOCs, MEOs, NADOs, future ITA)		✓	
	Leagues			✓
	Entities in charge of public health and/or player safety			✓
	Clubs			✓
Funding	Budget	✓		
	Public/private funding (parity basis) from sports movement and governments	✓		
	Financial contribution from leagues			✓
	Budget region allocation for governments (tailored calculation)			✓
	Additional funding necessary for supportive infrastructure	✓		

2 The World Anti-Doping Code (WADC) *and the International Convention against Doping in Sport (UNESCO Convention)*

The WADC (including its International Standards) and the *UNESCO Convention* provide interesting insights for the introduction of an International Standard for Concussion (eg, possibility to incorporate fragmented efforts into a more global system, signatories, outlines, implementation/compliance/enforcement, CAS). Again, some components (eg, stakeholders, disciplinary regulation, mandatory jurisdiction of CAS) have limited or no interest, or reveal gaps.

Components	WADC and UNESCO Convention	Relevant	Irrelevant	Not covered
Past efforts	Taking into account of past efforts	✓		
Code signatories	Ifs	✓		
	Leagues			✓
	Testing infrastructure (NOCs, MEOs, NADOs)		✓	
Code outlines	One main document, supplemented by schedules and model rules	✓		
Code content	Part III of the Code (role and responsibilities of signatories)	✓		
	Other parts of the Code and disciplinary regulation		✓	
	General principles on compliance and privacy	✓		
Code legal standard of care	Required standard of care towards athletes			✓
Code implementation, compliance and enforcement	Incorporation of principles and good practices into signatories' regulations and policies; monitoring	✓		
	Systematic monitoring (annual reports)			✓
	Respect by IFs prerequisite for Olympic participation and funding	✓		
	Flexibility in specific cases			✓
	Respect by national associations as a condition for membership and funding	✓		
	Monitoring national associations and clubs			✓
Convention signatories	Governments	✓		
Convention content	General obligations (eg, education, research)	✓		
	Obligations specific to doping		✓	
	Obligations specific to concussion			✓
	Fund to assist governments to develop education (and research) programs	✓		
	Compliance by governments by way of legislation, regulation, policies	✓		
Convention implementation and compliance	Withdrawal of financial support from non-compliant sports organisations	✓		
	Reports	✓		
	Reform-oriented recommendations or model legislation for governments, close monitoring, framework of consequences if no compliance, efficient resource mobilisation strategy (forthcoming)	✓		

(continued)

Components	WADC and UNESCO Convention	Relevant	Irrelevant	Not covered
CAS	Intervention of the CAS (compliance signatories and other proceedings)	✓		
	Flexibility			✓
	Proceedings against SGBs instead of athletes			✓

3 Main Hurdles

The obstacles that WADA and governments have faced also provide useful lessons for the area of concussion. They are discussed briefly here, and will be expanded upon in the conclusion.

The North American exception[285] demonstrates that any harmonised system, no matter how successful and expanded it may be, can never be absolute. It particularly emphasises the difficulty of convincing sports governed by collective bargaining and/or non-Olympic sports to submit to a common system, as well as the need to put in place appropriate means of pressure and compelling incentives. The Russian doping affair,[286] the Tübingen study[287] and the IOS report[288] serve as reminders that any regulatory system must not be set in stone, but should instead be able to adapt to new challenges and develop through experience. The Russian doping affair illustrates the reluctance that SGBs may have to uncover cases that may tarnish the reputation of the sport they want to promote. It shows the risks that may arise from self-governance, or at the very least from too much discretion given to sports organisations. Together with the IOS report, it triggered reviews of the WADC and *UNESCO Convention* aimed at addressing implementation/compliance/enforcement issues and, more generally, improving governance. Some of these reviews may be relevant to concussion regulation, it being specified, however, that the latter, although exposed in the past to concealment attempts,[289] does not carry the same risk of circumvention as the (punitive) measures that govern doping. Ultimately, the Tübingen study recalls the importance of cost-efficiency that, if neglected, prevents the measures in place from fully achieving their goal.

[285] See this chapter, Section IIIA6(b)(i).

[286] See this chapter, Section IIIA6(b)(ii).

[287] See this chapter, Section IIIA6(b)(iii).

[288] See this chapter, Section IIIA6(b)(iv).

[289] See in particular Chapter 3, Section IA1(a). See also Sections IB1, IIA1 and IIB1(a).

B Match-Fixing and Spectator Violence

The *Macolin Convention* and the recent measures taken by the IOC against match-fixing, contain additional interesting ideas (eg, risk assessment) that may be transposed into the area of concussion. They also highlight, by their limited scope, the difficulty of reaching a broad consensus, and the time required for any change. More specifically, they enable some of the objections that could be raised against a harmonised regulatory system of concussion to be anticipated (loss of prerogatives, financing).

Finally, the Conventions on Spectator Violence and Safety offer limited lessons, with interesting monitoring and promotion of best practice (eg, reports and signatory profiles), and emphasis on risk assessment.

C Towards a Reinforced Intervention of the International Olympic Committee (IOC)?

More generally, the strong involvement of the IOC in regard to anti-doping and match-fixing contrasts with the more discreet role that it currently plays in respect of concussion (despite valuable initiatives, such as the funding of the CISG).[290] For now, a major part of the concussion controversy certainly concentrates on sports leagues.[291] However, this controversy increasingly affects Olympic sports.[292] In addition, the IOC acts as the guarantor of international sport and holds significant experience in the implementation of major projects. Accordingly, one may legitimately expect the IOC to intensify its efforts, by being a catalyst for the implementation of the reforms that shall be discussed in the next sections.

[290] See Chapter 2 II. To this are added general measures regarding sports injuries, including the IOC injury surveillance system (see Chapter 3 IC1), conferences and the work undertaken by IOC Research Centres for Prevention of Injury and Protection of Athlete Health (on this latter point, see Caroline F Finch et al., 'Research Priorities of International Sporting Federations and the IOC Research Centers' (October 2016) 2 (1) *BMJ Open Sport and Exercise Medicine* 1, 1) (Finch et al., 'Priorities').

[291] See Chapter 3, Sections IA1(b) et seq (including subsequent case studies), Chapter 5, Sections IIA, VIB2, VIC4(a) and Chapter 6, Section IIIC.

[292] See Chapters 3 et seq (in particular football, water polo, rugby union and ice hockey, and footnotes 2 and 4). See also Chapter 1, Section II, footnote 5 (in particular skiing, ski jumping and tennis).

V A World Sports Safety Agency (WSSA), an International Standard on Concussion (ISC) and its Supporting Convention (*UNESCO Convention*)

WADA, the WADC and the *UNESCO Convention on Doping* are the foundations of the current anti-doping system. They also allow defining the contours of the WSSA, the ISC and its supporting *UNESCO Convention*, which are the key innovative measures of the harmonised regulatory framework for concussion proposed as part of this chapter.

As discussed in Part VI, WSSA would be established as a safety in sport guarantor at an international level. It would, in particular, be responsible for the creation, updating and monitoring of the ISC. The ISC would set up the regulatory mechanisms, duties and practical actions expected of IFs and sports leagues, while the *UNESCO Convention* would establish the duties of governments.

VI Proposed Reforms

A Preliminary Steps

The proposed innovative reforms aim high because they are intended to be implemented on a global scale.[293] The history of anti-doping regulation suggests that far-reaching harmonisation reforms regarding concussion will be difficult to achieve globally in the immediate future, but are more likely to develop in stages. One possible pathway is for a group of interested nations and private sector organisations (including the CISG) to give reform measures the necessary momentum. As discussed earlier in this chapter,[294] the current global regulatory framework for anti-doping owes much to earlier Council of Europe initiatives and sporting regulations promoted by the IOC. A similar staged pattern could be followed for concussion.

This chapter focuses on the final reforms rather than speculating on possible stepping-stones. As the example of doping demonstrates, reforms on a global scale are feasible, provided they are considered in the long term. It should be recalled that 10 years ago, no one had predicted that the issue of concussion, which started with a few dissenters in the US,[295] would generate such controversy and a wide variety of reforms. Yet, this controversy has continued to grow on a daily basis, further strengthening the need for harmonisation. A time is likely to be reached where the impetus for international agreement and major international harmonising reforms regarding concussion will become irresistible. This process can be seen at work in

[293]See this chapter, Section IIA.

[294]See this chapter, Section IIIA1.

[295]See Chapter 3, Sections IA1(b) and IA2.

the case for the institution of WADA, which rode an emerging climate favourable to reform dating from the deaths of two 'doped' cyclists in the 1960s[296] and culminating with events around the 1998 Tour de France.[297] Another example of this process is the case for the creation of a World Sports Integrity Agency which, following its initial proposal, was given impetus by the globalisation of sports betting and various corruption scandals,[298] but remains on hold.

The final reforms, discussed below, could take shape in the same chronological sequence as those implemented for doping, as follows.

B World Sports Safety Agency (WSSA)

The creation of a WSSA would be the first main reform. As already mentioned,[299] WSSA could be a combination of some elements of WADA and new features aimed at sports safety.

1 Creation and Mission

Like WADA,[300] WSSA could be established under the initiative of the IOC (drawing on the IOC's scope and international experience), and benefit from the support of governments.

WSSA would be tasked to coordinate and advocate for safety in sport internationally. It should place a strong emphasis on concussion, which is currently emerging as one of the biggest threats—if not the biggest threat—to player safety.[301] Its main mission in this regard would be to create, update and monitor the ISC.

In the medium to longer term, WSSA's activities could extend well beyond the issue of concussion. Through its contacts, infrastructure and resources, it would form a highly significant platform for the management of other types of injuries (eg, spinal/neck injuries, knee injuries)[302] and other closely related issues (eg, training techniques, use of painkillers). Broader public health and medical issues, such as

---

[296]See this chapter, Section IIIA1.

[297]See this chapter, Section IIIA2(a) and footnote 37.

[298]See this chapter, Section IIIB1.

[299]See this chapter, Section IVA1.

[300]See this chapter, Section IIIA2(a).

[301]See Chapter 1, Section I.

[302]About this latter point, see FIFPro website (<https://www.fifpro.org/news/alarming-number-of-ex-pros-suffer-knee-damage/en/>), which highlights the alarming number of serious knee injuries among professional football players.

sudden cardiac arrest, could also be considered.[303] In this context, WSSA's activities could include research, education, data storage/access, and assistance with developing and monitoring safety measures.

2 Structure and Governance

WSSA could either encapsulate WADA, or be created independently from it, with the latter option appearing more realistic, due to the profound changes that WADA is currently undergoing[304] and the different nature of its mission.[305] Close cooperation between the two agencies would, however, be beneficial, in view of their common threads (in particular public health).[306] It would also be advantageous as the two may face similar regulatory challenges.

Similar to WADA,[307] WSSA could have its seat in Lausanne, Switzerland, and be organised as a non-profit foundation under Swiss private law (or other legal systems that offer the same standards of corporate law). Its headquarters could be either in Switzerland (where the majority of IFs are located)[308] or in North America (which would allow it to be as close as possible to WADA's headquarters and the current concussion controversy).[309] It could also be assisted by regional offices on all continents.

WSSA would also be composed of a Foundation Board, an Executive Committee and Advisory Committees. The Foundation Board and the Executive Committee would share the main work within the Agency, and equally represent the sports movement and governments. In this case, the sports movement could include not only the Olympic Movement, but also the leagues governing non-Olympic sports, currently highly affected by the concussion controversy.[310] Advisory Committees and Commissions would provide support when specific expertise is needed (eg, athletes, education, medicine/research, policy, compliance, finance). A President and General Director would complete the picture.

The nomination of a neutral president and the addition of independent board members may assist in avoiding the internal conflicts of interest that were highlighted regarding WADA following the 'Russian doping affair'.[311] Stronger

[303]The examination of these areas is beyond the scope of this thesis. For more details, see Peter Brukner et al. (eds), *Brukner & Kahn's Clinical Sports Medicine* (McGraw Hill, 2017, 5th ed, Vol. I, 'Injuries', Part B, in particular Chapters 23, pp. 347–75 and 35, pp. 713–67; and Vol. II, 'The Medicine of Exercise', forthcoming publication).

[304]See this chapter, Section IIIA6(b)(ii).

[305]See this chapter, Sections IIIA2(a) and VIB1.

[306]See this chapter, Section IIA and Ibid.

[307]See this chapter, Section IIIA2(b).

[308]See Chapter 3, Section IIC1.

[309]See Chapter 3, Sections et seq and Chapter 5, Section IIIA2(b).

[310]See Chapter 3, Sections IA1(b) et seq (including subsequent case studies), Chapter 5, Sections IIA, IVC, VIC4(a) and Chapter 6, Section IIIC.

[311]See this chapter, Section IIIA6(b)(ii).

representation of the Athletes' Commission within the sports movement would also allow them to have a greater impact in the decision-making process.[312]

Entities in charge of public health and/or player representation, such as player and medical associations, as well as governmental agencies, should also be able to find their place in this configuration. Players' associations and governmental agencies could, respectively, be incorporated into the sports movement and governments, while medical associations could number among the independent members.

The main challenge, for the Olympic Movement and leagues, would be to not only wish to cooperate within a wider sports movement, but also to be able to do so effectively and in a unified way. To do this, an appropriate division of power should be found. It is difficult to predict such a division, which should result from political and financial negotiations and considerations. A good rapport should also be forged between the Athletes' Commission and players' associations, which may encounter difficulties working together and conciliating their viewpoints. Due to their large number, players' associations could be granted a voting right proportional to the number of athletes that they represent, or even be globally represented by the World Players Association.[313] The cooperation and the power sharing between governmental agencies in charge of public health and other governmental entities, in addition to those between medical associations and other independent members, seem to be less problematic at first glance, but should also be the subject of discussions.

3 Operation

WSSA would be in charge of overseeing sports safety internationally. Like WADA,[314] it could establish a general regulatory framework, and delegate the main operational aspects (eg, the adoption of regulations and their implementation) to other stakeholders.

However, unlike WADA, which has a strong focus on disciplinary matters,[315] WSSA's regulatory framework would focus on athlete safety. This structure could be achieved with the involvement of IFs (and their member associations) and leagues with, when needed, the support of clubs, various levels of government authorities, as well as player and medical associations.[316] The IOC could also support this process during Olympic Games.

---

[312]Ibid.

[313]The World Players Association, based in Switzerland, brings together 85 000 athletes across professional sport through more than 100 players' associations in over 60 countries (<http://uniglobalunion.org/sectors/world-players/about>).

[314]See this chapter, Section IIIA2(c).

[315]See this chapter, Section IIA and ibid.

[316]See this chapter, Sections VIC et seq and VIC4 et seq.

4 Funding

The funding necessary for WSSA's establishment and operation may be along the same lines as that of WADA,[317] but would have to be calculated with the specific functions of WSSA in mind. Again, like WADA,[318] it could be sourced equally from the sports movement and governments. Nevertheless, the financial contribution of the leagues within the sports movement and WSSA's regional budget allocation for governments would require specific negotiations. The financial contribution of leagues should correlate with the power they are granted within the sports movement. The regional budget allocation for governments could be established according to the level that each continent is affected by the issue of concussion, thus envisioning a substantial contribution from North America.

Annual agreements would determine the share of individual leagues and countries. Governments would then pay the required amount, with the sports movement matching their contributions through a joint fund managed by the IOC.

Players' associations and governmental agencies could be exempted from contributions, for the sake of simplification (they are traditionally funded, respectively, by SGB and governments, which would already be contributors themselves). This could equally be the case for medical associations, which generally have relatively limited financial means.

While the costs of maintaining WSSA's operation might be similar to those of WADA,[319] the total costs of a concussion safety system could be expected to be substantially less than those associated with doping,[320] because of the absence of disciplinary processes.

C International Standard on Concussion (ISC)

The ISC would form the core of the proposed reforms. It would establish the regulatory frameworks, duties and practical actions expected by IFs and sports leagues. Specifically, the ISC would address the issues, identified in Chapter 4, concerning rules of play, rules of the game and concussion management protocols, financial support for injured athletes, education, research and data collection ('six components'). WSSA would play a leading role in determining the ISC's content and operation. It would also arrange for the ISC's revision at regular intervals to take into account advances in medicine and technology, and the lessons gained from experience. The processes for establishing and revising the ISC would include consultation with (and potential approval by) key stakeholders, including IFs, sports leagues, the IOC, governments, independent medical authorities and players' associations.

---

[317]See this chapter, Section IIIA2(d).

[318]Ibid.

[319]Ibid, and Section VIB4.

[320]See this chapter, Section IIIA2(d).

While possessing its own character, to fit the demands of dealing with concussion, the ISC could adopt a structure resembling the WADC arrangements (ie, a main document, supplemented by various schedules and model rules). It could also draw from the experience of doping regulation regarding general principles on compliance by signatories and privacy.

As was the case with the drafting of the WADC,[321] the ISC would take previous comparable developments into account. The most important initiative to emerge so far, in relation to the issue of concussion worldwide, is the CISG's guidelines (and their implementation paper), which have become increasingly established as preeminent among the many medical guidelines available.[322] While the CISG's guidelines present only a partial solution to the problems identified earlier in this thesis,[323] they could be incorporated in the ISC and offer a valuable basis for some parts of it. However, as mentioned in Chapter 2, there are concerns over whether the guidelines are sufficiently independent of some influential stakeholders and if they represent best practice in all respects. To address these concerns, WSSA could engage a wider range of perspectives to specifically include government agencies, as well as medical and players' associations. Lessons from the case studies[324] and match-fixing and spectator violence regulation (including their successes and failures)[325] could also guide the development of the ISC.

It is envisaged that the ISC would contain the first authoritative and fully independent concussion guidelines applied on a global scale. It would provide guidance on issues already fully or partially covered by current medical guidelines, while also including previously unaddressed issues, such as financial support for injured athletes and data collection. It would also have the advantage of establishing (or at least guiding) a legal standard of care (or measure of good practice), thereby reducing legal uncertainty in litigation.[326]

A key role for WSSA would be supporting the implementation of the ISC with its six components. These components are classified (in full or in part) as mandatory, recommended or suggested. This classification is an attempt to prioritise the component according to its importance in safeguarding athletes from the occurrence or consequences of concussion bearing in mind vulnerability that may arise in the case of younger or concussed athletes. However, it also seeks to balance the autonomy of athletes to engage in risky sports and the autonomy, of sometimes very different sports, to govern their own affairs in a manner that is consistent across international boundaries while respecting local laws and conditions. Although this classification is not scientifically precise and would need refining, it presents a useful guide for the discussion.

[321] See this chapter, Sections IIIA1 and IIIA3(a).

[322] See Chapter 2, Section IX and Chapter 4, Section IIIB.

[323] See Chapter 2, Section IX.

[324] These lessons are set out at the end of each case study in Chapter 3.

[325] See this chapter, Sections IV et seq.

[326] See this chapter, Section VIC3.

Like doping regulations,[327] some components (eg, concussion management protocols) would be granted a regulatory status by IFs and thus have a trickle-down effect to national levels, which currently remain marked by substantial disparities. Appropriate monitoring systems could assure, control and enforce the procedures.[328]

The following consideration of the ISC is divided into four main parts: the content of the six components, the role of technical schedules and model rules, the legal status and issues of implementation, compliance and enforcement.

1 Main Content: The Six Components

(a) Rules of Play

The amendment of the rules of play is a key component of concussion prevention strategies.[329] Many SGBs, such as the NFL, World Rugby and FIFA,[330] have already used rule changes, at varying degrees. The numerous rule changes adopted in American football (among which the recent possibility of ejection for helmet-to-helmet contact),[331] the introduction of harsher penalties for high tackles in rugby union,[332] and the ban on tackles from behind in football,[333] are a testament to this fact. Others, like FINA,[334] have not yet undertaken a review of their rules. Efforts could still be made in all sports, knowing, however, that the sports deemed the most violent, like American football, have potentially the greatest scope for progress.[335] For sports where physical contact between players is mainly incidental (eg, football and baseball), there is less scope for progress through changing the rules of play.[336]

Based upon these findings, IFs and leagues that have this authority would be required to review the rules of their sport on a regular basis, with the view to minimising concussion and sub-concussion. To this end, they would rely on internal and external injury studies and data analysis, but also gather insights by means of consulting medical and players' associations and WSSA.

SGBs have so far not put in place a formal standard procedure directed towards the modification of their rules. However, the methodology used recently by World

---

[327]See this chapter, Section IIIA3(b).

[328]See this chapter, Sections VIC4 et seq.

[329]See Chapter 4, Section IIIA.

[330]See Chapter 3, Sections IA1(a) et seq, IA3, IIB1(a), IIB1(c), IC1 and IC3. See also Chapter 4, Section IIIA.

[331]See Chapter 3, Section IA1(e).

[332]See Chapter 3, Section IIB1(a).

[333]See Chapter 3, Section IC1.

[334]See Chapter 3, Sections ID2(a) and ID2(c). See also Chapter 4, Section IIIA.

[335]See Chapter 3, Section IA3 and Chapter 4, Section IIIA.

[336]See Chapter 3, Sections IC3 and ID1(c) and Chapter 4, Section IIIA. The assessment of the dangerousness of these sports will have to be fine-tuned once harmonised data on concussion is available (see this chapter, Section VIC1(f)).

Rugby must be highlighted. For the record, World Rugby conducted a video analysis of the causes of more than 600 instances of concussion, showing the dangerousness of high-tackles.[337] It then published its findings in a peer-review journal, and increased penalties on high tackles.[338] This 3-step action (study, publication and implementation) appears as an example of (evidence-based) good practice. It could be used by other SGBs, as is, or with variants (eg, analysis of physician-diagnosed concussion, publication of reports, etc).

The consultation with medical and players' associations, and WSSA could consist of the analysis of the data gathered by SGBs. It could also involve discussions of external studies, or more intuitive proposals likely to be made from all sides.

While mandatory, regular rule review is likely to lead to rule change, there is no guarantee that it will do so. Where a sport has a high level of concussion,[339] a more proactive approach may be required. WSSA could issue formal recommendations as to rule changes. Falling short of requiring rule change preserves the autonomy of the SGB to define the nature of the sport and the inherent risks of participation, while a formal recommendation identifies and places on record the need for specific action to preserve the health and safety of participants. The latter will have the effect of alerting interested parties such as medical and players' associations and perhaps pressuring the SGB to reflect carefully on the recommended change. Where a possible rule change might be less likely to reduce concussion and sub-concussion, it could be suggested rather than recommended.

Again, for sports with a high level of concussion, WSSA could suggest further information gathering and consultation that might inform a better approach to minimising concussion and sub-concussion.

Such a process would formalise, strengthen and accelerate the action of SGBs that already use rule changes as a way to improve player safety. These SGBs would benefit from a useful support, while preserving their freedom of choice as to possible rule changes to be made. It would also encourage SGBs that have not yet undertaken a review of their rules to finally take action.

Summary:

- Requirement: IFs and leagues would be required to review their rules of play on a regular basis with the view to minimising concussion and sub-concussion; they must also engage in discussions with medical/ players' associations, and WSSA;
- Recommendations and suggestions: IFs and leagues with a high level of concussion should consider formal recommendations and suggestions made by WSSA.

[337] See Chapter 3, Section IIB1(a).

[338] Ibid.

[339] What is a 'high level of concussion' may depend on each sport and its inherent risks.

(b) Rules of the Game and Concussion Management Protocols

There are currently numerous medical guidelines available to define, identify, treat and manage concussion.[340] Despite issues related to their content and, more generally, their lack of independence, the CISG's guidelines are considered to be preeminent at the international level.[341] They have contributed to improving player safety and harmonising concussion management, by providing SGBs with a foundation to adopt their concussion management protocols.[342]

The fact remains that athletes are subject, across sports and countries, to variable and sometimes inadequate standards once they sustain a concussion.[343] While SGBs are not always eager to share their practices,[344] it can be noted that some powerful leagues, such as the MLB,[345] still rely on other medical guidelines when creating and updating their concussion management protocols. In addition, IFs, like FIFA and FINA, just recommend the use of the CISG's guidelines.[346] Most have not adopted concussion management protocols for their sport. A frequent consequence of this is the absence of protocols, or even the adoption of disparate and/or flawed protocols, at national levels. The example of football is instructive in this regard. Out of the 211 national associations affiliated to FIFA, only The FA and the MLS (which is affiliated to FIFA through US Soccer) have adopted detailed concussion management protocols.[347] While The FA and MLS protocols each have their own specificities,[348] the MLS' protocols are the most open to criticism. The worst example is that the results of the advisory assessment performed by a neuropsychologist before return-to-practice are not communicated to the player.[349] Similarly, in water polo, USAWP's protocols are incomplete and may be seen to be flawed with room for improvement. Examples of which are the absence of baseline testing or stepwise return-to-practice protocols, the interruption of the game left to the referee's discretion, and the absence of specific medical background required for those who assess players.[350] The issues arise from failing to comply with the CISG's guidelines and/or gaps in the guidelines. To date, the most successful example of harmonisation of

[340]See Chapter 2, Sections II et seq and Chapter 4, Section IIIB.

[341]See Chapter 2, Section IX and Chapter 4, Section IIIB.

[342]Ibid.

[343]See Chapter 3, Sections IA1(e)et seq (including subsequent case studies).

[344]Many SGBs, such as the NHL, USAWP, the CFL, Rugby Australia, the NRL and the AFL have not published their concussion management protocols on their websites. Most also refuse to share them upon request [see footnotes 581, 990, 1060, 1089, 1217, 1303, 1350 and 1352, in Chapter 3; see also Bibliography and Chapter 4, Section VA].

[345]See Chapter 3, Sections ID1(a), ID1(c) and Chapter 4, Section IIIB.

[346]See Chapter 3, Sections IC1, IC3, ID2(a), ID2(c) and Chapter 4, Section IIIB.

[347]See Chapter 3, Sections IC, IC1 and IIC2. Note that a few SGBs, such as Football Federation Australia (FFA), have adopted some very brief protocols (<https://www.ffa.com.au/sites/ffa/files/2018-01/18-0102%20FFA%20Concussion%20Guidelines%20%28final%29.pdf>).

[348]See Chapter 3, Sections IC1 and IIC2.

[349]See Chapter 3, Sections IC1 and IC3.

[350]See Chapter 3, Sections ID2(a) and ID2(c). See also Chapter 4, Section IIIB.

protocols within one sport is World Rugby's HIA.[351] However, it only applies on a voluntary basis, and to a limited number of (international and national) competitions.[352] Coupled with this situation is the fact that the interpretation of the CISG's guidelines may differ substantially from one sport to another.[353]

IFs and leagues would be required to adopt concussion management protocols, or amend existing protocols, in order to incorporate current best practice and more effectively protect the health of athletes. IFs would also commit to incorporating their concussion management protocols into formal regulations, with a trickle down effect to national levels.

A major role for WSSA would be to clearly define and update best practice as well as to ensure their communication. The CISG's guidelines could be used as a starting point. Given the shared nature of the experience of concussion suffered by athletes, there should be little variation across sports and countries in the way concussion is defined, identified, treated and managed. Thus, the relevant concussion management protocols are particularly suited to a harmonised approach. Some adjustments are, however, inevitable, due to the different rules and playing conditions that characterise each sport, but also because of the different financial means available within each sport and country.

Bearing that in mind, WSSA could prepare mandatory model concussion management protocols for each of the most relevant sports (ie, the sports with high levels of concussion and/or which appear to be the most popular). The disparities identified in the case studies (eg, modified SCAT, person in charge of the test, independent contributors—eg, doctors, spotters, neuropsychologists—, baseline testing and substitution rules) will have to be reconciled as much as possible. This process could be an extension to the CISG's implementation paper.[354] In doing so, the characteristics of each sport will require a case-by-case approach. Also, the differences in the financial means could be dealt with by setting different requirements based on the capacities to implement them. Possible options include the coexistence of mandatory rules and recommended actions, as World Rugby already provides for the SGBs that wish to adhere to its HIA;[355] and/or the subdivision of SGBs/competitions into different classes for required protective measures, as provided by *Rowan's Law*.[356]

For sports with lower levels of concussion/popularity, which do not warrant the preparation of individual mandatory model concussion management protocols, it would be sufficient for WSSA's role to be confined to making recommendations and suggestions of either a general or specific nature.

---

[351] See Chapter 3, Sections IIB1(a), IIB1(c) and Chapter 4, Section IIIB.

[352] Ibid.

[353] See Chapter 2, Section IX, Chapter 3, Sections IA1(e) et seq (including subsequent case studies) and Chapter 4, Section IIIB.

[354] See Chapter 2, Section IX.

[355] See Chapter 3, Sections IIB1(a) and IIB1(c).

[356] See Chapter 3, Sections IIA1 and IIA3.

In all cases, national bodies would be free to set more demanding standards as local rules. This flexibility would serve to satisfy local laws while retaining a sense of international harmony.

By harmonising and improving best practice and protocols worldwide, the proposed standard would benefit athlete safety in all sports. The strongest and quickest impact should be felt in sports governed by IFs, which would be applied a single protocol on a global scale. This would also allow a better centralisation of efforts and cost rationalisation for SGBs.

Summary:

- Requirement: All IFs and leagues would be required to have concussion management protocols in place that comply with the best practice established by WSSA; IFs would also have to incorporate those protocols into formal regulations with a trickle down effect to national levels;
- Requirement: All IFs and leagues with high levels of concussion/popularity would be required to use the model concussion management protocols prepared by WSSA;
- Recommendations and suggestions: Other IFs and leagues should consider the recommendations and suggestions issued by WSSA.

(c) Financial Support for Injured Athletes

The question of concussion involves various complex financial issues that may affect player safety and welfare. SGBs should consequently take all of these issues into account.[357] Such matters include the prospect of lost income in the event of incapacity and early retirement, which may encourage players to ignore or not report their symptoms.[358] To this are added longer-term implications, such as the possible medical, residential and home care costs resulting from brain impairment.[359]

These issues point towards a common denominator: the need for adequate compensation and benefits.[360]

The efforts of a majority of North American leagues and all Australian leagues to have players' contracts that tend to be fully guaranteed against injuries have already been commended.[361] The NFL '88 Plan', which covers medical, residential and home care costs of former players with dementia, Parkinson's disease or ALS, has been highlighted.[362] This is also the case with Australian leagues' recent steps aimed at facilitating the internal resolution of disputes related to early retirements due to

[357]See Chapter 4, Section IIIC.

[358]Ibid.

[359]Ibid.

[360]Ibid.

[361]See Chapter 3, Sections IB1 and IB3 et seq (including subsequent case studies) and ibid.

[362]See Chapter 3, Sections IA1(c), IA3 and Chapter 4, Section IIIC.

concussion (through the payment of substantial lump sum fees, which do not discriminate against degenerative or pre-existing injuries).[363]

These measures have undoubtedly been taken in response to a real need.[364] The expediency of extending them to a wider international level, with or without adjustments and complementary measures, will vary depending on the specific (economic, structural and circumstantial) dynamic of each sport/country, as well as the development of medical science.[365]

It may be noted that the examples above are drawn from leagues governed by CBAs. SGBs that are not governed by CBAs currently act in a more opaque way, making it difficult to evaluate their practices.[366] Nevertheless, they should also provide players with adequate compensation and benefits.[367]

IFs (together with their national associations) and leagues would be advised to publicise their practices (through their websites, or at the very least by communicating directly with WSSA). They would be required to recognise that concussion and its effects carry financial implications, and commit to examining how to supply adequate financial coverage. Such coverage may result from new measures or adjustments in connection with CBAs, standard contracts, private insurance and disability schemes. This would complement legislative arrangements, such as workers' compensation and public disability schemes.

WSSA could promote this process by highlighting the efforts achieved and positive measures taken by some SGBs in response to players' financial needs. It could issue recommendations and suggestions for sports where players appear to be poorly protected. It could also help educate players as to financial costs and available benefits, in collaboration with players' associations.

By this means, better financial support would be provided to injured athletes. Concussion class actions (and other related proceedings) are constantly expanding, as illustrated by the past NFL and FIFA litigation, current NHL, CFL and USAWP litigation and the forthcoming AFL and NRL litigation.[368] This arouses growing apprehension in terms of risks. Consequently, SGBs can no longer restrict themselves to their reliance on private insurance and have to take greater responsibility.

---

[363]See Chapter 3, Sections IIB2(a), IIB2(c) and Chapter 4, Section IIIC.

[364]See Chapter 4, Section IIIC.

[365]Ibid.

[366]Ibid.

[367]Ibid.

[368]See Chapter 3, Sections IA2 et seq, IB2 et seq, IC2(b), ID2(b), IIA2, IIB2(b) and Chapter 4, Section II.

Summary:
- Requirement: IFs (together with their national associations) and leagues would be required to recognise that concussion and its effects carry financial implications and commit to examining how to supply adequate financial coverage;
- Recommendations: IFs and leagues should publicise their practices.
- Recommendations and suggestions: IFs and leagues, where players appear to be poorly protected, should consider formal recommendations and suggestions made by WSSA.

(d) Education

Educational campaigns help players become aware of the causes and nature of concussion, recognise their own symptoms and those exhibited by their team mates, and ultimately contribute to reducing the 'macho' culture in sport that has been linked to the dismissal of concussion as a serious issue or its portrayal as a 'badge of honour'.[369] Also, educational campaigns have value when they target other stakeholders, such as medical staff and coaches.[370]

Despite difficulties encountered while researching this thesis in ascertaining the precise terms of educational campaigns about concussion that have been offered to date, available evidence points to a lack of coordination between sports and countries.[371] Information on the possible long-term medical risks associated with concussion is regularly omitted,[372] with a notable exception being the NFL.[373] In the worst cases, campaigns are even used, like with the NHL,[374] to reassure players and brief them on the so-called 'misinformation' conveyed in the media and medical literature. IFs and leagues have a duty to educate players about the risks that they take. They should be required to support consistent educational campaigns, in collaboration with players' associations.

WSSA could promote best practice by providing guidance and resources for the education components. It could support harmonisation by encouraging, or mandating, the incorporation of these components into concussion management protocols, as done by World Rugby with its HIA, which includes online educational modules for all medical staff and information sessions for players and team management.[375] It could also issue a formal and independent position on CTE, in order to clarify current confusion.

[369] See eg, Chapter 4, Section IIID.

[370] See Chapter 4, Section IIID.

[371] Ibid.

[372] See Chapter 3, Sections IB1, IB3 et seq (including subsequent case studies) and ibid.

[373] See Chapter 3, Sections IA1(e), IA3 and Chapter 4, Section IIID.

[374] See Chapter 3, Sections IB1, IB3 et seq and Chapter 4, Section IIID.

[375] See Chapter 3, Sections IIB1(a), IIB1(c) and Chapter 4, Section IIID.

This would allow athletes to make an informed decision as to their participation in contact sports. It would also, indirectly, reduce the probability of concussion class actions, many of which have to date been triggered by the players' feeling that they have been insufficiently informed (or even misled) by their respective governing bodies as to possible risks. The best example of this is the NFL class action, based on negligence and fraud claims, where players reproached the league for not only having failed to warn them of the risks that they encountered, but also for having taken measures to hide those risks from them.[376] The NHL class action includes similar claims (negligence and fraud by omission).[377] Another example is the CFL class action, where players highlighted the misleading title of the article of Dr Tator, acting in partnership with the league, leading them to believe that no CTE cases had been diagnosed in Canadian football.[378]

Summary:
- Requirement: IFs and leagues would be required to support consistent educational campaigns for players, medical staff and coaches, which address the issues raised by concussion in both the short and long-term.

(e) Research

Research initiatives contribute to a better understanding and management of concussion.[379] A large range of medical and technological research activities is currently being undertaken.[380] All North American and Australian leagues do research on concussion.[381] Some of them, such as the NFL and the AFL, have even committed to spending a minimum amount on research through collective bargaining.[382] The NFL has already spent hundreds of millions of dollars on research, whereas the contribution of other leagues, such as the NHL, MLS and MLB, is much more modest (even when taking into consideration their revenues).[383] IFs are also heavily involved, but some entities, such as FINA, are, again, left behind.[384] Despite current efforts, there remain significant unanswered or disputed questions, in particular in relation with

---

[376] See Chapter 3, Section IA2(a)(i).

[377] See Chapter 3, Section IB2(a)(i) and footnote 601.

[378] See Chapter 3, Sections IIA1 and IIA2.

[379] See Chapter 4, Section IIIE1.

[380] Ibid.

[381] See Chapter 3, Sections IA1(a) et seq, IA3 et seq (including subsequent case studies) and ibid.

[382] See Chapter 3, Sections IA1(e), IA3, IIB2(a), IIB2(c) and Chapter 4, Section IIIE1.

[383] See Chapter 3, Sections IA1(a), IA1(e) et seq (including subsequent case studies) and Chapter 4, Section IIIE1.

[384] See Chapter 3, Sections IC1, IC3, IIB1(a), IIB1(c), ID2(a), ID2(c) and Chapter 4, Section IIIE1.

the potential long-term medical complications associated with concussion.[385] Independence and transparency issues are also recurrent among SGBs, with allegations ranging from simple preconceived ideas, to negligent misrepresentation, fraud/concealment and pressure exerted on institutions or researchers that have received a research grant.[386] In addition, there is insufficient coordination of research.[387]

IFs and leagues would be required to start or pursue their research, whether internally or externally, individually or in partnership with other sports, or even governments, and publicise their results. The sharing of results (through peer-reviewed journals, websites, press releases, or any other relevant means) would inform best practice, while putting an end to speculation over possible cover-ups.

WSSA could assist SGBs by identifying and recommending priority research areas, facilitating cooperation and information sharing, while overseeing the independence, transparency and quality of the research undertaken. It could negotiate a minimum percentage of revenue (or within a specified range) to be spent by each SGB, allowing expansion of research activities worldwide while recognising the different financial capacities and exposure to concussion in each sport. Ultimately, it could strongly encourage SGBs to act on their findings.

The list of current areas of research focus provided in the CISG's implementation paper[388] may help WSSA in developing a research framework and strategy.

These steps would facilitate the advancement of research on concussion and would avoid SGBs being able to hide behind scientific uncertainty to justify the status quo. SGBs, for their part, could bring forward both their financial efforts and the quality of the research projects undertaken. This would allow them to prevent (or defend themselves in) concussion litigation, it being specified, however, that their main purpose should be and must remain the safeguarding of athletes' interests.

Summary:
- Requirement: IFs and leagues would be required to either start or pursue research on concussion, and publicise their results;
- Requirement: IFs and leagues would be required to spend a minimum percentage of their revenues on concussion research;
- Recommendation: IFs and leagues should consider focusing their research on priority research areas identified by WSSA.
- Recommendation: IFs and leagues should act on their findings.

---

[385]See in particular Chapter 2, Section VII, Chapter 3, Section IA1(h), footnote 228, Chapter 4, Sections IIIE1 and IVD.

[386]For a summary, see Chapter 4, Section IIIE1.

[387]See Chapter 4, Sections IIIE1 and IVD.

[388]Patricios et al., above n 164 in Chapter 2, 639.

(f) Data Collection

Data collection helps assess the effectiveness of prevention strategies within one sport over time and comparisons between sports.[389] In the absence of guidance on how to collect and share data, current data on concussion is disparate and often difficult to access.[390]

IFs (together with their national associations) and leagues would be required to collect and share standardised data on concussion for the sport that they govern. It would be recommended that they publish annual concussion reports for national competitions, including detailed statistics for pre-season and regular season practices and games, by position/contacts. A similar approach could be used for international competitions, bearing in mind their shorter duration and lesser frequency and regularity.

WSSA could facilitate data standardisation through clear guidelines on data collection. These guidelines could be incorporated into concussion management protocols. They could draw upon practices already put in place by SGBs (in particular the NFL) to monitor concussion,[391] initiatives at the youth level (CDC, US youth concussion laws) or even wider scope projects (IOC injury surveillance system, EU IDB).[392] The guidelines should primarily provide common definition/thresholds, methods and observation periods, together with suggestions to facilitate comparisons (eg, instances of concussion per games). They should also contribute to harmonising circumstantial information in relation to injured players (age, gender, country of residence, club/sport, playing position, concussion history) and their injuries (date, mechanism, activity, number of games missed, treatment and follow-up).

WSSA would become the first centralised body for the collection and storage of concussion data worldwide. It could assist in the centralisation and access of the data, discussed above, by making a concussion registry available to SGBs. This registry could also extend its services to the centralisation of the data resulting from autopsies performed by forensic medicine centres.[393] This may include additional information about the deceased player (date of death, medical history, symptoms exhibited during lifetime) and stage of CTE (or other neurological disease).

The registry could take the form of an online database management system, possibly inspired by the mechanisms existing in doping (ADAMS).[394] Like ADAMs, it should require the highest data privacy protection standards, with, ideally, more flexibility regarding long-term data storage, in order to facilitate the study of concussion and its effects over the long term. Such storage might necessitate, beforehand, a compatibility study with the new *EU GDPR*,[395] in particular with

---

[389]See Chapter 4, Section IIIE2.

[390]Ibid.

[391]See in particular Chapter 3, Sections IA1(h) and IA3.

[392]See Chapter 3, Sections IA1(f), IC1, IIC2, as well as Chapter 4, Sections IIIE2 and IVD.

[393]See Chapter 3, Sections IA1(b) et seq and IA1(h) et seq (including subsequent case studies). See also Chapter 4, Section II.

[394]See this chapter, Section IIIA3(a)(ii).

[395]Ibid.

its Art. 17, which outlines the conditions allowing individuals to apply for data erasure.[396] Potential issues related to the data protection of deceased persons, which are currently left to member countries' discretion,[397] should also be examined.

The information gathered may be used by WSSA to perform risk assessments, and to identify the sports at high risk for concussion. Such methods to target problem areas are already well known under the *Macolin* and *Spectator Violence Conventions*.[398]

Summary:
- Requirement: IFs (together with their national associations) and leagues would be required to collect and share standardised data on concussion for the sport that they govern;
- Recommendation: They would be recommended to publish reports for national and international competitions.

2 Schedules and Model Rules

Like the WADC with its supporting International Standards,[399] the ISC could be supplemented by various schedules of a technical or procedural nature intended to flesh out best practice and expectations in various areas, including medical matters, education, data collection, protection of privacy and compliance. While those schedules would require drafting with the specific characteristics of concussion in mind, as described above,[400] the general standards and processes set in doping regulations could be used as guidance for privacy and compliance issues.

The schedule on privacy should, like WADA's ISPPPI (which regulates ADAMS),[401] ensure that all relevant parties involved in concussion management adhere to a set of minimum privacy protections when collecting, using and erasing athlete personal information. This includes compliance with data protection and

[396] Art. 17/1 *GDPR* lists six situations in which the data subject has the right to have his data erased: (a) the personal data is no longer necessary for the purpose for which they were collected or otherwise processed; (b) the data subject withdraws consent on which the processing is based; (c) the data subject objects to the processing of his data based on Art. 21/1 (legitimate interest of the controller), and there is no overriding legitimate interest to continue this processing, or the data subject objects to the processing pursuant to Art. 21/2 (marketing); (d) the personal data has been unlawfully processed; (e) the personal data has to be erased to comply with a legal obligation in Union or member state law to which the controller is subject; (f) the personal data has been collected to offer information society services to a child. Art. 17/3 *GDPR* provides for various exceptions, notably when data is processed in the public interest.

[397] See *GDPR*, Recital 27.

[398] See this chapter, Sections IIIB2 and IIIC1 et seq.

[399] See this chapter, Sections IIIA3(a)(i) and IIIA3(a)(ii).

[400] See this chapter, Section IIA.

[401] See this chapter, Section IIIA3(a)(ii).

privacy laws, the proportionality of the information processed, the consent of the participant, the implementation of security safeguards and the prohibition of public disclosure (apart from listed exceptions).[402]

The schedule on compliance, like WADA's ISCCS,[403] could describe signatories' rights and responsibilities, the supportive role of WSSA, and the process for determining and contesting non-compliance, as well as sanctions. Annual reports, the content of which should also be specified by WSSA, may be required from the signatories. These reports could then be used as a basis for the preparation of profiles aimed at advertising good practices, as for spectator violence.[404]

Model rules (such as model concussion management protocols, discussed above)[405] could be provided for the most relevant sports.

Both schedules and model rules could be published on the WSSA's website in order to ensure that they are widely communicated.

3 Legal Status

The legal status of the ISC would need determining, in conjunction with governments.[406] The ISC could be relevant to litigation by introducing a degree of certainty into the risk of liability. It could be set, in full or in part, as a mandatory standard by legislation that, if followed, could be a complete defence for SGBs to an allegation of negligence. Similar solutions could even apply to other stakeholders (eg, clubs/doctors compliant with concussion management protocols), while leaving the possibility open for claims in specific instances of mismanagement.

The conferring of legal immunity on those who adhere to the ISC would serve as encouragement for the adoption of state of the art practices and as reassurance for SGBs that need to function across international legal jurisdictions. This would preclude local courts from being involved in SGBs' decisions and rule making and, therefore, avoid disrupting international competitions, which depend on the existence of harmonised rules.

Guidance in this regard can be found in some US youth concussion laws,[407] which grant legal immunity to compliant schools (and their employees), excluding cases involving gross negligence or wilful/wanton misconduct.[408] Another

---

[402]Ibid.

[403]Ibid, and Section IIIA5.

[404]See this chapter, Section IIIC1.

[405]See this chapter, Section VIC1(b).

[406]See this chapter, Section VID.

[407]See Chapter 3, Section IA1(f).

[408]Ibid. See also *Sports Medicine Licensure Clarity Act* of 2017, Bill H.R. 302 — 115th Congress (2017–18). This law will provide legal protection for athletic trainers and sports medicine professionals who travel to other states with an athletic team to provide care for that team. For the purposes of liability, health care services provided by a covered athletic trainer or sports medicine professional to a student athlete, an athletic team or a staff member in a secondary state will be deemed to have occurred in the professional's primary state of licensure.

interesting example is the management and control of infectious diseases. In Australia, various states have adopted a standard for blood transfusion security.[409] Adherence to the standard confers legal immunity (subject to limited exceptions) on the Australian Red Cross, health services and other stakeholders involved in case of transmission of HIV or hepatitis to the recipient.[410]

A possible alternative to legal immunity would be to use the ISC as a measure of good practice that could inform any court ruling on reasonable care.

4 Implementation, Compliance and Enforcement

(a) Signatories: International Federations (IFs) and Leagues

Since the concussion controversy has emerged out of and remains largely focused on major sports leagues,[411] the ISC should aim, unlike the WADC,[412] to include the leagues as direct signatories, alongside IFs.

Otherwise, the mechanisms set by the WADC[413] could apply. Like the WADC, the principles and good practices established by the ISC should shape IFs' and leagues' regulations, policies and practices. Similarly, adherence to the ISC by IFs could be a prerequisite for Olympic participation and funding. Some flexibility may, however, be required for IFs governing sports which are relatively unaffected by concussion. These could be invited to have an 'observer' status within the system, or even be granted exemptions.

WSSA could monitor compliance based on signatories' annual reports and compliance schedule,[414] and investigate any alleged breaches found on this basis or brought otherwise to its attention.

(b) National Associations

Like in doping,[415] IFs should make sure that the commitments they undertake also penetrate to national levels. While their rules of play trickle down automatically, they should ensure that it is repeated for concussion management protocols, as well as education and data collection functions, by giving all three of them binding

---

[409] See eg, *Public Health and Wellbeing Act 2008* (Vic), Section 151 and Schedule.

[410] Exceptions to legal immunity include particular cases where the Red Cross had reasonable grounds for believing that a donor's declaration might be false or misleading and did not act; or negligence in administering blood that was in fact contaminated [ibid].

[411] See Chapter 3, Sections IA1(b) et seq (including subsequent case studies), this chapter, Sections IIA, IVC, VIB2 and Chapter 6, Section IIIC.

[412] See this chapter, Section IIIA3(b).

[413] Ibid.

[414] See this chapter, Section VIC2.

[415] See this chapter, Section IIIA3(b).

regulatory status (either separately, or within a single management protocol). More flexibility would be necessary for research and financial support for injured athletes. Here also, national associations could be required to comply to maintain their membership and related funding from IFs, as well as government funding.

FIFPro's proposal,[416] which would require each national association to submit its concussion management protocols and detailed reports on concussed players to FIFA, is worth considering (for all sports) in order to monitor national associations' compliance.

(c) Clubs/Teams

A specific feature of concussion management lies in the role of clubs and national teams, which are traditionally in charge of the implementation of concussion management protocols enacted by SGBs, as well as data collection.[417]

IFs (together with their national associations) and leagues should undertake to ensure that their concussion management protocols are complied with during their competitions. Besides the presence of independent contributors, the establishment of a systematic process to review incidents, coupled with punitive measures against non-compliant clubs/teams (eg, fines, loss of points) and responsible personnel (eg, suspension, deregistration), may be valuable.[418] These safeguards are already partly used by some SGBs, like the NFL,[419] which was notably the first one to put independent doctors in place during games, and to announce heavy fines in the case of protocol infringements.

Inappropriate reaction of SGBs in cases of specific instances of mismanagement could be monitored and reported to WSSA by federal or local authorities (eg, occupational health and safety agencies) and/or player and medical associations. The collaboration between WSSA and local authorities could be facilitated by memoranda of understanding and/or the legislation.

D UNESCO Convention

Like the WADC,[420] the ISC could receive governments' support through a *UNESCO Convention*. The Convention would formalise governments' commitment to improve concussion management. This might involve general obligations on governments drawn from anti-doping,[421] such as funding education (and research),

[416] See Chapter 3, Section IC3.

[417] See eg, Chapter 3, Sections IA1(e), IA1(h) and IIB2(a).

[418] See Chapter 3, Sections IA1(e), IA3, IIB2(a) and Chapter 4, Section IIIB.

[419] See Chapter 3, Sections IA1(e) and IA3.

[420] See this chapter, Sections IIIA3(a)(i) and IIIA4.

[421] See this chapter, Section IIIA4.

and withholding financial support (or other privileges) from non-compliant sports organisations. Additional areas of possible action include public insurance schemes (eg, workers' compensation, disability) and non-legislative parliamentary interventions (eg, hearings, roundtables, inquiries).[422] The legal status of the ISC[423] would also have to be determined, and the authorities in charge of monitoring inappropriate reactions of SGBs following specific instances of mismanagement by clubs/teams[424] officially appointed.

Of all the preceding domains, the issue of public insurance schemes seems to be particularly complex. It is, however, very topical, in light of increased concern surrounding athletes' health and the potential long-term risks they run. Governments could, for example, be invited to launch feasibility studies related to professional athletes' cover through workers' compensation (that, depending on the country, is either basic, like in the US,[425] or non-existent, like in Canada or Australia).[426] They could also be made aware of the possible legal issues that may arise in practice with regard to insurance law. A good example of this is provided by Switzerland,[427] where the potential long-lasting effects of sports concussion are an area of contention as to their legal standing (since they do not fall within the definition of 'illness' or 'accident' defined in legislation, and raise causality issues).

As with doping,[428] governments would comply with their treaty obligations by way of legislation, regulation, policies or any other relevant means, and provide reports on their activities.

The Convention could also provide a mechanism to assist governments to develop concussion education (and research) programmes through a fund managed by UNESCO, similar to the 'The Fund for the Elimination of Doping in Sport'.[429]

Finally, the reforms that are currently being implemented by UNESCO in doping[430] would be worth considering, in order to ensure that governments' declarations of intention are followed by concrete actions. This includes support by UNESCO Commissions to governments through reform-oriented recommendations or even model legislation, close monitoring and a framework of consequences in case of non-compliance, as well as an efficient resource mobilisation strategy.[431]

---

[422]See Chapter 4, Sections IV et seq.

[423]See this chapter, Section VIC3.

[424]See this chapter, Section VIC4(c).

[425]See Chapter 3, Sections IA2(b), IA3 and Chapter 4, Section IVA.

[426]See Chapter 3, Sections IIA1, IIA3, IIB1(a), IIB1(c) and Chapter 4, Section IVA.

[427]See Chapter 3, Section IIC1.

[428]See this chapter, Section IIIA4.

[429]Ibid.

[430]See this chapter, Section IIIA6(b)(iv).

[431]Ibid.

E The Court of Arbitration for Sport (CAS)

The last issue to be resolved in relation to the proposed reforms is the designation of the court(s) ultimately invested to enforce them.

The doping chapter highlights the importance of CAS, which has two main competences in this area: reviewing the disputes of signatories declared non-compliant by WADA; and reviewing the sanctions inflicted on athletes who have used prohibited substances. This raises the question of the role that CAS could play in the context of a harmonised system in the field of concussion.

In a similar line to the doping model, the ISC could allow signatories to go to CAS to challenge WSSA's decisions to declare them non-compliant.

The introduction of a wider compulsory recourse to CAS for personal injury claims would be much more problematic, not to say unrealistic. Certainly, the expertise of CAS would allow a particularly technical and consistent interpretation of the ISC. However, it would be highly contentious in the eyes of the major leagues (which have their own arbitration mechanisms, established by CBAs,[432] and which have no link with Switzerland). It may also attract controversy from certain IFs (whose regulations contain CAS clauses of varying scope)[433] as well as governments and players' associations (which generally resist all renunciation of state justice). In light of these considerations, the ISC should be applicable before CAS, but also other arbitration courts and state courts. This would allow leagues, if they wish to do so, to maintain their specific arbitration mechanisms, and IFs to continue to decide the scope of their CAS clauses, without alienating governments and players' associations. State courts could, for their part, intervene based on their residual jurisdiction.

---

[432]See Chapter 3, Sections IA2 et seq, IB2 et seq, ID1(b), IIA2 and IIB1(c), footnote 1255.

[433]See eg, Chapter 3, Sections 3 IC2(b), IIB1(b) and this chapter, Section IIIA5. See also Chapter 3, Sections IIC2 and IIC3.

Chapter 6
Conclusion

It always seems impossible until it's done.

Quote attributed to Nelson Mandela by numerous authors.

I Argument and Proposed Reforms

The concern articulated at the outset of this thesis related to the public health and legal risks associated with concussion. These risks are illustrated by the multiple CTE cases that are currently being diagnosed among professional athletes, and the legal proceedings filed against SGBs.

The thesis argues that harmonised reforms would be the most compelling way to reduce those risks, given the ongoing nature of the concussion controversy across countries and sports, and the need for sport to operate internationally. Using anti-doping regulation as a guiding thread, it proposes a series of reforms to achieve a harmonised regulatory framework. These reforms include an international standard on concussion (the 'ISC'), a supporting international convention ('*UNESCO Convention*'), a new World Sports Safety Agency (the 'WSSA') and some limited enforcement mechanisms.

Undertaking such reforms will take enormous effort, which is likely to face significant hurdles and resistance. However, any hurdles or resistance could be overcome, as was the case for anti-doping. In any event, the need for reforms is urgent and irrefutable, and the potential benefits are substantial.

A. Veuthey, *Concussion in Professional Team Sports: Time for a Harmonised Approach?*, https://doi.org/10.1007/978-981-15-1979-6_6

II Benefits

The WSSA would allow the ISC to be created, updated and monitored. The ISC, consistently implemented and enforced on a large scale, would drastically reduce the risk of immediate and long-term injury to professional athletes. It would ultimately contribute to improving the state of medical science through its registry, and constitute a valuable source in guiding the development of prevention and management strategies. By clarifying the requirements and improving safety, it would also significantly reduce the risk of litigation, and bring back some harmony at an international level. In case of litigation, it would introduce a degree of certainty into the risk of liability and could be a complete defence for SGBs to an allegation of negligence.

From a broader perspective, the reforms would improve transparency and collaboration between the stakeholders. The involvement of governments, justified by the public health issues involved, would guarantee that responses are made in a strong and united voice. Simultaneously, it would provide a means of pressuring SGBs that may otherwise be tempted to take a 'wait-and-see' approach.

Furthermore, the reforms, although primarily targeted at professional team sports, would benefit grassroots/youth sports. Thus, some of the measures prescribed by the ISC at a professional level, such as changes in the rules of play, would automatically trickle down to the grassroots/youth levels due to the pyramidal structure of sport.[1] Other measures could create a positive trend likely to have repercussions at lower levels,[2] or even be used as a barometer for the whole sports community.[3] The ISC could also be applicable in litigation, subject to the principle of reasonableness applicable in tort law/delict. The principle of reasonableness was developed through case law both in common law and civil law. It states that the expected standard of care is dependent upon the facts and what is reasonable in the circumstances.[4] Inevitably, the limited financial and medical resources available in grassroots/youth sport[5] would have to be taken into account. The absence of team doctors

[1]See Chapter 3 (introductory remarks).

[2]This hypothesis has already been confirmed in several countries and sports, where the adoption of protocols at the professional level has been accompanied, concomitantly or in a deferred way, by similar measures at the lower levels (see eg, Chapter 3. Sections IA1(f), IIA1, IIB1(a) and IIC2, footnote 1452; see in particular The FA's protocols that, although they prescribe additional obligations for the professional level, are intended to apply at all levels of play). The same phenomenon has been observed for educational campaigns (see Chapter 3, Sections IA1(e), IA1 (f), IB1, ID1(a), IIA1, IIB1(a) and IIB2(a)). It goes without saying that such campaigns, even targeted at the highest level, have the potential to change the macho culture that still prevails in sport, as professional athletes serve as role models to young people.

[3]This is the case of research and data collection undertaken at the professional level, whose results, without being directly transposable as such, could provide a trend regarding the risks of immediate and long-term injuries in community sport.

[4]See eg, *Vairy v Wyong Shire Council* (2005) 223 CLR 422, 426, paragraph 4.

[5]See Chapter 1, Section II, footnote 4.

should lead to the adoption of more rigid management guidelines (including the athlete's removal from the playing arena every time a concussion is suspected, and more conservative return-to-practice timeframes). Young players would need to be protected and cared for in a particularly cautious manner due to their potential longer recovery time, as well as their lower maturity and legal independence level.[6] The financial aspects strictly related to CBAs and workers' compensation exemptions would have no relevance. Finally, education, research and data collection initiatives should be processed depending on the means available, with an increased support from governments.

Similarly, the reforms would also have a beneficial impact on individual sports, or even other types of injuries.[7] The exact shape and extent of this impact provides an interesting scope for future research. Assuming that the WSSA undertakes to regulate all these areas directly, the benefits would be increased.

III Main Hurdles

A Funding

The example of match-fixing, and the unsuccessful negotiations surrounding the creation of a World Sports Integrity Agency,[8] is a reminder that the issue of funding is often an obstacle to the achievement of large-scale projects. The setting and maintaining of the proposed reforms would indisputably require substantial funds to be provided by SGBs and governments. However, this should not prevent these reforms from being introduced.

First, a major financial contribution is not unrealistic, especially when considering the amounts generated by the sports industry, estimated at USD800 billion per year.[9] Top level sports organisations and governments have, in the past, demonstrated their ability to jointly raise funds when needed. The current anti-doping system, which is supported annually by the Olympic Movement to the tune of USD300 million,[10] is instructive. There is no reason why the question of concussion,

[6]See in particular ibid, and Chapter 2, Section III. See also Chapter 3, Sections IC2(b) and ID2(b), which refer to the concussion class actions against FIFA and USAWP. These class actions included some minor plaintiffs, who had to be represented by their parents.

[7]The inherently violent nature of combat sports (see Chapter 1, Section II, footnote 5) would have to be considered. While blows to the head will be difficult to avoid, the standard of care expected by SGBs in case of concussion should not be reduced. The specific liability issues raised by less violent individual sports (see ibid) should also be dealt with. Other types of injuries could be regulated by WSSA (see Chapter 5, Section VIB1), when required.

[8]See Chapter 5, Sections IIIB1 and IVB.

[9]WADA website (<https://www.wada-ama.org/en/media/news/2015-10/speech-by-wada-director-general-david-howman-challenges-to-the-integrity-of-sport>).

[10]See Chapter 5, Section IIIA2(d).

which raises similar, or even more significant, public health concerns,[11] should not be able to attract sufficient financial support.

Furthermore, the contributions of SGBs and governments to funding the reforms must be put into perspective. They would not be as onerous to implement as may be intially imagined, as some of the expenditure would represent a redirection or reallocation of funds already being distributed on a regular basis. As mentioned previously,[12] significant sums are already allocated individually by certain SGBs and, to a lesser extent, governments, to the issue of concussion.

Moreover, the centralisation and coordination of efforts, and information sharing, would limit these costs. For example, the creation of harmonised, precise concussion management protocols in football would prevent the 211 FIFA member associations[13] from theoretically having to separately examine the issue of concussion, thus incurring unnecessary expenses. Cooperation between sports and/or governments would have similar benefits.

It might be expected that with the reduction or avoidance of physical injury from concussion, there would be lower injury costs and compensation as well as associated savings in litigation expenses. As stated earlier,[14] injuries strain the budgets not only of clubs, but also, indirectly, SGBs and public communities, up to tens of millions of US dollars a year or even, if one includes grassroots sport, several billions. Similar amounts (lawyers' fees, possible personal injury damages) emerge from an examination of many legal proceedings filed against SGBs.[15] In addition, there is the possibility of reputational damage (which may lead to indirect financial losses)[16] and, for public authorities, the costs of court systems. Also, in the worst-case scenario exposed in the introduction of this thesis, namely the end of contact sports, the whole sports financial system would experience immense adverse pressure.

Finally, the systematic imposition of fines by SGBs on non-compliant clubs and/or undisciplined players constitutes an obvious source of funding.[17] Such fines are already regularly imposed by the NFL,[18] and are starting to be emulated in other

[11]It is recalled that concussion is an issue at all levels of sport, and is strictly related to public health. It differs from doping, which is mainly confined to professional and elite sport, and raises all sorts of questions, including the integrity and fairness of competitions (on this latter point, see Chapter 5, Section IIA).

[12]See eg, Chapter 3, Section IA1(e).

[13]See Chapter 3, Section IC.

[14]See Chapter 2, Section II, Chapter 3, Sections IA1(e), IB1 et seq (including subsequent case studies).

[15]The best example of this is the NFL, and its USD1 billion settlement that, in addition to the compensation granted to the players, covers the parties' attorney fees up to USD112.5 million (only in relation to settlement discussions) (see Chapter 3, Section IA2(a)(v)). The NHL, which refuses to compromise, exposes itself to even greater attorney fees (see Chapter 3, Sections IB2 et seq).

[16]See eg, Chapter 3, Section IA2(a)(v).

[17]See Chapter 4, Section IIIB.

[18]See Chapter 3, Sections IA1(e) and IA3.

leagues, such as the NRL and AFL.[19] They can sometimes be as much as hundreds of thousands of dollars.[20] Other mechanisms, inspired closely or remotely by the 'Russian doping affair' (fines for non-compliant SGBs, imposition of a small levy on broadcasters and sponsors)[21] could also be considered.

B Convince SGBs to Surrender Part of Their Authority

SGBs may be reluctant to surrender part of their authority, in favour of a more centralised, open system, managed jointly by governments. This reluctance was observed in match-fixing,[22] where the proposal to create a World Sports Integrity Agency was perceived as an intrusion, or even a wilful failure to acknowledge the good work already undertaken in the area by various interested parties.

It will, therefore, be necessary to persuade SGBs that, as was the case in doping,[23] the proposed reforms could not only be supportive, but also a confirmation and continuation of the efforts made so far. The reforms would allow SGBs to benefit from governments' substantive and financial inputs, while incorporating their good practices into a more global system.

In addition, the possibility for SGBs to be granted legal protection in case of compliance with the ISC[24] would act as a strong incentive for them to join. Efficiency gains and increased legitimacy stemming from better-coordinated action, endorsed by a broad consensus, may be influential.

Finally, SGBs must be aware that by maintaining the status quo, they run the risk of having domestic courts or legislatures impose rules and concussion management protocols on them. This situation, already observed in grassroots/youth sport,[25] would cause a loss of control of SGBs over the rules governing their sport with, as a consequence, the organisation of international competitions being rendered more complex or even restricted.

---

[19]See Chapter 3, Sections IIB2(a) and IIB1(c).

[20]See Chapter 3, Sections IA1(e) and IIB2(a).

[21]See Chapter 5, Section IIIA6(b)(ii).

[22]See Chapter 5, Sections IIIB1 and IVB.

[23]See Chapter 5, Sections IIIA et seq.

[24]See Chapter 5, Section VIC3.

[25]The best example of this is the US, where headers were prohibited in football for children as a result of the FIFA litigation and US Soccer settlement. All US states also adopted youth concussion laws, some of which will soon go as far as to prohibit tackles in contact sports (see Chapter 3, Sections IA1(f) and IC1 and IC2(b)). Other examples include Canada and Australia (see Chapter 3, Sections IIA1 and IIB1(a)). The first signs of 'external' regulatory intervention in professional team sport can be found in Canada, where the CFLPA filed grievance against the league, with the view to compensating injured players and impose specific rule and policy changes (see Chapter 3, Section IIA2).

C Attract Sports Leagues/Non-Olympic Sports

Sports leagues, which for the most part exist outside the constraints imposed by the IOC, in an environment dominated by collective bargaining,[26] will most likely be the most difficult to convince. The example of doping, and the WADC in particular,[27] which did not win the support of the North American leagues, and attracted strong controversy among Australian leagues before its adoption, tends to confirm this consideration. Additionally, it should be noted that certain leagues, already active within CISG,[28] might prefer to maintain the status quo.

The absence of such leagues would be particularly regrettable, since they currently crystallize a substantial part of the concussion controversy.[29] The possibility of being granted legal protections if compliant with the ISC[30] should, however, find particular resonance with them, because of the financial and reputational damage carried by concussion litigation. For the leagues that are, or have already been affected by litigation,[31] the advantage could lie in the possibility of restoring or maintaining their reputation.

When necessary, governments could exert financial pressure on leagues. This pressure would be justified by the strong public health concerns raised by concussion and the need to reduce the costs, which would otherwise be incurred, in the public health and legal systems. Such pressure is already exerted at grassroots level by some Australian states,[32] which subordinate the granting of subsidies to compliance with their respective recommendations. Another interesting precedent exists in Australia with doping,[33] where a federal regulation indirectly makes the granting of governmental funding to leagues conditional upon compliance with the WADC. In North America, where benefits and subsidies are usually granted by cities as a matter of local politics,[34] this could be achieved through national legislation, such as tax codes. In the US, an additional leverage may include the preservation of the lucrative antitrust exemptions.[35]

---

[26]See Chapter 3 (introductors remarks) and Section IA3.

[27]See Chapter 5, Sections IIIA3(b) and IIIA6(b)(i).

[28]See eg, Chapter 2, Section IX, footnote 163.

[29]See Chapter 3, Sections IA1(b) et seq (including subsequent case studies), and Chapter 5, Sections IIA, IVC, VIB2 and VIC4(a).

[30]See Chapter 5, Section VIC3.

[31]See Chapter 3, Sections IA2 et seq, IB2 et seq and IIA2.

[32]See Chapter 3, Section IIB1(a).

[33]See Chapter 5, Section IIIA3(b).

[34]For more details, see Barnes, 'Hockey', above n 490 in Chapter 3, 297–304.

[35]See Chapter 3, Section IA1(d) and footnote 92.

Even if the ISC was not directly adopted by leagues, its general tenor could indirectly contribute to improving safety standards, by virtue of political pressure and informal collaboration with WSSA.[36]

D The Challenge of Sustaining a Strong Effect and Impact

It will be important for the proposed reforms to have a strong, effective and ongoing impact on player safety. Otherwise, they will appear as window-dressing. To do so, it will first be necessary to ensure that their content is fit for purpose. Reasonable assurance is provided in this regard through the analysis conducted as part of the case studies,[37] as well as the prospect of broad consultations and regular evaluations.[38]

Another predictable sticking point lies in the implementation, compliance and enforcement of the reforms. The individual efforts of SGBs regarding concussion,[39] just like various harmonisation attempts in sport (US youth concussion laws, boxing federal legislation, doping),[40] have already encountered these problems. In doping, the deficiencies identified following the Russian affair and the IOS report triggered extensive reviews in relation to the WADC and the *UNESCO Convention*.[41] The lessons from the foregoing reviews,[42] as well as the addition of more specific safeguards,[43] should prevent the proposed reforms from being ineffectively enforced, or even deliberately circumvented.

Finally, cost efficiency, the importance of which was highlighted in doping by the Tübingen study,[44] will also have to be regularly evaluated.

Despite these challenges, the proposed reforms, when introduced in a sustainable way, will be essential in reshaping the future landscape of contact sport.

---

[36]Similar indirect effects were observed in the US with regard to doping and the WADC (see Chapter 5, Section IIIA6(b)(i)).

[37]See Chapters 3 et seq.

[38]See Chapter 5, Section VIC.

[39]See eg, Chapter 3, Sections IA1(e) et seq and IIB2(a).

[40]See Chapter 3, Sections IA1(f), IA3 and Chapter 5, Section IIIA6(b)(ii).

[41]See Chapter 5, Sections IIIA6(b)(ii) and IIIA6(b)(iv).

[42]See Chapter 5, Sections IVA et seq. See also Chapter 5, Sections VIB2, VIC2, VIC4(a) and VID, which refer to several steps directly inspired by the reforms triggered by the Russian affair and the IOS report, such as the introduction of independent members in WSSA's board, the adoption of a compliance schedule and the implementation of supportive measures for UNESCO Convention's signatories.

[43]See Chapter 5, Sections VIC4(a) et seq.

[44]See Chapter 5, Section IIIA6(b)(iii).

IV Securing the Future of Contact Sport

This thesis comes at a critical time in the regulation of concussion, which has become the object of awareness not only within the sports world but also in terms of the recognition by the general public. The proposed reforms would have immediate application to an issue fundamental to sport, as well as to society as a whole. By reducing the public health and legal risks associated with concussion, they would indirectly secure the future of contact sport, at a professional level, but also, indirectly, for grassroots sports. As argued throughout this thesis,[45] SGBs and governments have a crucial role to play in whether and how the reforms may be taken up.

All of the sports contributors must, however, be conscious of the importance of this issue. Clubs, which are traditionally in charge of the implementation of concussion management protocols and data collection,[46] deserve special mention. Provided that the necessary safeguards are put in place upstream,[47] they have the power to significantly improve the management and knowledge of concussion.

The action of players' associations, through collective bargaining or separate initiatives, must also be highlighted. This action is mainly relevant for sports governed by leagues.[48] It has, therefore, a limited geographical impact for some major sports, organised under the umbrella of an IF, such as football,[49] rugby union[50] and ice hockey.[51] However, it has already facilitated significant improvements in player safety. Players' associations have so far primarily focused their efforts on the financial support for injured athletes, by means of CBAs (payment of salary, lump sum fees in case of early retirement, reimbursement for medical, residential and home care costs)[52] and attempts to amend workers' compensation laws.[53] Sometimes invited to join concussion working groups,[54] they are now starting to take an interest in other components, such as concussion management protocols, education and research. Good examples of this include players'

[45] See in particular Chapter 1, Section II, Chapter 3, Sections IA3 et seq (including subsequent case studies), Chapter 5, Sections IVC and V et seq.

[46] See eg, Chapter 3, Sections IA1(e), IA1(h), IIB2(a) and Chapter 5, Section VIC4(c).

[47] See in particular Chapter 5, Section VIC4(c).

[48] See Chapter 3 (introductory remarks).

[49] See Chapter 3, footnote 3, as well as Sections IC et seq and IIC et seq.

[50] See Chapter 3 IIB1 et seq.

[51] See Chapter 3, footnote 2, as well as Sections IB et seq and IIC1.

[52] See Chapter 3, Sections IA1(c), IA2(a)(iv), IA3, IB1, IB3, IC1, IC3, ID1(a), ID1(c), IIA1, IIA3, IIB1(a), IIB1(c), IIB2(a), IIB2(c) (all CBAs) and Chapter 4, Section IIIC.

[53] See eg, Chapter 3, Sections IIA1, IIA3 (both about the CFLPA), IIB1(a), IIB1(c), IIB2(a) IIB2 (c) (all about the AAN) and Chapter 4, Section IVA.

[54] See eg, Chapter 3, Sections IB1, IB3, IC1, footnote 780, IC3, IIB1(a) and IIB1(c) (about the NHL, MLS and World Rugby Concussion Working Groups/Committees and their related activity).

associations contributing to the drafting[55] or even proper application[56] of protocols, taking part in educational campaigns,[57] allocating research grants[58] and supporting cross-code studies,[59] as well as former players' surveys.[60] Interestingly, the pressure exerted by players' associations in American football and Australian Rules football has also led to the inclusion of clauses in CBAs requiring the NFL and the AFL to spend, annually, a minimum amount on concussion research.[61] The role that players' associations can take in player safety is evolving and has potential. Among the proposed reforms,[62] WSSA could assist players' associations in developing this potential, by acting as a platform for negotiating and exchanging ideas, providing them with support and advice, and setting minimum standards to be applied by SGBs and governments.[63]

Last but not least, athletes, when fully informed,[64] can contribute to changing attitudes. They must realise that there is something that goes beyond the participation in a Grand Final or a World Cup: the ability to remember it once retired, and the media spotlight on them has ceased.

V Latest Updates

Concussion continues to be a dynamic and fluid area. At the time of concluding this research, in November 2018, the NHL reached a tentative settlement with its former players, of a total value of USD16.9 million.[65] Of that total, up to USD7 million will

[55]Due to their presence in concussion working groups (or related safety committees), and close relationships with leagues, player representatives may have some influence on concussion management protocols [see ibid, and Chapter 3, Section IA1(e), related to the NFLPA]. In addition, a few protocols are attached to CBAs [see in particular the MLS and MLB protocols, mentioned in Chapter 3, Sections IC1, IC3, ID1(a), ID1(c) and Chapter 4, Section IIIB].

[56]See eg, Chapter 3, Section ID1(a) (about the intervention of an MLBPA expert in the independent process applicable to concussed players for clearance to return-to-activity). See also Chapter 3, Sections IA1(e), IA3 and footnote 413 (about the fines imposed by the NFL on non-compliant clubs based on a separate document that, according to some commentators, is subject to the CBA process).

[57]See eg, Chapter 3, Sections IA1(e) (NFLPA video), IB1 and IB3 (both about the NHLPA).

[58]See eg, Chapter 3, Sections IA1(e), IB1, ID1(a) and IIC2 (about the NFLPA, NHLPA, MLBPA and PFA).

[59]See eg, Chapter 3, Sections IIB1(a), IIB1(c), IIB2(a), IIB2(c) (all about the AAN) and Chapter 4, Section VC.

[60]See eg, Chapter 3, Sections IIA1, IIB2(a) and footnote 1334 (about the CFLPA and AFLPA).

[61]See Chapter 3, Sections IA1(e), IA3, IIB2(a) and IIB2(c).

[62]See Chapter 5, Sections V et seq.

[63]See Chapter 5, Sections VIB et seq and VIC et seq.

[64]See in particular Chapter 5, Section VIC1(d).

[65]Settlement Agreement between the NHL and Plaintiffs' Counsel, pp. 11 and 13. This document is available on the 'NHL Concussion Litigation' website (<https://www.nhlconcussionlitigation.com/information.html>).

be distributed to the players who opt-in as settlement claimants (USD22 000 per player).[66]

Simultaneously, the US Ninth Circuit Court of Appeal revived the class action against USAWP,[67] which had been dismissed in 2016 by the US District Court for the Central District of California.[68] It acknowledged that USAWP owes a duty of care to athletes to set protocols for returning to play after suffering a potential concussion.[69]

The NHL settlement does not mean that brain injuries did not happen, or will not continue to happen. It just shows, once again, that courts are not the best instrument to resolve these issues.[70] The NHL will, hopefully, take its responsibilities, with the support of governments, and realise that there should be no such thing as a 'legal' hit to the head.[71]

The decision of the US Ninth Circuit of Appeal could be far-reaching, as it formally establishes that SGBs have a duty of care to protect athletes from concussion. It also confirms the risks that SGBs take by choosing a 'wait-and-see' approach.[72] This approach is not only likely to lead them to court: it could also give rise to a finding of liability, with substantial financial and reputational damaging effects.

Other significant events, such as the filing of a class action against the AFL, are also expected shortly. These events will, again, fuel controversy, increasing the relevance not only of the research within this thesis, but of future discussions on concussion reforms in sports law.

[66]Ibid, pp. 8 and 13.

[67]*Alice Mayall v USA Water Polo* (9th Cir, No. 16-56389, 28 November 2018), Opinion.

[68]See Chapter 3, Section ID2(b).

[69]Opinion, pp. 10–23 and 28.

[70]See Chapter 3, Sections IA2 et seq (including subsequent case studies).

[71]See Chapter 3, Sections IB1 and IB3.

[72]See Chapter 3, Sections IA1 et seq and IA2 et seq (including subsequent case studies; in particular Sections ID and ID2 et seq).

Bibliography

A. *Articles/Books/Reports*

Agronin, Marc E, *Alzheimer's Disease and Other Dementias: A Practical Guide* (E-book, Routledge, 2014)

Al-Kashmiri, Ammar and J Scott Delaney, 'Head and Neck Injuries in Football (Soccer)' (2006) 8 *Trauma* 189

All-Party Parliamentary Group, *Acquired Brain Injury and Neurorehabilitation, Time for Change,* Report, 2018 (<https://www.ukabif.org.uk/wp-content/uploads/2018/10/1533_40pp_APPG-on-ABI_Report_Time-for-Change_2018_AW_SINGLES_WEB.pdf>)

Amen, Daniel G et al., 'Impact of Playing American Professional Football on Long-Term Brain Function' (Winter 2011) 23(1) *Journal of Neuropsychiatry & Clinical Neuroscience* 98

American Academy of Neurology, 'Practice Parameter, The Management of Concussion in Sports (Summary Statement), Report of the Quality Standards Subcommittee of the American Academy of Neurology' (1997) 48 *Neurology* 581

Andenas, Mads Camilla Baasch Andersen and Ross Ashcroft, 'Towards a Theory of Harmonisation', in Mads Andenas and Camilla Baasch Andersen (eds), *Theory and Practice of Harmonisation* (Edward Elgar Publishing, 2012) 572

Andersen, Rune, IAAF Taskforce, Interim Report to IAAF Council, 17 June 2016 (<https://www.iaaf.org/news/press-release/iaaf-council-meeting-vienna>)

Anderson, April R, 'The Punch that Landed: The Professional Boxing Safety Act of 1996' (1998) 9 *Marquette Sports Law Journal* 191 (April Anderson, 'Punch')

Ando, Yuta, 'Harmonisation and International Approaches to Match-Fixing' in Stacey Steele and Hayden Opie (eds), *Match-Fixing in Sport: Comparative Studies from Australia, Japan, Korea and Beyond* (Routledge, 2017) 111

Areza-Fegyveres, Renata, et al., 'Dementia Pugilistica With Clinical Features of Alzheimer's disease' (2007) 65 *Arquivos de Neuropsiquiatria* 830

Aubry, M et al., 'Summary and Agreement Statement on the 1st International Conference on Concussion in Sport, Vienna 2001' (2002) 36 *British Journal of Sports Medicine* 6

Baglio, Scott, 'The Muhammad Ali Boxing Reform Act: The Fist Jab at Establishing credibility in Professional Boxing' (2000) 68 *Fordham Law Review* 2257

Bailes, Julian E, et al., 'Role of Subconcussion in Repetitive Mild Traumatic Brain Injury, A Review' (2013) 119 *Journal of Neurosurgery* 1235

A. Veuthey, *Concussion in Professional Team Sports: Time for a Harmonised Approach?*, https://doi.org/10.1007/978-981-15-1979-6

Barker, Caleb et al., 'NFL Concussions: The Current Situation and Policy Implications', A Section 6, Frontier Torts White Paper (Harvard Law School, 2012) (<http://learning.law.harvard.edu/frontiertorts/wp-content/uploads/2013/04/NFL-Concussions-White-Paper-2.pdf>)

Barnes, John, Sports Title, Canadian Encyclopedic Digest (Carswell/Thomson Reuters, 5th ed, 2016) (Barnes, 'Digest')

Barnes, John, *The Law of Hockey* (LexisNexis, 2010) (Barnes, 'Hockey')

Barrio, Jorge R, et al., 'In Vivo Characterization of Chronic Traumatic Encephalopathy Using [F-18]FDDNP PET Brain imaging' (2015) 112 *Proceedings of the National Academy of Sciences of the United States of America* 2039

Batten, Jack, *Lawyers* (Penguin, 1985)

Baugh, Christine et al., 'Chronic Traumatic Encephalopathy: Neurodegeneration Following Repetitive Concussive and Subconcussive Brain Trauma' (2012) 6 *Brain Imaging and Behavior* 244

Bell, Melissa, 'Time to Give Boxers a Fighting Chance: The Muhammad Ali Boxing Reform Act' (2000) 10 *DePaul-LCA Journal of Art and Entertainment Law* 473

Benson, BW et al., 'What Are the Most Effective Risk Reduction Strategies in Sport Concussion?' (2013) 47 *British Journal of Sports Medicine* 321 (Benson et al., 'Strategies')

Benson, Brian W et al., 'A Prospective Study of Concussions Among National Hockey League Players During Regular Season Games: The NHL-NHLPA Concussion Program' (2011) 183 *Canadian Medical Association Journal* 905 (Benson et al., 'Hockey')

Benson, Brian et al., 'Is Preventive Equipment Useful in Preventing Concussion? A Systematic Review of the Literature' (2009) 43 (Supplement 1) *British Journal of Sports Medicine* 56 (Benson et al., 'Prevention')

Berkow, Ira *Giants Among Men: Y.A., L.T., the Big Tuna and Other New York Giants Stories* (Triumph Books, 2015)

Bernstein, Amy, 'Into the Red Zone: How the National Football League's Quest to Curb Concussions and Concussions-Related Injuries Could Affect Player's Recovery' (2012) 22 *Seton Hall Journal of Sports and Entertainment Law* 271

Bey, Tareg and Brian Ostick, 'Second Impact Syndrome' (2009) 10 *The Western Journal of Emergency Medicine* 6

Bienik, Kevin F et al., 'Chronic Traumatic Encephalopathy Pathology in a Neurodegenerative Disorders Brain Bank' (2015) 130 *Acta Neuropathologica* 877

Blumenfeld, Robert S, 'The Epidemiology of Sports-Related Head Injury and Concussion in Water Polo' (June 2016) 7(98) *Frontiers in Neurology* 1

Boodman, Martin, 'The Myth of Harmonization of Laws' (1991) 39 *The American Journal of Comparative Law* 699

Boriboon, Kia, 'Concussion Management in Football: Don't Shake it Off' (February 2013) *PT in Motion* 18

Bramlett, Helen M and W Dalton Dietrich, 'Long-Term Consequences of Traumatic Brain Injury: Current Status of Potential Mechanisms of Injury and Neurological Outcomes' (2015) *Journal of Neurotrauma* 1834

Broglio, Steven P, et al., 'National Athletic Trainer's Association Position Statement, Management of Sport Concussion' (2014) *Journal of Athletic Training* 245

Brukner, Peter et al., (eds), *Brukner & Kahn's Clinical Sports Medicine* (McGraw Hill, 5th ed, 2017, Vol. I, 'Injuries', Part B; and Vol. II, 'The Medicine of Exercise', forthcoming publication)

Bunworth, Richard, 'Egg-Shell Skulls or Institutional Negligence? The Liability of World Rugby for Incidents of Concussion Suffered by Professional Players in England and Ireland' (2016) 16 *International Sports Law Journal* 82

Burstein, Devin, 'The Muhammad Ali Boxing Reform Act: Its Problems and Remedies, Including the Possibility of a United States Boxing Administration' (2003) 21 *Cardozo Arts & Entertainment Law Journal* 433

Byard, Roger W and Robert Vink, 'The Second impact Syndrome' (2009) 5 *Forensic Science, Medicine and Pathology* 36

Calandrillo, Steve P, 'Sports Medicine Conflicts' (2005) 50 *Saint Louis University Law Journal* 185
Camargo de Carvalho, Adolpho Julio, Chapter 3, Brazil in András Gurovits (ed), *The Sports Law Review* (Law Business Research, 2nd ed, 2016) 26
Cantu, Robert C and Alisa D Jean, 'Second-Impact Syndrome and a Small Subdural Hematoma: An Uncommon Catastrophic Result of Repetitive Head Injury with a Characteristic Imaging Appearance' (2010) 27 *Journal of Neurotrauma* 1557
Cantu, Robert C, 'Chronic Traumatic Encephalopathy in the National Football League' (2007) 61 *Neurosurgery* 223 (Cantu, 'CTE')
Cantu, Robert, 'Posttraumatic Retrograde and Anterograde Amnesia, Pathophysiology and Implications in Grading and Safe Return to Play' (2001) 36 *Journal of Athletic Training* 244 (Cantu, 'Amnesia')
Caron, Jeffrey G et al., 'Effects of Multiple Concussions on Retired National Hockey League Players' (2013) 35 *Journal of Sports & Exercise Physiology* 168
Carrabis, Andrew B, 'Head Hunters: the Rise of Neurological Concussions in American Football and its Legal Implications' (2011) 2 *Harvard Journal of Sports & Entertainment Law* 371
Carter, Tracey B, 'From Youth to Collegiate Athletics to Professional Leagues: Is There Really "Informed Consent" by Athletes Regarding Sports-Related Concussions' (2015) 84 *University of Missouri-Kansas City Law Review* 331 (Tracey B Carter, 'Consent')
Castellani, Rudy J, 'Chronic Traumatic Encephalopathy: A Paradigm in Search Evidence' (2015) 95 *Laboratory Investigation* 576
Cerra, David S, 'Unringing the Bell: Former Players Sue NFL and Helmet Manufacturers over Concussion Risks in Maxwell v NFL' (2012) 16 *Michigan State University Journal of Medicine & Law* 265
Chappelet, Jean-Loup and Brenda Kübler Mabbott, *The International Olympic Committee and the Olympic System*: The Governance of World Sport (Routledge, 2008)
Chappelet, Jean-Loup, 'Beyond Governance: the Need to Improve the Regulation of International Sport' (2018) 21 *Sport in Society* 724 (Chappelet, 'Governance')
Chappelet, Jean-Loup, 'The Olympic Fight Against Match-Fixing', (2015) 18 *Sport in Society* 1260 (Chappelet, 'Match-Fixing')
Chappelet, Jean-Loup, 'L'Agence Mondiale Antidopage: Un nouveau régulateur des relations internationales sportives' (Autumn 2002) Nr 111 *Relations Internationales* 381 (Chappelet, 'Agence')
Chio A et al., 'Severely Increased Risk of Amyotrophic Lateral Sclerosis Among Italian Professional Football Players' (2005) 128 *Brain* 472
Cifu, David X and Deborah Caruso, *Traumatic Brain Injury* (DemosMedical, 2010)
Clair, Bradley J, 'Why Federal Preemption Is Necessary to Create Uniform Professional Boxer Safety Standards' (2008) 73 *Brooklyn Law Review* 1173
Clausen, H, P McCrory and V Anderson, 'The Risk of Chronic Traumatic Brain injury in Professional Boxing: Change in Exposure Variables Over the Past Century' (2005) 39 *British Journal of Sports Medicine* 661
Collins, Michael W, et al., 'Statements of Agreement From the Targeted Evaluation and Active Management (TEAM) Approaches to Treating Concussion Meeting Held in Pittsburgh', October 15-16 2015' (2016) 79 *Neurosurgery* 912
Colorado Medical Society, *Report of the Sports Medicine Committee, Guidelines for the Management of Concussions (Revised)* (Colorado Medical Society, 1991)
Conte Stan, Christopher L Camp and Joshua S Dines, 'Injury Trends in Major League Baseball over 18 Seasons: 1998-2015' (2016) 45 *American Journal of Orthopedics* 116
Corsellis, J A, CJ Bruton and D Freeman-Browne, 'The Aftermath of Boxing' (1973) 3 *Psychological Medicine* 270
Craton, Neil and Leslie Oliver, 'Time to Re-think the Zurich Guidelines?: A Critique on the Consensus Statement on Concussion in Sport: The 4th International Conference on Concussion in Sport, Held in Zurich, November 2012' (2014) 24 *Clinical Journal of Sport Medicine* 93
Cusimano, Michael D et al., 'Assessment of Head Collision Events During the 2014 FIFA World Cup Tournament' (2017) 317 *Journal of the American Medical Association* 2548
Dahl, Jeffrey, 'The NFL and ERISA' (2010) 13 *Journal of Consumer & Commercial Law* 114

Damji, Faraz and Shelina Babul, 'Improving and Standardizing Concussion Education and Care: a Canadian experience' (October 2018) *Concussion* 1 (Online First)

David, Paul, *A Guide to the World Anti-Doping Code* (Cambridge, 2017)

Davis, Gavin A and Laura K Purcell , 'The Evaluation and Management of Acute Concussion Differs in Young Children' (2014) 48 *British Journal of Sports Medicine* 98

Davis, Gavin A and Michael Makdissi, 'Concussion Tests: Clarifying Potential Confusion Regarding Sideline Assessment and Cognitive Testing' (2012) 46 *British Journal of Sports Medicine* 959

Davis, Gavin A et al., 'International Study of Video Review of Concussion in Professional Sports' (September 2018; Online First) *British Journal of Sports Medicine* 1

Davis, Gavin A, Rudolph J Castellani and Paul McCrory, 'Neurodegeneration in Sport' (2015) 76 *Neurosurgery* 643

Davis, Timothy, 'Tort Liability of Coaches for Injuries to Professional Athletes: Overcoming Policies and Doctrinal Barriers' (2008) 76 *University of Missouri Kansas City Law Review* 571

Dehghani, S et al., 'Intracranial Meningioma At the Site of a Previous Cranial Penetrating Trauma Due to Shrapnel' (2014) 25 *Journal of Craniofacial Surgery* 125

Delaney, Jeffrey Scott et al., 'Why Professional Football Players Chose not to Reveal their Concussion Symptoms during a Practice or Game ' (2018) 28 Nr 1 *Clinical Journal of Sports Medicine* 1

Delaney, J Scott, 'Mechanisms of Injury for Concussions in University Football, Ice Hockey and Soccer' (2014) 24 *Clinical Journal of Sport Medicine* 233

Deubert, Christopher, Glenn I Cohen and Holly Fernandez Lynch, *Comparing Health Related Policies and Practices in Sports, the NFL and Other Professional Leagues* (Report Harvard Law School, 2017)

Deubert, Christopher R, et al., *Promoting and Protecting the Health of NFL Players: Legal and Ethical Analysis and Recommendations'* (Report Harvard Law School, 2016)

Diehl, Erika A, What's All the Headache?: Reform Needed to Cope with the Effects of Concussions in Football' (2010) 23 *Journal of Law and Health* 83

Donaldson, Alex et al., 'Translating Guidelines for the Diagnosis and Management of Sports-Related Concussion into Practice' (2016) 10 *American Journal of Lifestyle Medicine* 120

Donaldson, Laura, Mark Asbridge and Michael D Cusimano, 'Bodychecking Rules and Concussion in Elite Hockey' (2013) 8(7) *PlosOne* 1 (<http://www.ncbi.nlm.nih.gov/pmc/articles/PMC3714233/pdf/pone.0069122.pdf>)

Downie, Rachelle, 'Improving the Performance of Sports Ultimate Umpire: Reforming the Governance of the Court of Arbitration for Sport' (2011) 12 *Melbourne Journal of International Law* 315

Dvorak J, A Junge and P McCrory, 'Head Injuries' (2005) 39 (Supplement 1) *British Journal of Sports Medicine* 1

Ellemberg, Dave, *Les commotions cérébrales dans le sport* (Les Editions Québec-Livres, 2013)

Ehrlich, Sam C, 'Gratuitous Promises: Overseeing Athletic Organizations and the Duty of Care' (2018) 25 *Jeffrey S Moorad Sports Law Journal Sports Law Journal* 1

Ehrlichman, Brad, 'Is this Corner: An Analysis of the Federal Boxing Legislation' (2011) 34 *Columbia Journal of Law and The Arts* 421

Fainaru-Wada, Mark and Steve Fainaru, *The League of Denial: The NFL, Concussions, and the Battle for Truth* (2013, Crown Archetype) (Fainaru-Wada and Fainaru, 'Denial')

Finch, Caroline F and Peta White, 'The New Concussion in Sport Guidelines Are here. But How do We Get them out there? (2017) 51 *British Journal of Sports Medicine* 1734

Finch, Caroline F, Angela J Clapperton and Paul McCrory, 'Increasing Incidence of Hospitalisation for Sports-Related Concussion in Victoria, Australia' (2013) 198 *The Medical Journal of Australia* 427

Finch, Caroline F et al., 'Research Priorities of International Sporting Federations and the IOC Research Centers' (October 2016) 2 (1) *BMJ Open Sport and Exercise Medicine* 1 (Finch et al., 'Priorities')

Finch, Caroline F et al., 'Concussion Guidelines Need to Move From Only Expert Content to Also Include Implementation and Dissemination Strategies' (2013) 47 *British Journal of Sports Medicine* 12 (Finch et al., 'Guidelines')

Flint, Charles, Adam Lewis and Jonathan Taylor, 'The Fight Against Doping in Sport: the Regulatory Framework' in Adam Lewis and Jonathan Taylor, *Sport, Law and Practice* (Bloomsbury, 3rd ed, 2014) 135

Folick, Lorne, Michael Libby and Paul Dawson, *Sports and Recreation Liability Law in Canada* (Thomson Reuters, 2017)

Frémont, Pierre, 'In Response to: Time to Rethink the Zürich Guidelines? A Critique on the Consensus Statement on Concussion in Sport: The 4th International Conference on Concussion; Held in Zurich, November 2012' (2014) 24 *Clinical Journal of Sport Medicine* 520

French, Christopher C, 'A Battle for NFL vs Insurance Industry Re: Concussion Liabilities' (2016) 53 *San Diego Law Review* 901

Fuller, Colin W, et al., 'Evaluation of World Rugby Concussion Management Process: Results from Rugby World Cup 2015' (2017) 51 *British Journal of Sports Medicine* 64

Fuller, CW, A Junge and J Dvorak, 'A Six-Year Prospective Study of the Incidence, Aetiology and Causes of Head and Neck Injuries in International Football' (2005) 39 (Supplement 1) *British Journal of Sports Medicine* 1

Fyffe, Iain, *On His Own Side of the Puck* (2014, self-published)

Gabbett, Tim, et al., 'Applied Physiology of Rugby League' (2008) 38 *Sports Medicine* 119

Galland, Anne, 'Football Headers and Dementia: Five Minutes with Willie Stewart' (January 2018) Vol. 360 Issue 8137 *BMJ* 190

Gardner, Andrew J, et al., 'A Preliminary Video Analysis of Concussion in the National Rugby League' (2015) 29 *Brain Injury* 1182 (Gardner et al., 'Rugby League')

Gardner, Andrew J, et al., 'A Systematic Review and Meta-Analysis of Concussion in Rugby Union' (2015) 44 *Sports Medicine* 1717 (Gardner et al., 'Rugby Union')

Gardner, Andrew, Grant L Iverson and Paul McCrory, 'Chronic Traumatic Encephalopathy in Sport: A Systematic Review' (2014) 48 *British Journal of Sports Medicine* 84

Garner, Bryan A (ed), *Black's Law Dictionary* (Tomson Reuters, 10th ed, 2014)

Geddes, J F et al., 'Neuronal Cytoskeletal Changes Are An Early Consequence Of Repetitive Head Injury' (1999) 98 *Acta Neuropathologica* 171

Gerardi, Kristina M, 'Tackles that Rattle the Brain' (2011) 18 *Sports Lawyers Journal* 181

Giametta, Joseph, 'In re National Football League Concussion Litigation: An Examination of the Merits of Class Action and Certification' (2017) 20 *Quinnipiac Health Law Journal* 213

Giza, Christopher C et al., 'Summary of Evidence-Based Guideline Update: Evaluation and Management of Concussion in Sport, Report of the Guideline Development Subcommittee of the American Academy of Neurology' (2013) 80 *Neurology* 2250

Gould IV, William B, 'Football, Concussion and Preemption, The Gidiron of National Football League Litigation' (2012) 8 *FIU Law Review* 55

Gove, Jeremy P, 'Three and Out: the NFL's Concussion Liability and How Players Can Tackle the Problem' (2012) 14 *Vanderbilt Journal of Entertainment and Technology Law* 649

Graham, Robert et al (eds), *Sports Related Concussion in Youth, Improving the Science, Changing the Culture* (National Academy of Science, 2014)

Green, Gary A, et al., 'Mild Traumatic Brain Injury in Major and Minor League Baseball Players' (2015) 43 *American Journal of Sports Medicine* 1118

Greenhow, Annette, 'A Knock to the Head', *Law Institute of Victoria Journal*, 3 April 2018 (<https://www.liv.asn.au/Staying-Informed/LIJ/LIJ/April/A-knock-to-the-head>) (paywall) (Greenhow, 'Knock')

Greenhow, Annette and Jocelyn East, 'Custodians of the Game: Ethical Considerations for Football Governing Bodies in Regulating Concussion Management' (2015) 8 *Neuroethics* 65

Greenhow, Annette and Lisa Gowthorp, 'Head Injuries and Concussion Issues' in: Niko Schulenkorf and Stephen Frawley (eds), *Critical Issues in Global Sports Management* (Routledge, 2017) 93

Greenhow, Annette, 'Concussion Policies of the National Football League: Revisiting the "Sport Administrator's Charter" and the Role of the Australian Football League and National Rugby League in Concussion Management' (2011) *Sports Law eJournal* 1 (<https://research.bond.edu.au/en/publications/concussion-policies-of-the-national-football-league-revisiting-th>) (Greenhow, 'Charter')

Grinberg, Lea T et al., 'Chronic Traumatic Encephalopathy Presenting as Alzheimer's Disease in a Retired Soccer Player' (2016) 54 *Journal of Alzheimer's Disease* 169

Groschel, Cristina E, 'Down for the Count: 'The Muhammad Ali Boxing Reform Act and Its Shortcomings' (2002) 26 *Nola Law Review* 927

Guccione, John, 'Moving Past a Pocket Change Settlement: The Threat of Preemption and How the Loss of Chance Doctrine Can Help NFL Concussion Plaintiffs Prove Causation' (2014) 22 *Journal of Law and Policy* 907

Guerriero M, Christopher C Giza and Alexander Rotenberg, 'Glutamate and GABA Imbalance Following Traumatic Brain Injury' May (2015) 15(5) *Current Neurology and Neuroscience Reports* 1

Guskiewicz, Kevin, et al., 'Evidence-Based Approach to revisiting the SCAT 2: Introducing the SCAT 3' (2013) 47 *British Journal of Sports Medicine* 289 (Guskiewicz, 'SCAT 3')

Guskiewicz, Kevin M et al., 'Association between Recurrent Concussion and Late-Life Cognitive Impairment in Retired Professional Football Players' (2005) 57 *Neurosurgery* 719 (Guskiewicz, 'Impairment')

Gust, IV and Thomas Rockwell, 'The California Workers' Compensation Act: The Death Knell of NFL Player's "Concussion" Case' (2012) 44 *University of Toledo Law Review* 273

Hales, Chadwick et al., 'Late-stage CTE Pathology in a Retired Soccer Player with Dementia' (2014) 83 *Neurology* 2307

Hanna, Joseph and Daniel Kain, 'NFL's Shaky Concussion Policy Exposes the League to Potential Liability Headaches' (Fall 2010) 28(3) *Entertainment and Sports Lawyer* 9

Hanna, Joseph M, 'Ray Rice, Roger Goodell and Explosive Legal Showdown' (Fall 2014) *American Bar Association – Section Minority Trial Lawyer* (online review) (Hanna, 'Legal Showdown')

Hanna, Joseph M, 'Concussions May Prove to Be a Major Headache for the NFL' (2012) 84 *New York State Bar Association Journal* 10 (Hanna, 'NFL')

Harmon, Kimberley G et al., 'American Medical Society for Sports Medicine's Position Statement: Concussion in Sport' (2013) 47 *British Journal of Sports Medicine* 15

Hart, John Jr et al., 'Neuroimaging of Cognitive Dysfunction and Depression in Aging Retired National Football League Players' 2013 (70) *JAMA Neurology* 326

Hawley, Jessica Leigh, 'Class Certification Issues: In re: National Football League Concussion Injury Litigation' (2016) 6 *Pace Intellectual Property, Sports & Entertainment Law Forum* 185

Hazrati, Lili-Naz et al., 'The Absence of Chronic Traumatic Encephalopathy in Retired Players with Multiple Concussions and Neurological Symptomatology' (2013) 7 *Frontiers in Human Neuroscience* 1 (<https://www.ncbi.nlm.nih.gov/pmc/articles/PMC3662898/>)

Hay, Roy, 'A Tale of Two Footballs: The Origins of Australian Football and Association Football Revisited' (2010) 13 *Sport in Society* 952

Heard, Kelly A, 'The Impact of Preemption in the NFL Concussion Litigation' (2013) 68 *University of Miami Law Review* 221

Hecht, Alexander N, 'Legal and Ethical Aspects of Sports-Related Concussions: the Merrill Hoge Story' (2002) 12 *Seton Hall Journal of Sports and Entertainment Law* 17

Heiner, Jennifer Ann, 'Concussions in the National Football League: Jani v Bert Bell/Pete Rozelle NFL Player Ret. Plan and Legal Analysis of the NFL's 2007 Concussion Management Guidelines' (2008) *Seton Hall Journal of Sports and Entertainment Law* 255

Heshka, Jon and Kris Lines, 'A Proposed New Approach to Regulating Brain Injuries in Sport' (2013) 3 *International Journal of Sport and Society* 141

Heshka, Jon, 'Sports Law Expert Takes Closer Look at $200 Million CFL Concussion Lawsuit' (2015) *Professional Sports and the Law* 17 (Heshka, 'CFL')

Heshka, Jon 'Brain Injuries: A Shot Across the NHL's Bow' (2012) 36 *Law Now* 35 (Heshka, 'NHL')

Hohenstein, Andrew D, 'Team Physicians: Adhering to the Hippocratic Oath or Just Plain Hypocrites?' (2009) 19 *Marquette Sports Law Review* 579

Howard, Kelley C, 'Regulating the Sport of Boxing: Congress Throws the First Punch With the Professional Boxing Safety Act' (1997) 7 *Seton Hall Journal of Sports and Entertainment Law* 103

Huebinger, Jason, 'Beyond the Injured Reserve: the Struggle Facing Former NFL Players in Obtaining Much Needed Disability Assistance' (2009) 16 *Sports Lawyers Journal* 279

Hutchison, Michael G et al., 'A Systematic Video Analysis of National Hockey League (NHL) Concussions, Part II: How Concussions Occur in the NHL' (2015) 49 *British Journal of Sports Medicine* 552 (and previous publications) (Hutchison et al., 'Hockey')

Hutchison, Michael G, et al., 'Head Trauma in Martial Arts' (2014) 42 *American Journal of Sports Medicine* 1352 (Hutchison et al., 'Martial Arts')

Improving Sports Safety: A Multifaceted Approach: Hearing Before the House Comm. on Energy and Commerce, 113th Cong. 1 (2014) (retrieved from Heinonline)

Izraelszki, Jason, 'Concussions in the NHL: A Narrative Review of the Literature' (2014) 58 *The Journal of the Canadian Chiropractic Association* 346

James, Sarah, 'Ringing the Bell for the Last Time: How the NFL's Settlement Agreement Overwhelmingly Disfavors NFL Players Living with Chronic Traumatic Encephalopathy (CTE)' (2016) 11 *Journal of Health & Biomedical Law* 391

Johnson, Paul T, et al., 'The Contractual and Ethical Duty for a Professional Athlete to Be an Exemplary Role Model: Bringing the Sport and the Sports Person Into Unreasonable and Unfair Disrepute' (2013) 8 *Australian and New Zealand Sports Law Journal* 55

Junge, Astrid and Jiri Dvorak, 'Football Injuries during the 2014 FIFA World Cup' (2015) 49 *British Journal of Sports Medicine* 601 (Junge and Dvorak, 'FIFA')

Junge, Astrid and Jiri Dvorak, 'Injury Surveillance in World Football Tournaments 1998-2012' (2013) 47 *British Journal of Sports Medicine* 782 (Junge and Dvorak, 'World Football')

Junge, Astrid and Nina Feddermann-Demont, 'Prevalence of Depression and Anxiety in Top-Level Male and Female Football Players' (2016) 2(1) *BMJ Open Sport and Exercise Medicine* (online article)

Junge, Astrid et al., 'Injury Surveillance in Multi-Sport Events: The International Olympic Committee Approach' (2008) 42 *British Journal of Sports Medicine* 413 (Junge et al., 'Multi-Sport Events')

Junge, Astrid et al., 'Football Injuries during FIFA Tournaments and the Olympic Games, 1998-2001' (2004) 32 (Supplement 1) *American Journal of Sports Medicine* 80S (Junge et al., 'Football Injuries')

Kain, Daniel J, 'It's just a Concussion: the National Football League's Denial of a Causal Link between Multiple Concussions and Later-Life Cognitive Decline' (2009) 40 *Rutgers Law Journal* 697

Kajankova, Maria et al., 'Response of School Districts to the New York State Concussion Awareness and Management Act: Review of Policies and Procedures' (2017) 87 *Journal of School Health* 409

Kamba, WJ, 'Comparative Law: A Theoretical Framework' (1974) 23 *International and Comparative Law Quarterly* 485

Kelly, James P and Jay H Rosenberg, 'Diagnosis and Management of Concussion in Sport' (1997) 48 *Neurology* 575

Kent, Michael, *The Oxford Dictionary of Sports Science & Medicine* (Oxford University Press, 2006, 3rd ed)

Kerry ZY et al., 'Nine Year Risk of Depression Diagnosis Increases with Increasing Self-Reported Concussions in Retired Professional Football Players' (October 2012) 40(10) *American Journal of Sports Medicine* 2206

Kim, Theresa S, 'Tackling Head Injuries in Youth and Interscholastic Football with NFL Contract Reform' (2017) 24 *Sports Law Journal* 71

Kirby, Joanne, 'Employers' Liability and Concussive Injury in Professional Rugby Union: The Application of Health and Safety Legislation to Concussive Injury in Professional Rugby Union in the UK and Ireland' (2015) 13 *Entertainment and Sports Law Journal* (online review)

Kuhn, Andrew W and Gary S Solomon, 'Concussion in the National Hockey League: A Narrative Review of the Literature' (2015) 1(1) *Concussion* 1

Legal Issues Relating to Football Head Injuries (Part I and II): Hearing Before the House Comm. on the Judiciary, 111th Cong. 1 (2010) (<http://judiciary.house.gov/_files/hearings/printers/111th/111-82_53092.PDF>)

Legg, Michael, 'National Football League Players' Concussion Injury Class Action Settlement' (2015) 10 *Australian and New Zealand Association Sports Law Journal* 47

Letters to the Editor, 'In Response to: Time to Rethink the Zürich Guidelines? A Critique on the Consensus Statement on Concussion in Sport: The 4th International Conference on Concussion; Held in Zurich, November 2012' (2014) 24 *Clinical Journal of Sport Medicine* 520

Levy, Michael L et al., 'Concussions in Soccer: A Current Understanding' (2012) 78 *World Neurosurgery* 535

Lewis, Adam et al., *Challenging Sports Governing Bodies* (Bloombsbury, 2016)

Lincoln Quarie, Kenneth and Ian Robert Murphy, 'Towards an Operational Definition of Sports Concussion': Identifying a Limitation in the 2012 Zurich Consensus Statement and Suggesting Solutions' (2014) 48 *British Journal of Sports Medicine* 1589

Ling, Helen et al., 'Mixed Pathologies, Including Chronic Traumatic Encephalopathy Account for Dementia in Retired Association Football (Soccer) Players' (2017) 133 *Acta Neuropathologica* 337 (Ling et al., 'Pathologies')

Ling, Helen et al., 'Historical Evidence of Chronic Traumatic Encephalopathy in a Large Series of Neurodegenerative Diseases' (2015) 130 *Acta Neuropathologica* 891 (Ling et al., 'Series')

Lipsky, Brian, 'Dealing with the NFL's Concussion Problems of Yesterday, Today and Tomorrow' (2008) 18 *Fordham Intellectual Property, Media and Entertainment Law Journal* 959

Lipton, Michael L et al., 'Soccer Heading is Associated with White Matter Microstructural and Cognitive Abnormalities' (2013) 268 *Radiology* 850 (Lipton et al., 'Heading')

Lipton, ML et al., 'Robust Detection of Traumatic Axonal Injury in Individual Mild Traumatic Brain Injury Patients: Intersubject Variation, Change Over Time and Bidirectional Changes in Anisotropy' (2012) 6 *Brain Imaging & Behaviour* 329 (Lipton et al., 'Injury')

LoVelette, Brett Edwin, 'Mortal Kombat in Cleats: an Examination of the Effectiveness of the National Football League Disability Plan and its Impact on Retired Players' (2009) 36 *Pepperdine Law Review* 1101

Lueke, Lesley, 'High School Athletes and Concussions, More than a Game at Stake' (2011) 32 *Journal of Legal Medicine* 483

Luce, Robert, 'Proving a Mild Traumatic Brain Injury: A Complex but no Longer Impossible Task' (2012) 38 *Vermont Bar Journal* 12

Luis, Adam, Beth Wilkinson and Marc Henzelin, Independent Review on Integrity in Tennis, interim report, 2018 (<http://tennisirp.com/>)

Lydakis, Michael and Andrew Zapata, 'Tackling the Issues: The History of the National Football League's 2011 Collective Bargaining Agreement and What it Means for the Future of Sport' (2012) 10 *Willamette Sports Law Journal* 17

Maiolini, Danielle and Leila Barreto, '*Lesões no Esporte Profissional – a Jurisprudência Trabalhista sobre o Seguro Desportivo*' (2017) Nr 38 *Revista Síntese de Direito Desportivo* 81

Makdissi, Michael and Gavin Davis, 'Using Video Analysis for Concussion Surveillance in Australian Football' (2016) 19 *Journal of Science and Medicine in Sport* 958

Maroon, Joseph C et al., 'Chronic Traumatic Encephalopathy in Contact Sports, A Systematic Review of All Reported Pathological Cases' (February 2015) 10(2) *PlosOne* 1

Marrar, Mallika et al., 'Epidemiology of Concussions Among United States High School Athletes in 20 Sports' (2012) 40 *American Journal of Sports Medicine* 747

Marrs, Scott D and Sean P Milligan, 'Courts and Sports: Player Injuries – Assumption of the Risk or Illegal Foul? (2012) 50 *Houston Lawyer* 10

Martin, Tate, 'Wake up Call: How the Ray Rice Incident Opened the Public's Eyes to Domestic Violence in Professional Sports and the Need for Change' (2017) 24 Sports Law Journal 183

Martland, Harrison S, 'Punch Drunk' (1928) 15 *Journal of the American Medical Association* 1103

Mayer, Kayleigh R, 'This Is Football, You're Supposed to Get Hit: Tackling Concussions and Chronic Traumatic Encephalopathy ; Has the NFL Been Wrongful ?' (2014) 10 *DePaul Journal of Sports Law & Contemporary Problems* 31

McCrory, Paul, 'Does Second Impact Syndrome Exist?' (2001) 11 *Clinical Journal of Sport Medicine* 144

McCrory, Paul et al., 'Sports Concussion', in Brukner et al. (eds), *Brukner & Khan's Clinical Sports Medicine* (McGraw-Hill Australia, 5th ed, 2017, Vol. I, 'Injuries', Part B) 296 (McCrory et al., 'Concussion')

McCrory, Paul et al., 'Consensus Statement on Concussion in Sport: The 5th International Conference on Concussion in Sport Held in Berlin, October 2016' (2018) 51 *British Journal of Sports Medicine* 838 (McCrory et al., '5th Consensus')

McCrory, Paul et al., 'Consensus Statement on Concussion in Sport: The 4th International Conference on Concussion in Sport Held in Zurich, November 2012' (2013) 47 *British Journal of Sports Medicine* 250 (McCrory et al., '4th Consensus')

McCrory, P et al., 'Consensus Statement on Concussion in Sport: The 3rd International Conference on Concussion in Sport Held in Zurich, November 2008' (2009) 43 *British Journal of Sports Medicine* 76 (McCrory et al., '3rd Consensus')

McCrory, P et al., 'Summary and Agreement Statement on the 2nd International Conference on Concussion in Sport, Prague 2004' (2005) 39 *British Journal of Sports Medicine* 196 (McCrory et al., '2nd Consensus')

McCrory, Paul, Gavin Davis and Michael Makdissi, 'Second-Impact Syndrome or Cerebral Swelling After Sporting Head Injury' (2012) 11 *Current Sports Medicine Reports* 21

McCrory, Paul, Tscharni Zazryn and Peter Cameron, 'The Evidence for Chronic Traumatic Encephalopathy in Boxing' (2007) 37 *Sports Medicine* (Springer) 467

McGillivray, Heather, 'Where is the Awareness in Concussion Awareness: Can Concussed Players Really Assume the Risk in a Concussed State?' (2014) 21 *Jeffrey S Moorad Sports Law Journal Sports Law Journal* 529

McGowan, Carter Anne, 'The Other Skate Drops: The NHL Concussion Lawsuit' (2014) 25 *NYSBA Entertainment, Arts and Sports Law Journal* 23

McGowan Lowrey, Kerri and Stephanie R Morain, 'State Experiences in Implementing Youth Sports Concussion Laws: Challenges, Successes, and Lessons for Evaluating Impact' 2014 (42) *Journal of Law, Medicine and Ethics* 290

McGowan Lowrey, Kerri, 'State Laws Addressing Youth Sports-Related Brain Injury and the Future of Concussion Law and Policy' 2014 (10) *Journal of Business and Techonology Law* 61

McIntyre, James, 'Getting Schooled in the Hard Knocks of Concussion Liability' (2017) 99 *The ANZSLA Commentator* 2

McKee, Ann C, 'Chronic Traumatic Encephalopathy' in Bradford Dickerson and Alireza Atri (eds), *Dementia, Comprehensive Principles and Practice* (Oxford University Press, 2014) 160 (McKee, 'CTE')

McKee, Ann C, 'Chronic Traumatic Encephalopathy in Athletes Progressive Tauopathy after Repetitive Head Injury' (2009) 68 *Journal of Neuropathology & Experimental Neurology* 709 (McKee, 'Head Injury')

McKee, Ann C et al., 'The Neuropathology of Sport' (2014) 127 *Acta Neuropathologica* 29 (McKee et al., 'Neuropathology')

McKee, Ann C et al., 'The Spectrum of Disease in Chronic Traumatic Encephalopathy' (2013) 136 *Brain* 43 (McKee et al., 'Spectrum')

McKee, Ann C et al., 'TDP-43 Proteinopathy and Motor Neuron Disease in Chronic Traumatic Encephalopathy' (2010) 69 *Journal of Neuropathology and Experimental Neurology* 918 (McKee et al., 'Motor Neurone Disease')

McLaren, Richard, Independent Investigation Report Part I, 18 July 2016 (<https://www.wada-ama.org/en/resources/doping-control-process/mclaren-independent-investigation-report-part-i>) (McLaren, Report I)

McLaren, Richard, Independent Investigation Report Part II, 9 December 2016 (<https://www.wada-ama.org/en/resources/doping-control-process/mclaren-independent-investigation-report-part-ii>) (McLaren, Report II)

McLaren, Richard, 'Twenty-Five Years of the Court of Arbitration for Sport: A Look in the Rear-View Mirror' (2010) 20 *Marquette Sports Law Review* 305 (McLaren, 'Twenty Five Years')

McLaren, Richard, 'The Court of Arbitration for Sport: An Independent Arena for the World's Disputes' (2001) 35 *Valparaiso University Law Review* 379 (McLaren, 'Independent Arena')

Mecham, Shane C and Kevin M Guskiewicz, 'Head Case: an Agent's Guide to Protecting their NFL's Clients from Concussions and Associated Risks' (2008) 76 *University of Missouri-Kansas City Law Review* 699

Meehan, W P, *Kids, Sports and Concussion* (Praeger, 2011)

Meier, Timothy B, et al., 'Recovery of Cerebral Blood Flow Following Sports-Related Concussion' (2015) 72 *JAMA Neurology* 530

Mez, Jesse et al., 'Clinicopathological Evaluation of Chronic Traumatic Encephalopathy in Players of American Football' (2017) 318 *Journal of the American Medical Association* 360

Mielke, Michelle M et al., 'Head Trauma and in Vivo Measures of Amyloid and Neurodegeneration in a Population-Based Study' (2014) 82 *Neurology* 70

Mihalik, Jason P, et al., 'Measurement of Head impacts in Collegiate Football Players: Relationship Between Head Impact Biomechanics and Acute Clinical Outcome After Concussion' (2007) 61 *Neurosurgery* 1229

Miller, John J and Tom T Wendt, 'The Concussion Crisis in the National Hockey League' (2015) 9 *Journal of Contemporary Athletics* 1

Mills, Brian James, 'Football Helmets and Product Liability' (2001) 8 *Sports Lawyers Journal* 153

Millspaugh, J A, 'Dementia Pugilistica' (1937) 35 *US Naval Medical Bulletin* 297

Mitten, Matthew J and Hayden Opie, ' "Sports Law", Implications for the Development of international, Comparative law and Global Dispute Resolution', in Robert CR Siekmann and Janwillem Soek, *Lex Sportiva, What is Sports Law?* (Springer, 2012) 173

Mitten, Matthew, et al., *Sports Law and Regulation: Cases, Material and Problems* (Wolters Kluwer, 4th ed, 2017) (Mitten, 'Cases')

Mitten, Matthew J, 'Drug Testing of Athletes – An Internal, not External Matter' (2005) 40 *New England Law Review* 797 (Mitten, 'Drug Testing')

Mitten, Matthew J, 'Team Physicians as Co-Employees: A Prescription That Deprives Professional Athletes of an Adequate Remedy for Sports Medicine Malpractice' (2005) 50 *Marquette University Law School Review* 211 (Mitten, 'Team Physicians')

Mitten, Matthew J, 'Emerging Legal Issues in Sports Medicine' (2002) 76 *Saint John's Law Review* 5 (Mitten, 'Legal Issues')

Modery, Michelle M, 'Injury Time-Out: Justifying Workers' Compensation Awards to Retired Athletes with Concussion-Caused Dementia' (2011) 84 *Temple Law Review* 247

Molloy, Charlene et al., 'Is Traumatic Brain Injury A Risk Factor for Schizophrenia? A Meta-Analysis of Case-Controlled Population-Based Studies' (2011) 37 *Schizophrenia Bulletin* 1104

Monette, Michael, 'Heavy Hitting: Concussions and Safety Law' (2012) 184 *Canadian Medical Association Journal* 639

Murray, Stephanie A, 'Misnomer of the NFL's "Concussion Crisis": Don't Count on the NFL to Solve Football's Biggest Problem - and OSHA Regulation May not Save the Game Either' (2017) 56 *Washburn Law Journal* 181

Nehme, Marina and Catherine Ordway, 'Governance and Anti-Doping: Beyond the Fox and the Hen House' in Ulrich Haas and Deborah Healey (eds), *Doping in Sport and the Law* (Hart Publishing, 2016) 207

Nilsson, Michael et al., 'Head and Neck Injuries in Professional Soccer' (2013) 23 *Clinical Journal of Sports Medicine* 255

Norwood, Catherine, 'Clear Heads Needed on Concussion in Sport' (August 2012) 58(39) *Chronicle of Higher Education*, Monash Supplement 20

O'Brien, Sean D and Kenneth Ferguson, 'Traumatic Brain Injury and the Law: Introduction' (2015) 84 *University of Missouri-Kansas City Law Review* 287

Omalu, Bennet et al., 'Postmortem Autopsy-Confirmation of Antemortem [F-18]FDDNP-PET Scans in a Football Player With Chronic Traumatic Encephalopathy' (2018) 82 *Neurosurgery* 237 (Omalu et al., 'Scans')

Omalu, Bennet I et al., 'Chronic Traumatic Encephalopathy in a Professional American Wrestler' (2010) 6 *Journal of Forensic Nursing* 130 (Omalu et al., 'Wrestler')

Omalu, Bennet I et al., 'Chronic Traumatic Encephalopathy (CTE) in a National Football League Player: Case Report and Emerging Medicolegal Practice Questions' (2010) 6 *Journal of Forensic Nursing* 40 (Omalu, 'NFL Player III')

Omalu, Bennet I et al., 'Chronic Traumatic Encephalopathy in a National Football League Player: Part II' (2006) 59 *Neurosurgery* 1086 (Omalu et al., 'NFL Player II')

Omalu, Bennet I et al., 'Chronic Traumatic Encephalopathy in a National Football League Player' (2005) 57 *Neurosurgery* 128 (Omalu et al., 'NFL Player I')

Opie, Hayden and Elizabeth Toomey, 'Trans-Tasman Sport and Law – Some Observations' (2010) 16 *Canterbury Law Review* 155

Opie Hayden, 'The Sports Administrator's Charter: Agar v Hyde' (2002) 12 *Seton Hall Journal of Sport Law* 199

Patricios, Jon S et al., 'Implementation of the 2017 Berlin Concussion in Sport Group Consensus Statement in Contact and Collision Sports: A Joint Position Statement from 11 National and International Sports Organisations' (2018) 52 *British Journal of Sports Medicine* 635

Pearce, Alan et al., 'Neurophysiological and Cognitive Impairment following Repeated Sports Concussion Injuries in Retired Professional Rugby League Players' (2018) 32 *Brain Injury* 498 (Pearce et al., 'Rugby League')

Pearce, Alan J et al., 'The Long Term Effects of Sports Concussion on Retired Australian Football Players: A Study Using Transcranial Magnetic Stimulation' (2014) 31 *Journal of Neurotrauma* 1139 (Pearce et al., 'Australian Football')

Pellman, Elliot J and David Viano, 'Concussion in Professional Football: Summary of the Research Conducted by the National Football League's Committee on Mild Traumatic Brain Injury' (2006) 21 *Neurosurgery Focus* 1

Pellman, Elliot J et al., 'Concussion in Professional Football: Players Returning to the Same Game, Part 7' (2005) 56 *Neurosurgery* 79 (Pellman, 'Part 7')

Pellman, Elliot J et al., 'Concussion in Professional Football: Neuropsychological Testing, Part 6' (2004) 55 *Neurosurgery* 1290 (Pellman, 'Part 6')

Pellman, Elliot J et al., 'Concussion in Professional Football: Repeat Injuries, Part 4' (2004) 55 *Neurosurgery* 860 (Pellman, 'Part 4')

Pellman, Elliot J et al., 'Concussion in Professional Football: Epidemiological Features of Game Injuries and Review of the Literature, Part 3' (2004) 54 *Neurosurgery* 81 (Pellman, 'Part 3')

Piggin, Joe and Allyson Pollock, 'World Rugby's Erroneous and Misleading Representation of Australian Sports Injury Statistics' (2017) 57 *British Journal of Sports Medicine* 1108

Piquero, Alex et al., 'The National Felon League? A Comparison of NFL Arrests to General Population Arrests' (2015) 43 *Journal of Criminal Justice* 397

Pollack, Keshia M, 'Developing and Implementing Major League Baseball's Health and Injury Tracking System' (2016) 183 *American Journal of Epidemiology* 490

Pound, Dick, Independent Commission Report I, 9 November 2015 (<https://www.wada-ama.org/en/resources/world-anti-doping-program/independent-commission-report-1>) (Pound, 'Report I')

Pound, Dick, Independent Commission Report II, 14 January 2016, amended 27 January 2016 (<https://www.wada-ama.org/en/resources/world-anti-doping-program/independent-commission-report-2>) (Pound, 'Report II')

Price, Jo, Peter Malliaras and Zoe Hudson, 'Current Practices in Determining Return to Play following Head Injury in Professional Football in the UK' (2012) 46 *British Journal of Sports Medicine* 1000

Prien, A et al., 'Health Problems in Elite Female Football Players: Prevalence and Risk Factors' (2017) 27 *Scandinavian Journal of Medicine & Science in Sports* 1404 (Prien et al., 'Football')

Prien, Annika et al., 'Injury and Illness in Aquatic Sport: How High is the Risk? A Comparison of Results from Three FINA World Championships' (2017) 51 *British Journal of Sports Medicine* 278 (Prien et al., 'Aquatic Sport')

Prinz, Birgit, Jiri Dvorak and Astrid Junge, 'Symptoms and Risk Factors of Depression during and after the Football Career of Elite Female Players' (2017) 2(1) *BMJ Open Sport and Exercise Medicine* (online article)

Quénet, Jean-François, *Un cyclone nommé dopage* (Broché, 1999)

Raftery, Martin and Ross Tucker, 'Implementing a Worldwide Concussion Program, The World Rugby Strategy to Secure Player Welfare' (2016) 5 *Aspetar* 50

Reeb, Matthieu, 'The Role and Functions of the Court of Arbitration for Sport (CAS)' in Ian Blackshaw, Robert CR Siekmann and Janwillem Soek (eds), *The Court of Arbitration for Sport 1984–2004* (TMC Asser Press, 2006) 31

Reich, J Brad, When Getting Your Bell Rung May Lead to Ringing the Bell: Potential Compensation for NFL Player Concussion-Related Injuries (2013) 12 *Virginia Sports & Entertainment Law Journal* 198

Roberts, AH, *Brain Damage in Boxers: A Study of the Prevalence of Traumatic Encephalopathy Among Ex-Professional Boxers* (Pitman, 1969)

Roche, Blaine V, 'Congressional Involvement in Professional Sports' Drug-Testing Policies: Get Involved but Don't Infringe' (2010) 4 Phoenix Law Review 489

Romero, Melanie, 'Check to the Head: The Tragic Death of NHL Enforcer, Derek Boogaard, and the NHL's Negligence – How Enforcers Are Treated as Second-Class Employees' (2015) 22 *Jeffrey S Moorad Sports Law Journal Sports Law Journal* 271

Rowan's Law Advisory Committee, *Creating Rowan's Law*, Report, September 2017 (<https://www.ontariocanada.com/registry/showAttachment.do?postingId=27186&attachmentId=37751>)

Ruhe, Alexander, Axel Gänsslen and Wolfgang Klein, 'The Incidence of Concussion in Professional and Collegiate Ice Hockey: Are We Making Progress? A Systematic Review of the Literature' (2014) 48 *British Journal of Sports Medicine* 102

Russell, Kelly et al., 'Legislation for Youth Sport Concussion in Canada: Review, Conceptual Framework and Recommendations' (2017) 44 *The Canadian Journal of Neurological Sciences* 225

Rutherford, Andrew et al., 'Do UK University Football Club Players Suffer Neuropsychological Impairment as a Consequence of their Football (Soccer) Play?' (August 2009) 31 *Journal of Clinical & Experimental Neuropsychology* 664

Rütter, Heinz and Christian Schmidt, *The Economic Importance of International Sports Organisations in Switzerland*, Report, 2013 (<http://www.fifa.com/mm/document/affederation/footballgovernance/02/22/25/11/international_sports_organisations_report_en_ok_neutral.pdf>)

Saffary, Roya, Lawrence S Chin and Robert C Cantu, 'From Concussion to Chronic Traumatic Encephalopathy: A Review' (2012) 6 *Journal of Clinical Sport Psychology* 351

Samadani, Uzma et al., 'Eye Tracking Detects Disconjugate Eye Movements Associated with Structural Mild Traumatic Brain Injury and Concussion' (2015) 32 *Journal of Neurotrauma* 548

Savage, Jason, et al., 'The Incidence of Concussion in a Professional Australian Rugby League Team, 1998-2012' (2013) *Journal of Sports Medicine* 1 (<https://www.hindawi.com/journals/jsm/2013/304576/>)

Scheuerman, Sheila B, 'The NFL Concussion Litigation: a Critical Assessment of Class Certification' (2012) 8 *FIU Law Review* 81

Schmid, Samuel, IOC Disciplinary Commission Report to the Executive Commission, 2 December 2017 (<https://stillmed.olympic.org/media/Document%20Library/OlympicOrg/IOC/Who-We-Are/Commissions/Disciplinary-Commission/IOC-DC-Schmid/IOC-Disciplinary-Commission-Schmid-Report.pdf#_ga=2.174085026.1613046842.1515970842-402556292.1510806486>)

Schmidt, ML et al., 'Tau Isoform Profile and Phosphorylation State in Dementia Pugilistica Recapitulate Alzheimer's Disease' (2001) 101 *Acta Neuropathologica* 518

Schot, Natasha, 'Negligent Liability in Sport' (2005) *Sports Law e-Journal* 1 (<http://classic.austlii.edu.au/au/journals/SportsLaweJl/2005/1.html>)

Schwindel, Leslie E, et al., 'Epidemiology and Outcomes of Concussions in Major League Baseball' (2014) 2 *Annals of Orthopedics and Rheumatology* 1022

Shen, Francis X, Are Youth Sports Concussion Statutes Working? (2018) 56 *Duquesne Law Review* 7

Shahim, Pashtun, et al., 'Blood Biomarkers Could Help Guide Return to Play for Athletes After Concussion' (2014) 71 *JAMA Neurology* 684

Showalter, Brent D, Steroid Testing Policies in Professional Sports: Regulated by Congress or Responsibility of the Leagues?' (2007) *Marquette Sports Law Review* 651

Silver, Steven J, 'NFL Concussion Litigation Moves Closer to a Resolution' (2015) 13(5) *World Sports Law Report* (online review)

Simeoni, Manon and Pierre Wessner, 'L'acceptation du risque en responsabilité civile, un concept à géométrie variable dans la pratique de sports', in Antonio Rigozzi, Dominique Sprumont and Yann Hafner (eds), *Mélanges en l'honneur de Denis Oswald* (Helbing & Lichtenhahn, 2012) 259

Smith, Aynsley M, et al., 'Ice Hockey Summit II: Zero Tolerance for Head Hits and Fighting' (2015) 14 *Current Sports Medicine Reports* 135 (Aynsley M Smith, 'Summit')

Spaude, Lance K, 'Time to Act: Correcting the Inadequacy of Youth Concussion Legislation through a Federal Act' (2017) 100 *Marquette Law Review* 1093

Stern, Robert A et al., 'Clinical Presentation of Chronic Traumatic Encephalopathy' (2013) 81 *Neurology* 1122

Stewart, Walter F et al., 'Heading Frequency Is More Strongly Related to Cognitive Performance than Unintentional Head Impacts in Amateur Soccer Players' (2018) Vol. 9 Art. 240 *Frontiers of Neurology* 1 (Stewart et al., 'Soccer')

Stewart, W, et al., 'Chronic Traumatic Encephalopathy: A Potential Late and Under Recognized Consequence of Rugby Union? (2016) 109 *QJM: An International Journal of Medicine* 11 (Stewart et al., 'Rugby Union')

Strain, Jeremy F, et al., 'Imaging Correlates of Memory and Concussion History in Retired National Football League Athletes' (2015) 72 *JAMA Neurology* 773

Straueme-Naesheim, Truls M et al., 'Do Minor Head Impacts in Soccer Cause Concussive Injury? A Prospective Case Control Study' (2009) 64 *Neurosurgery* 719

Stricker, Claude and Amandine Bouzigue, *The Economic impact of International Sports Organisations in Switzerland* (2008–13), Report, 2015 (<https://www.aists.org/sites/default/files/publication-pdf/aists_economic_impact_study-english-web.pdf>)

Strong, Michael J (ed), *Amyotrophic Lateral Sclerosis and Frontotemporal Dementias* (Oxford University Press, 2012)

Sungwon, Kim et al., 'Legislative Efforts to Reduce Concussions in Youth Sports: An Analysis of State Concussion Statutes' (2017) 27 *Journal of Legal Aspects Sport* 162

Sullivan, Shea, 'Football Helmet Product Liability, a Survey of Cases and Call for Reform' Sports 3 (1996) *Lawyers Journal* 233

Tagge, Chad A et al., 'Concussion, Microvascular Injury, and Early Tauopathy in Young Athletes after Impact Head Injury and an Impact Concussion Mouse Model' (2018) 141 *Brain* 422

Taylor, Jefferson C, 'The War on Soccer Hooliganism: The European Convention on Spectator Violence and Misbehaviour at Sports Events' (1987) 27 *Virginia Journal of International Law* 603

Telis, Michael, 'Playing Through the Haze: The NFL Concussion Litigation and Section 301 Preemption' (2014) 102 *The Georgetown Journal* 1841

Thorpe, David et al., *Sports Law* (Oxford University Press, 3rd ed, 2017)

Toy, Ozan, Mill Etienne and Ronald Bogdasarian, 'Consequences of Traumatic Brain Injury in Male Ice Hockey Players' (P5.319)' (2014) 82 *Neurology* No 10 Supplement

Thorndike, Augustus, 'Serious Recurrent Injuries of Athletes – Contraindications to Further Competitive Participation' (1952) 247 *New England Journal of Medicine* 554

Tucker, Ross, et al., 'A Video Analysis of Head Injuries Satisfying the Criteria for a Head Injury Assessment in Professional Rugby: A Prospective Cohort Study' (2017) 51 *British Journal of Sports Medicine* 1147

Tuominen, Markku et al., 'Concussion in the International Ice Hockey World Championships and Olympic Winter Games between 2006 and 2015' (2017) 51 *British Journal of Sports Medicine* 244

Ugolini, Joel Michael, 'Even a Violent Game has its Limits: a Look at the NFL's Responsibility for the Behavior of its Players' 39 (2007) *University of Toledo Law Review* 41

Ulrich, Rolf et al., 'Doping in Two Elite Athletics Competitions Assessed by Randomized-Response Surveys' (2018) 48 *Sports Medicine* 211

UNESCO Director-General, Final Report on the Preparation of the International Convention Against Doping in Sport (Paris, February 2005) (<http://unesdoc.unesco.org/images/0013/001388/138831e.pdf>)

UNODC IOC Study, *Criminal Law Provisions for the Prosecution of Competition Manipulation*, 2017 (<https://www.unodc.org/documents/corruption/Publications/2017/UNODC-IOC-Study.pdf>)

US House of Representatives, Committee on Energy and Commerce, Ranking Member Franck Pallone Jr, Democratic Staff Report, 'The National Football League's Attempt to Influence Funding Decisions at the National Institutes of Health', May 2016 (<https://democrats-energycommerce.house.gov/sites/democrats.energycommerce.house.gov/files/Democratic%20Staff%20Report%20on%20NFL%20NIH%20Investigation%205.23.2016.pdf>)

Veuthey, Alexandra, 'Match-Fixing and Governance in Cricket and Football: What is the Fix?' (2014) 14 *International Sports Law Journal* 82 (Veuthey, 'Match-Fixing')

Veuthey, Alexandra, 'Quelle protection pour les athlètes blessés? Analyse du cas de la National Football League à la lumière du droit suisse' (27 January 2014) *Jusletter* (online review) Rz1 (Veuthey, 'Droit suisse')

Veuthey, Alexandra, *Concussion in the National Football League: What Can we Learn?* (E-book, Weblaw, 2013) (Veuthey, 'NFL')

Veuthey, Alexandra, 'Racism in English Premier League: Is Football Operating in a Cocoon?' (2013) 13 *Sweet & Maxwell International Sports Law Review* 76 (Veuthey, 'Racism')

Wadas, MJ et al., 'Detection of Traumatic Brain Injury Protein Biomarkers With Resonant Microsystems' (December 2017) 1(6) *Sensors Letters* 1

Weiner, Myron F and Anne M Lipton (eds), *Clinical Manual of Alzheimer Disease and Other Dementias* (American Psychiatric Publishing, 2012)

Wendt, John T and John J Miller, ' "Ref, Is This the Final?" Concussion Issues at the 2014 FIFA Men's World Cup: A Case Study' (2015) 25 *Journal of Legal Aspects of Sport* 1

Wennberg, Richard et al., 'Is Concussion a Risk Factor for Epilepsy?' (2018) 45 *The Canadian Journal of Neurological Sciences* 275

Wetjen, Nicholas M, Mark A Pichelmann and John LD Atkinson, 'Second Impact Syndrome: Concussion and Second Injury Brain Complications' (2010) 211 *Journal of the American College of Surgeons* 553

Wilson, Marie-France, ‘Young Athletes at Risk: Preventing and Managing Consequences of Sports Concussions in Young Athletes and the Related Legal Issues’ (2010) 21 *Marquette Sports Law Review* 241 (Marie-France Wilson, ‘Youth Athletes’)

Withnall, Christopher et al., ‘Effectiveness of Headgear in Football’ (2005) 39 (Supplement 1) *British Journal of Sports Medicine* 40

Wood, James, David Howman and Ray Murrihy, Report of the Review of Australia’s Sports Integrity Arrangements, 2018 (<http://www.health.gov.au/internet/main/publishing.nsf/Content/63F0A5D7BDA5A0B5CA2582CF0005E6F9/$File/HEALTH-RASIA-Report-Acc.pdf>)

Wood, Jennifer A, ‘Dirty Game: Trusting the National Hockey League to Play Judge, jury and Executioner’ (2012) 13 *Texas Review of Entertainment and Sports Law* 185

Wong, Glenn, *Essentials of Sports Law* (Praeger, 4th ed, 2010)

Yang, Jingzhen et al., ‘New and Recurrent Concussions in High School Athletes before and after Traumatic brain Injury Laws’, 2005–16 (2017) 107 *American Journal of Public Health* 1916

Zhang, Marsha R et al., ‘Evidence of Cognitive Dysfunction after Soccer Playing with Ball Heading Using a Novel Tablet-Based Approach’ (2013) 8(2) *Plos One* 1 (<http://www.plosone.org/article/info:doi/10.1371/journal.pone.0057364>)

B. *Cases*

I) State Courts

- Australia

Agar v Hyde (2000) 201 CLR 552
Green v Australian Rugby Football League Ltd and Ors [2002] NSWSC 749
Haylen v New South Wales Rugby Union Ltd [2002] NSWSC 114
McManus v Knights Rugby League Pty Ltd [2017] NSWSC 1101
Vairy v Wyong Shire Council (2005) 223 CLR 422
Woods v Multisport Holdings (2002) 208 CLR 460

- Brazil

Altair da Silva v Sadia S.A, Paraná Regional Labour Court, 28 September 2010
Federação Nacional dos Atletas Profissionais de Futebol (FENAPAF) v Confederação Brasileira de Futebol (CBF), Labour Court of Campinas, 12 June 2017
Thiago Dutra Regis v Joinville Esporte Clube, Superior Labor Court of Santa Catarina, 7 March 2014

- Canada

Agar v Canning [1965] 54 W.W.R. 302
Arland Richard Bruce v Mark Steven Cohon, Leave to appeal refused, March 15, 2018 (S.C.C.)

Bruce v Cohon 2017 BCCA 186
Bruce v Cohon 2016 BCSC 419
Levita v Crew (2015), 2015 CarswellOnt 13326 (Ont. S.C.J.)
Robitaille v Vancouver Hockey Club Ltd (1981) 124 DLR (3d) 228
Smith v Horizon Aero Sports Ltd [1981] 130 D.L.R. (3d) 91 B.C.S.C.
Zacchardo v Chartis Insurance Company of Canada. 2016 QCCS 398

- England

Watson v BBBC [2001] QB 1134

- New Zealand

Gatland v Fairfax New Zealand Limited [2016] NZHC 970

- US

Alice Mayall v USA Water Polo (9th Cir, No. 16-56389, 28 November 2018), Opinion
Alice Mayall v USA Water Polo, (CD Cal, No 8:15-cv-00171, 30 March 2016), Order
Alice Mayall v USA Water Polo, (CD Cal, No 8:15-cv-00171, 8 June 2015), Order
Alice Mayall v USA Water Polo (CD Cal, No 8:15-cv-00171, 4 May 2015), Order
Ballard v National Football League Players' Association (ED Mo) (2015) WL 4920329
Beauty Time Inc v VU Skin System, 118 F3d 140 (3d Cir. 1997)
Boogaard v NHL, 126 F. Supp. 3d 1010 (N.D.III.2015)
Dean v Handy & Harmon, 961 F. Supp. 798 (M.D. Pa. 1997)
Dent v National Football League, N.D. Cal., 2014 US Dist. LEXIS 174448
Duerson v National Football League, N.D. III, 2012 WL 1658353
Flood v Kuhn, 407 US 258 (1972)
In re: *National Hockey League Players' Concussion Injury Litigation* (D Minn, MDL No. 14-2551, 13 July 2018), Court Memorandum Opinion and Order
In re: *National Hockey League Players' Concussion Injury Litigation* (D Minn, MDL No. 14-2551, 26 April 2017), Court Memorandum Opinion and Order
In re: *National Hockey League Players' Concussion Injury Litigation*, (D Minn, MDL No. 14-2551, 18 May 2016), Court Memorandum Opinion and Order
In re: *National Hockey League Players' Concussion Injury Litigation* (D Minn, MDL No. 14-2551, 25 March 2015), Court Memorandum Opinion and Order
Kline v Security Guards, Inc., 386 F.3d 246 (3d Cir. 2004)
Maxwell v National Football League (C.D. Cal., No. 11-CV-08394, 8 December 2011), Order
Mehr et al. v. Fédération Internationale de Football Association et al (9th Cir, No. 15-16622, 22 September 2015), Order
Mehr et al. v. Fédération Internationale de Football Association et al (N.D., Cal., 16 July 2015, No. 14-cv-3879-PJH), Order
N. Am. Soccer League v NFL, 670 F.2d 1249, 1252 (2d Cir. 1982)
Peisino v Riddell Corporation, Wilmington, Delaware Superior Court, 1992

Sandage v. Bankhead Enters., Inc., 177 F.3d 670, 675 (8th Cir. 1999), cert. denied, 528 U.S. 1019 (1999)
Stringer v National Football League, 474 F. Supp. 2d 894 (S.D. Ohio 2007)
Walker v Schutt Sports Sales Group, Grayson Court, April 2000
Williams v National Football League, 582 F.3d 863 (8th Cir. 2009)
Yarusso v Bell Helmets, Delaware Superior Court, September 2000

- Switzerland

Lucien Favre & Gabet Chapuisat, judgment of the Indictment Chamber of Geneva of 1 September 1986 (SJ 1987 119)
Lucien Favre & Gabet Chapuisat, judgment of the Court of justice of Geneva of 7 March 1988 (unpublished)
STF 134 IV 26
SFT 121 III 350

II) Court of Arbitration for Sport

CAS 2013/A/3280, *Eishockey club Olten & Keller vs Schnyder & SIHF*
CAS 2005/A/952, *Ashley Cole v Football Association Premier League (FAPL)*

C. *Legislation*

- Australia

Australian Sports Anti-Doping Authority (ASADA) Regulations 2006 (including *National Anti-Doping (NAD) Scheme*)
Civil Proceedings Act 2011 (Qld)
Civil Procedure Act 2005 (NSW)
Federal Court of Australia Act 1976 (Cth)
Limitations Act 1958 (Vic)
Public Health and Wellbeing Act 2008 (Vic)
Supreme Court Act 1986 (Vic)

- Brazil

Brazilian Civil Code (CC)
Brazilian Constitution
Brazilian Labour Code
Complementary Law 75/93

Law 7347/85
Law 9615/98 ('Pelé Law')

- Canada

Limitation Act 2012, S.B.C. 2012 (British Columbia)
Limitations Act 2002, S.O. 2002 (Ontario)
Rowan's Law Advisory Committee Act, 2016, S.O. 2016, chapter 11 [repealed 2016, chapter 11, section 3] (Ontario)
Rowan's Law (Concussion Safety), 2018, S.O. 2018, chapter 1 (Ontario)

- England

Civil Procedure Rules & Practice Directions (UK)
Limitation Act 1980 (UK)

- Switzerland

Federal Act on Private International Law (1987) *(PILA)*
Lugano Convention on Jurisdiction and Enforcement of Judgments in Civil and Commercial Matters (1988) (Lugano Convention, *LC*)
Swiss Civil Code (CC)
Swiss Code of Obligations (CO)

- US

Air Transportation Safety and System Stabilization Act of 2001, 49 USC § 40101 et seq.
American Law Institute, *Restatement (Second) of Torts* (1965) § 402A and 323
American Law Institute, *Restatement (Second) of Torts* (1979) § 904
American Law Institute, *Restatement (Thirds) of Torts* (1997) § 2
American Law Institute, *Restatement (Thirds) of Torts* (2010) § 6 cmt. b
American Law Institute, *Uniform Commercial Code (UCC)* (2002) § 2
Black Lung Benefits Act of 1973, 26 USC § 9501 et seq. (2018)
District of Columbia Statutes of Limitations, DC Code § 12-301(8) (2018)
Employee Retirement Income Security Act (ERISA) of 1974, 29 USC § 1001 et seq. (2018)
Federal Rules of Civil Procedure (FED.R.CIV.P.), 12b and 23e
Labor Management Relations Act (LMRA) of 1947, 29 USC § 185 (2018)
Minnesota Statutes of Limitations, Minn Stat § 541.05 (2018)
Muhammad Ali Boxing Reform Act ('Ali Act') of 2000, 15 USC § 6301 (2018)
New York Statutes of Limitations, NY CPLR 214(5) (McKinney, 2018)
Occupational Safety and Health Act of 1970 (OSHA), 29 USC § 651 et seq. (2018)

Pennsylvania Statutes of Limitations, PA Cons Stat § 5524 (West, 2018)
Pennsylvania Workers' Compensation Act, PA Cons Stat § 411(2) and 565 (West, 2018)
Pennsylvania Comparative Negligence Law, PA Cons Stat § 7102 (West, 2018)
Professional Boxing Safety Act (PBSA) of 1996, 15 USC § 6304 and 6309 (2018)
Sports Broadcasting Act of 1961, 15 USC 1291 (2018)
Sports Medicine Licensure Clarity Act of 2017, Bill H.R. 302 — 115th Congress (2017–18)
United States Constitution, Art. 1 § 8
Youth sports — Concussion and head injury guidelines — Injured athlete restrictions ('Zackery Lystedt Law'), Wash Rev Code § 28A.600.190 (West, 2009) (and subsequent state laws)

D. *Treaties / International Conventions / EU Regulations*

European Union's General Data Protection Regulation (GDPR), opened for signature 27 April 2016 (entered into force 25 May 2018)
The Council of Europe Convention on an Integrated Safety, Security and Service Approach at Football Matches, opened for signature 3 July 2016, CETS 218 (entered into force 1 November 2017)
The Council of Europe Convention on the Manipulation of Sports Competitions ('the Macolin Convention'), opened for signature 18 September 2014, CETS 215 (not yet into force)
The Council of Europe's Anti-Doping Convention, opened for signature 16 November 1989, CETS 135, (entered into force 1 March 1990)
The European Convention on Spectator Violence and Misbehaviour at Sports Events and in Particular at Football Matches, opened for signature 19 August 1985, CETS 120 (entered into force 1 November 1985)
The International Convention against Doping in Sport, opened for signature 19 October 2005, 2419 UNTS (entered into force 1 February 2007)
New York Convention of 10 June 1958 on the Recognition and Enforcement of Foreign Arbitral Awards (New York Convention), opened for signature 10 June 1958, 330 UNTS 38 (entered into force 7 June 1959)

E. *Sports Regulations and Documentation*

- AFL

AFL Anti-Doping Code (2015) (<http://s.afl.com.au/staticfile/AFL%20Tenant/AFL/Files/AFL%20Anti-Doping%20Code%202015-FINAL.pdf>)
AFL Collective Bargaining Agreement 2017–22 (<http://www.aflplayers.com.au/wp-content/uploads/2017/08/2017-2022-CBA.pdf>) (and previous CBAs)
AFL Concussion protocols 2017–18 (unpublished, but copy on file with author)
AFL Respect and Responsibility policy 2017 (unpublished, but copy on file with author)
AFL Information Paper, 'Responsible Approach to Concussion in the AFL', May 2012 (<http://www.aflcommunityclub.com.au/fileadmin/user_upload/Coach_AFL/Injury_Management/ResponsibleApproachConcussionintheAFL.pdf>)

- AIBA

AIBA Open Boxing (AOB) Competition Rules (2017) (<http://d152tffy3gbaeg.cloudfront.net/2015/02/AIBA-AOB-Competition-Rules-April-26-2017.pdf>)

- ARLC

ARLC Constitution (unpublished)

- ASF

ASF statutes (2013) (<http://www.football.ch/fr/Portaldata/1/Resources/dokumente/offizielle_dokumente_/2013/juli/STATUTEN_F_20130507.pdf>)

- ASUA

ASUA Constitution (2015) (<https://www.teamunify.com/uana/UserFiles/File/Bylaws/UANA-CONSTITUCION2011(EngSept).pdf>)

- CAS

Code of Sports-Related Arbitration (CAS Code, 2017) (<http://www.tas-cas.org/fileadmin/user_upload/Code_2017_FINAL__en_.pdf>)
CAS statutes: see CAS Code

- CBF

CBF statutes (2017) (unpublished, but copy on file with author)
CBF statutes (2015) (unpublished, but copy on file with author)

- CFL

CFL Collective Bargaining Agreement (CBA) 2014–19 (<http://www.bcbargaining.ca/content/1665/CFL_CFLPA.pdf>) (and previous CBAs)
CFL Concussion protocols (2017) (unpublished, but copy on file with author)
CFL Domestic violence policy (unpublished)

- CONCACAF

CONCACAF Gold Cup Regulations 2017 (<https://res.cloudinary.com/concacaf-production/image/upload/v1498764762/goldcup-prod/assets/2017_Regulations_English_Edition.pdf>)

- CONCACAF & CONMEBOL

CONCACAF & CONMEBOL Copa Americana Centaênario Regulations 2016 (unpublished, but copy on file with author)

- FFA

FFA Concussion Guidelines 2018 (<https://www.ffa.com.au/sites/ffa/files/2018-01/18-0102%20FFA%20Concussion%20Guidelines%20%28final%29.pdf>)

- FIFA

FIFA Laws of the Game 2018–19 (<https://img.fifa.com/image/upload/khhloe2xoigyna8juxw3.pdf>)

FIFA Statutes (2018) (<https://resources.fifa.com/image/upload/the-fifa-statutes-2018.pdf?cloudid=whhncbdzio03cuhmwfxa>)

- FINA

FINA Constitution (2017) (<https://www.fina.org/sites/default/files/1._fina_constitution_approved_by_the_fina_congress_on_22.07.2017_final.pdf>)

FINA Water Polo Rules 2017–21 (<https://www.fina.org/sites/default/files/2017_2021_wp_rules_07022018_colour.pdf>)

- IIHF

IIHF Medical Care Guide (2018) (<https://www.iihf.com/IIHFMvc/media/Downloads/Medical/Medical%20Care%20Guide%202018/2018-IIHF-Medical-Care-Guide-FINAL.pdf>)

IIHF Medical Regulations (2019) (not published yet, but copy on file with author)

IIHF Medical Regulations (2016) (<https://www.iihf.com/IIHFMvc/media/Downloads/Medical/Medical-Regulations-2016.pdf>)

IIHF Rulebook 2018–22 (<https://www.iihf.com/IIHFMvc/media/Downloads/Rule%20Book/IIHF_Official_Rule_Book_2018_Web_v2.pdf>)

- IOC

IOC Anti-Doping Code (1998) (unpublished) (and previous regulations)
Olympic Movement Code on the Prevention of the Manipulation of Competitions (2015) (<https://stillmed.olympic.org/media/Document%20Library/OlympicOrg/IOC/Who-We-Are/Commissions/Ethics/Good-Governance/olympic_movement_code_on_the_prevention_of_the_manipulation_of_competitions-2015-en.pdf#_ga=2.37936038.447501667.1520204391-402556292.1510806486>)
Olympic Charter (2015) (<https://stillmed.olympic.org/Documents/olympic_charter_en.pdf>)

- MLB

MLB Collective Bargaining Agreement (CBA) 2017–21 (<http://www.mlbplayers.com/pdf9/5450407.pdf>) (and previous CBAs)
MLB concussion protocols: see Attachment 36 CBA
MLB domestic violence and sexual assault policy: See Attachment 52 CBA
MLB Official Baseball Rules (2018) (<http://mlb.mlb.com/documents/0/8/0/268272080/2018_Official_Baseball_Rules.pdf>)

- MLS

MLS Collective Bargaining Agreement (CBA) 2015–20 (1 February 2015) (<https://s3.amazonaws.com/mlspa/Collective-Bargaining-Agreement-February-1-2015.pdf?mtime=20180213190926>) (exhibits unpublished)
MLS Concussion Evaluation and Management Protocols: See Exhibit 12 CBA (unpublished, but copy on file with author)
MLS Medical Policies and Procedures Manual 2016 (unpublished, but copy on file with author)
MLS Player Substance Abuse and Behavioral Health Program and Policy (SABH): See Exhibit 5 CBA (unpublished, but copy on file with author)

- NCAA

NCAA Ice Hockey Rules and Interpretations 2016–17 and 2017–18 (<http://www.ncaapublications.com/productdownloads/IH18.pdf>)

- NFL

NFL Collective Bargaining Agreement (CBA) 2011–20 (August 2011) (<https://nfllabor.files.wordpress.com/2010/01/collective-bargaining-agreement-2011-2020.pdf>) (and previous CBAs)

NFL Head, Neck and Spine Committee's Concussion Diagnosis and Management Protocol' (2018) (<https://www.playsmartplaysafe.com/wp-content/uploads/2018/08/nfl-concussion-protocol-2018.pdf>)
NFL On-Field Code of Conduct and Schedule of Fines (no date) (<http://operations.nfl.com/football-ops/fines-appeals/>)
NFL Personal Conduct Policy (December 2014) (<http://static.nfl.com/static/content/public/photo/2014/12/10/0ap3000000441637.pdf>)
NFL Personal Conduct Policy (June 2013) (<https://nfllabor.files.wordpress.com/2013/06/personal-conduct-policy.pdf>)
NFL Rulebook (2018) (<https://operations.nfl.com/media/3277/2018-nfl-rulebook_final-version.pdf>) (and previous regulations)

- NHL

NHL Concussion Evaluation and Management Protocol (2017–18) (unpublished, but copy on file with author)
NHL Concussion Evaluation and Management Protocol (2016–17) (<http://cdn.agilitycms.com/nhlpacom/2016-17_ConcussionProtocol.pdf>) (and previous versions)
NHL Rulebook (2018–19) (<http://www.nhl.com/nhl/en/v3/ext/rules/2018-2019-NHL-rulebook.pdf>) (and previous regulations)
NHL Collective Bargaining Agreement (CBA) 2013–22 (February 2013) (<http://www.nhl.com/nhl/en/v3/ext/CBA2012/NHL_NHLPA_2013_CBA.pdf>) (and previous CBAs)
NHL Constitution and By-Laws (extracts, date not mentioned) (<https://democrats-judiciary.house.gov/letter/letter-nhl-domestic-violence-practices-and-policies>)

- NRL

NRL Anti-Doping Policy (2015) (<https://playnrl.com/media/2308/2015-leagues-anti-doping-policy.pdf>)
NRL Collective Bargaining Agreement 2017–22 (and previous CBAs) (unpublished)
NRL Concussion protocols (unpublished)
NRL Respectful Relationships Education Manual (unpublished, but copy on file with author)

- Oceania Rugby

Oceania Rugby Constitution (2018) (unpublished, but copy on file with author)

- OHL

OHL Rulebook 2017–18 (<http://ontariohockeyleague.com/ohl-rule-book/>)

- Rugby Australia (formerly ARU)

Rugby Australia Collective Bargaining Agreement (CBA) 2018–20 (unpublished, but copy on file with author) (and previous CBAs)
Rugby Australia Concussion protocols (unpublished)
ARU Constitution (2016) (unpublished, but copy on file with author)
Rugby Australia Medical Policy (2017) (<http://www.rugbyau.com/about/codes-and-policies/all-codes-and-policies>)

- SFL

SFL contract template (<http://www.football.ch/sfl/fr/Portaldata/2/Resources/reglemente_f/Contrat_de_travail_joueur.pdf>)
SFL statutes (2018) (<https://www.sfl.ch/fileadmin/user_upload/Statuts_SFL_300518.PDF>)

- SIHF

SIHF brochure on concussion (2009) (<http://www.sihf.ch/media/4925/siha-broschuere-concussion-ed-24-11-09-2.pdf>)
SIHF statutes (2017) (<https://www.sihf.ch/media/8331/sihf_statuts.pdf>)

- The FA

The FA Handbook 2018–19 (<http://handbook.fapublications.com/#!/book/26>)
The FA's Concussion Guidelines (2015) (<http://www.thefa.com/get-involved/coach/concussion>)

- UEFA

UEFA statutes (2018) (<https://www.uefa.com/MultimediaFiles/Download/uefaorg/General/02/54/12/62/2541262_DOWNLOAD.pdf>)

- US Soccer

US Soccer Bylaws 2018–19 (<https://www.ussoccer.com/about/governance/bylaws>)

- USAWP

USAWP Codes of Conduct (no date mentioned) (<https://usawaterpolo.org/sports/2018/11/28/resources-codes-conduct-html.aspx>)
USAWP Concussion Protocols (2011) (unpublished)
USAWP Water Polo Rules 2015–18 (<http://grfx.cstv.com/photos/schools/uswp/genrel/auto_pdf/2015-16/misc_non_event/2015_2017Rules.pdf>)
USAWP Zone Policies and Procedures (2015) (<http://grfx.cstv.com/photos/schools/uswp/genrel/auto_pdf/2015-16/misc_non_event/USAWPZonePolicies_Procedures.pdf>)

- WADA

WADA Code (WADC) (2018) (<https://www.wada-ama.org/en/resources/the-code/world-anti-doping-code>)
WADA International Standards (<https://www.wada-ama.org/en/what-we-do/international-standards>)
WADA Statutes (2018) (<https://www.wada-ama.org/en/resources/legal/revised-statutes>)

- World Rugby

World Rugby Concussion Guidance (no date) (<http://playerwelfare.worldrugby.org/concussion>)
World Rugby Handbook (2017) (<https://www.world.rugby/handbook>)
World Rugby HIA Protocol (2018) (<http://playerwelfare.worldrugby.org/concussion>)
World Rugby Laws of the Game (2018) (<https://laws.worldrugby.org/>)

F. ***Other***

AAP, 'NFL Concussion Claims Eclipse $675 Mark', *Brisbane Times*, 31 July 2018 (<https://www.brisbanetimes.com.au/sport/nfl/nfl-concussion-claims-eclipse-675m-mark-20180731-p4zujd.html>) (AAP, 'NFL')
AAP, 'NRL to Tighten Shoulder Charge Law', *SBS*, 6 August 2015 (<http://www.sbs.com.au/news/article/2015/08/06/nrl-tighten-shoulder-charge-law?utm_source=Clearinghouse+for+Sport&utm_campaign=9a73618d6e-Daily_Sports_News_5_August_20158_4_2015&utm_medium=email&utm_term=0_3515f1cde2-9a73618d6e-316686657>) (AAP, 'NRL')

AAP, 'Luke Burgess Concerned Ian Roberts' Concussion Claims Will Scare Away Young Footballers', *ABC*, 11 March 2014 (<http://www.abc.net.au/news/2014-03-11/luke-burgess-concerned-brain-damage-claims-will-deter-kids-from/5313372?section=sport>) (AAP, 'Concussion Claims')

'Aaron Hernandez Criminal Cases Timeline', *FoxSport*, 14 May 2014 (<http://www.foxsports.com/nfl/story/aaron-hernandez-murder-case-timeline-051414>)

Addicott, Adam, 'Casey Dellaqua to Miss the Entire Australian Open Season Due to Concussion' *Ubitennis*, 4 December 2015 (<http://www.ubitennis.net/blog/2015/12/04/casey-dellacqua-to-miss-the-entire-australian-open-season-due-to-concussion/>)

AFL Injury Survey (2017) (<http://www.afl.com.au/staticfile/AFL%20Tenant/2017AFLInjuryReport.pdf>)

AFP, 'NFL Gets "Tough" in Bid to Save Reputation', *The Sydney Morning Herald*, 11 December 2014 (<http://www.smh.com.au/sport/nfl-gets-tough-in-bid-to-save-reputation-20141211-12561d.html>)

Alternative Dispute Resolution Center, press release, 29 August 2013 (<http://static.nfl.com/static/content/public/photo/2013/08/29/0ap2000000235504.pdf>)

Almond, Elliott, 'NFL is Funding Campaigns of Lawmakers Reviewing Concussion Issue' *Mercury News*, 23 March 2016 (<http://www.mercurynews.com/sports/ci_29676270/nfl-funds-campaigns-lawmakers-reviewing-concussions>)

Anderson, Jack, 'The Legal Implications of Concussion in Contact Sports', *Lawinsport*, 12 September 2016 (<https://www.lawinsport.com/articles/item/the-legal-implications-of-concussion-in-contact-sports?category_id=112>) (paywall) (Jack Anderson, 'Contact Sports')

Anderson, Jack, 'Symptom Free: Will the Law Strike a Knockout Blow on Concussion in Rugby' *Lawinsport*, 5 March 2015 (<http://www.lawinsport.com/blog/item/symptom-free-will-the-law-strike-a-knockout-blow-on-concussion-in-rugby?category_id=139&utm_source=LawInSport.com+Newsletter&utm_campaign=ae4efe45a2-Newsletter_06_03_2015&utm_medium=email&utm_term=0_85b8c26e66-ae4efe45a2>) (paywall) (Jack Anderson, 'Rugby')

Anderson, Paul D, 'NFL to Enforce Concussion Protocol Violations', '*NFL Concussion Litigation*', 26 July 2016 (<http://nflconcussionlitigation.com/?p=1900>) (Paul D Anderson, 'NFL')

Anderson, Paul D, 'Third Circuit Oral Argument Published', *'NFL Concussion Litigation'*, 23 November 2015 (<http://nflconcussionlitigation.com/?p=1827>) (Paul D Anderson, 'Third Circuit')

Anderson, Paul D, 'NFL Concussion Litigation Oral Argument Set for Nov. 20', *'NFL Concussion Litigation'*, 9 October 2015 (<http://nflconcussionlitigation.com/?p=1764>) (Paul D Anderson, 'Oral Argument')

Anderson, Paul D, 'Stabler's Death is a Stark Reminder About the Settlement Deficiencies', *'NFL Concussion Litigation'*, 10 July 2015 (<http://nflconcussionlitigation.com/?p=1756>) (Paul D Anderson, 'Settlement')

Anderson, Paul D, 'Judge Brody Orders Mediation', *'NFL Concussion Litigation'*, 8 July 2013 (<http://nflconcussionlitigation.com/?p=1467>) (Paul D Anderson, 'Mediation')

Anderson, Paul D, 'Exclusive: Concussion Kickoff — Oral Arguments held in NFL Concussion Litigation', *'NFL Concussion Litigation'*, 10 April 2013 (<http://nflconcussionlitigation.com/?p=1423>) (Paul D Anderson, 'Kickoff')

Anderson, Paul D, 'Report: Junior Seau had CTE', *'NFL Concussion Litigation'*, 10 January 2013 (<http://nflconcussionlitigation.com/?p=1345>) (Paul D Anderson, 'Report')

Anderson, Paul D, 'Latest Concussion Lawsuit Targets Teams', '*NFL Concussion Litigation*', 27 June 2012 (<http://nflconcussionlitigation.com/?p=899/>) (Paul D Anderson, 'Teams')

Anderson, Pauline, 'AAN, NFLPA Launch a Video on Concussion for Players', *Medscape*, 7 September 2016 (<http://www.medscape.com/viewarticle/868529>) (paywall) (Pauline Anderson, 'AAN')

A People's History - Episode 1: A Simple Game. Dir. Laine Drewery, prod. Wayne Chong. DVD. Canadian Broadcasting Corporation/Radio- Canada, 2006

'ARU Committed to Gender Equality', *Rugby.com*, 17 June 2016 (<http://www.rugby.com.au/news/2016/06/17/09/26/aru-joins-with-our-watch>)

Associated Press, 'Late Appeal Sends NFL Concussion Case to Supreme Court', *ESPN*, 1 September 2016 (<http://www.espn.com.au/american-football/story/_/id/17433451/late-appeal-moves-nfl-concussion-case-supreme-court>) (Associated Press, 'Supreme Court')

Associated Press, 'High School Sports Governing Body Sued Over Concussions', *The Washington Times*, 11 December 2015 (<http://www.washingtontimes.com/news/2015/dec/11/pennsylvania-school-sports-agency-sued-over-concus/>) (Associated Press, 'High School')

Associated Press, 'Judge Nixes First Class Action Lawsuit Over High School Concussions', *CBS*, 28 October 2015 (<http://www.cbsnews.com/news/concussions-lawsuit-against-illinois-high-school-association-dismissed-by-illinois-judge/>) (Associated Press, 'Judge')

Associated Press, 'NFL Makes Case to Appeals Panel for Peterson Suspension', *MPR News*, 19 October 2015 (<http://www.mprnews.org/story/2015/10/19/adrian-peterson>) (Associated Press, 'Peterson')

Associated Press, 'Former Players in Concussion Lawsuit Seek Deposition from Bettman', *The Global and Mail*, 26 March 2015 (<http://www.theglobeandmail.com/sports/hockey/former-nhl-players-in-concussion-lawsuit-seek-deposition-from-bettman/article23642872>) (Associated Press, 'Deposition')

Associated Press, "Illinois Group Says Concussions Lawsuit 'Threatens' Football" *ESPN*, 13 April 2015 (<http://espn.go.com/chicago/story/_/id/12679379/illinois-high-school-association-concussions-lawsuit-threatens-football>) (Associated Press, 'Illinois')

Associated Press, 'Youth Concussion Laws Lack Bite', *ESPN*, 28 January 2015 (<http://espn.go.com/nfl/story/_/id/12242612/youth-concussion-laws-pushed-nfl-lack-bite-according-associated-press-analysis>) (Associated Press, 'Youth Concussion Laws')

Associated Press, 'Ray Rice Wins Appeal, Suspension Vacated Immediately', *The Huffington Post*, 28 November 2014 (<http://www.huffingtonpost.com/2014/11/28/ray-rice_n_6237962.html?utm_hp_ref=sports>) (Associated Press, 'Ray Rice')

Associated Press, 'Judge Order on NFL Concussion Settlement', 29 August 2013 (<http://www.nfl.com/news/story/0ap1000000235517/printable/judges-order-on-nfl-concussion-settlement>) (Associated Press, 'Order')

Associated Press, 'Colo. Court Finds Riddell Negligent in Helmet Suit', *CBS*, 14 April 2013 (<http://www.cbsnews.com/8301-201_162-57579537/colo-court-finds-riddell-negligent-in-helmet-suit/>) (Associated Press, 'Riddell')

Associated Press, 'Junior Seau's Family Sues NFL for Wrongful Death after CTE Diagnosis' *The Guardian*, 24 January 2013 (<https://www.theguardian.com/sport/2013/jan/23/junior-seau-family-sues-nfl-cte>) (Associated Press, 'Junior Seau')

Associated Press, 'Michael Wayne Current Faced Charges', *ESPN*, 18 January 2012 (<http://espn.go.com/nfl/story/_/id/7474337/ex-lineman-michael-wayne-current-killed-self-faced-sex-charges>) (Associated Press, 'Michael Wayne')

Associated Press, 'Former Tampa Bay Buc Found Dead in Oregon Park', *The Herald Tribune*, 17 January 2012 (<http://www.heraldtribune.com/article/20120117/wire/120119596>) (Associated Press, 'Tampa Bay')

Associated Press, 'MLS Discusses Concussion Protocol', *ESPN*, 7 January 2012 (<http://www.espn.com/sports/soccer/news/_/id/7436065/mls-medical-staffers-target-concussion-protocol>) (Associated Press, 'MLS')

Axon, Rachel, 'Federal Judge Rejects Preliminary NCAA Concussion Settlement', *USA Today*, 18 December 2014 (<http://www.usatoday.com/story/sports/college/2014/12/18/ncaa-concussion-case-settlement-rejected/20574481/>)

Bachynski, Kathleen, 'Are Parents Morally Obligated to Forbid Their Kids from Playing Football', *The Conversation*, 2 June 2015 (<https://theconversation.com/are-parents-morally-obligated-to-forbid-their-kids-from-playing-football-39764?utm_medium=email&utm_campaign=Latest+from+The+Conversation+for+June+2+2015&utm_content=Latest+from+The+Conversation+for+June+2+2015+CID_33967ad959627>)

Baker, Grant and Michael Warner, 'Research Shows Full Extent of Concussion Problem within AFL', *The Herald Sun*, 30 August 2016 (<http://www.heraldsun.com.au/sport/afl/more-news/

research-shows-full-extent-of-concussion-problem-within-afl/news-story/7556a0ea7a5d1b72ebd79384f66f07ce>) (paywall)

Barrett, Paul M, 'Will Brain Injury Lawsuits Doom or Save the NFL?', *Bloomberg*, 21 February 2013 (<http://www.bloomberg.com/news/articles/2013-01-31/will-brain-injury-lawsuits-doom-or-save-the-nfl>)

Barry, Dan, 'An Athlete Felled by Concussions, despite Playing a "Safer" Sport', *The New York Times*, 21 June 2015 (<https://www.nytimes.com/2015/06/22/sports/an-athlete-felled-by-concussions-despite-playing-a-safer-sport.html?ref=international&_r=1>)

Bates, Mike 'MLB's Record on Domestic Violence Worse than NFL's', *SB Nation*, 28 July 2014 (<http://www.sbnation.com/mlb/2014/7/28/5936835/ray-rice-chuck-knoblauch-minnesota-twins-mlb-domestic-abuse-violence>)

Baxter, Kevin, 'Hope Solo Loses Bid to Have Domestic Violence Case Thrown Out', *The Los Angeles Times*, 6 June 2016 (<http://www.latimes.com/sports/la-sp-sn-hope-solo-domestic-violence-20160608-snap-story.html>)

Bellware, Kim, 'Nearly Half of Living NFL Veterans Show Signs of Brain Injury: Study' *The Huffington Post*, 12 April 2016 (<http://www.huffingtonpost.com.au/entry/nfl-veterans-brain-injury_us_570c19f0e4b014223249f6b8?ir=Sports&section=australia&utm_hp_ref=sports>)

Belson, Ken, 'Canadian Football's Big Steps to Reduce Hits, a Contrast to the N.F.L.', *The New York Times*, 24 November 2018 (<https://www.nytimes.com/2017/11/24/sports/football/canadian-footballs-big-steps-to-reduce-hits-a-contrast-to-the-nfl.html?rref=collection%2Fsectioncollection%2Fsports>) (Belson, 'Canadian Football')

Belson, Ken, 'Debilitated Players Accuse N.F.L. of Stalling on Settlement Payments', *The New York Times*, 13 November 2017 (<https://www.nytimes.com/2017/11/13/sports/football/nfl-concussion-lawsuit.html>) (Belson, 'Settlement')

Belson, Ken, 'N.F.L. Concussion Settlement Payments Can Begin After Supreme Court Defers', *The New York Times*, 12 December 2016 (<https://www.nytimes.com/2016/12/12/sports/football/nfl-concussion-settlement-payments-supreme-court.html>) (Belson, 'Supreme Court')

Belson, Ken, 'Appeals Court Won't Revisit N.F.L. Concussion Settlement', *The New York Times*, 1 June 2016 (<http://www.nytimes.com/2016/04/19/sports/football/nfl-concussion-lawsuit.html?_r=4>) (Belson, 'Appeals Court II')

Belson, Ken, 'Appeals Court Affirms Landmark N.F.L. Concussion Settlement', *The New York Times*, 18 April 2016 (<http://www.nytimes.com/2016/04/19/sports/football/nfl-concussion-lawsuit.html?_r=4>) (Belson, 'Appeals Court I')

Belson, Ken, 'Ivy League Moves to Eliminate Tackling at Football Practices', *The New York Times*, 1 March 2016 (<http://www.nytimes.com/2016/03/02/sports/ncaafootball/ivy-league-moves-to-eliminate-tackling-at-practices.html?emc=edit_th_20160302&nl=todaysheadlines&nlid=50808085&_r=2>) (Belson, 'Ivy League')

Belson, Ken, 'Concussion Report Highlights Field Maintenance', *The New York Times*, 29 December 2015 (<http://www.nytimes.com/2015/12/30/sports/football/concussion-report-highlights-field-maintenance.html>) (Belson, 'Field Maintenance')

Belson, Ken, 'Judge Approves Deal in N.F.L. Concussion Suit', *The New York Times*, 22 April 2015 (<http://www.nytimes.com/2015/04/23/sports/football/nfl-concussion-settlement-is-given-final-approval.html?_r=1>) (Belson, 'Deal')

Belson, Ken, 'Chris Borland, Fearing for Health, Retires From the 49ers. At 24.', *New York Times*, 17 March 2015 (<http://www.nytimes.com/2015/03/18/sports/football/49ers-linebacker-citing-injury-risk-joins-list-of-nfl-retirees.html?_r=1#http://www.nytimes.com/2015/03/18/sports/football/49ers-linebacker-citing-injury-risk-joins-list-of-nfl-retirees.html?_r=0>) (Belson, 'Chris Borland')

Belson, Ken, 'N.F.L Suspends Use of Helmet Sensors', *The New York Times*, 19 February 2015 (<http://www.nytimes.com/2015/02/20/sports/football/nfl-suspends-use-of-helmet-sensors.html?_r=0>) (Belson, 'Helmets')

Belson, Ken 'Family Sues Pop Warner Over Suicide of Player Who Had Brain Disease', *The New York Times*, 5 February 2015 (<http://www.nytimes.com/2015/02/06/sports/family-of-player-with-cte-who-killed-himself-sues-pop-warner.html?ref=sports&_r=3>) (Belson, 'Pop Warner')

Belson, Ken, 'Ray Rice Wins Reinstatement to NFL in Arbitration', *The New York Times*, 28 November 2014 (<http://www.nytimes.com/2014/11/29/sports/football/ray-rice-suspension-overturned-in-arbitration.html?ref=sports&_r=2>) (Belson, 'Ray Rice')

'Benoit's Brain Showed Severe Damage From Multiple Concussions, Doctor and Dad Say', *ABC*, 5 September 2007 (<http://abcnews.go.com/GMA/story?id=3560015&page=1>)

Benson, Andrew, 'Fernando Alonso: The Dangers of Concussion Explained', *BBC*, 27 February 2015 (<https://www.bbc.com/sport/formula1/31654193>)

Berkovic, Nikola, 'Australian Athletes Alliance Calls for Workers Compensation Law Revamp', *The Australian*, 18 July 2014 (<http://www.theaustralian.com.au/business/legal-affairs/australian-athletes-alliance-calls-for-workers-compensation-law-revamp/news-story/a3c63526e3b0ee86cdff402e5fde2ba8>) (paywall)

'Bettman Responds to C.T.E. Concerns', Gary Bettman's letter to US senator Richard Blumenthal of 22 July 2016, *The New York Times*, 26 July 2016 (<http://www.nytimes.com/interactive/2016/07/26/sports/hockey/27hockey-doc.html?_r=0/>)

Bleaney, Rob, 'Cillian Willis to Sue Sale Sharks Over Concussion Which Ended His Career', *The Guardian*, 23 August 2016 (<https://www.theguardian.com/sport/2016/aug/23/cillian-willis-sue-sale-sharks-concussion-saracens>)

Bogage, Jacob, 'High School Football Participation Continues to Drop as Concerns over Cost, Injuries Persist', *The Washington Post*, 28 August 2018 (<https://www.washingtonpost.com/news/early-lead/wp/2018/08/28/high-school-football-participation-continues-to-drop-as-concerns-over-cost-injuries-persist/?utm_term=.9da3f6fcd903>)

Bonomi, Amy E, 'Dear NFL: Put Your Money Where All the Concussions are', *The Huffington Post*, 29 July 2014 (<http://www.huffingtonpost.com/amy-e-bonomi/dear-nfl-put-your-money-where-all-the-concussions-are_b_5630392.html?utm_hp_ref=sports&ir=Sports>)

Boren, Cindy, 'The NFL Studied Every Concussion over Two Seasons. What Happens Next May Be up to Manufacturers', *The Washington Post* (<https://www.washingtonpost.com/news/early-lead/wp/2017/11/09/the-nfl-studied-every-concussion-over-two-seasons-what-happens-next-may-be-up-to-manufacturers/?noredirect=on&utm_term=.aafa26b0f89a>)

Boston University, 'Football And Progressive Brain Damage: Tom McHale Of NFL Suffered From Chronic Traumatic Encephalopathy When He Died In 2008' *ScienceDaily*, 27 January 2009 (<www.sciencedaily.com/releases/2009/01/090127165938.htm>)

Bradley, Bill, 'Independent Concussion Specialists Ready to Work NFL Sidelines', *NFL*, 3 September 2013 (<http://www.nfl.com/news/story/0ap1000000237739/article/independent-concussion-%20specialists-ready-to-work-nfl-sidelines>)

Brain Injury Australia, *Policy Paper: Concussion in Sport*, October 2012 (<https://www.braininjuryaustralia.org.au/wp-content/uploads/CONCUSSIONpolicypaperFINAL.pdf>)

Branch, John, 'Steve Montador Had C.T.E.; Family to Sue N.H.L.' *The New York Times*, 12 May 2015 (<http://www.nytimes.com/2015/05/13/sports/hockey/steve-montador-had-brain-trauma-family-to-sue-nhl.html?_r=0>)

Breech, John, 'Roger Goodell Admits that a Key NFL Play Could Be Eliminated Soon', 14 September 2016, *CBS Sports* (<http://www.cbssports.com/nfl/news/roger-goodell-admits-that-a-key-nfl-play-could-be-eliminated-soon/?ET_CID=12593&ET_RID=46461995&ttag=allsportsdailyheadline309142016>)

Breslow, Jason M, 'New: 87 Deceased NFL Players Test Positive For Brain Disease', *PBS*, 18 September 2015 (<http://www.pbs.org/wgbh/pages/frontline/sports/concussion-watch/new-87-deceased-nfl-players-test-positive-for-brain-disease/>) (Breslow, 'NFL Players')

Breslow, Jason M, 'What We've Learned from Two Years Tracking NFL Concussions', *PBS*, 4 February 2014 (<http://www.pbs.org/wgbh/frontline/article/what-weve-learned-from-two-years-of-tracking-nfl-concussions/>) (Breslow, 'NFL Concussions')

Brandt, Andrew, ‘The Conversation the NFL Does Not Want To Have’, *MMQB*, 11 June 2015 (<http://mmqb.si.com/2015/06/11/nfl-young-players-retirement-problem/>)

Brophy, Mike, ‘NHL, NHLPA Agree on Mandatory Visors’, *NHL*, 5 June 2013 (<https://www.nhl.com/news/nhl-nhlpa-agree-on-mandatory-visors/c-672983>)

Bucholtz, Andrew, ‘John Cornish Retiring at 31 Should be Another CFL Concussion Wake Up Call’, *Yahoo Sports*, 2 December 2015 (<https://ca.sports.yahoo.com/blogs/cfl-55-yard-line/jon-cornish-retiring-at-31-should-be-another-cfl-concussion-wake-up-call-201104913.html>)

Buist, Steve, ‘Collision Course: A Spectator Report on the Science of Hard Head Knocks’, *The Spectator*, 30 August 2017 (<https://www.thespec.com/news-story/7525066-collision-course-a-spectator-report-on-the-science-of-hard-head-knocks/>)

Burns, John F, ‘In Europe, Echoes of America as Concussions Spur Debate’, *The New York Times*, 5 April 2014 (<https://www.nytimes.com/2014/04/06/sports/in-europe-echoes-of-america-as-concussions-spur-debate.html>)

Butler, Nick, ‘Anti-Doping Claimed to Cost Sport $300 Million Each Year’, *Inside the Games*, 16 March 2017 (<https://www.insidethegames.biz/articles/1048181/anti-doping-claimed-to-cost-sport-300-million-each-year>)

Campisi, Jon, ‘Mediation Between Players and Helmet Maker Riddell Continues; No Word on Lawyers' Fees Following NFL Settlement’ *PennRecord*, 10 September 2013 (<http://pennrecord.com/stories/510553372-mediation-between-players-and-helmet-maker-riddell-continues-no-word-on-lawyers-fees-following-nfl-settlement>)

Carayannis, Michael, ‘State of Origin: NRL Appoints Independent Doctor to Help avoid Concussion Headache’, *The Sydney Morning Herald*, 23 May 2014 (<http://www.smh.com.au/rugby-league/league-news/state-of-origin-nrl-appoints-independent-doctor-to-help-avoid-concussion-headache-20140523-zrmh9.html>)

Carter, Lucy, ‘NRL Players’ Brains Shown to Be More Damaged than Brains of Non-Players, Says Scientist’, *ABC News*, 20 March 2017 (<http://www.abc.net.au/news/2017-03-20/nrl-players-brains-more-damaged-than-non-players:-study/8369226>) (Lucy Carter, ‘NRL’)

CAS, media release, 27 September 2018 (<http://www.tas-cas.org/fileadmin/user_upload/Media_Release_5921.pdf>)

CAS, media release, 9 February 2018 (<http://www.tas-cas.org/fileadmin/user_upload/Media_Release_AHD9_DecisionOG18_02_03.pdf>)

CAS, media release, 1 February 2018 (<http://www.tas-cas.org/fileadmin/user_upload/Media_Release__decision_RUS_IOC_.pdf>)

‘CFL Commissioner Jeffrey Orridge to Step Down in June’, *AP News*, 12 April 2017 (<https://apnews.com/4c175dee8f604151a8f9d210c0bdbc43/cfl-commissioner-jeffrey-orridge-step-down-june>)

CFL, media release, 28 April 2016 (<https://press.cfl.ca/new-canadian-football-league-player-health-and-safety-measures-for-2016-season>)

CFL Staff, ‘CFL Announces Violence against Women Policy’, *CFL*, 6 August 2015 (<http://www.cfl.ca/2015/08/06/cfl-announces-violence-against-women-policy/>)

CFL Staff, ‘CFL Teams Partner with NFL on Concussion Testing’, *CFL*, 6 August 2015 (<https://www.cfl.ca/2015/08/06/cfl-teams-and-nfl-partner-on-concussion-testing/>)

CFLPA, media release, 26 April 2017 (<https://cflpa.com/why-the-1playaway-push-for-expanded-rehab-coverage-matters-to-the-cfls-players/>)

CFLPA, media release, 23 August 2016 (<https://cflpa.com/35293-2/>)

CFLPA, media release, 22 August 2014 (<https://cflpa.com/concussion-prevention-in-the-cfl/>)

Charter, David, ‘FIFA Sleaze Claims Prompt Swiss to Change the Law’, *The New York Times*, 8 December 2014 (<http://www.thetimes.co.uk/tto/sport/football/international/article4290444.ece>)

Clarke, Mary and Pat Iversen, ‘The Most Interesting and Damning Details from the Unsealed Documents in the NHL Concussion Lawsuit’, *SB Nation*, 30 March 2016 (<http://www.sbnation.com/nhl/2016/3/30/11333286/nhl-concussion-lawsuit-unsealed-emails-gary-bettman-colin-campbell>)

Cohen, Jake, 'How Effective is FIFA's Concussion Protocol', *Lawinsport*, 8 October 2014 (<http://www.lawinsport.com/sports/football/item/how-effective-is-fifa-s-concussion-protocol>) (paywall)

Collett, Mike, 'FIFA Medical Officer Wants Strict New Rules on Concussion', *Reuters*, 9 September 2014 (<http://www.reuters.com/article/us-soccer-medical-concussion-idUSKBN0H422C20140909>)

'Concerns about Violence Spread in the NFL', *SBS*, 15 September 2014 (<http://www.sbs.com.au/news/article/2014/09/15/concerns-over-violence-spread-nfl>)

Concussion in Sport Australia, Position Statement, October 2018 (<https://concussioninsport.gov.au/position-statement>)

Conference of Parties to the International Convention against Doping in Sport, 25–6 September 2017, Resolution 6CP/15 (<http://unesdoc.unesco.org/images/0025/002592/259298E.pdf>)

Conway, Richard, 'Premier League to Introduce New Rules on Head Injuries', *BBC*, 5 August 2014 (<http://www.bbc.com/sport/football/28656263>)

Copenhagen Declaration on Anti-Doping in Sport (no date) (<https://www.wada-ama.org/en/resources/world-anti-doping-program/copenhagen-declaration>)

Council of Europe, Explanatory report of the Convention – CETS 218 – Integrated Safety, Security and Service Approach at Sports Events, 3 August 2016 (<https://rm.coe.int/CoERMPublicCommonSearchServices/DisplayDCTMContent?documentId=0900001680666d0d>)

Council of Europe, Explanatory Report of the Convention on the Manipulation of Sports Competitions – CETS 215 –, 18 September 2014 (<https://rm.coe.int/CoERMPublicCommonSearchServices/DisplayDCTMContent?documentId=09000016800d383f>)

Cripps, Tom, 'Ray Rice, Domestic Violence and the NFL's Personal Conduct Policy', *Lawinsport*, 7 October 2014 (<http://www.lawinsport.com/articles/item/ray-rice-domestic-violence-and-the-nfl-s-personal-conduct-policy?utm_source=LawInSport.com+Newsletter&utm_campaign=35bc3f9985-Newsletter_09_10_2014&utm_medium=email&utm_term=0_85b8c26e66-35bc3f9985-415816121>) (paywall)

Cronshaw, Damon, 'Sports Concussions Risk Brain Damage', *The Newcastle Herald*, 4 September 2014 (<http://www.theherald.com.au/story/2537836/sport-concussions-risk-brain-damage-poll/?cs=2373>)

Declaration of the 6th Olympic Summit, 28 October 2017 (<https://www.olympic.org/news/communique-of-the-olympic-summit>)

Declaration of the 5th Olympic Summit, 8 October 2016 (<https://www.olympic.org/news/declaration-of-the-5th-olympic-summit>) (and subsequent updates)

'Decoding the N.F.L. Database to Find 100 Missing Concussions', *The New York Times*, 24 March 2016 (<http://www.nytimes.com/2016/03/25/sports/football/at-least-100-concussions-left-out-of-nfl-studies.html?version=meter+at+2&module=meter-Links&pgtype=article&contentId=&mediaId=&referrer=https%3A%2F%2Fwww.google.com.au%2F&priority=true&action=click&contentC>)

Delessio, Joe, 'Injury Status: Unknown', *Sports on Earth*, 26 February 2013 (<http://www.sportsonearth.com/article/41962374/the-nhls-injury-policy-forces-fans-and-the-media-to-speculate-wondering-why-for-example-the-new-york-rangers-rick-nash-has-been-out-for-over-a-we>)

Delsohn, Steve, 'OTL: Belcher's Brain Had CTE Signs', *ESPN*, 30 September 2014 (<http://espn.go.com/espn/otl/story/_/id/11612386/jovan-belcher-brain-showed-signs-cte-doctor-says-report>)

Dingus, Sheila and Derek Helling, 'What's Next for Retired NHL Players in their Quest for Brain Injury Accountability?', *Advocay for Fairness in Sport*, July 2018 (<http://advocacyforfairnessinsports.org/current-litigation/whats-next-for-retired-nhl-players-in-their-quest-for-brain-injury-accountability/>)

Dokoupil, Tony, 'NFL Player Was Accused of Rape on Saturday, Played on Sunday: Lawyer', *NBC News*, 26 September 2014 (<http://www.nbcnews.com/storyline/nfl-controversy/nfl-player-was-accused-rape-saturday-played-sunday-lawyer-n212756>)

Dolman, Matthew, 'Naturally Occurring Hormones May Treat Traumatic Brain Injuries', *DolmanLaw*, 26 April 2013 (<https://www.dolmanlaw.com/naturally-occurring-hormones-treat-traumatic-brain-injuries/>)

Drohan, Ryan, 'Are We Taking the NFL's Future for Granted?', *Sports Rants*, 17 March 2015 (<http://sportsrants.com/nfl/2015/03/17/are-we-taking-the-nfls-future-for-granted/>)

Dryden, Ken, 'A Concussion Lawsuit Has Been Settled. A Commissioner's Legacy Is Unclear.', *The New York Times*, 16 November 2018 (<https://www.nytimes.com/2018/11/16/sports/hockey-concussions-settlement-bettman.html?rref=collection%2Fsectioncollection%2Fsports&action=click&contentCollection=sports&region=rank&module=package&version=highlights&contentPlacement=5&pgtype=sectionfront>)

Droz, Daniel, 'Le CIO aimante les fédérations', *L'Express*, 29 December 2014 (<http://www.arcinfo.ch/fr/en-continu/articles/index.php?idContent=1393307>) (paywall)

Dudzic, Kelly, 'Former Sabre Joins Class Action Lawsuit Against the NHL', *WGRZ*, 10 February 2016 (<http://www.wgrz.com/sports/nhl/sabres/former-sabre-joins-class-action-lawsuit-against-the-nhl/39687531>)

Earle, Richard, 'AFL Facing Concussion Armageddon', *The Advertiser*, 29 November 2017 (<https://www.adelaidenow.com.au/subscribe/news/1/?sourceCode=AAWEB_WRE170_a_GGL&dest=https%3A%2F%2Fwww.adelaidenow.com.au%2Fsport%2Fopinion%2Fafl-facing-concussion-armageddon%2Fnews-story%2F95a84d454f652f780e6f387f33874828&memtype=anonymous&mode=premium>) (paywall)

Edwards, Drew, 'CFL, Partners Take Aim at Concussions' *The Hamilton Spectator*, 4 May 2011 (<http://www.thespec.com/sports-story/2202717-cfl-partners-take-aim-at-concussions/>)

Egelko, Bob, 'USAWP Can Be Sued for Concussion-Related Injury, Court Rules', *San Francisco Chronicle*, 29 November 2018 (<https://www.sfchronicle.com/bayarea/article/USA-Water-Polo-can-be-sued-for-concussion-related-13429789.php>)

Emison, Brett, 'More Players Join Lawsuits Against NFLPA', *The Legal Examiner* (Kansas City), 13 August 2014 (<http://kansascity.legalexaminer.com/head-brain-injuries/more-players-join-con cussion-lawsuits-against-nflpa//>)

English, Tom, 'Rugby's Concussion Reviews "Are not Fit for Purpose", Says Brain Expert', *BBC*, 21 April 2017 (<http://www.bbc.com/sport/rugby-union/39630540>)

Fainaru, Steve and Mark Fainaru-Wada, 'Congressional Report Says NFL Waged Improper Campaign to Influence Government Study', *ESPN*, 24 May 2016 (<http://espn.go.com/espn/otl/story/_/id/15667689/congressional-report-finds-nfl-improperly-intervened-brain-research-cost-tax payers-16-million>) (Fainaru and Fainaru-Wada, 'Congressional Report')

Fainaru, Steve and Mark Fainaru-Wada, 'Study: New Cases of CTE in Players', *ESPN*, 3 December 2012 (<http://espn.go.com/espn/otl/story/_/id/8697286/boston-university-researchers-discover-28-new-cases-chronic-brain-damage-deceased-football-players>) (Fainaru and Fainaru-Wada, 'CTE')

Fainaru, Steve, 'NFL Acknowledges, for First Time, Link between Football, Brain Disease', *ESPN*, 16 March 2016 (<http://espn.go.com/espn/otl/story/_/id/14972296/top-nfl-official-acknowledges-link-football-related-head-trauma-cte-first>)

Felder, Adam, 'Battering the Batter', *The Atlantic*, 5 May 2015 (<https://www.theatlantic.com/entertainment/archive/2015/05/no-more-battering-the-batter/391991/>)

Fendrich, Howard and Eddie Pells, Associated Press, 'States Youth Concussion Laws Vary in Strength', *Albuquerque Journal*, 30 January 2015 (<http://www.abqjournal.com/533408/sports/states-youth-concussion-laws-vary-in-strength.html>)

Fendrich, Howard, 'Members of Congress Ask NFL to Hold Teams Accountable For Domestic Abuse', *The Huffington Post*, 24 February 2015 (<http://www.huffingtonpost.com/2015/02/24/2-members-of-congress-wri_n_6744810.html?utm_hp_ref=sports&ir=Sports>) (Fendrich, 'Congress') (this link does not exist anymore – copy on file with author)

Fendrich, Howard, 'There Were at Least 111 Concussions in the NFL this Season', *HuffingtonPost*, 29 January 2015 (<http://www.huffingtonpost.com/2015/01/29/nfl-concussions-2014-season-

2015_n_6573260.html>) (Fendrich, 'NFL') (this link does not exist anymore – copy on file with author)

Finley, Patrick, 'Ex Bear Safety Craig Stelz Suing the NFL over Concussions: Report', *Chicago Sun Times*, 30 March 2018 (<https://chicago.suntimes.com/sports/ex-bears-safety-craig-steltz-suing-nfl-over-concussions-report/>)

Fiore, Kristina, 'PET Scan May Detect CTE Sooner', *MedpageToday*, 7 April 2015 (<https://www.medpagetoday.com/neurology/generalneurology/50859>)

Fitzgerald, Sean, 'List of NHL Enforcers Who Have Passed Away Gets Longer', *The Star*, 22 September 2015 (<https://www.thestar.com/sports/hockey/2015/09/22/list-of-nhl-enforcers-who-have-passes-away-gets-longer.html>)

Flood, George, 'FIFA Respond to Latest Football Dementia Study as FA Welcome New Research', *IB Times*, 15 February 2017 (<https://www.ibtimes.co.uk/fifa-respond-latest-football-dementia-study-fa-welcome-new-research-1606735>)

Florio, Mike 'Concussion Lawsuit Against the NFLPA Dismissed' *NBC Sports*, 18 August 2015 (<http://profootballtalk.nbcsports.com/2015/08/18/concussion-lawsuit-against-nflpa-dismissed/>) (Florio, 'NFLPA')

Florio, Mike, 'Cowboys Player Allegedly Involved in a Sexual Assault', *NBC Sports*, 1st October 2014 (<http://profootballtalk.nbcsports.com/2014/10/01/cowboys-player-allegedly-involved-in-a-sexual-assault/>) (Florio, 'Cowboys')

Florio, Mike, 'NFL Moving Closer to Using Helmet Sensors', *NBC Sports*, 4 September 2013 (<http://profootballtalk.nbcsports.com/2013/09/04/nfl-moving-closer-to-using-helmet-sensors/>) (Florio, 'Helmets')

Florio, Mike, 'Duerson Estate Sues for Wrongful Death', *NBC Sports*, 23 February 2012 (<http://profootballtalk.nbcsports.com/2012/02/23/duersons-estate-sues-nfl-for-wrongful-death/>) (Florio, 'Duerson')

Flurh, Howard et al., 'Report of the Segal Group to Special Master Perry Golkin', 2014 (<http://nflconcussionlitigation.com/wp-content/uploads/2014/09/6168-NFL-Report-to-Special-Master.pdf>)

Foer, Franklin and Chris Hughes, 'Barack Obama is not Pleased – The President on his Enemies, the Media and the Future of Football' *The New Republic*, 27 January 2013 (<https://newrepublic.com/article/112190/obama-interview-2013-sit-down-president>)

'Former NCAA Football Player Fires Lawyer in Class-Action Concussion Lawsuit', *CNN*, 10 June 2015 (<http://edition.cnn.com/2015/06/10/us/ncaa-class-action-concussion/>)

Ganim, Sara, 'Class-Action Lawsuit Filed Over High School Football', *CNN*, 2 December 2014 (<http://edition.cnn.com/2014/12/01/us/concussion-lawsuit-high-school-football/>)

Gibbons, Brett, 'Jeff Astle's Widow Accuses FA of "Lies" Over Albion Star's Death', *The Brimingham Mail*, 18 March 2014 (<http://www.birminghammail.co.uk/news/midlands-news/jeff-astles-widow-accuses-fa-6846102>)

Gibbs, Lindsay, 'NFL Ends Concussion Research Partnership $16 Million Short of $30million Commitment', *'Think Progress'*, 29 July 2017 (<https://thinkprogress.org/nfl-nih-end-concussion-research-8a5750ecf3fb/>)

Gilbert, Ewan, 'NRL Players May Face Life Bans if found Guilty of Domestic Violence', *ABC*, 17 July 2017 (<http://www.abc.net.au/news/2017-07-17/nrl-players-may-face-life-bans-if-guilty-of-domestic-violence/8715698?section=sport>)

Gill, Pete, 'Fernando Alonso Suffered "Temporary Memory Loss" After his Crash in Testing', *Skysports*, 29 March 2015 (<http://www1.skysports.com/f1/news/24184/9746706/fernando-alonso-suffered-8216temporary-memory-loss8217-after-his-crash-at-barcelona>)

Ginsburg, Steve, 'NFL Player Jovan Belcher Likely Had Brain Damage Before Murder-Suicide', *The Sydney Morning Herald*, 30 September 2014 (<http://www.smh.com.au/sport/nfl-player-jovan-belcher-likely-had-brain-damage-before-murdersuicide-20140929-10nv3y.html>)

Goff, Steven, 'Namoff's Lawsuit was Dismissed', *The Washington Post*, 14 January 2015 (<https://www.washingtonpost.com/news/soccer-insider/wp/2015/01/14/namoffs-lawsuit-was-dismissed/>)

Goldberg, Jamie, 'Portland Timbers no Longer Defendant in Eddie Johnson's Concussion Lawsuit, *The Oregonian*, 19 January 2017 (<https://www.oregonlive.com/timbers/index.ssf/2017/01/portland_timbers_no_longer_a_d.html>) (Goldberg, 'Lawsuit')

Goldberg, Jamie, 'Eddie Johnson $9.9 Million Lawsuit Against Portland Timbers Remains Ongoing', *The Oregonian*, 11 February 2016 (<http://www.oregonlive.com/timbers/index.ssf/2016/02/former_portland_timbers_forwar_3.html>) (Goldberg, 'Portland Timbers')

Goldman, Shayna, 'The NHL Adds "Central Spotters" to Concussion Protocols', *SportTechie*, 28 September 2016 (<http://www.sporttechie.com/2016/09/28/sports/nhl/the-nhl-adds-central-spotters-to-concussion-protocol/>) (Goldman, 'Central Spotters')

Goldman, Shayna, 'Hit or Miss: NHL Appoints Concussion Spotters', *SportTechie*, 25 September 2015 (<http://www.sporttechie.com/2015/09/25/hit-miss-nhl-appoints-concussion-spotters/>) (Goldman, 'Central Spotters')

Goldman, Shayna, 'Death of Former NHL Player Steve Montador Promotes Discussions of Concussions' *SportTechie*, 26 May 2015 (<http://www.sporttechie.com/2015/05/26/death-of-former-nhl-player-steve-montador-promotes-discussions-of-concussions//>) (Goldman, 'NHL')

Graf, Rachel, 'More Than 18K Players Register For NFL Concussion Settlement', *'Consider The Consumer'*, 7 August 2017 (<https://considertheconsumer.com/consumer-news/18k-push-nfl-concussion-settlement>)

Greenhow, Annette, 'Who Should Be Responsible for Brain injuries in Sport', *The Conversation*, 25 July 2016 (<https://theconversation.com/who-should-be-responsible-for-brain-injuries-in-sport-62285>) (Greenhow, 'Brain Injuries')

Grow, Nathaniel, 'Imagining a MLB Concussion Lawsuit', *Fangraphs*, 18 February 2015 (<http://www.fangraphs.com/blogs/imagining-an-mlb-concussion-lawsuit/>)

Hall, Vicki, 'Federal Government Announces $1.4M Investment to Develop National Concussion Management Guidelines', *The National Post*, 24 October 2016 (<http://news.nationalpost.com/sports/federal-government-announces-1-4m-investment-to-develop-national-concussion-management-guidelines>)

Hanna, Joseph M, 'WWE Cleared from all Concussion-Related Lawsuits Amid Plaintiff Attorney Sanctions', *Sports Law Insider*, 20 September 2018 (<https://sportslawinsider.com/wwe-cleared-from-all-concussion-related-lawsuits-amid-plaintiff-attorney-sanctions/>) (Hanna, 'WWE')

Hanna, Joseph M, 'NFL Concussion Litigation Settlement Results in a Flurry of Objections', *Sports and Entertainment Law Insider*, 1 May 2017 (<http://sportslawinsider.com/nfl-concussion-litigation-settlement-results-in-a-flurry-of-objections/>) (Hanna, 'Objections')

Hanna, Joseph M, 'Is a Football Player's Concussion an Intentional Injury? Arena Football Says No, Moves for Dismissal of Player's Concussion Lawsuit' *Lawinsport*, 3 February 2017 (<https://www.lawinsport.com/sports-law-news/item/is-a-football-player-s-concussion-an-intentional-injury-arena-football-says-no-moves-for-dismissal-of-player-s-concussion-lawsuit>) (paywall) (Hanna, 'Arena Football')

Hanna, Joseph M, 'Third Circuit Denies Rehearing NFL Concussion Settlement, Compensation Forthcoming' *Sports and Entertainment Law Insider*, 9 June 2016 (<http://sportslawinsider.com/third-circuit-denies-rehearing-nfl-concussion-settlement-compensation-forthcoming/>) (Hanna, 'Third Circuit')

Hanna, Joseph M, 'Riddell Concussion Update: Helmet Company Thrown Back Into NFL Suit', *Sports and Entertainment Law Insider*, 8 February 2016 (<http://sportslawinsider.com/riddell-concussion-update-helmet-company-thrown-back-into-nfl-suit/>) (Hanna, 'Riddell')

Hanna, Joseph M, 'Not Enough Evidence to Charge Winston in Rape Accusation', *Sport and Entertainment Law Insider*, 28 December 2014 (<http://sportslawinsider.com/not-enough-evidence-to-charge-winston-in-rape-accusation/>) (Hanna, 'Winston')

Hanna, Joseph M, 'NCAA Concussion Settlement Denied', *Sports and Entertainment Law Insider*, 27 December 2014 (<http://sportslawinsider.com/ncaa-concussion-settlement-denied/>) (Hanna, 'NCAA')

Hanna, Joseph M, 'Minnesota Will Play Host to NHL Concussion Litigation', *Sports and Entertainment Law Insider*, 23 August 2014 (<http://sportslawinsider.com/minnesota-will-play-host-to-nhl-concussion-litigation/>) (Hanna, 'Minnesota')

Hanna, Joseph M, 'Lawsuits Becoming a Headache for NHL as Fourth Concussion Suit is Filed' *Sports and Entertainment Law Insider*, 1 August 2014 (<http://sportslawinsider.com/lawsuits-becoming-a-headache-for-nhl-as-fourth-concussion-suit-is-filed/>) (Hanna, 'NHL')

Hanna, Joseph M, 'Former Players Accused Union of Conspiring to Conceal Risks of Head Injuries', *Sports and Entertainment Law Insider*, 21 July 2014 (<http://sportslawinsider.com/former-nfl-players-accused-union-of-conspiring-to-conceal-risks-of-head-injuries//>) (Hanna, 'Union')

Hanna, Joseph M, 'The Real Story Behind the NFL's Player Association "$100 Million Research Grant" to Harvard Medical School', *Sports and Entertainment Law Insider*, 13 March 2014 (<http://sportslawinsider.com/the-real-story-behind-the-nfl-players-association-100-million-research-grant-to-harvard-medical-school/>) (Hanna, 'Grant')

Hanna, Joseph M, 'Paying the Piper: NFL's Concussion Policy Results in Huge Class Action Lawsuit', *'Mosessport'*, 15 August 2012 (<http://www.mosessport.com/Paying_the_Piper_-_NFL_s_Concussion_Policy_Results_in_Huge_Class_Action_Lawsuit.pdf>) (Hanna, 'Class Action')

Hardy, Sarah 'A Comprehensive Timeline of Ezekiel Elliott's Domestic Violence Case', *SB Nation*, 30 November 2017 (<https://www.sbnation.com/2017/8/29/16151642/ezekiel-elliott-timeline-domestic-violence-police-report-nfl-suspension-appeal>)

Hauser, Thomas, 'No One is Enforcing the Federal Boxing Laws', *ESPN*, 25 September 2007 (<http://sports.espn.go.com/sports/boxing/news/story?id=3032059>)

Hanzus, Dan, 'NFL Places A.P. on Exempt List Pending Appeal', *Around the NFL*, 26 February 2015 (<http://www.nfl.com/news/story/0ap3000000474256/article/adrian-peterson-suspension-overturned-by-judge>)

Healy, Melissa, 'Could a Blood Test Detect Concussion With Lasting Disability', *The Los Angeles Times*, 20 November 2013 (<http://www.latimes.com/science/sciencenow/la-sci-blood-test-concussion-20131119-story.html/>)

Herman, Martyn, 'Ammann Recovering in Hospital After Serious Crash', *Reuters*, 7 January 2015 (<http://www.reuters.com/article/2015/01/07/us-ski-jumping-ammann-idUSKBN0KG1RM20150107/>)

Hodgekiss, Anna 'Headgear for Amateur Boxers to Be Banned in Bid to Reduce Head Injuries', *Daily Mail Australia*, 16 March 2013 (<http://www.dailymail.co.uk/health/article-2293803/Headgear-boxers-banned-bid-REDUCE-head-injuries.html>)

Holder, Gord, 'Head Injuries and the CFL: Grievance and Class-Action Suit Still Pending', *Ottawa Citizen*, 21 November 2018 (<https://ottawacitizen.com/sports/football/cfl/head-injuries-and-the-cfl-grievance-and-class-action-suit-still-pending>) (Holder, 'CFL')

Holder, Gord, 'Arland Bruce Files Concussion-Related Grievance Against CFL and Five Teams', *Ottawa Sun*, 6 April 2018 (<https://ottawasun.com/sports/football/cfl/arland-bruce-files-concussion-related-grievance-against-cfl-and-five-teams>) (Holder, 'Bruce')

Holder, Gord, 'Former CFLer Receiver Carrying Through with his Concussion-Related Lawsuit' *Ottawa Citizen*, 27 January 2017 (<http://ottawacitizen.com/sports/football/cfl/former-cfler-receiver-carrying-through-with-his-concussion-related-lawsuit>) (Holder, 'Receiver')

Honeysett, Stuart, 'Former Hawthorn Premiership Winner and Brownlow Medallist John Platten Joins AFL Concussion Lawsuit', *Nine*, 28 November 2017 (<https://wwos.nine.com.au/afl/former-hawthorn-browlow-medallist-john-platten-joins-afl-concussion-lawsuit/7e1b5173-cfc7-4a73-ad7b-105dac7c60e7>)

House of Commons, Culture, Media and Sport Committee, *Football Governance* (2010–12) (<https://publications.parliament.uk/pa/cm201012/cmselect/cmcumeds/792/792i.pdf>)

Howman, David, 'Time for a World Sports Integrity Agency', statement from WADA director general following the European Union Sports Forum Budapest, 24 February 2011 (<https://www.

wada-ama.org/en/media/news/2011-02/statement-from-wada-director-general-following-the-european-union-sports-forum>)

Hubbard, Dominic Bryce (Lord Addington) et al., *Concussion Can Kill - Cross Party Call for a Parliamentary Inquiry into Concussion in Sport*, Report, 2014 (<https://fr.scribd.com/document/229341836/Concussion-Can-Kill-Call-for-Inquiry>)

IAAF, press release, 17 June 2016 (<https://www.iaaf.org/news/press-release/iaaf-council-meeting-vienna>)

IAAF, press release, 13 November 2015 (<https://www.iaaf.org/news/press-release/iaaf-araf-suspended>)

IDB-Jamie Full Data Set (IDB-FDS), Data Dictionary, Version 1.3, 2014 (<http://www.eurosafe.eu.com/uploads/inline-files/IDB%20JAMIE%20FDS%20Data%20Dictionary%20MAR14.pdf>)

Illiakostas, Tony, 'How Effective is Major League Baseball's Domestic Violence Policy?', *Lawinsport*, 11 May 2016 (<http://www.lawinsport.com/articles/item/how-effective-is-major-league-baseball-s-new-domestic-violence-policy>) (paywall)

Interview of Matthieu Reeb, CAS General Secretary, in: *Le Temps*, 5 August 2016 (<https://www.letemps.ch/sport/2016/08/05/sportifs-ont-pris-lhabitude-dexplorer-toutes-voies-reglementaires-possibles>)

IOC Fact Sheet, 22 December 2017 (<https://stillmed.olympic.org/media/Document%20Library/OlympicOrg/IOC/Who-We-Are/Commissions/Disciplinary-Commission/2017/IOC-re-analysis-programme-Sochi-2014-22-december-2017-1.pdf#_ga=2.35280545.1613046842.1515970842-402556292.1510806486>)

IOC, press release, 28 February 2018 (<https://www.olympic.org/news/ioc-statement-2018-02-28>)

IOC, press release, 25 February 2018 (<https://www.olympic.org/news/decision-of-the-ioc-executive-board-2018-02-25>)

IOC, press release, 14 February 2018 (<https://www.olympic.org/news/international-testing-agency-appoints-director-general>)

IOC, press release, 5 February 2018 (<https://www.olympic.org/news/request-to-invite-15-athletes-and-coaches-to-pyeongchang-2018-for-the-olympic-athlete-from-russia-group-declined>)

IOC, press release, 18 January 2018 (<https://www.olympic.org/news/already-over-14-000-doping-tests-conducted-to-safeguard-pyeongchang-2018>)

IOC, press release, 5 December 2017 (<https://www.olympic.org/news/ioc-suspends-russian-noc-and-creates-a-path-for-clean-individual-athletes-to-compete-in-pyeongchang-2018-under-the-olympic-flag>)

IOC, press release, 12 October 2017 (<https://www.olympic.org/news/independent-testing-authority-on-track>)

IOC, press release, 16 February 2017 (<https://www.olympic.org/news/ioc-publishes-unprecedented-olympic-movement-code-for-preventing-competition-manipulation>)

IOC, press release, 9 December 2016 (<https://www.olympic.org/news/statement-of-the-ioc-regarding-the-independent-person-report>)

IOC, press release, 24 July 2016 (<https://www.olympic.org/news/decision-of-the-ioc-executive-board-concerning-the-participation-of-russian-athletes-in-the-olympic-games-rio-2016>)

IOC, press release, 17 December 2015 (<https://www.olympic.org/news/ifsi-forum-gets-full-support-and-commitment-from-participants>)

IOC, press release, 13 April 2015 (<https://www.olympic.org/news/first-international-forum-for-sports-integrity-adopts-roadmap-for-future-action-to-protect-clean-athletes>)

IOS Evaluation Office, *Evaluation of UNESCO's International Convention against doping in sport*, Report, August 2017 (<http://unesdoc.unesco.org/images/0025/002587/258739E.pdf>)

IRB staff, 'IRB Issues Statement on "Tip or Spear" Tackle', 16 October 2011 (<http://www.rugby.com.au/news/2016/02/10/irb-issues-statement-on-tip-or-spear-tackle>)

Jansen, Steve and Gus Garcia-Roberts, 'Concussion Take a Terrible Toll on America's Young Athletes', *LaWeekly*, 18 August 2011 (<http://www.laweekly.com/content/printView/2171689>)

Jerome, Amanda, 'B.C. Court of Appeal Dismisses Former Player's Concussion Lawsuit', *The Lawyer's Daily*, 16 May 2017 (<https://www.thelawyersdaily.ca/articles/3746/b-c-court-of-appeal-dismisses-former-cfl-player-s-concussion-lawsuit->)
Joint Statement Regarding Concussion Lawsuit Resolution, *US Soccer*, 2 November 2015 (<http://www.ussoccer.com/about/recognize-to-recover/concussion-guidelines/player-safety-campaign>)
Jones, Lindsay H, 'NFL Begins New Phase of Domestic Violence Education as Training Camps Open', *USA Today*, 27 July 2015 (<http://www.usatoday.com/story/sports/nfl/2015/07/27/domestic-violence-training-education-drunk-driving-intervention/30752175/>)
Kaplan, Daniel, 'Engineers to Assist NFL with Injury Prevention', *SportsBusinessDaily*, 23 February 2015 (<http://www.sportsbusinessdaily.com/Journal/Issues/2015/02/23/Leagues-and-Governing-Bodies/NFL-engineers.aspx>)
Kaszuba, Mike, 'What's to Learn from Lou Gehrig's Death?', *Star Tribune*, 9 October 2012 (<http://www.startribune.com/what-s-to-learn-from-lou-gehrig-s-death/172581481/?c=y&page=all&prepage=1#continue>)
Kelly, Caitlin, 'The Hope Solo Fiasco', *The New Yorker*, 12 June 2015 (<http://www.newyorker.com/news/sporting-scene/the-hope-solo-fiasco>)
'Kenny McKinley Found Dead at Home', *ESPN*, 21 September 2010 (<http://sports.espn.go.com/nfl/news/story?id=5598078>)
Kilgore, Adam, 'Aaron Fernandez Suffered from Most Severe CTE Ever Found in a Person of his Age', *The Washingon Post*, 9 November 2017 (<https://www.washingtonpost.com/sports/aaron-hernandez-suffered-from-most-severe-cte-ever-found-in-a-person-his-age/2017/11/09/fa7cd204-c57b-11e7-afe9-4f60b5a6c4a0_story.html?utm_term=.82d00d5fd2e1>)
Kirsch, Jesse, 'New NFL Game Plan Looks to Tackle Head Injuries', *ABC News*, 13 September 2015 (<http://abcnews.go.com/Sports/nfl-game-plan-tackle-head-injuries/story?id=33387925>)
Klayman, Ben, 'Concussion Treatment, Diagnosis Focus of World Sports Conference', *Reuters*, 22 October 2015 (<http://www.reuters.com/article/us-sport-concussions-idUSKCN0SG18520151022>)
Klein, Christopher, 'How Teddy Roosevelt Saved Football', *History*, 6 September 2012 (<http://www.history.com/news/how-teddy-roosevelt-saved-football>) (Christopher Klein, 'Roosevelt') (this link does not exist anymore, copy on file with author)
Klein, Jeff, 'With Stricter Rule on Hits to the Head, Some N.H.L. Stars Are Split on a Full Ban', *The New York Times*, 19 September 2011 (<http://www.nytimes.com/2011/09/20/sports/hockey/nhls-top-stars-weigh-in-on-hits-to-the-head.html?pagewanted=all>) (Jeff Klein, 'NHL')
Kozora, Alex, 'NFL Rule Change Now Makes Head To Head Contact Illegal', '*Steelers Depot*', 27 March 2018 (<https://steelersdepot.com/2018/03/nfl-rule-change-now-makes-head-to-head-contact-illegal-possible-ejection/>)
Lake, Ryan, 'The Effects of Fighting in Ice Hockey: An Overview of the Ongoing NHL Concussion Litigation', *Lawinsport*, 19 April 2016 (<http://www.lawinsport.com/sports/item/the-effects-of-fighting-in-ice-hockey-an-overview-of-the-ongoing-nhl-concussion-litigation?category_id=152>) (paywall)
Lausanne Declaration on Doping in Sport, 4 February 1999 (<https://www.wada-ama.org/en/resources/general-anti-doping-information/lausanne-declaration-on-doping-in-sport>)
Lazerus, Mark, 'Former Blackhawks Defenseman Steve Montador Dead at 35', *The Chicago Suntimes*, 15 February 2015 (<http://chicago.suntimes.com/sports/former-blackhawks-defenseman-steve-montador-dead-at-35/>)
'Leading Canadian Health Organizations Produce a Guide to Help Sport and School Organizations Implement Concussion Management Protocols', press release, *Lawinsport,* 7 September 2015 (<https://www.lawinsport.com/sports-law-news/item/leading-canadian-health-organizations-produce-a-guide-to-help-sport-and-school-organizations-implement-concussion-management-protocols>) (paywall)

Leslie, Cameron, 'Ian Roberts Brain Damage Revelations Are Cause for Concern for Football Codes', *ABC*, 13 March 2014 (<http://www.abc.net.au/news/2014-03-11/luke-burgess-concerned-brain-damage-claims-will-deter-kids-from/5313372?section=sport>)

Lukas, Paul, 'Alex Torres and the History of Headgear in Baseball', *ESPN*, 23 April 2015 (<http://www.espn.com/mlb/story/_/id/12741917/uni-watch-history-headgear-mlb-alex-torres>)

Malet, Maxime, 'La NFL secouée comme jamais', *L'Equipe*, 17 September 2014 (<http://www.lequipe.fr/Football-americain/Actualites/La-nfl-secouee-comme-jamais/499843>)

'Marcelo encaminhado para o hospital com concussão cerebral', *Record*, 24 February 2018 (<https://www.record.pt/futebol/futebol-nacional/liga-nos/rio-ave/detalhe/marcelo-encaminhado-para-o-hospital-com-concussao-cerebral>)

McCann, Michael, 'The Wins and Losses of the NHL's Tentative Concussion Lawsuit Settlement', *Sports Illustrated*, 12 November 2018 (<https://www.si.com/nhl/2018/11/12/nhl-concussion-lawsuit-settlement-wins-losses-former-players>)

Mihoces, Gary, 'FIFA Doctor at NFL Summit "not Alarmed" by Soccer's Concussion Data', *USA Today*, 25 August 2014 (<http://www.usatoday.com/story/sports/nfl/2014/08/25/nfl-fifa-concussion-think-tank-world-cup-christoph-kramer/14574077/>) (Mihoces, 'FIFA')

Mihoces, Gary, 'NFL Think Tank has Sports "Pooling Resources" *USA Today* in Concussion Battle', 25 August 2014 (<https://www.usatoday.com/story/sports/2014/08/25/nfl-concussions-olympics-fifa-soccer-nhl-ncaa/14593579/>) (Mihoces, 'NFL Think Tank')

Ministère de l'Éducation des Loisirs et du Sport du Québec, Protocole de Gestion des Commotions Cérébrales, 2017 (<http://www.education.gouv.qc.ca/fileadmin/site_web/documents/loisir-sport/Protocole_de_gestion_des_commotions_cerebrales_FR.pdf>)

'Miranda sofre concussão em choque com Alisson é cortado da Seleção Brasileira após perder memória', *Fox Sports*, 1 September 2017 (<https://www.foxsports.com.br/news/320799-miranda-sofre-concussao-em-choque-com-alisson-e-cortado-da-selecao-brasileira-apos-perder-memoria>)

MLB, press release, 29 March 2011 (<http://mlb.mlb.com/content/printer_friendly/mlb/y2011/m03/d29/c17181944.jsp>)

Muller, Vikram, 'Cal Men's Water Polo Athletes Participate in USA Water Polo National League Championship' *The Daily Californian*, 3 May 2016 (<http://www.dailycal.org/2016/05/03/cal-mens-water-polo-athletes-participate-in-usa-water-polo-national-league-championship/>)

Nash, Jonno and Charlie Happell, 'Front and Centre: Concussion in AFL Remains a Critical Issue', *ESPN*, 11 May 2017 (<http://www.espn.com.au/afl/story/_/id/19355678/front-centre-head-concussion-remains-critical-issue-afl>)

Naylor, Dave, 'CFL Immediately Ends Full-Contact Practices', *TSN*, 13 September 2017 (<http://www.tsn.ca/cfl-to-announce-immediate-end-to-full-contact-practices-1.855515>)

NCAA, *Self-Reported Concussion among NCAA Student Athletes, Executive Summary*, February 2014 (<https://www.ncaa.org/sites/default/files/Concussion%20%20GOALS%20Exec%20Summary_Feb_12_2014_FINALpost_0.pdf>)

NFL Annual Player Health and Safety Report (2018) (<https://www.playsmartplaysafe.com/newsroom/reports/nfl-annual-player-health-and-safety-reports/>) (and previous reports)

'NFL Commitment to Player Health and Safety, A Letter from Commissioner Roger Goodell', *NFL*, 14 September 2016 (<https://www.playsmartplaysafe.com/commitment-letter/>)

NFL Injury Data Report (2017) (<https://www.playsmartplaysafe.com/newsroom/reports/2017-injury-data/>)

'NFL, NFLPA Announce Policy to Enforce Concussion Protocol', *NFL*, 25 July 2016 (<http://www.nfl.com/news/story/0ap3000000676669/article/nfl-nflpa-announce-policy-to-enforce-concussion-protocol>)

'NHLPA Chief Seeks Ban on Hits to Head', *NHL*, 9 March 2009 (<https://www.nhl.com/news/nhlpa-chief-seeks-ban-on-hits-to-head/c-413060>)

NHLPA Staff, 'Smashfest Raises Over $500 000 in First Five Years For Concussion and Rare Cancer Research', *NHLPA*, 22 July 2016 (<http://www.nhlpa.com/news/smashfest-raises-over-500000-in-first-five-years-for-concussion-rare-cancer-rese>) (NHLPA Staff, 'Smashfest')

NHLPA Staff, 'NHLPA Gift to Support Concussion Research Announced at See The Line', *NHLPA*, 12 August 2015 (<http://www.nhlpa.com/news/nhlpa-gift-to-support-concussion-research-announced-at-see-the-line>) (NHLPA Staff, 'Gift')

NHL Public Relations, 'NHL Updates Concussion Protocols', *NHL*, 12 October 2015 (<https://www.nhl.com/news/nhl-updates-concussion-protocol/c-282571624>)

Nordrum, Amy 'Concussions Are Treatable, Experts Conclude at NFL-Sponsored Scientific Meeting', *International Business Times*, 16 October 2015 (<http://www.ibtimes.com/concussions-are-treatable-experts-conclude-nfl-sponsored-scientific-meeting-2144801?utm_content=buffer66d04&utm_medium=social&utm_source=linkedin.com&utm_campaign=buffer>) (Nordrum, 'NFL-Sponsored Meeting')

Nordrum, Amy 'NFL Underwrites Scientific Meeting to Set National Agenda for Concussion Treatment', *International Business Times*, 14 October 2015 (<http://www.ibtimes.com/nfl-underwrites-scientific-meeting-set-national-agenda-concussion-treatment-2137145>) (Nordrum, 'National Agenda')

'NRL Announces Historic CBA Deal', NRL website, 3 November 2017 (<https://www.nrl.com/news/2017/11/03/nrl-announces-historic-cba-deal/>)

'NRL Announces Plans to Increase Maximum Insurance Payouts to $1 Million for Players Sustaining Catastrophic Injuries', *The Telegraph*, 24 July 2014 (<http://www.dailytelegraph.com.au/sport/nrl/teams/nrl-announces-plans-to-increase-maximum-insurance-payouts-to-1-million-for-players-sustaining-catastrophic-injuries/news-story/763bac3b3896f4c1aff2e4c6e28ba4f7>)

NRL, media release, 24 May 2017 (<http://www.nrl.com/independent-expert-to-assess-origin-concussions/tabid/10874/newsid/107120/default.aspx>)

NRL, media release, 6 April 2017 (<http://www.nrl.com/nrls-head-injury-protocol-sanctions/tabid/10874/newsid/105412/default.aspx>)

'NRL to Conduct Interchange Rule Review to Reduce "Big Collisions"', *ABC*, 24 March 2015 (<http://www.abc.net.au/news/2015-03-25/nrl-to-conduct-interchange-rule-review-to-reduce-27big-collisio/6346064?section=sport>)

O'Connell, Elizabeth, 'NFL Announces Latest Partnership with International Concussion and Head Injury Research Foundation', *SportTechie*, 28 October 2015 (<http://www.sporttechie.com/2015/10/28/nfl-announces-latest-partnership-international-concussion-head-injury-research-foundation/>)

O'Keefe, Michael, 'Boston University Finds Possible Link Between Traumatic Brain Injuries and Domestic Violence', *New York Daily News*, 18 October 2014 (<http://www.nydailynews.com/sports/football/study-cte-linked-domestic-violence-article-1.1978936>) (O'Keefe, 'Boston University')

O'Keefe, Michael, 'Former Chief Player Jovan Belcher Showed Signs of CTE in Postmortem Brain Exam', *New York Daily News*, 29 September 2014 (<http://www.nydailynews.com/sports/football/chiefs-player-jovan-belcher-showed-signs-cte-post-mortem-brain-exam-article-1.1957229>) (O'Keefe, 'Jovan Belcher')

O'Keefe, Michael, 'Two Former Players Sue Union Over Concussions', *New York Daily News*, 18 July 2014 (<http://www.nydailynews.com/sports/football/nfl-players-sue-union-concussions-article-1.1872172>) (O'Keefe, 'Union')

O'Keefe, Michael, 'Congress Tells FIFA to Get its Act Together Over Concussion', Bill Pascrell Jr and Thomas Rooney's letter to Joseph Blatter of 15 July 2014d, *New York Daily News*, 16 July 2014 (<http://www.nydailynews.com/blogs/iteam/congress-tells-fifa-act-concussions-blog-entry-1.1869314>) (O'Keefe, 'FIFA')

'Olympics: IOC Confirms 169 Russians Cleared to Compete in Pyeongchang', *Reuters*, 28 January 2018 (<https://www.reuters.com/article/us-olympics-2018-russia-team/olympics-ioc-confirms-169-russians-cleared-to-compete-in-pyeongchang-idUSKBN1FG0Y6>)

Ontario Ministry of Education, Policy/Program Memorandum on Concussion (2014) (<http://www.edu.gov.on.ca/extra/eng/ppm/158.pdf>)

Palmer, Dan, 'Three-Time Olympian Bauer Sues Canandian Freesytle Association after Concussions', *Inside The Games*, 16 December 2015 (<https://www.insidethegames.biz/articles/1032583/three-time-olympian-bauer-sues-canadian-freestyle-ski-association-after-concussions>)

Parachute, Canadian Guideline on Concussion in Sport (2017) (<http://www.parachutecanada.org/downloads/injurytopics/Canadian_Guideline_on_Concussion_in_Sport-Parachute.pdf>)

Pelissero, Tom, 'NFL Toughens Domestic Violence Stance', *Athletic Business*, 29 August 2014 (<http://www.athleticbusiness.com/more-news/nfl-toughens-domestic-violence-stance.html?topic=5,100&eid=162250984&bid=921134>) (13 March 2015) (this link does not exist anymore – copy on file with author)

Pengilly, Adam 'States back in Charge of Concussion Calls', *The Sydney Morning Herald*, 31 May 2018 (<https://www.smh.com.au/sport/nrl/states-back-in-charge-of-concussion-calls-20180531-p4zimm.html>)

Penton, Kirk, 'CFL Introduces "Bold" Policy Dealing with Violence against Women', *Toronto Sun*, 6 August 2015 (<http://www.torontosun.com/2015/08/06/cfl-introduces-bold-policy-dealing-with-violence-against-women>) (30 May 2017)

Pepper, Ben, 'Jeff Astle Died from "Boxing" Brain Injury', *Lexology*, 3 June 2014 (<https://www.lexology.com/library/detail.aspx?g=7779a299-7a91-49e2-8405-b629b1549351>) (paywall)

Perez, AJ, 'NHL, NHLPA Launch Sexual Assault, Domestic Violence Training Initiative', *USA Today*, 5 January 2016 (<http://www.usatoday.com/story/sports/nhl/2016/01/05/nhl-sexual-assault-harassment-domestic-violence-training/78300616/>)

'Peter Gordon Doesn't Believe a Concussion Class Action against the AFL Would Be Successful', *The Herald Sun*, 14 September 2018 (<https://www.news.com.au/sport/afl/peter-gordon-doesnt-believe-a-concussion-class-action-against-the-afl-would-be-successful/news-story/2b774aafaf84e6a86c3bb1de9eb1d5b6>)

Peter, Josh, 'Former NFL Exec: Team Hid "Hundreds" of abuse incidents', *USA Today*, 9 October 2014 (<http://www.usatoday.com/story/sports/nfl/2014/10/09/jerry-angelo-chicago-bears-national-football-league/16981865/>)

Peters, Sam, 'After Three 1966 Heroes Are Revealed to Have Dementia, Jeff Astle's Family Ask Why the FA Have Yet to Tackle Sport's Silent Scandal', *MailOnline*, 16 April 2016 (<http://www.mailonsunday.co.uk/sport/concussion/article-3543806/After-three-1966-heroes-revealed-dementia-Jeff-Astle-s-family-ask-FA-tackle-sport-s-silent-scandal.html>)

Pettersson, Edvard, 'NFL Sued by Widow of Chargers Paul Oliver After Suicide', *Bloomberg Business*, 24 September 2014 (<http://www.bloomberg.com/news/articles/2014-09-24/nfl-sued-by-san-diego-chargers-paul-oliver-s-widow-after-suicide>)

Phillips, Rich, 'Former Football Player Paul Oliver Shot Himself in the Head, Police Says', *CNN*, 3 October 2013 (<http://edition.cnn.com/2013/10/02/us/georgia-football-player-suicide/index.html>)

Pierik, Jon, 'Sports Doctor Peter Larkins Calls for AFL to Consider Concussion Substitute', *The Age*, 29 May 2017 (<http://www.theage.com.au/afl/afl-news/sports-doctor-peter-larkins-calls-for-afl-to-consider-concussion-substitute-20170529-gwfjun.html>) (Pierik, 'AFL')

Pierik, Jon, 'Madden Ready to Donate Brain to Help Injury Research', *The Age*, 15 May 2012 (<http://www.theage.com.au/afl/afl-news/madden-ready-to-donate-brain-to-help-injury-research-20120514-1yn2w.html>) (Pierik, 'Madden')

Press Association, 'IOC Promises to Boost WADA's Funding if it Agrees to Anti-Doping Reform', *The Guardian*, 9 October 2016 (<https://www.theguardian.com/sport/2016/oct/08/ioc-wada-funding-anti-doping-reform>)

Ralph, Jon, 'AFL to Fund a Minimum of $250,000 a Year for Concussion Research', *News.Com*, 22 June 2017 (<http://www.news.com.au/sport/afl/afl-to-fund-a-minimum-of-250000-a-year-for-concussion-research/news-story/e95fe084d1bc8f9637acbf51ea00ea0b>) (Ralph, 'AFL')

Ralph, Jon, 'Peter Jess Says He Has Players with Evidence to Sue Over Concussion Management', *The Herald Sun*, 26 February 2016 (<http://www.heraldsun.com.au/sport/afl/more-news/peter-jess-says-he-has-players-with-evidence-to-sue-their-club-over-concussion-management/news-story/44e5f99663e5641139e04eac4f77d741>) (paywall) (14 June 2017) (Ralph, 'Peter Jess')

Read, Brent, 'Brett Horsnell to Claim that he Suffers from Disease that Cost NFL a Billion', *The Australian*, 13 May 2017 (<http://www.theaustralian.com.au/sport/nrl/brett-horsnell-to-claim-he-suffers-from-disease-that-cost-nfl-a-billion/news-story/00691cc2cdff35ebfa5c7ad22cec2d64>)

Red, Christian 'Meet the Doctors Trying to Solve NFL's CTE Issue' *New York Daily News*, 6 November 2017 (<http://www.nydailynews.com/sports/football/meet-doctors-solve-nfl-cte-issue-article-1.3613902>) (Red, 'Doctors')

Red, Christian, 'Judge Applies Abuse of Discretion Standard in Ray Rice Ruling' *New York Daily News*, 29 November 2014 (<http://www.nydailynews.com/sports/football/judge-applies-abusive-discretion-standard-ray-rice-ruling-article-1.2027285>) (Red, 'Ray Rice')

Rees, Paul, 'George North's Concussion Damaged Him and the Image of Rugby Union', *The Guardian*, 12 February 2015 (<https://www.theguardian.com/sport/2015/feb/12/breakdown-george-north-wales-concussion>)

Reuters, 'Concussion Protocol Altered after Recent Missteps', *Reuters*, 24 September 2017 (<https://www.reuters.com/article/us-football-nfl-concussion/concussion-protocol-altered-after-recent-missteps-idUSKBN1EI0JV>) (Reuters, 'Protocol')

Reuters, 'Science Catching up to Media Hype Around Concussions', *SBS*, 25 October 2015 (<https://www.sbs.com.au/news/science-catching-up-to-media-hype-around-concussions>) (Reuters, 'Science')

Riccio, David, 'NRL Beef Up Concussion Protocols Following Series of Ugly Head Knocks', *The Daily Telegraph*, 29 June 2017 (<http://www.dailytelegraph.com.au/sport/nrl/teams/nrl-beef-up-concussion-protocols-following-series-of-ugly-head-knocks/news-story/d0b7ec049b4f0e48f5df64f6906b6bb1>) (paywall)

Robertson, Justin, 'How Canadians Are Helping in the Fight Against Concussion in Sport', *Vice Sports*, 6 March 2017 (<https://sports.vice.com/en_ca/article/how-canadians-are-helping-in-the-fight-against-concussions-in-sport>)

Rosen, Dan, 'NHL, NHLPA Bolster Concussion Evaluation Process', *NHL*, 15 September 2015 (<https://www.nhl.com/news/nhl-nhlpa-bolster-concussion-evaluation-process/c-779135>) (Rosen, 'Process')

Rosen, Dan, 'Hybrid Icing Tops List of Rule Changes for 2013-14', *NHL*, 1st October 2013 (<https://www.nhl.com/news/hybrid-icing-tops-list-of-rule-changes-for-2013-14/c-684940>) (Rosen, 'Rule Changes')

Rosen, Dan, 'New Concussion Protocol Goes Into Effect Tonight', *NHL*, 16 March 2011 (<http://www.nhl.com/ice/news.htm?id=556289>) (Rosen, 'Protocol')

Rothenberg, Ben, 'Eugenie Bouchard and U.S.T.A. Reach Settlement', *The New York Times*, 23 February 2018 (<https://www.nytimes.com/2018/02/23/sports/tennis/bouchard-usta-lawsuit.html>)

Rothfield, Phil, 'Alex McKinnon Will Sue the NRL and Melbourne Storm Player Jordan McLean over Tackle that Left Him Paralysed', *The Daily Telegraph*, 18 December 2016 (<http://www.dailytelegraph.com.au/sport/nrl/alex-mckinnon-will-sue-the-nrl-and-melbourne-storm-player-jordan-mclean-over-tackle-that-left-him-paralysed/news story/1e2974c5426c70497eefd23b6c91f118>)

'Rugby Study Points to Link Between Concussion and Brain Function', *BBC*, 28 July 2015 (<http://www.bbc.com/sport/rugby-union/33686163>)

Russell Kennedy, 'The NRL to Keep Concussion Breaches Secret', *Lexology*, 31 May 2018 (<https://www.lexology.com/library/detail.aspx?g=d6cd4a3e-ddc9-410b-83ea-2b63fa1b7543&utm_source=lexology+daily+newsfeed&utm_medium=html+email+-+body+-+general+section&utm_campaign=australian+ihl+subscriber+daily+feed&utm_content=lexology+daily+newsfeed+2018-06-01&utm_term=>) (paywall)

Sanders, Markus, 'Jeremy Flores: It was a Nightmare', *Surfline*, 29 June 2015 (<http://www.surfline.com/surf-news/french-surfer-recounts-head-butting-the-reef-at-lakey-peak-which-resulted-in-35-stitches-and-two-hours-of-memo_128928/>)

Sarre, Rick, 'Why Boxing and Cage Fighting Should be Banned – but Won't Be', *The Conversation*, 27 March 2015 (<https://theconversation.com/why-boxing-and-cage-fighting-should-be-banned-but-wont-be-38901>)

Scarr, Lanai, 'Health Minister Greg Hunt has Unveiled $125Million of Funding into Medical Research Projects', *The Herald Sun*, 3 February 2015 (<http://www.heraldsun.com.au/news/national/health-minister-greg-hunt-has-unveiled-125-million-of-funding-into-medical-research-projects/news-story/8684f9a1c3017059ff7bf650215172a4>) (paywall)

Schmidt, Michael S, 'BATS; M.L.B. Names New Medical Director', *The New York Times*, 15 April 2010 (<https://archive.nytimes.com/query.nytimes.com/gst/fullpage-9404E6DE1438F936A25757C0A9669D8B63.html>)

Schmook, Nathan and Lee Gaskin, 'Players Get 20 Per Cent Pay Rise in New CBA', *AFL*, 20 June 2017 (<http://www.afl.com.au/news/2017-06-20/players-get-20-per-cent-pay-rise-in-new-cba>)

Schofield, Daniel, 'The Big Read: Sport Must Come Clean over Risks of Concussion', *New Zealand Herald*, 11 July 2016 (<http://www.nzherald.co.nz/sport/news/article.cfm?c_id=4&objectid=11672511>)

Setar, Cal, 'NHL Feels "No Desire" to Settle Concussion Lawsuit' (REPORT), *HNGN*, 1er October 2015 (<http://www.hngn.com/articles/135746/20151001/nhl-feels-no-desire-to-settle-concussion-lawsuit-report.htm>)

Schwarz, Alan, 'N.F.L.-Backed Youth Program Says It Reduced Concussion. The Data Disagrees', *The New York Times*, 27 July 2016 (<http://www.nytimes.com/2016/07/28/sports/football/nfl-concussions-youth-program-heads-up-football.html?nytmobile=0&_r=0&mtrref=undefined>) (Alan Schwarz, 'Youth Program')

Schwarz, Alan, 'Handling of Ray Rice Puts Roger Goodell Under Heightened Level of Scrutiny', *The New York Times*, 14 September 2014 (<http://www.nytimes.com/2014/09/15/sports/football/handling-of-ray-rice-case-puts-roger-goodell-under-heightened-level-of-scrutiny.html?ref=sports&_r=1&assetType=nyt_now>) (Alan Schwarz, 'Ray Rice')

Schwarz, Alan, 'Study Says Brain Trauma Can Mimic A.L.S', *The New York Times*, 18 August 2010 (<http://query.nytimes.com/gst/fullpage.html?res=9E0DE2D7143DF93BA2575BC0A9669D8B63>) (Alan Schwarz, 'ALS')

Schwarz, Alan, 'Dementia Risks Seen in Players in N.F.L Study', *The New York Times*, 29 September 2009 (<http://www.nytimes.com/2009/09/30/sports/football/30dementia.html?pagewanted=all&_r=0>) (Alan Schwarz, 'Dementia')

Schwarz, Joe, 'Major League Baseball and the Concussion Problem', *Viva El Birdos*, 2 February 2016 (<http://www.vivaelbirdos.com/2016/2/2/10892078/major-league-baseball-and-the-concussion-problem>) (Joe Schwarz, 'MLB')

Sessler, Marc, 'NFL Passes Automatic Ejection Rule for 2016 Season', *NFL*, 23 March 2016 (< http://www.nfl.com/news/story/0ap3000000646837/article/nfl-passes-automatic-ejection-rule-for-2016-season>)

Slot, Owen, 'Rugby Needs Confidence and Proof it is not a Health Risk', *The Australian*, 5 September 2017 (<http://www.theaustralian.com.au/sport/the-times-sport/rugby-needs-confidence-and-proof-it-is-not-a-health-risk/news-story/aa38a4200bff5e93a80013cda06a59be>) (paywall)

Shaw, Garrett S, 'NFL and NFLPA Implement Updated Concussion Protocol Procedures', *SportTechie*, 26 July 2016 (<http://www.sporttechie.com/2016/07/26/nfl-nflpa-implement-updated-concussion-protocol-procedures/>)

Shinzawa, Fluto, 'NHL Players' Fines to Help Others', *The Boston Globe*, 19 January 2014 (<https://www.bostonglobe.com/sports/2014/01/19/nhl-player-fines-put-good-use/AFCmu81UICfFfcwWGU8LBM/story.html>)

Shyr, Luna, 'NFL Looks to Helmet Technology to Combat Concussions', *National Geographic Daily News*, 1 February 2013 (<https://news.nationalgeographic.com/news/2013/13/130202-football-concussions-nfl-super-bowl-safety-head-injuries-health/>)

Siegel, Jonas, ‘NHL’s Gary Bettman Brushes off Attack from US Senator over Concussion’, *The Star*, 17 August 2016 (<https://www.thestar.com/sports/hockey/2016/08/17/gary-bettman-nhl-stance-on-concussions-sends-wrong-message-us-senator.html>)

Slater, Matt, ‘NFL Safety Boss Says the League Could Ban Helmets One Day’, *BBC Sport*, 18 June 2015 (<http://www.bbc.com/sport/0/american-football/33167457>)

Smith, Michael David, ‘NFL Passes Five Player Safety Rules’, *NBC Sports*, 24 March 2015 (<http://profootballtalk.nbcsports.com/2015/03/24/nfl-passes-five-player-safety-rules/>) (Michael David Smith, ‘Safety’)

Smith, Michael David, ‘Cardinals Deactivate Dwyer After Domestic Violence Arrest’, *NBC Sports*, 17 September 2014 (<http://profootballtalk.nbcsports.com/2014/09/17/cardinals-deactivate-dwyer-after-domestic-violence-arrest/related/>) (Michael David, ‘Domestic Violence’)

Smith, Michael David, ‘NFL Officiating Video Stresses New “Crown of the Helmet” Rule’, *NBC Sports*, 6 August 2013 (<http://profootballtalk.nbcsports.com/2013/08/06/nfl-officiating-video-stresses-new-crown-of-the-helmet-rule/>) (Michael David Smith, ‘Crown’)

Smith, Stephanie and Dan Moriarty, ‘First Major League Baseball Player Diagnosed with CTE’, *CNN*, 16 December 2013 (<https://edition.cnn.com/2013/12/15/health/baseball-ryan-freel-cte-suicide/index.html>)

Smith, Stephanie, ‘Ex-Falcons Lineman Had Brain Disease Due to Concussions’, *CNN*, 1 April 2011 (<http://edition.cnn.com/2011/HEALTH/04/01/brain.concussion.dronett/index.html?hpt=Sbin>) (Stephanie Smith, ‘Falcons’)

Sokoloski, Chris, ‘Howard High Legend Dead at 66’, *South Strand News*, 29 October 2015 (<http://www.southstrandnews.com/news/howard-high-legend-dead-at/article_89835109-9e05-5a2f-80b7-edf0f19cee38.html>)

Sports Medicine Australia, General Principles (WA, 2017) (<https://sportconcussion.com.au/>)

Sports Medicine Australia, Concussion in Sport Policy (NSW, 2018) (<https://sportandrecreation.nsw.gov.au/sites/default/files/sma-concussion-in-sport-policy.pdf/>)

Starkman, Randy and Rob Cribb, ‘Star Investigation: What Really Killed NHL’s Bill Masterton’, *The Star*, 28 May 2011 (<http://www.thestar.com/sports/hockey/2011/05/28/star_investigation_what_really_killed_nhls_bill_masterton.html>)

Starkman, Randy, ‘Concussion Epidemic Hits Women’s Water Polo Team before Olympic Qualifier’ *The Star*, 1 April 2012 (<https://www.thestar.com/sports/olympics/2012/04/01/concussion_epidemic_hits_womens_water_polo_team_before_olympic_qualifier.html>)

Steele, David, ‘Goodell’s New Medical Chief Isn’t a Concussion Expert’, *Sporting News*, 12 February 2015 (<http://snip.ly/RxOc#http://www.sportingnews.com/nfl/story/2015-02-12/elizabeth-nabel-nfl-medical-advisor-goodell-cardiologist-concussions-conflict-kraft-patriots>)

Strachan, Maxwell, ‘NFL Champions Steve Weatherford and Sidney Rice To Donate Brains to Science’, *The Huffington Post*, 3 March 2015 (<http://www.huffingtonpost.com/2015/03/03/steve-weatherford-brain-sidney-rice-nfl_n_6796068.html>)

Strauss, Ben, ‘Former Soccer Player Sues Illinois, Saying that Concussion was Mishandled’, *The New York Times*, 8 June 2015 (<http://www.nytimes.com/2015/06/09/sports/soccer/former-soccer-player-sues-illinois-saying-concussion-was-mishandled.html?ref=health&_r=2>)

Strom, Pete, ‘Will Concussions Bankrupt the NFL?’, *‘Strom Law Firm’* website (<http://stromlaw.com/6459/will-concussions-bankrupt-the-nfl/#>)

Swope, Rodante P.A., ‘An Overview of Riddell Class Action Lawsuits’ *Swope, Rodante P.A.*, 17 March 2014 (<http://www.swoperodante.com/overview-riddell-class-action-lawsuits/>)

Tannenwald, Jonathan, ‘U.S. Soccer Responds to Criticism from Senator; Jeramy Stevens Defends Hope Solo’, US senator Richard Blumenthal’s letter of 11 June 2015 and US Soccer President Sunil Gulati’s reply of 12 June 2015, *The Inquirer Daily News*, 13 June 2015 (<http://www.philly.com/philly/blogs/thegoalkeeper/US-Soccer-responds-to-criticism-from-senator.html>)

The Canadian Press, ‘CFL Players’ Association Files Grievance Against League over Safety’, *CBC*, 2 March 2018 (<http://www.cbc.ca/sports/football/cfl/cfl-players-association-grievance-safety-1.4585843>) (The Canadian Press, ‘Grievance’)

The Canadian Press, 'Sports Legends Push for National Standard for Concussion Treatment', *CBC Sports*, 6 December 2016 (<http://www.cbc.ca/sports/concussions-protocol-canada-conference-1.3883604>) (The Canadian Press, 'Standard')

The Canadian Press, 'Gary Bettman Says NHL Proactive About Off-Ice Conduct', *CBC Sports*, 22 September 2014 (<http://www.cbc.ca/sports/hockey/nhl/gary-bettman-says-nhl-proactive-about-off-ice-conduct-1.2774276>) (The Canadian Press, 'Off-Ice')

The Canadian Press, 'Pacioretty Injury Part of the Game: Bettman', *CBC Sports*, 10 March 2011 (<http://www.cbc.ca/sports/hockey/pacioretty-injury-part-of-game-bettman-1.1008959>) (The Canadian Press, 'Pacioretty')

The Dominion Post, press release, 'Clarification: WRU Concussion', *Stuff*, 21 August 2016 (<https://www.stuff.co.nz/sport/rugby/international/83256246/clarification-wru%2D%2Dconcussion>)

The Editorial Board, 'A Football Player's Safe Exit', *The New York Times*, 21 March 2015 (<http://www.nytimes.com/2015/03/22/opinion/sunday/a-football-players-safe-exit.html#http://www.nytimes.com/2015/03/22/opinion/sunday/a-football-players-safe-exit.html>)

The White House, Office of Science and Technology Policy, 'Fact Sheet: Obama Administration Proposes Over $300 Million in Funding for the Brain Initiative', *The White House*, February 2015 (<https://obamawhitehouse.archives.gov/sites/default/files/microsites/ostp/brain_initiative_fy16_fact_sheet_ostp.pdf>) (The White House, 'Support').

The White House, Office of the Press Secretary, 'Fact Sheet: President Obama Applauds Commitments to Address Sports-Related Concussions in Young People', *The White House*, 29 May 2014 (<https://www.whitehouse.gov/the-press-office/2014/05/29/fact-sheet-president-obama-applauds-commitments-address-sports-related-c>) (The White House, 'Young People')

The White House, Office of the Press Secretary, 'Fact Sheet: Brain Initiative', *The White House*, 2 April 2013 (<https://www.whitehouse.gov/the-press-office/2013/04/02/fact-sheet-brain-initiative>) (The White House, 'Brain Initiative')

Toor, Amar, 'Soccer's Rule Makers Consider Video Replay for Head Injuries', *The Verge*, 10 November 2016 (<http://www.theverge.com/2016/11/10/13582510/instant-replay-soccer-concussion-ifab>)

Tuckey, Ian, 'What is the difference Between Rugby League and Rugby Union?', *The Sun*, 3 March 2017 (<https://www.thesun.co.uk/sport/2238885/what-is-the-difference-between-rugby-union-and-rugby-league/>)

Ubelacker, Sheryl, 'NHL Hockey Concussions Take Centre Ice', *The Huffington Post* (<http://www.huffingtonpost.ca/2011/12/19/nhl-hockey-concussions_n_1158403.html>)

UEFA, press release, 18 May 2017 (<http://www.uefa.com/insideuefa/protecting-the-game/medical/news/newsid=2470859.html?redirectFromOrg=true>)

'UEFA to Launch Study Into Link Between Playing Football and Dementia', *BBC*, 16 February 2017 (<http://www.bbc.com/sport/football/38990953>)

University of Pennsylvania School of Medicine, 'Penn Researchers Identify Protein that Predicts Post-Concussion Severity in Professional Athletes', *EurekAlert*, 25 November 2014 (<http://www.eurekalert.org/pub_releases/2014-11/uops-pri112514.php>)

'Uruguaio do Sao Paulo bate a cabeza, repeta cena da Copa e volta ao juogo', *UOL Esporte*, 2 August 2014 (<https://esporte.uol.com.br/futebol/campeonatos/brasileiro/serie-a/ultimas-noticias/2014/08/02/uruguaio-do-sao-paulo-bate-a-cabeca-repete-cena-da-copa-e-volta-ao-jogo.htm>)

Vasquez, Thomas, 'NFL Concussion Liability Forecast', Report, 10 February 2014 (<http://nflconcussionlitigation.com/wp-content/uploads/2014/09/6167-Special-Master-Report.pdf>)

Voser, Nathalie and Benno Strub, 'Switzerland: Revision of the Statute of Limitations', *Mondaq*, 10 August 2018 (<http://www.mondaq.com/x/725456/Personal+Injury/Revision+of+the+Statute+of+Limitations>)

Vrentas, Jenny, 'NFL Safety is in her Hands', *MMQB*, 15 May 2015 (<http://mmqb.si.com/2015/05/15/betsy-nabel-nfl-health-medical-concussions-head-injuries/#>)

WADA Anti-Doping Rule Violations (ADRV) Report 2016 (<https://www.wada-ama.org/sites/default/files/resources/files/2016_adrvs_report_web_release_april_2018_0.pdf>)

WADA Anti-Doping Testing Figures Report 2017 (<https://www.wada-ama.org/sites/default/files/resources/files/2017_anti-doping_testing_figures_en_0.pdf>)

WADA, press release, 20 September 2018 (<https://www.wada-ama.org/en/media/news/2018-09/wada-executive-committee-decides-to-reinstate-rusada-subject-to-strict-conditions>)

WADA, press release, 25 February 2018 (<https://www.wada-ama.org/en/media/news/2018-02/wada-statement-regarding-the-iocs-decision-not-to-reinstate-the-russian-olympic>)

WADA, press release, 19 May 2016 (<https://www.wada-ama.org/en/media/news/2016-05/wada-names-richard-mclaren-to-sochi-investigation-team>)

WADA, press release, 18 November 2015 (<https://www.wada-ama.org/en/media/news/2015-11/foundation-board-media-release-wada-strengthens-anti-doping-worldwide>)

WADA, press release, 16 December 2014 (<https://www.wada-ama.org/en/media/news/2014-12/wada-announces-details-of-independent-commission>)

WADA statement on Al Jazeera's documentary, 28 December 2015 (<https://www.wada-ama.org/en/media/news/2015-12/wada-statement-on-al-jazeera-documentary>)

Wagner, Jodie, 'Football: Santaluces Withdraws Coaching Offer to Korey Banks Amid FHSAA Probe' *PalmBeachPost*, 19 January 2017 (<http://highschoolbuzz.blog.palmbeachpost.com/2017/01/19/football-santaluces-withdraws-coaching-offer-to-korey-banks-amid-fhsaa-probe/>)

Walsh, Dan, 'NRL Cracks Down on lifting Tackles', *NRL*, 16 April 2014 (<http://www.nrl.com/nrl-cracks-down-on-lifting-tackles/tabid/10874/newsid/77691/default.aspx>)

Walter, Brad, 'NRL Clubs Face Loss of Competition Points Over Concussion Breaches', *WAtoday*, 23 March 2015 (<http://www.watoday.com.au/rugby-league/league-news/nrl-clubs-face-loss-of-competition-points-over-concussion-breaches-20150323-1m5v3k.html>) (Walter, 'NRL')

Walter, Brad, 'Ian Roberts Says He Has Brain Damage', *Brisbane Times*, 9 March 2014 (<http://www.brisbanetimes.com.au/rugby-league/league-news/ian-roberts-says-he-has-brain-damage-20140309-34ez8.html>) (Walter, 'Ian Roberts')

Washchyshyn, Marika, 'Is the Canadian Football League Safer than the NFL?' *Complex Sports*, 25 November 2015 (<http://au.complex.com/sports/2015/11/cfl-concussions>)

Wawrow, John, 'NHL, Former Players in Mediation for Concussion Lawsuit', *CBC*, 11 September 2018 (<https://www.cbc.ca/sports/hockey/nhl/nhl-former-players-in-mediation-for-concussion-lawsuit-1.4819212/>)

Webeck, Tony, 'Concussion Guidelines Explained', *NRL*, 14 March 2014 (<http://www.nrl.com/concussion-guidelines-explained/tabid/10874/newsid/76791/default.aspx>)

Weinbaum, William, 'Pitchers to Debut New Protective Headwear in Spring Training', *ESPN*, 12 February 2016 (<http://www.espn.com/mlb/story/_/id/14765775/mlb-players-association-work-together-develop-more-protective-pitching-hat>)

Westhead, Rick 'NHL, Plaintiffs Agree Concussion Lawsuits Should Kick Off with Four Trials', *TSN*, 26 September 2018 (<https://www.tsn.ca/nhl-plaintiffs-agree-concussion-lawsuits-should-kick-off-with-four-trials-1.1181451>) (Westhead, 'Trials')

Westhead, Rick, 'Four Junior Hockey Players Diagnosed with CTE', *TSN*, 21 April 2017 (<https://www.tsn.ca/four-junior-hockey-players-diagnosed-with-cte-researcher-says-1.730445>) (Westhead, 'Junior')

Westhead, Rick, 'NHL Doctor Slams "Situational Ethics" on Concussions in Unsealed Lawsuit Documents', *TSN*, 28 March 2017 (<http://www.tsn.ca/nhl-doctor-slams-situational-ethics-on-concussions-in-unsealed-lawsuit-documents-1.708729>) (Westhead, 'Documents')

Westhead, Rick, 'Link between Fighting, Concussions, "Personal Tragedies" Discussed in Unsealed NHL' Emails', *TSN*, 28 March 2016 (<http://www.tsn.ca/link-between-fighting-concussions-personal-tragedies-discussed-in-unsealed-nhl-emails-1.460651?smid=tw-nytsports&smtyp=cur>) (Westhead, 'Fighting')

Westhead, Rick, 'NHL Concussion Study Group Folded Without Any Conclusions After Leadership Worries, PA "Roadblocks" ', *TSN*, 29 March 2016 (<http://www.tsn.ca/nhl-concussion-study-

group-folded-without-any-conclusions-after-leadership-worries-pa-roadblocks-1.461185>) (Westhead, 'Leadership')

Wetsman, Nicole, 'What if the NFL Were Regulated by OSHA?', *Deadspin*, 22 May 2018 (<https://deadspin.com/what-if-the-nfl-were-regulated-by-osha-1826080311>)

Wheildon, Lisa, '$1Million Granted to Sports Organisations to Prevent Violence Against Women and their Children', *Our Watch*, 30 July 2015 (<https://www.ourwatch.org.au/News-media/Latest-news/$1million-granted-to-national-sporting-organisatio>)

Whiteman, Honor, 'Brain Shrinkage, Poorer Memory Found in Retired NFL Players with History of Concussion', *Medical News Today*, 19 May 2015 (<http://www.medicalnewstoday.com/articles/294056.php>)

Wickelgren, Ingrid, 'The Blood Test That Could Revolutionize Concussion Treatment – And Pro Sports', *Salon*, 11 January 2015 (<http://www.salon.com/2015/01/11/the_new_blood_test_that_could_revolutionize_concussion_treatment_and_pro_sports_partner/>)

Wilkinson, James, 'Former Dallas Cowboys Linebacker is Arrested for Stabbing his Wife to Death, One Month after He Kidnapped his Son from School and Blamed it on "Football Injuries" ' *DailyMail*, 4 November 2017 (<https://www.dailymail.co.uk/news/article-5048969/Ex-Dallas-Cowboys-linebacker-stabbed-wife-death.html>)

Williams, Uwe et al., 'Repairing Shattered Lives – Brain Injury and its Implications for Criminal Justice', University of Exeter, 2012 (<http://www.barrowcadbury.org.uk/wp-content/uploads/2012/11/Repairing-Shattered-Lives_Report.pdf>)

Wilson, Caroline, 'AFL to Overhaul Policy Covering Treatment of Women', *The Age*, 26 February 2016 (<http://www.theage.com.au/afl/afl-news/afl-to-overhaul-policy-covering-treatment-of-women-20160226-gn4pb1.html>) (Caroline Wilson, 'AFL')

Wilson, Jeremy, 'Exclusive: Single Protocol Needed to Treat Brain Injuries in Sport, Urges Report', *The Telegraph*, 9 October 2018 (<https://www.telegraph.co.uk/sport/2018/10/09/exclusive-single-protocol-needed-treat-brain-injuries-sport/>) (Jeremy Wilson, 'Protocol')

Wilson, Jeremy, 'FA Finally Opens Study into Link between Football and Dementia in Victory for the Telegraph and Astle Family', *The Telegraph*, 30 March 2017 (<http://www.telegraph.co.uk/football/2017/03/30/fa-finally-opens-study-link-football-dementia-victory-telegraph/>) (Jeremy Wilson, 'Study')

Wilson, Jeremy, 'FA Invites Jeff Astle's Daughter to Join Panel on Head Injuries', *The Telegraph*, 28 July 2016 (<http://www.telegraph.co.uk/football/2016/07/28/fa-invite-jeff-astles-daughter-to-join-panel-on-head-injuries/>) (Jeremy Wilson, 'Panel')

Wilson, Jeremy, 'Football's Brain Injury Risk No Lower Now than in the Past', *The Telegraph*, 31 May 2016 (<http://www.telegraph.co.uk/football/2016/05/31/footballs-brain-injury-risk-no-lower-now-than-in-the-past-warn-m/>) (Jeremy Wilson, 'Risk')

Zak, Michaels, 'Top 15 Largest Prison Sentences for NFL Players', *The Sportster*, 26 April 2017 (<https://www.thesportster.com/football/top-15-largest-prison-sentences-for-nfl-players/>)

Zelkowich, Chris, 'Canadian Football Tackles Concussions Head-On', *The Toronto Star*, 4 May 2011 (<https://www.pressreader.com/canada/toronto-star/20110504/282595964479675>)

Zimmerman, Kevin, 'Judge Tosses WWE lawsuit; Attorney Wows Appeal', *Westfair Online*, 19 September 2018 (<https://westfaironline.com/106959/judge-tosses-wwe-concussion-lawsuit-attorney-vows-appeal/>)

The manufacturer's authorised representative in the EU is Springer Nature Customer Service Centre GmbH, Europaplatz 3, 69115 Heidelberg, Germany. If you have any concerns regarding our products, please contact ProductSafety@springernature.com

Printed and bound by CPI Group (UK) Ltd, Croydon, CR0 4YY

30/09/2026

02225290-0017